PSALMS A Devotional Commentary

D1563808

A Devotional Commentary

PSALMS

HERBERT LOCKYER, SR.

Author of the famous "All" series

kregel
PUBLICATIONS

Grand Rapids, MI 49501

To
our beloved son,
Herbert Lockyer, Jr.,
a faithful minister of the Word.

Psalms: A Devotional Commentary
by Herbert Lockyer, Sr.

Copyright © 1993 by Kregel Publications, a division of Kregel, Inc., P.O. Box 2607, Grand Rapids, MI 49501. All rights reserved. No part of this book may be reproduced, stored in a retrieval system, or transmitted in any form by any means—electronic, mechanical, photocopy, recording, or otherwise—without written permission of the publisher, except for brief quotations in printed reviews.

For more information about Kregel Publications, visit our web site at www.kregel.com.

Cover and book design: Alan G. Hartman

Library of Congress Cataloging-in-Publication Data
Lockyer, Herbert, 1886–1984.
    Psalms: A Devotional Commentary / Herbert Lockyer.
        p.   cm.
    1. Bible. O.T. Psalms—Commentaries. I. Title.
BS1430.3.L631992   223'.206—dc20   92-15243
                                                                    CIP

ISBN 0-8254-3137-9 (paperback)

Printed in the United States of America
2 3 4 / 04 03 02 01 00 99 98

Contents

6   **Contents**

Introduction

When we journey from home to explore hitherto unknown parts of our own country or to visit other lands, maps and guidebooks are essential to show us how to reach our objective in travel and also instruct us as to hospitable resting places on the way, and inform us as to the kind of people we may meet. Only thus can we expect to have a beneficial odyssey. It is thus with the Book of Psalms with their Oriental background. The whole Book has 150 stops, so that we can rest awhile after each stage on our spiritual pilgrimage, and reflect upon all we have read about our persons and facts, known and unrecognized before. But the 150 Psalms have been given a fivefold classification, namely, Book 1, Psalms 1-41; Book 2, Psalms 42-72; Book 3, Psalms 73-89; Book 4, Psalms 90-106; Book 5, Psalms 107-150. And these Books can be treated as guides of information as to what to expect as we wander over the continent of truth they contain.

A fact to be borne in mind is that our Lord and His Apostles looked upon the Psalms as one Book. Silencing the questioning Scribes, He said, "David himself said in the Book of Psalms," Luke 20: 42. Our Lord also classed this Book as the *chiefest*, with the Law and the Prophets next, Luke 24:44. Then, in the choice of Matthias, Peter reminded the assembled disciples gathered for the election of a successor to Judas of the prophecy regarding such in Psalm 69: 25, "It is written in the Book of Psalms." And in so far as the revelation of God and of His purposes are concerned, the whole Book of Psalms is indivisible. The production of different persons, and belonging to different periods, and emphasizing different aspects of truth, these Psalms were collected gradually over a period of nearly six centuries. The Psalter, as we now have it, was not made, but like Topsy "it just growed."

Evidently intended for the public worship of the ancient Church, each of the five Books may have existed in an independent hymnbook before the whole collection was bound together. In the A.V. this fivefold division of the Psalms is not given. The R.V., however, along with modern translations of the Old Testament recognize such a division. But from the Hebrew MSS, the Psalms have come down to us as Five Books, which is no fanciful arrangement, the product of man's ingenuity, because the whole collection is well marked by the repetition five times over of a Benediction, or closing formula, 41:13; 72:18, 19; 89:52; 106:48; 150:6.

7

Within these Five Books or sections, smaller groups of Psalms have been classified, description of which will be found in the course of our studies. Some scholars affirm that this fivefold division is artificial, arguing that the superscriptions found at the head of most of the poems of the Psalter show that there are several collections, which probably represent earlier stages before the final edition of the Book. Then attempts have been made to classify the Psalms chronologically, or group them by authors or themes. The Early Fathers, Ambrose, Jerome to Cyprian, all describe the Psalms as Five Books as one, and later on the five were dealt with as based upon and corresponding to the *historical* Pentateuch, and forming a poetical Pentateuch extending from Moses to Malachi. Christopher Wordsworth wrote of the whole Book of Psalms as "Hebrew set to music, an oratorio in five parts, with Messiah as its subject." Preachers and Students will find a good deal of helpful material on the comparison between the Pentateuch and The Psalms in Rotherham's *The Emphasized Bible.* What is evident is the way both Pentateuchs were used in Divine worship, and from the people's answer to God's address to them in the Law, namely, the expression of their feelings called forth by the Word of God (see page 12).

BOOK l.   Psalms 1 to 41.

Pearls of truth, precious and plentiful, can be found in this first group. For instance, the first three Psalms provide us with the keys to the whole collection.

Psalm 1 - *The Scriptures*
Psalm 2 - *The Messiah*
Psalm 3 - *The Believer's Experience*

These 41 Psalms are known as the Davidic-Jehovah Psalms, because of the way the Psalmist magnifies God as Jehovah.

According to the titles of these Psalms, there is no trace of any author but David. Altogether, out of the whole 150 Psalms, 80 of them are definitely assigned to David. Four Psalms in this first group are anonymous, but were in all likelihood composed by David. As for Divine names used—Jehovah, 279 times, Elohim, 45 times, some of which are connected with Jehovah, Who is presented as The Burning One, The Helper. A Doxology closes the section. See R.V, at Psalm 41:13.

BOOK 2.   Psalms 42 to 72.

Contained in the second Book are 17 Psalms attributed to David, 8 to Korah, 1 to Solomon, and 1 to Asaph. Four are titleless. As for Divine names—Elohim is used 262 times—twice in connection with Jehovah—and for this reason the group is referred to as the Elohim Psalms. El, 14 times, Jah, once.

Here we have Elohim, the wonder-working God. Forecasts of the Messiah's conflict, ending in His reign, appear most in Books 1 and 2. The Doxology at 72: 18, 19 is most expressive.

BOOK 3.   Psalms 73 to 89.

These seventeen Psalms have been given the title of "The Jehovah Psalms of David's Singers," seeing it contains—11 Psalms by Asaph, 4 by Korah, 19 by David, 1 by Ethan.

As for Divine names and titles employed—Jehovah, 65 times, Elohim 93 times, El, 5 times.

The general theme is that of the Lord as Elohim, Jehovah—The Mighty Helper, and the call to His ceaseless worship. The Doxology is short but sweet, "Blessed be Jehovah for evermore Amen and Amen," 89:52.

BOOK 4.   Psalms 90 to 106.

The burden of this portion is the fruit of Jehovah's victory and reign, and Israel's restoration after her pilgrim state. Fifteen of the Psalms are anonymous, one is by Moses, and two by David. They were probably compiled after Israel's captivity. Divine names used are:

Jehovah, 126 times.

Elohim, 31 times — 10 of which are combined with *Jehovah*.

El, 6 times.

Throughout the section, God is extolled as Jehovah, the Governing King, and as such should have submissive worship, as the *Hallelujah* Doxology indicates, 106: 48, R.V.

BOOK 5.   Psalms 107 to 150.

Used after Israel's Captivity, these Psalms are called The Songs of Degrees—the Ascents of the Lord's people going up from the wilderness leaning upon her Beloved, and their everlasting *Hallelujahs*. Of these last Psalms in the Psalter, 28 have no title; 15 are by David; one by Solomon. Prominence is given to God as Jehovah, 293 times; Elohim, 41 times—combined with Jehovah 4 times; El, 10 times; Elvah, twice.

In this concluding division the emphasis is on God as Jehovah, the Redeemer, Who merits the perfect worship of the redeemed, and Who expresses it in the jubilant *Hallelujah*, ending Psalm 150, as well as the entire Psalter, 150:6.

For the benefit of those who may not know the full meaning of the various Divine names cited in the foregoing lists, we are giving the following brief explanations based, more or less, upon those in E. W. Bullinger's *Companion Bible*. It sets forth:

Elohim. The first connection of this title connects it with Creation,

Genesis 1: 1, and carries with it the essential truth of God as *Creator.* It occurs some 2700 times in Scripture, and in the A.V. is given as GOD.

Jehovah. This is God in covenant relationship to those He created. Meaning "The Eternal and Immutable One," it is printed as Lord in the A.V. but as Jehovah in the R.V.

Jah. An abbreviation of Jehovah, this name represents Him in a special sense or relation. Its first occurrence is in Exodus 15:3 and implies, "The Becoming One."

El. As Elohim suggests strength or power, so El is the God who knows all, Gen. 14:18, 22; sees all, Gen. 16:13; performs all things for His people, Psalm 57:2. It portrays Jehovah as "the Almighty or Omnipotent One."

Eloah. Associated with worship, as its first use indicates, Deut. 32:15-17, this further name indicates, "Elohim Who is to be worshipped," and "The Living God," in contrast to inanimate dead idols.

Several attempts have been made to classify the Psalms according to their thematic motifs and uses; and such an order is beneficial to preachers desiring to expound the Psalter's various themes. Here is an outline to follow:

Praise Hymns,

Praise of the Lord of Nature, Pss. 8, 19, 29, 65, 67, 96, 148.

Praise of the Lord of History, Pss. 33, 46, 66, 68, 75, 76, 78, 89, 105, 106, 107, 113, 114, 115, 136, 149.

Praise of the Lord of Zion, Pss. 15, 24, 47, 84, 93, 94, 95, 97 to 99, 122, 125, 126, 132, 134, 135, 147, 150.

Crisis Prayers,

National Lamentations, Pss. 44, 60, 74, 79, 80, 83, 123, 137.

Personal Lamentations, Pss. 3, 4, 13, 35, 38, 39, 41 to 43, 54 to 57, 63, 64, 70, 71, 86, 102, 120, 141 to 143.

Faith Songs,

Personal Thanksgivings, Pss. 18, 30, 32, 34, 40, 118, 144 to 146.

Prayers of Communion, Pss. 11, 16, 17, 23, 26 to 28, 31, 36, 62, 103, 116, 121, 131, 138 to 140.

Meditations of Wisdom, Pss. 1, 12, 14 - see 53, 37, 49, 73, 90 to 92, 101, 111, 112, 119, 127 to 129.

Special Psalms,

Royal Hymns, Pss. 2, 20, 21, 45, 61, 72, 110.

Prophetic Oracles, Pss. 50, 81, 82.

Maledictions, Pss. 52, 58, 59, 109.

An Osyssey of the Psalms

STORIES OF THE INFLUENCE OF THE PSALTER

In his fascinating volume, *The Psalms in History and Biography*, a small volume deserving of a perpetual circulation, Dr. John Ker, says that in The Book of Psalms we have "a series of chambers where hearts and lives have left the records of their experience. They are very varied, but in all of them, prison or palace, this is a window towards the sun-rising." If one could gather all these records it would take volumes to present them, as Tholuck, the eminent theologian expressed it—

> What a record that would be, if one could write down—all the spiritual experiences, the disclosures of the heart, the comforts and the conflicts which men in the course of ages have connected with the words of the Psalms. What a history, if we could discover the place the Book has occupied in the inner life of the heroes of the Kingdom of God.

Multitudes of believers, not classed as *heroes,* have also found refuge in the dark and difficult hours of life in the majestic poetry of the Bible, with its broad humanity. The plenteous rain of the Psalms has watered, not only what we called the Garden of God, but has scattered drops far and wide "to satisfy the desolate and waste ground, and to cause the bud of the tender herb to spring forth." We can find verses from the Psalms quoted in strange places, and by unlikely lips. From sick beds, dungeons, scaffolds, lonely mountains and bleak moors; from poets, priests, and peasants; from exiles and martyrs come testimony to the comfort, encouragement and peace to be found in the language of the Psalms.

Those who are fortunate enough to possess the massive commentary on *The Psalms,* by C. H. Spurgeon (he named it *The Treasury of David),* will recall how replete this remarkable work is with stories of those who were greatly blessed by a particular Psalm, or verses from a Psalm. Familiar, as Spurgeon was, with the Early Fathers of the Church, he cites many telling illustrations of what the Psalms meant in the lives of those past stalwart defenders of the Faith. The following selection of illustrations, many of them from John Ker's interesting coverage, have been slightly adapted to bring them up-to-date for the reader. Pastors might find a basis for a series of enlightening and appealing messages on the general theme of *The Psalms, In Lives of Saints,* from these incidents. In this connection, we commend the most enlightening and readable volume by Rowland E. Prothero, *The Psalms in Human Life,* in which a different method is adopted from that of Dr. John Ker's work, in that he sets forth in chronological order, historical incidents connected with the Psalms. This remarkable literary volume is one of the most notable contributions to the literature on the Psalter it is possible to possess.

Psalms 1 and 2 are a key opening the door of the treasure-house containing the world's finest poetic works. Says John Ker, "As the First Psalm is the outer door of practical insight with a prophetic close, so the Second Psalm is the inner door of prophetic foresight with a practical close; and these two interchange and interpret each other through the whole book, in the one case the life-bestowing vision, in the other vision leading to life."

John Milton never lost the spell the Psalms threw over him in early life. Throughout his poems are scattered, more or less, allusions to the Psalms. In 1653, he wrote that eight more Psalms—1 to 8—were "done into verse." Frequent references will be found in the following pages to the influence of the Psalms in Milton's life and labors.

THE PSALMS AND THE PENTATEUCH TABULATED AND COMPARED

Book	Psalms	Doxology	Authors	Divine Names	Message	Pentateuch	Common Teaching
1	1—41	41:13	David, 37 Anon., 4	Jehovah, 279 x Elohim, 48 x	Jehovah – The Becoming One (Adoring Worship)	Genesis	Concerns the History of Man
2	42—72	72:18, 19	David, 18 Korah, 7 Anon., 4 Solomon, 1 Asaph, 1	Jehovah, 37 x Elohim, 262 x El, 14 x Jah, 1 x	Elohim – The Wonder-working God (Wondering Worship)	Exodus	Concerns the mattter of Redemption
3	73—89	89:52	Asaph, 11 Korah, 3 David, 1 Heman, 1 Athan, 1	Jehovah, 65 x Elohim, 93 x El, 5 x	Elohim – Jehovah—The Mighty Helper (Ceaseless Worship)	Leviticus	Concerns the Sanctuary
4	90—106	106:48	Anon., 14 Moses, 1 David, 2	Jehovah, 126 x Elohim, 31 x El, 6 x	Jehovah – The Governing King (Submissive Worship)	Numbers	Concerns the Earth
5	107-150	150	Anon., 28 David, 15 Solomon, 1	Jehovah, 293 x Elohim, 41 x Jah, 13 x El, 10 x Eloah, 2 x	Jehovah – The Redeemer (Perfected Worship)	Deuteronomy	Concerns the Word of God

Psalm 1

It was from his godly nurse that Lord Byron learned by heart the first Psalm, and other Psalms. John Ruskin included Psalm 1 in his selection of Psalms to be "well studied and believed, suffice for all personal guidance." Jerome had two favorite texts, "But his delight is in the law of the Lord; and in His law will he exercise himself day and night" Psalms 1:2; the other verse, Psalm 6:9.

Thomas Watson, renowned expositor of the 16th century who gave us that monumental compendium of theology, *Body of Divinity,* also wrote *Saints' Spiritual Delight,* in which he had this to say about the opening Psalm of the Psalter—

> As the book of the Canticles is called the Song of Songs by a Hebraism, it being the most excellent, so this Psalm may not unfitly be entitled, *The Psalm of Psalms,* for it contains in it the very pity and quintessence of Christianity. What Jerome saith on St. Paul's Epistles, the same may I say of this Psalm; it is short as to the composure, but full of length and strength as to the matter. This Psalm carries blessedness in its frontispiece, it being where we all hope to end: it may well be called a Christian's Guide, for it discovers the quicksands where the wicked sink down in perdition, and the firm ground on which the saints tread to Glory.

Among by-gone interpreters of Scripture, such as Augustus and Jerome, there was the conception that the first half of this first Psalm was intended to be descriptive of the character and reward of the *Just One,* namely, the Lord Jesus Christ Himself, Who is blessed forever.

Prothero informs us that it was in a reference to a Psalm that Boswell defended the minuteness of detail with which, throughout the most famous biography in the English language, he noted the conversations of Dr. Johnson. He quoted from Archbishop Secker, in whose tenth sermon there is the following passage—

> *Rabbi David Kimchi,* a noted Jewish commentator, who lived about five hundred years ago, explains that passage in the 1st Psalm, *His leaf also shall not wither,* from the rabbins yet older than himself, thus—That *even the idle talk,* so he expresses it, *of a good man ought to be regarded;* the most superfluous things he saith are always of value.

Cotton Mather, the Puritan minister and author of Boston, Mass., who became renowned for his crusade against *Witchcraft,* had a deep love for this verse. One of the most touching traits of his character was a consuming passion for usefulness, or, as he called it, *Fruitfulness*—passion which was not denied even in his own lifetime. His signet ring had for device a fruit-bearing tree with the words of Psalm 1:3 inscribed beneath it. When dying in 1728, and almost oblivious to the sight and hearing of earthly things, his son and successor asked him for one word to remember when he was dead, and the old warrior feebly whispered—*Fruitful! 1:3.*

The 6th verse contains a summary of the teaching, not only of the Psalms, but the whole of Scirpture—

> For the Lord knoweth the way of the righteous: But the way of the ungodly shall perish. (See Isa. 3:10-11).

An extension of these twin truths can be found in our Lord's message about the two ways, and their respective end.

> Strait is the gate, and narrow is the way, which leadeth unto life, and few there be that find it. The strait gate.

> Wide is the gate, and broad is the way, that leadeth to destruction, and many there be which go in thereat (Matt. 7:13-14).

There are only two classes, "the righteous" through grace and "the ungodly." If we are not in the first class, we must be in the second, for there is no middle class in God's estimate of the human race.

During the reign of James VI, a Scottish poet by the name of Alexander Montgomery, described by James Melville in his *Diary* as "A good, honest man, and the Regent's domestic," wrote many Odes and Sonnets, and gave us the earliest version of Psalm 1, in his native tongue. As can be seen, it has a close fidelity to the original beginning of The Psalter—

> Ode 1
>   That man is blest,
>   And is possessed.
>   Of truest rest,
> Who from ungodly counsel turns his feet;
>   Who walks not in
>   The way of sin
>   Nor comes within
> The place where mockers take their shameful seat;
>   But in God's law to go
>   He doth delight;

>And studies it to know
>Both day and night.
>That man shall be—like to a tree
>Which by the running river spreads its shade;
>Which fruit does bear—in time of year;
>Whose root is firm, whose leaf shall never fade.

Ode 2

>His actions all
>Still prosper shall;
>So doth not fall
>To wicked men, whom, as chaff and sand,
>Winds, day by day
>Shall drive away;
>Therefore I say
>The wicked in the judgment shall not stand;
>Neither shall sinners dare,
>Whom God disdains,
>To enter the assembly where
>The just remains.
>For God most pure, keeps records sure;
>He knows the righteous heart and converse aye;
>But like the fire—kindles his ire
>'Gainst wicked men, till they consume away.

Psalm 2

One of the favorite Psalms of Martin Luther was this 2nd Psalm, and his comment upon it brings out salient features in the character of a man whose very words were half-battles:

> The 2nd Psalm is one of the best Psalms. I love that Psalm with all my heart. It strikes and flashes valiantly among kings, princes, counselors, and judges. If what this Psalm says be true, then all the allegations and aims of the papists are stark lies and folly. If I were as our Lord God, and had committed the government to my son, or He to His Son, and these vile people were as disobedient as now they be, I would knock the world in pieces.

Messianic in nature, this triumphant poem is rightly named as *The Psalms of The King,* for God's King, even His Son, is seen as the universal Ruler—Rejected, Established, Reigning over the Nations. After the Messiah's death, resurrection, and ascension, this Psalm took on a deeper significance for the Apostles who fashioned it into the earliest Song of Thanksgiving and Prayer in the Christian Church. The Psalm is the beginning of that long history in which David, Christ, and the experience of the Church, are found so often re-appearing in union. In defiance of the authorities Peter and John continued with boldness to speak of the things they had seen and heard, and then came the united voice of the Church as with one accord those fearless saints sang their spiritual *Marseillaise* from Psalm 2—

> Lord, Thou art God, which hast made heaven and earth,
> And the sea, and all that in them is:
> Who by the mouth of Thy servant David hast said,
> Why did the heathen rage,
> And the people imagine vain things?
> The kings of the earth stood up,
> And the rulers were gathered together
> Against the Lord, and against His Christ.
> For of a truth, against Thy holy Child Jesus,
> Whom Thou hast anointed,
> Both Herod and Pontius Pilate, with the Gentiles,
> And the people of Israel, were gathered together,
> For to do whatsoever Thy hand and Thy counsel
> Determined before to be done.
> And now, Lord, behold their threatenings;

And grant unto Thy servants,
That with all boldness they may speak Thy Word,
By stretching forth Thine hand to heal;
And that signs and wonders may be done
By the name of Thy holy Child Jesus" (Acts 4:24-30).

Spurgeon calls this sublime Psalm—*The Psalm of The Messiah Prince*—because it sets forth in a wondrous vision, the tumult of the people against the Lord's anointed, the determinate purpose of God to exalt His own Son, and the ultimate reign of that Son over all His foes. We must read the Psalm with the eye of faith, beholding, as in a glass, the final triumph of our Lord Jesus Christ over those who oppose Him. Then Spurgeon goes on to quote Lowth who wrote of the second Psalm—

> The establishment of David upon his throne, notwithstanding the opposition made to it by his enemies, is the subject of this Psalm. David sustains in it a twofold character, literal and allegorical. If we read over the Psalm, first with an eye to the literal David, the meaning is obvious, and put beyond all dispute by the sacred history. . . . If we take another survey of the Psalm as relative to the person and concerns of the spiritual David, a noble series of events immediately rises to view, and the meaning becomes more evident, as well as more exalted.

As the First Psalm is the outer door of practical insight with a prophetic close, says Dr. Ker, so the Second Psalm is the inner door of prophetic foresight with a practical close.

The people imagine a vain thing, 2:1. A writer of the last century observed, "We have here a monument raised by Paganism, over the grave of its anguished foe. But is this, 'the people imagine a vain thing' so far from being deceased. Christianity was on the eve of its final and permanent triumph, and the stone guarded a sepulchre empty as the urn which Electra washed with her tears. Neither in Spain, nor elsewhere, can be pointed out the burial place of Christianity; it is not, for the living have no tomb."

The certainty and inevitability of Divine judgment upon those who seek to reject Divine authority, verses 5, 9, is borne out in ancient Rome, as Dr. W. R. Plumer observed, away back in 1867. Of 30 Roman Emperors, Governors of Provinces, and others in high office, who distinguished themselves in their zeal and bitterness in persecuting the Early Christians, one became blind, one became speedily deranged after some atrocious cruelty, one was slain by his own son, one was drowned, the eyes of one started out of his head, one was strangled, one died in a miserable captivity, one fell dead in a manner that will not bear recital, one died of a disease that several of his physicians were put to death because they could not abide the stench that filled his room, two committed suicide, a third attempted it, but had to call for help to finish the work, five were assassinated by their own people or servants, five others died the most miserable and excruciating deaths, several of them having an untold complication of diseases, eight were killed in battle, or after being taken prisoners.

Among the latter was the notorious Julian the Apostate, who in the days of his prosperity was said to have pointed his dagger to Heaven defying the Son of God whom he constantly called the Galilean. But when wounded in battle, Julian saw that all was over with him, he gathered up his clotted blood, threw it in the air, exclaiming, *"Thou* hast conquered, Thou Galilean!"

A further historical proof of Divine Justice comes from Voltaire who recorded the agonies of Charles IX of France, which drove the blood through the pores of the skin of that miserable monarch, after his cruelties and betrayal of the Huguenots.

Verses from this royal Psalm have brought consolation to saints down the ages. For instance, John Lambert, a stalwart for the faith in the 15th century, addressed a remonstrance to Henry VIII by quoting the words—

> Now, ye kings, understand, and ye which judge the earth be wise and learned. Serve the Lord with fear, and rejoice in Him with trembling.

Angered by the godly man's protest, the King ordered Lambert to be burned at the stake, and his martyrdom at Smithfield in 1538 has been described as "one of the most cruel of that time." But as he died, faith was victorious for he lifted up his fingers flaming with fire, and cried, *None but Christ,* none but Christ! 2:10, 11. One would like to know how many effective Gospel sermons have been preached from the closing invitation of this kingly Psalm—

> Kiss the Son, lest He be angry, and ye perish from the way?

Alas! Judas kissed the Son, but perished from the way. 2:12.

Psalm 3

The title of this Psalm informs us that it was written during David's poignant experience when he was forced to flee from Absalom his son. The French Protestants who, in times of persecution, adapted the Psalm to varied experience, used Psalm 3 for the stationing of sentinels to keep watch against sudden attack; when the danger was past, and they could worship again in safety, they would sing Psalm 122.

It was in words from this Psalm—*Lord, how are they increased that trouble me*—that the English nation expressed their fears of impending invasion, as five centuries before, they had, with the same words invoked Divine aid against the Norsemen. During the French Wars of religion, sentries from Conde's army were posted and relieved to the chant of Psalms. Psalm 3:1, "Lord, how are they increased that trouble me," gave the signal of danger.

Writing from India during the mutiny there, in 1857, Dr. A. Duff, in a letter form Calcutta, spoke of his reliance upon the Psalms, in the midst of panic, open mutiny, and secret disaffection. "I have a confident persuasion that, though this crisis has been permitted to humble and warn us, our work in India has not yet been accomplished, and that until it be accomplished, our tenure of the Empire, how brittle, is secure. Never before did I realize as now the literality and sweetness of the Psalmist's assurance—*'I laid me down and slept; I awaked; for the Lord sustained me. I will not be afraid of ten thousands of people, that have set themselves against me round about. Arise, O Lord, save me, O my God,'* 3:5.

Verses 3-6 of this Psalm born in heart-anguish formed the basis of a sermon the renowned Bishop Bedell preached to his fellow-prisoners during the Irish rebellion in 1642—

> "But Thou, O Lord, art a shield for me; my glory, and the lifter up of mine head. . . . I will not be afraid of ten thousands of people that have set themselves against me round about."

He loved the Irish language, and had the Bible translated into it. Ever assiduous in Christian service, he was conspicuous for his meekness and self-sacrifice.

Psalm 4

Believing that this Psalm has a special value, Augustine deemed it necessary to be sung aloud before the whole world as an expression of Christian courage, and as a testimony of the peace God can give in outward and inward trouble (see Psalm 9:4). James Neville quoted it with other Psalms when he lay dying. Rehearsing the prayer in Hebrew brought great comfort to his heart, "Lord, lift up the light of thy countenance upon me." Philip Doddridge in his biography of his friend, Colonel Gardiner, 1688-1745, tells us of the hold which the Psalms possessed on the Colonel's life. Mortally wounded in the Rebellion of 1745, he prayed that at *the hour of death* his glorious Redeemer would lift up upon him *"the Light* of His life-giving Countenance." 4:6. This was the same verse James Melville quoted when he was dying, for the comfort of his soul.

Few of us realize that natural sleep is a gift from God's bountiful hand, "So He giveth His beloved sleep," 4:8 with 127:2. Many have proved the preciousness of this provision when threatened with insomnia. Mrs. Thomas Carlyle, wife of the famous essayist, wrote in her Journal, "Sleep has come to look to me the highest virtue and the greatest happiness, that is, good sleep, untroubled, beautiful, like a child's."

Augustine, who was forever crying to God in the Psalms tells of how Psalm 4, especially, worked upon his mind. As he read, "When I called upon Thee, Thou didst hear me, O God of my righteouness: Thou has set me at liberty when I was in trouble; have mercy upon me, and hearken unto my prayer," 4:1, he mourned over the Manichees, pitying their blind rejection of the antidote which might have cured their madness— "Would they could have heard, without my knowing that they heard, lest they should have thought it was on their account I spoke, what I cried as I read these words! In truth I could not so have cried, had I felt that they were watching. Nor, indeed if I had used the very same words, could they have meant to them what they meant to me, as they poured from my heart in that soliloquy which fell on Thine ears alone. For I trembled with fear, and I glowed with hope and great joy in Thy mercy, O my Father. Yea, joy and hope and fear shone in my eyes and thrilled in my voice, while the good Spirit turned to us, and said—

> O ye sons of men, how long will ye blaspheme Mine honor; and have such pleasure in vanity, and seek after leasing? 4:2.

It is to be feared that the majority of people have never learned how to accustom themselves to soliloquies, or to have conferences with themselves which is what the Psalmist meant when he said, *Commune with your own heart.* What a famous answer that was which Antisthenes gave when he was asked what fruit he has reaped by all his studies. "By them," he said, "I have learned both to live and talk with myself." It has been said that "soliloquies are the best disputes; every good man is best company for himself of all the creatures; that when we have none to speak with, we can talk to ourselves."

How choice are the words, *I will both lay me down in peace and sleep: for Thou, O Lord, only makest me dwell in safety,* 4:8. Spurgeon tells us that apparently this 4th Psalm was meant to accompany the 3rd, seeing the two make a pair. If Psalm 3 can be entitled *The Morning Psalm,* Psalm 4 equally deserved the title of *The Evening Hymn,* seeing it contains the sweet song of rest as we retire to our repose—

> Thus with my thoughts composed to peace,
> I'll give mine eyes to sleep;
> Thy hand in safety keep my days,
> And will my slumbers keep.

Gorgonia, daughter of Gregory Naziangen, one of the grandest of poets, orators, and theologians of Eastern Christendom in the 3rd century, had a presentiment of death's approach, and when the end came, friends at her father's bedside heard her murmur, *I lay me down in peace, and take my rest.* Martin Luther left it on record that the concluding verses of Psalm 4 had been loved by him from his youth, and that it was his wish to hear their soothing words sung when he came to his last moments.

Nicholas Ridley, Bishop of London, in the 15th century, rejected the offer of a fellow-priest to spend the last hours before his execution with him. But Ridley refused, saying that he meant to go to bed and sleep as quietly as he ever did in his life: *I will lay me down in peace, and take my rest: for it is Thou, Lord, only, that makest me dwell in safety,* 4:8. The next day, as he burned at the stake, he cried with a loud voice, "Lord, Lord, receive my spirit."

How comforting are the lines of the poetess M'Cartree on God's gift of natural sleep—

> How blessed was that *sleep*
> The sinless Savior knew!
> In vain the storm-winds blew
> Till he awoke to others' woes,
> And hushed the billows to repose.

How beautiful is *sleep*—
The *sleep* that Christians know!
Ye mourners! cease your Woe,
While soft upon his Savior's breast
The righteous sinks to endless rest.

Psalm 5

The unvarying theme running through the first four Psalms, namely, the contrast between the position, character, and the prospects of the righteous and of the wicked is continued by David in the Psalm before us, with emphasis upon the contrast between himself made righteous by God's grace, and the wicked who opposed Him. There are expositors, like Spurgeon, who believe that to the devout mind there is presented in this Psalm a precious view of the Lord Jesus, of whom it is said that in "the days of His flesh, He offered up prayers and supplications with strong crying, and tears."

Saints, in succeeding ages, have been encouraged by David's example to maintain a morning watch—*My voice shalt thou hear in the morning, O Lord: in the morning will I direct my prayer unto thee, and will look up,* 5:3. Thrice blessed are they who make David's resolution, their own. Whether or no, it is true that "an hour in the morning is worth two in the evening," it is true that prayer is the key of the day and the lock of the night. Henry Vaughan, spiritual poet of the 16th century, gave the Church a most impressive poem founded on David's morning tryst with God, the first verse of which reads—

> When first thine eyes unveil, give thy soul leave
> To do the like; our bodies but forerun
> The spirit's duty; true hearts spread and heave
> Unto their God, as flowers do to the sun;
> Give him thy first thoughts, then, so shalt thou keep
> Him company all day, and in him sleep.

It was in July, 1270, that Louis IX took the Cross, and embarked for Africa, but before the walls of Tunis, both the climate and a raging plague did their deadly work, for Louis himself was struck down, and lingered for three weeks. On August 25, 1270, laid on a bed of ashes, he died, murmuring the words of David's personal decision, *As for me, I will come into Thine house, even upon the multitude of Thy mercy; and in Thy fear will I worship toward Thy holy temple,* 5:7.

How gracious it is of the Lord to compass the righteous with favor *as with a shield,* 5:12! Truly, this is a Divine promise of infinite length, of unbounded breadth, and of unutterable preciousness. When Martin Luther made his way into the presence of Cardinal Cajentan, who had commanded the Reformer to answer for his heretical opinions at Augsburg, he was asked by one of the Cardinal's officials, where he could find a shelter, if his patron, the Elector of Saxony, should desert him? Luther's reply was, "Under the shield of Heaven," and such an answer silenced the questioner, and he left the chamber.

Shields of old were made very large in order to protect and defend, not a particular part of the body, but the whole of it. Thus, because of its broadness, it was called a gate or door, because so long and large, it covered the whole person of the warrior. David would have us know that the lovingkindness of God is such a shield, defending every part of the believer's life. The sense of Divine favor is a protection for body and soul alike.

The necessity of beginning each day with God is enjoined in this product of David's mind and pen. C. E. Wyekoff, a well-known editor of the past century asked, "Did you ever search your Bible to find beautiful passages about the morning watch? Here is one: 'My voice shalt thou hear in the morning, O Lord: in the morning will I direct my prayer unto thee and look up.' 5:3."

Psalm 6

When in 1174, Henry II sought to do penance for the sacrilege of the murder of Thomas à Becket at Canterbury, December 29th, 1170, he entered the Cathedral, kissed the stone where Becket had fallen, and then recited this penitential cry in Psalm 6, against wrath. The king's humiliation was so profound that the chroniclers of the time appealed to the language of the Psalms to describe the impression produced—"The mountains trembled at the presence of the Lord"—"The mountains of Canterbury smoked before Him who touches the hills and they smoke." Bishop John Hooper included this same 6th Psalm in the collection of Psalms calculated to induce lessons of "patience and consolation" at times "when the mind can take no understanding nor the heart any joy of God's presence."

O Lord, rebuke me not in Thine anger, 6:1, was engraven in Latin on the florin of Edward III, in 1344. As for verse 2, *Have mercy upon me, O Lord, for I am weak,* Maine de Biran, 1766-1824, named as one of the greatest of French metaphysicians, who also was a lover of the Psalms, affirmed that without Divine aid, man would weary of the struggle, and ask for help in the words of the Psalmist. Jane Welsh Carlyle was one who cried for such help. As Prothero informs us, "On March 24th, 1856, she had resolved, in spite of weakness and ill-health, neither to indulge in vain retrospects of the past, nor to gaze into vague distances of the future, but to find the duty nearest to hand, and do it." Two days later, she had learned how much she was the creature of external circumstances, and wrote in her Diary—March 26, 1856—

> One cold, rasping savage March day, aided by the too tender sympathy of a friend, brought back all my troubles—Have mercy upon me, O Lord, for I am weak; O Lord, heal me for my bones are vexed. My soul is also sore vexed; But Thou, O Lord, how long? Return, O Lord, deliver my soul; O save me for Thy mercies sake. 6:2-4.

As we have indicated elswhere, it was to this Psalm that John Calvin turned, in mental troubles, as well as in the throes of pain and death. When in any anxiety of mind, he would repeat the words of David, *My soul is sore troubled: but, Lord, how long wilt Thou punish me?* 6:3.

William Langland, the 14th century poet of realistic power of spiritual intensity, in Section 15 of his *Vision of Piers Plowman,* which deals with

27

"Charity," wrote, "God purgeth men of pride, cleansing them in the Laundry with groans and tears—*I am weary with my groaning: all the night make I my bed to swim; I water my couch with my tears,* 6:6."

This Psalm is known as the first of The Penitential Psalms of which there are seven, the others being Psalms 22, 38, 51, 102, 130 and 143. Each of us, as penitents, can make the language of the initial Psalm of contrition our own, and express our sorrow, 6:3, 6, 7; our humiliation, 6:2, 4, and our hatred of sin, 6:8; for these are the unfailing evidences of the contrite spirit when it turns to God.

In the paragraph found in the Journal of Mrs. Thomas Carlyle, referred to under Psalm 4, this noble lady also added, "Ah me! Have mercy upon me, O Lord; for I am weak; O Lord, heal me; for my bones are vexed. My soul is also sore vexed: but Thou, O Lord, how long?" Ps. 6:2, 3. Another lady of refinement, Elizabeth Charlotte, niece of Sophia, Electress of Hanover, was a woman of remarkable abilities. Her marriage of convenience to the Duke of Orleans, brother of Louis XIV, arranged by her father, was fraught with disaster. The land she loved was devastated by French armies, and Elizabeth came to see that she had been cruelly sacrificed to a vain policy. In her *Letters,* profitable for the light they focused upon the Court of France at that time, she relates an experience associated with this Sixth Psalm.

One day, while walking in the orangery at Versailles, she sang a translation of this Psalm as an expression of her feelings. A noted artist of the time, warmly attached in heart to the Reformed religion, was engaged in painting the roof, and heard her: "Scarcely," she wrote, "had I finished the first verse of the Psalm, when I saw M. Rousseau hasten down the ladder and fall at my feet. I thought he was mad, and said, 'Rousseau, Rousseau, what is the matter?' He replied, 'Is it possible, Madam, that you will recollect our Psalms and sing them? May God bless you, and keep you in this good mind.' He had tears in his eyes." Broken-hearted in his old age by defeats and disappointments, Louis XIV, recognizing the godliness of Elizabeth Charlotte, came to rely heavily on her for comfort.

The third verse of this Psalm, so dear both to Elizabeth Charlotte and Mrs. Thomas Carlyle was also the common expression of John Calvin when he was in trouble—*Tu Domine usque quo?* "Thou, O Lord, how long?" John Ker remarks that the Psalm might have a history to itself.

> It has a wail of pain and sorrow, deepening into anguish, running through it; but comfort dawns at the close, like an angel turning the key of the prison. It is the first of the Seven Penitential Psalms, the others being the 32nd, 38th, 51st, 102nd and 143rd.

Dr. Ker then goes on to give us this historical reference—"One of the strangest, though not the happiest, in the records of history, is that Psalm

6 along with Psalm 142, was the choice of Catherine de Medici, the Jezebel and Athaliah of the French monarchy." She was irreligious, superstitious, profligate and devoured by ambition: and the fact that she had no children seemed likely to deprive her of the control which she hoped to gain in the counsels of the kingdom. The 6th Psalm was the expression of her worldly disappointment. Ultimately, she became the mother of Francis II—the first husband of Mary Stuart—and of Charles IX, whose character she corrupted by ministering to his vices, and whom she urged to the massacre of St. Bartholomew. Says a French historian, "Her desire was realized for the misery of Francis; and that family, which then took pleasure in the Psalms, put to death thousands of the Reformed for singing them."

Psalm 7

The heading of this Psalm furnishes the historical occasion for its composition. It was the song David composed and sang unto the Lord, "concerning the words of Cush the Benjamite." The *words* in question were those Cush had used when he accused David to Saul of treasonable conspiring against his royal authority. Because of his jealous hatred of David, and the good relationship existing between himself, as the son of Kish, and this Cush, or Kish, the Benjamite, Saul readily believed the lie told him concerning David. This episode, then, was the occasion for the Psalm, Spurgeon calls *The Song of the Slandered Saint,* and then adds—

> What a blessing would it be if we could turn even the most disastrous event into a theme for song, and so turn the tables upon our great enemy. Let us learn a lesson from Martin Luther, who once said: 'David made Psalms; we also make Psalms, and sing them as well as we can to honor our Lord, and to spite and mock the Devil.'

There is, however, the broader outline of the real subject of the Psalm which is the Messiah's appeal to God against false accusations of His enemies; and the predictions which it contains of the final ingathering of souls, and of future judgment, are clear and explicit.

Lest he tear my soul like a lion, rending it in pieces, 7:2. David describes his enemy as having strength and ferocity, yet he knew that God is able to deliver him from all injurious slander, even as he, when a shepherd-lad, had delivered the defenseless lamb from the lion that had pounced upon it. The Italians say that a good reputation is like the cypress—once cut, it never puts forth leaf again. A character damaged by slander does not easily regain its former verdue. Wounds of the tongue cut deeper than the flesh, and are not soon cured. "If God was slandered in the Garden of Eden, we shall surely be maligned in this land of sinners."

Tear my soul like a lion! What a horrifying simile David used! It is said that tigers enter into a rage upon the scent of fragrant spices. In like manner, ungodly men cannot stand the blessed savor of godliness. It has also been reported that some barbarous nations in the past became so enraged when the sun shone upon them, that they would shoot up their arrows against it. Is this not similar to wicked men when they encounter the light and heart of godliness? Away back in the Garden of Eden, God said, "I will put enmity between thy seed and her seed."

Confident of his own innocence in the matter of Cush's false accusation David yet said, *O Lord, my God, if I have done this, if this be iniquity in my hands,* 7:3. The early Christians were under great reproach. For instance, in Tertullian's day, the heathen would paint the God the saints worshiped with an ass's head, and a book in his hand, to signify that though they pretended learning, yet they were unlearned, rude and ignorant. Then Josephus, the Jewish historian, tells us of Apollinaris, who affirmed that both Jews and Christians were more foolish than barbarians. As for Augustine, did he not say, "Any one that begins to be godly, presently he must prepare to suffer reproach from the tongues of adversaries"?

Paulus Fagius told the story of an Egyptian, who tore into the reputation of Christians saying that they were "a gathering together of a most filthy, lecherous people." Because they kept the Sabbath, he went on to say, "they had a disease that was upon them, and they were fain to rest on the seventh day because of that disease." Cyrian, his foes called *Coprian,* which means, one that gathers up dung, because they said that all the excellent things he had dealt with in his writings were but dung. Well, does not the Bible warn us?—*Beware when all men speak well of thee.*

In his appeal to the dread tribunal of God, David tells Him that if he was guilty of the words of Cush then, *let my enemy tread down my life upon the earth, and lay mine honor in the dust,* 7:5. Doubtless the allusion here is to the manner in which the vanquished were often treated in battle, when they were ridden over by horses, and trampled by oncoming foes in the dust. David declared himself ready to suffer the utmost indignity and scorn if what Cush had said to Saul was true. As for the illustration of honor being trodden in the dust, we know that when Achilles dragged the body of Hector in the dust around the walls of Troy, he did but carry out the usual manners of the barbarous times in which he lived. One needs to have a golden character who dares, as David did, to challenge such an ordeal.

The phrase, *The Lord trieth the hearts and reins,* 7:9, gave Francis Quarles, unique poet of the early 16th century, his inspiration for the lines—

> I that alone an Infinite, can try
> How deep within itself thine heart can lie,
> Thy seaman's plummet can but reach the ground,
> I find that which thine heart itself ne'er found.

Illiricus tells a story that illustrates the conception David gives us of Divine judgment upon the godless. *He hath also prepared for him the instruments of death; he ordaineth his arrows against the persecutors,* 13. It concerns one Felix, Earl of Wartenberg, one of the captains of the

Emperor Charles V, who swore in the presence of many at supper, that before he died he would ride up to the spurs in the blood of the Lutherans. Here was one eaten up by malice, but God had His arrows to shoot at him, for that very night the Divine hand struck him, and he strangled and choked in his own blood, and did not ride out to bathe himself in the blood of the Lutherans, as he boasted he would do, but in his own blood as he died.

It would seem as if Cush was paid back in his own coin under the figure David gives of a man digging a ditch for someone else to fall into, but drops into it himself. *He made a pit, and digged it, and is fallen into the ditch which he made, 7:15.* The practice of making pits in ancient times was a stratagem used, not only for ensnaring wild beasts, but also for the trapping of the enemy in time of war. David's thought is that having made a pit for man or beast, and covered it over so completely as to disguise the danger, the digger himself inadvertently treads on his own trap, and suffers the agony he had meant for another.

Then the proverb that "curses are like young chickens, they always come home to roost," is behind the further, appealing description David gives of the wrongdoers' retribution. *His mischief shall return upon his own head, and his violent dealing shall come down upon his own pate, 7:16.* The story of Phalaris's bull invented for the torment of others, but serving afterwards for himself, is notorious in heathen history, but fittingly illustrates the idea the Psalmist expresses. Then it was a voluntary judgment which Archbishop Cranmer inflicted on himself when he thrust that very hand into the fire, and burnt it, with which he had signed the popish articles, crying out, *Oh, my unworthy right hand!* Mischief returned upon his own head. Men have burned their own fingers when they were hoping to brand their neighbor's.

Psalm 8

This marvelous Psalm is another John Ruskin includes in his section of Psalms, summing up all the wisdom of society and of the individual. It is rightly styled *The Song of the Astronomer,* for David's remarkable description of the aerial heavens has never been excelled. As Dr. A. Chalmers, the famous Scottish editor of the early 18th century beautifully expressed it—

> There is much in the scenery of a nocturnal sky, to lift the soul to pious contemplation. That moon, and these stars, what are they? They are detached from the world, and they lift us above it. We feel withdrawn from the earth, and rise in lofty abstraction from this little theatre of human passions and human anxieties. The mind abandons itself to reverie, and is transferred in the ecstasy of its thought to distant and unexplored regions. It sees nature in the simplicity of her great elements, and it sees the God of Nature invested with the high attributes of wisdom and majesty.

These must have been the feelings of David when, one cool evening, he looked up at the starry heavens and found himself lost in wonder and praise, and then wrote this hymn of delight, in which he extolled the Lord's greatness, and declared His condescension toward man.

Chaucer has few quotes from the Psalms, and when he does cite them, he places his quotations in the mouths of persons like the Prioress, who begins the prologue of her tale with the lines—

> 'O Lord, our Lord, Thy name how marvelous
> Is in this large worldly-sprad,' quod she. 8:1, 2.

The first and last verses of the Psalm present the same note of exclamation. *O Lord our Lord, how excellent is thy name in all the earth,* 8:1, 9. Repetition in Scripture usually implies Divine emphasis, and stress is laid in the Psalm upon the whole of creation being radiant with the excellency of God's power.

Martin of Tours, 316-96, whose influence on French history has been accepted by most secular historians, found himself favored by the inhabitants of Tours as their Bishop. But a few, led by another Bishop, Defensor by name, objected to the meanness of Martin's personal appearance, his unkempt hair, and his squalid garments. It was by a verse from the Psalms, however, that the election was decided. A bystander, opening the Psalter at hazard, read the verse, "Out of the mouth of very babes and sucklings hast Thou ordained strength, because of Thine enemies; *That Thou mighest still the enemy and the avenger,"* 8:2. The words were hailed as an omen. Defensor and his adherents were confounded, and Martin was consecrated as Bishop of Tours in 372. It was he who founded *Marmontier,* the most celebrated of French monasteries.

When Jesus was here on earth the proud Pharisees were silent, but the children cried, Hosannah! In his gruesome *Book of Martyrs,* Fox tells how a valiant believer by the name of Lawrence was burned at Colchester who, when he was carried in a chair to the fire to be burned, because, through the cruelty of the Papists, he could not stand upright, several young children gathered around the fire, and prayed as well as they could—"Lord, strengthen thy servant, and keep thy promise." God answered the cry out of the mouths of those babes and sucklings, and Lawrence died firmly and calmly for his Master.

George Wishart, the great Scotch martyr, was once told by a Popish chaplain that he had a devil in him, but a child standing nearby cried out, "A devil cannot speak such words as yonder man speaketh." George Whitefield, the renowned evangelist in one of his letters, detailed the persecution he received when he first preached in Moorfields in this way—

> I cannot help adding that several little boys and girls, who were fond of sitting around me on the pulpit while I preached and handed me people's notes—though they were often pelted with eggs and dirt, thrown at me— never once gave way; but on the contrary, every time I was struck, turned up their little weeping eyes, and seemed to wish they could receive the blows for me. God make them, in their growing years, great and living martyrs for Him who, out of the mouths of babes and sucklings, perfects praise.

There may be a vast contrast between the glory of the heavens, and the little mouths of babes and sucklings, yet by both the name of the Lord is made excellent.

What a captivating phrase that is, "When I consider *thy heavens, the work of thy fingers!* 8:3." It was this magnificent description that inspired Edward Young to pen the lines—

> This prospect vast, what is it?—weigh'd aright,
> 'Tis nature's system of divinity,
> And every student of the night inspires.
> 'Tis elder Scripture, writ by God's own hand:
> Scripture authentic! uncorrupt by man.

Bernard Palissy, the Huguenot potter, who invented *Palissy Ware,* with its lustrous glaze and lifelike reproductions of natural objects, was mocked by his neighbors, and bitterly reproached by his family for beggaring them in his wanderings to observe the beauty and variety of nature that, with his marvelous skill, he could imitate. One day he compared the infinite power and wisdom and goodness of God to his own petty cares and trials, and said, "I have fallen on my face, and adoring God, cried unto Him in spirit, *What is man that Thou art mindful of him?*" 8:4. Several poets have put into verse that question of the Psalmist, *What is man?* We have chosen the stanza Edward Young, poet of the 17th century, gave to the world—

> How poor, how rich, how abject, how august,
> How complicate, how wonderful is man!
> How passing wonder HE who made him such!
> Who centered in our make such strange extremes!
> How different natures marvelously mix'd,
> Connexion exquisite of distant worlds!
> Distinguish'd link in being; endless chain!
> Midway from nothing to the Deity!
> A bean ethereal, sullied and absord'd,
> Though sullied and dishonor'd, still divine!
> Dim miniature of greatness absolute!
> An heir of glory! a frail child of dust!
> *Helpless*, immortal! Insect *infinite*!
> A worm! a god! I tremble at myself,
> And in myself am lost.

Dungeons in the Tower, London, still record the power of the Psalms to soothe "sorrow, sighing" of Roman Catholics who suffered for their faith. Philip Howard, Earl of Arundel, in 1587 inscribed upon the walls, "Thou madest him lower than the angels; to crown him with glory and worship," 8:5. Lovers of Scripture have found in verses 5, 6, 7, 8, the lowly position Jesus assumed for our sakes, and yet His coming universal providential dominion. Manhood's glory is the glory of our nature in the Person of the Lord Jesus. That Christ is the principal Subject of this Psalm, is interpreted by Him, both by our Lord Himself, Matt. 21:16, and by the Apostle Paul, 1 Cor. 15:27; Heb. 2:6, 7.

Rule over the material world, and also of the intellectual or spiritual creation is implied in the phrase, *Thou hast put all things under his feet,* 8:6. Hermodius, a nobleman born, upbraided the valiant captain Iphicrates for that he was but a shoemaker's son. "My blood," said Iphicrates, "taketh beginning at me; and thy blood, at thee now taketh her farewell"; intimating that he, not honoring his house with the glory of his virtues, as the house had honored him with the title of nobility, was but as a wooden knife put into an empty sheath to fill up the place; but for himself, he, by his valorous achievements was now beginning to be the raiser of his family. Thus, in the matter of spirituality, he is but gentleman that is the best Christian. Ancient trade guilds have found in the Psalms the legend of their Charter of Incorporation. For instance, the *Butchers Company* chose Psalm 8:6, 7—*Omnia subgleisti sub jedibus, oves et boves.*

Psalm 9

Among the various interpretations of the heading of this Psalm perhaps the most feasible is that of the Chaldee explanation that "it concerns the death of the Champion who went out between the camps"—a reference to Goliath of Gath, or some other mighty Philistine, on account of whose death this Psalm was likely written in after years by David. Mystically, we have a reference to the victory of the Son of God over the champion of evil, even the enemy of souls, 9:6. This Psalm is evidently a triumphal hymn which should strengthen the faith of the valiant soldier of Christ, and likewise stimulate the courage of the timid saint as he thinks of Him on whose vesture and thigh is written, King of kings and Lord of lords! We are justified, then, in calling the Psalm *The Song of the Conqueror.*

The abundant theme of praise is *all thy marvelous works,* 9:1. Creation, Scripture, Providence, and Redemption, are all marvelous, as exhibiting the attributes of God in such a degree as to excite the wonder of all God's universe. *I will be glad, and rejoice in thee,* 9:2. Here gladness and joy are combined because they form the appropriate spirit in which to praise the goodness of the Lord. A writer of the 18th century reminds us that sailors give a cheery cry as they weigh anchor; the ploughman whistles in the morning as he drives his team; the milkmaid sings her rustic song as she sets about her early task: when soldiers are leaving friends behind them, they do not march out to the tune of *Dead March in Saul,* but to the quick notes of a lively air. Thus a praising spirit accomplishes for us all what their songs and music did for them. As the evil spirit in Saul yielded to the influence of the harp of the son of Jesse, so the spirit of melancholy often takes flight, when we take up the song of praise and thus glorify God.

The Lord also will be a refuge for the oppressed, 9:9. It was to be said that the Egyptians, living in the fens, and being vexed with gnats, used to sleep in high towers. As the troublesome insects could not soar so high, the people were delivered from their sting. When we would be bitter with cares and fear, what a high, safe refuge God is to which to flee.

The Name, so highly praised in the previous Psalm, still rings in the ear of the sweet singer of Israel. *They that know thy name shall put their trust in thee,* 9:10. *Name,* emphasizing all God is in Himself, celebrates the confidence of those who "know" that "name" as if its fragrance still breathed in the atmosphere around. This precious verse presents the triad of Knowledge, Faith, and Experience.

Sing praises unto the Lord, 9:11. In all revivals in Church history, there has been a sudden outburst of the spirit of song. Luther's Psalms and Hymns were in all men's mouths, and in later revivals under Wesley and Whitefield the strains of Charles Wesley, Toplady, Hart, Newton, and others were the outgrowth of restored piety. The singing of the birds of praise fitly accompanies the return of the gracious spring of Divine visitation through the preaching of the Gospel of the Happy God.

An historical illustration of the affirmation, *The wicked is snared in the work of his own hands,* 9:16, can be found, not only in Haman on the gallows he had prepared for Mordecai, but also in the French Revolution, when, of its horrors we read that "within nine months of the death of the Queen Marie Antoinette by the guillotine, every one implicated in her untimely end, her accusers, the judges, the jury, the prosecutors, the witnesses, all, every one at least whose fate is known, perished by the same instrument as their innocent victims—a further confirmation of the verse—"In the net which they had laid for her was their own foot taken—into the pit which they digged for her did they themselves fall."

There is no more solemn pronouncement in Scripture than the emphatic one David uses in this Psalm of *the wicked shall be turned into hell,* 9:17. Men may try to explain away the final abode of torment; but it is still there. John Milton describes it—

> *Hell,* their fit habitation, fraught with fire
> Unquenchable, the house of woe and pain.

Only a Divine schoolmaster can teach men who grow so vain, that they are but men, whose breath is in their nostrils, the Creator can withdraw at any moment. Rulers are apt to forget that the crowns they wear leave them *but men:* that degrees of the eminent learning make their owners not more than *men,* valor and conquest cannot elevate beyond the dead level of *but men;* and all the wealth of Croesus, and the wisdom of Solomon, the power of Alexander, the eloquence of Demosthenes, if added together, would leave the possessor but a man.

Psalm 10

Henry Martyn, who was welcomed to India by Dr. William Carey, in turn, at the end of his career, blessed Alexander Duff who had come to take over his sphere. Tottering, and with outstretched hands he gladly welcomed Duff to the land he had given his life for. Martyn's *Journal*—a missionary classic—has the entry, "It was Psalm 10 that he was reading to Lydia Grenfell when he was hastily summoned to rejoin his ship, and they parted forever on earth. During his long and tedious voyage, surrounded by uncongenial companions, it was the Psalter that he turned to for comfort."

Titleless, this 10th Psalm is thought by some to be a fragment of Psalm 9, but, being complete in itself, we should treat it as a separate composition. Because its prevailing theme appears to be the oppression and persecution of the righteous by the wicked, we can entitle the Psalm *The Cry of the Oppressed for Deliverance*. Augustine, however, thought of it as *The Psalm of the Antichrist*.

Many are the historical incidents emphasizing the literality of the teachings of this Psalm. Saints have gathered comfort from it while smarting under the hand of proud sinners. Take verse 2—*The wicked in his pride doth persecute the poor: let them be taken in the devices that they have imagined.* That famous persecutor of believers, Domitian, like others of the Roman Emperors, assumed Divine honors, and heated the furnace seven times hotter against Christians because they refused to worship his image. Further, many of the Popes of Rome decorated themselves with the blasphemous titles of *Masters of the World* and *Universal Fathers,* while at the same time they let loose their bloodhounds upon the faithful. Pride with them, and others, became the egg of persecution.

Take another delineation of the wicked who, *through the pride of his countenance will not seek after God: God is not in all his thoughts,* 10:4. The Athenians were not far from the truth when they ordained that men should be tried in the dark lest their countenances should weigh with the judges; for there is much more to be learned from the motions of the muscles of the face than from the words of the lips. Honesty shines in the face, Spurgeon says, but villainy peeps out at the eyes. As for God not being in all the thoughts of men whose countenance betrays them, some read the passage *All his thoughts are, there is no God.* Those who do not seek after God become practical atheists.

Seneca, heathen though he was, said that there are no atheists, though there would be some: if any say there is no God, they lie; though they say it in the day time, yet in the night when they are alone they deny it; howsoever some desperately harden themselves, yet if God doth but show himself terrible to them they confess him. Diagoras, a grand atheist of his time, when troubled with the strangullion, acknowledged the Diety he had denied: How blessed we are if we have God in all our thoughts, and controlling our whole life!

Is there not an allusion to certain venomous reptiles said to carry bags of poison under their teeth with which, with great subtlety they inflict the most deadly injuries to those within their reach, in the Psalmist's phrase, *Under his tongue is mischief and vanity,* 10:7? As for those who sit in *the lurking places of the villages,* 10:8, Arab robbers used to lurk like a wolf among sand-heaps, springing out suddenly upon the solitary traveler, robbing him with swiftness, then plunging again into the Wilderness of the reedy downs where pursuit was fruitless. The whole imagery of verses 8-10 bid us beware of those evil forces lying in wait to rob us of heavenly treasures as we travel through the wilderness of this world. Hungry lions are crouching in every den to catch us as Quarles warns us in his memorable lines—

> The close pursuers' busy hands do plant
> Snares in thy substance; snares attend thy wants;
> Snares in thy credit; snares in thy disgrace;
> Snares in thy high estate; snares in thy base;
> Snares tuck thy bed; and snares surround thy board;
> Snares watch thy thoughts; and snares attack thy word;
>
> Snares in thy quiet; snares in thy commotion;
> Snares in thy diet; snares in thy devotion;
> Snares lurk in thy resolves; snares in thy doubt;
> Snares lie within thy heart, and snares without;
> Snares are above thy head, and snares beneath;
> Snares in thy sickness; snares are in thy death.

Andrew Bonar, commenting on the verse *The Lord is King for ever and ever: the heathen are perished out of the land,* 10:16, says that "such confidence and faith must appear to the World strange and unaccountable. The story is told of a man that his powers of vision were so extraordinary, that he could see distinctly the fleet of the Carthaginians entering the harbor of Carthage, while he stood himself at Lilyboeum, in Sicily. But many of his friends failed to believe he had such a power. A man seeing across an ocean, and able to tell of objects so far off! He could feast his vision on what others saw not. Even thus does faith now stand at its Lilyboeum, and see the long tossed fleet entering safely the desired haven, enjoying the bliss of that still distant day, as if it was already come."

That the tears of the poor appeal for vengeance from God, is illustrated for us by Hugh Latimer, who was burned as a martyr, in his observation on God as the judge of *the fatherless and the oppressed,* 10:18. Cambyses was a great Emperor, having many lord deputies, lord presidents, and lieutenants under him. Representing him in his dominions was a deputy who was a briber, a gift-taker, a gratifier of rich men, who followed gifts as fast as he that ran; a handmaker in his office, to make his son a great man, as the old saying has it, "Happy is the child whose father goeth to the Devil." The cry of a poor widow came to the Emperor's ear, and caused him to slay the deputy, and lay his skin on his chair of judgment, that all judges who should give judgment afterward, should sit on the same skin which became a goodly sign of justice. God is ever the Judge of widows, and the Father of the fatherless, and hears the cry of the oppressed as they turn to Him.

Psalm 11

Mary, Queen of Scots, who was executed at Fotheringay in 1587 was entreated by her executioner to forgive him for having been ordered to kill her. "I forgive all," she cried. After a handkerchief was bound over her eyes she "kneeled down upon the cushion resolutely, and without any token of fear of death," repeated aloud this precious Psalm, and said aloud several times, "Into Thy hands I commend my spirit."

John Welsh, the renowed Scottish warrior for the cause of Christ, was brought along with other prisoners from Blackness, on the Firth of Forth, to appear before the Court at Linlithgow. As they walked by night under guard to their trial, they sang this Psalm, in the old version which begins—

> I trust in God, how dare ye then
>   Say thus my soul untill;
> Flee hence as fast as any fowle,
>   And hid you in your hill?

It was while Welsh and his fellow-sufferers were lying in their dungeon, deep and dark, below the level of the sea, that they received a letter from Lady Melville, of Calcross, one of the noblest women of her time, bidding them be thankful that they were only "in the darkness of Blackness, and not in the blackness of darkness."

Among the various explanations of the historicity of this short, sweet Psalm we give preference to that of Charles Simeon, a very safe and spiritual commentator of a past generation. Herewith is his most excellent Summary of this *Song of the Stedfast*—

> The Psalms are a rich repository of experimental knowledge. David, at different periods of his life, was placed in almost every situation, in which a believer, whether rich or poor, can be placed; in these heavenly compositions he delineates all the workings of the heart. He introduces, too, the sentiments and conduct of the various persons who were necessary either to his troubles or his joys; and thus sets before us a compendium of all that is passing in the hearts of men throughout the world. When he penned Psalm 11, he was under persecution from Saul, who sought his life, and hunted him, "as a partridge upon the mountains." His timid friends were afraid for his safety and recommended him to flee to some mountain where he had a hiding-place and then to conceal himself from the rage of Saul. But David,

being strong in faith, spurned the idea of resorting to any such pusillanimous
expedients, and determined confidently to repose his trust in God.

David's holy confidence in the hour of trial comes in the opening
phrase of the Psalm—*In the Lord put I my trust.* Before Anne Askew was
burned at the stake at Smithfield in 1546, she composed and sang a heart-
moving ballad of this first verse of Psalm 11, made up of 14 stanzas, 4 of
which we quote—

> Like as an arméd knight,
> Appointed to the field,
> With this World will I fight,
> And Christ shall be my Shield.

> Faith is the weapon strong,
> Which will not fail at need;
> My foes, therefore, among,
> Therewith will I proceed.

> More enemies now I have
> Than hairs upon mine head;
> Let them not be deprave,
> But fight Thou in my stead.

> On these my care I cast,
> For all their cruel spite;
> I set not by their haste;
> For Thou art my delight.

Martyrs of old would not accept deliverance from their sufferings on
base terms. No fleeing away as birds to the mountains for them. They
scorned to fly away for the enjoyment of rest except it were with the
wings of a dove, covered with silver innocence. The tormentors who grew
tired of torturing Blandian, protested, "We are ashamed, O Emperor! The
Christians laugh at your cruelty, and grow the more resolute." Those persecutors counted such martyr-courage as obstinacy, because they were
ignorant of the secret armor saints wear about their hearts.

Birds are prominent in the description given of David in his trials and
triumphs. The feathered creation is rich in symbolic teaching.

> In prosperity, when in full control of himself and his nation, David
> was an *Eagle*—
> In adversity, when condemned, he was like an *Owl*—
> In devotion, when alone, he was as a *Pelican*—
> In solitariness, when deserted, he was as a *Sparrow*—
> In persecution, when fearing the company of foes, he was like a
> *Partridge*.

Here, in the opening verse of Psalm 11, David's enemies urge him to *flee as a bird to the mountain,* which he did in a real sense when he speedily betook himself to Him Who is our hiding-place in the storms of life, for in Him alone was succor and security.

Because His children are precious to Him, God refines them with afflictions. He does not spare them trials, seeing that trial is the channel of many blessings as William Cowper emphasizes in his poem on the announcement, *The Lord trieth the righteous,* 11:5.

> 'Tis my happiness below
>> Not to live without the cross;
> But the Savior's power to know,
>> Sanctifying every loss
>
> Trials make the promise sweet;
>> Trials give new life to prayer;
> Trials bring me to his feet—
>> Lay me low, and keep me there.
>
> Did I meet no trials here—
>> No chastisement by the way—
> Might I not, with reason, fear
>> I should prove a cast-away?
>
> Bastards may escape the rod,
>> Sunk in earthly vain delight;
> But the true-born child of God
>> Must not—would not, if he might.

God's judgment upon the wicked is terrible to contemplate—*He shall rain snares, fire and brimstone, and an horrible tempest,* 11:6. The combatants at the Lake Thrasymene are said to have been so engrossed with the conflict, that neither party perceived the convulsions of nature that shook the ground—

> An earthquake reeled unheedingly away,
> None felt stern nature rocking at his feet.

Is it not thus with the godless who fail to realize the terrible judgment awaiting them? For those who are in Him Who is their Refuge, there is no fear of such convulsions. The phrase, *the portion of their cup,* means, the allotment of their cup, and was the expression used in connection with the custom of distributing to each guest his mess of meat. At the Great White Throne, each among condemned sinners will receive his just portion of judgment.

Psalm 12

One of the best known hymns Martin Luther wrote for the German people was founded in the first verse, "Help, Lord: for the godly man ceaseth." The hymn commences, "Ah, Lord, from Heaven look down and see."

John Ruskin included this Psalm of David in the first half of the Psalter which sums up all the wisdom of society and of the individual. In his volume, *Our Fathers Have Told Us,* Ruskin says that Psalms 1, 8, 12, 14, 15, 19, 23 and 24, well studied and believed, suffice for all personal guidance; Psalms 48, 72 and 75 contain the law and the prophecy of all just government.

At least two incidents are recorded as to the influence of verse 5 of this Psalm. "For the oppression of the poor, for the sighing of the needy, now will I arise, saith the Lord; I will set him in safety from him that puffeth at him." The first historical account concerns a ship carrying religious exiles, driven by a fearful storm on to the coast of Barbary. Facing either death by the lashing waves or captivity among the Moors, they sang this Psalm and as they reached the 5th verse, the ship went to pieces, and most of them perished in the sea, or passed through the sea to Glory.

The second story of this same verse is that it was the text Fabricius preached from before Gustavus Adolphus, after he had taken Augsberg after a severe fight. A solemn thanksgiving was held in the principal church, and religious liberty was proclaimed in the city of the famous Confession, while the ferocious Tilly, after his defeat, retired breathing out threatenings and slaughter.

In this further Psalm of David, we have a title almost identical to that given to Psalm 6. Reading the Psalm as a whole it would seem to be a song of complaining faith in the light of the Lord's coming to break in pieces the oppressor. It was probably written while Saul was persecuting and pursuing David, and those who were his supporters. *Good Thoughts in Bad Times,* is the heading Spurgeon gives to the Psalm.

With a double heart do they speak, 12:2. The Chinese consider a man of two hearts to be a very base man, and we are safe in reckoning all flatterers to be such. Those who only extol us to our face, only show one side of their heart. "He who puffs up another's heart, has nothing better than wind in his own." "Flattery is the sign of the tavern where duplicity is the host." But destruction awaits those of flattering lips, and tongues speaking proud things. 12:3. These free-talkers, who are usually free-thinkers, will be silenced one day by Him Who is indeed Lord over them.

The philosopher Bion being asked what animal he thought the most hurtful replied, "That of wild creatures a tyrant, and of tame ones a flatterer." Raleigh, himself a courtier, who was initiated into the whole art of flattery, discovered in his own career and fate its dangerous and deceptive power, its deep artifice and deeper falsehood, and came to write, "A flatterer is said to be a beast that boteth smiling. But it is hard to know them from friends—they are so obsequious and full of protestations; for as a wolf resembles a dog, so doth a flatterer a friend."

If God is provoked by those of flattering lips and tongues then He has the prerogative *to cut them off,* 12:3, 4. There may be an allusion here to those terrible but suggestive punishments which Oriental monarchs were wont to execute on criminals. Lips were cut off and tongues torn out when offenders were convicted of lying or stealing. Infinitely more terrible is the punishment of those who sin both by life and lip.

There are those who still think that with *their tongues they can prevail,* 12:4. There is the historical account of twelve poor and unlearned men on the one side, all the eloquence of Greece and Rome arrayed on the other. From the time of Tertullius to that of Julian the Apostate, every species of oratory, learning, wit, was lavished against the Church of God, and the result, like the well-known story of that dispute between the Christian peasant and the heathen philosopher, when the latter, having challenged the assembled fathers of a synod to silence him, was put to shame by the simple faith of the former—"In the name of our Lord Jesus Christ, I command thee to be dumb."

What a sterling tribute to the veracity of Scripture is the positive declaration, *The words of the Lord are pure words,* 12:6. Montesquieu said of Voltaire, "When Voltaire reads a book, he makes it what he pleases, and then writes against it what he has made." It is no difficult matter to besmear and blot the pages of the Bible, and then impute the foul stains that men of corrupt minds have cast upon it, to its stainless Author. But if we honestly look at it as it is, we shall find that like its Author, it is without blemish and without spot.

> The words of Jehovah are pure words—
> Silver refined in the crucible—
> Gold, seven times washed from the earth.

This Psalm closes with the lament that *the wicked walk on every side, when the vilest men are exalted,* 12:8, of which history affords striking examples. For those of us, however, who are saved and safe through Christ, we can sing this mournful song of David's with hearts in full accord with its mingled melody of lowly mourning and lofty confidence.

Psalm 13

John Calvin, who introduced the chanting of the Psalms into the public worship of the Reformed Church, in Geneva in 1541, always turned to the Psalms in mental troubles. Dying in the throes of pain, he repeated Psalm 6:3 and 19:10, and his last words were a fragment from Psalm 13:1, "How long, O Lord?"

Gregory of Decapolis told the story of a noble Saracen, converted by a vision of the Lamb of God, and who, under a Christian teacher, learned all the Psalms by heart, and returned to his own land to preach the Christ he had found. But his own countrymen refused to listen to his message, and stoned him to death. In his final agony he repeated the words, "Lighten mine eyes, that I sleep not in death," 13:3.

Humorously, Spurgeon says, "We have been wont to call this the *How Long Psalm*. We had almost said the *Howling Psalm,* from the incessant repetition of the cry *how long.*" The man after God's own heart, who has not yet found occasion to use the language of this brief ode, will do so before long, seeing that it expresses the feelings of the people of God in those ever-returning trials besetting them. All attempts to find a birthplace of the Psalm in David's history, are only guesses. It is the language of every much tried man of God.

When grief is prominent we are apt to play most on the worst string. "We set up monumental stones over the graves of our joys, but who thinks of erecting monuments of praise for mercies received? We write four books of *Lamentations* and only one of *Canticles* and are far more at home in wailing out a *Miserere* than in chanting a *Te Deum.*" But the writer of this doleful Psalm goes on to say, *Those that trouble me rejoice when I am moved,* 13:4, that is, they compose comedies out of our tragedies. James Thomson, poet of the 17th century gave us this stanza on such rejoicing troublers—

> Ah! can you bear contempt; the venom's tongue
> Of those whom ruin pleases, the keen sneer,
> The lewd reproaches of the rascal herd:
> Who for the self-same actions, if successful,
> Would be as grossly lavish in your praise?
> To sum up all in one—can you support
> To mournful glances, the malignant joy,
> Or more detested pity of a rival—
> Of a triumphant rival?

47

That the Lord is able to give us songs in the night, as well as in the day-time, is the testimony of the writer of this 13th Psalm with its mournful sighs—*I will sing unto the Lord,* 13:6. John Philpot, sufferer for Christ's sake, had every reason to be sad after being imprisoned for so long in the Bishop of London's coal-house, in the 16th century. One day the Bishop sent for him and asked him why he was so merry in prison, rejoicing in his naughtiness, when he should have been sorry and full of lament. Philpot replied, "My lord, the mirth which we make is but singing certain Psalms, as we are commanded by Paul, to rejoice in the Lord, singing together hymns and psalms, for we are in a dark, comfortless place, and therefore, we thus solace ourselves. Though we are in misery, yet we refresh our selves with such singing." Then Philpot was carried back to his coal-house where as he said, "I, with my six fellow prisoners, do rouze together in the straw, as cheerfully—I thank God—as others do in their beds of down."

A notable feature of this 13th—this number is ominous because of the associations of such a figure—is that although it begins with a sigh it ends with a song. Moaning gives way to music, *I will sing unto the Lord,* 13:6. The six verses of the Psalm show the stages from grousing to gladness, two verses for each, *mourning, praying, rejoicing.* It would seem as if the Psalm had been composed by two men of contrary feelings, one sad, the other glad. But David, after weeping, cleared his throat for a song, believing that—

Sorrows remembered sweeten present joy.

Avowing his confidence, *I have trusted in thy mercy,* the Psalmist proved that as the shipwrecked mariner clings to his mast, so he had clung to his faith in God, and so rejoiced in His salvation and in His bounty.

Psalm 14

Who but a fool, and a corrupt one at that, as the context shows, could say in his heart and utter with his lips, that "There is no God," or, "No God for me!" How full the world is of avowed and practical atheists! Fear has ever ruled in the hearts of the people, and on the throne and all implied in its stability, as Queen Elizabeth did in the 15th century. Her love for the Psalter is revealed in her version of this 14th Psalm, which begins—

> Fooles, that true fayth yet never had,
> Sayeth in their hartes, there is no God!
> Fylthy they are in their practyse,
> Of them not one is godly wyse.

Henry Martyn had the item under 4th September, 1812, in his *Journal,* "I beguiled the hours of the night thinking of Psalm 14." Prothero remarks that "the genius of Bacon is one of the glories of the Elizabethan age." He also studied and quoted the Psalm. In his essay *On Atheism,* he comments on the first verse of Psalm 14, that the fool who said in his heart, *There is no God,* "saith it rather by rote to himself, as that he would have then what he can throughly believe it or be persuaded of it."

Baldwin, Archbishop of Canterbury in the 11th century, who led Crusaders, became horror-stricken at the licentiousness prevalent among the host, and his horror was summed up by his Chaplain in the words of the 2nd verse of this Psalm, "God is not in the camp. There is none that doeth good, no not one."

A peculiarity of this Psalm is that it appears twice in the Psalter, for the 14th and 53rd Psalms are the same, with the alterations of one or two expressions at the most. Then, with instructive alterations, Paul transcribes the greater part of it in his argument that both Jews and Gentiles are under sin, Romans 3:10-12. Spurgeon would give this admirable ode the heading, *Concerning Practical Atheism,* seeing that it displays the atheist as a *fool,* pre-eminently, and a fool universally.

The word for "fool" used here is *Nabal,* which takes us back to David's association with Abigail, whose wealthy husband was Nabal, and who, because he refused food to David's men in time of need earned the Psalmist's displeasure, so much so, that he threatened to kill Nabal. Abigail, pleading for the life of her worthless husband said to David, "Let not my lord regard this man of Belial, even Nabal: for as his name *is,* so *is* he; Nabal is his name, and folly is with him," 1 Sam. 25:25. What Abigail actually said was, He's a fool by name, and a fool by nature.

The word David used for *fool* has the significance of fading, dying, or falling away, as a withered leaf of flower, and used of a person indicates that he has lost the juice and sap of wisdom, reason, honesty, and godliness. John Trapp calls such a man, "that sapless fellow, that carcase of a man, that walking sepulchre of himself, in all religion and right reason is withered and wasted, dried up and destroyed." Atheism, The Creed of Fools, robs those who embrace it of all nobility of character. *They are corrupt.* Of this, we are certain, such a Creed is not accepted in Hell.

> On earth are atheists many,
> In Hell there is not any.

The Italian poet of a past century, Giovanni Cotta, composed the following stanza based on the opening statement of this Psalm—

> "There is no God," the fool in secret said:
> There is no God that rules or earth or sky.
> Tear off the band that binds the wretch's head,
> That God may burst upon his faithless eye!
> Is there a God?—The stars in myriads spread,
> If he look up, the blasphemy deny;
> While his own features, in the mirror read
> Reflect the image of Divinity.
> Is there a God?—The stream that silver flows,
> The air he breathes, the ground he treads, the trees,
> The flowers, the grass, the sands, each wind that blows,
> All speak of God; throughout one voice agrees,
> And eloquent, his dread existence shows:
> Blind to himself, ah, see him, fool, in these.

Rejecting God, the fool becomes *altogether filthy*, 14:3. The Hebrew for "filthy" means, *stinking*. A Roman satirist describes those of this our age thus—

> Nothing is left, nothing, for future times
> To add to the full catalogue of crimes,
> The baffled sons must feel the same desires,
> And set the same mad follies as their sires,
> Vice has attained its zenith.

A further trait of these godless fools is, *They eat up my people as they eat bread,* 14:4. Daily and duly, as they eat bread, so with the same eagerness and voracity they become man-eaters, cruel cannibals, who are ready to destroy God's people as they are to eat a good meal when hungry. As quaint John Trapp expressed it—

> Like pickerels in a pond, or sharks in the sea, they devour the poorer, as these do the lesser fishes; and that many times with a plausible, invisible consumption; as the usurer, who, like the ostrich, can digest any metal; but especially money."

Plundered, shamed, and mocked, the righteous although poor, had the Lord as their refuge, and when He turned their captivity into blessed freedom they confessed, *We are like unto them that dream*, 14:7. Their release, however, was no dream, but a glorious reality, so beautifully expressed by one of the greatest poets of the early 16th century, Giles Fletcher in his poem *Christ's Triumph Over Death*—

> No sorrow now hangs clouding on their brow,
> No bloodless malady impales their face:
> No age drops on their hairs his silver snow;
> No nakedness their bodies doth embrace;
> No poverty themselves and their disgrace;
> No fear of death the joy of life devours;
> No unchaste sleep their precious time deflowers;
> No loss, no grief, no change, wait on their winged hours.

Psalm 15

Included in Ruskin's selections of Psalms to be well studied and believed and deemed sufficient for all personal guidance, is Psalm 15, which, along with Psalm 16 is mentioned by Henry Martyn in his *Journal*, "September 10—All day at the village, writing down notes on the 15th and 16th Psalms."

Sir Charles Warren, past General in the British Army, who was responsible for excavations at Jerusalem for the *Palestine Exploration Fund* and author of *Underground Jerusalem*, and who also commanded the troops against the Bechuanas, left this testimony on record—

> As a child my father taught me to repeat every morning the 15th Psalm: "Lord, who shall abide in Thy tabernacle?" etc. That chapter is still with me at any time wherever I may be, and I should say that its possession at all times has been a blessing to me.

John Wilson, who, under the pen-name of Christopher North wrote *Lights and Shadows of Scottish Life,* chose this Psalm to be sung at "the elder's death-bed," for, "it was the custom in Scotland that the ransomed of the Lord returned and came to Zion with songs." Down the centuries, men in every walk of life who have been an honor and strength to the Church, and country were those who lived in the spirit of this Psalm.

> Within Thy tabernacle, Lord,
>   Who shall abide with Thee?
> And in Thy high and holy hill
>   Who shall a dweller be?
> The man that walketh uprightly,
>   And worketh righteousness,
> And as he thinketh in his heart,
>   So doth he truth express.

William Langland who, in the 14th century, was the Dante of the English people, had a grandeur of conception and nobility of execution that made this English poet the rival of Dante in realistic power. With his love of the Psalm it is not surprising that he should clothe much of his *Vision of Piers Plowman* with their language. In spite of what David said of those who take bribes—"Lord, who shall dwell in Thy tabernacle? He that hath not taken reward against the innocent," Psalm 15:1, 6, Langland yet deemed bribery to be all-powerful.

This remarkable Psalm, bears a striking resemblance to Psalm 24, the composition of both being connected with the removal of the Ark to the holy hill of Zion. Because some unauthorized person had contacted the Ark, David was unable on the first occasion to fulfill his desire of bringing the Ark to Zion. On his second effort, however, he was more careful about who should carry the Ark, and those who should minister in the house of the Lord. As we shall later indicate, the Psalm points to the historical Christ, Who came as the perfect Man, and in Him all who through grace are conformed to His image.

Because the first verse asks a question, and the following verses give both positive and negative answers, the Psalm can be called *Question and Answer Psalm*. It is profitable to see as in a mirror, in both question and answer, the sincerity and holiness of Jesus.

He that walketh uprightly, 15:2. Pomponius is said to have been so true, that he never made lie himself, nor suffered a lie in another. Aristides was so just in his government that he would not tread awry for any respect to friend or despite of foe. Curtius at Rome, Menaeceus at Thebes, Codrus at Athens, exposed themselves into voluntary death, for the good of their neighbors and country. What we are within, is seen in our walk. The inner quality of a tree is judged by its fruit. It is only when the wheels of a clock move within, that the hands on the dial will move without. We judge a spring by the water running from it.

The inner source of character is borne out by the next phrase, *Speaketh the truth in his heart.* Anatomists have observed that the tongue in man is tied with a double string to the heart. Speaking the truth implies the necessity of our agreeing with our heart and thoughts. If we speak the truth as from the heart, then our tongue will not *backbite* others, 15:3. The Hebrew word for "backbiteth" means *to play the spy,* and so metaphorically, a backbiter, after the manner of a spy, notes the faults and defects of others, and speaks of them in a malicious way. Backbiting is a malicious defamation of a man behind his back. Those who pry into the secrets of others, divulge them, and often represent them in a false light, take their place among the worst of men.

Richard Turnbull, Biblical expositor of the 16th century, wrote that "That scorpion hurteth none but such as he touched with the tip of his tail; and the crocodile and basilisk slay none but such as either the force of their sight, or strength of their breath reacheth. The viper woundeth none but such as it biteth; the venomous herbs or roots kill none but such as taste, or handle, or smell them, and so come near unto them; but the poison of slanderous tongues is much more rank and deadly, in that it can spread far and wide."

Contemn, means, to scornfully regard, and so to *contemn* the wicked and honor the godly are opposite one to the other. To the man abiding in the Tabernacle of the Lord, to contemn, or flatter the ungodly is not seemly. Augustine so manifested the hatred he had toward tale-bearers and false reporters of others, that he had the lines written on his table—

> He that doth love with bitter speech the absent to defame,
> Must surely know that at this board no place is for the same.

The other side of the coin in this fourth verse is what all of us should strive for—*He honoreth them that fear the Lord.* George Fox, being asked whether he remembered a poor servant of God who had received succour from him in time of trouble replied, "I remember him well; I tell you, I forgot the Lords and Ladies, to remember such." It was in this respect that John Calvin's resolution concerning Martin Luther was most admirable. These two theological giants differed about the actual presence of Christ in the Sacrament, and Luther being of vehement spirit wrote bitterly against those, like Calvin, who did not hold his views.

But wisely, Calvin did not answer Luther in the same tart manner. Instead the Reformer wrote to a fellow-theologian, most highly respected, and persuaded him to show all due respect to Luther, and consider his worth and excellency, even though he had acted so roughly toward himself. Said Calvin, "Although Luther should call me a devil, yet he would do him honor, to acknowledge him a choice servant of the Lord."

Another portrait of the godly man is the one *that sweareth to his own hurt, and changeth not,* 15:4—a reputation Shakespeare expressed in the lines—

> His words are bonds, his oaths are oracles;
> His love sincere, his thoughts immaculate;
> His tears pure messengers, sent from his heart;
> His heart as far from fraud as heaven from earth.

The Man Christ Jesus is the only One Who perfectly corresponded to such a delineation of unchanging security. It is because of all He is in Himself, and in the life He lived among men, that He can never be moved.

Psalm 16

One of the victims of Government vengeance inflicted upon insurgents was a young Scotsman of twenty-six, Hugh McKail, a well-connected and well-educated young man of fervid poetic ability. Licensed to preach during the reign of Charles II, McKail's last sermon was preached in the High Church of Edinburgh as 400 Presbyterian ministers were being driven from their churches, September 8, 1662. Speaking of the persecutions of the Church he dearly loved McKail said, "She has suffered from an Ahab on the throne, a Haman in the State, and a Judas in the Church."

The prison trials of this scholarly Covenanter were heavy for his tender nature to bear. The torture of the boot, for example, shattered the leg causing terrible pain, yet in such agony McKail had a sense of humor for being asked how his tortured leg was, he replied, "The fear of my neck maketh me forget my leg." Many appeals were made for the sparing of his noble life but all in vain. The evening before his execution in the Grassmarket of Edinburgh, Psalm 16 was the last Scripture to be read by him, and after reading it he said to his father, and those about him, "If there were anything in this world sadly and unwillingly to be left, it were the reading of the Scriptures. I said, *I shall not see the Lord, even the Lord, in the land of the living.* But this needs not make us sad; for, where we go, the Lamb is the Book of Scripture, and the light of that city, and, where he is, there is life— even the river of the water of life, and living springs."

The next day, December 22nd, 1666, at two o'clock in the afternoon, Hugh McKail was carried to the scaffold, and ere he was executed he sang part of Psalm 31, and was encouraged to die triumphantly as he came to the 6th verse in the old metrical rendering—

> Into Thy hands I do commit
>   My spirit; for Thou art He,
> O Thou, Jehovah, God of truth,
>   Who has redeemed me.

Another historical association of Psalm 16 is connected with the departure of William Carey as a missionary to India. He vowed, as he took his farewell to England, that he would never return. The text which supplied the sermon preached at Kettering, in October, 1792, at his dedicatory service was, "They that run after another God shall have great trouble," 16:4. Eternity alone will reveal what this consecrated cobbler accomplished for God among the millions of India.

In mediaeval times ancient families sought their Mottoes in the Psalms. The Beauchamps, for instance, chose *Fortuna mea in bellow campo*, founded on Psalm 16:7.

James Melville found the Psalms the expression of his sorrow, his gratitude, or his triumph, and at the moment of death their message gave him strength and courage. Dying in great pain, he was content as he thought of the sight of the face of God in glory; and rehearsing the twelfth verse of this Psalm in the old Scotch vernacular—"Thow wilt schaw me the path of lyffe; in thy sicth are fulness of all joyes, at thy right hand is the plentie of pleasures for ever," he was comforted.

Because of the influence this Psalm has exerted in the lives of so many, and also because of the value of its contents, we can readily understand why it has been named *The Golden Psalm*. Its matter is as the most fine gold, thus earning the commendation as "David's Jewel." The title *Michtam* is said to mean "golden," or "precious jewel," and so the margin has it, *A Golden Psalm of David*. The works of some of the most excellent Arabian poets were called *Golden* because they were written in letters of gold, and this 16th Psalm, being of surpassing excellence, is worthy of being written in letters of gold.

Some scholars think that *Michtam* is probably a simple derivation of a word signifying "to hide," thereby suggesting a secret or mystery, which suggested to Spurgeon the title—*The Psalm of the Precious Secret*. What makes it most valuable is the way the Apostles referred to it as a prophecy of the Messiah, in which His passion, victory over death and the grace and His subsequent exaltation to the right hand of God are all foretold. Jerome said, "The Psalm pertains to Christ, Who speaks in it . . . It is the voice of our King, which He utters in the human nature that He had assumed, but without detracting from his divine nature . . . The Psalm belongs to His passion." Augustine had a similar interpretation—"Our King speaks in this Psalm of the human nature that he assumed, at the time of his passion, the royal title inscribed will show itself conspicuous."

Doubtless the Early Fathers were influenced by the way Peter, by the Holy Spirit, declared of the Psalm, "David speaketh concerning HIM," Acts 2:25. Then in his memorable sermon Peter unequivocally related the closing part of the Psalm to the Savior he saw crucified and yet raised again from the grave, Acts 2:29-31. Paul, likewise by the same infallible inspiration of the Spirit, saw no man in this Psalm save Jesus only. The Apostle testified that David wrote of the Man through whom is preached the forgiveness of sins, Acts 13:35-38. Surely these historical occasions mark the Psalm out as a prophetic portrait of David's greater Son!

The Saints that are in the earth, 16:3. We can only become saints, and excellent, and a delight to the Lord as the result of the Savior's mediatorial work. All who are saved by Grace are saints, but some are more saintly than others. Isaac Watts sums up the infinite mercy of God in the lines—

> Oft have my heart and tongue confess'd
> How empty and how poor I am;
> My praise can never make the blest,
> Nor add new glories to thy name.
> Yet, Lord, thy saints on earth may reap
> Some profit by the good we do;
> These are the company I keep,
> These are the choicest friends I know.

Sinners are different from Saints in that they *hasten after another god.* But as Matthew Henry pithily puts it—"They that multiply gods multiply griefs to themselves; for whosoever thinks one god too little, will find two too many, and yet hundreds not enough."

That Saints *excel* sinners is evident from David's description of them as *The Excellent.* Ingo, an ancient king of the Draves, making a stately feast, appointed his nobles, at that time pagans, to sit in the hall below, and commanded certain poor Christians to be brought up into his presence-chamber, to sit with him at his table, to eat and drink of his kingly cheer. At this many wondered. He said, he accounted Christians, though never so poor, a greater ornament to his table, and more worthy of his company than the greatest peers unconverted to the Christian faith; for when these might be thrust down to hell, those might be his comforts and fallen princes in Heaven. How privileged are the saints to sit together in heavenly places with Christ Himself.

David blessed the Lord as the Giver of Counsel, and goes on to say that often such guidance came *in the night seasons,* 16:7. Antonine often thanked the gods for directing him in his sleep to answers for many problems. The Psalmist, believing that God was ever with him, experienced what it was to receive admonition in his dreams, or at least during his waking thoughts by night. We have a saying that "the pillow is the best counselor," which is especially true if we commit ourselves to God, and take the prayerful spirit with us to bed. Think of the terrible massacre the Jews were saved from because a king could not sleep in Esther's day!

What a marvelous conclusion this 16th Psalm has! *Pleasure for evermore,* 16:11. Saints in Heaven prove that their joy never ends, or fades. "Their joy lasts for ever whose objects remain for ever." Austin, of the Early Church, said, "Lord, I am content to suffer any pains and torments in this world, if I might see Thy face one day, but alas! were it only a day, then to be ejected from heaven, it would rather be an aggravation of misery." But we have the Divine assurance "forever with the Lord." *Fullness of joy* awaits those who have chosen the path of life leading to Heaven!

Psalm 17

In the 17th century, prison cells were filthy holes, cramped and badly ventilated, in which prisoners were confined without exercise or employment, and jail fever and smallpox raged. It was while John Howard was visiting some of these vile dens that he himself caught fever, which ultimately resulted in his death in 1789, at Kherson. Some time previously he had chosen the inscription for his monument—"O let the sorrowful sighing of the prisoners come before thee," Psalm 79:11—and even selected the text for the sermon which his friend and pastor would preach on the event— "As for me, I will behold thy face in righteousness: I shall be satisfied, when I awake, with thy likeness," Psalm 17:15. Said Howard, "That text is the most appropriate to my feelings of any I know; for I can indeed join with the Psalmist in saying, 'As for me, I shall behold thy face.'"

John Gibson, one of the gallant Covenanters betrayed by a traitor along with four other fellow-Covenanters, was alone permitted to pray before he was shot, and sang part of the Prayer of David found in Psalm 17, telling his mother and sister that it was the most joyful day of his life. The rest were shot "without being allowed to pray separately."

Visiting fever-stricken prisons had no terrors for John Howard. Often his visits were paid in peril of his life, and the text encouraging him to persevere was Psalm 17:5—"Hold up my goings."

Woven into the biography of David Livingstone are the familiar words of the Psalter that Mrs. Mary Moffat, mother-in-law of this renowned missionary to Africa, sent him—"My dear son Livingstone, unceasing prayer is made for you. When I think of you, my heart will go upward: 'Keep him in the apple of thine eye.' Psalm 17, 'Hold him in the hollow of thine hand. . . .'"

Another record of the influence of this marvelous verse is connected with Julius Hare who, with Neander, was among the Cambridge liberals who sought for the reconciliation of revelation with intellect. Hare especially delighted in Psalm 17:15. Whewell, his old college friend at Trinity, Cambridge, wrote, "When the Psalm was read to him before his spirit departed, he thanked those who had thus chosen the words of Scripture which he so especially delighted in; with these sounds of glory singing in his ears, 'I will behold Thy presence in righteousness; and when I awake up after Thy likeness, I shall be satisfied in it.' our dear friend fell into that sleep from which he was to awake in the likeness of Christ."

In his Preface to this Psalm, C. H. Spurgeon, dealing with its Title *A Prayer Of David*, remarked—

> David would not have been a man after God's own heart, if he had not been a man of prayer. He was a master in the sacred art of supplication. He flies to prayer in all times of need, as a pilot speeds to the harbor in the stress of tempest. So frequent were David's prayers that they could not all be dated and entitled; and hence this Psalm simply bears the author's name, and nothing more. The smell of the furnace is upon this present Psalm, but there is evidence in the last verse that he who wrote it came unharmed out of the flame. We have in the present plaintive song, *An Appeal to Heaven,* from the persecutions of earth. A spiritual eye may see Jesus here.

Gathering boldness from the strengthening influence of prayer, the Psalmist entreats the Judge of all the earth to pronounce sentence upon his case, *Let my sentence come forth from thy presence,* 17:2. Is not the hymn writer's holy boast ours?—

> Bold shall I stand in that great day;
> For who aught to my charge shall lay?
> While, through thy blood, absolved I am
> From sin's tremendous curse and shame.

As a parent bird completely shields her brood from evil, so our condescending God has promised to *Keep me as the apple of the eye,* 17:8. In Hebrew the *pupil* of the eye is expressed as "the daughter of the eye." No part of the body is more precious, more tender, and more carefully guarded than the eye; and of the eye, no portion is more peculiarly to be protected than the central apple, or the pupil. Our all-wise Creator has placed the eye in a well-protected position; it stands surrounded by projecting bones like Jerusalem encircled by mountains. It is also compassed about with the hedge of the eyebrows, the curtain of the eyelids, and the fence of the eyelashes. What a superb illustration of God's care of His own!

That God often allows the wicked to have all their sensual appetites crave for, is hinted at in the phrase, *Whose belly thou fillest with thy hid treasures,* 17:14. But their *portion* is only *in this life.* Like Passion in "Pilgrim's Progress," they have their best things first, and revel during their little hour. Martin Luther was always afraid lest he should have his portion here, and therefore frequently gave away sums of money he had received as gifts. God allows swine the husks they hunger for, as Richard Mant indicated in the verse—

> Thou from thy hidden store,
> Their bellies, Lord, hast fill'd:

Their sons are gorg'd, and what is o'er,
To their sons' sons they yield.

On what a blessed note David finishes his prayerful Psalm! *I shall be satisfied, when I awake, with thy likeness,* 17:15. Henry Ward Beecher gave us this telling illustration of the Psalmist's blessed hope—The old Pope, when he had Michaelangelo employed in decorating the interior of that magnificent structure, the Sistine Chapel, demanded that the scaffolding should be taken down so that he could see the glowing colors that with matchless skill were being laid on.

Patiently and assiduously did that noble artist labor, toiling by day, and almost by night, bringing out his prophets and sibyls and pictures wondrous for their beauty and significance, until the work was done. The day before it was done, if you had gone into that Chapel and looked up, what would you have seen? Posts, planks, ropes, lime, mortar, dirt. But when all was finished the workmen came, and the scaffolding was removed. And then, although the floor was yet covered with rubbish and litter, when you looked up, it was as if Heaven itself had been opened, and you looked into the courts of God and angels.

Now, the scaffold is kept around men long after the fresco is commenced to be painted; and wondrous disclosures will be made when God shall take down this scaffolding body, and reveal what you have been doing. When God's work is complete, and we stand before Him, with hearts full of praise and gratitude we shall say, *I am satisfied!*

Psalm 18

The comprehensive title given to this Psalm provides us with the historical occasion of its composition. With significant variations the Psalm is found in 2 Samuel 22. The humility of David, its composer, is seen in that although he was King of Judah at the time, he called himself, "the servant of the Lord." As he has no mention of his royalty, it could seem as if he deemed it a higher honor to be God's servant than Judah's King. As a servant, he addressed God as his *Lord,* and ascribed deliverance from all his foes to Him. Whenever he reviewed his own remarkable history, David recognized the hand of God in all the events and crises encountered and broke forth into song.

Of all the Psalmist's enemies, Saul was the chiefest, yet as he looked back he saw the gracious hand of God, and His manifold and marvelous mercies in the deliverances experienced. David was conscious of his debt of honor and gratitude and he paid such a debt in full as he thought of the Divine preservation afforded him. Thus, a fitting heading for this Psalm, with its backward look is, according to Spurgeon, *The Grateful Retrospect.*

A further historical association of the Psalm is the fact that hundreds of years later, its 2nd and 49th verses came to be quoted in the New Testament, and declared to be not only the words of David, but of the Lord Jesus. Thus, a greater than David is in this lengthy Psalm, and it is not difficult for the spiritual eye to trace Him in His sorrows, deliverance, and triumphs, in the marvelous poetic song which the Psalmist wrote (See Rom. 15:9; Heb. 2:13).

One cannot read this great Psalm without being impressed with its abundance of striking, apt metaphors, which seem to trip over each other as they leave the lips of such a poetic genius. *The Lord is my rock and fortress,* 18:2. When forced to escape the malice of Saul and live as a fugitive, David dwelt among the crags and mountain caves, and came to know them well as places of concealment and security. As he hid in the clefts of a rock, he thought of himself, hunted like a partridge, safe in God, and hidden from all outside peril. When high up on a rocky eminence beyond the reach of Saul, the happy poet blessed God for being his *High Tower.* Succeeding verses are replete with the gift David had in describing his experiences of God's protecting power in rich, poetical language.

Floods of ungodly men that made David afraid, 18:4, is most expressive.

As a most courageous man, hoping for the best, he yet feared the worst, as he did after his marvelous defeat of Goliath. C. H. Spurgeon whose strong and eloquent evangelical preaching drew thousands to hear him, illustrates this torrent of ungodliness David depicts, in what overtook him on the night of the lamentable accident in the Surrey Music Hall, packed with listeners, some of whom were killed. "The floods of Belial were let loose on me, and the subsequent remarks of a large portion of the Press were exceedingly malicious and wicked. Our soul was afraid as we stood encompassed with the sorrows of death and the blasphemies of the cruel. But, oh, what mercy was there in it all, and what honey of goodness was extracted by our Lord out of this lion of affliction."

David then goes on to employ four arresting metaphors to depict his hopelessness—

> He was bound like a malefactor for execution,
> He was overwhelmed like a shipwrecked mariner,
> He was surrounded and standing at bay like a hunted stag,
> He was captured in a net like a trembling bird—yet God covered His servant's defenseless head in response to his cry of distress, 18:6.

There went up smoke out of His nostrils, 18:8. The ancients believed that the seat of anger was in the nose, or nostrils; because when it grows warm and violent, it discovers itself by a heated vehement breath, that proceeds from them. The metaphor David used was a violent oriental method of expressing wrath, and he felt the figure fittingly portrayed the anger of the Almighty against those who dared to injure His children. Such grandeur of description was captured by Bishop Maud in the verse—

> Smoke from his heated nostrils came,
> And from his mouth devouring flame;
> How burning coals announced his ire,
> And flashes of careering fire.

What inimitable imagery David uses to picture God, majestic in His flight, to help and relieve His own—*He rode upon a cherub, and did fly,* 18:10. John Milton in *Paradise Lost* wrote of the cherubim often represented as the chariot of God—

> He on the wings of cherubim
> Uplifted, in paternal glory rode
> Far into chaos,
> He on the wings of *cherub* rode sublime
> On the crystalline sky.

As the cherub is represented as having the countenance of man, the lion, the bull, and the eagle—combining in itself, as it were, the intelligence, majesty, strength, and life of nature—was a symbol of the powers of nature serving God, as He rode on them to aid His beleagured servant.

> In his descent, bow'd heaven with earth did meet,
> And gloomy darkness roll'd beneath his feet;
> A golden winged cherub he bestrid,
> And on the swiftly flying tempest rid.

Several times David thought his destruction by Saul was almost unavoidable, but God was ever near in *the day of calamity,* and was the Psalmist's *stay,* 18:18. When Henry the VIIIth had spoken and written bitterly against Martin Luther, the renowned Reformer replied, "Tell the Henries, the Bishops, the Turks, and the Devil himself, do what they can, we are the children of the kingdom, worshipping of the true God whom 'they, and such as they spit upon and crucified.'" And of the same spirit were many martyrs. Basil affirms of the primitive saints that they had so much courage and confidence as they suffered, that many of the heathen around them seeing their heroic zeal and constancy, became Christians.

A bow of steel is broken, 18:34. The drawing of a mighty bow by a warrior was a mark of great skill and slaughter, as Alexander Pope indicated in his lines translated from Homer—

> So the great master drew the mighty bow,
> And drew with ease. One hand aloft display'd
> The bending horns, and one the string essay'd.

How verses 38-40 ring with David's triumph over all his foes. *They are fallen under my feet*—a victory William Cowper cast in poetic form in the stanza—

> Oh, I have seen the day,
> When with a single word,
> God helping me to say,
> "My trust is in the Lord."
> My soul has quelled a thousand foes,
> Fearless of all that could oppose.

Esau, finding no place of repentance, though he sought it carefully with tears, had successors in those who cried, but *there was none to help them,* 18:41. The historian who wrote of Antiochus said though he vowed in his last illness "that also he would become a Jew himself, and go through all the world that was inhabitated, and declare the power of God," yet for all this his pains would not cease, continues the historians, for the just judgment of God was come upon him, 2 Macc. 9:17, 18.

The Lord liveth, 18:46. All die—even our foes, but He is alive forevermore. The story is told of a godly woman who, having buried one of her children, sat alone in her sadness, yet had ease of heart when she read *The Lord liveth.* Then another child died, still she remained calm and trustful, as she said, "Comforts die, but God lives." Then the heaviest blow of all fell upon her, for her beloved husband died, and she became almost overwhelmed with sorrow. But her surviving child, having observed what before she spoke to comfort herself, said to her disconsolate mother, "Is God dead, mother? Is God dead?" This reached the sorrowing woman's heart, and her former confidence in a *living* God returned.

It is God! Is this not a reassuring statement, 18:47? It was on June 14, 1645, that Oliver Cromwell wrote to the Speaker of the House of Commons, after the battle of Naseby—

> Sir, this is none other then the hand of God; and to Him alone belongs the glory, wherein none are to share with Him. The General served you with all faithfulness and honor; and the best commendation I can give him is that I dare say he attributes all to God and would rather perish than assume himself.

It was thus with David as he recalled all of his deliverances from Saul's evil pursuit. He gave God all the glory.

As we read verses 46 to 50 of this God-honoring Psalm, our thoughts go from David to his Greater Son, for with evident prophetic foresight of the glorious triumphs of the Messiah, the Psalmist extols Him Who, at His coming to reign, will subdue all people under Him.

This song of deliverance from all his enemies David sang unto the Lord has been a favorite one of saints all down the ages. Shakespeare had a fascinating way of weaving sentences from the Psalms into his literary masterpieces which prove his familiarity with the Psalter. For example, in his address of Romeo to Juliet, where Shakespeare compares her to "a winged messenger of Heaven"—

> When he bestrides the lazy-lacing clouds
> And sails upon the bosom of the air,—

brings to mind sentences like, "Magnify Him that rideth upon the Heavens," Ps. 68:4, or "Who maketh the clouds His chariot, and walketh upon the wings of the wind," Ps. 18:10.

Four sons of the Huguenots who suffered much in the cause of Christ sang upon the scaffold the verses—

> He delivered me from my strong enemy, and from them which hated me: for they were too strong for me.
> They prevented me in the day of my calamity: but the Lord was my stay.
> He brought me forth also into a large place; he delivered me because he delighted in me.—Psalm 18:17-19.

These same verses were sung by the last martyrs of the desert, Francis Rochette, and three brothers of the name of Grenier, who suffered as late as 1762, under the reign of Louis XV, when the stones of cities were watered by the precious faith of those who proclaimed with unconquerable fidelity their faith in Christ.

During the terrible days of religious rivalry in Ireland during the 16th century, the Protestants of the North fleeing from the army of King James found refuge in Londonderry. But much cowardice and treachery were at work, and many deserted their leaders. In desperation to garrison those, Rev. George Walker, as one of the governors, in his Diary describes the fearful experiences endured during the siege lasting from April 17th to July 31st. In a remarkable sermon Walker preached to bolster the courage of the starving host, he urged them to cleave fast to the Rock of their salvation, for it is said, "With the merciful Thou wilt show Thyself merciful. And with an upright man, Thou shalt show Thyself upright; with the pure Thou shalt show Thyself pure; with the forward Thou shalt show Thyself forward. For Thou wilt save the afflicted people, but wilt bring down high looks," Psalm 18:25-27.

Mention has been made of James Melville's deep love for the Psalms. Those associated with *light* had a special attraction for him and in the English of the 15th century we find him saying—

> The candell being behind his bak, he desyred that it should be brought before him, that he might sie to die (Psalm 23:4). Be occasionne quhairof that pairt of the Scripture was rememberit, "Light aryses to the righteous in the middes of darkness," Psalm 112:4; and Psalm 18, verse 28, "The Lord will lighten my candell; He will inlighten my darkness."

As we are discovering in these Stories of the Psalter, this portion of Scripture was the constant source of inspiration of the Scottish Covenanters. True to the spirit of these brave men and women whose—

> Tales
> Of persecution and the Covenant
> Whose echo rings through Scotland to this hour.

Walter Scott has embodied in his novels the influence of the Psalms in their lives. It was a Pslam that nerved Manse Headrigg to leap her horse over a wall, Psalm 18:29.

This Psalm was also connected, at an early period, with the history of France with the emergence of the Frankish Kingdom. Clovis, Founder of the French monarchy, whose name in the form of Louis descended to many kings, was marching southward from Paris in 507 A.D. to meet the formidable Visigoths in battle, and, anxious for a forecast of the result, sent a messenger to consult the shrine of St. Martin of Tours, the oracle of Gaul. As they entered the church in which the bones of St. Martin rested, the choir was chanting the words—

> "Thou hast girded me with strength unto battle;
> Thou hast made mine enemies also to turn their backs upon me;
> And I shall destroy them that hate me." Psalm 18:39, 40.

Encouraged by this omen, Clovis pressed on and many foes fell into his hands, and the Frankish Kingdom grew in power and influence.

Psalm 19

D. C. Gilman, who became the first President of Johns Hopkins University, in 1875, once said, "As my favorite text of Scripture, I name the 19th Psalm and the Sermon on the Mount." Another well-known American in the past century, G. W. Summer, Rear Admiral of the US Navy, who was conspicuous in naval battles during the Civil War, wrote, "My favorite chapter is the 19th Psalm. My attention was especially called to it many years ago from hearing and seeing it read by the blind preacher, Milburn."

Joseph Addison's famed paraphrase of Psalm 19, which was an essay on confirming faith in God, closes with the description of "The spacious firmament on high," Psalm 19:1-6. Ruskin included this Psalm in his first half of the Psalter in which there is to be found all the wisdom for society and the individual. Then we have Shakespeare's lines—

"See how the morning opes her golden gates,
And takes her farewell of the glorious sun"

—which is a reminiscence of David's emblem of the sun rejoicing "as a giant to run his course," 19:5. In *Grace Abounding to the Chief of Sinners,* John Bunyan presents with vivid realism the struggle of a Christian as a transcript of his own spiritual conflict. Feeling he had yielded to the satanic suggestion to sell Christ, he thought he had committed the great offense David mentions—regarding "great transgressions," 19:13. Bunyan says that he was made conscious of his error by "the deeply sensible prayer of David," who asked God to hold him back from sin, "So shall I be undefiled, and innocent from the great offence."

The title of this unique Psalm gives no hint whatever of its biographical connection with David its author. Doubtless in his earlier days after his victory over Goliath the Giant, while keeping his father's flock, he had time for quiet meditation in the open fields, and gave himself up to a study of God's two massive volumes, namely, the beautiful world above and around him, and the perfect Word of God.

> David has so thoroughly entered into the spirit of these two only volumes in his library that he was able with a devout criticism to compare and contrast them, magnifying the excellency of the Author as seen in them both.

Plutarch, Greek philosopher of the 1st century wrote, "The world resembleth a divinity school, and Christ, as the Scripture telleth, is our doctor, instructing us by his *works,* and by his *words.* It is said that Aristotle had two sorts of writings, one called *Exoterical,* for his common auditors, and another named *Acromatical,* for his private scholars and familiar acquaintances. From Psalm 19 we learn from David that God has two sorts of books—The book of His creations, a commonplace book for all in the world to read, 19:1-6. The other volume is Scripture, a statute-book for His domestical auditory—The Church—The Law is an undefiled law, 19:7-8. Paul must have had these two volumes in mind when he wrote that God's *invisible things* are His eternal power and Godhead, *are clearly seen* by the creation of the world, *being understood by the things that are made.* That the invisible God makes Himself visible in His created works was expressed by the spiritual poet, Du Bartas, centuries ago—

> Therein our fingers feel, our nostrils smell,
> Our palates taste his virtues that excel,
> He shows him to our eyes, talks to our ears,
> In the ordered motions of the spangled spheres.

Some there are who fail to trace the goings forth of Jehovah in *Creation* was well as in *Grace.* They appear to be too heavenly to consider the heavens and are in danger of becoming too heavenly minded as to be of any earthly use. Further, there have been those daring enough to set the *Works* of God against the *Word* of God, spending their wits trying to find discrepancies and contradictions between the two volumes, separating, thereby, two parties that ought to live in closest union. But Spurgeon expresses it—

> We may rest assured that the true *Vestiges of Creation* will never contradict Genesis, nor will a correct *Cosmos* be found at variance with the narrative of Moses. He is wisest who reads both the *World-Book* and the *Word-Book* as two volumes of the same work, and feels concerning them, 'The Father wrote them both.'

Although we heartily agree with the above sentiments, it would seem as if this 19th Psalm is *A Psalm of Three Books,* for while verses 1-6 declare the glory of God in Nature, and verses 7-11 magnify the nature and influence of Scripture, verses 12-14 make bare the heart of man, and its need for deliverance from sin. Thus, we have three volumes, Creation, Scripture, and Man.

Words and metaphors drawn from earth utterly fail to fully express the loftiest thoughts of God as revealed in Creation and Scripture and Grace. Yet they help in some measure to instruct us in their grandeur.

The heavens declare the glory of God, 19:1. Millions of words had been written on this opening verse declaring as it does that the great fabric around us was fashioned by God for His glory. Costing us nothing to read and study, the Book of Nature has three chapters—*Heaven—Earth—Sea,* of which Heaven, or Heavens constitute the first and most glorious, for by its aid we are able to see the beauties of the other two. "Any book without its first page would be sadly imperfect, and especially the great Natural Bible, since its first pages, the sun, the moon, and the stars, supply light to the rest of the volume, and are thus the keys, without which the writing which follows would be dark and undiscerned."

During the French Revolution, Jean Bon St. André, the notorious Vendean revolutionist, said to a godly peasant,

> I will have all your steeples pulled down, that you may no longer have any object by which you may be reminded of your old superstitions.

The peasant defiantly replied, "But *you cannot help leaving us the stars.*" While a literal reading of the first two verses of the Psalm is given as—

> The heavens are *telling* the glory of God,
> The firmament displaying the work of his hand;
> Day unto day *welleth forth* speech,
> Night unto night *breathes* out knowledge—

poets have vied with each other in their lyrical expressions of the wonder and glory of God's created works. Here is John Milton's tribute—

> These are thy glorious works, Parent of good,
> Almighty! Thine this universal frame,
> Thus wondrous fair; Thyself how wondrous, then!
> Unspeakable, who sitt'st above these heavens
> To us invisible, or dimly seen
> In these thy lowest works; yet these declare
> Thy goodness beyond thought, and power divine.

Effectively and without ambiguity, the glorious heavens and firmament *sheweth knowledge,* 19:2. The differing measure in which natural objects convey knowledge to men of differing mental and spiritual capacity is illustrated for us in the story of our great English artist, Turner. While he was engaged upon one of his immortal masterpieces, a lady of rank standing by remarked, "But, Mr. Turner, I do not see in nature all that you describe there." The artist simply replied, "Ah, Madam, do you not wish you could?"

In them he hath set a tabernacle for the sun, 19:4. What a wonderful simile David uses in this phrase! "In the midst of the heavens the sun encamps, and marches like a mighty monarch on his glorious way. He has no fixed abode, but as a traveler pitches and removes his tent, a tent which will soon be taken down and rolled together as a scroll. As the royal pavilion stood in the center of the host, so the sun in his place appears like a king in the midst of attendant stars."

Does not the Psalmist's ability to use most fittingly metaphorical ability amaze you? He goes on to describe the sun as a *bridegroom* coming out of his chamber, and then as a joyful *strong man* running a race, 19:5. Yet even the glorious sun shines in light borrowed from the Great Father of Lights.

> Thou sun, of this great world both eye and soul,
> Acknowledge Him thy greater; sound His praise
> Both when thou climb'st, and when high noon hast gained,
> And when thou fall'st.

Coming to the third book in this Psalm of David, we find several evangelical phrases worthy of notice. *Converting the soul,* 19:7. Clemens Alexandrinus was not afraid to say that if the fables of Orpheus and Anphion were true—that they drew birds, beasts, and stones, with their ravishing melody—the harmony of the Word is greater, seeing it translates men from Helicon to Zion, which softens the hard heart of men obdurate against the truth, that raises up children to Abraham of stone—who became *living stones* in God's temple.

Sweeter than honey and the honeycomb, 19:10. Although we may not observe any difference between the delicacy of honey in the comb and that which is separated from it, Dr. Halle, writing on the diet of the Moors of Barbary, said that they esteemed honey a very wholesome breakfast. "The most delicious that which is in the comb with the young bees in it, before they come out of their cases, whilst they still are mild-white." Thus the distinction made by David is perfectly just and conformable to custom and practice.

Moreover by them is thy servant warned, 19:11. It is recorded that a certain Jew had formed a design to poison Martin Luther, but was disappointed by a faithful friend, who sent Luther a portrait of the man, with a warning against him. It is so with the Word of God as it reveals the face of those that Satan employs to poison our soul.

Cleanse thou me from secret faults, 19:12. This phrase, which was a principle text of the Reformers against the auricular confession of Roman Catholics, is a petition for deliverance from committing acts which it will be necessary to conceal—a thought emphasized in a most remarkable poem by Hood, called *The Dream of Eugene Aram.* Aram had murdered a man and cast his body into the river—"a sluggish water, black as ink, the depth was so extreme." The next morning Aram visited the scene of his guilt—

> And sought the black accursed pool,
> With a mild misgiving eye;
> And he saw the dead in the river bed,
> For the faithless stream was dry.

Next Aram covered the corpse with heaps of leaves, but a mighty wind swept the wood and left the secret bare before the sun—

> Then down I cast me on my face,
> And first began to weep,
> For I knew my secret then was one
> That earth refused to keep;
> On land or sea though it should be
> Ten thousand fathoms deep.

Thus in plaintive notes Aram prophesied his own discovery. Then he buried his victim in a cave and trod him down with stones, but when the years had run their weary round, the foul dead was discovered and the murderer put to death. How true it is that Guilt is a *grim chamberlain.* May we be saved from the misery of secret sins.

Acceptable in thy sight, O Lord, 19:14. All wish to please, if only it is to please themselves. But David's passion was to please *God,* and his last prayer in this blessed Psalm reveals his humility, affection, recognition of duty, and a regard to self-interest. The Psalmist expressed the harmony of heart and lips most needful for Divine acceptance.

Psalm 20

This militant Psalm, of which David the King was the sweet Psalmist of Israel, was both its subject and composer, is cast as a kind of *National Anthem,* fashioned to be sung at the outbreak of war, when the monarch was girding on his sword for the fight. We cannot give any particular occasion for this song in the history of David, for during his day, Israel was almost always at war. If David himself had not been associated with some of his nation's wars, we would never have been blessed with a Psalm like this one, in which a joyful people plead with loving hearts to Jehovah for their valiant sovereign—*God save the King!*

The spiritual mind, however, is not long in perceiving that this hymn of prayer, as the drums beat, is prophetical of Him Who was born a King. "It is the cry of the ancient Church on behalf of her Lord, as she sees Him in vision enduring a great fight of afflictions on her behalf. The militant people of God, with the great Captain of their Salvation at their head, may still in earnest plead that the pleasure of the Lord may prosper in His hand."

By the *name* of God is meant all that He is in Himself. *The name of the God of Jacob defend thee,* 20:1. Joseph Irons, writing away back in the 18th century, described a visit he paid to Ireland, and one day was goaded by a Roman Catholic to try some of the supposed miracles if only certain conditions were fulfilled. "A silly Irish papist told me, in his consummate ignorance and bigotry, that if a priest would but give him a drop of holy water, and make a circle with it around a field of wild beasts, they would not hurt him.

"I retired in disgust at the abominable trickery of such villains, reflecting, what a fool I am that I cannot put such trust in my God as this poor deluded man puts in his priest and a drop of holy water! And I resolved to try what *the name of the God of Jacob* would do, having the Father's fixed decrees, the Son's unalterable responsibility and the Spirit's invincible grace and operation around me. I tried it and felt my confidence brighten. O brethren, get encircled with covenant engagements, and covenant grace, and covenant promises, and covenant securities; then will *the Lord hear you in the time of trouble, and the name of the God of Jacob will defend you.*"

Long ago, the setting up of a banner signified open avowal of allegiance, declaration of war, index of perseverance, claim of possession, signal of triumph. *In the name of our God we will set up our banners,*

20:5. Samuel Burden in his *Oriental Customs*, written in 1812, spoke of a custom with the Soobak in Tibet to ascend a hill every month, set up a white flag, and perform his religious ceremonies, to conciliate the favor of a *dewta*, or invisible being, the genius of the place, who was said to hover about the summit, dispensing at his will, good and evil to everything around him.

In religions, as well as warlike processions, people carried banners— even industrial strikers today carry them! Of old, on the pinnacles of sacred spires, on the domes or gateways of temples, and on the roof of a new house, could be seen the banner of the caste or sect floating in the air. Siva, the Supreme, is described as having a banner in the celestial world. But saints celebrate their victories in His name. Their banners are lifted up in triumph, and they set up their trophies *in the name of our God*. He alone must have all the glory of our triumph. No instrument must have any part in the honor due to Him, our Glorious Victor, Prince Divine.

Numa, being told that his enemies were coming after him as he was offering sacrifices, thought it was sufficient for his safety that he could say, "I am about the service of my God." Was this not the spirit of David when he wrote, *But we will remember the name of the Lord our God*, 20:7. Augustus Herman Franke, 1662-1727, wrote of an experience he had about the time of *Michaelmas* when he was in utmost extremity. Contemplating the manifested power of God in the created world around, his heart was strengthened in faith, and here is what he thought within himself—

> What an excellent thing it is when we have nothing, and can rely upon nothing, but yet are acquainted with the living God, Who made heaven and earth, and place our confidence alone in him, which enables us to be so tranquil even in necessity!

"Although I was well aware that I required something that very day," he recalled, "yet my heart was so strong in faith that I was cheerful, and of good courage. On coming home I was immediately waited upon by the overseer of the workmen and masons, who, as it was Saturday, required money to pay their wages. He expected the money to be ready, which he wished to go and pay, but enquired, however, whether I had received anything.

'Has anything arrived?' asked he. I answered,

'No, but I have faith in God.'

Scarcely had I uttered these words when a student was announced, who has brought me thirty dollars from someone, whom he would not name. I went into the room again, and asked the overseer how much he required from the workmen's wages. He answered *Thirty dollars!* Here they are, I said, and enquired at the same time, if he needed any more? He replied,

No, which very much strengthened the faith of both of us, since we so wisely saw the miraculous hand of God Who had remembered us and sent at the very moment all that was needed."

Richard Mant left us the lines—

> Some of their warrior horses boost,
> Some their chariots' marshall'd host;
> But our trust will we proclaim
> In our God Jehovah's name.

Cyrus Hamlin, for many years missionary to Turkey, and founder of Robert College in Constantinople, and author of *Among the Turks,* and *My Life and Times,* who died in his 90th year, wrote a few months before he died, "My favorite text is the 20th Psalm. I have often read it to the afflicted and to those in any danger."

The famous Edinburgh physician, Sir James Y. Simpson, discoverer of chloroform, the godly son of a pious mother, was greatly influenced by this Psalm. Left a widow early in her married life, Mrs. Simpson had many a sore struggle in providing bread for her children. When hard pressed and wondering what to do she would sit down and repeat this 20th Psalm, and rise refreshed. Her children learned to call it *Mother's Psalm.*

A touching story is related of a coal pit disaster, near Musselburgh, Scotland, when 13 miners were imprisoned in a narrow space. Here they prepared for death, and prayed and sung together the first four verses of this Psalm, and their hope of a brighter world was strengthened. But by a miracle they were delivered and this last verse of the Psalm they sung seemed prophetic.

> In thy salvation we will joy;
> In our God's name we will
> Display our banners; and the Lord
> Thy prayers all fulfill.

A famous monastic institution in Wales was Llancarvan of which Cadoc the Wise was the first Abbot. It was with a Psalm that turned Gwynllia the Warrior, father of Cadoc, from a life of violence and banditry to the austerities of a monastery anchorite. Won by Christ by the example of his son, the robber chieftain did penance for his sins, chanting, "The Lord hear thee in the day of trouble," 20:1. He retired from the world and lived such a holy life that he became commemorated as St. Woolos, the Patron Saint of Newport, Mon.

Born in the lifetime of the renowned Early Father, Origen, a young, rich orphan, Antony, 251-256 A.D. became an outstanding example of godly asceticism, giving up all his possessions to help the poor. Sometimes the world and the flesh swept over him with all their fury, but the Psalms were the weapons enabling him to overcome his evil tendencies. Psalm 20 was his paean of victory, for words like "Some put their trust in chariots, and some in horses; but we will remember the Name of the Lord our God" 20:7, put Satan to flight. It was also this verse that St. Patrick chanted as he followed the Druids to the place of Tara, and then before the assembled Hosts spoke of the Kingdom founded upon the King of kings, and of Him Who reigns from the Cross. No wonder the power of the Druids was broken! A further story of the use of this 7th verse is associated with Adelme, Abbot of the Benedictine House of Chaise-Dieu, who accompanied the army of Alphonse the Valiant, first King of Castile, who in 1085 had driven the Moors from Toledo. Prothero records that "at the passage of the Tagus, the Christian soldiers recoiled from entering the swollen flood." But Adelme, mounted on his ass, rode into the stream, singing the 7th verse of Psalm 20—"Some put their trust in horses," etc. Adelme's courage shamed the hesitating soldiers; they plunged into the stream, and the whole Christian army crossed the river, and victory followed. The Moors were defeated at Oran in 1510, and the Cardinal who led the victors through the streets, chanted—

> Not unto us, O Lord, not unto us, but unto Thy Name give the praise, Psalm 115.

That the Psalms are inextricably mingled with our national, as well as our private lives, is evident from the fact that both in spirit—"Save, Lord; let the king hear us when we call," Psalm 20:9—and language, "Let God arise, let his enemies be scattered," 68:1, they form the basis of the British *National Anthem.*

Psalm 21

The martial air pervading this *Royal Triumphal Ode,* links it to the previous one. Psalms 20 and 21 make good companions. The former Psalm anticipates what the latter one regards as realized. As Perowne reminds us, "Psalm 20 was a litany before the king went forth to battle. Psalm 21 is apparently a *Te Deum* on his return." Jerome has a similar notation, "He who in the preceding Psalm was prayed for as having taken the form of a servant, in this is King of kings, and Lord of lords." Several writers see Christ as the Messiah in Psalm 20 in the day of His trouble, and in Psalm 21, in His ultimate triumph. Throughout the Psalm before us, the *King* is most prominent, and our meditation of Him will be sweet if we constantly see Him as such as we read its thirteen verses.

The title affirms the Psalm to be of David's composition—one he wrote, sung, and meant to magnify God for his triumphs, yet intended by him to reach its fullest significance in his heavenly King, Who must be crowned with the glory of our salvation—praised because of His redeeming love—extolled because of His emancipating power. God has indeed made Him most blessed forever.

He asked life of thee, 21:4. We read of how Alexander the Great gave a poor beggar a city; and that he sent his schoolmaster a ship full of frank-incense, and bade him sacrifice freely. Hezekiah asked but one life, and God gave him fifteen years, which we reckon two lives and more. How true it is that God is better to His people than their prayers! They ask for a life of blessing, He adds an eternity of bliss!

Honor and majesty hast thou laid upon him, 21:5. The hymnist has expressed how a glorious crown will rest upon the lofty brow once marred with thorns—

> Let him be crowned with majesty
> Who bowed his head to death,
> And be his honors sounded high
> By all things that have breath.

Thou shalt make them as a fiery oven . . . the fire shall devour them, 21:9. It has been said that a frown of Queen Elizabeth killed Sir Christopher Hatton, the Lord Chancellor of England. If this was so, then what will the frowns of the King of nations? If the rocks rend, and mountains melt, and the foundations of the earth tremble under His wrath, how will the ungodly appear when He comes in all His royal glory to take vengeance on those who despised and rejected His proffered mercy?

As a fiery oven, is a phrase describing something extremely hot without relief of any cool refreshment. Bishop Horsley remarks, "It describes the smoke of Messiah's enemies perishing by fire, ascending like the smoke of a furnace." How awfully grand is that description of the ruins of the cities of the plain, as the prospect struck Abraham's eye on the fatal morning of their destruction! *"And he looked toward Sodom and Gomorrah, and toward all the land of the plain, and beheld, and lo, the smoke of the country went up as the smoke of a furnace."* John Milton has the lines—

> Overhead the dismal hiss
> Of fiery darts in flaming volleys flew,
> And flying vaulted either host with fire.

What lamentations there must have been in Rome when it burnt for seven days together; what shrieks where heard in Troy, when it was wholly consumed with flames; what howling and astonishment in Pentapholis, when those cities were destroyed with fire from heaven; what weeping there must have been in Jerusalem, when they beheld the house of God, the glory of their kingdom, the wonder of the world, involved in fire and smoke!

When it comes to the final judgment of the wicked, the remembrance of where they could have been if only they had repented and believed the Gospel, will be sufficient to make them throughout Eternity, a fiery oven to themselves. As Augustine put it, "Thou shalt make them on fire within, by the consciousness of their ungodliness, in the time of Thy manifestation." The judgments of God are called *thine arrows,* 21:12, because they are sharp, swift, sure, and deadly. How dreadful to contemplate the ungodly as the *butt,* at which these Divine arrows are directed!

Henry of Navarre, a prisoner at Court of Charles IX, urged the young king to throw in his lot with him and fight their common enemy. On a dark and wintry night, Henry fled from Paris, and joined the Protestants assembled at Alencon. The next morning he attended Divine service, at which the Psalm appointed to be sung was Psalm 21—"The king shall rejoice in thy strength, O Lord," etc. This picture of a true king seemed a propitious omen, and Henry asked whether the Psalm had been selected to welcome him to the camp, but finding that it came in the regular course, he was much impressed.

Sung throughout England by the overtrustful Presbyterians at the restoration of Charles II, this 21st Psalm is a noble coronation Psalm when raised to the praise of Him Who has a right scepter and an eternal throne.

> The King in Thy great strength, O Lord,
>   Shall very joyful be:
> In Thy salvation rejoice
>   How veh'mently shall he!

Psalm 22

It is with some trepidation that we approach this solemn Psalm, seeing that the place whereon we stand is holy ground. Many have set forth their estimation of the Psalm as a whole, but none so forcibly as Martin Luther, who wrote—

> This is a kind of gem among the Psalms, and is pecularly excellent and remarkable. It contains those deep, sublime, and heavy sufferings of Christ, when agonising in the midst of the terrors and pangs of divine wrath and death, which surpass the human thought and comprehension. I know not whether any Psalm throughout the whole book contains matter more weighty, or from which the hearts of godly men can so truly perceive those sighs and groans, inexpressible by man, which their Lord and Head, Jesus Christ, uttered when conflicting for us in the midst of death, and in the midst of the pains and terrors of hell. Wherefore this Psalm ought to be most highly prized by all who have any acquaintance with temptations of faith and spiritual conflicts.

What a striking contrast there is between the last Psalm, when we were introduced to the steps of the royal throne, and this Psalm, leading us to the foot of the Cross. Yet the Cross is the only way to the Throne. The heading of this ode of singular excellence composed by David, says that it was handed over to *the chief Musician,* the most excellent of the temple songsters. "The Chief among ten thousand is worthy to be extolled by the chief Musician." Interpretations and conjectures as to the meaning of Aijeleth Shahar are numerous. The margin in the A.V. gives the interpretation, "Concerning the hind of the morning"; and the *hind* is a very appropriate emblem of the suffering One portrayed in this Psalm. Hengstenberg remarks that "the *hind* may be a figurative expression significant of the suffering innocence, is put beyond a doubt by the fact that the wicked and the persecutors in this Psalm, whose peculiar physiognomy is marked by emblems drawn from the brute creation, are designed by the terms *dogs, lions, bulls.*"

From Wood's informative book on *Bible Animals* we learn that according to the curious natural history given by some old authors, there exists a deadly enmity between the deer and the serpent, and the deer by its warm breath draws serpents out of their holes in order to devour them. The old grammarians derived *Elaphas,* meaning, Hart, from a phrase signifying, the drawing away all snakes. If a snake had escaped the hart after being drawn out by the hart's breath, it was said to be more vehemently poisonous than before. Even the burning of a portion of the deer's horns was said to drive away all snakes. The timidity of the deer was ascribed to the great size of its heart, in which the ancients thought was a bone shaped like a Cross.

Faith has no difficulty in finding Jesus in the Hind of the Morning, David—who had an intimate knowledge of the animal creation—sang about. Often referred to as the *Hind,* such a beautiful poetic metaphor of the cruel huntings, so pathetically described in this Calvary Psalm, force us to believe He alone is *The Morning Hind.* It will be noted that this Psalm of the Cross begins with, "My God, My God, why hast thou forsaken me?" and ends, as some Hebrew scholars affirm from the original, with "It is finished." For all that we know, Jesus may have actually repeated word by word this Psalm when He was hanging on the tree.

Spurgeon had no doubt as to the historical fulfillment of the Psalm in the finished work of the Cross. Here is this notable expositor's wonderful tribute to it—

> For plaintive expressions uprising from unutterable depths of woe we may say of this Psalm, *There is none like it.* It is the photograph of our Lord's saddest hours, the record of his dying words, the lachrymatory of his last tears, the memorial of his expiring joys. David and his afflictions may be here in a very modified sense, but as the star is concealed by the light of the sun, he who sees Jesus will probably neither see nor care to see David. Before us we have a description both of the darkness and of the glory of the Cross, the sufferings of Christ and the glory which shall follow. Oh for grace to draw near and see this great sight!

I am a worm, and no man, 22:6. The abasement of the Lord of Glory is seen in this feeling of Himself as being comparable to a helpless, powerless, down-trodden worm, passive while crushed, and unnoticed and despised by those who trod upon Him. How wonderful it was of Him to select the weakest of His creatures, which is all flesh, yet becomes, when crushed under foot, writhing, quivering flesh, utterly devoid of any might except strength to suffer.

Among the Hindus, when a man complains and abhors himself, he asks: "What am I? A worm! A worm!" "Ah, the proud man! he regarded me as a worm, well should I like to say to him, 'We are all worms.' Worms crawl out of my presence." The Chaldee paraphrase renders the word in verse as a *weak worm.*

Strong bulls of Bashan beset me round, 22:12. Bashan was a fertile country, and its cattle were fat and strong, Deut. 32:13. The bulls of this area were remarkable for the proud, fierce, and sullen manner in which they exercised their great strength. They were thus fitting symbols of the persecutors surrounding our Lord at the Cross, who were both human and hellish foes and all distinguished by the proud, fierce manner in which they attacked Jesus.

Dogs have compassed me, 22:16. So great and varied was the malignity exhibited by our Lord's enemies at Calvary that the combined characteristics of two species of ferocious animals were not adequate to fully represent their determination to destroy Him. *Bulls* and *Lion* are now joined by *Dogs* who with unfailing scent track down their victim, and run it to death. These dog-like enemies of Jesus *compassed* Him about. The Oriental mode of hunting, both in ancient and modern times, is murderous and merciless in the extreme. A circle of several miles in circumference is beat around; and the men, driving all before them, and narrowing as they advance, enclose the prey on every side. Having thus made them prisoners, the cruel hunters proceed to slaughter at their convenience. It was thus with our Lord's enemies who, from the time of His entrance into His public ministry, used the most treacherous plans to silence Him, and at Calvary came in for the kill.

The meek shall eat and be satisfied, 22:26. Bonaventure, the Seraphic Doctor, and Italian philosopher of the 12th century, had the sweet saying of our Lord's—*Learn of me, for I am meek and lowly in heart,*—in an engraved form in his study. If we are among the number redeemed by the blood of the Cross, may such a message of meekness be engraved upon our foreheads, and our hearts. What a spiritual banquet the saints are invited to as the result of the Savior's sacrifice, Who, as He expired, thought of the joy of those exhibiting His meekness as the Lamb Who was slain.

With this poignant Psalm, so dear to the heart of the Lord Jesus we come to an impressive Messianic triad, for Psalms 22, 23, and 24 form a threefold cord that cannot be broken.

In Psalm 22, we have the *Cross* with the Messiah as *Savior*
In Psalm 23, we have the *Crook* with the Messiah as *Shepherd*
In Psalm 24, we have the *Crown* with the Messiah as *Sovereign.*

John Hooper, who, in 1551, was consecrated Bishop of Gloucester. met with unflinching courage the torture of fire at the stake for his noble witness, loved the Calvary Psalm 22, and while in prison awaiting death wrote an exposition of it, as well as of other Psalms. Psalm 22 was among those Hooper recommended for the lessons of "patience and consolation," at times "when the mind can take no understanding, nor the heart any joy of God's promise."

The opening words of the Psalm Jesus used when He died upon the Cross were the words Richard I poured out in indignation, when he found himself deserted by his followers and knew that his crusade had failed—*My God, why hast Thou forsaken me?*

The words of verses 4 and 5—"Our fathers trusted in thee: they trusted, and thou didst deliver them. They cried unto thee, and were delivered; they trusted in thee, and were not confounded"—were linked on to one of the most celebrated responsive chants of the Middle Ages: *Media vita in morte sumus*—"In the midst of life we are in death," and then transferred to the Anglican litany.

The phrase in verse 12 of this 22nd Psalm—"The fat bulls of Bashan," and the "hill of Bashan," 68:5, must have been in Shakespeare's mind when he composed Antony's prayer in *Antony and Cleopatra*—

> Oh, that I were
> Upon the hills of Basan, to outroar
> The horned head! for I have a savage cause.

The horns of the unicorn of Psalm 22:21 are taken to represent the supporters of the Royal Arms in British history, just as the Coronation services from Egbert to Edward VII, with their symbolic ceremonies, were taken from the Psalms—The oil of gladness above his fellows; the sword girded on the thigh of the most Mighty One; the crown of pure gold; the scepter of righteousness, and the throne of judgment.

Already we have mentioned the love Henry Martyn had for the Psalms, drawing from them unfailing encouragement in his missionary enterprise. Under December 10th, 1805, he quoted in his *Journal* the words of Psalm 22:27, "All the ends of the earth shall remember, and be turned to the Lord," and then remarked—

"Sooner or later, they shall remember what is preached to them, and though missionaries may not see the fruits of their labors, yet the memory of their words shall remain, and in due time shall be the means of turning them unto the Lord."

Psalm 23

It is quite understandable that this much-loved Psalm has been preached on, and written about, more than any other in the Psalter, and the following historical associations prove this Shepherd Psalm has a continuous and abiding influence. Spurgeon's testimony is, "This is the Pearl of Psalms whose soft and pure radiance delights every eye; a Pearl of which Helicon need not be ashamed though Jordan claims it. Of this delightful song it may be affirmed that its piety and poetry are equal, its sweetness and its spirituality are unsurpassed."

Although this surpassing Ode is titleless who else but David, the one-time shepherd, could have written it? Since it has no heading as to any historical event associated with it, this means that every believer can take the Psalm to his own heart. Spurgeon gives it the title of *Heavenly Pastoral,* and then goes on to describe David's early days, sitting under a spreading tree, with his flock around him, singing this unrivalled Pastoral with a heart as full of gladness as it could hold; or, if the Psalm be the product of his after years, we are sure that his soul returned in contemplation to the lovely water-brooks which rippled among the pastures of the wilderness, where in his early days he had been wont to dwell.

Another feature worthy of consideration is the position of the Psalm, following, as it does Psalm 22, in which the woes and agonies of the Shepherd are revealed, and in which there are no green pastures, no still waters. But the cry of the crucified Shepherd, *My God, My God, why hast thou forsaken me?* now results in the joy of a redeemed flock, *The Lord is my shepherd, I shall not want*—or, what more do I want? "We must by experience know the value of blood-shedding, and see the sword awakened against the Shepherd, before we shall be able truly to know the sweetness of the good Shepherd's care."

Henry Ward Beecher, the famous American preacher, wrote of this Psalm as "the nightingale of the Psalms. It is small, of a homely feather, singing shyly out of obscurity; but, oh! it has filled the air of the whole world with melodious joy, greater than the heart can conceive. Blessed be the day on which that Psalm was born! . . . It has charmed more griefs to rest than all the philosophy of the world. . . Nor is the work done. It will go singing to your children and my children, and to their children, through all generations of time; now will it fold its wings till the last pilgrim is safe, and time ended: and then it shall fly back to the bosom of God, whence it issued, and sound on, mingled with all those sounds of celestial joy which make Heaven musical forever."

Spurgeon, however, ventures to compare this Psalm to the lark, which sings as it mounts, and mounts as it sings, until it is out of sight, and even then is not out of hearing. As for Augustine, he is said to having beheld, in a dream, the 119th Psalm rising before him as a tree of life in the midst of the Paradise of God, and the 23rd Psalm as some of the fairest flowers growing around that tree.

I shall not want, 23:1. Curate John Stevenson, renowned expositor of the 18th century, tells the story of a poor member of the flock of Christ reduced to circumstances of the greatest poverty in his old age, yet he never murmured. "You must be badly off," said a kind-hearted neighbor to him one day when they met out walking, "you must be badly off; and I don't know how an old man like you can maintain yourself and your wife, yet you are always cheerful." "Oh, no," the aged man replied, "we are not badly off. I have a rich Father, and He does not suffer me to want, and always takes care of me." These aged Christians were daily pensioners on the Providence of God, and He never failed them. Don Crawford, the African missionary who wrote the classic, *Thinking Black,* faced many scarcities but said that "God always heard the scraping of the bottom of the barrel," and produced what was necessary.

Lie down, 23:2. A short but touching epitaph is frequently seen in the Catacombs at Rome—*In Christe, in pace*—In Christ, peace. To realize the constant presence and guidance from the Shepherd means a peace the world cannot give, nor take away.

The valley of the shadow of death, 23:4. When the godly wife of a missionary in Bombay was dying, a friend said to her that he hoped the Savior would be with her as she walked through the dark valley of the shadow of death. "If this," she replied, "is a dark valley, it has not a dark spot in it, all is light." She had, during most of her sickness, bright views of the perfection of God. "His awful holiness," she said, "appeared the most lovely of all His attributes." At one time she said she wanted words to express her views of the glory and the majesty of Christ. "It seems that if all other glory were annihilated and nothing left but His bare self, it would be enough; it would be a universe of glory!" was one of her last utterances.

Thou anointest my head with oil, 23:5. In the East no entertainment could be without this service, and is given for bodily refreshment. An English lady sailing on an Arabian ship which touched at Trincomalee recorded how an Arabian female came to her cabin and poured perfumed oil on her head. The unguents of Egypt were used to preserve bodies from corruption, ensuring them a long duration in the dreary shades of the sepulchre. The precious perfumed oil of grace and gladness, the Shepherd mysteriously pours upon our souls, purifies and strengthens them.

I will dwell in the house of the Lord, forever, 23:6. What celestial notes, more fitting for the eternal mansions than for these dwelling places below the clouds, the last verse contains. May the Shepherd Himself enable us to live in the spirit of this comforting Psalm, thereby causing us to experience days of Heaven upon earth, before we leave earth for Heaven. Among the 150 Psalms forming the Psalter, the Shepherd Psalm carries the prize for being the best-loved poem from the inspired pen of David, the one-time shepherd lad, whose early life among sheep constituted the background of his famous 23rd Psalm. It would take a weighty volume all its own to record all the stories and incidents regarding its influence in human lives. Testimonies abound as to its worth. Doubtless the majority of saints today can repeat it from memory. Since David wrote it millennia ago, it has filled a very large place in the history of God's children. As one historian says of this fearless Psalm—

> It has sung courage to the army of the disappointed. It has poured balm and consolation into the hearts of the sick, of captives in dungeons, of widows in their pinching grief, of orphans in their loneliness. Dying soldiers have died easier as it was read to them; ghastly hospitals have been illuminated; it has visited the prisoner, and broken his chains, and, like Peter's angel, led him forth in imagination, and sung him back to his home again. It has made the dying Christian slave freer than his master.

If the 6th Psalm may be called a *Well of Marah* into which the tree is at last thrown which sweetens the waters, then the 23rd Psalm is, from first to last, as the *Waters of Siloah* that go softly, having its source in the holy place of the tabernacles of the Most High. In many a tongue the Psalm of the Crook has shown its power when the *Good Shepherd* speaks through it to those who know His voice. In Scotland, the Psalms occupy a very prominent place in congregational singing, and in particular, the 23rd Psalm, every line and every word of which has been engraven for generations on Scottish hearts. It has accompanied them from childhood to old age, from their homes to all seas and lands where they have wandered, and has been to a multitude no man can number, the rod and staff of which it speaks, to guide and guard them in dark valleys, and, at last, they go to dwell in the house of the Lord forever. That the history of this notable Psalm sparkles to the daylight in numerous records, the following stories we have culled is striking proof. Eternity alone, however, will reveal all the secret, but not sunless, resting-places the Psalm has had in hidden hearts all down the ages. In our bewildered age, society needs as never before the guidance and grace of Him Who died as the Good Shepherd, and is to return as the Great Shepherd.

Prothero reminds us that "the language of the Psalm was ever on the lips of those who, in the early history of Christianity suffered violent deaths for or in the faith." This was why Augustine, Church father and Bishop of Hippo, 306-430, fitly chose Psalm 23 as the Hymn of Martyrs.

Francis of Assisi, Italian monk and founder of the Franciscan Order, 1182-1226, going out alone, bareheaded and barefooted, to convert the Sultan, kept up his spirit by chanting this Psalm.

Quaint George Herbert, English divine and poet, 1593-1633, was inspired by David's spirit to pour out his soul in verse. It was to him that Bacon dedicated his *Certaine Psalms,* and his hymn, "The God of Love my Shepherd is," is one of the most popular versions of Psalm 23.

Bishop John Hooper, who, from the time of the accession of Queen Mary, was a marked man, but could have escaped capture by those who hated his witness. But as a true shepherd of his flock in Gloucester he refused saying, "I am thoroughly persuaded to tarry, and to live and die with my sheep." In September of 1553, Hooper was committed to the then Fleet prison to "a vile and stinking chamber," with nothing for his bed but "a little pad of straw" and "a rotten covering." Yet in such appalling conditions he wrote an exposition of Psalm 23, and also of Psalms 62, 73, and 77.

Joseph Addison, English essayist and poet, 1672-1719, owed no considerable portion of his fame to paraphrases of the Psalms. Writing in the *Spectator* in 1712, he said, "David has very beautifully expressed his steady reliance on God Almighty in his 23rd Psalm, which is a kind of pastoral hymn, and filled with those allusions which are usually found in that kind of writing" . . . Then follows the well-known version of the Psalm—*The Lord my pasture shall prepare.*

Heinrich Heine, German poet and critic, 1796-1856, in one of his poems recalled the image of the Shepherd Guide whose "Pastures green and sweet, refresh the wanderer's feet." Dr. John Ker tells us that Heine had been a pantheist and a scoffer but had to lay for years on what he called his *mattress sepulchre,* and took to reading the Bible, especially the Psalms. Almost his last poem, addressed to his much loved wife, bears traces of the Shepherd-Song of God's flock, which David gave to the World. Although the poem lacked the sparkle of Heine's early genius, it is redeemed by its softened tenderness—

> My arm grows weak, Death comes apace,
> Death pale and grim; and I no more
> Can guard my lamb as heretofore
> O God! into thy hands I render
> My crook; keep thou my lambkin tender.
> When I in peace have laid me down,
> Keep thou my lamb, and do not let
> A single thorn her bosom fret

And guide where pastures green and sweet
Refresh the wanderer's weary feet.

John Welsh, the son-in-law of John Knox, who took a prominent part
in the development of the Reformed Church, both in Scotland and France,
had the distinction of being the first graduate and licensed preacher sent
out by the University of Edinburgh. After his banishment to France, he
never returned to Scotland. As he left at 2 in the morning, along with other
Ministers of the Reformed Faith and a large company of friends and
acquaintances, John Welsh joined in the joyful singing of Psalm 23, in the
old version—

The Lord is only my support,
And he that doth me feede;
How can I then lack anie thing
Whereof I stand in need?

Welsh's wife besought the King for her husband, and was offered his
liberty on condition that he preach and teach no more. The brave daughter of John Knox lifted her apron with her hands and said, "I would rather
receive his head here than his liberty at such a price."

Among the courageous Covenanters in Scottish history were two
young women, Marion Harvey and Isabel Hamilton, "honest, worthy lasses," as Alexander Peden called them. Marion was a servant girl in
Borrowstounness, and only 20 years of age. Isabel belonged to Perth and
was of private means. Both girls were apprehended for hearing Donald
Cargill preach, and for helping him escape from the authorities. Both were
executed and no murder was more universally condemned than that of
these two women. On their way to the scaffold for the honor and name of
Jesus, Marion and Isabel were annoyed by the priests who wished to
thrust their prayers on them, and Marion said, "Come, Isabel, let us sing
the 23rd Psalm," which they did. At the scaffold, they sang the 84th Psalm
and Marion said, "I am come here today for avowing Christ to be the
Head of His Church, and King in Zion. O seek Him, sirs, seek Him, and
ye shall find Him."

As for Isabel, her last word was, "Farewell all created comforts;
farewell sweet Bible in which I delighted most, and which has been sweet
to me since I came to prison; farewell Christian acquaintances; now into
thy hands I commit my spirit, Father, Son, and Holy Spirit." Whereupon
the hangmen ushered her into Eternity.

James Inglis, a devout saint of the 18th century had the 23rd Psalm
read to him, and then said, "You will understand me as not speaking
boastfully of myself when I say that every word you have read is personal
to me, personal to my faith, personal to my soul. And now I will rest and
afterwards we will talk about God's mercies." Very similar was the death

of the Indian missionary, Dr. Alexander Duff, who, apparently unconscious and dying, yet responded at the end of each verse as his daughter
read Psalm 23 to him.

Edward Irving, one time assistant to Dr. Thomas Chalmers, and founder
of the Catholic and Apostolic Church, became one of the most famous
men of his time. With his conspicuous figure, sonorous voice, and noble
features, his personal magnetism was heightened, so much so that brilliant
members of London society crowded to hear his mystic eloquence and
prophetic outpourings. Spellbound, large congregations listened to Irving
as he expounded his theories of the Second Advent, and his prophecies of
"The Coming of the Messiah in Glory and Majesty." It was for the first
time in his church at Regent Square that in 1831, speaking in unknown
tongues was heard. Dismissed from his city pulpit in 1832, he was deposed
from his ministry in the Presbyterian Church because of heresy. Although
he was re-ordained by apostles of his church he founded, Irving never
recovered from the blow he received at being cast out of the denomination
in which he had been reared. As he neared his end, he wrote on October
12th, 1834, "How in the night seasons the Psalms have been my consolations against the faintings of flesh and spirit." At the end he was heard
repeating to himself in Hebrew the 23rd Psalm. His dying voice swelled
in glorious conviction as he uttered the word, "Though I walk through the
valley of the shadow of death, I will fear no evil." Irving's last articulate
words were, "If I die, I die unto the Lord, Amen!" and with them he ended
the days of his life on December 7th, 1834.

Lord Byron, who called himself "half a Scot by birth," spent his earliest years at Aberdeen where, from his godly nurse, he gained a love and
knowledge of the Bible which he never lost. He learned many of the
Psalms, with the 1st and the 23rd being among his favorites.

John Ruskin, who founded much of his aesthetic teaching on the Psalms,
included Psalm 23 among those as being sufficient for all personal guidance.
As soon as he was able to read, he studied the Bible by his mother's side,
and learned by heart this Shepherd Psalm, along with other Psalms.

John D. Long, Secretary of the United States Navy Dept., 1897-1900,
during the Spanish War, who affirmed that a study of the Psalms would
give people "a better style and use of our language," also wrote that the
23rd Psalm was his favorite chapter: "With me, as with many others, it
is associated with the earliest period of my life. I was taught it earlier
than I can remember, and taught to repeat it, as was my mother before
me."

Dr. Howard Taylor, son of Hudson Taylor who founded the China
Inland Mission, and who became its Medical Director, often said that
David's universally loved Shepherd Psalm was his favorite.

The great German theologian, Neander, who died in July, 1850, was greatly loved by his students who celebrated his last birthday, January 6th, 1850, by singing to him Psalm 23 in the German language.

Anstice Abbot, who accomplished a great work as a missionary in Bombay, India, wrote to a friend, "I will mention the 23rd Psalm as one of the portions dearest to me, and particularly the third verse."

Sir William Hamilton, who was perhaps the greatest of Scottish philosophers, died repeating, "Thy rod and thy staff they comfort me" 23:4. Another Scot, James Melville, we have previously noted, quoted in his last moments this same verse, "Albeit I walket through the valley of the shadow of death, yet will I fear none evill, because God is with me."

This same verse was brought to the notice of the missionary Alexander Duff, while traveling in the Himalayas where he watched a native shepherd protect his sheep from wolves and other dangerous animals infesting the region. With his long rod the shepherd would strike a wolf such a blow as to make it flee. Thus the words, "Thy rod and thy staff they comfort me," saved the passage as Duff thought from the charge of tautology, the staff referring to God's hold on the sheep, the rod to his defense against enemies, seeing that the Indian shepherd had a long rod, with a thick bar of iron twisted round its lower half.

With the landing of Augustine in England, there began the Benedictine Rule, and the religious history of Saxon England is to a great extent bound up in the progress of the Order. Novices were admitted into the Order with a Psalm. A child, whose hands had been wrapped up in the white folds of the altar-cloth, grew up in the monastic school, and at length came to give himself up to God repeating, "Here will I dwell forever," Psalm 23:6.

The Covenanters were closely associated with Bothwell Bridge, Scotland, where a monument stands to their unflinching courage in defense of the Faith. Among the numbers who approved *The Declaration,* in which was renounced allegiance to the king, defiance of his laws, and a call to him to forfeit his throne, was Richard Cameron. Charles II was disowned as a tyrant and usurper, and "under the standard of our Lord Jesus Christ, Captain of our Salvation," war was declared upon the king. Richard Cameron was captured and killed, his head and hands "hagged off with a dirk," were thrown into a sack and carried to Edinburgh for display at the City Port. When these gruesome remains were first shown to Richard's father, then a prisoner at the Tolbooth, Glasgow, he was asked if he knew to whom they belonged. The old man, kissing the cold, blood-despattered brow of his fair-haired son replied, "I know them, I know them, they are my son's, my dear son's." Then he added words recalling Psalm 23:6, "It is the Lord; good is the will of the Lord who cannot wrong me nor mine, but has made goodness and mercy to follow us all our days."

Psalm 24

Patrick Delany, well-known divine of the 17th century, said of this anthem of praise that, "I have no notion of hearing, or of any man's ever having seen or heard anything so great, so solemn, so celestial, on this side the gates of Heaven." The early saints appropriated this 24th Psalm to the Lord's Day, believing that it was intended to celebrate the Resurrection of the Messiah, and His Ascension into Heaven, there to sit as a Priest upon God's throne, and from thence to return bringing blessings and mercies to His people.

The title heralds it as *A Psalm of David,* and leads us to meditate upon the wonderful operations of the Spirit upon Israel's sweet singer, enabling him to touch the mournful string in Psalm 22—The Psalm of the Cross: to pour forth gentle notes of peace in Psalm 23—The Psalm of the Crook, and here to utter such majestic and triumphant strains in Psalm 24—the Psalm of the Crown.

If the Psalm has any historical connections, it can be related to being sung when the Ark of the Covenant was taken up from the home of Obed-edom, to remain behind curtains upon the hill of Zion. David, however, looked beyond the upgoing of the Ark to the sublime ascension of the King of Glory. Thus, this precious ode can be called *The Song of the Ascension.* It will be found that Psalm 15 and Psalm 24 make an impressive pair.

The earth is the Lord's, v. 1. The first part of this verse is engraven upon the Royal Exchange, London, and will one day be written in letters of light across the sky.

Lift up your heads, O ye gates, 24:7. Doors were often taken from their hinges when Easterners would show welcome to a guest, and some doors were drawn up and down like a portcullis, and may possibly have protruded from the top, thus literally lifting up their heads. The picture the Psalmist gives us is, of course, highly poetical, and reveals how wide Heaven's gate is set by the Ascension of our Lord. The ancient gates of the eternal Temple are personified and addressed in song by the attending cohort of rejoicing spirits—

> Lo his triumphal chariot waits,
>> And angels chant to solemn lay,
> "Lift up your heads, ye heavenly gates;
>> Ye everlasting doors give way."

Several poets have expressed in moving verse the triumphs of the Lord of Glory to be found in this Psalm. Here is a stanza of James Scott on verses 7 to 10—

> Lift up your heads, ye gates, and, O prepare,
> Ye living orbs, your everlasting doors,
> The King of Glory comes!
> What King of Glory? He whose puissant might
> Subdued Abaddon, and the invernal powers.
> Of darkness bound in adamantine chains:
> Who, wrapp'd in glory, with the Father reigns,
> Omnipotent, immortal, infinite!

For the sheep of the fold who have known the love, care, provision and protection of the crucified Shepherd all the days of their life, there is the glorious prospect of seeing Him in Heaven, crowned with glory and honor. As John Ker expresses it, "The Psalm of the *Lord the Shepherd* is followed by that of the *Lord the King,* for the door of mercy leads into the throne-room of power, and places those who enter it under the shadow of the Almighty."

Principal Carstairs, who became celebrated as the restorer of the Scottish Church at the Revolution, had a godly father who was a man of warm devotional character, and suffered severely in the time of the 28 years of persecution in Scotland. At one time, while conducting the Sacrament for a brother minister, a remarkable emotion overtook the hearers as they listened to his sermon. Then Carstairs, Sr., gave out for singing the 24th Psalm—

> He from th' Eternal shall receive
>   The blessing him upon,
> And righteousness, ev'n from the God
>   Of his salvation.
> This is the generation
>   That after Him inquire,
> O Jacob, who do seek Thy face,
>   With their whole heart's desire.

While singing the whole of this Psalm, the whole gathering was marvelously affected, and it seemed as if glory filled the house as the bread and wine were served in a kind of rapture.

At one time there spread all over South-Western France the popular legend, that on Easter Day, when the words, "Lift up your heads, O ye gates," Psalm 24:7, were being sung in church, the treasure-houses marked by dolmens, cromlechs, and menirs, or concealed, as at Brussac, in the walls of castles, spring open, and men could, for a brief space, enter and enrich themselves unharmed by their infernal guardians.

Other interesting references to this Psalm, Ruskin included among the first half of the Psalter as being beneficial to all are as follows. In the Great Exhibition of 1851, sanction for such a huge project was the text, "The earth is the Lord's, and all that therein is, the compass of the world, and they that dwell therein."

Protestant worship was not authorized in Paris till the Edict of Nantes, 1598. It was in this year that Catherine of Navarre assembled a large company in the Palace of the Louvre, which had been the center of the massacre of St. Bartholomew. The Psalm first sung was the 24th, and with deep feeling the remnant sang, "The earth is the Lord's, and the fullness thereof; the world, and they that dwell therein."

We wonder how many Londoners know that across the portico of *The Royal Exchange* in the heart of their city the words are inscribed, "The earth is the Lord's, and the fullness thereof." A wag, reading this inscription once remarked: "The earth is the Lord's, and the fullness thereof belongs to *The Royal Exchange.*"

In this Coronation Psalm of David, no one but the King of Glory is worthy to stand in God's holy place, seeing that He only had clean hands, and a pure heart, and in the days of His flesh, never lifted up His soul unto vanity, nor swore deceitfully, Psalm 24:3-4.

William Langland, poet of the 14th century, whose "tender sympathy redeems the harshness of his rugged lines, and gives to his racy vigour and homely language something of spiritual intensity," and who clothes much of his *Vision of Piers Plowman* in the language of the Psalms, in Section 17 of this work, refers to Psalm 24:7-10 as being expressive of the Resurrection of Christ—"Lift up your heads, O ye gates," etc. After his death, the devils in Hell saw a soul "hitherward sailing with glory and with great light," and knew the coming of the King of Glory. Then the *Dukes* of that *dymme place* are bidden to undo the gates—

> That Christ may come in
> The Kynges sone of hevene.

There is also an echo of these same verses of the Psalm in Milton's *Paradise Lost* where in Book VII we have the stanzas—

> Heav'n open'd wide
> Her ever during gates, harmonious sound
> On golden hinges moving to let forth
> The King of Glory in His powerful Word
> And Spirit coming to create new worlds.

—and, as God returns heavenward, His creative work accomplished:

> Open, ye everlasting Gates, they sung,
> Open, ye Heav'ns, your living doors; let in

> The great Creator, from his Work return'd
> Magnificent, his six days' work—a World.

During the Danish invasions of England, the land was devoured as if by locusts. There was, however, one signal triumph over the Danes, and "Saxon legend inseparably associated the Psalms with the person of St. Neot, who every morning said the Psalter through, and every midnight chanted a hundred Psalms." When he died, full of years and honor, there was no one of equal sanctity to take his place. But legend has it that when, in 878 A.D. King Alfred lay in his tent at Iley, on the eve of the battle of Ethendun that St. Neot appeared to Alfred, "like an angel of God, his hair white as snow, his raiment, white, glistering, and fragrant with the scents of heaven." Neot promised the King victory and recited the verse, "The Lord shall be with you, even the Lord strong and mighty in battle, who giveth victory to kings," Psalm 24:8. Next day, the battle turned in favor of King Alfred, and a majestic figure the Saxons recognized as St. Neot, led the victorious Saxons, and peace came to the land with many of the Saxons becoming Christians.

Psalm 25

T he historical setting of the second of the seven Penitential Psalms is not too difficult to state. As David refers to the sins of his youth, it is evidently a production of his latter days. Then as he has painful references to the craft and cruelty of his many foes, it is more than likely that he had in mind the period when his much-loved son, Absalom, headed a massive rebellion against him. As a whole, the Psalm is a true portrait of the writer's holy trust, his many trials, his great transgression, his bitter repentance, and deep distresses—a true mark of "a man after God's own heart" whose sorrows remind him of his sins, and whose sorrow for sin drives him to God.

Thomas Fuller, spiritual expositor of a past century, drew attention to the four Psalms immediately following one another, in which David is presented in four postures of piety, namely, *lying, standing, sitting,* and *kneeling.*

"In Psalm 22, he is *lying* all alone, falling flat on his face, low groveling on the ground, even almost entering into a degree of despair, speaking of himself in the history of Christ in the mystery, 'My God, My God, why hast thou forsaken me?'

"In Psalm 23, he is *standing*, and though God's favor, in despite of his foes, trampling and triumphing over all opposition; 'The Lord is my Shepherd, therefore shall I lack nothing.'

"In Psalm 24, he is *sitting,* like a doctor in his chair, or a professor in his place, reading a lecture of divinity, and describing the character of that man—how he must be accomplished—'Who shall ascend into the holy hill?'—and hereafter be a partaker of happiness.

"In Psalm 25, he is *kneeling*, with hands and voice lifted up to God, and on these two hinges that whole Psalm turneth; the one is a hearty beseeching of God's mercy, and the other a humble bemoaning of his own misery."

A most peculiar feature of this Psalm is the fact that it is the first specimen of the acrostic mode of writing, once so fashionable among Jews, as numerous instances in their compositions prove. The twenty-two verses of this alphabetical song begin in the original with the letters of the Hebrew alphabet in their proper order. Andrew Bonar and C. H. Spurgeon both reckoned that this method was adopted by David to assist memory; and that the Holy Spirit, Inspirer of all David's Psalms, may have employed the method to show that the graces of style and the arts of poetry may lawfully be used in God's service. "Why should not all the wit and ingenuity of man be sanctified to noblest ends by being laid upon the altar of God?"

Unto thee, O Lord, do I lift up my soul, 25:1. Cyprian tells us that in primitive times the minister was wont to prepare people's minds to pray, by announcing *Sursum corda*—"Lift up your hearts." The Jews used to write upon the walls of their synagogues a Hebrew phrase, meaning, *A prayer without the intention of the affection is like a body with a soul.* Through the prophet God sighed, "This people draweth nigh unto me with their lips, but their heart is far from me," Isa. 29:13.

For they have been ever of old—or, "from eternity," 25:6. When we plead with the Lord to bestow His tender mercies and loving-kindnesses upon us, we can urge it as a custom of the most ancient kind. In courts of law men make much of precedents, and we may plead them at the throne of grace. As one writer expresses it, "Faith must make use of experiences and read them over to God, out of the register of a sanctified memory, as a recorder to him who cannot forget."

The sins of my youth, 25:7. Two aged saints met one day, and the younger said to his older fellow-pilgrim, "Well, how long have you been interested in the things of God?" "Fifty years," was the reply. "Well, have you ever regretted that you began when young to devote yourself to God?" "Oh, no," said he, and the tears trickled down his furrowed cheeks; "I weep when I think of the sins of my youth; it is this which makes me weep now." God has promised to remember our sins no more, whether committed in youth or afterwards, if only they are all under the blood.

O Lord, pardon my iniquity; for it is great, 25:11. William Secker has the comment on this verse, "Esau mourned not because he sold his birthright, which was his sin, but because he lost the blessing, which was his punishment. This is like weeping with an onion; the eye sheds tears because it smarts. A mariner casts overboard that cargo in a tempest, which he courts the return of when the winds are silenced. Many complain more of the sorrows to which they are born, than of the sins with which they were born; they tremble more at the vengeance of sin, than at the venom of sin, one delights them, the other affrights them."

The great Vieyra, whose dramatic preaching gave him the reputation of being the first preacher of his age, delivered a sermon of tremendous spiritual power at a Fast on the occasion of the threatened destruction of the Portuguese dominion in Brazil by the Dutch. Taking the 11th verse of this Psalm as the basis of his message, Vieyra said, "I confess, my God, that it is so; that we are all sinners in the highest degree. But so far am I from considering this any reason why I should cease from my petition, that I behold in it a new and convincing argument which may influence thy goodness. All that I have said before is based on no other foundation than the glory and honor of thy most holy name. And what motive can I offer more glorious to that same Name, that our sins are many and great?"

Mine eyes are ever toward the Lord, 25:15. John Calvin's remark is apt—"As the sense of sight is very quick, and exercises an entire influence over the whole frame, it is no uncommon thing to find all the affections denoted by the term *eyes.*" *He shall pluck my feet out of the net*—An unfortunate dove, whose feet are taken in the snare of the fowler, is a fine emblem of the soul entangled in the cares or pleasures of the world; from which she desires, through the power of grace, to fly away, and to be at rest, with her glorified Redeemer.

I am desolate and afflicted, 25:16. David uses no less than six words all descriptive of woe—*Desolate, Afflicted, Troubles, Distresses, Affliction, Pain.* The Lord Jesus, in the days of His flesh experienced such a condition; none could enter into the secret depths of His sorrows, He trod the winepress alone, and therefore He is able to succour in the fullest sense those who tread the solitary path.

> Christ leads me through no darker rooms
>   Than he went through before;
> He that into God's kingdom comes,
>   Must enter by this door.

Let me not be ashamed; for I put my trust in thee, 25:20. This verse reminds us of Coriolanus betaking himself to the hall of Attius Tullur, and sitting as a helpless stranger there, claiming the king's hospitality, though aware of his having deserved to die at his hands. Here, the Psalmist throws himself on the compassions of an injured God with similar feelings; *I trust in thee!*

This further Psalm from *God's Poet Laureate* is another that figures in the history of the Covenanters. These touching words began the dying-song of Margaret Wilson, as the sea slowly rose and covered her body at Blednock, Wigtown—

> My sins and faults of youth
>   Do thou, O Lord, forget:
> After thy mercy think on me,
>   And for thy goodness great.

Margaret was only 20 years of age, but dearly loved to gather with the saints in field and house coventicle. Captured and condemned to be drowned, she was tied to a stake within the tide-mark, where the Solway waters come up swift and strong into the channel of the Blednoch. Her persecutors gave her a last chance of denying the Covenant, but defying them she shouted back, "Never, I am Christ's, let me go!" Faithful unto the death this blameless martyr illustrated the truth of this precious Psalm which she sang until the rising tide choked her—

> O do thou keep my soul
> Do thou deliver me:
> And let me never be asham'd,
> Because I trust in thee.

The Mass for the first Sunday in Advent began with the opening words of Psalm 25, "Unto Thee, O Lord, will I lift up my soul. My God, I have put my trust in Thee." It was on this calendar day that Louis of France was crowned in 1226. Joinville, the historian, who notes the fact, observed that even in his death the King had perfect trust in God. Having regulated his life by Psalm 106:3, he died with Psalm 5:7 on his lips, August 25th, 1270.

Pico della Mirandola, one of the most brilliant scholars of the Italian Renaissance, bosom-friend of Savonarola, left the words—

> Let no day pass but thou once, at the least wise, present thyself to God by prayer, and falling down before Him flat on the ground . . . not from the extremity of thy lips, but from the inwardness of thine heart cry these words of the Psalmist, 'O remember not the sins and offenses of my youth; but according to thy mercy think upon me, O Lord, for Thy goodness,' Psalm 25:6.

During the Indian Mutiny of 1857, William Edwards was the magistrate and collector in the Rohilkund district. Along with other fugitives, he experienced many harrowing experiences. Merciless massacres by natives, and plagues of flies brought Edwards moments of despair. The Psalms, however, proved to him and friends with him, great comfort. On August 5, 1857 he wrote in his Diary—

> There is not a day on which we do not find something that appears as if written especially for persons in our unhappy circumstances, to meet the feelings and wants of the day. This morning, for instance, I derived unspeakable comfort from the 13th and 16th verses of the 25th Psalm. 'The secret of the Lord is among them that fear Him; and He will show them His covenant,' and 'The sorrows of my heart are enlarged: O bring Thou me out of my troubles'; and in the evening, from the 14th, 15th and 16th verses of Psalm 27:16—'O tarry Thou the Lord's pleasure; be strong, and He shall comfort thine heart; and put thou thy trust in the Lord.'

St. Francis de Sales, Bishop of Geneva, 1567-1622, one of the godliest of men in his time, had a mind steeped in the Psalms and thus his thoughts naturally clothed themselves in their language. It was on the

Feast of St. John, 1622, that he was struck down by a paralytic seizure, which left his mind unclouded. A friendly visitor expressed regret at his condition, but Sales replied—

> "Father, I am waiting on God's mercy: *Expectans, expectavi Dominum et intendit mahi"*—"I waited patiently for the Lord, and He inclined unto me, and heard my calling." One of the watchers by his bedside asked Sales if he feared the last struggle, and he replied, "Mine eyes are ever looking unto the Lord, for He shall pluck my feet out of the net," Psalm 25:15. He died in the evening of the Holy Innocents' Day, 1622.

Psalm 26

Although this Psalm was composed by David, and taken up as it is with his enduring reproach, the title gives us no clue as to its historical association in the Psalmist's career. It is thought that the Psalm was David's appeal to Heaven at the time of the assassination of Ishbosheth, by Baanah and Rechab, to protect his innocence of all participation in that treacherous murder. David called upon God the supreme Judge, the testimony of good conscience bearing him witness, to believe that he had no part in such a foul crime. A forceful illustration of such an appeal to Heaven appears in the life of George Whitfield, that mighty evangelist of the 17th century—

> However some may account me a mountebank and an enthusiast, one that is only going to make you methodically mad; they may breathe out their invectives against me, yet Christ knows all: he takes notice of it, and I shall leave it to him to plead my cause, for he is a gracious Master. I have already found him so, and am sure he will continue so. Vengeance is his, and he will repay it! *Judge me, O Lord!* 26:1.

Dissemblers, 26:4. Thomas Adams of the Victorian Age describes those who hide themselves to do evil in this unique fashion—"The hypocrite has, much angel without, more devil within. He fries in words, freezes in works; speaks by ells, doth good by inches. He is a stinking dunghill, covered over with snow; a loose-hung mill that keeps great clacking, but grinds no grist; a lying hen that cackles when she hath not laid."

I will wash mine hands in innocency, 26:6. Gotthold, preacher of the early 16th century, had a gift of using striking emblems in his sermons. One morning, when pouring water into a basin to wash his hands, he recalled these words of David which revealed how diligently he had endeavored to walk blamelessly and habitually in the fear of God. Upon the verse Gotthold mused, and then said—

> Henceforth, my God, every time I pour out water to wash with, I will call to mind that it is my duty to cleanse my hands from wicked actions, my mouth from wicked words, and my heart from wicked lusts and desires, that so I may be enabled to lift up holy hands unto thee, and with unspotted lips and heart worship thee to the best of my ability . . . My first care shall be to maintain a blameless walk; my next, when I have thoughtlessly

defiled myself, to cleanse and wash away my stain, and remove mine iniquity from thine eyes.

Their right hand is full of bribes, 26:10. Walking in his integrity, David condemned those who took bribes for favors desired. To quote Thomas Adams again, "They that see furthest into the law, and most clearly discern the cause of justice, if they suffer the dust of bribes to be thrown into their sight their eyes will water and twinkle, and fall at last to blind connivance. It is a wretched thing when justice is made a hackney that may be backed for money, and put on with golden spurs, even to the desired journey's end of injury and iniquity. Far be from our souls this wickedness that the ear should be open to complaints should be stopped with the earwax of partiality. Alas! poor truth, that she must now be put to the charges of a golden earpick, or she cannot be heard!"

My feet standeth in an even place, 26:12. In his uprightness, David testified that his walk was not haltingly but uncomely as those who in unequal ways, hobbling up and down, or as those Solomon described—"legs of the lame are not equal," and so cannot stand in an even place, because one leg is longer than the other. "The hypocrite, like the badger, hath one foot shorter than another; or, like a foundered horse, he doth not stand, as we say, right on all fours: one foot at least you shall perceive he favors, loth to put it down. If our feet are evenly and firmly fixed on the Rock of Ages we need have no fear that our adversaries will triumph over us.

During the reign of Louis XIV, Protestant ministers were driven from France, but the people were forbidden to leave. Many of them suffered greatly, and despair drove many a godly Protestant inhabitant to attempt every means of escape, and thrilling stories are told of those who managed to reach friendly frontiers. Reaching a land willing to welcome them they thanked God for the freedom and safety their own country had denied them. Pineton of Chambrun, one of the exiles, wrote that when he and his companions came in sight of Geneva, they sang with tears of joy Psalm 26, which from verse 8 to the end of the Psalm seemed so descriptive of their experiences—

> Lord, I have loved the habitation of thy house, and the place where thine honor dwelleth. Gather not my soul with sinners, nor my life with bloody men . . . But as for me, I will walk in mine integrity; redeem me, and be merciful unto me. My foot standeth in an even place; in the congregation will I bless the Lord, 26:8-12.

Peter Abelard, during 1114, was the most famous teacher in the then most renowned school in Paris. Near Troyes he built the Oratory of the Paraclete, which ultimately he made over to his much-loved Heloise and her nuns. Between Abelard and Heloise there was a deep affection, but it is doubtful if they ever met again once she entered convent life. In a letter to her he exhorted her to patience and resignation and much prayer. Quoting Psalm 26:2—"Examine us, O Lord, and prove us," Abelard wrote, "It is as if the psalmist asked for himself, 'Examine the strength there is, and suit the burden to it.' O Lord, that which Thou hast severed in the world, join forever unto Thyself in Heaven, Amen!" The severance of these lovers meant pain to both.

During the 15th century, in the spirit of the Psalms, monastic builders lavished their genius and devotion on beautiful monasteries for there was the desire to adore the habitation of God, and prepare dwelling-places for His honor. Hugh of Cluni was one of these, and, according to his biographer, he took as his incentive the verse, "I have loved the habitation of Thy house, and the place where Thine honor dwelleth," Psalm 26, and thus devoted his means entirely to the decoration of his church, and to the good of the poor.

William Langland, the people's *Dante* of the 14th century we have previously mentioned, in his renowned *Vision of Piers Plowman,* discussing the matter of Bribery has the comment, "God sees also that Justice and Favor are bestowed on men in whose hands are wickedness," provided that "their right hand is full of gifts," Psalm 26:10.

Psalm 27

Common to many of the Psalms is the short, plain announcement, *A Psalm of David,* with some of them not intimating the occasion of its composition in the life of the Psalmist. Usually, however, from the language of such Psalms, we can gather clues as to the historical connection, as in this 27th Psalm, when in verses 2 and 3 as David was pursued by enemies, the writer was shut out from the house of the Lord, verse 4; telling us of his recent parting from his parents, verse 10, and then having slander cast upon him, verse 12. All of these experiences would seem to be connected with the occasion when Doeg the Edomite betrayed and spoke against David to Saul. But this Psalm of cheerful hope has been a benediction to saints all down the ages who, in seasons of trial, learned how to rest upon the Almighty arm. The language David used of himself is likewise applicable to the Church, and also to her Lord.

The Lord is my light and my salvation; whom shall I fear . . . the strength of my life, 27:1. The fearlessness faith begets is wonderfully illustrated for us in the experience of Alice Driver, martyr, when at her examination she put all the examiners to silence, so that they had not a word to say, but looked at one another in amazement. Then she said, "Have you no more to say? God be honored, you be not able to resist the Spirit of God, in me, a poor woman. I was an honest poor man's daughter, never brought up at the University as you have been; but I have driven the plough many a time before my father, I thank God, yet, notwithstanding, in defense of God's truth, and in the cause of my Master, Christ, by his grace I will set my foot against the foot of any of you all in the maintenance and defense of the same; and if I had a thousand lives they should go for payment thereof." The Chancellor, however, condemned her to death, and she returned to the prison joyful.

The Lord is my Light. Making all things visible, light was the first made of all visible things. St. Bernard, who loved this simile of the Lord, said of this opening phrase of the Psalm—

> Adorable Sun, I cannot walk without thee; enlighten my steps, and furnish this barren and ignorant mind with thoughts worthy of thee. Adorable fullness of light and heat, be thou the true noonday of my soul; exterminate its darkness, disperse its clouds; burn, dry up, and consume all its filth and impurities. Divine Sun, rise upon my mind, and never set.

That will I seek after, 27:4. Holy desires must lead to resolute action. An old proverb says, "Wishers and woulders are never good housekeepers." Another saying reads, "Wishing never fills a sack." In his trying circumstances, David might have been expected to seek repose and safety, but no, he had his heart set on the pearl and was determined to find it. *One thing.* Divided aims tend to distraction. Alexander Pope has the lines—

> One master passion in the breast
> Like Aaron's serpent, swallows up the rest.

That I may dwell in the house of the Lord all the days of my life, 27:4. The word *dwell* used here implies to reside continually there, not to come for a spurt or a fit. The godly mother of St. Austen knew how to *dwell* in the house of the Lord, seeing that she came so duly and truly twice a day, which led her son to record, "That she, in thy Scriptures might hear, of God, what thou saidst to her, and thou, in her prayers, what she said to thee." In another place St. Austen spoke of Christians as "the *emmets* of God"—"emmet" being an old English term for *dial.* "Behold the emmet of God it riseth every day, it runneth to God's Church, it there prayeth, it heareth the lesson read, it singeth a psalm, it ruminateth what it hearest, it meditateth thereupon, and hoardeth up within itself the precious corn gathered from that barn-floor."

To behold the beauty of the Lord, and to enquire in his temple, 27:4. Once David felt himself in a safe and secure position, what was his main purpose? Not as Pyrrhus, King of Epirus, to sit still and be merry, when he had overcome the Romans and all his enemies, as he sometime said to Cyneas, the philosopher, but to improve his rest to perpetual piety, in going from day to day to God's house, as Hannah of old did. Pyrrhus found solace of his soul in the beauty of the sanctuary, as David before him had found.

He shall hide me, 27:5. The word used here for *hide* means to hide, secrete, and then to defend and protect. It is a word that could be properly applied to those who had fled from oppression, or impending evil, and *secreted* themselves in a cavern, and thus were safe from pursuers. Doubtless when David used this metaphor, he had in mind the ancient custom of offenders, who would flee to the tabernacle, or altar, where they esteemed themselves safe. The word *pavilion* comes from a word meaning a *butterfly,* and signifies a *tent* of cloth stretched out on poles, which in form resembles in some measure the outstretched wings of a butterfly.

Wait on the Lord, be of good courage, 27:14. The Greek for "good courage," implies, "be comfortable," "hold fast," "be manly," or "quit thee as a man," which is the translation Paul gives us in 1 Corinthians 16:13.

This challenging verse, warning us against fear, remissness, faintness of heart, and other infirmities was embodied in Bishop Thomas Ken's stirring poem—

> Stand but your ground, your ghostly foes will fly—
> Hell trembles at a heaven-directed eye;
> Choose rather to defend than to assail—
> Self-confidence will in the conflict fail.
> When you are challenged you may dangers meet—
> True *courage* is a fixed, not sudden heat;
> Is always humble, lives in self-distrust,
> And will itself into no danger thrust.
> Devote yourself to God, and you will find
> God fights the battles of a will resigned.
> Love Jesus! love will no base fear endure—
> Love Jesus! and of conquest rest secure.

The Rev. George Walker was a noble Protestant who defied King James in his siege of Londonderry when the forces of the garrison dwindled owing to treachery, sickness, famine, or words. Walker and his officers clung to their post with the tenacity of despair, and preached a remarkable sermon on *Constancy,* which Cathedral Sermon is still in existence. A sentence of this stirring call reads, "Therefore let a good Christian consider that his strength is in the Lord. And if God hear his side, he need not be afraid though danger beset him round about, but be comforted and made valiant by the words of the kingly prophet—

> The Lord is my light and my salvation, whom shall I fear?
> The Lord is the strength of my life; of whom shall I be afraid?
> When the wicked, even mine enemies and my foes, came upon me
> to eat up my flesh, they stumbled and fell.
> Though a host should encamp against me, my heart shall not fear;
> though war shall arise against me, in this will I be confident, Psalm
> 27.

Sunday, July 28th, 1689, was a memorable day. Says Ash, the biographer: "It was to be remembered with thanksgiving by the besieged of Derry as long as they live, for on this day we were delivered from famine and slavery." On the 31st of July, 1689, the enemy decamped, and the cause of the Revolution was saved in Ireland.

George John Romanes, one of the ablest of modern biologists, wrote a *Sonnet* on Psalm 27, the first of which reads—

> I ask not for Thy love, O Lord; the days
>   Can never come when anguish shall atone,
>   Enough for me were but Thy pity shown,

To me as to the stricken sheep that strays,
With ceaseless cry for unforgotten ways—
O lead me back to pastures I have known
Or find me in the wilderness alone,
And slay me, as the hand of mercy slays.

James Hannington, the first Bishop of Equatorial Africa, in the 18th century, endured many bitter experiences when fierce persecution of Christians broke out in the country. Consumed with fever, and at times delirious from pain, devoured by vermin, and menaced every moment by death, the resolute Bishop found strength in the Psalms, and in his Diary, October 28th, he wrote, "I am quite broken down and low. Comforted by Psalm 27. Word came that Mwanga had sent three soldiers, but what news they bring, they will not let me know. Much comforted by Psalm 28." Shortly after this, at the early age of 37, Hannington was killed.

In India, too, there was the groundswell of the terrible mutiny of 1857. Sir John Lawrence, the then British representative, had done much for the preservation of the Indian Empire, who could not quit his post, conceded that his wife should return to their children in England. Afterwards, Lady Lawrence wrote, "When the last morning of separation, January 6, 1858 arrived, we had our usual Bible reading, and I can never think of Psalm 27, which was the portion we then read together, without recalling that sad time." As one peruses the Psalm they he see what springs of comfort must have opened in every verse for those two troubled hearts.

It was from the first verse of this Psalm that the University of Oxford took its motto—*Dominus illuminatio mea*—"The Lord is my light," Psalm 27:1. Savonarola, who had a great love of the Psalms, in the hours of his terrible torture, wrote, "Bowed at the feet of the Lord, my eyes bathed with tears, I cried, *The Lord is my light and my salvation; of whom shall I be afraid?*"

St. Francois de Sales, Bishop of Geneva, we have previously mentioned, was sometimes beset by midnight terrors, and as a preparation against their approach he would repeat, "I am 'safe under his feathers', Psalm 91:4; and 'The Lord is my light and my salvation . . . of whom, then, shall I be afraid?'" Psalm 27:1.

Pope Gregory the Great had a mind immersed in the Psalms which consoled his heart in troubled times. When made Pope in 590 A.D., he seemed to be lamented by the change of his monastic life for it seemed to thrust him far from the face of God, and back into the world, and so he wrote: "I panted for the face of God, not in words only, but from the inmost marrow of my heart, crying, My heart hath talked of Thee, Seek ye my face; Thy face, Lord, will I seek," Psalm 27:9.

A touching story is told of Commander Gardiner who found himself, in 1826, free to devote his life to missionary work. For years he labored among the Zulus in South Africa and the Indians in South America. In 1850 he sailed with six like-minded companions for Tierra del Fuego where they hoped to establish a mission, but were stranded on Picton Island, and great trials overtook the brave little band. One by one they sickened and died, except Gardiner, whose body later on was found unburied on the shore. He dearly loved the Psalms and facing starvation wrote in his Diary, "June 4, 1851, 'Wait on the Lord, be of good courage, and He shall strengthen thine heart. Wait I say on the Lord,'" Psalm 27:14. A lucky shot, fired with almost the last grain of powder, killed five ducks, and gratitude for a good meal found expression in the promise, "He will regard the prayer of the destitute, and not despise their prayer," Psalm 102:17.

To all young people studying history, the tragedy that overtook Lady Jane Dudley's reign and her death on the scaffold on Monday, February 12th 1554, is well known. Losing her crown, her palace became her prison when she stoutly refused to embrace the Roman faith. Her last hours were spent writing to her father, bidding him not to reproach himself for her death, and exhorting him to remain firm in his faith. She also wrote an appeal to Chaplain Harding in which she reproached him for his apostasy urging him to lay certain Scriptures to heart, including Psalm 27:14, which had greatly comforted her own heart.

Psalm 28

Here is another of those spiritual odes bearing the general title, *A Psalm of David*, with no indication as to the historical occasion that gave it birth. Spurgeon, is his preface to an exposition of this 28th Psalm, wrote that "its position, following Psalm 27, seems to have been designed, for it is a most suitable pendant and sequel to it. It is another of those *songs in the night* of which the pen of David was so prolific. The thorn at the breast of the nightingale was said by the old naturalists to make it sing; David's grief made him eloquent in holy psalmody. The main pleading of this Psalm is that the suppliant may not be confounded with the workers of iniquity for whom he expresses the utmost abhorrence; it may suit any slandered saint who, being misunderstood by men, and treated by them as an unworthy character, is anxious to stand upright before the bar of God. The Lord Jesus may be seen here pleading as the representative of his people."

My Rock, 28:1. This oft-repeated metaphor so expressive of the safety and security to be found in God, has comforted countless numbers of saints down the ages. In the early 18th century, the Rev. John Rees, the well-known minister of Crown St, Soho, London, was visited on his death-bed by the Rev. John Leifchild, who, because he was a very close friend of Rees, asked him to describe his real state of mind. This seemed to make the dying lamp glow, and raising himself up and looking his friend in the face, Rees, with great dignity and determination said: "Christ is his person, Christ is the love of his heart, Christ is the power of his arm, is the Rock on which I rest: and now" (reclining his head gently on the pillow) "Death, strike!"

Be not silent unto me, 28:1. Samuel Rutherford, speaking of the Savior's delay in responding to the request of the Syrophenician woman, said, "he *answered* not a word, but it is not said, he *heard* not a word. These two differ much. Christ often heareth when he doth not answer—his not answering *is an answer,* and speaks thus—'Pray on, go on and cry, for the Lord holdeth his door fast bolted,' not to keep you out, but that you may knock, and knock, and it shall be opened." The two phrases, "I *lift* up my hands toward thy holy temple," and "*Lift* them up forever," 28:2, 9 provide a profitable meditation.

Give them according to their deeds, 28:4. History is replete with illustrations of men being paid back in their own coin, as we say. Think of the following instances—

The *Egyptians* killed the Hebrew male children—God smote the first born of Egypt.

Sisera, who thought to destroy Israel with his iron chariots, was himself killed with an iron nail, struck through his temples.

Gideon slew forty elders of Succoth—his sons were murdered by Abimelech.

Abimelech slew 70 sons of Gideon upon one stone—his own head was broken by a piece of millstone thrown by a woman.

Saul slew the Gibeonites—seven of his own sons were hung up before the Lord.

Joab having killed Abner, Amasa, and Absalom, was put to death by Solomon.

Daniel saw his accusers thrown into lion's den they had meant for him.

Haman hung upon the gallows he had designed for Mordecai.

The history of later years, after the Bible, testifies to the same law of retribution—

Bajazet was carried about by Tamerlane in an iron cage, he had intended for Tamerlane.

Mazentius built a bridge to entrap Constantine, and was overthrown himself on that very spot.

Alexander VI was poisoned by the wine he had prepared for another.

Charles IX made the streets of Paris to stream with Protestant blood—soon after blood streamed from all parts of his body in a bloody sweat.

Cardinal Beaton condemned George Wishart to death, and soon after died a violent death himself. He was murdered in bed, and his body was laid out in the same window from which he had looked upon Wishart's execution.

Bishop Hannington, in the hour of extreme need and facing massacre wrote in his Diary: "Much comforted by Psalm 28." Quotations from the Psalms have supplied inscriptions fro ancient coins, like those of the Black Prince in Guienna, who had the words of Psalm 28:8 inscribed on them in Latin, *Dominus Ajutor Menus Et Protector Meus*—"The Lord is the saving strength of his anointed," 28:8.

Psalm 29

A part from the intimation that this was *A Psalm of David,* we have no knowledge what prompted such a sublime song. Perhaps he was inspired to compose it when overtaken by a thunderstorm, and thus led by the Spirit to express in such descriptive language the glory of God in the peal of thunder, and in the mighty floods an equinoctial tornado can produce. We cannot read the eleven verses of the Psalm without seeing how they march to the time of thunderbolts. Spurgeon suggests that as "the 8th Psalm should be read by moonlight, when the stars are bright, so this 29th Psalm can be best rehearsed beneath the black wing of tempest, by the glare of the lightning, or amid that dubious dusk which heralds the war of elements. God is everywhere conspicuous, and all the earth is hushed by the majesty of His presence."

As to the application of this turbulent Psalm to life and experience, Spurgeon described true ministers of the Gospel as songs of thunder, through whom the voice of God in Christ Jesus is full of majesty. Thus, God's Works and God's Word are joined together, and no man can put them asunder by the false idea that Theology and Science can by any possibility oppose each other. There is also the prophetic aspect of the Psalm in which we can behold the dread tempests of the latter days, and the security in such for those who worship the Lord in the beauty of holiness. That there is no phenomenon in nature so awful as a thunderstorm, almost every poet from Homer and Virgil down to Dante and Milton, has so graphically described.

A seasoned traveler, writing of a tempest he experienced in the neighborhood of Baalbeck, said, "I was overtaken by a storm, as if the floodgates of Heaven had burst; it came in a moment, and raged with a power which suggested the end of the world. Solemn darkness covered the earth; the rain descended in torrents, and sweeping down the mountainside, became by the fearful power of the storm transmuted into thick clouds of fog." (See Matt. 7:27)

Give. . . Give . . . Give, 29:1, 2. These three *Gives* are a triad revealing how unwilling men usually are to give God His right, or suffer a word of exhortation to this purpose. The Rabbins observed that God's holy name is mentioned 18 times in this Psalm: that great men especially may give Him the honor of His name, that they may stand in awe, and not sin, that they may bring presents to Him Who ought to be feared, since He is a great King, and stands much upon His seniority.

The powerful voice of God overturning mountains, and dividing the heavens causing them to send their torrents upon the earth as depicted in verses 3-10, is cast in poetic form by James Montgomery, the godly poet of the early 18th century—

> The voice of the Lord on the ocean is known,
> The God of Eternity thundereth abroad;
> The voice of the Lord from the depth of his throne,
> In terror and power,—all nature is awed.
> The voice of the Lord through the calm of the Wood
> Awakens its echoes, strikes light through its caves;
> The Lord sitteth King on the turbulent flood,
> The winds are his servant, his servants the waves.

The voice of the Lord is powerful, 29:4. How true this is both in Grace and Nature. In the latter an irresistible power attends the lightning of which thunder is the report. In a moment of time, when the Creator wills it, the force of electricity produces amazing results. An authority on this subject speaks of these results as including a light of the intensity of the sun in his strength, a heat capable of fusing the compactest metals, an instant force paralyzing the muscles of the most powerful animals; a power suspending the all-pervading gravity of the earth, and an energy capable of decomposing and recomposing the closest affinities of the most intimate combinations. In his *Hand and the Book,* Thompson speaks of "the unconquerable lightning as seeing it is the chief of the ways of God in physical forces, and none can measure its power. It is so in Grace for when God utters His voice, hard hearts melt."

The voice of the Lord breaketh the cedars, 29:5. Ancient expositors declared that the breaking of the *cedar trees* by the winds was a figure of the laying low of the lofty and proud things of the world—the Lord being able by the Wind of the Spirit to uproot those who have long resisted His mercy. And the mighty trees, which for ages stood the force and fury of tempests, became objects of destruction under the fury of God's lightning. Dr. Philip Francis' translation of Homer's lines is apt—

> When high in the air the pine ascends,
> To every ruder blast it bends.
> The palace falls with heavier weight,
> When tumbling from its airy height;
> And when from heaven the lightning flies,
> It blasts the hills that proudest rise.

He maketh them also to skip like a calf, 29:6. The animal creature is used to symbolize how the mountains move as though they frisked and leaped like young bulls or antelopes. David heard the crash and roar among the ranges of Libanus, and so describes the tumult in graphic terms, as a Welsh poet of a past century does of a similar experience in his own country—

> Amid Carharvon's mountains rages loud
> The repercussive roar; with mighty crash
> Into the flashing deep, from the rude rocks
> Of Penmaen Mawr, leaps hideous to the sky,
> Tumble the smitten cliffs; and Snowdon's peak,
> Dissolving, instant yields his wintry load.
> Far seen, the heights of healthy Cheviot blaze,
> And Thule bellows through her utmost isles.

How grateful we are that the glorious Gospel of this God of Thunder has more than equal power over the rocky obduracy and mountainous pride of man!

The voice of the Lord maketh the hinds to calve, 29:9. "The voice of the Lord" is a common Hebrew phrase denoting *thunder*. In fierce storms, the animal creation has Divine protection. "The birth of the hinds dost thou guard," Job 39:1. According to Suetonius, Augustus, the Roman Emperor, was so terrified when it thundered that he wrapped a sealskin round his body, with the view of protecting it from lightning and concealed himself in a secret corner till the tempest ceased.

The tyrant Caligula, who sometimes affected to threaten Jupiter himself, covered his head, or hid himself under a bed; and Horace confesses he was reclaimed from Atheism by the terror of thunder and lightning, the effects of which he described with his unique felicity. The phrase, however, that David used is eloquent of God's providence, conspicuous in the care of the mother and her fawn. If what Pliny and later naturalists affirm is true, God has been graciously pleased to provide certain herbs, which greatly facilitate the birth of calves, and that, by instinct the hind finds, then feeds on them until the time of gestation ends. The Psalmist seems to imply that God by the thunder promotes the parturition of the hind, by awakening her fears, and agitating her by such an atmospheric convulsion.

The Lord will bless his people with peace, 29:11. After God is magnified in all the terrible grandeur of His power in the universe, it is fitting that this Psalm closes with the assurance that the omnipotent Jehovah will give both strength and peace to His people. Heaven and earth may pass away, but God's overshadowing of His own is forever. The Bible speaks of a threefold Peace—*Externa, Interna, Aterna*—a temporal, spiritual, and eternal peace. There is the outward peace, *the blessing;* inward peace, *the grace;* eternal peace, *of glory.* As in a stately palace there is a lodge or court that leads into the inmost goodly rooms, so external peace is the entrance or introduction to the inward lodgings of the sweet peace of con-science and of that eternal rest in which our peace in Heaven is perfect, inasmuch as external peace affords as many accommodations and help to the gaining and obtaining both the one and the other.

What a noble Psalm, then, is this one with its cool calm after the storm, tranquility after the thunder! It is indeed a Psalm to sing in stormy weath-er, actually or metaphorically. Is grace ours to sing when the thunder rolls? We have a popular ditty today called *Singing in the Rain.* It is more coura-geous, however, to be found singing when the tempest is raging, and the billows are tossing high.

George Herbert, 1593-1632, a man of saintly piety, at once an ascetic and a mystic, yet had the courtly grace and refined instincts of the high-bred gentleman. Like David, God's *Poet Laureate,* Herbert poured out his soul in verse, and adorned his poetry with the quaint conceits and fancies of the Elizabethan Age, of which he was a part. The motto of his *Sacred Poems and Private Ejaculations,* published at Cambridge in 1633, was "In His Temple Doth Every Man Speak Of His Honor," and this same 8th verse of Psalm 29, suggested for his book the title of *The Temple.*

John Ker informs us that in some of the old versions of the Psalter, in the 17th century, there is an arrangement of the Psalms according to the months of the year, forming what may be called a Calendar of Nature yielding its fruit of praise every month—

Psalm 29 is taken for *July,* the season of thunderstorms, for in this Psalm, seven thunders utter their voices. *April* has the latter part of Psalm 65; and the showers and springing verdure of *May* have Psalm 104:13, 14. Psalm 90, suggesting the flight of time, is placed against December; while Psalm 147:16, 17, is chosen for the snow and ice of January.

Psalm 30

The biographical setting of this song of faith is given by Spurgeon as being composed "on the floor of Ornan, where the poet received the inspiration which glows in this delightful ode," the title of which should read, *A Psalm: A Song of Dedication for the House, By David.* Evidently it was meant to be sung at the building of the house of cedar David erected for himself, when he was no longer forced to hide himself in the Cave of Adullah, but had become Israel's illustrious King. But there is a larger application of the song, seeing it refers to the Temple laid in store for the site of which David purchased from Ornan. For the Psalmist, however, his song was one of faith for he never lived to see the Temple built.

God is extolled for all deliverances vouchsafed, and throughout the Psalm pardon follows repentance over the sin of presumption, and after David's chastening, God's mercy is glorified, and becomes the Object of eternal praise.

Weeping may endure for a night, but joy cometh in the morning, 30:5.

All down the ages, multitudes of saints have experienced the literal truth of these words. They proved that their *mourning* only lasted till *morning.* Grief was turned into gladness—Sighing into singing— Misery into music—Winter into Summer.

> When in our Father's happy land
> We meet our own once more,
> Then we shall scarcely understand
> Why we have wept before.

Weeping appears to be personified by the figure of a wanderer who leaves in the morning the lodging into which he had entered the previous evening. After him another guest arrives whose name was Joy.

Unto the Lord I made supplication, 30:8. St. Bernard, in fable form, looked upon the kings of Babylon and Jerusalem as signifying the state of the world and the Church, always warring together; in which encounter at length it fell out that one of the soldiers of Jerusalem had fled to the castle of *Justice.* Siege was laid to the castle, and a multitude of enemies entrenched round about it, and *Fear* gave over all hope, but *Prudence* ministered her comfort.

"Dost thou not know," she said, "that our king is the King of Glory; the

113

Lord strong and mighty, even the Lord mighty in battle? Let us therefore despatch a messenger that we may inform him of our necessities." *Fear* replied, "But who is able to break through? Darkness is upon the face of the earth, and our walls are begirth with a watchful troop of armed men, and we are utterly inexpect of the way into so far a country." Whereupon, *Justice* is consulted. "Be of good cheer," said *Justice.* "I have a messenger of special trust, well known to the King and his court, *Prayer* by name, who knoweth the address herself by ways unknown in the stillest silence of the night, till she cometh to the secrets and chamber of the King himself." Forthwith she goeth, and findeth the gates shut, knockest saying, "Open ye gates of righteousness, and be ye opened ye everlasting doors, that I may come in and tell the King of Jerusalem how our case standeth."

During the fierce governorship of the cruel Alca, in the Netherlands, many were brutally massacred. Among them was one, John Herwin, whose biographer wrote of him—

> In prison he was wont to recreate himself by the singing of the Psalms, and the people used to flock together to the prison door to hear him. At the place of execution, one of the company gave his hand and comforted him. Then he began to sing Psalm 30. A friar tried to stop him, but Herwin finished the Psalm, the people joining in the singing of it.

Then he said to him sympathizers, "I am now going to be sacrificed; follow you me when God of His goodness shall call you to it."

At first the valiant soul was strangled, and then burned to death. But what faith was his to look through death, and close his song and his life with the words of this Psalm—"Thou hast turned for me my mourning into dancing: thou hast put off my sackcloth, and girded me with gladness; to the end that my glory may sing praise unto thee, and not be silent. O Lord, my God, I will give thanks unto thee forever."

Dr. John Brown, the renowned Bible commentator, was another who found continued consolation in the Psalms. As he died he was heard to repeat the 5th verse of this 30th Psalm—"His anger is for a moment; his favor is for a life; weeping may endure for a night, but joy cometh in the morning." Psalm 30 was likewise included among the Psalms recommended by John Hooper in the reign of Henry VIII for lessons of "patience and consolation" at times "when the mind can take no understanding, nor the heart any joy of God's promises." Bishop Hannington was another who found "patience and consolation" in reading this Psalm before his martyrdom. In his Diary he wrote, "October 29th. Thursday— eighth day in prison—I can hear no news, but was held up by Psalm 30, which came with great power. A hyena howled near me last night, smelling a sick man, but hope it is not to have me yet." This was his last entry, for on the same day, at the age of 37, Hannington was killed.

Psalm 31

Of all the Psalms this *Psalm of David* figures conspicuously in the lives of saints called upon to suffer and die for their precious Lord. As we shall find from following historical events and incidents, the dying voice of the Lord heard in verse 5 has inspired many to endure martyrdom for His dear sake. David himself often faced death in the cause of truth, and knew experimentally what it was to commit his spirit to God, and, believing that his times were in His hands, appealed to Him for help with much confidence, and then magnified Him for His goodness in undertaking for him.

The place and the occasion for this song of mingled measures and alternate strains of grief and woe are hard to determine. Some have felt that it was born in the heart of David during the treachery of the men of Keilah. Others place it at a later day, possibly during the period when Absalom, his son, rebelled against him, and his courtiers fled from him, and lying lips spread a thousand malicious rumors against him. But amid his mournful experience, the Psalmist affirmed his confidence in God and cried to Him for deliverance. We are in full agreement with the sentiment that it is as well that we have no expressed statement as to the precise occasion associated with this Psalm, otherwise we might have been guilty of applying it to David only, forgetting its suitability to our trials and grief.

Francis Quarles gives us an excellent, poetic setting of verses, 1, 2, 3, in these lines—

> Shadows are faithless, and the rocks are false;
> No trust in brass, no trust in marble walls;
> Poor cots are e'en as safe as princes' halls.
>
> Great God! there is no safety here below;
> Thou art my fortress, thou that seem'st my foe,
> 'Tis thou, that strik'st at the stroke, must guard the blow.
>
> Thou art my God, by thee I fall or stand
> Thy grace hath given me courage to withstand
> All tortures, but my conscience and thy hand.
>
> I know thy justice is thyself; I know,
> Just God, thy very self is mercy too;
> If not to thee, where, whither shall I go?

115

Into thine hand I commit my spirit, 31:5. As the illustrations we have gathered and presented prove, these living words of David became our Lord's dying words, and have been frequently repeated by His redeemed ones in their hour of departure.

Thou hast considered my trouble, 31:7. To quote dear old Francis Quarles again, here is his stanza on this phrase—

> Man's plea to man, is, that he never more
> Will beg, and that he never begg'd before:
> Man's plea to God, is, that he did obtain
> A former suit, and, therefore sues again.
> How good a God we serve; that when we sue,
> Makes his old gifts the examples of his new!

I am forgotten as a dead man out of mind, 31:12. We have a striking instance of how even the greatest princes are forgotten in death, in the death-bed scene of Louis XIV. "The Louis that was, lies forsaken, a mass of abhorred clay; abandoned to some poor persons, and priests of the *Chapelle Ardente,* who make haste to put him in two lead coffins, pouring in abundant spirits of wine." Thomas Carlyle in his *French Revolution* goes on to say—"The new Louis with his court is rolling towards Choisy, through the summer afternoon: the royal tears still flow; but a word mispronounced by Monseigneur d'Artios sets them all laughing, and they weep no more."

The mournful verses 12-15, in which David vehemently pleads for Divine deliverance, are summarized by George Sandys in his lines—

> Forgot as those who in the grave abide,
>   and as a broken vessel past repair,
> Slandered by many, fear on every side,
>   Who counsel take and would my life ensnare.
>
> But, Lord, my hopes on thee are fixed: I said,
>   Thou art my God, my days are in thy hand;
> Against my furious foes oppose thy aid,
>   And those who persecute my soul withstand.

I have heard the slander of many, 31:13. Among the accusing voices causing David grief of heart was Shimei who cried after the king, "Go up, thou man of blood." "All Beelzebub's pack of hounds may be in full cry against a man, and yet he may be the Lord's anointed." What a depth of meaning is the phrase of William Shakespeare—"Be thou as chaste as ice, as pure as snow, thou shalt not escape calumny."

My times are in thy hands, 31:15. How slow we are to learn that

His hand holds *all* our times! The famous lines of Robert Browning form a fitting exposition of this view of life—

> I report as a man may of God's work—all's love, but all's law.
> In the Godhead I seek and I find it, and so shall it be
> A face like my face that receives thee, a Man like to me.
> Thou shalt love and be loved by me forever, a hand like this hand
> Shall throw open the gates of new life to thee;
> > *See the Christ stand!*

This precious Psalm looms largely in the lives of saints all down the ages. In 1498, Savonarola, the great Dominican preacher, who for five years held within the hollow of his hand the destinies of Florence, and became one of the most fascinating figures in history, suffered a cruel fate at the hands of those who hated his spiritual witness. Repeated tortures were his. Near his end, his torturers broke his left arm and crunched the shoulder bone out of its socket, but his right arm was left whole in order that he might sign his so-called confessions. He used it, however, to write his meditations on Psalms 51 and 31, but the latter was never finished. Only three verses of Psalm 31 were completed, commencing with the comment—

> Sorrow hath pitched her camp against me. She hath hemmed me in on every side. Her men of war are strong and many. She hath filled my heart with the shout of battle and the din of arms. Day and night she ceaseth not to strive with me. My friends have become my foes, and fight under her standard.

Cardinal John Fisher, victim of the Protestant Reformation in England, was Bishop of Rochester, 1459-1535. Erasmus, his friend, wrote of him in 1510, "Either I am much mistaken, or Fisher is a man with whom none of our contemporaries can be compared, for holiness of life and greatness of soul." After a long imprisonment in the Bell Tower of the Tower of London, Fisher was sentenced to death on June 17, 1535, and on the following Tuesday, June 22nd, he was beheaded on Tower Hill, so weak and emaciated that he could hardly stand. At the foot of the scaffold his strength seemed to revive, and as he mounted the steps alone, the south-west sun shone full in his face. Lifting up his hands, he murmured the words of Psalm 34:5—"They had an eye unto him, and were lightened; and their faces were not ashamed." On the scaffold, he knelt down in prayer, and repeated Psalm 31—"In Thee, O Lord, have I put my trust." Then, as Prothero expresses it, with the joyful mien of a man who receives the boon for which he craves, he received the blow of the axe upon his slender and feeble neck, and so passed to his rest.

St. Francis Xavier had an ambition to carry the Gospel message to

China, even though it was death for foreigners to enter the Empire at that time. On December 2nd, 1552, Xavier lay dying of the island of San Chan, half a day's sail from Canton. Winged by pity, armed by faith, and fired by love, he had traveled seas and explored lands that were only known to Europe by vague report. The way he braved dangers and endured privations was almost superhuman, as he literally compassed sea and land to win a single human soul to Christ. But fever struck him down, and to mortal eyes he was alone in his death-agony. Yet to his unclouded vision, he saw the blessed Master standing with outstretched arms to welcome His faithful servant. With a ray from the Divine Presence lighting up his face, he fixed his eyes upon his crucifix, and, gathering all his strength uttered the words, "In Thee, O Lord, have I put my trust; let me never be put to confusion"—Psalm 31:1—and breathed his last.

Mère Angélique Arnauld, one of the purest and most devoted women of France, died August 6th, 1661, with these same words, which Xavier had also used at the end of his toilsome career, "In Thee, O Lord, have I put my trust." Dante, who made much use of the Psalms, directly or symbolically, beheld Beatrice, white-veiled, olive-crowned, strewn with flowers, and clad in the mystic colors of Love, Faith and Hope (*Purgatorio,* canto XXX, 11.82-5, and Psalm 31:1-9). In the eyes of Beatrice are reflected the twofold nature of Christ, and she bids Dante mark her well; but his gaze shrinks from her stern pity.

> And, suddenly, the angels sang,
> "In Thee, O gracious Lord! my hope hath been"
> But went no further than "Thou, Lord, hast set
> My feet in ample room."

It would seem that Psalm 31:5 is the most frequently quoted verse from the Psalms used by saints at the end of the road. History records the extraordinary place it has had among dying believers—"Into Thy hand I commit my spirit"—are words that have risen from saint after saint. Possibly it is because these were the last words upon the lips of our Lord as He died; and the words which Stephen, the first martyr of the Church Jesus founded, uttered as he was stoned to death. No wonder, "this Psalm sparkles all through with lamps which have lighted the steps of men in dark places," as John Ker expresses it. "Above all, the 5th verse has given the closing words to many a life."

Many of the Early Fathers, like Polycarp, Basil, St. Louis, doubtless inspired by the example of Jesus, made His final word on the Cross their own, as they came to cross the narrow sea of death. As Paul and Silas encouraged themselves by singing Psalms throughout the night in their dark, damp dungeon, so multitudes of saints died with the language of the Psalms, particularly the 5th verse of Psalm 31, upon their lips. Herewith is mention of a few instances of the succour succeeding saints gathered from David's committal, "Into thine hand I commit my spirit."

Possidius, biographer of St. Augustine, describing the plain and barely furnished room in which this famous son of Hippo lay dying, says that his eyes were fixed upon the Seven Penitential Psalms, which Augustine had ordered to be written out and placed where he could see and read them, thus passed into his rest, August 28th, 430 A.D. He found consolation in the last cry from the Cross. Previous to Augustine was Basil the Great who died at Caesarea, January 1st, 379, with his death-bed surrounded by citizens who were ready to shorten their own lives, if so they might lengthen the days of their beloved Bishop.

Charlemagne, hailed by the Pope as his champion, and by the people as their deliverer, had a love for the Psalms, his favorite one being Psalm 68, "Let God arise." As he died at Aix-la-Chapelle on January 28th, 814, he repeated with his last breath, "Into Thy hand I commend my spirit." It was because of his pleasure in the Psalms that he loved to be called among his friends by the name of *David.*

The sacrilege of the murder of Thomas à Becket in Canterbury Cathedral, December 29th, 1170, ever remains a dark spot in Church history. We all know how the soldiers of Henry II suddenly forced their way into the north side of the Cathedral, as Becket mounted the fourth step of the staircase leading from the Chapel of St. Benedict to the choir of the Church. Firzurse, leader of the knights in full armor, ordered Becket to descend into the transept, and in his white rochet, a cloak and hood thrown over his shoulders, Becket obeyed and faced his murderers. A blow on the head from Tracy, one of the knights, drew blood, and as the Archbishop wiped the stain from his face he repeated the familiar words, "Into Thy hands I commend my Spirit." Thus the foul deed was accomplished.

Another conspicuous figure in the Church's Roll of Martyrs is John Hus, who, at the Council of Constance, July 6th, 1415, presided over by Sigismund, King of the Romans was found guilty of heresy and handed over to the secular arm of the Council for immediate execution. A stake was prepared on the road from Constance to Gottlieben, and when Hus reached the spot, dressed up with a paper cap of blasphemy, adorned with "three devils of wonderfully ugly shape," and inscribed with the word *Heresiarcha,* he fell on his knees and prayed, chanting Psalm 31. As he died, choked by the flames, he repeated with "a merry and cheerful countenance," the precious words, "Into Thy hands, I commend my spirit."

It was on the same spot about a year later, May 30th, 1416, that Jerome of Prague was burned to death. Described as being, "tall, powerfully built, graceful of speech, and one of the most brilliant laymen of the day," Jerome had come to the Council of Constance to plead the cause for which his friend, John Hus, had died. After an imprisonment of six months, he was still adamant regarding the justice of the sentence passed upon Hus. The price he paid for his defense of his friend was to perish in the same way as he did, and like him, with his last breath he repeated the same words, "Into Thy hands I commend my spirit."

Philip Melancthon, close friend of Martin Luther, was another who, as he died on April 19th, 1560, committed his soul to God in the same words Hus and Jerome had uttered, "Into Thy hands I commend my spirit."

What schoolboy is not thrilled with the story of Christopher Columbus, who, although the scholar of the Renaissance, was yet a man of action, and his the fame of discovering the New World of America, which he spoke of as being the fulfillment of Divine design. The name Christopher means *Christ-bearer*, and Columbus thought of himself as such. It was in a wretched hired lodging at Valladolid, dressed in the Franciscan habit, and fortified by the rites of his Church, that on the eve of Ascension Day, May 20th, 1506, he died with the familiar words on his lips, "Into Thy hands I commend my spirit."

John Haughton, Prior of the London Charterhouse in the 15th century, was a zealous servant of God who governed his community by example rather than by precept. Before the accession of Henry VIII, he had been a monk for 20 years, but did not meddle in the question of the King's marriage. When he appeared, however, in 1533 before the Commissioners and was asked his opinion on the divorce of Catherine of Arragon, he courageously said that he could not understand how a marriage, ratified by the Church, and so long unquestioned, could now be undone. But when Henry assumed the title of Supreme Head of the Church, Haughton knew that his end was near. In the chapel he preached a sermon from the text, "O God, Thou hast cast us out, and scattered us abroad," Psalm 60:1, and concluded his discourse with the words—

> It is better that we should suffer here a short penance for our faults, than be reserved for the eternal pains of Hell hereafter.

Haughton, and the Priors of two daughter Houses, refused to acknowledge the new title of the King as Supreme Head, and were tried and found guilty of treason. On May 4th, 1535 there were executions at Tyburn, accompanied with all the barbarities of the time. Haughton suffered first, and said, "Pray for me, and have mercy on my brethern, of whom I have been the unworthy Prior." Kneeling down, he recited the opening verses of Psalm 31, and calmly resigned himself into the hands of the executioner. Those who were condemned with him died with the same tranquility and unflinching courage.

Added to what we have already written about John Hooper is the fact that it was not till February 9th, 1555, that through his death at the stake, he passed from the winter of his cruel imprisonment into the summer of eternal life. Sending him to Gloucester for execution, his enemies hoped that the Bishop would weaken, and recant, but he faced with unflinching courage the tortures of the fire which were needlessly protracted for almost an hour by the greenness and insufficiency of the material used. Hooper resigned himself to terrible death, uttering the words, "Into Thy hands I commend my spirite; Thou haste redeemed me, O God of truthe."

Nicholas Ridley, Bishop of London, 1500-55, whose favorite Psalm was the 101st, was another brave heart condemned to perish in the flames. Chained to a stake in the town ditch, opposite the south front of Ballicol College, Oxford, in 1555, as the flames rose around him exclaimed "with a wonderful loud voice," *In manus tuas, Domine, commendo spiritum meum; Domine, recife spiritum meum,* and then in English, "Lord, Lord receive my spirit."

In the history of Robert Southwell, a Jesuit and an Elizabethan poet, born in 1560, the power of the Psalms is illustrated in fullest detail. How he loved the Psalter. In his lonely misery, tortured 13 times without uttering a word, he compared himself like David to the sparrow and the pelican, Psalm 102:6, 17. He lingered in prison in a filthy cell in the Tower, London, but toward the end was allowed the books he had asked for—The Bible, and the works of St. Bernard. It was on February 21st, 1595, that he faced death. Rising up in the cart that had brought him from Newgate to Tyburn, with bound hands and a rope round his neck, Southwell briefly addressed the crowd who had gathered to witness his death by hanging. With his eyes rais'd up to Heaven, he repeated with great calmness of mind and countenance the words of David, "Into Thy hands, O Lord, I commend my spirit." Prothero reminds us that the effect of courageous death forced the bystanders to prevent the executioner from cutting the rope till Southwell was dead, in order that the ghastly formalities of disembowelling and quartering might not be carried out on his living body.

Lady Jane Dudley, who saw the mangled body of her husband, Lord Guildford Dudley, thrown into a cart, did not weaken in her own firm resolution to die for what she believed. On February 12th, 1554, she was taken from the Tower prison to the scaffold. Overcome by the sight of an innocent lady dying in such a way, the hangman kneeled down and asked her forgiveness, which Lady Jane gave most willingly. She then asked him to dispatch her quickly. Laying her head down on the block, and stretching out her body, she prayed, "Lorde, into Thy hands I commende my spirite." So the end came, and the trumpets sounded for her on the other side.

The Duke of Suffolk, father of Lady Jane Dudley who feared that her father might fall from the Protestant Faith, was beheaded at Tower Hill, a few days after his daughter's death. Fox the historian says that the Duke, "kneeled down upon his knees, and repeated the Psalm *Miserere mei, Deus,* holding up his hands and looking up to Heaven." And when he had ended the Psalm, he said, *In manus tuas, Domine, commendo, spiritum meum*—"Into Thy hands I commend my spirit." At the first blow of the axe his head fell from the block.

Lamorel, Count of Egmont and Prince of Gavre, was sentenced without a trial to death on June 2nd, 1568. In an appeal to Philip asking for compassion to be shown to his wife and children he concluded by saying—

> *Ready to die*, this 5th June, 1568. Your Majesty's very humble and loyal vassal and servant.   —Lamoral D'Egmont.

The scaffold was raised in the center of the famous Grande Place of Brussels, and on the morning of June 5th, as the bells tolled from churches and gloom hung over the city as if, as a contemporary put it, "the day of judgment is at hand," Egmont walked with steady step on to the scaffold. Then stripping himself of his mantle and robe, knelt down, and drawing a silk cap over his eyes, repeated the words, "Lord, into Thy hands I commend my spirit." A few minutes later, Count Horn, his friend in whom he had inspired confidence, was led to the same scaffold, and died with the same courage and with the same words from Psalm 31 on his lips. With the senseless massacre of these two noble men began the revolt of the Netherlands.

On the morning of her death at Fotheringay, Mary, Queen of Scots, awoke early and had read to her some of her favorite book, *The Lives of Saints*. Then dressing with unusual care, she retired to pray, and at the appointed hour on February 8th, 1587, was led to the scaffold where the executioner, on his knees, begged her forgiveness. "I forgive all," was her reply. Then, with a handkerchief bound over her eyes—to quote a chronicler of the time—"She kneeled downe upon the cushion resolutely; and, without any token of feare of deathe, sayde allowde in Lattin the Psalme, *In te Domine confido,* Psalm 31." Another authority states that the Queen said aloud several times, "Into Thy hands I commend my spirit."

Bishop Jewel, well-known in the 15th century for his massive theological works, died a peaceful death at Monckton Farleigh in Wiltshire, on September 23rd, 1571. On his death-bed he desired that Psalm 71 might be sung, and when the singers reached the words, "Cast me not off in time of age," Jewel exclaimed—"Every one who is dying, in truth, old and grey-headed, and failing in strength." The Psalm ended, he broke forth in frequent ejaculations—"Lord, now lettest Thou Thy servant depart in peace"; "Lord, suffer Thy servant to come to Thee"; "Lord, receive my spirit"—and so entered the eternal realm.

George Herbert, who had something of David's spirit as he poured out his soul in verse, and who found continual comfort in the Psalms, uttered with his latest breath, "Forsake me not when my strength faileth," Psalm 71:2, and then committed his soul to God in the familiar words, "Into Thy hand I commend my spirit."

Conspicuous in the history of the Covenanters is George Wishart, whose personal fascination marked him out as the leader of the religious movement, and who paid dearly for his witness to the truth. Convicted of heresy, he was burned at the stake, March 1st, 1546, at the foot of the Castle Wynd, opposite the castle gate, in St. Andrews. John Knox, Wishart's most devoted disciple, says of the leader he loved, "When he came to the fire he sat down upon his knees, and rose up again, and thrice said the words: 'O Thou Savior of the world, have mercy upon me! Father of Heaven, I commend my spirit into Thy holy hands.' Then as a sign of forgiveness he kissed the executioner on the cheek, saying, 'Lo, here is a token that I forgive thee. My harte, do thy office.'" How nobly these warrior-saints of old could die for the Master they so loyally served.

In November, 1572, John Knox, who triumphed in the cause of which George Wishart suffered martyrdom, was a man of iron will, passionate eloquence, and grim self-reliance. Some 25 years after Wishart's death, Knox saw the leadership of the Sovereign and the nobility swept away, and the Scottish tie with Rome forever broken, and in his home at Netherbow Port, of Edinburgh, as the reformer lay, to all appearances asleep, he was often heard repeating to himself the words, "Come, Lord Jesus, sweet Jesus, into Thy hands I commend my spirit."

Almost a hundred years after the death of John Knox, there appeared another gifted martyr in Hugh McKail, a young man of only 26 years of age, who was supposed to have incurred the personal hatred of the Primate, to whom he had given the name of *Judas*. Appeals were made to save his life, but in vain. One of his legs was tortured in an iron boot to make him confess. As he took hold of the ladder to go up the scaffold, he said, "I care no more to go up this ladder, and over it, than if I were going to my Father's house." Then he called to his friends and fellow-sufferers below—

Be not afraid. Every step of this ladder is a degree nearer Heaven.

On December 22nd, 1666, at two in the afternoon he died singing part of the old metrical rendering of Psalm 31—

Into Thy hands I do commit
My spirit; for Thou art He,

> O Thou, Jehovah, God of truth,
>   Who hast redeemed me.

With the murder of Archbishop Sharp on Magus Moor, May 3rd, 1679, there came a renewal of the open struggle between the Covenanters and the Government. Fresh efforts were made to surprise the Covenanters in the Coventicles and destroy them, and many godly men perished, their blood running like water, as at Bothwell Bridge, June 22nd, 1679. Among these was Donald Cargill, successor to Richard Cameron, whose name became immortalized in the *Cameronians,* the stricter Covenanters. The only remaining preacher at field-coventicles, Cargill was a marked man, and a high reward was placed upon his head. On July 11th, 1681, he was captured, and hurried, his legs tied hard under a horse's belly, to Edinburgh, where he was executed at the Cross, on July 27th, 1681. On the scaffold he sang his favorite Psalm—the 118th—and his last words were "Welcome, Father, Son, and Holy Ghost! Into Thy hands I commend my spirit."

The last of the Cameronians who suffered on the scaffold was James Renwick who, young though he was, started to preach in 1683. He was not long in becoming the soul of the movement among the Cameronian Societies who disowned the authority of King James, and declared war against him a the subverter of the religion and liberty of Scotland. When captured in January, 1688, Renwick was charged, not only with denying the power of the King, but for teaching the unlawfulness of paying a tax called *cess,* and for exhorting the people to carry weapons at the field-gatherings. Admitting the charges, he was sentenced to death, and on February 17th, 1688, was executed in the Gran-market, Edinburgh. He tried to chant Psalm 103, but his words were drowned by the drums. As he turned over the ladder, his last words were, "Lord, into Thy hands I commend my spirit; for Thou hast redeemed me, O Lord, Thou God of truth."

A further evidence of the tremendous influence of the Psalmist's prayer, Jesus used as His last cry on the Cross, is seen in the fact that more than half of the great army of *witnesses* who died on the scaffold between Hugh McKail in 1666 and James Renwick in 1688, like the Savior, made it their dying prayer. Since then, in many renowned Poets the influence of the Psalms is manifest. For instance, Newman in *Dream of Gerontius,* has some striking passages which are echoes from the Psalms. As Gerontius died, he murmurs the much-loved words—

> *Novissima Lora est:* and I fain would sleep.
> The pain has wearied me . . . Into Thy hands,
> O Lord, into Thy hands . . .

Readers will recall our previous reference to Henry Martyn, the brilliant Cambridge scholar, who devoted his life and abilities to missionary work.

While awaiting news of a definite appointment to the Indian Chaplaincy, he made the following entry in his Diary—

"So closes the easy part of my life," enriched by every earthly comfort, and caressed by friends, I may scarcely be said to have experienced trouble; but now, farewell ease, if I might presume to conjecture. "O Lord, into Thy hands I commit my spirit! Thou hast redeemed me, Thou God of truth! May I be saved by Thy grace, and be sanctified to do Thy will, and to all eternity; through Jesus Christ."

Eight years later, in Shiraz, Persia, where he hoped to translate the Bible into Arabic, on the 16th October, 1812, only 31 years of age, alone among strangers, Henry Martyn entered Heaven and saw Jesus in His glory. Macaulay's Epitaph of him will ever remain a masterpiece:

Here Martyn lies. In Manhood's early bloom
The Christian Hero finds a Pagan tomb.
Religion, sorrow o'er her favorite son,
Points to the glorious trophies he won,
Eternal trophies! not with carnage red.
Not stained with tears by hapless Captives shed,
But trophies of the Cross! for that dear name,
Through every form of danger, death, and shame,
Onward he journeyed to a happier shore,
Where danger, death, and shame assault no more.

During the Reign of Terror in France, in 1794, hundreds of men and women died on the scaffold, committing their spirits into the hands of God, in the language of the Psalms. Among them was Madame de Noailles, and her father-in-law, the Duc de Noailles-Mouchy, Marshal of France, who, at the age of 80, mounted the scaffold for his God, as, at 16, he had mounted the breach for his king. From the touching prison letters of Madame de Noailles we learn, not only something of the beauty of her character and the depth and purity of her faith, but also her deep love and concern for her three children. Thinking that death was near she made her will dispossessing of her personal effects, ending the codicil with the words—

In the name of the Father, the Son, and the Holy Ghost. Accept, O Lord, the sacrifice of my life. Into Thy hands I commend my spirit. My God haste Thee to help me. Forsake me not when my strength faileth me.

But her prayer was heard—and answered—in a way she least expected for when on the way, with other prisoners, to the scaffold, all received absolution from M. Carrichon, and the women died with unflinching courage.

It would be interesting to have a fuller catalogue of martyrs and saints all down the ages to the present century who found consolation in their last hours in the prayer of David. Thomas Jefferson, third President of the United States, had the final word, "I resign my spirit to God and my daughter to my country." Edward the Sixth, son of Henry the Eighth finished his course praying, "Lord, take my spirit." Michaelangelo, who, as he died, admonished his relatives in their life and death to think on the sufferings of Jesus Christ, uttered, as his last word, "My soul I resign to God."

Psalm 32

In his great chapter on Justificaton through grace, by faith, Paul quotes three verses from this gloriously evangelistic Psalm, to illustrate his thesis that the man to whom the Lord will not impute sin because of the covering of the blood, is indeed *blessed,* Romans 4:6-8. This Psalm of spiritual instruction can therefore be rightly named, *The Psalm of Matchless Grace.* David had been guilty of a terrible sin, but a deep repentance brought him Divine forgiveness and a blissful peace of mind, leading him to pour out his gratitude in the soft music of this choice song of mercy.

Several writers have pointed out that, historically, this 32nd Psalm follows the 51st Psalm in which David promised, as a forgiven sinner, to teach transgressors the Lord's ways, and in the Psalm before us he does this most effectively. Included among the Penitential Psalms, Psalm 32 was sung on the annual day of the Jewish expiation, when a general confession of sin was made. It is recorded that one day Martin Luther was asked which, of all the Psalms, he loved best, and his reply was, *Psalmi Paulini.* When pressed what these Psalms might be he replied, "The 32nd, 51st, 130th, and 143rd, for they all teach that the forgiveness of our sins comes, without the law, and without works, to the man who believes, and therefore I call them *Pauline Psalms."*

This is the first Psalm, after Psalm 1, to begin with *Blessed.* Like the Sermon on the Mount, it begins with beatitudes. The first Psalm describes the result of holy blessedness in the life of a child of God, and Psalm 32 gives the source and cause of such belssedness. "He who in the first Psalm is a constant reader of God's Book, is here, in Psalm 32, a suppliant at God's throne accepted and heard." In the original, the word *Blessed* is in the plural—BLESSEDNESSES—and for the sinner whose transgression, sin, and iniquity are forgiven there are multiplied joys, bundles of happiness, and mountains of delight.

M. Montague, in his work on *The Seven Penitential Psalms,* informs us that when Galileo, the ancient astronomer, was imprisoned by the Inquisition at Rome, for asserting the Copernican System, he was enjoined, as a penance, to repeat the Seven Penitential Psalms every week for 3 years. This must have been intended to extort from him the confession of his guilt, and acknowledgment of the justice of his sentence. In same, however, there certainly was some cleverness and, indeed, humor, however adding to the iniquity—or foolishness—of the proceeding. Otherwise it is not easy to understand what ideas of pain or punishment the good fathers could attach to a devotional exercise such as this, which, in whatever way, could only have been agreeable and consoling to their prisoner.

Selah . . . Selah . . . Selah, 32:4, 5, 7. This frequently used exclamatory term of the Psalmists, is said to indicate a pause in the music. As many of the Psalms were set to music and sung as songs, pauses were necessary to meditate upon the great truths being sung. They were not to be hurried over. At the heart of *Selah* is the idea—*Think of that!* And what a glorious truth the forgiveness of sins is to constantly think about.

> *Pause,* my soul, adore and wonder,
>   Ask, O why such love to me?
> Grace has put me in the number
>   Of the Savior's family.
>   Hallelujah!
> Thanks, eternal thanks to thee.

I will confess . . . and thou forgivest, 32:5. David makes it plain that remission of sins is undoubtedly annexed to confession. Said St. Austin, *"Pec-Ca-Vi,* these three syllables in the Latin, three words in English are of great force when uttered with a contrite heart"—*I have sinned!*

Surely in the floods of great waters they shall not come nigh unto him, 32:6. Many saints have lost their goods, and suffered much in mind and body, yet the "floods of great waters" did not affect their inner life in God. Anaxarchus, when as Nicocreon the tyrant commanded that he should be beaten to death in a mortar, said to his executioner, "Beat and bray as long as thou wilt Anaxarchus his bag or satchel (as he called his body), but Anaxarchus thou canst not touch."

When Amyelas the pilot was greatly afraid of the tempest he said to Julius Caesar that he feared what might happen on the angry sea. Caesar replied, "What meanest thou to fear, base fellow? dost thou not know that thou carriest Caesar with thee?" Which meant to say, "Caesar's body may be drowned, as any other man's may; but his mind, his magnanimity, his valor, his fortitude, could never be drowned."

I will guide thee with mine eye, 32:8. Among the fables contained in natural history books of a past century is the one of certain creatures which hatched their eggs only by looking at them. What cannot the eyes of God produce in us! The margin expresses the sense of the Hebrew, the literal meaning being, "Mine eyes shall be upon thee," or "my eye shall be directed towards thee." Comments Albert Barnes,

"The *idea* is that of one who is telling another what way he is to take in order that he may reach a certain place; and he says he will watch him, or will keep an eye upon him; he will not let him go wrong."

Be ye not as the horse, or as the mule, 32:9. The Early Fathers and later expositors have given us several interpretations of the opposite natures of these two animals. St. Jerome thought that fierceness and rashness are presented in the horse, and sloth in the mule. But St. Augustine carried these qualities farther, saying that in the fierceness of the horse are represented by those who ran far from the knowledge of Christianity; and by the laziness of the mule the Jews, those who came to nothing so fast, as they were invited by their former helps to the embracing thereof. Samuel Horsley's explanation is more reasonable—

> The admonition given by the Psalmist to his companions, is to submit to the instruction and guidance graciously promised from Heaven, and not to resemble, in a refractory disposition, those ill-conditioned colts which are not to be governed by a simple bridle; but, unless their jaws are confined by a muzzle, will attack the rider as he attempts to mount, or the groom as he leads them to the pasture and the stable.

Shout for joy, all ye that are upright in heart, 32:11. When the poet Carpani enquired of his friend Haydon how it happened that his church music was so cheerful, the great composer framed a most beautiful reply. "I cannot," he said, "make it otherwise, I write according to the thoughts I feel: when I think upon God, my heart is so full of joy that the notes dance and leap, as it were, from my pen: and, since God has given me a cheerful heart, it will be pardoned me that I serve him with a cheerful spirit." How blest we are if in spite of the troublesome sea of the world, we can *Rejoice in the Lord.*

> O sing unto this glittering glorious King,
> O praise his name let every living thing;
> Let heart and voice, like bells of silver, ring
> The comfort that this day doth bring.

All who have experienced the joy of sins forgiven love and live in this Instruction Psalm of David who himself knew the blessedness of having his transgression forgiven. What precious truths there are for our hearts in all the eleven verses of this Psalm!

Ever since his baptism by Ambrose at Milan on Easter Sunday, April 24th, 387, when Psalm 43 was sung, Augustine set out on his life-long study of the Psalms, and came to write two commentaries on them. Above his bed was the inscription of Psalm 32, that his eyes might rest upon the words at the moment of waking. When it came to the closing scene of his life on the wall of his bare room within the walls of beleagured Hippo, the same words consoled his heart. One biographer reminds us that "with weeping heart and eyes, and before his death he had the 32nd Psalm written upon the wall which was over against his sick bed, that he might be exercised and comforted by it in his sickness." Augustine's own words, "The beginning of knowledge is to know thyself to be a sinner," could be prefixed to this Psalm. A countless host have loved this as a fitting motto.

When Martin Luther was asked which were the best Psalms, he replied, *The Pauline Psalms,* and being asked to name them he gave these four belonging to *The Penitential Psalms*—the 32nd, 51st, 130th, and 143rd. In time of deep spiritual need the heart feels its way to these in its extremity.

This Psalm was a great favorite of Alexander Peden, conspicuous in Scottish history of the Covenanters. From upper Clydesdale and Nithsdale to the Solway, was peculiarly the land of the Covenant, and the name of Alexander Peden who, when hard pressed by the troopers and brought to a breathless stand would rest and pray that God would "cast the skirt of His cloak over him"—which He did, in the form of mist and cloud. This still permeates the covenanting country so we have *Peden's Cave—Peden's Pulpit—Peden's Bed.* Although he died at last in one of his hiding places, his persecutors, discovering his body, hung it on a gibbet at Cummock. One who accompanied Peden when pursued wrote that "on one occasion when a service was ended, he and others that were with him lay down in the sheep-house, and slept." Rising early, he went to the burnside for a season of meditation and when he returned he sang Psalm 32 from verse 7 to the end.

> Thou art my hiding place, thou shalt
>   From trouble keep me free:
> Thou with songs of deliverance
>   About shalt compass me.

When Peden had finished singing, he repeated the 7th verse again, and said, "These and what follow are sweet lines which I got at the burnside this morning, and I will get more tomorrow, and we shall have daily provision."

Dante, who, as we have already noted, made much use of the Psalms, especially in his *Purgatorio,* describes Matilda returning from her earthly Paradise, like an enamoured dame to sing her song (Canto XXIX, 11:1-3) "Blessed is he whose unrighteousness is forgiven, and whose sin is covered," Psalm 32:1.

William Langland, called the 14th century's *Dante,* in his *Vision of Piers Plowman,* Section V, describes the dreamer seeing the "field full of folk," where the sinners are induced to confess and repent. *The Deadly*

Sins make their penitential confession, and *Repentance* prays for the penitents, and *Hope* seizing a horn, blows upon it—"Blessed is he whose unrighteousness is forgiven; and whose sin is covered," Psalm 32:1.

The Bishop of Sanderson, Robert Sanderson, 1587-1662, was a peaceful yet shining light during the Civil Wars. Sorrow and imprisonment were his but he told his friend and biographer, Isaak Walton, how his sorrows but deepened and enlarged his love of the Psalter—*the treasury*—as the Bishop called it. At the conclusion of his charming biography of the Bishop, Walton said. "It is now too late to wish that my life might be like his; for I am in the eighty-fifth year of my age; but I may humbly beseech Almighty God, that my death may, and do as earnestly beg . . . any reader to say Amen. *Blessed is the man in whose spirit there is no guile,"* Psalm 32:2.

Psalm 33

Doubtless you have observed that this Psalm is coupled with the previous one by the *catchword* with which it opens, which is a repetition of the exhortation with which the preceding Psalm ends, "Be glad in the Lord, and rejoice," 32:11, and "Rejoice in the Lord, O ye righteous," 33:1. When and why, and by whom, this eucharistic Psalm was written we are not told, for it comes to us without title, to teach us "to look upon Holy Scripture as altogether inspired of God, and not put a price upon it for the writers thereof." Its 22 verses constitute a sacred song of Jehovah, for all that He is in Himself, and for all He is able to accomplish.

Praise is comely for the upright, 33:1. Joy is the soul of praise, but unless we are among the righteous and the upright we cannot praise God as we ought. As Spurgeon expresses it, "God has an eye to things which are becoming. When saints wear their choral robes, they look fair in the Lord's sight. A harp suits a bloodwashed hand. No jewel more ornamental to a holy face than sacred praise. Praise is not comely from unpardoned professional singers; it is like a jewel of gold in a swine's snout. Crooked hearts make crooked music, but the upright are the Lord's delight. Praise is the dress in Heaven. It is meet that they should fit it on below."

Praise the Lord with the harp, 33:2. This is the first mention of musical instruments in the Psalms. The Early Fathers almost with one accord protested against their use in churches; as they were forbidden in the Eastern Church up to a late date. Justin Martyr recorded that the use of singing with instrumental music was not received in the Christian churches as it was among the Jews in their infant state, but only the use of plain song. The writer of these lines can remember being in Scottish churches where no instruments were used, but in which the singing was led by a *Precentor.*

The word of the Lord is right, 33:4. In work and word, God agrees with Himself and the purest truth. "God writes with a pen that never blots, speaks with a tongue that never slips, acts with a hand which never fails." *All his works* are done in truth. William Thomas Bacon gave us the admirable poem exalting God for His unerring revelation—

> *Truth* is in each flower
> As well as in the solemnest things of God;
> *Truth* is the voice of nature and of time—

> *Truth* is the startling monitor within us—
> Nought is without it, it comes from the stars,
> The golden sun, and every breeze that blows—
> *Truth*, it is God! and God is everywhere!

The waters of the sea, 33:7. Wrote one who had witnessed the heavings of a prodigious bulk of waters—"A troubled ocean, to a man who sails upon it, is, I think, the biggest object that he can see in motion, and consequently gives his imagination one of the highest kinds of pleasure that can arise from greatness." For those of us who have traveled over the ocean several times, seasickness for most of the time did not produce imagination of the greatness of the rolling waves. Calmer waters were longed for.

He spake and it was done, 33:9. The Latin reads *Dictum Factum,* meaning *Said Done,* no delay having interposed. This was so at Creation. The universe and man appeared immediately as the effects of the Divine will, and the fruits of intelligence, design, and counsel.

The Lord bringeth the counsel of the heathen to nought, 33:10. The more men oppose the truth, the more it prevails. Richard Younger wrote that "the Reformation in Germany was much furthered by the Papists' opposition; yea, when two kings, amongst others, wrote against Martin Luther, namely Henry VIII of England, and Ludovicus of Hungary, this kingly title being entered into the controversy—making me more curious to examine the matter—stirred up a general inclination towards Luther's opinions."

An horse is a vain things for safety, 33:17. Military strength among the Orientals lay much in horses and scythed chariots, but the Psalmist calls them a lie, a deceitful confidence. Surely the knight upon his gallant steed may be safe, either by valor or by flight? Not so, his horse shall bear him into danger or crush him with its fall. Pharaoh's horses and chariots found it disastrous to pursue the Lord's anointed.

There is no king save by the multitude of a host, 33:16. At the battle of Arbela, the Persian hosts numbered between 500 thousand and a million men, but they were utterly put to the rout by Alexander's band of 50,000; and the once mighty Darius was soon vanquished. Napoleon led more than half-a-million men into Russia—

> Not such the numbers, nor the host so dread,
> By northern Bren, or Scythian Timour led.

But the terrible winter encountered left the massive army a mere wreck, and their proud leader was soon a prisoner on the lone rock of St. Helena. All along the line of history down to Adolph Hitler's day, this verse has been verified. The strongest battalions melt like snowflakes when God is against them.

He is our help, 33:20. Antigonus, king of Syria, being ready to give battle near the Isle of Andreos, sent out a squadron to watch the movements of his enemies, and to descry their strength: return was made that they had more ships, and were better manned than he was. "How?" said Antigonus, "that cannot be; for how many dost thou reckon me?" intimating that the dignity of a general weighed down many others, especially when poised with valor and experience. But where is valor and experience to be found if not in God? He is the Lord of Hosts, whether they be heavenly, human, or hellish.

When, with the landing of Augustine in England, the Benedictine Rule was introduced, and the religious history of Saxon England to a great extent became bound up in the progress of the Order, the lives of monks and nuns were regulated by the spirit, if not by the letter, of the Psalms. The rule, or vow, of silence, for instance, was founded upon the words, "I said, I will take heed to my ways, that I offend not with my tongue," Psalm 39:1. One of the first duties of those under monastic rule was to learn the Psalter by heart. Sanction for the use of the organ in divine service was found in the words, "Praise the Lord with harp, sing praises unto Him with the lute, and instrument of ten strings," 33:2.

The central point of interest in the third and last of the civil wars in France was the siege of Rochelle in 1627-8, when the dreaded Richelieu drew round the doomed city his girdle of famine which claimed a daily death-roll of 400. During these terrible days when starving people fed on corpses of the dead, and a woman died gnawing her own arms, a widow named Prosnir helped starving neighbors from her own dwindling supply of food. Her sister-in-law, Madam de la Goute, rebuked her, asking what she would do when her store was gone. "The Lord will provide," was her reply, and then she repeated the words of the Psalmist, "Behold the eye of the Lord is upon them that fear Him, and upon them that trust in His mercy; to deliver their soul from death, and to feed them in time of dearth," Psalm 31:17, 18.

The siege continued, and Madame Prosni with her four children were in sore straits. Her sister-in-law refused to help her, and taunted her over the lack of Divine supply in spite of her faith. Prosni became dejected but resolved to meet death with patience. As she reached home after visiting her callous relative, her children met her at the door dancing with joy, for a stranger had knocked at the door, thrown in a sack of wheat and departed. The identity of the benefactor was never discovered. His gift, however, supported the family until the siege was over, with Prosni proving that no promise of God can possibly fail.

Psalm 34

The title of this second alphabetical Psalm in the Psalter leaves us in no doubt as to its association in David's eventful career. He composed it to commemorate his design to escape an attack upon his life as he "changed his behavior before Abimelech; who drove David away, and he departed." The casting of this heading to the Psalm in the original suggests that the Psalmist did not compose it at the time of his escape from Achish, the King or Abimelech of Gath, but later, as a song of gratitude to God for His goodness in delivering him. See 1 Samuel 21.

Although the transaction in playing the fool with singular dexterity reflects no credit upon David's memory, in his Psalms he did not refer to any of the unusual incidents in connection with his escape, but only upon the blessed fact that God heard him in his hour of peril, and saved him out of all his troubles. "Guilty of playing the fool before Abimelech, David was not so real a fool as to sing of his own exploits of folly. We may learn from his example not to parade our sins before others, as some vain-glorious professors are wont to do."

That David, in view of the special peril from which he was rescued, took great pains to write his song of praise, is found in the way he wrote it to correspond to the letters of the Hebrew alphabet. Nine in number, these Alphabetical Psalms were called *Psalmi Abcedaric,* by the Latin Fathers. The Hebrew has only 22 letters to our 26; and of the 22, a considerable number have no fellows in our alphabet. On the Psalm, as a whole, it divides itself into two general divisions, in which David having expressed his gratitude to God turns to address His children. In verses 1-10, then, we have a *Hymn of Praise;* and in verses 11-15, *A Sermon of Exhortation.*

I will bless the Lord at all times, 34:1. When Bradford, the martyr, spoke of Queen Mary, at whose cruel mercy he then lay, he said, "If the Queen be pleased to receive me, I will thank her; if she will imprison me, I will thank her; if she will burn me, I will thank her." The attitude of everyone should be, "Let God do with me what He will, I will be thankful."

I sought the Lord, and he heard me, 34:4. William Gurnall, unique 18th century expositor, wrote that, "Meditation is like the lawyer's studying the case in order to his pleading at the bar, when, therefore, thou hast viewed the promise, and affected my heart with the riches of it, then fly thee to the throne of grace, and spread it before the Lord."

The angel of the Lord encampeth round about them that fear him,
34:7. According to the observation of D'Arvieux, the practice of the
Arabs was to pitch their tents in a circular form; the prince being in
the middle and the Arabs about him, but so as to leave a respectful
distance between them. Tenvenot also describes a Turkish
encampment near Cairo, and noticed the leader, Bashaw's spacious
tent, and adds, "Round the pale of his tent, within a pistol shot, were
above 200 tents, pitched in such a manner that the doors of them all
looked towards Bashaw's tent; and it was ever so, that they may have
their eye always upon their master's lodging, and be in readiness to
assist him if he be attacked." Angels are guardians of the saints,
protecting them, as well as ministering unto them.

They that seek the Lord shall not want any good thing, 34:10. In a
sermon of his, preached in 1682, Alexander Peden, the renowned
Covenanter, said, "I remember as I came through the country, that
there was a poor widow woman, whose husband fell at Bothwell: the
bloody soldiers came to plunder her house, telling her they would take
all she had. 'We will leave thee nothing,' they said, 'either to put in
thee, or on thee.' 'I care not,' she replied, 'I will not want as long as
God is in the heavens.'"

The last afternoon Columba spent on earth, he was found transcribing
the Psalms of David. Having come to this passage in Psalm 34, "They that
seek the Lord shall not want any good thing," he said, "I have come to the
end of a page, and I will stop here, for the following verse, 'Come, ye
children, hearken unto me. I will teach you the fear of the Lord,' will better suit my successor to transcribe than me. I will leave it, therefore, to
Baithen." As usual, the bell was rung at midnight for prayers, and
Columba was the first to hasten to the Church. On entering it soon after,
Dermid found him on his knees in prayer, but evidently dying. As the
brethren entered, and saw Columba in this dying condition they wept
aloud. Columba heard them, and opened his eyes and tried to speak, but
his voice failed. He lifted up his hands as if to bless them, immediately
after which he breathed out his spirit. His countenance retained in death
the expression it wore in life, so that it seemed as if he had only fallen
asleep.

Evil shall slay the wicked, 34:21. St. Peter Damiano, of the 10th
century wrote of this verse—

> Conscience' self the culprit tortures, gnawing him with pangs
> unknown;
> For that now amendment's season is forever past and gone,
> And that late repentance findeth pardon none for all her moan.

Both Cyril and Jerome, prominent among the Early Fathers, mention this Psalm as being usually sung by the Church of Jerusalem at the time of Communion, being deemed appropriate seeing it contains the passage which John applied to Jesus, "He keepeth all his bones; not one of them is broken," John 19:36 with Psalm 34:20.

William Law's call to devotion, *Serious Call,* published in 1729 exercised a profound influence over many. Dr. Johnson said it was the first book which made him think "in earnest of religion." In his book Law advocated the Psalms as a great aid to devotion and dedication.

> Do but so live that your heart may truly rejoice in God, that it may feel itself affected with the praises of God, and then you will find, that the state of your heart will neither want a voice, nor ear to find a tune for a psalm.

Law then goes on to say that Psalm 34, along with Psalms 96, 103, 111, 146, and 147, are such as wonderfully set forth, "the glory of God, and, therefore, you may keep to any one of them at any particular hour as you may like; or you may take the finest parts of any Psalms, and so, adding them together, may make them fitter for your own devotion."

Among the noble band of martyrs who found consolation and courage in the language of the Psalms in an age of persecution was Theodore the Martyr, the young soldier who rashly burned to the ground the Temple of the Mother of Gods at Amasea in 306 A.D. Condemned, he found strength to endure severe torture by chanting, "I will always give thanks unto the Lord; His praise shall ever be in my mouth," Psalm 34:1.

Upon one of the old houses that existed in Edinburgh, the inscriptions were found, *"He that tholes* (endures) *overcomes,* and, O, magnify the Lord with me, and let us exalt His name together," Psalm 34:3.

Cardinal John Fisher, to whom we have already referred, who possessed one of the best private libraries in England, in the 15th century, spent 14 months of imprisonment in the Tower of London, and then on Thursday, June 17th, 1535, was sentenced to death. The following Tuesday, June 22nd, weak and emaciated, he was executed on Tower Hill. As he mounted the steps of the scaffold, he murmured the words, "They had an eye unto him, and were lightened; and their faces were not ashamed," Psalm 34:5. For this brave man, the things of earth became strangely dim, in the light of His glory and grace.

There can be no doubt about the popularity of the 10th verse of this Psalm among the saints of succeeding ages. "The young lions do lack, and suffer hunger; but they that seek the Lord shall not want any good thing." Columba, famous for his 34 years of labor in Iona, Scotland, felt death coming upon him, yet remained diligent until the end. Blessing the grain in the monastery one day, he thanked God because there would be enough for the brethren. Returning from the barn, he went to his library to continue his studies on The Psalms, and when he came to the words, "They that seek the Lord shall not want any good thing," 34:10, Columba rose from his work and said, "This ends the page, and I will cease here. Baithen may write what follows." Baithen, whom he chose as his successor, did complete Columba's notes. Columba's last words were addressed to the brethren at the monastery, "This is my last commandment to you, little children, that ye should love one another sincerely, and be at peace." He died on the morning of the Lord's Day, June 9, 597 A.D., in his beloved Iona.

Commander Gardiner, whose ambition, after he left the Royal Navy in 1826, was to establish a mission in Tierra del Fuego, has already found a place in our stories of the Psalms. His body, along with the corpses of three of his companions, was found unburied on the shore, and it seemed as if his had been a useless sacrifice in a helpless cause for he achieved no results at all in Tierra del Fuego. On June 16th, 1851, Gardiner wrote in his Diary, "They that seek the Lord shall not want any good thing," Psalm 34:10. Then on his birthday a week later, June 28, there was the entry, "They who seek the Lord shall want no manner of thing that is good." But his prayer for himself and companions that the Lord might be pleased "to provide that which is needful" was not answered.

In the Benedictine Rule, we mentioned under Psalm 33, the Psalm before us seems to strike the keynote of the Rule, for, said Benedict—

> The Lord Who seeketh His servant in the midst of the people, still saith to him, "What man is he that lusteth to live, and would fain see good day?" If at that word thou answerest, "It is I," then will the Lord say unto thee, "If thou wouldest have life, keep thy tongue from evil, and thy lips that they speak no guile. Eschew evil, and do good; seek peace, and pursue it." And that being done, "Then shall My eyes be upon you, and My ears shall be open to your cry. And even before thou callest Me, I shall say to thee, Here am I," 34:12-14.

Among the noble band of godly men executed in Edinburgh during 1679, were two ploughmen from Galloway, Andrew Sword and John Clyde, both of whom had been condemned for attending a gathering of Covenanters at Bothwell, and also for participating in the death of Archbishop Sharp although neither of them had ever seen him. As these two men of simple faith came to the place of execution they sang this Psalm, the 19th verse of which brought them much consolation.

> The troubles that afflict the just
>   In number many be;
> But yet at length out of them all
>   The Lord doth set him free.

Psalm 35

All we can learn from the heading of this Psalm, which the spiritual mind knows goes beyond David to David's greater Son, is that David composed it. Internal evidence, however, provides an historical setting for it. Such an appeal to Heaven of a bold heart and a clear conscience, irritated beyond measure and malice, places the composition of the Psalm during those troublous times when Saul hunted David over hill and dale, and when those who professed allegiance to the cruel king slandered the innocent object of Saul's wrath, or it may refer to the unquiet days of frequent insurrections in David's old age. Andrew Bonar entitled the Psalm —*The Awful Utterance of the Righteous One Regarding Those That Hate Him Without Cause.*

A noticeable feature in the division of this Psalm is its triple character for its *plea, prayer* and *promise of praise* are repeated with remarkable parallelism three times even as our Lord prayed three times in the Garden, using the same words.

Draw out the spear and stop the way, 35:3. The Hebrew for "draw" means *empty,* or *unsheath.* In the day of David the spear was a favorite weapon. A valiant man bravely defending a narrow pass might singly with his lance keep back a pursuing host, and give time for his friends to escape. Very remarkable were the feats of valor of this sort performed in Oriental warfare. David wanted God as his heroic Defender, making his enemies pause in pursuit.

Say unto my soul, I am thy salvation, 35:3. Note the pronouns, *My—Thy.* Martin Luther once said that "there is great divinity in pronouns." It is assuring to believe that Jesus came as the Savior of the World, but this avails nothing to me unless mine is the pronoun of a personal salvation, "Behold God is *my* Salvation!"

For without cause, 35:7. Twice over David asserts in one verse that his enemies plotted against him "without cause." In no way did he injure, assail, or provoke his adversaries. Fair warfare belongs to honorable men, but the assailants of God's Church prefer mean, ungenerous schemes, and so prove their nature and their origin.

Let his net that he hath hid catch himself, 35:8. Goliath, slain with his own sword, proved that the wicked are often undone by their own doings. Maxentius built a false bridge to drown Constantine, but was drowned himself. Henry III of France was stabbed in the very chamber where he schemed the cruel massacre of the Protestants, while his brother, Charles IX, who delighted in the blood of the saints had blood given him to drink. Thus, those devising evil for others, fall at last into their own pit, and the most cunning find themselves caught by what they had prepared for others.

All my bones shall say, 35:10. Both here, and in Psalm 51:8, exulting joy is attributed to the bones. Franz Delitzsch, in his *Biblical Psychology* developed the idea that ordinary experience shows that the intestines have sympathy with our passionate excitements, but we have no consciousness of the bones becoming sympathetically sensitive. The expression of David, therefore, is highly poetical, and indicates that the joy intended would be far beyond ordinary and common delight; it would be so profound that even the most callous part of the human frame would partake of it. Doubtless the poetry has a basis of truth in it, for though we may not perceive it, there is most assuredly a true and real sympathy with our mental state in every particle of bone and muscle, as well as in those tender organs which are more apparently affected.

As one that mourneth for his mother, 35:14. Mahomet was once asked what relation had the strongest claim upon our affection and respect, and he instantly replied, "The mother, the mother, the mother." Spurgeon reminds us that because of "the plurality of wives in an Eastern household, the sons are usually far more attached to their mother than their father. Their father they share with a numerous band of half-brothers, who are envious of them, and of whom they are jealous, but their mother is all their own, with her they are brought up in childhood; she takes their part in youth, in the numerous battles of the harem; and on their part when they are grown up, they love her intensely, and hence their mourning at her decease is of the bitterest kind."

They opened their mouth against me . . . O Lord, keep not silence, 35:21, 22. For the utterance of great lies wide mouths are needed. These two verses were given poetic form by Sir John Davies, in the lines—

> They gap and drawe their mouths in scornful wise,
> And crie, fie, fie, wee sawe it with no eyes.
> But thou their deed, O Lord, doest also see;
> Then bee not silent soe, nor hart frome mee.

My God and my Lord, 35:23. With a slight difference in the words this was the cry of Thomas, when he gazed upon the wounds of Jesus, *My Lord and my God!* Nouet, in his exposition of these words used by Thomas, exclaimed, "Oh, sweet word, I will say it all my life long; I will say it in the hour of death; I will say it in eternity." Here, again, we have the pronoun of personal possession—*My, My!*

Let them be clothed with shame and dishonor that magnify themselves against me . . . Let the Lord be magnified, 35:26, 27. The Romans being in great distress were put so hard to it that they even took the weapons out of the temples of their spoils to fight with their enemies, and so overcome them: so when the people of God have been hard put to it by reason of afflictions and persecutions, the weapons that they have fled to have been prayers and tears, and with these they have overcome their persecutors. And prayers are still the arms the saints have recourse to in the dark and difficult hours of life.

The science, literature, and history of the Middle Ages came under the sway of the Psalms, and of the monastic spirit in literature during the period was *The Imitation of Christ,* by Thomas Haemmerlein, who became better known as Thomas à Kempis. Of him his biographer said that he was a simple man given over "to the interior life and devotion." It was his habit in solitude and silence to bow himself before the Savior he loved, so that he might catch the faintest whisper of His voice, and conform his entire life to its slightest command. The fruit of such close personal communion forms the basis of *The Imitation of Christ,* which, although it throbs as the spiritual heart of mediaeval Christianity, is a spiritual classic widely treasured by believers in the 20th century.

Contrary to what one would expect, the thought, feeling, and language of Thomas à Kempis's renowned devotional book is largely based upon the Psalms, rather than the New Testament. In it the Psalms are cited more often than the Gospels, and illustrations from the Psalms outnumber all the passages quoted from the four records of our Lord's life upon earth. In his *Soliloquy of the Soul* he gives us the history of his inner life, which is but an impassioned expression of texts taken from the Psalms, among them being—

> "Say unto my soul, I am Thy salvation," 35:3.
> "All my bones shall say, Lord, who is like unto Thee?" 35:10.

From our history lessons at school we learned all about Spain's determination to crush Protestant England, in the 15th century, and how she prepared *The Invincible Armada,* as it was named, to carry a Holy War against heretics. Among the 30,000 men forming the Armada was a son from every noble family in Spain sent to fight for Christ and Our Lady. The ships were named after Apostles and Saints, and the crews were under a vow to abstain from vice and evil speaking. From the standard of the flagship San Martin was unrolled the motto, *Exsurge, Deus, et vindica causam taum*—"Awake, and stand up to judge my quarrel: avenge Thou my cause, My God, and my Lord," Psalm 35:23. The rest of the story is known by many. God released strong winds which scattered and destroyed the proud and costly fleet, causing a renowned Spaniard to say, "To princes belong all that is on the earth, save only the wind." As for the English, their fears of impending invasion and death were expressed in the words of another Psalm—

"Lord, how are they increased that trouble me," Psalm 3.

Psalm 36

As we are discovering, not all the Psalms have historical connections. All who bear the easy yoke of Jesus can join in singing this *Song of Happy Service*. It was simply an outburst of praise to Jehovah for the honor of being called His "servant." David only uses this title *The Servant of the Lord* here, and in Psalm 18, and in both Psalms it is deemed fitting, as a servant, to describe God's dealings both with saints and sinners. The wicked are contrasted with the wicked, and the Lord is extolled for His righteouness, and rebellion against His claims is plainly condemned.

In a striking fashion, David depicted how the wicked person makes his bed a hot-bed for poisonous weeds, 36:3-4, as Robert Pollock, of the early 18th century, poetically described—

> Yet did he spare his sleep, and hear the clock
> Number the midnight watches, on his bed
> Devising mischief more; and early rose,
> And made most hellish meals of good men's names.
> From door to door you might have seen him speed,
> Or placed amid a group of gaping fools.
> Peace fled the neighborhood in which he made
> His haunts; and, like a moral pestilence,
> Before his breath the healthy shoots and blooms
> Of social joy and happiness decayed.
> Fools only in his company were seen,
> And those forsaken of God, and to themselves
> Given up. The prudent shunned him and his house
> As one who had a deadly plague.

Thy righteousness is like the great mountains; thy judgments are as great deeps, 36:6. As winds and hurricanes cannot shake an Alp, so the righteousness of God can never be affected by circumstances. It is always firm and unmoved, lofty and sublime. Further, the providential dispensations of God are far and wide, terrible and irresistible like an ocean, yet they can appear as peaceful as the lake Jesus calmed while here below. As none can discover the springs of the sea, so man cannot comprehend the providence of the Eternal.

> Undiscovered sea!
> Into thy dark, unknown, mysterious caves,
> And secret haunts unfathomably deep,
> Beneath all visible, retired, none went
> And came again to tell the wonders there.

"Yet as the deep mirrors the sky, so the mercy of the Lord is seen reflected in all the arrangements of His government on earth; and over the profound depth the covenant rainbow casts its arch of comfort, for the Lord is faithful in all that He doeth."

Under the shadow of thy wings, 36:7. This common figure in the Psalms, taken immediately from the wings of the cherubim overshadowing the mercy-seat which covered the ark, is more remotely associated with birds which defend their young from the solar rays by overshadowing them with their wings. While a prisoner in Antwerp in 1551, Jeronimus Segerson wrote to his wife, Lysken, including these lines in his letter—

> In lonesome cell, guarded and strong I lie,
> Bound by Christ's love, his truth to testify,
> Though walls be thick, the door no hand unclose,
> God is my strength, my solace, and repose.

They shall be abundantly satisfied with the fatness of thy house, 36:8. The story is told of a father who, when he removed his family to a new house where accommodation was much more ample, and the substance much more rich and varied than that the family had been accustomed to, that his youngest son ran round every room and scanned every article with ecstacy, and then called out in childish wonder, "Is this ours, father? and is this ours?" The joyous child did not say *yours* but *ours,* and one could read in the father's glad eye that the child's confidence in appropriating as his own all his father had, was an important element in his satisfaction.

Fatness means, the best, the prime of everything, and what are the silks of Persia, the spices of Egypt, the gold of Ophir, and the treasures of both Indies, to the glory and provision of the Father's home on high? The joys of Heaven are inconceivable and unexpressible, and when we reach there our confession will be, "The half was not told us."

Bearing the title, "A Psalm of David, the servant of the Lord," this Psalm figures in Section V of William Langland's *Vision of Piers Plowman,* in which the dreamer sees again the "field full of folk" where sinners are induced to confess and repent. Then altogether, saints in glory and men on earth, cry upward "to Christ and to his moder" in the words of David, "Thou, Lord, shalt save both man and beast; how excellent is Thy mercy, O God," 36:7.

Psalm 37

Nathaniel Hardy, in a Funeral Sermon based on this Psalm, and preached in 1649, said that it could be styled, "The good man's cordial in bad times; a sovereign plaister for the plague of discontent; or, a choice antidote against the poison of impatience." Although this song or meditation, which David evidently wrote in his old age, 37:25, contains no direct allusion to the Psalmist's own circumstances of persecution or distress, it yet remains invaluable as a record of one who had a varied experience. Akin to the Book of Proverbs, Psalm 37 contains many sentential and pithy, concise gems of truth. It contains eight great precepts, is twice illustrated by autobiographical statements, and abounds in remarkable contrasts. It is also another alphabetical Psalm, which was a poetical invention to help one's memory.

As to the main subject of this Psalm, Spurgeon's explanation is as choice as it is concise—"The great riddle of the prosperity of the wicked, and the affliction of the righteous, which has perplexed so many is here dealt with in the light of the future; and fretfulness and repining are most impressively forbidden. It is a Psalm in which the Lord hushes most sweetly the too common repinings of his people, and calms their minds as to his present dealings with his chosen flock, and the wolves by whom they are surrounded."

Fret not . . . neither be thou envious, 37:1. This precept opening the Psalm is also a positive command. The word *fret* means, "burn not thyself with anger or grief." To fret is to have heartburn, which alas! is all too common among us as we see law-breakers riding in limousines, and obedient subjects walking in the mire. Queen Elizabeth envied the milkmaid when she was in prison; but if she had known what a glorious reign she would have had afterwards for 44 years, she would not have envied her. Why envy the wicked when the candle flickers into everlasting darkness?

Commit thy way unto the Lord, 37:5. Both the Hebrew and the margin give us "Roll thy way upon the Lord," as one who lays upon the shoulders of one stronger than himself a burden which he is not able to bear. Here we have one of the doubles of the Psalm; *commit—trust.* Our destiny is joyfully accomplished if we confidently entrust all to Him, Who is the length of our days.

> Thy way, not mine, O Lord,
> However dark it be;
> O lead me by thine own right hand,
> Choose out the path for me.

A little that a righteous man hath is better than the riches of many wicked, 37:16. Is not this proverb illustrated for us in the King of Spain, the greatest prince in Christendom, who extended his kingdom far and wide, so much so that he could truly say that the sun ever shone on his dominions? Yet he chose this motto for himself, *Totus non sufficit orbis*—"The world is not sufficient." Contentment finds *multum in parvo*—much in little—while for a wicked heart the whole world is too little. Better feed on scant fare with the prophets in Obadiah's cave than riot with the priests of Baal. That emperor certainly understood verses 16 and 17 of this Psalm who said of his crown, as he looked on it with tears, "If you knew the cares that are under this crown you would never stoop to take it up."

The seed of the wicked shall be cut off, 37:28. One commentator has said, "Like the house of Jeroboam and Ahab, of which not a dog was left. Honor and wealth ill-gotten seldom reach the third generation; the curse grows ripe before many years have passed, and falls upon an evil house. Among the legacies of wicked men the surest entail is a judgment on their family."

Spreading himself like a green bay tree, 37:35, 36. We wonder if Shakespeare, in *Henry VIII,* had these verses in mind when he wrote?

> —Today he puts forth
> The tender leaves of hopes, tomorrow blossom,
> And bears his blushing honors thick upon him:
> Third day comes a frost, a killing frost;
> And—when he thinks, good easy man, full surely
> His greatness is a ripening—nips his root,
> And then he falls, as I do.

Mark . . . Behold, 37:37. Herodotus mentions a custom among the Ethiopians of selling the dead bodies of their friends in glazed sepulchres, that their proportions might be obvious to strangers. Although a needless custom, it is doubtless no more than just that the pious lineaments of their minds who die in the Lord should be presented to the living in the mirror of art. Mary's name is ever remembered because of the box of ointment she poured on the head of the Master she loved.

The end of that man is peace, 37:37. The memorable Melancthon just before he died, chanted in his sleep the words, "I will not any more eat thereof until it be fulfilled in the kingdom of God." He seemed restless, and on being asked by one near him, "whether there were anything more he desired?" replied, *Aliud nihil nisi calum*— Nothing more unless it be heaven!

Martin Luther, in his Exposition of this Psalm, closed it with the sentence, "Oh, shame on our faithlessness, mistrust, and vile unbelief, that we do not believe such rich, powerful, consolatory declarations of God, and take up so readily with little grounds of offense, whenever we hear the wicked speeches of the ungodly. Help, O God, that we may once attain to right faith." The following biographical items prove how many were consoled by the Psalmist's varied declarations of God.

This further Psalm David sang occupies a prominent place in the life and experience of many saints through history. It achieved great notoriety when Paul Gerhardt made it the basis of his German hymn, *Befiehl du dene Wege,* which became well-known in our language through John Wesley's translation:

> Commit thou all thy griefs,
>> And ways into his hands,
> To his sure truth and tender care,
>> Who heaven and earth commands.

The origin of Gerhardt's hymn is related to his banishment from Berlin by the Elector of Brandenberg, because he conscientiously refused conditions attached to his ministry. Cast adrift with his wife and children, and seeing how deeply distressed his wife was, he quoted to her the words all of us can repeat from memory, "Commit thy way unto the Lord; trust also in him, and he shall bring it to pass," 37:5. Then Gerhardt went into the garden, composed his hymn and read it to his wife for comfort. Without doubt, this hymn comforting the hearts of so many in troubled times was the expression of Gerhardt's own character and life. Later on he became Archdeacon of Luebben. Later on, it became the custom of high schools in Germany, when pupils were leaving at the close of their course, to accompany them to the gate of the town singing the German composer's hymn.

Other associations of this hymn, written in grief, are worthy of notice. When the first Lutheran Church was opened in Philadelphia, Pennsylvania, in 1743, it was with Gerhardt's song on Psalm 37. Then when Queen Louisa of Prussia in 1806 received news of the disastrous battle of Jena, she sat down, after her first burst of weeping, and sang this song softly at the piano, and rose, her eyes clear and her spirit calm.

Among different verses from Psalm 37 appearing in the history and biography of various Christians, some have interesting connections. The son of the famous Wolseley, at one time Commander of the British Army, Sir George B. Wolseley, who served on the staff of the British Army in

India was a devout believer, and once wrote, "Psalm 37:3—'Trust in the Lord, and do good: so shalt thou dwell in the land, and verily thou shalt be fed'—a verified dream!" The story of this verse we like best is that connected with early Methodism in England when there was a preacher named Samuel Bradburn, of whom John Wesley held a high opinion. At one time Bradburn was in financial straits, and Wesley sent him five one pound notes with the following brief, scriptural letter—

> Dear Sammy—"Trust in the Lord, and do good: so shalt thou dwell in the land, and verily thou shalt be fed," Psalm 37:3.
> Yours affectionately,
>
> —John Wesley.

Preacher Bradburn wrote back—

> Rev. and Dear Sir,
> I have often been struck with the beauty of the passage quoted in your letter, but I must confess that I never saw such useful expository *notes* upon it before. I am, Rev., and dear sir, your obedient and grateful servant.
>
> —S. Bradburn

The precious verse commencing Wesley's setting of Gerhardt's hymn carries further stories of its influence in human lives. For instance, David Livingstone, as a Scot, would be expected to have a mind saturated with the language of the Psalms—which he did have. On the morning he left his humble home in Blantyre, Scotland for Africa, he read Psalms 121 and 135 and then prayed. When, after 30 years toiling to explore the continent, abolish slavery, and evangelize the native races Livingstone came to die, it was a Psalm that sustained him. In his explorations, facing death by savages, sickened by the atrocities of slavery, enduring fever, hunger, and bodily pain, this intrepid missionary found his daily strength in the words—"Commit thy way unto the Lord, and put thy trust in him; and he shall bring it to pass," 37:5. Livingstone himself confessed that it was this very verse that sustained him at every turn of his "course of life in Africa, and even in England." The promise which was his sheet-anchor has also been a source of inspiration to multitudes in life's crises.

Sir Walter Scott, true to the spirit of the Covenanters, had embodied in his novels the permanent influence of the Psalms. It was Psalm 37:16, 25, that the daughter of a Covenanter, Jeanie Deans, marked with her *kylevine pen* for her lover, Reuben Butler, on the eve of her adventurous journey to plead for her sister's life, and it was Psalms 42:14, 15 and 43:5, 6, that she repeated in her hour of peril when she was at the mercy of desperate ruffians.

A great multitude of the aged no man can number have said a loud *Amen!* while reading verse 25 of this Psalm—

> I have been young, and now am old; yet have I not seen the righteous forsaken, nor his seed begging bread.

This was the promise a great-grandson of John Knox, Robert Baillie of Jerviswoode, left to his son George when his estate was confiscated, and he was condemned to death at Edinburgh, December 24, 1684. On the scaffold at the Old Cross he could not deliver the speech he had prepared because of the beating drums. Baillie bade his son George, who visited him the night before his execution, to trust in the testimony of the Psalmist, "I have been young and now am old, yet have I not seen the righteous forsaken, nor his seed begging bread." Evidently young George laid this promise up in his hand for he proved to be a son honoring his father's memory. He rose to high office in the State after the Revolution, and the descendants of Robert Baillie who gave his son the promise of the Psalmist were found among some of the noblest families in the kingdom who verified the testimony of David.

It is not generally known that the bells of Westminster Abbey, London, chime hourly a sweet, simple melody, to which are allied the words—

> All through this hour,
> Lord be my Guide,
> And through Thy power
> No foot shall slide (Psalm 37:31).

Psalm 38

The reason David wrote this Psalm was *To bring remembrance,* but what to remember, he did not go on to say. Psalm 70 is given the same title, and in both Psalms David pours out his complaint that his sorrows made him feel as if God had forgotten him. In this 38th Psalm, the Psalmist engages in a long tale of sorrow, and pours out a flood of griefs for God to hear. There are many good things, however, we can keep alive in our memories. When we remember that any experience driving us to God is a blessing, and that anything weaning us from confidence is the arm of flesh, to lean wholly upon God, then memory becomes a Paradise from which we need not be driven.

It is not easy to fix the historical setting of the Psalm. One commentator says that David was on his death-bed as he thought, and he said, "It shall be a Psalm of Remembrance to bring sin to remembrance, to confess to God my uncleanness with Bathsheba, to bring to my remembrance the evils of my life." Spurgeon suggests that the Psalm may be a commemoration of David's own sickness and endurance, or on the other hand, it may have been composed by him for use by sick and slandered saints, with special reference to himself.

Thy hand presseth me sore, 38:2.   Homer called the hands of Jupiter, hands whose praise could not be sufficiently spoken—hands inaccessible, irresistible for strength: all the gods in heaven could not ward off a blow of Jupiter's hand. His hand never strikes but for sin; and where sin is mighty his blow is heavy. Divine palmistry is a most fascinating Bible study.

Neither is there any rest . . . because of my sin, 38:3.   Quicksilver has a principle of motion in itself, but not of rest, and, too often, our Christian life resembles quicksilver: we are never quiet, but like a ship upon the waves. As long as we live in unforgiven sin, there is motion without rest. Not until Christ and the sinner meet can there be rest. Everything is in motion till it comes at the center; Christ is the Center of the soul; the needle of the compass trembles till it comes to the North Pole.

I go mourning all the day long, 38:6.   John Bunyan in *Grace Abounding* shares the continual moan of David. "And now was I both a burden and a terror to myself, nor did I ever so know, as now, what it was to be weary of life, and yet afraid to die. Oh, how gladly now would I have been anybody but myself! Anything but a man! and in any condition but mine own! for there was nothing did pass more frequently over my mind than that it was impossible for me to be forgiven my transgression, and to be saved from wrath to come."

My groaning is not hid from thee, 38:9. How blessed to remember that the good Physician understands the symptoms of our disease and sees the hidden evil which they reveal, hence our case is safe in His hands.

> He takes the meaning of our tears,
> The language of our groans.

Our sorrow and anguish can never be hid from Him Who became the Man of Sorrows, and that One acquainted with human grief.

My heart panteth, 38:10. The language David used here signifies "to travel," or "wander hither and thither," and has come to mean the agitation or disquietude which distress of heart engenders when we know not what to do. John Calvin goes on to say that it is so with the heart that is disquieted within, and thus turns about on all sides, or runs to and fro.

For in thee, O Lord, do I hope, 38:15. Thomas Cole, devotional writer of the 16th century, used the following illustration in his work, *Morning Exercises.* "A man that is to go down into a deep pit he does not throw himself headlong into it, or leap down at all adventures, but fastens a rope at top upon a cross beam or some sure place, and so lets himself down by degrees: so let thyself down into the consideration of this sin hanging upon Christ; and when thou art gone so low that thou canst endure no longer, but art ready to be overcome with the horror and darkness of thy miserable estate."

I will be sorry for my sin, 38:18. Pliny wrote of some families that had private marks on their bodies peculiar to those of that line, and every man had, as it were, a private sin, which is most justly called his. But if we will confess our sins aright, we must not leave out that sin. Our chiefest spite must be against it, according to David's resolve, for he not only declared *his* sin but was sorry for it. Thus, he came to experience that the Lord was his salvation, 38:22. Faith the suppliant became faith triumphant.

The intriguing title given to this Psalm reads, *A Psalm of David, to bring to remembrance.* But it does not say remembrance of what? As we have a penitent's plea in the Psalm, it may be that as David remembered his sin, he was sorry, and turned to the Lord for his forgiving mercy. Bishop John Hooper included Psalm 38 in the Psalms he recommended for their lessons of "patience and consolation," at times, "when the mind can take no understanding, nor the heart any joy of God's promises." This would seem to be the feeling of David when he composed this 38th Psalm.

Maine de Biran, 1766-1824, was known as one of the greatest of French metaphysicians. Not only was he a soldier and politician, but a solitary thinker of the facts of his inner consciousness. His *Journal* lays bare the mental stages by which he became a believer in Christianity. The last entry is dated May 17th, 1824, and was made when he felt the rapid approach of the disease that was to end his earthly course, and was in the form of a comment on Psalm 38:7. It is worth quoting in full.

> In my weakness and in my moral and physical, I cry aloud upon my cross, 'Have mercy upon me, O Lord, for I am weak. My loins are filled with a sore disease; and there is no whole part in my body.' Woe to the man who is alone. Unhappy too is the man, however powerful his intellect, or however great his human wisdom, who is not sustained by a strength and a wisdom higher than his own. The true wisdom, the true strength, consists in feeling the support of God. If he has not this, woe to him, for he is alone. The Stoic stands alone. The Christian walks in God's presence and with God, through this world and the next.

It was a quotation from this Psalm that quaint George Herbert who, when he retired from the Court and Holy Orders, and died as the parish priest of Bemerton, in view of the tapering spire of Salisbury Cathedral, took as the burden of his admirable poem, *The Quip*. It was verse 15— "Thou shalt answer me, O Lord my God."

Psalm 39

The renowned Biblical scholar, H. Ewald, called this Psalm, "the most beautiful of all the elegies in the Psalter." Written by David, it was dedicated *to Jeduthun,* and given over to him, as one of the great masters of the temple service, to prepare as a hymn of praise for the presence of God. Called "the king's seer," Jeduthun was the medium of Divine guidance to David, 2 Chron. 35:15. His name also appears at the heading of Psalms 62 and 77. As his name means, "praising," or "celebrating," it was a most appropriate one for a leader in sacred psalmody.

David, then, left this sorrowful ode in Jeduthun's hands because he thought him most fit to set it to music, or because he would distribute the sacred honor of same among all the musicians, who, in their turn, presided in the choir. Biographically, it was the kind of song that David's checkered life would be sure to produce, for in it we have the fit effusions of a man sorely tempted, strong in his passions, yet firm in his faith.

I said, I will take heed, 39:1. No lesson is so hard to learn as that of holding our tongue. Yet David promised that his would be a wise and discreet government of his lips. Socrates reported of one Pambo, an honest, well meaning man, who came to his friend; desiring to teach him one of David's Psalms, he read him this verse. Pambo answered, "This one verse is enough, if I learn it well." Nineteen years later, he said, in all that time he had hardly learned that one verse. May God deliver you and me from fruitless talking!

I held my peace, 39:2. A Christian being asked what fruit he had by Christ, answered: "Is this not fruit, not to be moved at your reproaches?" In cases of this nature, we must refer all to God; if thou hold thy peace, God speaks for thee; and if God speaks for us, it is better than we can speak for ourselves. David said, "I held my peace, for it was thy doing."

I was musing, 39:3. Gersom called *Meditation,* "the nurse of prayer." Says Thomas Watson, the Puritan divine, "Meditation is like oil to the lamp; the lamp of prayer would soon go out unless meditation cherish and support it. Meditation and Prayer are like two turtles, if you separate one the other dies; a cunning angler observes the time and season when the fish bite best, and then he throws in the angle, when the heart is warmed by meditation, now is the best season to throw in the angle of prayer, and fish for mercy."

William Gurnall, another Puritan stalwart, gives us this further illustration of *musing*. "Meditation is prayer in bullion (gold), prayer is the ore, soon melted and run into holy desires. The laden cloud soon drops into rain, the piece charged soon goes off when fire is put to it. A meditating soul is in *proxima potentia* in prayer. This was an ejaculatory prayer shot from David's soul when in the company of the wicked."

Lord, make me to know mine end—how frail I am, 39:4. The Emperors of Constantinople, in their inauguration, on their coronation days, had a mason come and show them several marble stones, and ask them to choose which of those should be made ready for the gravestones. Joseph of Arimathea had his tomb in his garden, to check the pleasures of the place. Between Walsall and Iretsy, in England's beautiful Cheshire, was a house built in 1636, of thick oak framework, filled in with brick. Over the window of the taproom, the following inscription cut in oak was there for all to read—"You would weep if you knew that your life was limited to one month, yet you laugh while you know not but it may be restricted to a day." The brevity of life is emphasized in the next verse—

My days as an handbreadth, 39:5. An "handbreath" is one of the shortest kind of measures. There is an *ell,* a *cubit,* and a *palm,* or *handbreath,* whereof there are two kinds, the greater and the less. The greater handbreadth is the whole space betwixt the top of the thumb and the little finger, when the hand is extended, called a *span,* in account near 12 inches. The lesser handbreath is a more proper and strict signification, just the breadth of the four fingers of the hand closed together, here chiefly intended, this interpretation but agreeing with the original of verse, 5, and complying most with the Psalmist's mind.

Walked in a vain shew . . . heapeth up riches, 39:6. When Edmund Burke put up for Parliament in the Bristol election, his competitor died suddenly, and Burke said, "What shadows we are, and what shadows we pursue." How impressive is the poetic setting of this verse Shakespeare has given us in these lines—

> Tomorrow, and tomorrow, and tomorrow,
> Creeps in this petty pace from day to day,
> To the last syllable of recorded time;
> And all our yesterdays have lighted fools
> The way to dusty death. Out, out, brief candle!
> Life's but a walking shadow; a poor player,
> That struts and frets his hour upon the stage,
> And then is heard no more; it is a tale
> Told by an idiot, full of sound and fury,
> Signifying nothing.

A similar thought was expressed by Edmund Layfields well over a century ago—"The plentiful showers of tears which stand in our eyes when we come from the womb, and when we draw to the tomb, are faithful witnesses of man's vanity. We bid the world *good morrow* with grief, and *goodnight* with a groan."

And now, Lord, what wait I for? 39:7. David, disgusted with all things around him, knowing that they are vain and soon pass away, longed to cut all cords binding him to earth, and was ready to sound, "Boot and saddle, up and away." Was this not the same longing George Herbert had in mind when he gave us this verse?

> O loose this frame, this knot of man untie,
> That my free soul may use her wing,
> Which is now pinioned with mortality,
> As an entangled, hamper'd thing.
> What have I left that I should stay and groan?
> The most of me to heaven is fled;
> My thoughts and joys are all pack'd up and gone,
> And for their old acquaintance plead.

I was dumb . . . because thou didst it, 39:9. God has His own ways of educating His children for Eternity, and while they may think that at times His discipline is harsh and stern, and His strokes severe, His is ever the training of love. The true feelings of a saint in the hour of bitterness is illustrated for us in the case of Richard Cameron's father. This aged, covenanting saint was in prison "for the Word of God and for the testimony of Jesus Christ." The bleeding head of his martyred son was brought to him by his callous persecutors who asked him derisively if he knew it. "I know it, I know it"—said the father, as he kissed the mangled forehead of his fair-haired son—"it is my son's, my own dear son's! It is the Lord: good is the will of the Lord, who cannot wrong me or mine, but who hath made goodness and mercy to follow us all our days."

The last words of John Calvin were, "I held my tongue, because thou, Lord hast done it—I mourned as a dove—Lord, thou grindest me to powder, but it sufficeth me because it is thy hand." That the ways of God are past finding out is likewise emphasized by the attitude of a little girl who, in the providence of God, was born deaf and dumb. She was received, and instructed, at an institution established for those afflicted ones. One day, a visitor requested to examine the children thus sadly laid aside from childhood's common joys. Several questions were asked, and quickly answered by means of a slate and pencil. At length the visitor wrote on a board, *Why were you born deaf and dumb?* A look of anguish clouded for the moment the expressive face of the little girl; but it quickly passed

Psalms: *A Devotional Commentary*

as she took her slate, and wrote, *Even so, Father; for so it seemeth good in Thy sight.*

Thou makest his beauty to consume away like a moth, 39:11. The apparent truth David declares in the use of this simile is that as a moth crumbles into dust under the slightest pressure, or to the gentlest touch, so man dissolves with equal ease, and vanishes into darkness, under the finger of the Almighty. While they live, moths spend their time eating clothes, as I realized when I was about to sit down to pen these lines. I went to put on an old jacket I had almost forgotten about, and lo! it was riddled with gaping holes. *Wax old,* Isa. 51:6, and *consumed,* probably refer to a moth-eaten garment. See Psalm 6:7; 31:9. George Horne would have us know that the body of man is a *garment* to the soul: in this garment sin hath lodged a *moth,* which, by degrees, fretteth and weareth away, first the beauty, then the strength, and, finally, the contexture of its parts.

Among the Early Fathers was Ambrose, Bishop of Milan, who baptized Augustine. As his was a life-long study of the Psalms it was fitting that he should write his treatise on the Duties of the Clergy, by patience, simplicity, and contempt for riches based on Psalm 39.

Socrates, ecclesiastical historian of the 5th century, tells of a plain man named Pambo who came to a saintly, scholarly man, Antony, and asked him to teach him one of the Psalms, and who began to read to Pambo Psalm 39: "I said, I will take heed to my ways, that I sin not with my tongue." After this first sentence, Pambo left saying that he would make this his first lesson. But he did not return and, when ten months later the teacher met him and asked if he had mastered the first lesson yet, Pambo had to say—No. Some 49 years later, he had to give a like answer, which offers us a good illustration of the saying of James, "The tongue can no man tame." Perhaps Pambo might have succeeded better had he allowed his teacher to go on to verse 7 of the Psalm, "And now, Lord, what wait I for: my hope is in thee"; or had he sought, as the Apostle James puts it, "the wisdom from above, which is first pure and then peaceable."

Under Psalm 33, a reference will be found to the opening verse of Psalm 39. Among passages from the Psalms which Shakespeare uses is the 8th verse of this Psalm, "Truly my hope is even in Thee." As for verse 9, it has several impressive associations. The last days of John Calvin were heavy with severe bodily suffering, forcing from the Reformer involuntary moans. Friends around his bed heard him repeat the words of Hezekiah, "I did mourn as a dove: mine eyes fail looking upward," followed by those of this Psalm, "I was dumb, I opened not my mouth; because thou didst it," 39:9.

When the well-known minister of St. George's, Edinburgh, Dr. Thomson fell dead at the door of his own house in the city, the blow was thought to be irreparable by the evangelical party in the Church of Scotland. His bosom friend, Dr. Jones, of Lady Glanorchy Church, who was the man who discovered the genius of Thomas Chalmers, and brought him to the fore, was called to preach the funeral sermon at St. George's Church. Shutting himself up in privacy, he did not appear till the Sabbath, when he preached with powerful effect. The first Psalm Jones gave out for singing sent a thrill through the immense congregation—

> Dumb was I, opening not my mouth,
> Because this work was thine.

Psalm 40

After His Resurrection, our Lord told His disciples that all things written *in the Psalms,* and other Old Testament Scriptures, concerning Him had been fulfilled. We can imagine how He would linger over Psalm 40 as He opened this portion to his awestruck followers, for David, by the Holy Spirit, was led into the region of prophecy, and was thus honored to write of Someone far greater than himself. The writer to the Hebrews had no difficulty in seeing Jesus in this Psalm, for in verses 5-7 of chapter 10, he quotes verses 6-8 of Psalm 40 as being spoken by Him concerning Himself. The title, *David's Psalm,* or, as Henry Ainsworth puts it, "A Psalm concerning David, that is, Christ who is called *David* in the Prophets, Hosea 3:5; Jeremiah 30:9; Ezekiel 34:23, 24." Says Spurgeon, "Jesus is evidently here, although it might not be a violent wrestling of language to see both David and his Lord, both Christ and the Church, the double comment might involve itself in obscurity, and therefore we shall let the sun shine even although this should conceal the stars."

He brought me up also out of a horrible pit, 40:2. Positive misery is indicated by this figure, just as the absence of solid comfort is suggested by the *miry clay.* Give a man a good foothold, and a burden is greatly lightened, but to be loaded and to be placed on slimy, slippery clay, is to be tried doubly. Some pits referred to in the Bible were like prisons, in which there were no openings except a hole at the top, which served for both door and window. Isaiah called the same a "pit of corruption," 38:17, and they were pits of putrifaction and filth, and often deep in mud. The Hebrew for "horrible pit" is a "pit of noise," so called because of water falling into it, making a roaring noise, or because of the outcries those cast into them made. In His Resurrection, Jesus was brought out of both the horrible pit and the miry clay, and His feet set upon an eternal rock.

Mine ears hast thou opened. 40:6. The literal translation reads, "Mine ears hast thou digged, or pierced, through," and is an allusion to the custom of masters boring the ear of a slave, who had refused his offered freedom, in token of retaining him, Exodus 21:6. The phrase, then, implies, "Thou hast accepted me as thy slave." Such a mark of perpetual servitude is also observed by other nations marking and stigmatizing their servants' bodies. James Merrick, in the 17th century applied the custom of the true servant of God—

158

> Nor sacrifice thy love can win,
> Nor offerings from the stain of sin
>   Obnoxious man shall clear.
> Thy hand my mortal frame prepares,
> (Thy hand, whose signature it bears),
>   And open my willing ear.

Saintly Bishop Handley taught the same when he wrote of himself as a "glad vassal of a Savior's throne"—

> My Master, lead me to Thy door;
> Pierce this now willing ear once more . . .
> And pierced ears shall bear the tone
> Which tells me Thou and I are one.

Then said I, Lo, I come, 40:7. Often, when we refer to our birth we say, "I came into the world on such and such a date," but actually none ever came into the world, save Jesus. The stupendous thought behind the miracle of His Incarnation is the fact that *He lived before He was born.* "I come" speaks of a pre-existence. Jesus often spoke of having come from the Father, and one only properly *comes* who comes from some other place. *He* only had a place He lived in before He came. Further, "Lo, I come," means *to appear before thee,* and was a phrase used to indicate the coming of an inferior into the presence of a superior, or of a slave before his master, Numbers 23:38; 2 Samuel 19:26, and was generally expressive of willingness, all of which is applicable to Him Who came to do His Father's will.

Therefore my heart faileth me, 40:12. None of the ransomed will ever know how dark was the night their Lord passed, nor how deep the waters were He crossed, before He found the sheep that was lost. What agony was His in the Garden, when all strength seemed to leave Him—

> There my God bore all my guilt,
> This through grace can be believed;
> But the horrors which he felt
> Are too vast to be conceived.
> None can penetrate through thee,
> Doleful, dark, Gethsemane.

I am poor and needy; yet the Lord thinketh upon me, 40:17. One of the sons of Caesar Malon, well-known spiritual leader and writer who died in 1864, wrote of his brother Jocelyn, who, years prior to his death, was the subject of intense bodily suffering: "One striking feature in his character was his holy fear of God, and reverence for his will. One day I was repeating a verse from Psalm 40, 'As for me, I am poor and needy, but the Lord careth for me.' He said, 'Manina, I love that verse, all but the last bit, it looks like a murmur against God, He never *tarries* in my case.'"

Without doubt, this is one of the great Messianic Psalms, Psalm 41 being the next in order. Who among us, confident that we have been saved by grace, has not found expression of our salvation in the opening verses of this great Psalm? Attention has already been drawn to the inspiration St. Francis de Sales, Bishop of Geneva, 1567-1622, gathered from the Psalms. It was also in his death that he turned to them for expressions of his confidence and hope. On the Feast of St. John, 1622, Sales was struck down by a paralytic seizure, which left his mind unclouded. A friendly visitor expressed regret at his condition, but he replied, "I am waiting on God's mercy: *Expectans, expectavi, Dominum et intendit mihi*—"I waited patiently for the Lord, and He inclined unto me, and heard my calling," Psalm 40:1.

St. Francis of Assisi, who made active love the source of his religion, lived in the Psalms, to which he came "with great trembling and reverence" for the love of Him that is called "The Rock," ever repeating the words, "Thou didst set my feet upon the rock," 40:2. Robert Southwell, a Jesuit and Elizabethan poet, born in 1560, experienced something of the anguish expressed in this Psalm. As he awaited his fate for the crime of being a Roman Catholic, he wrote a letter describing the horrible death of two priests, "hung up, for whole days, in such a manner that they can but just touch the ground with the tips of their toes. They are kept in a prison, and truly live in the horrible pit, in the mire and clay," 40:2.

The unceasing love for the Psalter that Queen Elizabeth had is seen in her constant quotations from it. On the death of Queen Mary, relieved from constant dread of execution, she expressed her gratitude in the words, "This is the Lord's doing; and it is marvellous in our eyes," 118:23. Stamped on her silver was the Latin inscription—*Posni Deum adjutorem meum*—adapted from Psalm 40:21—"Thou art my helper . . . O my God."

Robert Rollock, the first Principal of the University of Edinburgh, who died in 1599, found much comfort in his last illness in the Psalms. Often he would repeat, *Deus meus, ne tardaveris*—"Make no tarrying, O my God," 40:17. At the end, he broke out with the words, "Come, Lord, make no delay; come, Lord Jesus, tarry not. I am wearied with my loathing day and night. Come, Lord Jesus, that I may come to Thee."

Psalm 41

The frequently used title, *A Psalm of David,* reminds us, yet once again, that its composer made his own experience the basis of a prophetic song, for, as with the previous Psalm, a far greater than David is set forth. Without doubt, the Psalmist himself had a wide range of experience, and had spiritual unction to edify the future ages, and become a type of his Greater Son, Jesus Christ. Yet the bitterness David faced has proved to be a fountain of unfailing succor to many generations of the redeemed. In his introduction to this Psalm, Spurgeon says that "Jesus Christ betrayed by Judas Iscariot is evidently the great theme of this Psalm, but we think not exclusively. He is the antitype of David, and all his people are in their measure like him. Such as receive a vile return for long kindness to others, may read this song with much comfort, for they will see that it is alas! too common for the best of men to be rewarded for their holy charity with scorn and cruelty; and when they have been humbled by falling into sin, advantage has been taken of their low estate, their good deeds have been forgotten and the vilest spite has been vented upon them."

He considereth the poor, 41:1. The *Syriac* says of the title, "It was a Psalm of David, when he appointed overseers to take care of the poor." The opening verse does not say "commiserate" the poor, but *consider* them. But do we make them our special consideration and objects of compassion? George Crabbe, the much-loved spiritual poet who died in 1832, left this poetic exposition on this verse—

> An ardent spirit dwells with Christian love,
> The eagle's vigour is the pitying dove.
> 'Tis not enough that we with sorrow sigh,
> That we the wants of pleading men supply,
> That we in sympathy with sufferers feel,
> Nor hear a grief without a wish to heal;
> Not these suffice—to sickness, pain, and woe,
> The Christian spirit loves with aid to go:
> Will not be sought, waits not for want to plead,
> But seeks the duty—nay, prevents the need;
> Her utmost aid to every ill applies,
> And plants relief for coming miseries.

Thou wilt make his bed in his sickness, 41:3. That bed must be soft
which God will make. Oriental beds have no need to be made up in
the same sense as our own, seeing they are no more than mattresses or
quilts thickly padded, and turned when they are uncomfortable—
which is the idea in this verse. Paxton Hood told the story of visiting
his beloved friend, Benjamin Parsons, as he lay dying. "How are you
today?" I asked; and he replied, "My head is sweetly resting on three
pillows—infinite power, infinite love, and infinite wisdom." Preaching
in Canterbury Hall, Brighton many months after this event I was
requested to call upon a poor but holy young woman, apparently
dying. She said, "I felt I must see you before I died, I heard you tell
the story of Benjamin Parsons and his three pillows; and I went
through a surgical operation, and it was very cruel. I was leaning my
head on the pillows, and as they were taking them away I said,
'Mayn't I keep them?' The surgeon said, 'No, my dear, we must take
them away.' 'But,' said I, 'you can't take away Benjamin Parsons'
three pillows, I can lay my head on infinite power, infinite love, and
infinite wisdom.'"

Herein is love, indeed, that God turns bedmaker to His sick children.
A bed soon becomes hard, if the body is weary with tossing to and fro
upon it, but grace gives patience, and God's smile gives peace, and the
bed is made to feel soft because the sufferer's heart is content; the pillows
are downy because the head is peaceful.

If he came to see me, he speaketh vanity, 41:6. Visits of sympathy
are visitations of mockery. "When the fox calls on the sick lamb his
words are soft, but he licks his lips in the hope of a carcass." Jeremy
Taylor wrote of a pretty apologue Bromiard told. "A fowler, one
sharp, frosty morning, having taken many birds for which he had long
watched, began to take up his nets, and nipping the birds on the head
laid them down. A young thrush seeing the tears trickling down his
cheeks by reason of the extreme cold, said to her mother, that certainly
the man was very merciful and compassionate who wept so bitterly
over the calamity of the poor little birds. But her mother told her more
wisely that she might better judge of the man's disposition by his hand
than by his eye; and if the hands do strike treacherously, he can never
be admitted to friendship, who speaks fairly and weeps bitterly."

Mine own familiar friend, 41:9. How prophetic this was of the
villainy of Judas Iscariot, treasurer of the apostolic college. The
original runs, "The man of my peace." When stabbed by his closest
friend, the dying Caesar cried, *Et tu Brute?* "The kiss of the traitor
wounded our Lord's heart as much as the nail wounded his hand,"
says Spurgeon. "What Ahithophel was to David, Judas was to our
Lord. The traitor was an apostle, admitted to the privacy of the Great

Teacher, hearing His secret thoughts, and, as it were, allowed to read His very heart," but such confidence was betrayed. Where we place great trust an unkind act is the more severely felt.

Both the poor in worldly possessions, and the poor in bodily health have found consolation in one of the *Blesseds,* the Bible is so full of, and which provides a grand opening for this Psalm. "Blessed is he that considereth the poor; the Lord will deliver him in time of trouble. . . . The Lord will strengthen him upon the bed of languishing, thou wilt make all his bed in sickness." Thomas Fuller tells how Queen Mary of England, abstracted from her evil counsellors, had good features of character. For instance, she erected again the hospital of the Savoy which had been founded by her grandfather, Henry VII; and her maids, out of their own wardrobe, furnished it with beds, blankets, and sheets; and then Fuller adds, "Were any of those ladies still alive, I would pray for them in the language of the Psalmist: *The Lord make all their bed in their sickness.* And He is a good bed-maker indeed, who can make it fit the person, and please the patient. But seeing such are all long since deceased, it will be no superstition to praise God for their piety, and commend their practice to the imitation of posterity."

Psalm 42

The historical events and incidents associated with this soul-moving Psalm indicate how precious it has been to many pilgrims who found themselves, like David, in the Slough of Despond. While there is no clue as to the authorship of this Psalm, as far as the title is concerned, it must be the offspring of his pen, seeing it is so Davidic in expression. "It smells of the son of Jesse, and bears marks of his style and experience in every letter. We would sooner doubt the authorship of the second part of *Pilgrim's Progress* than question David's title to be the composer of this Psalm."

Further, no stated declaration of the circumstance occasioning the Psalm is given in its heading. It is thought to have been composed by David when forced to flee from his son, Absalom. If this is so, then the ode is a most instructive one, as it details the trials of a thoroughly gracious and much afflicted saint. It has as its dominant theme the sob of a soul far removed from the outward ordinances and worship of God, sighing for the long-loved house of God; and has been the voice of many a spiritual believer, deeply depressed, longing for the renewal of the Divine Presence, struggling with doubts and fears, but yet holding his ground by faith in the living, ever-present God.

Dedicated to *The Chief Musician,* the Master of Sanctuary Music, this instructive song was to be sung by the choice band of singers, *The Sons of Korah,* who were the spared ones of sovereign grace, seeing that their father and his associates were swallowed up alive because of their sin of deceit, Numbers 26:11. Having been delivered from going down into the pit, these sons were qualified to lead the sacred music of the house of God, and also because they were descendants of a Levitical family of singers. Heman, one of the three famous musicians of the time, was a Korahite, 1 Chronicles 25. See 1 Chronicles 6:16-33. Like warlike bishops of latter times, the Korahites knew how to lay aside priestly vestments for the soldier's armor, and their hands could wield the sword as well as strike the harp, 1 Chronicles 12:6. Medieval writers loved to dwell upon the will of God in raising up saints where they could have been least looked for. Who would have imagined that from the posterity of him who said, "Ye take too much upon you, ye sons of Aaron," should have arisen those whose sweet Psalms would be the heritage of the Church of God to the end of time?

The hart panteth after the water-brooks, 42:1. This animal must have been one of Solomon's favorites, seeing he used it often as a metaphor to express his thought. Thomson, in his *Hand and the Book,* remarks, "What elegant creatures these gazelles are, and how gracefully they bound! . . The sacred writers frequently mention gazelles under the various names of harts, roes, and hinds . . . I have seen large flocks of these panting harts gather round the water-brooks in the great deserts of Central Syria, so subdued by thirst that you could approach quite near before they fled." David, now a banished man, yearned for his return to the house of God, of which he said he would rather be a doorkeeper than dwell in the tents of wickedness. Driven from the house of God, he felt he was also driven from God Himself—*When shall I come and appear before God?*

My soul thirsteth for God, 42:2. Bradford, that holy saint and martyr, said that he could not leave *confession* till he found his heart touched and broken for sin; nor *supplication,* till his heart was affected with the beauty of the blessings desired; nor *thanksgiving,* till his soul was quickened in return of praise; nor *any duty,* until his heart was brought into a duty frame, and something of Christ was found therein. Augustine wrote that he came to cease loving Tully's elegant orations because he could not find *Christ* in them: "nor doth a gracious soul love empty duties." Isaac Watts in one of his sermons, quoted one of his poems founded on the opening verses of this Psalm. The opening stanza reads—

> When I am banished from thy house
>   I mourn in secret, Lord;
> "When shall I come and pay my vows,
>   And hear thy holy word?"

Where is thy God?, 42:3. The ungodly are ever ready to shake the faith of a mind already dejected, and to upbraid him for having a God forsaking him in trouble.

> "Where is now thy God!" Oh, aid me,
>   Lord of mercy, to reply—
> "He is HERE—though foes invade me,
>   Know his outstretched arm is nigh,"
> Help me thus to be victorious,
>   While the shield of faith I take;
> Lord, appear, and make thee glorious,
>   Help me for thy honor's sake.

A teacher of atheistic outlook wrote on the blackboard—GOD IS NOWHERE! but a bright girl who knew and loved God, spoke up and said, "Please, sir, you have made a mistake in your last word for it should read—GOD IS NOW HERE!

With a multitude that kept holy day, 42:4. The crown of David's sorrow was the remembrance of companying with those who spent God's Day in God's House. In his forced absence from the Sanctuary, he maintained his private devotions, but how he longed for the happiness of gathering again with the Lord's people in public worship. George Herbert, in *The Temple*, poetically described such a longing—

> Though private prayer be a brave design
> Yet public hath more promises, more love;
> And love's a weight to hearts, to eyes a sign.
> We all are but cold suitors; let us move
> > Where it is warmest. Leave thy six and seven;
> > Pray with the most: for where most pray is Heaven.

Why art thou cast down, O my soul? 42:5. Three times over the Psalmist uses this word to describe this dejected feeling, 42:5, 6, 11; 43:2. But, as Spurgeon asks, "Why this deep depression, this faithless fainting, this chicken-hearted melancholy?" Old John Trapp said of this phrase, "David chideth David out of the dumps." It was only right that he should rebuke himself for such a mournful dirge. Athanasius counseled his friend that when any trouble should fall upon him, he should give himself to the reading of this Psalm; for there was a way, he thought, of curing by the like, as well as by the contrary; for 'tis observed that when two instruments are tuned to the same unison, if you touch the strings of the one, the strings of the other will move too, though untouched, if placed at a convenient distance. The word the Psalmist used for our English word *disquieted,* litterally means, "tumulcasted," a word frequently applied to the roaring and tumult and tossing of the sea, Isaiah 7:12; Jeremiah 3:22; 6:23. What deep agitation is behind his—*Why?*

But after chiding his soul for its misery, David cried, *I shall yet praise him.* Among those imprisoned in Canterbury Castle for their faith in Christ was a noble woman, Alice Benden, who by the Bishop's order was let down into a deep dungeon where none of her friends could come to her. There she was fed with a halfpenny bread, and a farthing for a day, neither would they allow her any more for her money. Her bed was a little straw, between a pair of stocks and a stone wall. This made her to grievously bewail and lament her estate, reasoning with herself, why her Lord did in so heavy a wise afflict her, and suffered her thus to be sequestered from the sweet society of her loving prison-fellows. In this extremity of misery, and in the midst of these dolorous mournings she continued, till on a night, repeating that of the Psalmist—*Why art thou so heavy, O my soul? And why art thou so cast down within me? Still trust in God,* she said, "God's right hand can change all this," which gave her comfort in her sorrows, and she continued joyful until she was released.

Deep calleth unto deep at the noise of thy waterspouts, 42:7. As in a waterspout, the deeps above and below clasp hands, so it seemed to David that heaven and earth united to create a tempest around, causing his woes to become incessant and overwhelming. Yet he called them, *"Thy* waves and *Thy* billows," recognizing, thereby, the truth that the Divine heart permitting his waters of affliction, would achieve their beneficial design in his life.

> Deep to deep incessant calling,
>   Tossed by furious tempests' roll,
> Endless waves and billows falling,
>   Overwhelm my fainting soul.
> Yet I see a Power presiding
>   Mid the tumult of the storm,
> Ever ruling, ever guiding,
>   Love's intentions to perform.
> Yes, mid sorrows most distressing,
>   Faith contemplates thy design,
> Humbly bowing, and confessing
> All the waves and billows THINE.

David passes from the deriding question, *Where is thy God?* to the affirmation, *God my Rock,* v. 9. As a fugitive, with little means of defense, and continually pursued by enemies as he was, he came to appreciate the natural hollows and excavated caves in the mountainous country he knew so well. Such an idea of shelter and defense, associated in David's mind with that of a rock, it was natural for him to apply the figure to God, and seek in Him the preservation he desired. *Hope thou in God!* Hope is like the sun, which, as we journey towards it, casts the shadow of our burden behind us. Melancholy within his heart gave David's face a ghastly look, and so he praises God Who is *the health of my countenance.* The martyr Stephen became so occupied with Jesus that in the midst of his persecutors, and death so imminent, he had a face which "shone as the face of an angel." If our countenance is sad and sickly looking, because of an agitated heart, the only way we can shine with the joy of the Lord is to trust and hope in Him.

This familiar Psalm is well-named as an *Instruction* one, seeing it is heavy with lessons conducive to the development of our spiritual life. It was this Psalm that brought much consolation to the heart of Daniel McMichael, a Scottish covenanter who, on January 1, 1685, as his captors led him out into the fields to be shot, died singing part of it.

The opening verse, "As the hart panteth after the water-brooks," giving the key-note to the Psalm as a whole, was often in the thoughts of early Christians in the time of persecution. This is why the *hart* was a common emblem on the walls of the Catacombs where they found refuge, and why they sang the entire Psalm at the close of the Lord's Supper.

Orison Sweet Marden, the American author of a past generation who wrote *Architects of Fate, Pushing to the Front,* and other books, said of the first verse of this Psalm, "It has always been my favorite and I cannot remember the time when I was not impressed by it." Before his day, "George Beisley, Priest," as he is described, and who perished for his religious convictions in the dungeons of the Tower, London, in the 15th century, had inscribed on his shield, in Latin, the same opening verse of Psalm 42.

Henry II caroled Psalm 42—"Like as a hart desireth the water brooks"—as he hunted the stag in the Forest of Fontainebleau, riding by the side of Diane de Poitiers, for the motto of whose portrait as a huntress he chose the first verse of this, his favorite Psalm.

When Francis de Sales, Bishop of Geneva, came to die, the Psalms he greatly loved in life were on his lips. Among the verses he was heard to murmur was Psalm 42:2, "When shall I come to appear before the presence of God?" It was on the evening of the Holy Innocents' Day, 1622, that this saint was called to appear in the presence of God, and to remain there forever.

The narrative of the death of Bohemian martyrs, who suffered at Prague in 1621, is replete with stories of those who, in the hour of death found comfort in the Psalms. For example, there is the item, "John Schultis was the next, who on the scaffold said, 'Why art thou cast down, O my soul? hope thou in God, for I shall yet praise Him,' Psalm 42:5. The righteous seem in the eyes of men to die, but indeed they go to their rest." Then kneeling down, Schultis said, "Come, come, Lord Jesus, and do not tarry," and so he was beheaded.

From Purcell's *Life of Cardinal Henry Manning,* we read that it was a text from the Psalm that haunted him as an undergraduate at Oxford when his religious opinions were yet not formed, and his ambitions still centered on political life. As Cardinal and Archbishop, the same words bore to him their daily message. "The Psalms and the Lessons," he said in an autobiographical note on the years 1829-31, "were always a delight to me. The verse, 'Why art thou cast down, O my soul,' (Psalm 42:6) always seemed a voice to me. Every day in the daily Mass it comes back to me." How expressive of our feelings when we have felt somewhat low has this same verse been!

For the wanderers during the days of the Covenanters, the beautiful pass called Dalveen, between Nithsdale and Clydesdale, has the famous defile of the Enterkin which, with its sequestered character and ready doors of escape, was a favorite refuge. It was here, in the summer of 1685 that Covenanter Daniel McMichael was surprised by the troopers and told to prepare for death. His calm reply was, "If my life must go for His cause I am willing; God will prepare me." Daniel was shot in the presence of some of his relatives while singing part of this Psalm—

> His loving-kindness yet the Lord
>   Command will in the day;
> His song's with me by night; to God,
>   By whom I live, I'll pray
>   *—Psalm 42:8.*

Daniel's friends carried his body to the romantic churchyard at Durisdeer—"the door of the oak forest"—where he was buried under a rude stone with the epitaph—

> Daniel was cast into the lions' den
> For praying unto God, and not to men;
> Thus lions cruelly devoured me
> For bearing unto truth my testimony;
> I rest in peace till Jesus rend the cloud,
> And judge 'twixt me and those who shed my blood.

When Vladimir Monomarkus became the Great Prince at Kieff in 1113, he was instructed by the Patriarch Nicephorus in his duties as a ruler. Vladimir had to learn by heart Psalm 101, meditate upon it, and by it fashion his government. It was in the spirit of this Psalm that he ruled his subjects. In his dying injunctions to his son, Vladimir concluded by opening the Book of Psalms, and reading with deep stirring of heart Psalm 42:11—

> Why art thou so vexed, O my soul, and why art thou so disquieted within me? Put thy trust in God. I will confess my faults, and He is gracious.

Verses 14, 15, of this Psalm were among the passages quoted by Jeanie Deans, on the eve of her adventurous journey to plead for her sister's life, and which she repeated in her hour of peril when she was at the mercy of the desperate ruffians on Gunnerley Hill. (See under Psalm 37).

Psalm 43

Because of the similarity of structure of this Psalm with the one just considered, some expositors have wrongly suggested that Psalm 43 is but a continuation or supplement, of Psalm 42, and that they should be united to make one Psalm—which has been done in some MSS. We believe, however, that Psalm 43 is complete in itself and one of the small pearls in the setting of the Psalter. We concur with the assertions of Spurgeon that, "the fact is that the style of poetry was pleasant to the writer, and therefore in after life he wrote this supplemental hymn after the same manner. As an appendix it needed no title. David complains of his enemies, and asks the privilege of communion with God as his surest deliverance from them."

The deceitful and unjust man, 43:1. Whether David had in mind Doeg or Ahithophel, both of whom fit such a description, matters little, for such double distilled villains are plentiful, and the only way of dealing with them is to refer them to the righteous Judge of all. What troubled David, however, was the feeling that the God, pleading his cause, and being his strength, had cast him off—*Why dost thou cast me off?*, 43:2. We can hardly imagine the state of a soul professing to have God as its strength, yet treated by Him as a cast-off! Because of His dark providential dealing, it may appear as if God has cast us off, but we must never mistake our fears for actualities. Permitting mysterious trials to overtake us, God can best expound their design to us.

> Blind unbelief is sure to err,
> And scan his work in vain;
> God is his own interpreter,
> And he will make it plain.

Hope in God! 43:5. This phrase can mean *Wait for God!* The season of complaint will end, and that of praise begin. There is need of patience, but there is ground for hope. "Come, my heart, look out of the window, borrow the telescopic glass, forecast a little, and sweeten thy chamber with sprigs of the sweet herb of hope." A motto of the world is, "A bird in hand is worth two in the bush," meaning, give me today, and take tomorrow whoso will. But the motto of the trusting saint is *Shero Meliora*—My hopes are better than my present possessions.

On Easter Sunday, April 24, 387, Augustus after a severe and prolonged spiritual conflict, was baptized by Ambrose, his spiritual father, at Milan, and at this baptism this 43rd Psalm was sung, and doubtless begot in Augustine his life long study of the Psalms. In the 15th century to win the favor of Henry II, the gentlemen of the Court begged him to choose for each a Psalm. Anthony, King of Navarre, was similarly requested and chose for himself Psalm 43—"Give sentence with me, O God."

In the religious history of Scotland no event since the Reformation created so profound an impression as the succession of the Free Church ministers, May 18th 1843, when the Psalms figured prominently in the speeches of succeeders. Prominent among them was Thomas Chalmers who presided as Moderator over the 470 ministers who had resigned their livings to form the Free Church of Scotland, in the Tanfield Hall, Edinburgh. After gathering, a heavy thundercloud darkened the building, but Dr. Chalmers gave out Psalm 43 to be sung—

> O send thy light forth and thy truth;
>   Let them be guides to me,
> And bring me to thy holy hill,
>   Even where thy dwellings be.

During the lusty singing of this Psalm, the cloud passed—the sun poured forth—the somber shade became dazzling light—an omen for those men of conscience who knew not what the future held for them.

Martin Luther, who clung to the Psalter as a tried and trusted friend, had moments when even he felt something akin to despair, and asked with the Psalmist, "Why art thou cast down, O my soul?" 43:5. It was in such hours that he would say to his friend, Melancthon, "Come, Philip, let us sing the 46th Psalm" (See more fully under this Psalm). In the hour of her peril, Jeanie Deans repeated verses 5 and 6 of this Psalm.

Psalm 44

Although the title gives no indication as to who composed this song, rehearsing as it does the mighty works of the Lord, we seek for no other father of anonymous Psalms when David will suffice. "Therefore we are loathe to ascribe this sacred song to any but the great Psalmist, even although we hardly know any period of his life which it could fairly describe." Historically, the Psalm may refer to "some Israelitish patriot fallen on evil times, who sings in mingled faith and sorrow, of his country's ancient glory and her present griefs, her traditions of former favor and her experience of pressing ills." Because of the nature of this song it was well fitted for the voices of the saved by grace, Sons of Korah. As a further *Maschil,* or instruction Psalm, it was to these singers, as well as for us all, full of spiritual teaching, and can best be understood if put into the mouth of the Church when persecution, peculiarly severe, overtakes her.

Ambrose, in his far-off day, observed that in former Psalms we have prophecies of the Passion, Resurrection, and Ascension of Christ, and of the coming of the Holy Spirit, but that in Psalm 44 we are taught that we ourselves must be ready to struggle and suffer, in order that these truths may profit us. Human will must work together with Divine grace.

We have heard with our ears . . . our fathers have told us, 44:1. The word for *hear* implies that they both heard and heeded with utmost attention and affection what they had heard of the heroism of their ancestors. Among the godly Israelites the biography of their nation was preserved by oral tradition, with great diligence and accuracy. What is heard with the ears affects us more sensitively than what we read with the eyes. "Our fathers have *told* us." There are no better schoolmasters than godly fathers. By nature and grace they are the best instructors of their children. Basil's comment on this verse is apt—

> Hear this, ye fathers that neglect to teach your children such things as may work his fear and love in them, and faith to rely upon and seek to him in all times of danger. They made their mouths, as it were, books, wherein the mighty deeds of the Lord might be read to his praise, and to the drawing of their children's hearts unto him.

Command deliverances for Jacob, 44:4. Although Jacob had been dead a long time when this Psalm was composed, yet such an historical reference to the patriarch indicates that his long life crowded with trials and deliverances, as it was, his descendants are here called by his name, as if to typify the similarity of their experience to that of their great forefather. He who would win the blessings of Israel must share the sorrows of Jacob.

Through thee will we push down our enemies, 44:5. The phrase, *through thy name,* represents all the mighty Victor is in Himself. The metaphor about pushing down our enemies is taken from an ox or bull tossing dogs into the air which attack him. "We will toss them into the air with our horns." We may be as weak as babes in ourselves, yet by Divine grace and power, we can set our feet upon the necks of our foes. Bunyan, in his description of Christian's fight with Apollyon, has the couplet—

> The man so bravely played the man
> He made the fiend to fly.

Thou hast put them to shame that hated us, 44:7. God enabled His people to defeat their foes in such a manner as to make them ashamed of themselves that they had been overcome by such puny adversaries as the Israelites were deemed to be. This double action God makes possible of saving His people from their enemies, and then giving them confusion of face, has historical illustrations in Pharaoh being drowned, as Israel passed though the sea—as Amalek being smitten, while the tribe rejoiced—in the heathen being chased from their homes, while the sons of Jacob rested beneath their vines and fig-tree.

Thou sellest thy people for nought, 44:12. Referring to the siege of Jerusalem by Titus, Eusebius wrote that, "Many were sold for a small price; there were many to be sold, but few to buy."

Thou makest us by a byword, 44:14. "Byword" literally means *a similitude.* The misery of Israel was so great that people would figuratively call a miserable man *a Jew,* just as liars were called *Cretans;* wretched slaves, *Sardians.*

All this is come upon us, 44:17. Yet amid all the grief endured, the sufferings, one did not forget God, or deny the covenant. In his narration of the cruelties inflicted upon the *Christians* by Eastern tyrant, Maximinus, Eusebius said—

> He prevailed against all sorts of people, the Christians only excepted who contemned death and despised his tyranny. The men endured burning, beheading, crucifying, ravenous devouring by beasts, drowning in the sea, maiming and broiling of the members, goring and digging out of the eyes, mangling of the whole body; moreover famine and imprisonment; to be short, they suffered every kind of torment for the service of God rather than they should leave the worship of God, and embrace the adoration of idols.

Women also, not inferior to men through the power of the Word of God, put on a manly courage, whereof some suffered the torments with men, some attained unto the like masteries of virtue.

All down the ages, true believers, called upon to suffer much persecution for Christ's sake, resemble the *moon,* which emerges from her eclipse by keeping her motion, and ceases not to shine because the dogs bark at her.

Stretched out our hands to a strange god, 44:20. The stretching out of hands was the symbol of adoration and of entreaty in prayer. Israel bore witness that she had not acted thus toward any of the idols of the heathen. Pitts, in his account of the religious manners of the Mohammedans, recounts that when they set out on a voyage, they hold up their hands begging the marabbot's (Mohammedan saint) blessing, and a prosperous voyage. In like manner, when leaving the *Beat,* or holy house at Mecca, after their devout pilgrimage, "they hold up their hands towards the *Beat,* making earnest petitions."

Killed all the day long . . . as sheep for the slaughter, 44:22. In this and the following verses we clearly hear the martyr's cry. From Piedmont and Smithfield, from St. Bartholomew's massacre and the dragoonades of Claverhouse, this appeal goes up to Heaven, while the souls under the altar continue their solemn cry for vengeance.

Divine inaction in time of peril is likened unto a God Who sleeps. The closing verses of this Psalm are mirrored in John Milton's famous lines on the massacre of Protestants among the mountains of Piedmont. But this Bard of Paradise bids us join our voices in the great martyr cry, and sing—

> Avenge, O Lord, thy slaughtered saints, whose bones
>   Lie scattered on the Alpine mountains cold;
>   Even those who kept thy truth so pure of old,
>   When all our fathers worshipped stocks and stones,
>   Forget not: in thy record book their groans
>   Who were thy sheep.

Our soul is bowed down to the dust, 44:25. Such a metaphor expresses depth of misery and also of sorrow and humiliation, and allusion being to a man overcome in battle, or mortally wounded, and tumbling to the dust, or to a dead man laid in the earth—brought to *the dust of death,* Psalm 22:15. When Herod Agrippa died, the people put on sackcloth and lay upon the dust of the earth weeping.

Arise for our help! 44:26. This short but sweet and comprehensive prayer closes this memorable Psalm. Faithful sufferers who had not forgotten their God plead for mercy, and man will never be able to find a better plea than *for thy mercies sake.*

> Were I a martyr at the stake,
> I'd plead my Savior's name,
> Intreat a pardon for his sake
> And urge no other claim.

This further instruction Psalm for the Sons of Korah is also a Psalm, as John Ker suggests, "wherein the depressed and almost hopeless state of the Church is contrasted with the great history of God's doings for it in the past, closing with a piercing cry for a new interposition." James Melville in his Diary, 1572, includes the item—"Our Primarius (Principal of the University of St. Andrews), Mr. James Wilkie, a guid, peaceable, sweet auld man, caused sing commonly this year the 44th and 79th Psalms, which I learned by heart, for that was the year of the bloody massacres in France and great troubles in this country." John Knox died this same year, with firm faith in God, but with his spirit clouded by the dark signs of the time in Scotland as well as France.

That the Apostle Paul knew this Psalm by heart is proven by the fact that he quoted verse 22 of it in his triumphant hymn of victory—

> For thy sake we are killed all the day long;
> We are accounted as sheep for the slaughter,
> Nay, in all these things we are more than conquerors through him
> who loved us, Romans 8:36, 37.

These same inspiring words were sung by the noble Bohemians who were executed in the midst of a terrible persecution of the Protestants by Ferdinand of Austria, in the Grosser Ring at Prague, June 21, 1621, when 47 were executed on two separate days, and among them were those men of the nation most distinguished for rank, learning, and piety. As the first passed on to their death, those still in prison sang to them, "Yea, for thy sake are we killed all the day long, we are counted as sheep for the slaughter." With undaunted hearts these brave men went to their death dressed in their best apparel as if going to a marriage feast.

Almost the last labor of Ambrose of Milan, in 397, was a Commentary on this 44th Psalm. He wrote, "It is painful to wait so long for the day when mortality shall be swallowed up of Life; but, happily the torch of the Word of God does not quit mine eyes." Ambrose died as he preached, "Up, Lord, why sleepest thou; awake and be not absent forever," 44:23.

Psalm 45

Among all the Messianic Psalms, this Christ-exalting one is *par excellence*. How fragrant it is with His presence and glory! It is short-sightedness to limit the subjects of this magnificent Psalm to any historical reference it may have to the union between Solomon and Pharaoh's daughter, for this is no wedding song of earthly nuptials but one describing the marriage of the Heavenly Bridegroom and His elect spouse, the Church. Not only is the person and work of *The King* set forth in the Psalm, but the truth more precious than gold of the mystical union between Christ and His redeemed people. A fitting title for the Psalm, then, would be—*The Nuptial Song of Christ and the Church*. Through grace we are joined to Him in a union surviving the everlasting hills.

My heart is inditing a good matter, 45:1. *The good matter,* the Psalmist wrote of was not a mere romantic ballad, but an instructive ode to be spiritually understood, a Psalm of holy teaching, *a Song of Loves,* not "a carnal sentimental love song, but a celestial canticle of everlasting love fit for the tongues and ears of angels." The word for *inditing* means "boileth or bubbleth up," and denotes the language of a heart full and ready for utterance. Erasmus said of Origen that he was ever earnest, but most of all when he discoursed of Christ. Then it was reported of Johannes Mollias, a Bononian, that whenever he spoke of Christ, his eyes dropped, for he was fraught with a mighty fervency of God's Holy Spirit; and like John the Baptist, he was first a burning, or boiling, and then a shining light.

As we slowly read this glorious Psalm we can feel the warmth of "the writer's heart, the fulness of his heart, and the consequent richness and glow of his utterance. The writer was not one who frigidly studied the elegancies and proprieties of poetry, his stanzas are the natural outburst of his soul, comparable to the boiling jets of the geysers of Heela." Then, mixing metaphors, he goes on to say, *My tongue is the pen of a ready writer.* Matthew Henry says, "We call the prophets the *penmen* of Scripture, whereas they were but the *pen*." From a work on this Psalm published away back in 1706 we have the comment, *"My tongue* shall be like the pen of one that takes minutes or writes shorthand: for I shall speak briefly, and not in words at length, or so as to be understood in a literal sense, but in figures and emblems." An exposition of the literary implication of this phrase about the tongue being the pen of a ready writer, given by Spurgeon, is the most satisfying we have come across—

> It was not so much for rapidity, for the tongue always has the preference, but for exactness, elaboration, deliberation, and skillfulness of expression. Seldom are the excited utterances of the mouth equal in rich weight and accuracy to the *verba scripta* of a thoughtful, accomplished penman: but here the writer, though filled with enthusiasm, speaks as correctly as a practical writer; his utterances therefore are no ephemeral utterances, but such as fall from men who sit down calmly to write for Eternity.

The *good matter,* goodspell, or gospel, he wrote about concerned *The King,* yet not exclusively of him, as almost one-half is directly addressed to the Queen. But it relates to the King inasmuch as it relates to his family. Christ ever identifies Himself with His people; so that, whatever is done to them, is done to Himself. Their interests are His.

Thou art fairer than the children of men, 45:2. Of Moses we read that he was exceeding fair, and of David, that he was ruddy, and of a beautiful countenance. Josephus reported that all who saw David were amazed at and enamoured of his beauty. But their beauty is not comparable to Christ's, seeing He combined all the beauty and loveliness of both Heaven and earth. The beauty of Heaven is God, the beauty of earth is man, and the beauty of Heaven and earth together is the possession of this God-Man, the King. The Hebrew has it, "Thou art *double fairer.*" In one of his sermons to the congregation at Herrnhut, Count Zinzendorf exclaimed, "I have a passion, and it is He—He only."

> All human beauties, all divine,
> In our Redeemer meet and shine.

Grace is poured into thy life, 45:2. The last words of Jesus when He was with His disciples are words of love, tender and amiable, so much so that it is reported of Peter in Ecclesiastical History that after Christ's Ascension he wept so abundantly that he was always seen wiping his face from tears. Being asked why he wept so, he replied that he could not choose but weep as often as he thought of that most sweet conversation of Jesus Christ before His death.

O most mighty, 45:3. Might became the King's, through the girding on of His sword, which was reckoned a part of the ceremony of royal inauguration. According to ancient custom the sword was hung on a belt put around the shoulders, and reached down to the thigh. The weapon was not literally bound on the thigh, but hung in a girdle at the back of the thigh. If David's reference to the sword was associated with some special occasion of solemn and official character, then same was the custom observed. A traveler abroad observed that when a Persian or an

Ottoman *ascends the throne,* he girds on his sabre. "Mohammed Jaffer, for example, was proclaimed by the Khan, governor *pro tempero,* till the arrival of his brother, and was invested with this dignity by *the girding of a sword upon his thigh,* an honor which he accepted with a reluctance not wholly feigned." Girded thus, the Messiah is qualified as King and worthy of receiving honor and power as Lord of all.

Anointed thee above thy fellows, 45:7. At Oriental feasts it was the custom to pour oil on the heads of distinguished and welcome guests. Here, God is pictured as anointing His beloved Son, as He sits at the heavenly feast, thus honoring and rewarding Him for all His pain and anguish as the Redeemer.

All thy garments smell of myrrh . . . out of the ivory palaces, 45:8. One can almost smell the aroma of these fragrant, gladdening, choice unguents as they read the Psalmist's description of them. Myrrh, aloes, and cassia were celebrated for their peculiar fragrance. Myrrh and cassia were two of the spices composing the holy anointed oil, and were therefore deemed sacred, Exodus 30:23, 24. It was because of this that the Israelites were forbidden to pour it upon man's flesh, or to attempt any imitation of it in their own perfumes. Ivory, in ancient times, was rare and costly, and for palaces of ivory, the richest perfume in the greatest profusion was used. Over a century ago, Bishop Horsley suggested that there should be a slight change in the A.V. translation, so that the idea of abundance would be connected, not with the fragrance arising from the anointing, but with the anointing itself. Thy garments are all myrrh, aloes, and cassia, excelling the palaces of ivory, excelling those which delight in thee.

This literal as well as poetical translation is comparatively free from obscurity, and visibly sets forth, under the most expressive imagery, the super eminent fullness of anointing conferred on our Lord above His fellows. *Thy garments are all myrrh* which means that they were not merely richly perfumed, but that they consisted of the very articles which entered into the composition of the most precious and odoriferous unguents mentioned. The strength of our perfumes evaporates, and their fragrance diminishes, but His garments retain a permanent as well as plentiful fragrance.

> Myrrh, aloes, and cassia, are all thy garments,
> From ivory palace of Minaea they have made thee glad.

Upon thy right hand did stand the queen in gold of Ophir, 45:9. The *right* hand signified the place of love, honor, and power. It is written of Empress Matilda that she was the daughter of a king, the mother of a king, and the wife of a king. David, in his *Song of Loves,* depicts the Church as the daughter of a King—"The king's daughter is all glorious within,"

45:13—and the mother of a King, "Instead of thy fathers shall be thy children, whom thou mayest make princes in all the earth," 45:16—and the wife of a King—"Upon thy right hand did stand the queen," 45:6—the spiritually wedded wife of the King of Glory. What else can we do but mark the solemn pomp of the verses 6-9!

> The King is seen with rapture, he girds himself as a warrior, robes himself as a monarch, mounts his chariot, darts his arrows, and conquers his foes. Then he ascends his throne with his scepter in his hand, fills the palace hall with perfume brought from his secret chamber, his retinue stand around him, and, fairest of all, his bride is at his right hand, with daughters of subject princes as her attendants. Faith is no stranger to this sight, and every time she looks she adores, she loves, she rejoices, she expects.

Forget also thine own people, 45:10. Themistocles desired rather to learn the art of forgetfulness than memory. Philosophy is an art of remembering. Divinity includes in it an art of forgetting. It is said that the first lesson Socrates taught his scholars was—*Remember.* He thought that knowledge was nothing else but a calling to remembrance of those things which the mind knew ere it knew the body. But the first lesson God's scholars have to learn is—*Forget.* "Forget thine own people." If set on reaching Canaan, we must forget the flesh-pots of Egypt.

Remember in all generations . . . the people praise thee forever and ever, 45:17. Our history books make it clear that names renowned in one generation are unknown to the next era. Their bearers have no undying fame and remembrance and praise. But our King has eternal fame, as well as a continuous progeny. His fame, His character, His person, will ever be dear to His people, and they will praise His worth and work forever.

> Let earth's wide circle round,
> In joyful notes resound,
>   May Jesus Christ be praised.
>
> Be this the eternal song
> Through all the ages long;
>   May Jesus Christ be praised.

What a fitting title this Psalm bears—*The Song of Loves!* It is a Psalm eloquent of God's love to us, and of our love for Him. It was this Psalm Columba sang near the fortress of the king of the Northern Picts, by the mouth of the river Ness, Scotland, near to the fortress of King Brude. Druids gathered to prevent the singing of Columba, but with a voice pealing like thunder, heard some 1,000 paces away, which struck the king and the people with amazement and fear, the saint echoed forth Psalm 45.

This Psalm also had a special place in the heart of Edward Irving, who, with his deep, finely modulated bass voice and profound feeling, read it to a crowded audience in the West Church of Edinburgh. Psalm 45 is one of those Psalms of majesty and tenderness which appeals to the spirit of mingled power and pathos both Columba and Irving possessed. The Psalm compasses a prophetic stanza—

> O thou that art the mighty One,
>> Thy sword gird on thy thigh;
> Even with thy glory excellent,
>> And with thy majesty.

> Thy name remembered I will make
>> Through ages all to be.
> The people, therefore, evermore
>> Shall praises give to thee.

Gregory VII, the vehement champion of papal supremacy, was elected Pope in 1073, with ambitions for the Papacy rather than for himself, and the history of his Papacy was full of dramatic experiences. In 1084, he became a prisoner in St. Angelo, but was rescued by Robert Guiscard, and such a downfall broke Gregory's heart. In the Castle of Salerno, under the protection of the Normans, he died on 25th May, 1085. His last words, taken from this 45th Psalm, breathe the tragic fullness of his bitter disappointment—

> I have loved righteousness, and hated iniquity; and therefore I die in exile.

Psalm 46

Here is another noble ode dedicated to the Sons of Korah who were a division of the Levites who took their turn in serving at the temple. "All the works of holy service ought not to be accomplished by one order of talent, each company of believers should in due course enjoy the privilege. None ought to be without a share in the service of God." The Chaldean version refers to *Coreh,* or the English Korah, stating that the name means *hidden* or *swallowed up,* and, originally, is connected with Korah, who was swallowed up by the earth, although these sons escaped such a doom. Thus the whole Psalm is associated with this historical incident, which is suggested by the phrase, "Though the earth be removed," the paraphrase of which reads, "When our fathers were changed from the earth."

Further, the stipulation that the song should be sung *Upon Alamoth,* is peculiar, implying says Andrew Bonar, "a choir of *virgins,* as if this virgin-choir were selected to sing a Psalm that tells of perils and fears and alarms abounding, in order to show that even the feeble virgins may in that day sing without dread, because of *The Mighty One* on their side." These Hebrew virgins, with their soprano voices, danced and sang the praises of David when he slew Goliath, and it was fitting that they should be chosen to make merry when the glorious victories of Jehovah became their theme. Only those with virgin hearts can praise Him with understanding and sincerity.

A very present help in trouble, 46:1. "Present," means that He is at hand whenever need arises. We do not have to call Him to our aid, for He is at our side, ready to succour. This is why we can sing with Martin Luther in his own characteristic version of the Psalm—

> A sure stronghold our God is He,
> A timely shield and weapon;
> Our help He'll be, and set us free
> From every ill can happen.

Therefore, though the earth be removed, 46:2. David had delight in using his *Therefores,* which imply that the unique poetry was no poetic rapture without rhyme or reason, but as logical as a mathematical demonstration. *Therefore* can be broken up and the question asked, What is it *there for?* What the Psalmist went on to say was an answer, for the rea-

181

son of his theme is that *faith* and *fear* cannot exist together. The one impairs the other. Though all visible things and the firmest of created objects suffer "the wreck of matter and the crash of worlds," in God we have an indestructible Refuge amid any convulsion. It was on March 8, 1750, when an earthquake shook London. John Wesley, who was preaching in Hyde Park at the time, made effective use of this second verse. After this experience, his brother Charles composed his great hymn containing this verse—

> How happy then are we,
>   Who build, O Lord, on Thee!
> What can our foundation shock?
> Though the shatter'd earth remove,
> Stands our city on a rock,
> On the rock of heavenly love.

There is a river, 46:4. What a wonderful range of metaphors David used in his Psalms to illustrate Divine truth! In verse one we have a *Refuge,* and here a *River.* Jerusalem has been described as being well supplied with water because of its surrounding mountains, and therefore is an appropriate simile of the Church of God as a well-watered city surrounded with mighty mountains of truth and justice, and garrisoned by Omnipotence. Out of her there flow rivers of water to refresh the ends of the earth.

God is in the midst of her, 46:5. When Popery was powerful, and Philip Melancthon was fearful lest the infant Reformation might be stifled in its birth, Martin Luther would comfort him with these words, "If we perish, Christ must fall too—He is in the midst of us—and if it be so, be it so; I had rather perish with Christ that great Ruler of the world, than prosper with Caesar." Spurgeon says that this Psalm might be called *The Song of Holy Confidence,* but because of the great Reformer's love for this soul-stirring hymn, it could be best remembered as *Luther's Psalm.*

The Lord of Hosts is with us, 46:7. The plural suggests that He is Ruler over *all* hosts—Angelic, Stellar, Natural, Human, and Hellish. The marvel is that this Generalissimo of the forces of the land, and the Lord High Admiral of the seas is our august ally, our shelter in the time of storm. *Selah!* Think of that!

Come, behold the works . . . desolations, 46:8. That God destroys destroyers and desolators is evident in the ruined cities of Assyria, Babylon, Petra, Bashan, and Canaan, and other nations of a later date. Their ruins are our instructors teaching us that in the tables of decayed stone we have the record of the judgment-work of the Lord. In Britain dismantled castles and ruined abbeys stand as memorials of Divine victories over oppression and superstition.

Ye gloomy piles, ye tombs of living men,
Ye sepulchres of womanhood, or worse;
Ye refuge of lies, soon may ye fall,
And mid your ruins may the owls, and bat,
And dragon find congenial resting place.

The victor who succeeds in destroying all the instruments of war is the one well-qualified to make peace. Peace is made in two ways. First, by taking up the differences and reconciling the spirits of men. Secondly, by breaking autocratic power, and taking from the combatants all provisions of war. David depicts the Lord making peace by both these ways, or by either of them. All sorts of weapons are piled heap on heap, and He destroys them all. See Joshua 11:6.

He maketh wars to cease, 46:9. God quiets the tumult of war, and when He crushes great powers, His people experience a profound repose.

He breaketh the bow. Prominent in David's time, and most effective in war, this sender of swift-winged death, God is able to render useless.

He cutteth the spear in sunder. Fighters feared this destructive weapon, yet even this lance of mighty warriors God is able to smash in pieces.

He burneth the chariot in the fire. The proud war-charoits of ancient times had death-dealing scythes, yet even this instrument of wholesale murder was consigned to ignominious destruction. When the Romans, well after David's day, had given their idea of peace to a nation, by slaughtering the greatest part of its miserable inhabitants, they would collect the weapons of the vanquished and reduce them to ashes. A medal, struck by Vespasian, the Roman Emperor, on ending his wars in Italy, and other parts of the world, represented the goddess of peace holding an olive branch in one hand, and with a lighted torch in the other, setting fire to a heap of armor. This custom was alluded to by Virgil—

O that Jupiter would restore to me the years that are past! Such as I was, when under Praeneste itself, I routed the foremost rank of the enemy, and victorious set fire to heaps of armour!

The Lord of Hosts is with us, 46:11. A biographer of John Wesley has given us this description of the great revivalist's last moments—

On Tuesday Mr. Wesley could with difficulty be understood, though he often attempted to speak. At last, with all the strength he had he cried out, "The best of all is, God is with us." Again, raising his hand, and waving it in triumph, he exclaimed with thrilling effect, "The best of all is, God is with us." These words seemed to have expressed the leading feature of his whole life. God had been with him from early childhood; His providence had guided him through all the devious wanderings of human life: and now, when he was entering "the valley of the shadow of death," the same hand sustained him.

Selah! What a great word with which to end a great Psalm! The Psalmist must have loved it, seeing he used it some 70 times throughout the Psalter. In this Psalm, this solemn, stately, peaceful note of rest fitly stands at the end of verses 3, 7, and 11, dividing the Psalm, thereby, by inspired authority into the parts we have suggested. For the singers of the Psalm, *Selah* meant a pause for them to take breath, but for ourselves, it implies an occasion for meditation.

> *Selah* bids the music rest,
> Pause in silence soft and blest;
> *Selah* bids uplift the strain,
> Harps and voices tune again;
> *Selah* ends the vocal praise,
> Still your hearts to God upraise.

Conspicuous in the history and biography of God's people down the ages is this grand Psalm made up as it is with the Power of God the Father, The Presence of God the Spirit, and The Peace of God the Son. Then the threefold *Selah* dividing the Psalm—an exclamation meaning, *Think of that!*—calls upon us to meditate upon the Three Persons of the Blessed Trinity and upon the respective characteristics of each Person. References to the influence of the Psalm in the lives of saints are most numerous. Without doubt, the Psalm was popularized by Martin Luther in his paraphrase of it in *Eine feste Burg,* translated for us in the well-known words—"A fortress strong is God our Lord"—and which became known as the *Marseillaise of The Reformation.* During the dark days of the Reformation, when Luther felt somewhat downcast he would say to his friend Melancthon, "Come, Philip, let us sing the forty-sixth Psalm." When the Protestant cause seemed to be losing ground, Luther could be heard singing it "to the lute every day, standing at the window and looking up to Heaven."

When Luther and Melancthon and other Reformers were sent into banishment, and were entering Weimar in a great despondency, they heard a girl singing this triumphant Psalm. "Sing on, dear daughter mine," said Melancthon, "thou knowest not what comfort thou bringest to our hearts." Luther's notable hymn founded upon Psalm 46 "breathes the force of battles, faces fearlessly the fire and the scaffold, and thrills in every line with unconquerable faith and Christian heroism." This was why before the battle of Leipzig, Sept. 17, 1631, Gustavus Adolphus asked his whole army to sing it, and after the victory he thanked God that the word was made good. "The field He will maintain it."

Another tribute to the influence of this battle-Psalm is traced in the reign of Emperor Joseph II, who, before the Edict of Toleration in 1781, joined in the singing of this Psalm. The Protestants were torn from their families and banished to Transylvania, and in their bitter grief they sang with tears—

> Take, if you will, our life,
> Goods, honor, children, wife,
> Yet is their profit small,
>   The city of God remaineth.

In 1380, the Tartar hordes advanced upon Moscow, and the people beggared by Mongol domination were urged to look upon the conflict facing them as a *Holy War*. Blessed by Sergius, the hermit of Holy Trinity, Demetrius advanced to meet Mamai and the Mongol invaders on the banks of the Don, Sept. 8th, 1380. Although the heart of Demetrius quailed at the numbers of the enemy, a Psalm renewed his courage and nerves. After reading aloud Psalm 46, he plunged into the fight, which ended in the total defeat of the Tartars at Koulikoff. Literature, pictures and sculptures in the Donskoi and Simonoff monasteries are reminders of the national gratitude associated with the name of Sergius and of Demetrius of the Don.

The people of Moscow, long before the atheistic philosophy of Communism covered Russia, used this same 46th Psalm as their memorial song of triumph for that night on which 20,000 of Napoleon's horses perished by frost, and the French Army was driven back by an unseen hand into its disastrous defeat.

During a shock of earthquake that threw London into panic and terror, John Wesley preached on this Psalm with great effect. In fact when this founder of Methodism came to die his triumphant death, he was heard to repeat verse eleven of the Psalm—The Lord of hosts is with us, the God of Jacob is our refuge. Then he repeated several times, "The best of all is, God is with us."

When the Huguenots and the Covenanters of Scotland were in trouble—as they often were because of their Christian witness—they were wont to say, "Come and let us sing Psalm 46—

> God is our refuge and our strength,
>   In straits a present aid;
> Therefore, although the earth remove,
>   We will not be afraid.

When, on the 17th of September, 1656, Oliver Cromwell rode in state from Whitehall to the Abbey Church of Westminster to open the second Parliament of the Protectorate, there went before his coach "hundreds of gentlemen and officers, bareheaded—the Life Guards—and his pages and lacqueys richly clothed." He returned to Whitehall with the same pomp, and once within the Painted Chamber, Cromwell delivered a speech to the newly assembled members which in part was an exposition of Psalm 46 and Psalm 85. Part of the Lord Protector's speech as he exhorted Parliament to set their hearts to the work facing them, reads—

> If you set your hearts to it, then you will sing Luther's Psalm (46). That is a rare Palm for a Christian! and if he set his heart open, and can approve it to God, we *shall* hear him say, "God is our refuge and strength, a very present help in trouble" . . . If Pope and Spaniard, and devil, and all, set themselves against us—yet in the name of the Lord we should destroy them. The Lord of Hosts is with us; the God of Jacob is our refuge.

In 1860, when the German armies marched on the French Capital, Martin Luther's version of Psalm 46 was their battle march. For Great Britain, India was the romance of her 19th century history. But a heavy toll in the massacre of British soldiers was part of the price Britain had to pay for her control of the continent. No disaster of such magnitude had ever befallen the British Army in the East as on January 13th, 1842, at the walls of Jellabad. Peril faced the whole garrison, and the Sunday before the assault of the Cabal force, all within the threatened walls gathered for Divine Service. As there was no Chaplain, the service was conducted by a gray-haired captain, of slight, well-knit figure, whose clear strong voice made every word of Psalm 46 clear. Giving out the Psalm, the captain said, "Luther was wont to use this Psalm in seasons of peculiar difficulty and depression," and the words of the Psalm were well suited to the desperate circumstances of the garrison, and expressed their eagerness and determination to defend the battlements to the last extremity—which they did. There is no better basis of confidence than this noblest of all classic utterances—

> Should the strong firmament in ruins break,
> Fearless the just man stands amid the wreck.

We have also discovered some heart-moving incidents related to particular verses of this much loved 46th Psalm. For instance, in 1132, the Archbishop of Canterbury, as Legate of the Apostolic See, was urged to further the desire of some of the Cistercians who sought to follow the fullest meaning of the vows of their profession. Said the Archbishop, "God is our hope and strength, a very present help in trouble," 46:1, as he arranged for the way of escape from the world.

The sermon is still in existence that the Rev. George Walker preached on the 28th of July, 1689, to the remaining sick and wounded of the garrison's fighting force at Londonderry. In his exhortation to the crowd of starving men and women, the Governor said, "Let but God arise and His enemies shall be scattered . . . God is our refuge and strength, a very present help in trouble. Therefore will we not fear though the earth be moved, and though the mountains be carried into the midst of the sea; though the waters thereof roar and be troubled," Psalm 46:1-3. Walker went on quoting from this Psalm and other Psalms, and their language cast a strange spell over the distressed garrison. God did help, and that right early, for Sunday, July 28th, 1689, was a thanksgiving day for the besieged of Derry from famine and slavery.

The conviction of everlasting endurance amid decay, that God's City, in the midst of an ephemeral world, stands forever, is found in the inscription within the Cathedral of Saint Sophia at Kieff, the oldest church in Russia, built by Yaroslaf in 1037. On the mosaics behind the altar is a colossal figure of the Virgin, bearing the verse, "God is in the midst of her, therefore shall she not be removed," Psalm 46:5. Needless to say, this is a gross misinterpretation of such a passage, for by *her*, "the tabernacles of the most High," is meant.

In the middle ages, mediaeval cosmogonists wrongly argued that the earth was not in motion, suspended in mid-air; rather was it firmly fixed, and its center was Jerusalem in which the column in the Holy City, at midday, casts no shadow, and "God is in the midst of her, therefore she shall not be removed," 46:5. Here is another misapplication of Scripture.

Vincentius of Herins, in the 15th century, and other monks like him, went out with a Psalm to choose sites for monasteries, exorcise the demons of mountains, lake or wood. Vincentius, himself, loved to quote—

Be still, and know that I am God, I will be exalted among the heathen, I will be exalted in the earth, 46:10.

This was the same verse the renowned Covenanter, Richard Cameron preached on near Drumclog, Scotland, July 17, 1680, three days before his martyrdom. Eight years later another Covenanter, James Renwick, was executed in Edinburgh, and on him was found notes of his two last sermons, one of which was on Psalm 46:10. "Be still then, and know that I am God," etc. As already indicated when John Wesley came to die he repeated verse 11 of this Psalm. "The Lord of hosts is with us, the God of Jacob is our refuge."

Psalm 47

This short Psalm of only 9 verses is another bearing the title *For the Sons of Korah,* which does not imply that they wrote, but simply that they sang them, and, as we have already indicated, they were fit singers of the Psalms carrying their name, because past history reminded them of sin, whose existence was a proof of sovereign Grace and power, and whose name has a close connection with the name of Calvary. As to the authorship of the Psalm, who else could have written such a jubilant, triumphant ode but David, the sweet Psalmist of Israel? "Our ear has grown accustomed to the ring of David's compositions, and we are morally certain that we hear it in this Psalm."

Scholars differ as to the historical setting of the Psalm. Some feel that its immediate subject is the carrying up of the Ark from the house of Obed-Edom to Mount Zion. Others, however, say that it might have been composed to celebrate a memorable victory. What is clear is that both the present sovereignty of Jehovah, and His ultimate triumph and dominion are fully hymned. It also has a prophetic aspect, in that it looks down the vista of the ages and describes Christ's Ascension, and His Second Advent. We are bidden gaze upon the Mighty One seated peacefully on His Throne, as Psalm 45 likewise depicts.

The Voice of Triumph, 47:1. Clapping and shouting may be demonstrative ways of magnifying the Lord, but He does not censure them. These most natural and most enthusiastic tokens of exultation come from *all* nations. Israel may lead the van, but all the Gentiles are to follow in the march of triumph, for in Christ there is neither Jew nor Gentile. Many are human languages, yet the nations triumph as with one voice. "The prospect of the universal reign of the Prince of Peace is enough to make the tongue of the dumb sing."

He is the King over all the earth, 47:2. Omnipotence, terrible to crush, yet almighty to protect is emphasized in this revelation of the self-existent One, Jehovah. David knew that as he reigned over Judea, that one day His reign would have no boundary. God is no local deity, no petty ruler of a tribe, "The Lord God omnipotent reigneth," and His absolute dominion will be visible when He appears as the sole Monarch of the earth, King of kings, and Lord of lords. Not a hamlet or an islet well be excluded from His universal domain. No wonder we have in the middle of this panorama of the greatest of all monarchies, a pause on the part of the songsters to meditate upon a reign so blessed and gracious—*Selah!*

> Muse awhile, obedient thought,
> Lo, the theme's with rapture fraught;
> See thy King, Whose realm extends
> E'en to earth's remotest ends!
> Gladly shall the nations own
> Him their Lord and God alone;
> Clap their hands with holy mirth,
> Hail him *Monarch of the earth.*
> Come, my soul, before him bow,
> Gladdest of his subjects thou;
> Leave thy portion to his choice,
> In his sovereign will rejoice,
> His thy purest, deepest bliss,
> He is thine and thou art his.

Sing ye praises with understanding, 47:7. Augustine says that this instructive way of singing, when *sense* and *sound* go together, and *hearts* and *heads* blend with *voices,* is an evidence of God's reality. "If they had sung *with understanding,* they had not adored stones. When a man sensible, sang to a stone insensible, did he sing *with understanding?*"

The shields of the earth belong unto God, 47:9. Shields used to represent the insignia of pomp, the emblems of rank, and the weapons of war. Bishop Reynolds, commenting upon this last verse of the Psalm says—

> A shield is a *merciful* weapon, none more so,
> A shield is a *venturous* weapon, a kind of surety, which bears the blows and receives the injuries which were intended for another.
> A shield is a *strong* weapon, to repel the darts of wickedness and break them in pieces.
> A shield is an *honorable* weapon, none more: taking away the shields was a sign of victory, preserving them a sign of victory.
> Remember, a shield must ever *have an eye to guide it* from the shields, the law the eye.

From the narrative it would seem as if the shields are personified; that the rulers of the earth, not only belong to God, but are His shields, having a duty to protect others. Thus dignity and duty were combined. An ancient writer observed that, "magistrates are said to *bear the sword,* not to be swords; and they are said *to be shields,* not be bear shields; and all this to show that protection and preservation are more essential and intrinsical to their office than destruction and punishment are."

Psalm 48

John Ruskin included this Psalm, with others, seeing it contained the law and the prophecy of all just government. Among the passages from the Psalms, Shakespeare quotes "Our guide unto death," 48:13. C. H. Spurgeon, whose fragile health in his later years necessitated brief seasons of treatment in the city of Lucerne, has a telling illustration of the 12th verse of this Psalm in his Commentary on the Psalms—*Walk About Zion.* "The city of Lucerne, encircled by its ancient walls, adorned with a succession of towers, is a visible illustration of this figure; and as we have gone around it, and paused at each picturesque tower, we have realized the loving, lingering inspection which the metaphor implies."

On verses 5 and 6, Spurgeon quotes the comment of George Horne, "The potentates of the world saw the miracles of the Apostles, the courage and constancy of the Martyrs, and the daily increase of the Church, notwithstanding all their persecutions; they beheld with astonishment the rapid progress of the faith through the Roman Empire; they called upon their gods, but their gods could not help themselves, idolatry expired at the foot of the victorious Cross."

The distinguished Biblical scholar, Lightfoot, affirms that "the constant and ordinary Psalm for the second day of the week was the forty-eighth." It is a Psalm all who believe in "the sweet Omnipotence of Love" should read every day of the week. What a God-honoring Psalm it is, even though its author and date are unknown! Named as *A Song and Psalm,* it is indeed a Song for joyfulness and a Psalm for reverence. Alas! every song is not a Psalm, for poets are not all heaven-born, and every Psalm is not a song, for in coming before God we have to utter mournful confessions, as well as exulting praises.

It would be dogmatic to associate this Psalm, the Sons of Korah were happy to sing, to any particular, historical event in Jewish history. Spurgeon says that "it records the withdrawal of certain confederate kings from Jerusalem, their courage failing them before striking a blow. The mention of the ships of Tarshish may allow us to conjecture that the Psalm was written in connection with the overthrow of Ammon, Moab and Edom in the days of Jehoshaphat; and if the reader will turn to 2 Chronicles 20, and note especially verses 19, 25, and 36, he will probably accept the suggestion." But the Psalm has a prophetic and an historic connection, for the great and glorious God revealed is to be our Guide unto death.

In the city of our God, 48:1. The city in question was Jerusalem, where He was great, and greatly to be praised. In His wisdom, God chose this city as His peculiar abode as the God of Israel. It was the seat of theocratic government, and the center of prescribed worship. But the Church is also likened unto a "holy city of God," and as such she is the medium of Divine manifestation.

Beautiful for situation, 48:2. Naturally, this was true of Jerusalem, and thus styled "The Queen of the East," and became the world's star, for whatever light lingered on earth was borrowed from the oracles preserved by Israel. Thomson in his *Hand and the Book* justifies this high eulogium of David, concerning Jerusalem. "The situation is indeed eminently adapted to be the platform of a magnificent citadel. Rising high above the deep valley of Gihon and Hinnom, on the west and south, and the scarcely less deep one of the Cheesemongers on the east, it could only be assailed from the side of the north. It was magificently beautiful and fortified by walls, towers, and bulwarks, the wonder and terror of the nations." The heavenly Zion, the New Jerusalem, will have a beauty and joy out-matching those of the temporal Zion.

Other translations read, *Beautiful in climate,* being situated as a fair and lovely climate. *Beautiful in extension,* meaning in the prospect which it extends to the eye. John Milton in *Paradise Regained,* has the lines—

> Fair Jerusalem,
> The Holy city, lifted high her towers,
> And higher yet the glorious temple rear'd.
> Her pile, far off appearing like a mount
> Of alabaster, topt with golden spires.

Pain, as of a woman in travail, 48:6. This strong expression of a mother in her pangs of childbirth was commonly employed by Orientals to set forth the extremity of anguish. When the Lord arises for the defense of His Church, her foes are to be full of pain as a trembling woman. Of verses 5 and 6, George Horne says that "the potentates of the world saw the miracles of the Apostles, the courage and constancy of the Martyrs, and the daily increase of the Church. Notwithstanding all their persecutions, they beheld with astonishment the rapid progress of the faith through the Roman Empire; they called upon their gods, but their gods could not help themselves; idolatry expired at the foot of the victorious Cross."

Walk about Zion . . . tell her towers . . . mark her bulwarks, 48:12, 13. Subject to constant ill-health, Spurgeon often went to Lucerne for rest and medical treatment, and under these verses in the Psalm, says that the city he dearly loved, was "encircled by its ancient walls, adorned with a suc-

192 Psalms: *A Devotional Commentary*

cession of towers, is a visible illustration of the figures used by David. As we have gone around it, and paused at each picturesque tower we realized the loving lingering inspection which the metaphors imply." In a spiritual sense, the *towers* and *bulwarks* of Zion are those Christian doctrines which are the strength and glory of the Church, which are to be maintained in their soundness and stability against the assaults of those heretical teachers, seeking to destroy them.

He will be our guide even unto death, 48:14. Emphasis in this last verse of the Psalm is on the words, "For *this* God is *our* God." The God of Israel's past history is to be their everlasting God, resulting in an eternity of bliss. The infallible Guide throughout life, He is present as His own pass through the valley of the shadow of death. "Thou art with me." *Unto death* is explained as meaning *over death,* or beyond it. "Our guide leading us over death." He Who swallowed up death in victory is with us in the last hour enabling us to trample on death, and follow Him into Glory, where there is no death.

Psalm 49

When Gregory Nazianzen began his *Apologia* against the Emperor Julian, it was with a quotation from this further Psalm for the Sons of Korah. The great evangelical verse of the Psalm—"None of them can by any means redeem his brother, nor give to God a ransom for him," 49:7, was the one Matthew Arnold quoted to express his melancholy sense of dumbness of Christ's death-place, the silence of the sacred land, and isolation of man and his inability to rise out of philosophic calm into the exaltation of unquestioning faith. Here are his lines—

> From David's lips this word did roll,
> 'Tis true and living yet;
> *No man can save his brother's soul,*
> *Nor pay his brother's debt.*
>
> Alone, self-poised, henceforward man
> Must labor, must resign
> His all too human creeds, and scan
> Simply the way divine.

How expressive is Spurgeon's comment on this 7th verse! "A king's ransom would be of no avail, a Monte Rosa of rubies, an America of silver, a world of gold, a sun of diamonds, could all be utterly contemned. O ye boasters, think not to terrify us with your worthless wealth, go ye and intimidate death before ye threaten men in whom is immortality and life."

Describing fools, the Psalmist says, "Their inward thought is that their houses shall continue forever," Psalm 49:11. The failure of the worldling to realize the fleeting nature of all earthly possessions is well illustrated in the life of William Beckford, and the unending character of gorgeous fabrics in the ruin of his famous Babel, Fonthill Abbey.

The term *Selah,* meaning, "think of that!" appears after a verse in which there is some striking truth we should pay particular attention to. Is it not something to think about that, "this their way is folly; yet their posterity approve their saying." Selah, 49:13? Dr. Leifchild in his work on *Remarkable Facts* records the following incident illustrative of this verse. A man of property who had been accustomed regularly to attend Leifchild's church, but had always manifested a covetous disposition. "I was sent for to offer to him consolation of religion as he lay upon his dying bed," says this Pastor. "What was my surprise, after having conversed and prayed with him, to find that he was unwilling to take my hand, muttering that he knew that he had not done what was right in reference to the support and furtherance of religion, but intended to amend in that respect. How could I reply, but by exhorting him to repent, and relinquishing all further thoughts of a worldly nature, to betake himself to the sacrifice and mediation of the Son of God for pardon, safety, and salvation in that world which he was to all appearances about to enter.

"He gazed at me with a look of disappointment. Upon a hint being given me to inquire into his thoughts at that moment, I questioned him very pointedly, and to my astonishment and horror, he reluctantly disclosed to me the fact that, while thus seemingly about to breathe his last his hands were under the bedclothes grasping the keys of his cabinet and treasures, lest they should be taken from him! Soon after, he died, and there was, alas! reason to fear that together with his property, he had transmitted somewhat of his fatal passion to those who survived him. It was distressing to me to reflect that a hearer of mine should quit this world with his fingers stiffened in death around the keys of his treasures. How strong, how terrible, was the ruling passion in the death of this man!"

In his helpful work on the Psalms, J.M. Neale says of this whole Psalm, "Strange it is that two Psalms so near together, as this and Psalm 45 should, and should alone imitate, or be the forerunner of, two works of Solomon, David's son: Psalm 49—*Ecclesiastes*—Psalm 45—*The Song of Solomon*. All that we can learn from the title is that the Psalm was given to the chief musician to arrange suitable music for it, and then left for the Sons of Korah to sing. Mention of the harp in verse 4, identifies the Psalm as another of David's wonderful odes. Here, the renowned poet-musician sings, to the accompaniment of his much-loved harp, the burden of his song being the despicable character of those who trust in their wealth, and the Divine consolation oppressed believers can expect.

Give ear, all ye inhabitants of the world, 49:1. This parable and dark saying, David put into song, concerned all men, whether low or high, poor or rich. No matter where men dwell, or in what age they live, all are equally embraced in the universality indicated by this verse. The laws of Providence are the same in all lands; therefore, that which concerns all men throughout history concerns *me*.

I will open my dark saying upon the harp, 49:4. When David said, "I will incline mine ear to a parable," he meant that he would diligently attend not to sing anything ungracefully. The metaphor is taken from musicians who bring their ear close to the harp, or any other stringed instrument in order to ascertain the harmony of the sound. Unafraid of the most profound topics, David knew how to open the treasures of darkness, and to win attention and cast his proverbial philosophy into the form of a song, and tuned his harp to the solemn tone of the theme. He left the chorus for the Sons of Korah to sing in the temple.

> Wherefore should I fear in the days of evil, when the iniquity of my heels shall compass me about? They that trust in their wealth, and boast themselves in the multitudes of their riches: None of them can by any means redeem his brother, nor give to God a ransom for him; (For the redemption of their soul is precious, and it ceaseth forever;) That he should still live forever, and not see corruption, 49:5-9.

The uselessness of wealth to redeem a soul from a sin was embodied in a hymn Dr. B. Hall Kennedy, of Cambridge, composed in 1860—

> Why should I fear the evil hour,
>   When ruthless foes in ambush lie,
> Who revel in their pride of power,
>   And on their hoarded wealth rely?
>
> A brother's ransom who can pay,
>   Or alter God's eternal doom?
> What hand can wrest from death his prey,
>   Its banquet from the rotten tomb?

They that trust in their wealth, 49:6. This Psalm has been well-named as *The Covetous Man's Soliloquy.* The folly of many rich men is that in any extremity overtaking them, money is their only trust. Rich men may be able to do great things, but one thing they cannot do is to redeem another. His silver and gold cannot obtain a ransom for a sinner. Some animals devoted to God could be redeemed at a price, but all the wealth of the world could not be paid for a ransom. Only the precious blood of God's Son could procure same.

Likewise the fools . . . perish . . . and leave their wealth to others, 49:10. Fools, as well as brutes, perish. Folly has no immunity from death, jollity cannot laugh off the dying hour. Death, visiting the university, does not spare the tavern where brutal men are found. Thoughtlessness and brutality meet their end, as surely as does the student's cap, none being able to take a mite with them as they pass from time into eternity. What assets they have, often left for others to fight over, they cannot carry over the great divide.

He is like the beasts that perish, 49:12. The boastful fools the Psalmist describes add to their folly by supposing that their houses and honor continue forever. Although they dwell in marble halls they never dream that a notice to quit will be served upon them, and that any eminence they may have bought or won will vanish from them, and they at last go down—

> To the vile dust from whence they sprang,
> Unwept, unhonor'd and unsung.

Death doth feed on them, 49:14. In some ancient stories are descriptions of grim giants who fed on men they enticed to their caves. Here, death the monster feeds on the flesh and blood of the rich and mighty, who only ruled till night fell, and then, because they were ungodly, had no prospect of a joyous life beyond the grave. As Keble expressed it—

> Even as a flock arrayed are they
> For the dark grave; Death guides their way,
> Death is their Shepherd now.

The fleeting nature of all earthly pleasures, and of their utter inability to redeem or save the soul is well illustrated for us in the life of William Beckford, and the unenduring character of gorgeous fabrics in the ruins of his famous Babel, Fonthill Abbey. Lord Byron sang of Beckford's palace in Spain, in language most applicable to Fonthill, England.

> There, too, thou Vathek! England's wealthiest son—
> Once formed thy Paradise, as not aware
> When wanton wealth her mightiest deeds have done,
> Meek Peace voluptuous lures was ever wont to shun.
> Here didst thou dwell; her schemes of pleasure plan,
> Beneath yon mountain's ever beauteous brow.
> But now, as if a thing unblest by man,
> Thy fairy dwelling is as lone as thou!
> Here giant weeds a passage scarce allow,
> To halls deserted, portals gaping wide;
> Fresh lessons to the thinking bosom, how
> Vain are the pleasurances on earth supplied,
> Swept into wrecks anon by Time's ungentle tide!

When he dieth, he shall carry nothing away, 49:17. St. Augustine well said that "the form of money agrees well with the condition of it; it is stamped round, because it is so apt to run away. Could we be rich so long as we live, yet that was uncertain enough, for life itself is but a dream, a shadow, but a dream of a shadow." If thieves do not rob a man while he live, Death waits to strip him bare. It is with us in this world, as it was in Jewish fields and vineyards of old: *pluck and eat* they might what they would while they were there; but they could not pocket any to carry away with them.

> You will carry none of your riches, fool, to the waters of Acheron,
> You will be ferried over quite naked in the infernal boat.

Men will praise thee, when thou doest well to thyself, 49:18. We live in an age when men worship success, no matter how it is gained. As Spurgeon put it—"The color of the winning horse is no matter; it is the winner, and that is enough. *Take care of Number One,* is the World's proverbial philosophy, and he who gives heed to it is a *clever fellow, a fine man of business, a shrewd common-sense tradesman, a man with his head put on the right way.* Get money, and you will be *respectable, a substantial man,* and your house will be *an eminent firm in the city,* or *one of our best country families.* To do good wins fame in Heaven, but to do good *to yourself* is the prudent thing among men of the world.

"Yet not a whisper of worldly congratulation can follow the departing millionaire; they say he died worth a mint of money, but what charm has that fact to the cold ear of death! The banker rots as fast as the shoeblack, and the peer becomes as putrid as the pauper. Alas! poor wealth, thou art but the rainbow coloring of the bubble, the tint which follows the morning mist, but adds no substance to it."

Psalm 50

This is the first of the Psalms of Asaph, but whether this eminent musician wrote it, or that it was dedicated to him by another scribe is hard to determine. But it matters little as to whether Asaph wrote and sang it, or used another's poem, for poet and musician are near akin, and if one composes words and another sets them to music, they rejoice together before the Lord.

There used to be mystery shrouding the authorship of that wonderful hymn *Dies Irae*—"Day of Judgment," "Day of Burning," but now it is generally ascribed to Thomas of Celano who lived in the 13th century. The first verse of this hymn represents the heathen prophetess as joining David in looking forward to the consummation of all things in the fire of the final day. It is felt by many that the hymn is related to the sublime words—

> Our God shall come, and shall not keep silence: a fire shall devour before him, and it shall be very tempestuous round about him. He shall call to the heavens above, and to the earth that he may judge his people, 56:3-4.

The opening five verses of this Psalm form Isaac Watts' majestic poem—

> No more shall atheists mock his long delay;
> His vengeance sleep no more; behold the day!
> Behold!—the Judge descends; his guards are nigh,
> Tempests and fire attend him down the sky.
> When God appears, all nature shall adore him.
> While sinners tremble, saints rejoice before him.
> Heaven, earth and hell, draw near; let all things come,
> To hear my justice, and the sinner's doom;
> But gather first my saints (the Judge commands),
> Bring them, ye angels, from their distant lands.
> When Christ returns, make every cheerful passion,
> And shout, ye saints; he comes for your salvation.

William Gurnall, a prominent commentator of two centuries ago, writing on the phrase, "Made a covenant with me," 50:5, remarked that "formerly soldiers used to take an oath not to flinch from their colors, but faithfully to cleave to their leaders; this they called *Sacramentum mil-*

itare—a military oath; such an oath lies upon every Christian. It is so essential to the being of a saint, that they are described by this, *Gather my saints together unto me, those that have made a covenant with me.* We are not Christians till we have subscribed this covenant, and that without reservation. We take upon us the profession of Christ's name, we enlist ourselves in his muster-roll, and by it do promise that we will live and die with him in opposition to all his enemies. . . . He will not entertain us till we resign ourselves freely to his disposal that there may be no disputing with his commands afterwards, but, as one under his authority, go and come at his word."

Prothero contends that "no figure in the early history of the Church is more attractive than that of Origen, 185-253. The son of a martyr, the master of disciples who braved martyrdom, himself a confessor who endured imprisonment and the torture of the chain, the collar and the rack, he dominated the century as much by his character as by his genius." From infancy Origen sang and loved the Psalms, and wrote an impressive commentary on them. Persecuted by the State as a Christian, he was also condemned as a heretic by many in the Church. Driven from Alexandria, he ultimately came to Jerusalem, and under pressure was forced to sacrifice unto Caesar. Remorse overwhelmed him when he was entreated to preach, seeing he had burned incense upon the altar. Taking the Psalter in his hands, however, Origen prayed, and, opening the book, read the words—"But unto the ungodly said God: Why dost thou preach My laws, and takest My covenant in thy mouth?" 50:16. He closed the book, sat down speechless, and burst into tears. "The prophet David himself shut the door on my lips," was his bitter lament, as he applied to his apostasy another verse, "The wild boar out of the wood doth root it up, and the wild beasts of the field devour it," 80:13.

Daniel Burgess, 1645-1713, in his volume *The Golden Snuffers,* writing on the verse "Unto the wicked God saith, what hast thou to do to declare my statutes?" etc. 50:16, asked, "Are unclean beasts fit to be made lord-almoners, and sent to bestow the king's favors? Are swine fit to cast pearls, and the very richest pearl of God's royal word?" Burgess then goes on to speak of the Duke of Alva who was said to complain that "his king sent him in fetters to fight for him; because that without his pardon given him, and while he was a prisoner, he employed him in war." Then Burgess makes the pointed application—"But the supreme King is a more merciful one, and orders our charity to begin at home; making it our first duty to break off our sins: and then when we have put off these our shackles, go to fight his battles."

I will reprove thee, and set them in order before thine eyes, 50:21. When God opens His register, forgetful spirits see the record of their forgotten sins. When a printer presses clean paper upon his oiled irons, it receives the print of every letter: so when God stamps the minds of the godless with His register, they see all their former sins at once. The mysterious hand was ever writing against Belshazzar, as he was ever sinning, though he saw it not till the cup was filled: so is it to the wicked; their sins are numbered, and themselves weighed, and see not till they be divided by a fearful awakening.

Lest I tear you in pieces, 50:22. This dread warning is a metaphorical expression taken from the strength and fury of a lion, from which the interference of the shepherd can apply no protection, or defense, for his flock. May we be found among the number offering praise, glorifying to God, and ordering our conversation, or manner of life, as under the eye of God. True believers are like Solomon's temple—gold within and without.

Psalm 51

Martin Luther said of this penitential Psalm that no other is more often sung or prayed in the Church. And no wonder, seeing it has been fitly called *The Sinner's Guide,* showing all who have sinned and come short of the glory of God, the way back to His side. The early father, Athanasius, recommended to Christians to repeat this Psalm when awake at night. Thomas Chalmers said of it that "this is the most deeply affecting of all the Psalms, and I am sure the one most applicable to me. It seems to have been the effusion of a soul smarting under the sense of a recent and great transgression. My God, whether recent or not, give me to feel the enormity of manifold offenses, and remember not against me the sins of my youth. What a mine of rich matter and expression for prayer!"

The title of this matchless Psalm, David-like all over, provides us with its historical connection, namely the occasion when he received the stern rebuke of Nathan the prophet after his grievous sin concerning Bathsheba and her husband. As the result of the Divine message, David's conscience was aroused and he realized the enormity of his guilt, and wrote this Psalm drenched with penitential tears. Spurgeon's description of the history of the Psalm is worthy of repetition—

> David has forgotten his psalmody while he was indulging the flesh, but he returned to his harp when his spiritual nature was awakened, and he poured out his song to the accompaniment of sighs and tears. The great sin of David is not to be excused, but it is well to remember that his case has an exceptional collection of specialities in it. He was a man of very strong passions, a soldier and an Oriental monarch having despotic power, no other king of his time would have felt any compunction for acting as he did, and hence there were not around him those restraints of custom and association which, when broken through, render the offense more monstrous. He never hints at any form of extenuation, nor do we mention these facts in order to apologize for his sin, which was detestable to the last degree; but for the warning of others, that they reflect that the licentiousness in themselves at this day might have been a graver guilt in the then erring King of Israel. When we remember his sin, let us dwell most upon his penitence, and upon the long series of chastisements which rendered the after part of his life such a wonderful history.

Chalmers is right in assuming that this whole Psalm was the effusion of a soul smarting under a deep sense of sin, for the tragic title of the

Psalm reveals the reason for David's outpouring of soul. All of its verses are drenched with repentant tears for his double sin of adultery and planned murder. Without bitter tears of conviction, confession and repentance this unique Psalm was not written, and without similar tears on our behalf it cannot be understood. Victorinus Strigelius, 1524-1569, said of the 51st Psalm, "It is the brightest gem in the whole book, and contains instruction so large, and doctrine so precious, that the tongue of angels could not do justice to the full development of it." David-like all over, the Psalm is suitable for the loneliness of individual penitence, and each of us have daily need of its confessions and plea for pardoning grace. Saints in succeeding ages have added their tears of repentance to those of David's while reading his matchless Psalm.

Savonarola, the great Dominican preacher of the 14th century, repeatedly tortured for the truth's sake, had his left arm broken and his shoulder bone crunched out of its socket. His torturers left his left arm whole in order that he might sign a confession of heresy on his part, but he used it to write a meditation on Psalm 51—which Martin Luther published in 1523—and which was the Psalm that gave strength and courage as he met his death, in silence and dignity, in the open space before the Palazzo Vecchio. It was from the verse, "Then shall I teach Thy ways unto the wicked; and sinners shall be converted unto Thee," 51:13, that the motto is taken for Michaelangelo's picture of Savonarola.

Sir Thomas More, who refused to acknowledge the validity of the marriage between Henry VIII and Catherine, was committed to the tower in London in April, 1534, and while there for over a year found in the Psalms much strength and solace, his long confinement in a "a close, filthy prison, shut up among rats and mice." On July 1st, 1535, More, broken in body, he was sentenced to death, and executed, July 6th, on Tower Hill. As he knelt on the scaffold, More repeated the plea, "Have mercy upon me, O God," for Psalm 51 had always been his favorite prayer.

Lady Jane Dudley, who witnessed the throwing of her husband's blood-bespattered body into a cart after his execution, was not shaken in her resolution to die courageously, for her Protestant faith. When she came to the scaffold, she said to Feckenham who had followed her to the scaffold, "Shall I say this Psalm?" He answered, "Yea," so she read the *Miserere*—Psalm 51—in English to the end. The Psalm ended, she stood up, gave her gloves and handkerchief to her maiden Mistress Tylney, and the Book to Master Brydes, brother to the Lieutenant of the Tower. The Book is a small manual of prayers on vellum which is preserved in the British Museum, London.

Eleven days after Lady Jane's execution, her dear father, the Duke of Suffolk, who resisted all efforts to turn him from the Protestant faith, was beheaded at Tower Hill, February 23rd, 1554. Like his daughter, he, too, died with Psalm 51 on his lips. Fox, the historian says, "The Duke kneeled down upon his knees, and said the Psalm (51) *Miserere mei, Deus,* unto the end, holding up his hands and looking up to Heaven. Then his head fell with the first blow of the axe."

Among those we have already mentioned who found great consolation in the Psalm was Lamoral, Count of Egmont and Prince of Gavre, who perished at the hands of a hangman. Reaching the place of execution, Egmont made his way to the block, repeating aloud verses from Psalm 51, and praying for all to hear. When his head was severed from his body, it was set on one of the spikes and a cloak was thrown over his mutilated trunk.

In 1525, the year in which the Inquisition was established in France, Wolfgang Schual, the Lutheran preacher in Lorraine, was burned alive at Nancy, and as he died, was heard to repeat the words of Psalm 51. Another who sang this same Psalm as he died for the Protestant faith was a young man, studying for Holy Orders, François Benezet, who was executed, January 1752, on the esplanade at Montpellier. His youth, his courage, and the fact that he left a widow and child, created a profound impression among fellow believers. His fate is commemorated in one of the rude songs which, through their uncouth stanzas, breathe the fervent piety and indomitable resolution of the Protestants of that time.

John Bunyan, whose great Puritan allegory has undying charm because of its reflection of his own spiritual experience, gives us in his *Pilgrim's Progress,* truth in allegorical form in the sphere of personal life. To the tinker of Bedford, the mountain was God's Church—the sunshine, His merciful face—the wall, the world—the gap, Jesus Christ. In his vehement desire to be of the number of those who sat in the sun, he would often sing Psalm 51, which gave him momentary assurance.

George Wishart, the Scottish martyr, died, even as he had lived, namely, with unshaken confidence in the God he nobly served. The night before his death was spent with the laird of Ormiston and other friends, and after supper the company sang together Psalm 51, in Wedderburn's version—

> Have mercy on me now, good Lord,
>   After thy great mercie;
> My sinful life does me remord,
>   Which sore has grieved me.

Although he passed to his bedroom that night with the words, "God grant quiet rest," it was during that night that he was seized by Earl Bothwell, and carried to the "Sea Towers of St. Andrews." Convicted of heresy, he was burned, March 1st, 1546, at the foot of the Castle Wynd, opposite the castle gate.

The following incidents show how different verses of this *Sinner's Guide* have wielded their influence over human lives. For instance, verse 1—"Have mercy upon me, O God, according to thy loving kindness," 51:1, supplied the *neck verse* of mediaeval justice, which afforded the test of benefit of clergy. William Carey, who, in December 1823, thought he was dying, wrote—

> I had no joys, nor any fear of death or reluctance to die; but never was I so sensibly convinced of the value of an Atoning Savior as then. I could only say, "Hangs my helpless soul on Thee," and adopt the language of the first and second verses of the 51st Psalm, which I desired might be the text of my funeral sermon—"Have mercy upon me, O God, after Thy great goodness: according to the multitude of Thy mercies do away with mine offences. Wash me thoroughly from my wickedness, and cleanse me from my sin."

Carey, however, survived this illness for nearly eleven years. Nevertheless, the verses he chose were used at his funeral.

The plea for heart-purity—"Purge me with hyssop, and I shall be clean; wash me, and I shall be whiter than snow," 51:7—has some interesting connections. During the expedition of Sir George Nares to the Arctic Sea, in the ship *Alert,* a member of the crew died and was buried in the brow of a hill near Cape Beechy. A large stone covers the grave, and, on a copper tablet at the head, the words are engraved, "Wash me, and I shall be whiter than snow."

William Langland, in Section 15 of his *Vision of Piers Plowman,* says of the Lord, "He purgeth men of pride, cleansing them in the laundry, with groans and tears (Psalm 6:6). With warm water from his eyes, he washes them whiter than snow (51:7), singing with his work, and sometimes weeping, for he knows that a broken and contrite heart, O God, shalt Thou not despise," 51:17.

Shakespeare in *Hamlet* had the prayer of David before him, "Thou shalt wash me, and I shall be whiter than snow," 51:7, when he made the king ask—

> What if this cursed hand
> Were thicker than itself with brother's blood,
> Is there not rain enough in the sweet heavens
> To wash it white as snow?

Henry Martyn's *Journal,* as we have previously stated, has quotations from the Psalms scattered throughout its pages, and also comments on their power to soothe and encourage. Assailed by failing health, sleepless nights—and temptation—Martyn yet strained after purity of heart, and his "hope and trust" were in the words, "Purge me with hyssop, and I shall be clean; wash me, and I shall be whiter than snow."

The fascinating story of St. Teresa, born in 1515, at Avila, who made the lives of saints her nursery tales, and her doll's house, a nunnery, came to establish 16 nunneries of the Reformed Carmelites and 14 foundations of Friars belonging to the same Rule. Ever a lover of the Psalms, when she came to die, a worn-out woman at Alba, October 4th 1582, on her lips were the words, "Make me a clean heart, O God, and renew a right spirit within me. Cast me not away from Thy presence, and take not Thy Holy Spirit from me. The sacrifice of God is a troubled spirit, a broken and contrite heart, O God, shalt Thou not despise," Psalm 51:10-11, 17.

Thomas Arnold, the great headmaster of Rugby, repeated as he lay on his deathbed in the torture of *Angina Pectoria,* the words, "O give me the comfort of Thy help again; and establish me with Thy free spirit," Psalm 51:12.

Augustine, who came to study the Old Testament through the eloquent preacher, Ambrose, turned from the lofty idealism of Plato to the Bible, for, in the pages of the Platonic writers he could find no trace of "the humble and contrite heart," no "sacrifice of the broken spirit," Psalm 51:17.

As Psalm 51 was read to Henry V, on his death-bed, verse 18, "O be favorable and gracious unto Sion; build Thou the walls of Jerusalem," the dying king was reminded of his cherished hope of rescuing the Holy City from the hands of Mussulman. Another connection of this same verse is to be found in the first presbytery of the Irish Presbyterian Church, constituted in Carrickfergus, Ireland by immigrants from Scotland on June 10, 1642. There were five ministers and as many elders. The sermon was from Psalm 51:18. "Do good in thy good pleasure unto Zion; build thou the walls of Jerusalem." On the anniversary, 200 years afterwards, every one of the 500 ministers preached from the same text.

This Psalm was also the last prayer of Oecola-mpadius, who had his sickness aggravated and his death hastened by the untimely end of his friend Zwingle in 1531. Calling the ministers of the churches around him, he exhorted them to fidelity and purity of doctrine, then, before he died, prayed earnestly in the words of Psalm 51.

Then the story is a long one of all the Protestants in France who made this Psalm their death-song, during that long agony in which it is difficult to say whether we wonder most at the cruelty of the persecutors or the constancy of the sufferers. One of the earliest to be burned in 1550 was Pierre Milet; and more than 200 years later, on March 27, 1752, Francis Benezet met a similar fate, but both men met their cruel death with this Psalm on their lips.

Psalm 52

No preacher, who loves to preach on *The Psalms,* can afford to work without Spurgeon's massive work at his side. *The Treasury of David* is *par excellence* when it comes to commentaries on *The Psalms,* in which so many incidents related to human life can be found. Spurgeon's brief introduction to each Psalm is always rich in suggestion. Dealing with the title of Psalm 52, the prince of preachers says, "Even short Psalms, if they record but one instance of the goodness of God, and rebuke but briefly the pride of man, are worthy of our best minstrelsy. When we see that each Psalm is dedicated to *The Chief Musician,* it should make us value our psalmody, and forbid us to praise the Lord carelessly."

Then drawing attention to the fact that this is an *Instruction* Psalm, Spurgeon goes on to say that "even the malice of a Doeg may furnish instruction to a David. David was the prime object of Doeg's doggish hatred, and therefore the most fitting person to draw from the incident the lesson concealed within it." Dealing with the item of information found in the title, "Doeg the Edomite came and told Saul, and saith unto him, David is come to the house of Abimelech," Spurgeon has the biographical comment, "By this deceitful tale-bearing, he procured the death of all the priests at Nob: though it had been a crime to have succoured David as a rebel, they were not in their intent and knowledge guilty of the fault. David felt much the villainy of this arch-enemy, and here he denounces him in vigorous terms; it may be also that he has Saul in his eye."

When Charles I had his power broken at Marston Moor, and he became a hostage or a prisoner in the Scottish Camp at Newark, triumphant ministers insulted their royal captive by ordering Psalm 52 to be sung—"Why boastest thou thyself, thou tyrant that thou canst do mischief; whereas the goodness of God endured yet daily?" It was in an appeal to the Psalms that Charles robbed the insult of its sting. His only reply was to ask for Psalm 56—"Be merciful unto me, O God, for man goeth about to devour me; he is daily fighting and troubling me. Mine enemies are daily in hand to swallow me up; for they be many that fight against me, O Thou Most High."

Psalm 53

One cannot take up the study of any Psalm without agreeing with John Calvin's assessment of the Psalms as a whole—"There is no movement of the spirit which is not reflected here as in a mirror. All the sorrows, troubles, fears, doubts, hopes, pain, perplexities, stormy outbursts by which the hearts of men are tossed have been depicted here to the very life." How true this sentiment of the Psalm before us, which is a repeat of Psalm 14! Such an almost verbatim repetition is not a vain repetition, for repeated truth in Scripture means Divine emphasis. It will be found that Psalm 53 is not an exact copy of Psalm 14, but another edition by the same author, emphasized in certain parts, and re-written for another purpose. We are slow to learn and need *line upon line.*

The word, *Mahalath,* in the title of the Psalm signifies "disease," and truly this Psalm is *The Song of Man's Disease*—the mortal, hereditary taint of sin reiterated, for the evil nature of man is here brought before our view a second time, in almost the same inspired words as Psalm 14. Thus as Spurgeon concludes in his exposition of the Psalm before us, "Holy Writ never repeats itself needlessly, there is good cause for the second copy of this Psalm; let us read it with more profound attention than before. If our age had advanced from 14 to 53, we shall find the doctrine of this Psalm more evident than in our youth."

This was the Psalm which along with Psalm 51, John Hus repeated at the place of execution near Constance. Psalm 51 was the expression of his own personal experience, while Psalm 53 marked the character of his time, and his hope of the triumph of truth—"O that the salvation of Israel were come out of Zion! When God bringeth back the captivity of his people, Jacob shall rejoice, and Israel shall be glad," 53:6. How the universal Church is indebted to John Hus for the light he kindled at the torch of Wycliffe, and handed on to Martin Luther. As Erasmus said of Hus, "burned, not confuted."

An addition worthy of note can be found in verse 5. The original copy of the Psalm simply says, "There were they in great fear," 14:5, but Psalm 53 adds, *Where no fear was.* Most of our fears are imaginary or in some cases superstitions. As John King, renowned preacher who died in 1621, put it—"Men are afraid of their shadows, as Pisander was afraid of meeting his own soul; and Antenor would never go forth of the doors, but either in a coach closed in upon the sides, or with a target borne over his head, fearing, I guess, lest the sky should fall down upon it, according to that in the Psalm, 'They fear where no fear is.' So why fear—it may never happen?"

Psalm 54

In this further brief Psalm of David, we have, in its title, an indication of its cause. It was the cry of the Psalmist's heart when he was forced to flee as a fugitive from Saul who sought his life. It was a Psalm born in the hour of pain, for David had come to the Ziphims to dwell quietly among them, hoping for a respite in his many flights from Saul. But they betrayed David, and in order to curry favor with Saul were guilty of gross inhospitality. Forced to flee again, David turned to God in prayer, "and so strong was his faith that he soon sang himself into delightful serenity."

Although we do not have any interesting stories to illustrate this Psalm, the first clause of verse 7, "For he has delivered me out of all trouble," has been the confession and exclamation of the newly pardoned penitent, the cry of the delivered saint, the song of the ripe Christian, and the shout of the glorified believer. This is a verse to hug to your heart if any kind of trouble has assailed you.

Psalm 55

Henry Stuart, Earl of Darnley, on whom his wife Mary, Queen of Scots, conferred the title of king, turned out to be as dissolute as he was handsome, and his insolence and caprice made him many enemies. Much has been written about the checkered life both husband and wife lived, and whether Mary was guilty of connivance in her husband's assassination. What is evident is the fact that after protracted illness, on the night before his tragic death by an explosion caused by gunpowder, restless and weak, and chilled by a sense of his loneliness and a vague foreboding of evil, Darnley opened the Book of Psalms, at Psalm 55, and these were the last words that he read on earth. With what force must these words have struck into his heart, if he suspected his impending doom, and his wife's probable complicity in a crime to get rid of him—

"My heart is disquieted within me; and the fear of death is fallen upon me," etc.

Lord Byron, whose love and knowledge of many of the Psalms he learned by heart, we have previously mentioned, was subject from boyhood to fits of melancholy. He could find expression for his mood in the paraphrased version of verse 6—

> Fain would I fly the haunts of men—
>   I seek to shun, not hate mankind;
> My breast requires the sullen glen
>   Whose gloom may sait a darken'd mind.
>
> Oh! that to me the wings were given,
>   Which bear the turtle to her nest!
> Then would I cleave the vault of Heaven,
>   To flee away, and be at rest.

Augustus M. Toplady, author of one of the world's most popular hymns *Rock of Ages*, died in London at the age of 38. Although he had the brightest prospects before him, he was fully prepared to die, and almost exultant at the future before him in Heaven. He repeated as he died, "Oh, that I had wings like a dove! for then would I fly away, and be at rest," 55:6.

Jerome, who was born in 346, at Stridon in Dalmatia, renowned for his love for Scripture, as well as his practice of asceticism, had two favorite texts—"But his delight is in the law of the Lord; and in His law will he exercise himself, night and day," Psalm 1:2, and "O that I had wings like a dove! for then would I flee away, and be at rest," 55:6. Where else, except in solitude, could he gratify his longing or follow the law of the Lord night and day?

Robert Browning, in *Ring and the Book,* assigned to Pompilia, as, before her flight, she sat at the Carnival, with her tyrant husband crouching behind in the shadows, verse inspired by David's poem—

> There is a Psalm Don Celestine recites,
> "Had I a dove's wings, how I fain would flee!"
> The Psalm runs not, "I hope, I pray for wings,"—
> Not "if wings fall from heaven, I fix them fast,"
> Simply, "How good it were to fly and rest,
> Have hope now, and one day expect content!
> How well to do what I shall never do!"
> So I said, "Had there been a man like that,
> To lift me with his strength out of all strife
> Into the calm, how I could fly and rest!"

When the fame of the Cistercians, who came from Europe and settled in 1128 and settled in Waverly, Surrey, penetrated the precincts of the Benedictine Abbey of St. Mary at York, the piety of these newcomers stirred the Benedictines from their lethargy, and dormant energies. Thus stirred, they wearied of the fret and fever of men and cities and sighed for "the wings of the dove," that they "might flee away, and be at rest." They longed to wander "afar off, and remain in the wilderness," Psalm 55:6, 7.

Prior Richard, whom Furstin blessed as the first abbot while at Ripon had monks, but no monastery. Beneath an elm tree, the brethren thatched a shelter to serve as church and home, only too conscious that they had "nowhere to lay their heads" and no hiding-place in which to escape the "stormy wind and tempest," 55:8.

The Messianic aspect of this Psalm is to be found in verses 12-15, which, without doubt, refer to the deceitful way in which Judas sold Jesus to the Pharisees. Spurgeon comments, "This is not a mere personal hymn, there is teaching in it for us all, and where our Lord shines through David, His personal type, there is a great depth of meaning. The man of many conditions, much tried and much favored, persecuted but delivered and exalted, was from experience enabled to write such precious verses in which he sets forth not only the sorrows of common pilgrims, but of the Lord of the way Himself."

Prothero, dealing with the influence of the Psalms in the 16th century remarks that it was from the treasure-house of the Psalter that Roman Catholics and Protestants alike drew inspiration, and that it was this common bond that led Bishop John Hooker to use the words, "We took sweet counsel together: and walked in the house of God as friends," 55:13, in his argument that community of worship forges the chains of human love.

Once admitted to the Benedictine Order, the lives of monks and nuns were more or less regulated by the spirit, if not by the letter, of the Psalms. Thus the canonical hours in the monastery were regulated by the Psalms—"In the evening and morning, and at noonday, will I pray, and that instantly," Psalm 55:18. Other regular periods found in Psalm 119:62, 164, were also observed.

One of the passages from the Psalms that consoled Commander Gardiner, who set out to evangelize Tierra del Fuego, but who met with terrible calamities on the way in 1851, was the promise—

Cast thy burden upon the Lord, and He shall sustain thee, 55:22.

The Psalms often appear in the naval war between the Spaniards and the English when in 1598, the question arose regarding peace with Spain. After a hot debate in Elizabeth's Council, the Earl of Essex, supported by the envoys from the States-General of Holland, warmly urged the continuance of the war, but Burghley as strongly pleaded for peace, and in the midst of the debate took from his pocket a Prayer-book, and read to Essex the verse, "The bloodthirsty and deceitful men shall not live out half their days," 55:23. Three years later, on February 25th, 1601, Essex was led to the high court, above Caesar's Tower, in the precincts of the Tower of London, and there beheaded.

Psalm 56

Spurgeon suggests that this blessed Psalm is a reflection of a previous one. "This is the second golden Psalm. We had the first in Psalm 16, to which this Psalm has a great likeness, especially in its close, for it ends in the joyful presence. A golden mystery, the gracious secret of a life of faith is in both of these Psalms most sweetly unveiled, and a pillar is set up because of God's truth."

The title tells the story behind this Psalm—"When the Philistines took David in Gath." During such captivity he was like a dove in stranger's hands, and when escaped he recorded his gratitude. The phrase *Upon Jonath-elemrechokim,* was probably the title of the tune *The Chief Musician* arranged, and seems to mean, "the silent dove in distant places," which was certainly descriptive of David when in the hands of the Philistines. One cannot read this Psalm so intimately related to the Psalmist's history without agreeing with Spurgeon's comment, "There is such deep spiritual knowledge in this Psalm that we may say of it, 'Blessed art thou David Bar-jonas, for flesh and blood hath not revealed this unto thee.' When David plays the Jonah he is not like the prophet of that name; in David the love of the dove pre-dominates, but in Jonah its mourning and complaining are most notable. . . ."

Among the precious gems in this Psalm is verse 3, which has generated confidence and hope in many a fearful heart in an hour of need. Commentator, Albert Barnes, says of the challenge this verse holds—

> It is a good maxim with which to go into a world of danger;
> a good maxim to go to sea with;
> a good maxim in a storm;
> a good maxim when in danger on the land;
> a good maxim when we are sick;
> a good maxim when we think of death and judgment.

What time I am afraid, I WILL TRUST IN THEE. Then how inspiring is the rumination of John Bunyan on this same verse—

"There is nothing like faith to help at a pinch; faith dissolves doubts as the sun drives away the mists. And that you may not be put out, know that your time for believing is always. There are times when some graces may be out of use, but there is no time wherein faith can be said to be so. Wherefore faith must always be in exercise. Faith is the eye, is the mouth, is the hand, and one of these is in use all the day long. Faith is to see, to receive, to work, or to eat; and a Christian should be seeing, or receiving, or working, or feeding all day long. Let it rain, let it blow, let it thunder, let it lighten, a Christian must still believe. At that time," said the good man, "I am afraid, I will trust in Thee."

The lament of David concerning his captors was, "Every day they wrest my words," (verse 5), or give them a meaning he never intended. Dr. Jewell, Bishop of Salisbury in a past century, died most godly and patiently and at the point of death used the versicle of the Hymn—*Te Deum*—"O Lord, in thee have I trusted, let me never be confounded," whereupon, his enemies, suppressing the rest of the hymn published that this principal champion of the heretics in his very last words cried he was confounded—a sense the Bishop never dreamed of.

All of us are agreed that the most tender phrase in this Psalm is that where David reminds God that He knew all about his wanderings, and then prayed, "Put thou my tears into thy bottle: are they not in this book?" 56:8. This was the verse frequently in the mouth of Archbishop Ussher, one of the godliest and most learned men of his time. He was the one who gave us the chronological dates found in the A.V. of the Bible. Born in Dublin 1586, he was driven to and fro through England and Ireland amid the troubles in Church and State, during one of the most troublous times in our history. In such wanderings, it consoled his heart to know that the God he faithfully served was storing up his tears. After preaching the Gospel for 55 years, he found the rest he often sighed for at Reigate, England, where he died in 1655.

John Gadsby, preacher in the 18th century, wrote of a friend of his in Cairo who had a unique collection of curios including a *lachrymatory,* or tear bottle, which had been found in a tomb at Thebes. In ancient times in the East, when a person was ill or in great distress, it was the custom for his friends to go to see him, and take with them a tear bottle. Then, as the tears rolled down the cheeks of the sufferer, they were caught in these bottles, sealed up, and preserved as a memorial of the event. This custom was in David's mind when he implored God to put his tears in His bottle. Such a figure of speech, of course, suggests God's remembrance of His people's affliction. It is blessed to know that if God has a *bottle* for our tears, He also has a *bag* for our transgressions.

Psalm 57

In his Diary, Commander Gardiner, who left the Royal Navy to do missionary work in the 18th century, records the fearful trials he and his little party had to endure when they landed on Picton Island. Facing the prospect of starvation, the brave Commander still retained his confident trust, and had this item in his Diary, "16th June—Be merciful unto me, O God, be merciful unto me, for my soul trusteth in Thee. Yea, in the shadow of Thy wings, will I make my refuge until these calamities are over past," 57:1.

When, in 1870, the German armies marched on the French Capital, chanting Luther's version of Psalm 46, the little village of Bourget was the scene of desperate struggles, lasting for three days. When the conflict and pillage was over, there was found, on the bullet-pierced altar of the church, a copy of the Psalter open at Psalm 57. "Be merciful unto me, O God, be merciful unto me, for my soul trusteth in Thee; and under the shadow of Thy wings shall be my refuge, until this tyranny is overpast."

Robert Sanderson, Bishop of Lincoln, in the 16th century had his sorrows deepened and enlarged by his love for the Psalter, which was his treasury of Christian comfort, fitted for all persons and all necessities. When he came to die, at the age of 85, he spent his last hours constantly repeating, "My heart is fixed, O God; my heart is fixed where true joy is found," 57:7.

It is interesting to observe that the title of this Psalm—Al-taschith—means "Destroy not," and the historical connection of such a phrase is worthy of notice. David had said *destroy not*, in reference to Saul, when he had him in his power in the cave, and he now takes pleasure in employing the same words in supplication to God. There are four of these *Destroy not* Psalms, namely the 57th, 58th, 59th, and 75th, and in all of them there is a distinct declaration of the wicked and the preservation of the righteous. But the particular application of Psalm 57 must not be lost sight of, for, as the title reminds us, the Psalm came from David "when he fled from Saul in the cave." Thus, "this is a song from the bowels of the earth, and, like Jonah's prayer from the bottom of the sea, it has a taste of the place. The poet is in the shadow of the cave at first, but comes to the cavern's mouth at last, and sings in the sweet fresh air, with his eye on the heavens, watching joyously the clouds floating therein."

Psalm 58

In our personal study of the Psalms it is most important to give consideration to the titles introducing them, seeing they are the keys opening not only the door of application to the Psalmist himself, but also for our personal appropriation. Although David had his own case in his mind's eye in the Psalms he composed, "yet he wrote not as a private person, but as an inspired prophet, and therefore his songs are presented for public and perpetual use." As Dr. Joseph Hertz, Chief Rabbi in Britain says, "The Psalms translate into simple speech the spiritual passion of the scholar and give utterance, with the beauty born of truth, to the humble longing and petition of the unlettered peasant. *They are the hymnbook of humanity.*"

The term we considered in the previous Psalm is before us again—*Altaschith,* meaning *Destroy not.* In this Psalm, the wicked are judged and condemned, but over the godly the sacred *Destroy not* is solemnly pronounced. *Michtam* signifies, "a prayer," and this is the fourth of the Psalms of such a Golden Secret, and the second of the *Destroy nots.* Of course, we are not always to look for a meaning in these superscriptions, but to treat them as we would the titles of poems, or the names of tunes. As Spurgeon observes, "Men give names to their horses, jewels, and other valuables, and these names are meant not so much to describe as to distinguish them, and in some cases to set forth the owner's high esteem of his treasure; after the same fashion the Oriental poet gave a title to the song he loved, and so aided his memory, and expressed his estimation of the strain."

As to historical uses of Psalm 58, when Shakespeare made Hector tell Paria in *Troilus and Cressida*—

> Pleasure and revenge
> Have ears more deaf then adders to the voice
> Of any true decision—

the poet must have had verse 4 in mind—"Their poison is like the poison of a serpent."

John Milton, over whom the Psalms threw their spell in early life, in *Samson Agonistes,* when he makes the blind Samson reject the appeal of Delilah, refers to the *deaf adder* of this same fourth verse of Psalm 58—"They are like the deaf adder that stoppeth her ear"—

215

I know thy trains,
Though dearly to my cost, thy gins, and toils;
Thy fair enchanted cup, and warbling charms.
No more on me have power; their force is null'd;
So much of adder's wisdom I have learn'd,
To fence my ear against thy sorceries.

On verse 5, where David speaks of the serpent "not hearkening to the voice of charmers, charming never so wisely," travelers to the East have described for us how reptiles can be charmed by music. François Auguste in the early 18th century wrote of a rattlesnake that entered their Canadian settlement one day, and of how a native who could play the flute, and by a few sweet and simple notes, calmed the snake to such an extent as to make both natives and Europeans wonder at the effect of harmony as they saw the snake follow the player. But experienced and skillful as serpent-charmers may be, there are fatal terminations to their exhalation of this psychic art, occasionally, when they encounter "deaf adders, which will not hearken to the voice of charmers." Preachers call and call, and call in vain to sinners to repent, till the arm of the Lord is revealed. This is at once their guilt and danger. They ought to hear but will not, and because they will not hear, they cannot escape the damanation of Hell.

You can call spirits from the vasty deep,
But will they come when you do call for them?

How suggestive are the figures of speech David uses in this Psalm, as he applies them to human life and character! Think of the way he describes the godless as having their lion-like teeth broken, as water running away, as archers cut in pieces, as the untimely birth of a woman, and "as a snail which melteth," 58:6-8. J. G. Wood, in *Bible Animals,* informs us that the Jewish Bible renders the passage in a way explaining the idea prevailing at the time the Psalms were composed—"As a snail let him melt as he passeth on." The ancients had an idea that the slimy track made by a snail as it crawled along was substracted from the substance of the body, and that in consequence the farther it crept the smaller it became until at last it wasted away entirely.

David's application of this metaphor declares that the godless, malicious person eats out his own strength while he proceeds upon his malevolent designs, and then disappears. To destroy himself by envy and chagrin is the portion of the ill-disposed. His character is shapeless, life never come to ripeness, and the graceless wretch is finally hidden away in an unknown grave.

What a striking phrase David uses at the end of his Psalm where he speaks of the righteous as washing their feet in the blood of the wicked, 58:10. William Greenhill, Bible expositor of the 16th century, refers to one Waldus, a man of note in Lyons who, seeing one struck dead in his presence, washed his hands in his blood, and then gave alms to the poor, instructed his family in the true knowledge of God, and exhorted all that came to him to repentance and holiness of life. The spiritual message of this figure of speech seems to be that the righteous triumph over the wicked, and that their overthrow is final and fatal, but the deliverance of the righteous is complete and crowning. The ultimate condemnation of sinners will not mar the eternal happiness of saints.

Psalm 59

The same title introducing the previous Psalm begins the one before us, but with the addition of the historical connection—"When Saul sent, and they watched the house to kill David." What a fervent heart-prayer this is! How appropriate it is to the circumstances mentioned in its title. How expressive is the introduction C. H. Spurgeon has to this Psalm as a whole—

> Strange that the painful events in David's life should end in enriching the repertoire of national minstrelsy. Out of a sour, ungenerous soil spring up the honey-bearing flowers of psalmody. Had he never been cruelly hunted by Saul, Israel and the Church of God in after ages would have been without song. The music of the sanctuary is in no small degree indebted to the trials of the saints. Affliction is the tuner of the harps of sanctified songsters.

Here is another *Al-taschith,* or *destroy not,* Psalm, and its historical association reminds us that all whom God preserves Satan cannot destroy. "The Lord can even preserve the lives of His prophets by the very ravens that would naturally pluck out their eyes." Although Saul had the house where David lodged closely watched, so that, at an opportune moment, he could kill his young successor to the throne, David had a friend within the house to help him in his peculiarly dangerous situation. It was Saul's own daughter, Michal, who loved David.

The double reference to *Dogs,* as symbolizing wicked transgressors, is used by David with great effect, 59:7, 14, 15. Writing in 1850, Albert Smith described in *A Month at Constantinople,* his experience there. Evidently it was the pitiful condition of dogs that interested him most—

> The noise I heard then I shall never forget. To say that if all the sheep-dogs in going to Smithfield on a market-day, had been kept on the constant bark and pitted against the yelping curs upon all the carts in London, they could not have given any idea of the canine uproar that now first astonished me, would be to make the feeblest of images. The whole city rang with one vast riot. Down below me, at Tophane; over about Stamboul; far away at Scutari; the whole 60,000 dogs that are said to overrun Constantinople, appeared engaged in the most active extermination of each other, without a moment's cessation. The yelping, howling, barking, growling, and snarling, were all merged into one uniform and continuous even sound, as the noise of frogs becomes, when heard at a distance. For hours there was no lull. I went to sleep

and woke again, and still, with my windows open, I heard the same tumult
going on; nor was it until daybreak that anything like tranquility was restored.

The foes of David, particularly Saul, were like a herd of Oriental dogs,
unhoused, prowling about seeking prey they cannot find. It was thus with
the servants of Saul who waited in vain hope of satisfying their malice and
their master. How the city must have laughed when they heard the story
of the image and the goats' hair laid on the bed! "The warrior poet hears
in fancy the howl of rage in the council of his foes when they found their
victim clean escaped out of their hands." How gifted the Psalmist was in
comparing his foes to Eastern dogs, loathsome and despised and hungry,
and in representing them as howling with disappointment, because they
cannot get the food they seek. "Vain were their watchings, the victim had
been delivered, and that by the daughter of the man who desired his blood.
Go, ye dogs, to your kennels and gnaw your bones, for this good man is
not meat for your jaws."

There is a further sentence in the Psalm which, at first sight, seems contrary to David's first desire, "Slay them not." It is in verse 13, "Consume
them in wrath, that they may not be." David's indignation at his foes
flamed forth, and cried to God against them. If they continue as mad dogs
in a city, then let them cease to be.

R. A. Bertram, reporting on atrocities in the 18th century, wrote, "I hear
of sad doings in Poland, of villages burnt down, of peaceable men deport-
ed to Siberia by hundreds, of women flogged: and when I look away to
that Warsaw market-place where a woman, nearly naked, is being publicly
beaten, and when I see cruel Mouravieff smile as blood jets forth from the
scourged soldiers, I will not deny that I feel very much tempted to say,
'Happy man, whose bullet in fair fight should empty that saddle!' Am I
blood-thirsty in this? Am I vindictive? Do you condemn me for this feeling?" Is this not our sentiment, in this supposedly civilized twentieth
century, as we daily read of heartless brutes who murder the innocent in
this and other countries, and who hijack planes resulting in terrible loss
of life and property? Of these destructive forces of Hell, how else can we
cry but "Consume them, O God, in Thy wrath"? This judgment Psalm
ends on a high note—"But I will sing of thy power; yea, I will sing aloud
of thy mercy in the morning: for thou hast been my defense and refuge in
the day of trouble," Psalm 59:16, 17. David could sing songs in the night
of his trial. His enemies might howl like dogs, but the Psalmist could sing
his choice song. And "my soul would sing in defiance of all the dogs of
Hell. Away, away, ye adversaries of my soul, the God of my mercy will
keep ye all at bay—

> Nor shall th' infernal rend
> Whom He designs to keep."

Psalm 60

That this warlike song is prominent in the history and biography of saints can be seen in the following uses made of it. Cuthbert, missionary of the seventh century, was first heard of as a shepherd boy on the hills of Gala Water, then known as Wedale. The religious revival among the Celtic races under Columba and his followers laid hold of the Saxons, and Cuthbert became the Apostle of the glens of the south of Scotland and the north of England. Numerous legends have gathered around his life and labors, and the wanderings of his body after his death, till the saint found a resting place in Durham Cathedral. Cuthbert's retirement was spent in the Ferne Islands, where he died. Friends who visited him sang Psalm 60, and the same Psalm was included in the burial service, March 20, 687. Accents of this Psalm and the wail for the dead were carried, with the signal of two lighted torches, across the sea to Lindisfarne where friends awaited such a preconcerted signal.

It was also in 685, during Cuthbert's time, that the Pictish monarch, after a great victory over the Saxons, crossed the Forth, took possession of Edinburgh and the Lothians, and prepared the way for an independent nationality, Scotland is again striving after, and for the Covenanting struggle of the Church of John Knox. The 60th Psalm appears in one of the incidents of such a history, for Robert Douglas gave it out to be sung when he preached the coronation sermon of Charles II, at Scone January 1st, 1651, the Marquis of Argyle putting the crown on the head of the ungrateful monarch who afterwards sent him to the block.

Then this 60th Psalm is likewise memorable in the history of the Secession Church of Scotland, for when Ebenezer Erskin in 1740, had to leave his church, an immense crowd followed him to Stirling Castle, and there sang the first five verses of this Psalm in the Scottish version—

> And yet a banner thou hast given
> To them who do thee fear;
> That it by them, because of truth,
> Displayed may appear.

> That thy beloved people may,
>> Delivered be from thrall,
> Save with the power of thy right hand,
>> And hear me when I call.

David's Psalm with its ring of battle, was also the favorite one of Erskine's friend, Wilson of Perth, as he faced similar circumstances. Both of these leaders were children of the Covenanters. When, in 1847, the Secession and Relief Churches were united in Tanfield Hall, Edinburgh, during 1847, the 60th Psalm was again sung, and with it Psalm 147:1-3, division ending in reconstruction.

> God doth build up Jerusalem,
>> And he it is alone
> That the dispersed of Israel,
>> Doth gather into one.

That this Psalm should be chosen as a rallying call in times of strife and turmoil in the history of the Church, is in harmony with the implication of its somewhat lengthy title. *Shushan-eduth* means, "The Lily of Testimony." Psalm 45 is one about the *Lilies,* and represented the kingly warrior in his beauty going forth to war. Here in Psalm 60 we see the king dividing the spoil and bearing testimony of the glory of God. In war-songs *Roses* and *Lilies* are often mentioned, as in Macaulay's *Song of the Huguenots.*

> Now by the lips of those ye love, fair gentlemen of France
> Charge for the golden lilies now, upon them with the lance.

The combined Aramean tribes sought to destroy Israel, but Joab signally defeated them, and in the *Valley of Salt* smote 12,000 of them. The power of the enemy was utterly broken, and well did the Lord who aided His people deserve this song from David.

When in 1535 King Henry VIII assumed the title of Supreme Head of the Church, Prior John Haughton of the London Charterhouse angered the King by boldly affirming that he could not understand how the King's marriage to Catherine of Arragon, ratified by the Church, could be dissolved. Sensing that his end was near, he preached in the Chapel from the text, "O God, Thou hast cast us out, and scattered us abroad," Psalm 60:1, and ended his sermon with the words, "It is better that we should suffer here a short penance for our faults, than be reserved for the eternal pains of Hell hereafter." Along with other Priors maintaining Haughton's position, all were tried for treason, and on May 4, 1535, were executed at Tyburn, Haughton being martyred first, and dying with the same calm and unflinching courage he had manifested in rebuking the King.

It was in the spirit of the Psalms, as they interpreted them, that the brethren of the Pilgrim Fathers, the Puritans who remained behind in England, fought out their quarrel with Charles I. For instance, it was from Psalm 60:2—"Thou hast moved the land, and divided it: heal the sores thereof, for it shaketh," that godly Bishop Hall appealed for peace in the Lent Sermon he preached in 1641 before Charles I at Whitehall, London.

John Howard, notable for his Prison Reform, found much in the language of the Psalms to console and encourage him in the crises of his troubled career. His memorandum books, in which he jotted down his pious ejaculations and secret aspirations, couched in the words of the Psalms, prove his love for them. An entry in his Diary made when he was very ill at the Hague in 1778 reads—

> May 13th—In pain and anguish all Night . . . help, Lord, for vain is the help of Man, Psalm 60:11.

Psalm 61

In this brief Psalm of David, sung with the accompaniment of a musical instrument which he himself played, we meet a title encountered before in Psalms 4, 6, 54, and 55, but with this shade of difference—the term *Michtam* is in the singular number, indicating that the Psalm is very personal and well suited for the private devotion of any saint. It is a pearl of a Psalm, as blessed as it is brief. Composed by David after he had come to his throne, 61:6, it has furnished consolation for many a mourner, providing speech when the mind was unable to think and speak for itself. Delitzsch, the renowned German theologian, says of the Psalm that it is, "Prayer and thanksgiving of an expelled King on his way back to his throne." John Newton said of the first clause of verse 5—"For thou, O God, hast heard my vows"—"About this time I began to know that there is a God who hears and answers prayer." On the verse as a whole we have the enlightening comment reiterated by Theophylus—"It is an inheritance, to shew that no man obtaineth the kingdom by his own good works, for no man hath so lived as to render himself worthy of the kingdom, but all is of the grace of God."

The first clause of verse 4—"I will abide in Thy tabernacle forever," produced the comment of an unknown preacher—

> Where the priest presented the sacrifice;
> Where the law as laid up in the ark is fulfilled;
> Where the light of the Spirit's candlestick shines;
> Where the manna abides;
> Where the glory is above the mercy-seat;
> Where no enemy can enter;
> Where I commune with a covenant God.

Psalm 62

John Hooper, who, in 1551, became the Bishop of Gloucester, while in prison for the religious principles he zealously advocated, wrote an *Exposition* of this Psalm, along with Psalms, 23, 63, and 67. Because of the sixfold repetition of the word "only," Psalm 62 used to be called *The Only Psalm*. It comes to us as another of David's matchless songs, and if it had not carried the royal signature, we would have been certain from the nature of internal evidence that he alone had penned the stanzas. *Jeduthun* or Etham, has this and other Psalms dedicated to him. Evidently, the sons of Jeduthun were porters, or doorkeepers of the sanctuary, 1 Chronicles 16:42. "Those who serve well make the best of singers, and those who occupy the highest posts in the choir must not be ashamed to wait at the posts of the doors of the Lord's house."

When, under the influence of Ambrose, Augustine turned from Plato to the Bible, he wrote of Platonic writings, "No one sings there. Truly my soul waiteth upon God; from Him cometh my salvation; He is my strong tower, I shall not be greatly moved," Psalm 62:1, 2.

A biography of Philip Doddridge, the famous preacher of the 17th century, who had much to do with the spiritual education of Colonel Gardiner, whose death is described in *Waverley,* relates how the Colonel carried a conviction of a speedy death, constantly dwelt with special delight on the words—"My soul, wait thou still upon God," 62:5. Allen Gardiner—no connection with the above—one-time Navy Commander, was the means of forming the Patagonian Missionary Society. He urged his friends in his last painful hour not to neglect the object for which he so gladly sacrificed his life. He also found consolation in phrases of this Psalm.

This Psalm, in which David, in his true and sole confidence in God, laughs to scorn all his enemies, is vibrant with the music of triumphant faith which is always in season, especially in the hour of trial. *"Trust in him at all times,"* 60:8—not sometimes, but *all* times. Such trust in One Who does not fail is an abiding duty and a perpetual privilege. The time of trusting in God cannot be lapsed. One remembers reading, many years ago, the newspaper report of a tragic disaster in one of our British coalmines. Many miners perished, and in one pocket the searchers came across four or five miners all huddled together in death. But before they died, they scratched on a board, *We are all trusting in Christ,* and added their names.

A perusal of any hymnbook reveals how many hymns there are founded upon the language of the psalmody of Scripture. An illustration of this can be gathered from L. A. Bennett's hymn *Trust Him*, which is but an expansion of the Psalmist's counsel—

"Trust in Him at all times."

Trust Him; He is ever faithful;
   Trust Him; for His will is best;
Trust Him; for the heart of Jesus
   Is the only place of rest.

Psalm 63

In this further Psalm of David, the Psalmist seems to feel that not only does he belong to God, but that God belongs to him. Theodore de Beza, 1519-1605, colleague of John Calvin at Geneva and author of the metrical version of Psalm 68 which was the battle-song of the Huguenots, was the one who devoted the best years of his life translating the Psalms into French verse, and into Latin prose and Latin verse. During sleepless nights, Beza used to repeat to himself the morning hymn of eastern Christians, the favorite Psalm of St. Chrysostom, "O God, Thou art my God; early will I seek Thee," Psalm 63:1.

Thomas à Kempis, whose *Soliloquy of the Souls* is made up in great part of impassioned expansion of verse drawn from the Psalms, included the phrase, "My soul hangeth on Thee," 63:9. How expressive is David's pursuit after God, found in the phrase, "My soul followeth hard after Thee," 63:8. The title tells us that David wrote this Psalm when he was in the wilderness of Judah, whether when fleeing from his much-loved son, Absalom, or at a time when as King (63:11) he was hard pressed by those who sought his life. When foes were following hard after him, he was found following hard after God. Spurgeon's comment is so apt at this point, for he wrote—

> David did not leave off singing because he was in the wilderness, neither did he in slovenly idleness go on repeating Psalms intended for other occasions; but he carefully made his worship suitable to his circumstances, and presented to his God a wilderness hymn when he was in a *wilderness*. There was no desert in his heart, though there was a desert around him. We too may expect to be cast into rough places as we go hence. In such season, may the Eternal Comforter abide with us and cause us to bless the Lord at all times, making even the solitary place to become a temple for Jehovah.

Spurgeon further remarks that this Psalm "is peculiarly suitable for the bed of sickness, or in any constrained absence from public worship."

Psalm 64

We cannot approach a Psalm like this without realizing that the chief appeal of the Psalter as a whole is in its themes—life and death, good and evil, justice and mercy—all contained in one overriding theme, the marvelous ways of God with man. God is the personal God of every individual. In the Psalm before us David's life was pictured as one of conflict, and very seldom does he finish a Psalm without mentioning his enemies—who were many! In this 64th Psalm, David's thoughts are wholly occupied with prayer against his foes, with judgment upon them causing the righteous to be glad in the justice of God.

On *arrows* poisoned with *bitter words,* 64:3, 4, C. H. Spurgeon relates a visit he paid to the Museum at Venice, where he saw an instrument with which one of the old Italian tyrants was accustomed to shoot poisoned needles at the objects of his wanton anger, which reminded the great preacher of gossips, backbiters, and secret slanderers who wished that their mischievous devices might come to a speedy end. "Their weapons of innuendo, shrug, and whisper," Spurgeon goes on to say in his *Feathers for Arrows,* "appear to be as insignificant as needles; but the venom which they instill is deadly to many a reputation."

It was the first clause of verse 8, "So they shall make their own tongue to fall upon themselves," that Shakespeare embodied in the lines—

> In these cases,
> We still have judgment here that we but teach
> Bloody instructions, which, being taught, return
> To plague the inventor; This even-handed justice
> Commends the ingredients of our poisoned chalice
> To our own lips.

Psalm 65

*G*race and *Nature* are the twin truths poetically described by David in this beautiful song of his inverting the order of Psalm 19 in which Nature comes first. Taking early possession of the heart of the Christian Church there is a prayer, evidently with Egypt in mind, inspired by verses 9-13 of the Psalm which has come down to us from the Church of Alexandria, alluded to by Origen in the first half of the 3rd century. It reads—

> Send rain out of thy treasures upon those places which stand in need of it.
> Renew and make glad the face of the earth by its descent that it may bring forth and rejoice in the rain-drops.
> Raise the waters of the river to their just height; renew and make glad the face of the earth by its ascent; water the furrows and increase their produce.
> Bless, O Lord, and crown the year with the riches of thy goodness, for the sake of the poor, the widows, the fatherless, and the stranger.

Spoken of as "A Lyrical Poem," this combination of *Psalm* and *Song* is surely one of the most delightful hymns in any language. In it the inspired singer dwells upon the glory of God in His sanctuary, and in the realm of nature. It is thus a song both of grace and providence. The first word of the Psalm is *Praise,* and its last word *Sing,* the song sung being looked upon as a *Vow*, 65:1. A modern writer defines a vow as "a religious promise made unto God in a holy manner." Peter Martyr, a man of repute and of spiritual influence in England in the days of King Edward VI, spoke of the *vow* as "a holy promise, whereby we bind ourselves to offer somewhat unto God." Such a vow must be of things lawful and possible. The Psalmist's vow was carried out in the expression of praise.

Addressing God as the One Who hears prayer the Psalmist says that HE is the One to Whom "all flesh must come," 65:2, affirming that He is the only source of salvation for every sinner and carnal man. The Grecian priest in ancient times, when approaching to receive the sacrifice, used to exclaim, *Who comes there?* and the reply was, *Many and good.* But God receives the bad as well as the good, publicans and sinners, and also those without guile are invited to His banquet. By *flesh* is meant man in his own utter weakness and need.

Whether the final verses of the Psalm were meant to commemorate a remarkably plentiful harvest, or simply the composition of a harvest hymn for all ages, we cannot say. What is apparent is that it seems to have been written after a violent rebellion had been quelled, 65:7, and foreign enemies subdued by a signal victory, 65:8.

Robert Southwell, Elizabethan poet born in 1560, alluded in a letter to the martyrdom of two saints, Bayles and Horner, and of the effect which their tragic yet holy end produced upon the people. Southwell wrote:

> With such dews as these the Church is watered, *ut in stillicidiis hujasmodi laetctur germinans*—"Thou crownest the year with thy goodness; thy paths drop fatness," 65:11. We also look for the time—if we are not unworthy of so great a glory—when our day—like that of the hired servant—shall come.

Southwell did not have long to wait for in 1592 he was betrayed by a woman, Anne Bellamy, into the hands of Topcliffe, who boasted that "he never did take so weighty a man, if he be rightly considered."

On the phrase, "Thy paths drop fatness," 65:11, Spurgeon says, "When the conqueror journeys through the nations, his paths drop blood; fire and vapor are in his tracks, and tears, and groans, and sighs attend him. But where the King of kings journeys He enriches the land. When kings of old made progress through their dominions, they caused famine wherever they tarried because their greedy courtiers ate up all the good things." But the paths of our heavenly King "drop fatness."

When John Wesley came to die on March 2nd, 1791, at Chapelhouse in City Road, London, he was greatly exhausted. One of the friends at the bedside wetted Wesley's parched lips and heard him say, "It will not do we must take the consequences; never mind the poor carcase." Pausing a little, he cried, "Thy clouds drop fatness," 65:11.

As for the concluding verses of the Psalm, 9-13, Barton Bouchier, devotional writer of the 18th century, wrote of them—

> I do not know any picture of rural life that in any measure comes up to the exquisite description here brought before us, and which every one's heart at once recognizes as so true to nature in all its branches. In the brief compass of five verses we have the whole scene vividly sketched, from the first preparation of the earth or soil . . . then the crowning of the whole year in the appointed weeks of harvest, and men's hearts rejoicing before God according to the joy in harvest.

Psalm 66

Although David's name does not introduce this Psalm, it is Davidic in style. It may be far wrong to attribute all the anonymous Psalms to David, as some writers suggest. Like the previous Psalm, this one is also defined as a Psalm and a Song—*A Psalm* to be read—and what a marvelous poem it is to recite: A *Song* to be sung, and when set to suitable music, it must have been one of the noblest strains ever heard by the Jewish people!

John Bunyan's masterpiece of a spiritual biography, *Grace Abounding to the Chief of Sinners,* bears the motto taken from this 66th Psalm— "Come and hear all ye that fear God, and I will declare what he hath done for my soul," 66:14. With a pen of iron and in letters of fire, Bunyan tells us what God did for his soul in his own passage from death to life. Two phrases can be brought together, *Come and see,* and *Come and hear,* 66:5, 16. How blessed are those who have seen the Lord, and daily hear His voice! But if they regard iniquity in their heart, the Lord will not hear them when they pray, 66:18.

Psalm 67

This is the fifth Psalm having the title, *Neginoth,* meaning, "upon stringed instruments," and like the others was so composed as to be sung with the accompaniment of "harpers harping upon their harps." It is also another lyric introduced as *A Psalm or Song,* suggesting the unity of solemnity and vivacity. "A *Psalm* is a *song,* but all *songs* are not Psalms: this is both the one and the other. Then it is another anonymous Psalm, but he would be a bold man who should not attempt to prove that David did not write it. We will be hard pushed before we will look for any other author upon whom to father these anonymous odes which lie side by side with those ascribed to David, and wear a family likeness to them."

Franz Delitzsch says of the whole Psalm, "There are seven stanzas; twice three two-line stanzas, having one of three lines in the middle, which forms the clasp or spangle of the septiad, a circumstance which is strikingly appropriate to the fact that the Psalm is called *Old Testament Paternoster,* by some old expositors."

C. S. Lewis, in his most refreshing study, *Reflections on the Psalms,* has a chapter on *"Judgment* in the Psalms," in which, quoting verse 4 of the Psalm before us, "O let the nations rejoice and be glad, for thou shalt judge the fold righteously," Lewis was greatly surprised to discover that the Psalmist looked upon Divine judgment as apparently an occasion of universal rejoicing. "People ask for it, and are glad when He administers it."

Some ancient expositors called this Psalm, *The Lord's Prayer of the Old Testament,* because like the New Testament, this one has seven divisions. The first three verses and the last three are linked by a longer one in the middle, and the third and fifth verses are in the same words. It is by special distinction *The Missionary Psalm.*

In 1644 the Corporation of London invited the two Houses of Parliament to a grand banquet, in proof of the union of their cause and in celebration of their victory. The Westminster Assembly of Divines and the Scottish Commissioners were also invited, and Stephen Marshall, a noted preacher of that time, selected most appropriately as his text, 1 Chronicles 12:38-40, and the feast ended with the singing of Psalm 67, which, said a chronicler of the time, "was a religious precedent worthy to be imitated by all godly Christians in both their public and private meetings."

Psalm 68

Historical references to this marvelous Psalm or Song of David abound. What an unceasing inspiration it has been in the lives of the saints down the ages! This most soul-stirring hymn was adopted by many warriors in their battle-song. It was known among the Huguenots as *The Song of Battle,* and was raised by them in many a bloody and desperate conflict. It was the massacre of the Huguenots which finally provoked the Wars of Religion, and when once the sword was drawn, their Psalms became the war-songs. On the battlefields of Coligny and Henry of Navarre could be heard the chants of Psalms 75 and 118, or, above all the metrical version of Psalm 68, composed by Theodore de Beza, 1519-1605. In 1589 when the Huguenots gained a victory at Dieppe, the roll of cannon marked the time of the austere melody of Psalm 68, by which they had marched.

At the siege of Montauban in August, 1621, one night, a Protestant soldier serving in the king's army played under the battlements of the town the familiar tune of Psalm 68, "Let God arise and let his enemies be scattered." It was a signal that the siege was raised. The next day the camp was struck, and the royalists retired.

This is not to be wondered at for the Psalm itself is one of "wonderful power and compass, of living fire and dramatic picturesqueness, ranging from the remote past with its triumphs, onward to a final and irresistible victory in the future; with figures which startle us by their sternness (v. 23), and others (v. 30), that teach us the spirit in which we should read the whole." Garments rolled in blood result in the conquest of the King of righteousness and peace, and "the sword in the Psalm is that which God permits, in His righteous government, the sword with which sin executes judgment on itself; the peace is that which Christ promises as His legacy and gift, and which is more fully described in Psalm 72."

Antony, 251-356, the most famous example of the ascetic principle, was often beset by evil tendencies, but rejoiced when Satan was put to flight. There was a time when a Psalm was his paean of victory, for high and clear rose Antony's voice, as he chanted Psalm 68, in triumph over his spiritual foes.

It would seem as if Browning used this Psalm in the same way as Antony, for as *Guiseppe Caponsacchi* watches by the side of Pompilia, hears her moaning in her restless, fevered dreams, and sees her fade away

232

from some evil spirit that threatens her, Browning in *The Ring and the Book,* hears Caponsacchi cry—

> Oh, if the God, that only can, would help!
> Am I his priest with power to cast out fiends?
> "Let God arise and all his enemies
> Be scattered!" By morn, this was peace, no sigh
> Out of the deep sleep.

Charlemagne, named by Pope Hadrian as his champion and by the people as their deliverer, ultimately received from Pope Leo III, "the diadem of the Caesars," with the people praying for long life and victory to "Charles, the most pious Augustus, crowned by God, the peace-giving Emperor." Fourteen years later on January 28th, 814, he died at Aix-la-Chapelle, and although with his last breath he repeated the prayer, "Into Thy hands I commend my spirit," Psalm 31:6, Charlemagne's favorite Psalm was Psalm 68.

It was on April 7th, 1498 that a crisis occurred that sealed Jerome Savonarola's fate. Along with his brother monks, he chanted Psalm 68 as they marched into the Piazza of Florence to meet the trial of fire—a Franciscan friar had challenged Savonarola to prove the truth of his preaching. "Let God arise, and let His enemies be scattered," was a hollow chant, for the episode resulted in Savonarola's execution on May 22nd, 1498.

It was in 1653 that the Barebones Parliament, London, was constituted, and on July 4th as Oliver Cromwell was standing by the window of the Council Chamber, he delivered a speech to his army officers which was loaded with references to Psalm 68. In his exposition, Cromwell said, "God is bringing His people out of deep waters. Kings of armies have fled, and the spoil has been divided. Indeed the triumph of this Psalm is exceeding high and great; and God is accomplishing it. And the close of it—that closeth with my heart, and I do not doubt yours—The Lord shaketh the hills and mountains, and they reel. And God hath a hill too; an high hill as the Hill of Bashan; and the chariots of God are 20,000, even thousands of angels; and God will dwell upon this hill forever."

In Russian history, September 1812 is a momentous date to remember for that was when the French Army entered Moscow, and after burning the city, there came the retreat which marked the turning-point in the fortunes of Napoleon. At the Church Service held to celebrate the retreat of the French, the Metropolitan of Moscow preached from "Let God arise, and let His enemies be scattered," 68:1. What a supreme moment of triumph that was for the people who were left in the smoking ruins of their city!

Generally, the British people do not know that the language of Psalm

68:1 is the basis of their National Anthem. In July 1650, when Oliver Cromwell had trouble with Scotland, he encountered hard and difficult times. The Scottish General, however, failed to drive back the Covenant forces, as they marched and shouted their watchword, *The Lord of Hosts.* From Cromwell's lips came the triumphant cry, "Let God arise, and let His enemies be scattered," 68:1. It was this same verse that the covenanter, Patrick Walter, used to encourage his followers in 1685 when preaching in the night-time in a barn at Garrick upon that text, Psalm 68:1, 2, "Let God arise, and let His enemies be scattered; let them also that hate Him flee before Him. As smoke is driven, so drive Thou them." Walker made the following application of these verses—

> The Duke of York, and now King of Britain, a known enemy of God and godliness; it was by the vengeance of God that he ever got that name; but as you see me throw away that chaff, so that the wind of vengeance shall blow and drive him off that throne; and he, nor no other of that name, shall ever come on it again.

Psalm 68 was the war-cry of the Britons at Mold, of the Knights Templars, of Demetrius of the Don.

That Shakespeare was familiar with this same Psalm is evident from his description of God in *Richard II,* as the "widow's champion and defense," taken from the Psalmist's description, "Father of the fatherless, and defendest the cause of the widow," 68:5. Then the sentence, "Magnify Him that rideth upon the heavens, as it were upon an horse," 68:4 finds an echo in the address of Romeo to Juliet, where he compares her to "a winged messenger of Heaven"—

> When he bestrides the lazy-pacing clouds
> And sails upon the bosom of the air.

From the annals of the Covenanters we read that in February, 1685, Alexander McRobin was hanged upon an oak tree near the Kirk of Irongray. At the tree-foot, a friend asked him if he had any word to send to his wife. "I leave her and the two babies upon the Lord," answered McRobin, "and to his promise; a father to the fatherless, and a husband to the widow, is the Lord in His holy habitation," 68:5. His biographer says that this brave convenanter died "in much composure and cheerfulness."

During the Indian Mutiny in 1857, a most conspicuous figure was William Edwards, the magistrate and collector of Budaon in the Rohilkund district, who became a fugitive and was forced to leave his wife and child as Nynee Tal. Facing harrowing experience, Edward wrote in his Diary August 16th, after a sleepless night, devoured by mosquitoes, and depressed in mind because his wife was ignorant of his fate:

It is at such times I feel what the real blessing of the Psalms are. They never fail to give peace and refreshment, when all is dark and gloomy without and within. The circumstances under which many of them were written, seasons of danger and almost despair—David fleeing and hiding from bloodthirsty enemies, as we are—render them peculiarly suitable to our case. This morning I felt the 5th verse of the 68th Psalm most soothing, in the assurance it gives me that, if I am cut off, my God will be with my widow and fatherless children. He is a Father of the fatherless, and defendeth the cause of the widows, even God in His holy habitation.

During the Ecumenical Conference of Foreign Missions, New York, 1900, a delegate, Ethel E. Baldwin, made a profound impression upon the Assembly when in the course of her address she said,

I call Psalm 68:11 my resurrected text, it being only in the Revised Version, 'The Lord giveth the word; the *women* who publish the tidings are a great host.' Strangely enough this text was resurrected just as the doors opened in heathen lands calling for a host of women, and they are at work under this renewed commission.

John Bunyan in *Grace Abounding,* describing the discouragement that overtook him for more than two years, and vehemently desiring to know whether there was indeed hope for him, these words came rolling into his mind and brought him much consolation, "Thou hast received gifts for men, yea, even for Thine enemies," 68:18, and so he asked, "If God had gifts for His enemies, why not for me?"

Psalm 69

As for this 69th Psalm, Bishop John Hooper included it among those Psalms he recommended for their lessons of "patience and consolation," at times "when the mind can take no understanding, nor the heart any joy of God's promises," and we should give heed to its teaching, seeing it enabled the Bishop to be burned at the stake with unflinching courage. We cannot do better than ponder over Spurgeon's apt introduction to Psalm 69, in which he reminds us how fragrant it is because of its prophetic portrait of the Messiah. The title word *Shoshannim,* means, "upon the lilies," and in the Psalm "we have Jesus, the Lily of the Valley, the lily among thorns, fair and beautiful, blossoming in the Garden of Gethsemane."

Of the pre-signature, *A Psalm of David,* the famous Baptist preacher asks, "Of whom speaketh the psalmist?, of himself, or of some other man?" We would reply, "Of himself, and of some other Man." Who that other is we need not be long in discovering; it is the Crucified alone who can say, "In my thirst they gave me vinegar to drink." "His footprints all through this wonderful song have been pointed out by the Holy Spirit in the New Testament and therefore we believe, and are sure, that the Son of Man is here. Yet it seems to be the intention of the Spirit, while He gives us personal types, and so shows the likeness of the first-born which exists in the heirs of salvation, to set forth also the disparities between the best of the sons of men, and the Son of God, for there are verses here that do not apply. We almost shudder when we see our brethren attempting to do so, for instance verse 5. Especially do we note the difference between David and the Son of David in the imprecations of the one against his enemies, and the prayers of the other *for* them. We commence our exposition of this Psalm with much trembling, for we feel we are entering with our Great High Priest, into the most holy place."

John Gadsby, in *My Wanderings,* vividly describes an experience he had while walking along the banks of the Nile. He came across a boatman sinking in the thick water, and who was almost drowned, had it not been for his deathlike grip on his boat. Then Gadsby goes on to say, "How I thought of poor David! Had he really witnessed a similar scene to this literally when, speaking of the feelings of his soul, spiritually, he said, *I sink in deep mire, where there is no standing; I am come into deep waters, where the floods overflow me,* 69:2. Oh what an agonizing state to be in."

Without a cause, 69:4, is the phrase used of Jesus in the affirmation of His innocency of the crime for which His enemies said, "He was worthy to die." It is well known what Tertullian relates of Socrates, when his wife met him after his condemnation and spoke to him with a woman's tears, *Thou art unjustly condemned, Socrates.* His reply was, *Wouldst thou have me justly?* Iniquities done to the innocent in his sufferings are not laid to the charge of the sufferer, but to him who inflicts suffering.

David's vehemence for Heaven boiled up into a fervent passion, *The zeal of thine house hath eaten me up,* 69:9. The Greek word for *zeal* signifies "to stretch out the neck," a metaphor taken from racers who strain every limb, and reach forward to lay hold upon the prize. We read of the Prophetess Anna that "she departed not from the temple, but served God with fastings and prayers, night and day." It is said that Martin Luther spent three hours a day in prayer, and that for holy Bradford, preaching, reading the Word, and prayer were his whole life. It was certainly true of Jesus that a zeal for God's glory and honor consumed Him.

When, in the 16th century Archbishop Laud was imprisoned in the Tower of London, and slanders and abusive ballads were used against him by his opponents, he comforted himself with the thought that he was "in the same case as the Prophet David"—*They that sit in the gate speak against me; and the drunkards make songs upon me,* 69:12. Laud was executed at Tower Hill, January 10th 1645, in his seventy-second year of life.

Although sackcloth was his garment, David made the personal vow, "But as for me, my prayer is unto Thee, O Lord, in an acceptable time," 69:13—which decision is embodied in a German stanza—

> The heavier the cross, the heartier the prayer;
>   the bruised herbs most fragrant are.
> If sky and wind were always fair,
>   The sailor would not watch the star;
>   And David's Psalm had ne'er been sung
>   If grief his heart had never wrung.

Recompense for inhumanity and cruelty is wrapped up in the sentiment, "Let their table become a snare," 69:22. Michaelis the historian tells us how exactly these words were fulfilled in the history of the final siege of Jerusalem by the Romans. Many thousands of Jews had assembled in the city to eat the Paschal Lamb, when Titus unexpectedly made an assault upon them. In the siege, the greater part of the inhabitants of Jerusalem miserably perished.

Christopher Wordsworth emphasizes the historical illustration of the Divine retribution the Jews suffered. "They gave gall and vinegar as food and drink to Christ; and their own spiritual food and drink has become a snare to them. His eyes were blindfolded; their eyes were darkened. His loins were scourged; their loins were made to shake."

C. S. Lewis, in his study on *The Psalms,* has a profitable chapter on "The Cursings" in this portion of Scripture. "In some of the Psalms the spirit of hatred which strikes us in the face is like a heat from a furnace mouth. In others the same spirit ceases to be frightful only by becoming— to a modern mind—almost comic in its naiveté." Dealing with Psalm 69:22—"Let their table become a snare to take themselves withal; and let the things that should have been for their wealth be unto them an occasion of failing." Lewis says that here "we get the refinement of malice."

Psalm 70

What a charming title this five-verse Psalm has!—*A Psalm of David, to bring to remembrance,*—a title corresponding to the contents of its counterpart, Psalm 40, of which Psalm 70 is a copy with variations. "David appears to have written the full-length Psalm (40)," says Spurgeon, "and also to have made this excerpt (Psalm 70) from it, and altered it to suit the occasion. It is a fit pendant to Psalm 69, and a suitable preface to Psalm 71." This Remembrance Psalm can rightly be called the poor man's memorial, for in it David personally pleads with God that he may not be forgotten, but David's Lord may be heard here also. "Even if the Lord seems to forget us, we must not forget Him. This memorial Psalm acts as a connecting link between the Psalms of supplicatory expostulation, and makes us with them a precious triad of song." A commentator of a previous century said that, historically, the Psalm as a whole applies to the state of the Christian Church after the Resurrection and Exaltation of Christ, and would put its words in the mouths of the faithful of that time.

Certainly the watchword of this Psalm—*Make Haste*—was the watchword of the Early Church as they thought of the promised return of Jesus. Spurgeon's own original hymn on the watchword is worthy of attention—

> Make haste, O God, my soul to bless!
> My help and my deliv'rer thou;
> Make hast, for I'm in deep distress,
> My case is urgent; help me now.

> Make haste, O God! make haste to save!
> For time is short, and death is nigh;
> Make haste ere yet I'm in my grave,
> And with the lost forever lie.

> Make haste, for I am poor and low;
> And Satan mocks my prayers and tears;
> O God, in mercy be not slow,
> But snatch me from my horrid fears.

> Make haste, O God, and hear my cries;
> Then with the souls who seek thy face,
> And those who thy salvation price,
> I'll magnify thy matchless grace.

Psalm 71

Mary, Queen of Scots, is supposed to have written some Latin lines on this great Psalm before her execution at Fotheringay on February 8th, 1589. Bishop Jewell, who confessed, "I rejoice that my body is exhausted in the labors of my holy calling," and who wrote, in 1562, *Apology For The Church Of England,* requested on his deathbed that Psalm 71 might be sung—and it was. When the singers came to the words, Thou, O Lord, art my hope and my trust from my youth up, Jewell cried out: "Thou, O Lord hast been my *only* hope." Then, as the singers reached the passage "Cast me not off in time of age," Jewell exclaimed, "Every one who is dying is, in truth, old and grey-headed, and failing in strength." The Psalm ended, the dying saint broke forth with frequent exclamations, "Lord, now lettest Thou Thy servant depart in peace"—"Lord, suffer thy servant to come to Thee—Lord, receive my spirit"—and so he died peacefully on September 23rd, 1571.

Slave emancipator, William Wilberforce, loved to study the Psalms, and when violently attacked by those involved in slavery, would turn to the Psalter for consolation. "The 71st Psalm, which I learned by heart lately, has been a real comfort to me," he wrote in a letter to his wife.

Origen, notable among the Early Fathers, loved this 71st Psalm and said of it, "This is my Scripture." Robert Blair, one of the most distinguished of the Covenanters, who died at Aberdour in 1666, broken by age, infirmity, and anxiety for the public interest, cherished this Psalm, and was accustomed to calling it "My Psalm." Just before he died, he repeated the whole of it and with much feeling repeated, "Now also when I am old and the grey headed, O God, forsake me not."

Philip de Morny, known as Plessis de Morny, a man of illustrious rank, chivalrous spirit, and sincere piety and who identified himself with the brave Huguenots and stood by them in every extremity, desired Psalm 71 to be read to him as he came to his deathbed, and it gave him infinite pleasure because of his experience of some of its expressions. One of the titleless Psalms of the Psalms, we can understand why it has been named *The Prayer of The Aged Believer.* John Howard of Prison Reform fame was a man who knew a great deal about the impact of the Psalms upon his life and work. In various crises he faced, the Psalms were his refuge. An entry from his Diary, when he was lying ill at the Hague in 1778, reads—

May 13th. In pain, and anguish all Night . . . help, Lord, for vain is the help of man. In Thee do I put my trust, let me not be confounded, 71:1.

Seneca, although reckoned as a heathen, could yet say, "Youth well spent is the greatest comfort of old age," which in Biblical language reads, "Thou art my trust from my youth," 71:5. When the proconsul bade Polycarp deny Christ and swear by the Emperor, he defiantly answered, "I have served Christ these 86 years, and he has not once injured me, and shall I now deny him?" When Geroge Herbert came to die in 1832, with his latest breath he repeated, "Forsake me not when my strength faileth," 71:9. Robert Sanderson, Bishop of Lincoln, the peaceful yet shining light of the Church during the Civil Wars, on the day before he died requested his chaplain to give him absolution, and the chaplain recorded, "After this desire of his was satisfied, his body seemed to be more at ease, and his mind more cheerful: and he repeated, Lord, forsake me not now my strength faileth me; but continue thy mercy, and let my mouth be filled with thy praise," 71:8.

No one can look upon a person tottering with years and broken down with infirmities—one whose sight and hearing are gone—one who is alone amidst the graves of all the friends possessed in early life—one who is a burden to himself and to the world—one who has reached the "last scene of all that ends the strange, eventful history"—that scene of

> Second childishness, and mere oblivion,
> Sans teeth, sans eyes, sans taste, sans everything

—that scene when one is heard to murmur—

> I have lived long enough; my way of life
> Is fallen into the sear, the yellow leaf;
> And that which should accompany old age,
> As honor, love, obedience, troops of friends,
> I must not look to have—

without praying with the Psalmist not to be cast off or forsaken in old age, but to have grace to grow old gracefully, bringing forth fruit to God's glory even in our old age. In this truth we can rest that God will not forsake us as we near the end of the race for He has promised never to leave us alone.

Sir Robert Grant left us a most impressive poem on the care of God till traveling days are done, the first and last verses we herewith cite—

> With fears oppressed, with sorrow worn,
> Dejected, harassed, sick, forlorn,
>   To thee, O God, I pray;
> To thee my withered hands arise,

To thee I lift these failing eyes:
 Oh, cast me not away.

Yea, broken, tuneless, still, O Lord,
This voice, transported, shall record
 Thy goodness tried so long;
Till, sinking slow, with calm decay,
Its feeble murmurs melt away
 Into a seraph's song.

During the Reign of Terror in France during the 18th century, Madam de Noailles, daughter-in-law of the then Marshal of France, was a lady of great beauty and character as well as depth of faith and love to God. Even the codicil of her will was laden with quotations from the Psalms. Precious to this noble handmaiden of the Lord, as she died with unflinching courage on the scaffold, July 22nd, 1794, was the prayer of David, "Forsake me not when my strength faileth me," 71:8, 10—which prayer was heard for this gracious lady died as magnificently as she had lived.

It was Canon Walter J. Edmonds of Exeter Cathedral, England, who at the beginning of the 19th century confessed—

> *Text of life-long helpfulness*—"I will go in the strength of the Lord God: I will make mention of Thy righteousness, even of Thine only," 71:16.

How wonderful it is to have God as a Teacher from the bloom of youth to old age! Such was the experience of David who could say, "Thou hast taught me from my youth," 71:17. Seneca, who certainly did not have God as his instructor yet said, *Virtue is a hard thing to youth, it needs a ruler and guide; vices are acquired without a master.* As for Plato, one of his literary gems reads, *There is nothing more divine than the education of children.* Plato in his treatise on the sacrifice of Cain and Abel wrote that, "Masters cannot fill the mind of their pupils as if they were pouring water into a vessel." But when God, the Fountain of Wisdom, communicates knowledge to a willing recipient, He does it without delay, in the twinkling of an eye.

Psalm 72

A thanasius, Archbishop of Alexandria, in the 3rd century made the Psalms his constant study as his two volumes, *Exposition of the Psalms* and *Titles of the Psalms*, as well as the numerous allusions to the Psalms in his other works, reveal. In hours of his own danger, as well as in crises facing his people, and Archbishop would quote his favorite Psalm which was the 72nd, and say, "Against all assaults upon thy body, thine estate, thy soul, thy reputation, and all temptations, tribulations, plots and slanderous reports this Psalm is thy refuge." Athanasius had proved it to be so in his own turbulent experience.

John Ruskin includes Psalm 72 among the Psalms, "containing the law and the prophecy of all just government." That he believed they contain a compendium of human life is emphasized in his lines on the Psalmist's work—

> That which he hath writ
> Is with such judgment labor'd, and distill'd
> Through all the needful uses of our lives,
> That could a man remember but his lines,
> He should not touch at any serious point
> But he might breathe his spirit out of him.

The title informs us that this is *A Psalm For Solomon*. Scholars have debated whether it should be *For* or *By* Solomon. Although it is declared that it is a Psalm Solomon likely wrote yet from verse 20, it seems as if David uttered it in prayer before he died. Spurgeon suggests that "the spirit and matter of the Psalm are David's but that he was too near his end to pen the words, or cast them into form. Solomon, therefore, caught his dying father's song, fashioned it into goodly verse, and without robbing his father made the Psalm his own. It is, we conjecture, the Prayer of David, but the Psalm of Solomon."

A striking feature of the Psalm is its Messianic outlook, for He Who came as the Messiah is here, beyond doubt, in the glory of His reign, both as He now is, and as He shall be revealed in the latter-day glory. Readers of *The Scofield Bible* will check this foot-note, along with a serviceable outline on this Psalm—"As a whole it forms a complete vision of Messiah's kingdom so far as O. T. revelation extended. All David's prayers will find their fruition in the Kingdom, 72:26 with 2 Samuel 23:1-4."

The prophecy that "the mountains shall bring peace to the people," 72:3, has received this fitting explanation—

> That the steep mountains on the frontier, strongly garrisoned, shall secure the land from hostile invasion; and the hills cleared of the banditti, which in the rude ages were accustomed to inhabit them, under the government of the King, intended in this Psalm, should be the peaceful seats of a useful, civilized peasantry.

Merrick has caught the sense of the passage in the lines—

> Peace, from the fort-clad mountain's brow,
> Descending, bless the plains below;
> And justice from each rocky cell,
> Such violence and fraud expel.

The declaration that men "shall fear Messiah as long as the sun and morn endure," 72:5, is proved by the unceasing homage He has received through succeeding ages. Since Jesus ascended from earth to His throne above well-nigh two millenniums ago, His dominion has not been recognized though "the mightiest of Empires have gone like visions in the night. We see on the shores of time the wrecks of the Caesars, the relics of the Moguls, and the last remnants of the Ottomans. Charlemagne, Maximillian, Napoleon, and Hitler, how they flit like shadows before us! They were but are not; but Jesus is forever is. Many rulers have had their hour: but the Son of David has all hours and ages as his own."

The humiliating action, "His enemies shall lick the dust," 72:9, reflects a custom with many nations that when individuals approached their kings, they kissed the earth and prostrated their whole body before them. This was the custom especially throughout Asia. No one was allowed to address the Persian kings unless he prostrated himself on the ground and kissed the footsteps of the king. Spurgeon's forceful comment on the phrase says, "Truly no sign is too humiliating to denote the utter discomfiture and subjugation of Messiah's foes. Tongues which rail at the Redeemer deserve to lick the dust. Those who will not joyfully bow to such a Prince rightly merit to be hurled down and laid prostrate; the dust is too good for them, since they trampled on the blood of Christ."

In Christian Art the conventional representation of the Wise Men of the East, who sought out the infant Jesus as three kings, is founded on the Kings of Tharbis, Saba, and Arabia, as found in 72:10-11.

The proverb that "God helps those that help themselves," does not bear the light of David's affirmation that, "God shall deliver the needy when he crieth; the poor also, and him that hath no helper," 72:13, 14. It is more true to say that God helps those who cannot help themselves, nor find help in others. Thomas à Kempis, in his *Soliloquy of the Soul*, includes the phrase, "Blessed be the name of His majesty forever," 72:19, among his texts taken from the Psalms.

Psalm 73

Crude pictures, still to be seen on the walls of subterranean Rome, tell the story of the infancy of Christianity when the persecuted saints met secretly at night or at early dawn to worship the Lord. At their gatherings the Psalms were prominent, and special Psalms were soon appropriated for special occasions, such as Psalm 73 for morning worship and Psalm 141 for the evening worship. John Hooper, Bishop of Gloucester, while in prison wrote an exposition of this Psalm and of its opening verse, "Truly God is loving unto Israel, even unto such as be of a clean heart." This courageous martyr said, "We must learn to say this verse whether it be winter or summer, pleasure or pain, liberty or imprisonment, life or death." Writing from prison where his bed was but "a little pad of straw," Hooper bade his wife, Anne, to read Psalm 77 because of the "great consolation" which it contains for those who are "in anguish of mind."

When Coligny was carried off the field after his defeat at Montcontous in 1569, his thoughts turned to the Psalms. Almost suffocated by the blood of three wounds pouring into his closed visor, a close friend who was being carried wounded beside Coligny heard him repeat the opening words of this Psalm—*Si est-ce que Dieu est très doux*—"Truly God is good to Israel." An historian of the time wrote, "That great captain confessed afterwards that this short phrase refreshed him, and put him in the way of good thoughts and firm resolutions for the future." If the whole Psalm is read, it will be seen to be singularly suited to such an emergency, as Dr. John Ker's observation indicates "and so well were Psalms then known, that the first verse called up the whole."

Dryden's stanza on the first clause of 73:1 is apt—

> Yet sure the gods are good: I would think so,
> If they would give me leave!
> But virtue in distress, and vice in triumph,
> Makes atheists of mankind.

Life is replete with examples of "the prosperity of the wicked," 73:3, but we are not to be envious of their ill-gotten gains. Actius Sincerus, a man of rare wit and great reputation, when in the presence of King Frederic, witnessed a discussion among physicians on what would most effectually sharpen their eyesight! The fumes of fennel, said some; the use of glass, said others; some one thing, some another: "but I, said he, replied—*Envy*. The doctors were astonished, and much amusement afforded to the audience at their expense. Then I continued: Does not *Envy* make all things seem larger and fuller? And what could be more to your purpose than that the very faculty of seeing should itself be made greater and stronger."

It is said that Socrates, being asked what would be vexatious to good men, replied, *The prosperity of the bad*. What would vex the bad, *The prosperity of the good*. Diogenes, the heathen cynic, seeing Harpalus, a vicious fellow, still thriving in the world, was bold to say that wicked Harpalus's living long in prosperity was an argument that God had cast off His care of the world, that He cared not which end went forward. We know, of course, that God does care, and that while He may not pay His accounts at once—at last He pays.

The description the Psalmist gives of the prosperous wicked, "Therefore pride compasseth them about as a chain," 73:5, often appears in the godless who because of their ill-gotten gains think they have a license to ride roughshod over others. Plato said of Protagoras that he boasted whereas he had lived 60 years, he had spent 40 years in corrupting youth. The Lord have mercy on those who brag of that which they ought to bewail.

Many of the facts of life troubled the Psalmist and gave him pain, "until he went into the sanctuary of God; then understood he their end," 73:17. Writing in 1871, Thomas Jones said, "Providence is often mysterious and a source of perplexity to us. Walking in Hyde Park, London, one day, I saw a piece of paper on the grass. I picked it up; it was a part of a letter; the beginning was wanting, the end was not there; I could make nothing of it. Such is Providence. You cannot see beginning or end, only a part. When you can see the whole, then the mystery will be unveiled."

David's definition of God as one awaking out of a dream is somewhat bold, yet the conception is somewhat subtle, and seems to have been shrewdly penetrated by Shakespeare, who makes the Plantagenet prince—affecting, perhaps the airs of a ruler in God's stead—say to his discarded favorite in *Henry IV*—

> I have long dreamt of such a kind of man,
> So surfeit swelled, so old and so profane,
> But being awake I do despise my dream

Among the illustrious women of Rome in the 3rd century who learned *Hebrew* that they might sing the Psalms in the native tongue, and Greek, that they might study the Gospel, was Paula, who figures largely in Jerome's writings. It was to Paula's daughter, Eustochium, that he addressed his first code of Christian Virginity; and to Paula's step-daughter, Loeta, his first treatise on the Christian Education of women. Paula and Eustochium wandered through Palestine with Jerome, and finally settled in Bethlehem and built a monastry of which Jerome became the head; a convent, presided over by Paula; a church, and a hospice for pilgrims. When the two ladies tried to induce Marcella, a young and wealthy Roman widow, to leave Rome and settle in the Holy Land, Jerome supported their appeal with a letter which closed with the words,

> For ourselves who are here, we think it good to trust God for all, to rest our hope on Him; that when we exchange the poverty of this world for the riches of Heaven, we may be able to cry with David, "Whom have I in Heaven but Thee? and there is none upon earth that I desire in comparison of Thee." 73:24.

But Marcella remained in Rome.

Charles Wesley, brother of John Wesley, wrote some 6,500 hymns, some of which are unsurpassed in beauty and rank among the finest in the English language. On his death-bed in March 1788, the train of Charles' thought was around Psalm 73:25, 26. "My flesh and my heart faileth; but God is the strength of my heart, and my portion forever." Verse took shape, and calling his wife to his side, he dictated this last exercise of his wonderful gift—

> In age and feebleness extreme,
> What shall a sinful worm redeem?
> Jesus, my only hope thou art,
> Strength of my failing flesh and heart;
> O could I catch a smile from thee,
> And drop into Eternity.

That no Christian stands alone is affirmed by David's assurance, "God is the strength of my heart, and my portion forever," 73:26. The Hebrew is most expressive. "God is the rock of my heart," that is, a sure, strong, and immovable foundation to build upon. The phrase *And my portion* is a metaphor taken from the ancient custom among the Jews of dividing inheritances whereby every one had his allotted portion; as if he had said, God is not only my rock to defend me from those tempests which assault me, and, thereby, my freedom from evil; but He is also my portion, to supply my necessities, and to give me the fruition of all good.

David's personal assertion, "It is good for me to draw near to God," is one that all believers have proved, 73:28. The Epicurean, says Augustine, is wont to say, *It is good for me to enjoy the pleasures of the flesh!* The Stoic is wont to say, *For me it is good to enjoy the pleasures of the mind.* The Apostle used to say—not in words, but in the sense—*It is good for me to cleave unto God.* To draw near to God Who is our wisdom, our honor, our safety, our peace, our spiritual riches, is an imperative approach.

Psalm 74

When, under Louis XIII and Louis XIV, there were successive edicts forbidding the use of Psalms in homes and Protestant houses of worship and the Huguenots were compelled to continue the singing of them in caves or forests, these severely persecuted saints had to endure the hardship of a winter journey across the Alps. Yet, with voices choked by exhaustion and misery, they sang, "O God, wherefore art Thou absent from us so long? Why is thy wrath so hot against the sheep of Thy pasture?" Psalm 74:1. The exiles streamed into Geneva where the words were re-echoed by the crowds who thronged the streets of the City of Refuge.

Three years later, in 1689, this same Psalm was chanted in triumph by seven hundred of the exiles, who, led by their pastor, Henri Arnaud, had fought their way back to their homes. Their enthusiasm was inexpressible, as they sang the 74th Psalm to the clash of arms, as the people settled again in their ancient and rightful settlement.

The Pentland Rising, in 1666, brought Patrick Walker to the fore as leader of an "honest zealous handful," as he called them. Armed resistance to forces alien to witness of the Covenanters failed to curb the onward march of Dalzell's well-appointed troops. As Walker retreated with his diminished numbers, hopelessly overmatched, the defeated company raised their appeal to God in the metrical version of this 74th Psalm—

> O God, why hast Thou cast us off?
>   Is it for evermore?
> Against Thy pasture-sheep why doth
>   Thine anger smoke so sore?

Over the grave of those who perished in this struggle was a stone inscribed with rugged lines beginning thus—

> A cloud of witnesses lie here
> Who for Christ's interest did appear.
> And to restore true liberty,
> O'erturned them by tyranny;
> These heroes fought with great renown
> By falling got the martyr's crown.

We can fully understand why tortured saints turned to this Psalm in their agony, seeing it contains the cry of a people on the brink of despair, calling upon God Who seems to stand with face averted and arms inactive. The appeal to Him was bold beyond measure, yet deep in its humility. Agonizing is the feeling of forsakenness and neglect, the troubled were yet full of faith, and Jacob-like cried, "We will not let thee go."

Whether this instructive Psalm by Asaph is a prophetic Psalm, intended for us in troubles unseen, or whether it was written by a later Asaph after the invasion of Sennacherib or during the Maccabean Wars, is hard to determine, is Spurgeon's observation on the historical background of the Psalm. In times of dire distress and fiery trials before us, no strange thing is happening unto us, for we are but following the trial of the host of God who have failed to see Him in the thick darkness.

Henry H. Milman, historian of the 18th century, in his *History of the Jews*, applies Psalm 74:4-7 to the persecution under Antiochus in 168 B.C.

> Athenaeus proceeded to Jerusalem, where, with the assistance of the garrison, he prohibited and suppressed every observance of the Jewish religion, forced the people to profane the Sabbath, to eat swine's flesh and other unclean food, and expressly forbade the national rite of cricumcision. The Jewish Temple was dedicated to Jupiter Olympus; the statue of that deity was erected on part of the altar of burnt offerings, and sacrifice daily performed. . . . As a last insult, the feasts of Bacchanalia, the license of which, as they were celebrated, in the latter ages of Greece, shocked the severe virtue of the older Romans, were substituted for the national festival of Tabernacles. The reluctant Jews were forced to join in these riotous orgies, and to carry the ivy, the insignia of the God. So near was the Jewish nation, and the worship of Jehovah to total extermination.

They set up their ensigns for signs, 74:4. Josephus, the renowned recorder of Jewish history around the time of Christ, wrote that the Romans, upon the flight of the Jews, burned their holy house and all buildings associated with it, and brought their own Roman ensigns and set them up over against the eastern-gate; and there offered sacrifices to them, and there made Titus *imperator,* with the greatest acclamation of joy.

The perverted use of the axe, found in the verse *Now they break down the carved work thereof at once with axes and hammers,* 74:6, had a fulfillment when Demetrius took a picture by Protogenes from the suburbs of Rhodes, and was besought by the Rhodians to be lenient towards their art, fearing that he would destroy the famous picture. He replied that he would sooner burn the statues of his father than so great a work of art. But not all barbarian invaders are willing to spare famous buildings and treasures for art's sake. Their ferocity finds vent in ruthlessly destroying sculptured edifices, polished with the greatest skill.

How lamentable was the sign, *We see not our signs*—those visible tokens of the miraculous God they served! 74:9. The signs in question, the Psalmist could not see and mourned over, were certain memorials that God was with His people and would continue to bless them. It is said that there were five things in Solomon's temple destroyed by Nebuchadnezzar which were not in the second temple erected after the Babylonian Captivity. Five memorials, tokens, or signs of God's special presence were lacking. They were—

The Ark of the Covenant

The Fire from Heaven upon the Brazen Altar

The Shechinah, or cloud resting upon the Mercy Seat

The Urim and Thummim which were in the breast-plate of the High Priest

The Spirit of Prophecy, ceasing with Malachi and reappearing with John the Baptist.

The Divine law of alternation is expressed in the phrase, *The day is Thine, the night is also Thine,* 74:16. God's hand that rules the world in its orbit, makes it fulfill its course through light and shade, is governing our lives for a higher than earthly end. *Day—Night,* each had its time and use. How illustrative of this verse, and how touching are the verses taken from *The Circle of the Year.*

> Ah! don't be sorrowful, darling,
> And don't be sorrowful, pray—
> Taking the year together, my dear,
> There isn't more night than day.
>
> And God is God, my darling,
> Of night as well as day;
> And we feel and know that we can go,
> Wherever He leads the way.
>
> A God of the night, my darling
> Of the night of death so grim,
> The gate that leads out of life, good wife,
> Is the gate that leads to Him.

Psalm 75

As the Psalter is made up of 150 Psalms, with Psalm 75 we come to the last one in the first equal section of the Psalter. John Ruskin names it last in the Psalms he marks out as containing "the law and the prophecy of all just government." Bearing the title, *Al-taschith*, we have here another of the DESTROY NOT Psalms. This mid-way Psalm was composed as a check upon the natural fierceness of the oppressed, or a taunt for the savage foe who, in the Psalm, is bitterly bidden to destroy not, because the nation is well aware that he cannot. The virgin daughter of Zion despises her foe, and laughs him to scorn. It would seem as if the destruction of Sennacherib's army is a striking and notable illustration of this sacred song which is entitled, *A Psalm or Song of Asaph.* Spurgeon's rich comment on such is that the Psalm is "for reading or singing. A hymn to God and a song for His saints. Happy were the people who having found a *Milton* in *David* had an almost equal songster in Asaph; happiest of all, because these poets were not inspired by earth's Castalian fount, but drank of the fount of every blessing."

From verses 6 to 10 of Psalm 75, we learn that the rise and fall of nations is ascribed to God Who has the prerogative, as the Creator of the ends of the earth, to exalt one empire and put down another at His pleasure. None can stay His hand, and ask, What doest Thou? Usually, when nations or individuals are prosperous, glorious, and powerful, they ascribe all glory to themselves or to fortune. But it is God Who raised them to eminence. When nations boast of their expansion, He can humble them as He did in World War II under the Hitler regime. The Psalmist would have us remember, then, that God is the Governor of the World, punishing the wicked and pouring out judgments on His enemies. Often the ministers of Providence executing wrath are war, pestilence, and famine. In days of national, or personal glory, it is as well to remember the lines of Isaac Watts—

> Here He exalts neglected worms
> To scepters and a crown;
> Anon the following page He turns,
> And treads the monarch down.

Psalm 76

What a stirring Psalm this is! It begins with God having a great name in Israel and concluded with Him being "terrible to the kings of the earth." "The Psalm is indeed a most jubilant war-song, a paean to the King of Kings, the hymn of a theocratic nation to its Divine Ruler." The *faith* in the previous Psalm, sung of victories to come, here becomes a song of triumphs achieved. When beset by fears of impending invasion by the Norsemen in the 11th century, it was with this Psalm that the English invoked Divine aid feeling that it voiced their faith in, and gratitude for, a decisive victory over the invaders. Psalm 76 was also one of the war-songs of the Huguenots, chanted on the battlefields of Coligny or Henry of Navarre.

Other historical appearances of the Psalm prove its continuing influence in the lives of those prominent in the cause of Truth. For instance, the Scottish Covenanters loved to sing this Psalm when Governmental activities were directed against their freedom of worship. If they gathered elsewhere than where the Government dictated, they were shot where found, and their bodies left to rot where they fell. This was the period James Renwick described when fields, "flowered the mosses with martyrs." June 1st, 1679, was an historical day at Drumclog. It was a Sunday, and the Covenanters met for worship in a forbidden place. "Bloody Claverhouse," as he was known because of his slaughter of the Covenanters, heard of the meeting, and with his dragoons, came upon the gathered company. One of the group, however, who acted as sentry saw Claverhouse approach, gave the alarm, and the armed men drew out from the surprised congregation to meet the foe. Although poorly armed, they were skillfully led and resolute of heart. Meeting the dragoons, the Covenanters raised their challenge in the words of this Psalm to the tune of *Martyrs*—

> In Judah's land God is well known,
>> His name's in Israel great;
> In Salem is his tabernacle;
>> In Zion is his seat.
>
> There arrows of the bow he brake,
>> The shield, the sword, the war,

> More glorious thou than hills of prey,
>   More excellent art far.
>
> Those that were stout of heart were spoiled,
>   They slept their sleep outright;
> And none of those their hands did find,
>   That were the men of might.

After this noble burst of triumph which in Bible times, celebrated the overthrow of Sennacherib and his host, Claverhouse escaped with great difficulty, being carried off the field by some of his men with his "guts hung out half an ell," from a pitchfork thrust in his belly.

Almost a century before this defeat of Government forces, this same Psalm 76 was sung at the Market Cross, Edinburgh, by Robert Bruce, descendant of the great King Robert, when the news came of the defeat and dispersion of the proud Spanish Armada. Bruce, like his royal name-sake, was such a man of majesty and power that John Livingstone who heard him said, "there had been no such preacher since the days of the Apostles, and never would be again . . . Everyone of his prayers seemed like a strong bolt shot up to Heaven."

Doubtless Drumclog was ever in the memory of the Covenanters who succeeded those who defeated Claverhouse. Then years after Bruce led the large audience in the singing of the battle-hymn of Psalm 76, Alexander Shiels, author of *The Hind Let Loose,* led a chorus of Covenanters, at Market Cross, Douglas, in celebration of the Revolution.

The venerable Charles Kingsley had a special love for Psalm 76. When voyaging up the Rhine in August, 1851, and looking on the hills crowned with the ruined strongholds of freebooters, he wrote in his Diary—

> How strange that my favorite Psalm about the hills of robbers—hills of prey—should have come in course the very day I went up the Rhine.

Then, as Prothero reminds us, it was "to the singing of Psalms that the sails of the *Mayflower* were set to catch the winds that wafted the Pilgrim Fathers to the white sandbanks of Cape Cod; and to their music were laid the foundations of the United States of America." *In Salem is His taber-nacle,* 76:2, were the words which suggested to John Endicott's company the name of their first settlement. It is not generally known that until the end of the 18th century, the Psalms were exclusively sung in the churches and chapels of America.

The stouthearted are spoiled, 76:5. They came to spoil, but became the *spoil* of those they attacked. What a scene that must have been when Sennacherib's host was utterly destroyed in one night. The hands which were furious to pull down the walls of Jerusalem could not even be raised from the sod, the most valiant warriors were as weak as the palsied cripples at the temple gate. Their eyes they could not open, a deep, deep sleep sealed their vision in everlasting darkness. *They have slept their sleep.* Not Sennacherib, nor Nisroth his god, but Jehovah alone, who with a silent rebuke had withered all the monarch's host. *Thou, even Thou, art to be feared,* 76:7.

> Fear Him, ye saints, and then ye shall
> Have nothing else to fear.

He shall cut off the spirit of princes, 76:12. Sennacheribs, Caesars, Napoleons, and Hitlers fall unto God's power as the boughs of the tree beneath the woodman's axe. How expressive are the verses of George Gordon—Lord Byron—on the manifestation of Divine power emphasized by the Psalmist, 76:5, 6.

> For the Angel of Death spread his wings on the blast,
> And breathed in the face of the foe as he passed;
> And the eyes of the sleepers waxed deadly and chill,
> And their hearts but once heaved, and for ever were still.
>
> And there lay the steed with his nostril all wide,
> But through it there rolled not the breath of his pride;
> And the foam of his gasping lay white on the turf,
> And cold as the spray of the rock-beating surf.
>
> And there lay the rider distorted and pale,
> With the dew on his brow and the rest on his mail;
> And the tents were all silent, the banners alone,
> The lances uplifted, the trumpet unblown.

Vow and pay unto the Lord your God, 76:11. These were the words the Archbishop of Canterbury used, when in 1132, some 13 associates of the Cistercian Order begged for protection, which the Archbishop was able to give as Legate of the Apostolic See. He urged them, in the words of the Psalmist, to follow the vows of their profession, "Promise unto the Lord your God, and keep it; pay the vows unto the most Highest; I will pay thee my vows which I promised with my lips." The Archbishop knew that the luxury of the surroundings had choked the spiritual aspirations of those who had sought his aid.

Behind the phrase, *He shall cut off the spirit of princes,* 76:12, is speed of action, as when one cuts off immediately a bunch of grapes from the vine. Sudden changes have overtaken many who boasted of their royalty, honors, and wealth. Victorious Henry the Fourth was a prince suddenly cut off. Although he had fought 52 pitched battles, he became poverty-stricken before he died and was forced to petition the Church of Spier to maintain him in his old age.

Another historic illustration of the Psalmist's fiat is the reports of King Gillimer by Procopious. A potent King of the Vandals, Gillimer was brought so low as to intreat his friend to send him a sponge, a loaf of bread, and a harp; a sponge to dry his tears, a loaf of bread to sustain his life, and a harp to solace himself in his misery.

Yet again the Psalmist's word about cutting off princes had a fulfillment in what Philip de Comines reported of a Duke of Exeter, who though he married Edward the Fourth's sister, yet he saw him in the Low Countries begging barefoot. Bellisarius, the chief man living in his time, having his eyes put out, was led at last on a string, crying, "Give a halfpenny to Bellisarius."

Psalm 77

Three Psalms are dedicated to Jeduthun, namely, 39, 62, 77. Originally known as *Ethan* (See 1 Chron. 9:16 etc.), Jeduthun was a Levite, and a chief singer and instructor; and it was but fitting that Asaph should append the musician's name to his Psalm, set somewhat in the minor key. There was a touch of sadness about thoughtful Asaph that imparted a tonic flavor to his songs. As to the position of the Psalm, perhaps it was meant to be a prelude to the next one, which would account for its sudden close. The hymn now before us is for experienced saints only, but to them it will be of rare value as a transcript of their own inner conflicts. All students of the Psalms are familiar with J. J. Stewart Perowne's most valuable Commentary on them. Of the contents of Psalm 77, he says: "The allusions to national history may indeed show that the season was a season of national distress, and that the sweet singer was himself bowed down by the burden of time, and oppressed by the woes which he had no power to alleviate, but it is his own sorrow, not the sorrow of others under which he sighs, and of which he has left the pathetic record."

It was this Psalm, Bishop John Hooper urged his wife, who had escaped to the Continent, to read. In a letter to her, written on October 13th, 1553, Hooper said that phrases like "I will cry unto God with my whole voice," were of "great consolation" to those "in anguish of mind." François de Sales, Bishop of Geneva, 1567-1622, had a mind so steeped in the Psalter that his thoughts naturally clothed themselves in the words of the Psalms. Among these was the verse, "When I am in heaviness, I will think upon Thee." 77:3.

John Bunyan was another who lived, moved, and had his being in the Psalms, as his great Puritan allegory reveals. In his *Grace Abounding,* which is a reflection of Bunyan's own nature, he was so sin-stricken at one time, and desired to know whether there was any hope for him. Then the words came rolling in his mind from Asaph's Psalm—

> Will the Lord absent Himself forever; and will He be no more intreated? Is His mercy clean gone forever; and is His promise come utterly to an end for evermore? Hath God forgotten to be gracious, and will He shut up His lovingkindness in His displeasure? 77:7-9.

Great deliverance came to the troubled, struggling conscience of

Bunyan when suddenly the sentence fell upon his soul, *Thy righteousness is in Heaven.*

The lament, yet the action, *This is my infirmity: but I will remember the years of the right hand of the most high,* 77:10, suggests that the bent and inclination of the soul is right, but either through some violence, corruption or strength of temptation, a person is diverted and turned out of the way. As the needle in the seaman's compass, you know if it be right if it will stand always northwards, the bent of it will be toward the North Pole, but being jogged and troubled, it may sometimes be put out of frame and order, yet the bent and inclination of it is still northward; this is an infirmity.

The description the Psalmist gives us of Divine Providence—*Thy footsteps are not known,* 77:19—prompts us to say that where we cannot *trace* God we can certainly *trust* Him. When Martin Luther encountered an affair of great importance occurring in some providential dispensation, he was very importunate at the Throne of Grace to ascertain the mind of God in it, and he would hear the Divine voice say, "I am not to be traced." That was a fine sentiment of Flavel—"Some providences, like Hebrew letters, must be read backwards."

> Not now—but in the coming years,
> We'll read the meaning of our tears—

and then bless the Hand that guided, and the Heart that planned. Meantime, let us rest with assurance that "God is His own interpreter, and He will make it plain."

Psalm 78

This long Psalm rightly earns the title of an *instruction* Psalm. How full of knowledge and wisdom it is! Historically, it may recapitulate for us important events in Israel's past, but the Psalm has a wider significance as a parable displaying the conduct and experience of believers in all ages. An instance of this is evident in the Archbishop of Canterbury's reply to those who forsook the Cistercian Order in 1132, and sought the Legate's advice, who, with the question in mind, *Can He give bread also?* 78:30, replied, "You long to flee from the fate of the Israelites in the desert, who 'did eat and were filled, for he gave them their own desire; they were not disappointed to their lust.' If you felt that you could not live uprightly so long as you stayed where you were, it was wrong for others to compel you to return."

Then verses 4 to 8 of the Psalm, containing a strong and striking appeal for the spiritual instruction of the young, have a few historical references to prove the value of training children in the way that they should go. The Children of Merindal, of a past century, so answered one another in the matters of Religion, before the persecuting Bishop of Cavailon, that his associate remarked, "I must needs confess I have often been at the disputations of the doctors in the Sorbonne, but I have never so much as by these children." Seven children at one time suffered martyrdom with Symphrosin, a godly matron, their mother. Julia the Apostate, who determined to hinder the increase of Christianity, ordered that children must not be taught either human or Divine learning. Philip was glad that Alexander was born while Aristotle lived, so that he might be instructed by Aristotle in philosophy. It is not a greater mercy that children born in our age can be nurtured in the blessed truths of the Gospel?

The inhabitants of Mitylene, sometimes lords of the seas, if any of the neighbors revolted, inflicted this punishment upon them—forbade them to instruct their children, esteeming this a sufficient revenge. Jewish Rabbis used to countenance a very strict custom and method for their children according to their age and capacity—

> At five years of age they were *filli legis,* sons of the Law, to read it.
> At thirteen they were *filli pracepti,* sons of the precept, to understand the Law.
> At fifteen they were *Talmuditae,* and went to deeper points of the Law, even to Talmudic doubts.

This was the goodly practice of God's ancient people, and still is to some degree; but what of us who live in an age with its full and final revelation of God in Christ? Are our children being brought up in the fear of the Lord? As parents, will it be our joy to hear our offspring say some day that we did not hide from them the glories and grace of Jesus? Let us arise and declare to our children the benefit and blessing of keeping God's commandments.

Ephraim stood condemned because, as a nation, she *refused to walk in His law,* 78:9. At Athens there used to be *Lepa odos,* "the sacred way," by which, as Harpocratic relates, the priests of the mysteries traveled to Elenxin. At Rome also there was a way which was called *Via Sacra.* To us also there is a way to Heaven, provided by Him who came as "The Way," and also consecrated for us by the footsteps of the saints. How incumbent it is upon us not to loiter, but to be ever walking in the light, even as He is in the light, and "The Light."

How expressive is the brevity of life as indicated by the Psalmist in the phrase, *A wind that passeth away, and cometh not again,* 78:39. Something of the same sentiment is found in the poem by old Francis Quarles—

> The secret wheels of hurrying time to give
> So short a warning, and so fast they drive,
> That I am dead before I seem to live.
>
> And what's a life? a weary pilgrimage,
> Whose glory in one day doth fill thy stage
> With childhood, manhood, and decrepit age.
>
> And what's a life? the flourishing array
> Of the proud summer meadow, which today,
> Wears her green plush, and is tomorrow hay.
>
> And what's a life? a blast sustained with clothing,
> Maintained with food, retained with vile self-loathing,
> Then weary of itself, again to nothing.

From following the ewes great with young He brought him to feed Jacob His people, 78:71. Although David became Israel's illustrious Poet-King, he never forgot those early days when, as the shepherd lad, he cared for his father's sheep. It is said that a learned doctor of Oxford, in the long ago, hung up his leathern breeches in his study for a memorial to visitors of his mean original calling. History tells us of Agathocles who rose from a potter to be king of Sicily, and who would be served in no other plate at his table but earthenware, to remind him of his former drudgery. Then it would be well if some would remember whose shoes they have cleaned, whose coals they have carried, and whose money they have borrowed, and deal gratefully with their creditors, as the good Lord Cromwell did by the Florentine merchant in the time of Henry the Eighth, when Wolsey like a butcher, forgot the king his master.

Gipsy Smith, the famous British evangelist, always carried an old knife with him to remind him of his boyhood days when he was in gipsy camp, and he had to cut down wood for fires. "King David, too, never forgot his lowly past. His golden scepter pointed to his wooden book, and he plays the old lessons of his oaten pipe upon his Algum harp, and spreads his Bethlehem tent within the marble palace on Mount Zion."

Psalm 79

What a Psalm of sighs, complaints, and moans this is! It might have come from the pen of the weeping Prophet, Jeremiah, amid the ruins of the beloved city of both Psalmist and Prophet. Its thirteen verses are associated with times of invasion, oppression, and national overthrow. As for its composer, Asaph was a patriotic poet who was never more at home than when he rehearsed the history of his nation. We sadly lack national poets whose song is of the Lord. The case Asaph presented to the Lord was a deplorable one, but he was an excellent advocate, and gave a graphic description of the calamities he could not fail to see, and which elicited his sympathy. Wonderful to know that we have a still mightier Intercessor above, Who never ceases to urge our suit before the eternal throne!

Delitzsch observes that this 79th Psalm, in every respect, is the pendant of Psalm 74, for both Psalms have the same Asaphic stamp, namely, the sending forth of their complaints out of the same circumstances of the time concerning a destruction of the Temple and of Jerusalem. The points of contact are not merely matters of style, the mutual relationships lie still deeper. Because of its nature, this Psalm has been wonderfully used to express the feelings of sorrow by patriots over national disaster. For instance, Psalm 79 was one which came closely home to the hearts of Britishers in the dark days of the Indian Mutiny, who would read it amid the horrors of Cawnpore and Lucknow.

At Meaux, in 1546, fifty-seven Protestants were taken prisoners and their friends in the crowd joined in singing Psalm 59 as they were led to prison; and it was the same Psalm fourteen of them who were condemned to death sang on their way to the scaffold—

> O God, the heathen are come into thine inheritance.

The priests and monks tried to drown the voices of the martyrs but their song was silenced only by the flames. While some of the sufferers chose Psalms with the cry for pardon for sin, and others the hope and joy of the Divine vision, there were those again who, as with these fourteen noble martyrs, appealed to God for His persecuted truth. Crespin, the early French martyrologist, tells of one of these, Jean Raba, "put to death with indescribable cruelty, at Angiers, in 1556, but who continued to sing this Psalm till he had scarcely the form of a man, and gave up his soul to God."

Psalm 79 was the one used by the Jews, every Friday, in lamentation over the ruins of Jerusalem. Prothero tells us that the same Psalm was applied alike to the zealous excesses of the Huguenots or the Puritans, and to the profane outrages of the French Revolution. It was used of the Carthusians of Woburn Abbey at the time of the dissolution of the monasteries, when Abbot Hobbs called the brethren together and bade them, "for the reverence of God," to pray devoutly and recite Psalm 79. Further, it was while a Protestant congregation was singing the Psalm in the grange at Vassey, in 1562, that Guise gave the signal for the massacre of the Huguenots which finally provoked the Wars of Religion.

James Melville, nephew of John Knox, the Presbyterian leader, during his studies at the University of St. Andrews, Scotland, noted in his Diary that—

> The primarius—James Wilkie—a guid, peaceable, sweet auld man, who luiffed me weill, . . . causit sing, commonlie the 44 and 79 Psalmes, quhilk I lernit *par couer,* for that was the yeir of the bludie massacres in France, and grait troubles in this country.

O God, the heathen are come into Thy inheritance, 79:1. When Jerome was in a cave at Bethlehem, wrestling with the difficulties of the Prophet Ezekiel, he found in this Psalm, especially its first verse, the best expression of a horror which, as he said, made him forget his own name.

Among the legendary or historical records of the persecuted Church down the ages, the Psalms are associated with signal triumph of native Christians over their heathen invaders. It was so in the 7th century when the English were forced back in their mountain fortresses, taking with them the national forms of their Christian worship, which they jealously guarded as symbols of their independence. It was a period of darkness, with few and uncertain glimmerings of light, that Bede, or like the historian of the Vandals of Africa, saw the words of this Psalm verified, *O God, the heathen are come into Thine inheritance,* 79:1-4.

J. L. Porter, traveler and historian of the 18th century, who wrote *The Great Cities of Bashan,* described a visit to the old part of Jerusalem, and found himself at the "Jews' place of Wailing," where the people meet to wail over the fallen temple, whose dust was dear to them, and in whose stones they still took pleasure, Verses 1, 4, and 5 of this Psalm again recited by them.

The dead bodies of thy servants have they given to be meat for the fowls of the air, 79:2. This is the motto chosen by the Jesuit Parsons for his book, *De perseutione Anglicana,* published in 1581, and was also used by Luisa de Carvaja as he witnessed Roman Catholics being executed in London in 1608, and who wrote, "We can hardly go out to walk without seeing heads and limbs of our dear and holy ones stuck up on gates that divide streets, and the birds of the air perching on them, which makes me think of the verse, 'The dead bodies of thy servants have they given to be meat for the fowls of the air.'" The Christians, who were slain at Pharsalia, scorned their persecutors as they came to die with the taunt, "Thou effectest nothing by this anger; what matters whether disease dissolve the body, or the funeral pile, or devoured by the fowls of heaven and beasts of earth." We are told in Jurieu's Letters that the Protestants of Metz sang this second verse when they lifted from a heap of refuse where it had been cast for the birds to devour the body of one of the brethren, a judge of the city, and carried it away to interment.

We are become a reproach, a scorn and derision, 79:6. Those the Psalmist describes were like the Apostles at a later period, who were counted as "the offscouring of all things." Chrysostom, writing on this verse said, "This was more grievous to them than stripes and wounds, because these being inflicted upon the body are divided after a sort betwixt soul and body, but scorns and reproaches do wound the soul only." Cicero commented, "scorn and derision leave a sting behind them."

When Augustine came under the influence of Ambrose, his life changed. Great soul struggles were experienced. A crisis came in September 386 when he was 33 years of age. Throwing himself down under the shade of a figtree in a retired corner of his garden in Milan, Augustine gave way to a flood of tears and moaned: *How long, O Lord, how long? Oh remember not our old sins!* 79:5, 8. Shortly after this, relief came when he heard a voice say, "Take and read! take and read!" and opened the Bible at random and read Romans 13:13, 14.

Pour out thy wrath upon the heathen that have not known thee. 79:6. At times it would appear as if Providence deals much more severely with the righteous than with the wicked, and this verse has been used as a bold appeal by many a persecuted saint, founded upon such an appearance. The Psalmist seems to say, "Lord, if thou must empty out thy vials of wrath, begin with those who have no measure of regard for thee, but are openly up in arms against thee; and be pleased to spare thy people, who are thine notwithstanding all their sins."

O remember not against us former iniquities: let thy tender mercies speedily prevent us: for we are brought very low, 79:8. These were the last words of godly John Own, who died August 24, 1683, when things looked very dark in England and Scotland for the cause of religious truth and freedom. It was the time of which the poet Waller wrote—

> Bold is the man who dares engage
> For piety in such an age.

Just before Owen died, he was told that his last and most remarkable of all his works, the spiritual classic, *Meditations on the Glory of the Redeemer,* had just come off the press. Hearing this, the dying saint lifted up his hands and said, "I am glad to hear it, the long wished-for day is come at last, in which I shall see that glory in another manner than I have ever done, or was capable of doing, in this world." Crispin and Crispinian, two brothers who, for love of Christ, renounced all honors of birth and made shoes for the poor, suffered during the Diocletian persecution at Soissons in 288. In their prolonged sufferings they were sustained by the words, *Help us, O God of our salvation, for the glory of Thy name . . . Wherefore do the heathen say, Where is now thy God!* After their martyrdom, these valiant brothers became the Patrons of Shoemakers. The story goes that their bodies were thrown in the river and carried out to sea, and that the waves, for love of the Blessed Feet which once walked upon them, wafted the mangled bodies of His martyrs to the shores of Romney March, where the inhabitants received them in joy, and built in their honor the church of Lydd.

Augustus wondered at a person sleeping quietly that was very much in debt, and sent for his pillow saying, "Surely there is some strange virtue in it, that makes him so secure." *Thou rememberest former iniquities against us.* Old debts vex most; the delay of payment increases them by interest; and the return of them being unexpected, a person is least provided for them. Christ, by His victory at Calvary, cancelled all our debts, and now assures us that our sins and iniquities He will remember no more against us forever.

We thy people . . . will give thee thanks forever . . . show forth thy praise to all generations, 79:13. On the tablets of the Church are memorials of her lasting and deep gratitude, and records of her great deliverances, which, as long as she lasts, her sons will rehearse with delight. Such a history will survive all other records.

The sighing of the prisoner, 79:11. Such a sigh is prominent in Scripture, and represents all of us in the world who are prisoners of one sort or another. "When a captive gazes through the bars of iron which night and day stand like mute sentinels before the narrow window of his cell, and when his eyes fall upon the green fields and groves beyond, he sighs, and turns away from the scene with a wish. He spake not a word, yet he wished. That sigh was a wish that he could be set free, for every sigh is an *unexpressed declaration."* God hears the sighs of His own dear children, and understands the wishes they represent. They always come up before Him.

> Though not a human voice he hears,
> And not a human form appears
>   His solitude to share,

He is not all alone—the eye
Of Him who hears the prisoner's sigh
    Is even on him there.

The motto on the title page of John Howard's *Account of Lazarettos* are the words of this verse, chosen by him after noticing their effect on the minds of the prisoners in Lancaster Gaol.

Preserve thou those that are appointed to die, 79:11. One had read of a Christian lady who kept a record of all who had been sentenced to death, so far as she heard of them, and prayed for them every day till their end came. Was not such a service in sympathy with the heart of God Who ever cares for those condemned to die?

Sevenfold into their bosoms, 79:12. This unique expression, in which punishment far exceeds the fault, is associated with an expression which originally seems to have had reference to the practice of holding things in the lap, or the front-fold of the flowing oriental dress, and has in usage the accessory sense of retribution or retaliation.

Psalm 80

John Milton, who revelled in the Psalms and wove fragments of them into his remarkable poems, in 1648 translated from the original *into meter* nine Psalms, 80-88, and in 1653, eight more Psalms, 1-8, were "done into verse." The title of this 80th Psalm claims our attention, seeing it is the fourth Psalm constituting a song upon *Shoshannim,* or the lilies, the other Psalms being 45, 60, and 69. Spurgeon thought that the most probable translation of this term is *upon the lilies,* and that it is either a poetical title given to a noble song after the Oriental manner, or it may relate to the tune to which it was set, or to the instrument which was meant to accompany it. Spurgeon, himself, inclined to the first explanation, seeing it is easy to follow the fitness of borrowing a name for truth so beautiful. In wedding garlands much use was made of lilies, the emblem of purity and loveliness, and which adorned Solomon's temple. This 80th Psalm is parallel to Psalm 44 and 60 in that it presents a plaintive lament of the church in distress and a supplicating cry for deliverance. While it is not easy to trace why this title of *Shoshannim* is given in every case, the delightfully poetical form of the Psalm before us justifies the use of such a charming word. Linked on to it is *Eduth,* signifying "testimony," and thus fittingly introduces such a testimony of the church as "a lily among thorns."

Referred to as *A Psalm of Asaph,* doubtless another by this same name is meant who, having the unhappiness to live like the "last minstrel" in evil times, his sacred song was not lightly esteemed in the days of old. If, on the other hand, it was written by the previous Asaph, then it was written in the spirit of prophecy, seeing it sings of times unknown to David.

Give ear, O Shepherd of Israel, 80:1. It is part of a shepherd's calling to give ear to the bleatings and cries of the sheep, to call them to mind, and run readily to their help. It was in this way that God led and cared for Joseph like a flock.

The Lord God of Hosts is angry, 80:4. What a great title this is! They talk of Tamerlane that he would daunt his enemies with the very looks of his countenance. What will it be like when the reprobates call to the rocks to hide them from the wrath of the Lamb?

Thou feedest them with the bread of tears, 80:5. The poetess, Elizabeth Barrett Browning, like her husband, knew how to weave the language of the Psalms into her poems. In *The Measure* she has this verse drawn from the above passage—

> Shall we, then, who have issued from the dust,
> And there return—shall we, who toil for dust,
> And wrap our winnings in this dusty life,
>   Say, "No more tears, Lord God!
>   The measure runneth o'er."

A vine which the Lord had planted, 80:8, 15. Theodosius, who lived in the 3rd century, in his work *De Situ Terrae Sanctae,* tells how "a vine which the Lord had planted," close to the field where He had Himself ploughed a furrow, regularly provided the wine for the Pentecostal communion. Mant's version of verses 8-19, most exquisite, and deserves to be quoted in full. Here is the first stanza setting forth verses 8-11—

> Thy hands from Egypt brought a goodly vine,
> And planted fair in fertile Palestine;
> Clear'd for its grasping roots the unpeopled land,
> And gave it high to rise, and firm to stand.
> Far o'er the eternal hills her shadow spread,
> The tendrils wreath'd the cedar's towering head;
> And, as the center of the land she stood,
> Her branches reach'd the sea, her boughs the eastern flood.

Didst cause it to take deep root, and it filled the land, 80:9. The analogy used here of Israel can be applied to every believer in Christ. All who are His have been planted by Him, and growing downward, "rooting roots," by His grace bear fruit upward, and as the Dresser of His vineyard, He causes the branches to spread far and wide.

The wild boar out of the wood doth root it up, 80:13. Origen, deemed a heretic by the Church, overwhelmed by remorse, turned to the Psalms for comfort but found himself silenced. "The prophet David himself shut the door on my lips," was his bitter lament as he applied to his apostasy the words, "The wild boar out of the wood doth root it up; and the wild beasts of the field devour it."

Then the description of the approach of Alcibiades which Shakespeare has in *Timon of Athens* is an echo of this verse—

> Who, like a boar too savage, doth root up
> His country's peace—

No image of a destructive enemy could be more appropriate than that of a wild boar the Psalmist used. Little foxes may spoil the vines, but wild boars break their way through fences, root up the ground, tear down the vines, and trample them under feet. Inhabitants of countries where these fearful animals flourish would as soon face a lion as a wild boar, the stroke of whose razor-like tusks is made with lightning swiftness, and which is sufficient to rip up a horse and cut a dog asunder. Pope, in Homer's Iliad, embodies the destructiveness of this animal in the lines—

> In vengeance of neglected sacrifice,
> On Oeneus' fields she sent a monstrous boar,
> That levell'd harvests and whole forests tore.

Upon the son of man whom thou madest strong for thyself, 80:17. History records that nations rise or fall largely through the instrumentality of powerful individuals: by a Napoleon the kingdoms are scourged; by a Wellington nations were saved from the tyrant. It will be by the Man Christ Jesus that fallen Israel will yet rise and reign with Him.

Psalm 81

In the previous Psalm, the people of God are represented under the figure of a Vine, and it is somewhat apt that this Psalm before us bears the title *upon Gittith,* which literally means, "upon the winepress." Whether the expression refers to a musical instrument, or to a particular tune is hard to determine. When Jesus came to use the figure of a vineyard to represent His Church, He spoke of her as a winepress dug in it, Matthew 21:33. The same figure of a winepress as expressive of final judgment upon the ungodly is found in Revelation 14. This is another *Psalm of Asaph,* in which the godly poet dwells upon the history of his country; his great forte being the rehearsal of the past in admonitory psalmody. "He is the poet of the history and politics of Israel. A truly national songster, at once pious and patriotic." As for the Psalm as a whole, Asaph calls for praise for some memorable day, perhaps, the Passover, and then for Divine deliverance out of Egypt. In the last half, the poet chides the people for their ingratitude, and concludes by describing their happy estate if only they had been obedient to their God of deliverances.

Make a joyful noise unto the God of Jacob, 81:1. The gods of Greece and Rome may be worshipped well enough with classical music, but Jehovah can only be adored with the heart, and that music is the best for His service which gives the heart most play. Here, the God of their father Jacob was extolled in gladsome music by Israel.

Blow upon the trumpet, 81:3. The sound of the trumpet is often employed in Scripture as a symbol of the voice or word of God (See Rev. 1:10; 4:1). The Jews affirm that the blowing of trumpets was in commemoration of Isaac's deliverance, a ram being sacrificed for him, and therefore they sounded with trumpets made of rams' horns. Another interpretation is that the use of the trumpet here was in remembrance of the trumpet blown at the giving of the Law.

I removed his shoulder from the burden, 81:6. God alone set the nation free from bondage. "Other peoples owe their liberties to their own efforts and courage, but Israel received its Magna Charta as a free gift of Divine power." As for the phrase, *Delivered from the pots*—bricklayer's baskets—*burden baskets* (Exod. 6:6, 7), hanging one at each end of a yoke laid across the shoulders is what is meant.

Open thy mouth wide, and I will fill it, 81:10. In Persia, the custom persisted for a long time that when the king wished to do a visitor, an Ambassador for instance, special honor, he would ask him to open his mouth wide, and then the king would cram it with delicious sweetmeats, and sometimes with jewels. Doubtless it is this custom Asaph applies to God's benevolence, Who fills the mouth, not with baubles of jewels, but with far richer, eternal treasure.

Hear, O my people . . . I am the Lord thy God, which brought thee out of the land of Egypt, 81:6-16. This whole section was the passage forming the beginning of the appeal of the Scottish exiles in Newcastle August 10, 1584, who were compelled to leave their country owing to the oppressive measures which continued in Church and State for almost 100 years during the reign of the later Stuarts. Leading the exiled party were Andrew Melville and his nephew James, who drew up a system of government for the Church of Scotland which fought its way to a definite triumph in the Glasgow Assembly of 1638. Then, as John Ker goes on to say, "Andrew Melville took up the standard from the dying hand of John Knox, and, instead of Frankfort and Geneva, the shelter of the refugees was found in Berwick and Newcastle. The common interest of the Reformation was now drawing England and Scotland more closely together, especially on the side of the Puritans, and preparing the way for the union of the kingdoms."

Honey out of the rock, 81:16. Summer travelers to Palestine have been impressed with the abundance of honey the bees of the land store up in the hollow of trees and in crevices of rocks. The thought of God extracting honey out the rock indicates that He is able to bring the sweetest pleasure from the hardness of afflictions. Out of the Rock of Ages at Calvary came a priceless salvation for a lost world.

The finest of the wheat, 81:16. The margin has it, "with the fat of wheat." God sought to feed His people, not with wheat only, but with the finest of the wheat, which is the best. They should not have had the bran, but the finest of the flour; not only honey, but honey out of the rock, which, naturalists say, is the best and purest honey. God spares no cost, nor thinks anything too costly for those who are truly His. When He spared not His Son for the World's salvation, He parted with the best of Heaven for the worst of earth.

Psalm 82

This brief Psalm made up of eight short verses is another from the poet of the temple, Asaph, who is here seen acting as a preacher to the court and to the magistracy. In his sermon to the judges, Asaph speaks very plainly, and his message is characterized by strength rather than by sweetness. "We have here," says Spurgeon, "a proof that all psalms and hymns need not be direct expressions of praise to God; we may, according to the example of this Psalm, admonish one another in our songs. Asaph no doubt saw around him much bribery and corruption, and while David punished it with the sword, he resolved to scourge it with a prophetic Psalm. In so doing, the sweet singer was not forsaking his profession as a musician for the Lord, but rather was practically carrying it out in another department. He was praising God when he rebuked the sin which dishonored Him, and if he was not making music, he was hushing discord when he bade rulers dispense justice with impartiality"—counsel, judges of any age should follow.

God standeth in the congregation of the mighty; he judgeth among the gods, 82:1. When the Puritans who remained behind in England, as their brethren, the Pilgrim Fathers, went to the New World, fought out their quarrel with Charles I, it was this verse which Bishop Andrews used as he protested against the intrusion of churchmen into secular affairs. Of those who pervert justice, Spurgeon's forceful remark is most apt—"Village squires and magistrates would do well to remember the Judges shall be judged, and to Justices justice shall be meted out. Some of them had need to go to school to Asaph till they have mastered this Psalm. . . . A higher authority will criticize the decisions of petty sessions, and even the judgment of our most impartial judges will be revised by the high court of Heaven."

What is most impressive in this opening verse is the attitude of the heavenly Judge Who *standeth.* It is customary with us for the judge to sit, and for the litigants or accused to stand. Even "Moses *sat* to judge the people, and the people *stood* by Moses." But God *stands*, because of His immutability, His power, His abiding presence, and also because of His promptness to act, to decide for the right, and to defend His own as He did when He stood up for Stephen.

Do justice to the poor and needy, 82:3. It is said of Francis the First, of France, that when a woman kneeled to him to beg justice, he bade her stand up; for, said he, "Woman, it is justice that I owe thee, and justice thou shalt have; if you beg anything of me, let it be mercy." Commendable is the Court where Justice is not extorted, but drops as kindly as honey from the comb—where Justice holds scales in her hand, not to weigh gold, but equity.

Ye shall die like men, 82:7. The priest who went before the bier of Saladin, that mighty monarch of the East, said, "He is gone, and hath carried no more along with him than ye see, that is, a shirt hung up for that purpose." Bringing nothing into the world, it is certain we can carry nothing out of it. Death quickly unrobes, not only judges, but all men. No position in society is too high for death's arrows, for it can bring down birds from the tallest trees.

Arise, O God, 82:8. Behind this last call to God, as the Judge, to mete out true justice, is the common gesture of judges, whose usual manner is to sit while they are hearing of cases; then to arise and stand when they come to give sentence. When the Judge of all the earth arises for the final judgment, He will do that which is right.

Psalm 83

President Kruger, of South Africa, prominent leader of the Boers, frequently appealed to the Psalms, arrogating to himself many of their promises, even although some of his actions were not consistent with religious sincerity. But when he addressed his burghers in the language of the Psalm he reached their hearts. In his speech, opening the Volksraads on May 7, 1900, he applied the words of this 83rd Psalm to his struggle with the British Empire, and dwelt especially on verse 4, where the enemies of God say, "Come, and let us root them out, that they be no more a people; and that the name of Israel may be no more in remembrance." Then Kruger went on the argue—"Psalm 83 speaks of attacks of the Evil one on Christ's Kingdom, which must no longer exist. And now the same words come from Salisbury, for he too says, 'This people must not exist,' and God says, 'This people shall exist.' Who will win? Surely the Lord."

Then, later on, in a circular dispatch sent to his officers, dated from Machadodorp, June 20, 1900, Kruger returned to the same passage saying, "According to Psalm 83, the enemies of old said that the people shall not exist in Christ's Kingdom. Salisbury and Chamberlain stand convicted by their own words: 'They shall not exist'; but the Lord says, 'The people shall exist,' and Christ is our Commander-in-Chief, Who leads us with His Word." A month later, Kruger sent a final dispatch to his officers from Machadodorp, which ended with the appeal, "See Psalm 83, how the evil spirit of the air said that the valiant fighter named Israel must not exist, or to use his own words, 'I will not permit your nation to continue to be a nation.' Dear brothers, through God's Word I am sure of this, that the victory is ours." But the writer of these lines, as a youth of 14, witnessed the homecoming of British soldiers from South Africa after the defeat of Kruger!

Returning, however, to a coverage of the Psalm itself, we gather from its title that it was, "A Song or Psalm of Asaph"—the last ode to come from this eloquent penman. When the two words, Song—Psalm appear together, the meaning seems to be *a lyric poem appointed to be sung.* "Asaph, the patriotic poet and seer, was well aware of the serious dangers arising from the powerful confederate nations, but his soul in faith stays itself upon Jehovah, while as a poet-preacher he excites his countrymen to prayer by means of this sacred lyric."

It is somewhat difficult to determine the exact historical setting of this Psalm, even though the array of proper names seems to offer an easy identification with some definite historical event. But as Ellicott goes on to say, "Our records nowhere speak of a confederation composed of all the tribes enumerated here; so that if we are to be governed by literal exactness, it is impossible to refer the Psalm to any known period of Israelite history." The probable origin of the poem is the period of which we have a detailed account in 1 Macc. 5. Spurgeon thought that the Asaph, who penned this song, was in all probability the person referred to in 2 Chronicles 20:14—*Jahaziel*—for the internal evidence referring the subject of the Psalm to the times of Jehoshaphat is overwhelming. The division in the camp of confederate peoples in the wilderness of Tekoa not only broke up their league, but led to a mutual slaughter, which crippled the power of some of the nations for many years after. They thought to destroy Israel and destroyed each other.

Keep not thou silence, O God: hold not thy peace, 83:1. When Benedict, to whom England owes a vast debt, came to his end worn out by labors, and paralyzed in his limbs, through sleepless nights, he would listen to the repetition of Psalms, in which he was himself too weak to join. He died on January 12, 690, when those who watched by him were repeating the words, "Hold not thy tongue, O God; keep not still silence."

They have holpen the children of Lot, 83:8. Romanism and Ritualism make common cause against the Gospel, says Spurgeon. They have come to the aid of Moab and Ammon, which two nations were among the fiercest in the conspiracy. There were ten to one against Israel, and yet she overcame all her enemies. Her name is not blotted out; but many, nay, most of her adversaries are now a name only, their power and their excellence are alike gone.

They became as dung for the earth, 83:10. History records that in 1830 more than a million bushels of "human and inhuman bones" were imported from the continent of Europe into the port of Hull, England. The neighborhood of Leipsic, Austerlitz, and Waterloo, where the principal battles were fought some 15 or 20 years before, were swept alike of the bones of the hero, and the horse which he rode. Thus collected from every quarter, they were shipped to Hull, and thence forwarded to the Yorkshire bone-grinders, who, by powerful machinery, reduced them to a granual state. In this condition they were sent chiefly to Doncaster, one of the largest agricultural markets of the country, and were there sold to the farmers to fertilize their lands. The oily substance gradually evolving as the bone calcines makes better manure than almost any other substance—particularly human bones. It is quite probable that the flesh and bones of the 6 million Jews Adolph Hitler massacred met a similar fate.

Make them like a wheel, 83:10, 13. The word given as *wheel* implies "a rolling thing"—possibly the wild artichoke named *gulgal,* which is as stubble before the wind, that can sit nowhere, rest at nothing, but turn about from one uncertainty to another. The margin in Isaiah 17:13 gives "thistle down." Thomson in *Land and the Book* says of these masses of dry weeds that "at the proper season thousands of them come suddenly over the plain, rolling, leaping, bounding with vast racket, to the dismay of the horse and rider." To this day the Arabs call it *akhub,* and employ it in a figurative way—

"May you be whirled like àkhub before the wind."

When great calamities befall sinners they are tossed with perpetual disquietude, and run hither and thither seeking various remedies, but only weary themselves thereby, and plunge deeply in their woes. They are ignorant of the deep, settled peace Jesus alone can impart when out on a troubled sea.

The fire . . . the flame . . . thy tempest . . . thy storm, 83:14-15. The mountains are pre-eminently the *pastures,* Psalm 50:10; 147:8. To quote Thomson again on the similes used here, "Before the rains came the whole mountainside was in a blaze. Thorns and briars grow so luxuriantly here that they must be burned off always before the plough can operate. The peasants watch for a high wind, and then the fire catches easily, and spreads with great rapidity." Thus will it be with the nations that fail to recognize God as Jehovah, the most high over the earth.

That men may know that thou, whose name alone is Jehovah, 83:18. Josephus, the Jewish historian, tells us that the great Alexander, when on his triumphant march, being met near Jerusalem by the Jewish high priest, on whose mitre was engraved the name of *Jehovah,* "approached by himself, and adored that name," and was disarmed of his hostile intent. There was significance and power in the glorious old name as written by the Jews. But the name of Jesus—Jehovah Jesus—is now far more mighty in the world than was the name Jehovah in those earlier ages.

Psalm 84

What a wonderful Psalm this is! Spurgeon praised it most highly and wrote of it, "This sacred ode is one of the choicest of the collection; it has a mild radiance about it, entitling it to be called *The Pearl of Psalms.*

> If the 23rd Psalm be the most popular,
> the 103rd Psalm the most joyful,
> the 119th Psalm the most deeply experimental,
> the 51st Psalm the most plaintive
> then the 84th Psalm is one of the most sweet of the
> Psalms of Peace."

By whom, and when, this precious Psalm was written, is not stated. "It exhales to us a Davidic perfume, it smells of the mountain heather and the lone places of the wilderness, where King David must have often lodged during his many wars." Because of the nature of this Psalm it well deserved to be committed to the noblest of the sons of songs, and thus is named, *A Psalm for the sons of Korah*. It was given to the chief musician to set to music of which none could be too sweet for its theme, or too exquisite in sound to match the beauty of its language. The term *Gittith* means "wine-press," but "sweeter than the joy of the wine-press is the joy of the holy assemblies of the Lord's house; not even the favored children of grace, who are like the sons of Korah, can have a richer subject for song than Zion's sacred festivals."

The Psalm praises the provision of tabernacles, and lays stress upon the longing desire of saints to journey to them to meet God. Such pilgrimages were a great feature of Jewish life. Spurgeon's comment reads—

> Pilgrimages to the shrine of Thomas of Canterbury, and our Lodge of Walsingham, were so general in our country as to affect the entire population, cause the formation of roads, the erection and maintenance of hostelries, and the creation of special literature; this may help us to understand the influences of pilgrimages upon the ancient Israelites. Families journeyed together, making bands which grew at each halting place; they camped in sunny glades, sang in union along the roads, toiled together over the hill and through the slough, and, as they went along, stored up happy memories which would never be forgotten. One who was debarred the holy

276

company of the pilgrims, and the devout worship of the congregation, would find in this Psalm fit expression for his mournful spirit.

In *German Choral Music,* the whole Psalm has been set forth in poetic form, and of the seven verses we cite the first—

> O Lord of hosts, how lovely in mine eyes
>   The tents where thou dost dwell!
> For thine abode my spirit faints and sighs;
>   The courts I love so well.
>
> My longing soul is weary
>   Within thy house to be;
> The world is waste and dreary,
>   A desert land to me.

Then, this Psalm, as we are to discover, is rich in its historical associations. The ancient monks, as shrines for the Psalter, built their abbeys and churches, and as they sprinkled the chosen sites with holy water, they chanted Psalm 84. In January, 1681, two *honest, worthy lasses* as Alexander Peden called them, Isabel Alison and Marion Harvie, were hanged at Edinburgh. On the scaffold they sang together, to the tune of *Martyrs,* Psalm 84. "Marion," said Bishop Paterson, "you would never hear a curate; now you shall hear one," and he called upon one of his clergy to pray. "Come, Isabel," was the girl's answer—she was but 20 years of age—"let us sing Psalm 23," and thus they drowned the voice of the curate.

Foxe in his *Book of Martyrs,* under the year 1554, during the reign of Queen Mary, gives the record of one William Hunder who, although only 19 years of age, was pursued to death for the Gospel's sake. When brought to the stake, he recited Psalm 84, while being bound. When the fire was kindled, he cast his Psalter into his brother's hands, who said, "William, think of the holy passion of Chirst, and be not afraid." William replied, "I am not afraid." Then, lifting up his hands to heaven, he cried, "Lord, Lord, Lord, receive my spirit," and as his head dropped into the smothering smoke, he yielded up his life for the truth, sealing it with his blood to the praise of God.

When Thomas Halyburton was dying, he asked those around him to read the 84th Psalm, and to sing the latter part of it—

> Lord God of Hosts, my prayer hear;
> O Jacob's God, give ear,
> See God our shield, look on the face
> Of thine anointed dear.

Halyburton joined in singing, and, after prayer, said, "I had always a mistuned voice, a bad ear, but, which is worst of all, a mistuned heart. But, shortly, when I join the temple service above, there shall not be, world without end, one string of the affections out of tune." He died in 1712, at the age of 38, and left behind a well-known record perfumed with the grace and holiness of the Lord he loved most deeply.

How amiable are thy tabernacles, O Lord of hosts! 84:1. The Hebrew word for "amiable" combines both senses of *How loved and how lovable.* The high-born Paula, whose family had Jerome as both spiritual guide and historian, built a monastery in Bethlehem, of which Jerome became the head, remaining there until he died in 420. When Paula herself came to die, and her last moments approached, the watchers heard her murmur the words of those Psalms, seldom far from her lips, "Oh how amiable are thy dwellings, O Lord of Hosts." "I had rather be a doorkeeper in the house of my God, than to dwell in the tents of wickedness," 84:1, 11.

St. Vincent de Paul, who labored for the Catholic faith in his native land, while studying law at Padua, in 1591, was seized with rheumatic fever, and his life was despaired of. Awaiting the end with resignation, he kept on repeating verses 1 and 2 of Psalm 84. However, he recovered, and two years later was ordained as a missionary, much to the sorrow of his father, who desired him, as his eldest son and heir, to take his place in the world. He died in 1622, and in death turned again to the Psalms for the expression of his hope.

What was it about those tabernacles of old that made them so lovely, dear, and beloved by the Israelites of old? They were not edifices conspicuous for skill and cost bestowed them. Solomon's Temple, of course, was one of extraordinary beauty, but the tabernacle in the wilderness Moses created was not at all lovely to look at from the outside, and not all becoming for the Lord Himself. Yet the people gathered to it because it was the dwelling place of Him Who loves to dwell in temples not made by hands.

My soul longeth . . . fainteth . . . crieth, for the living God, 84:2. We have just mentioned St. Vincent de Paul, and his love for the Psalms. As he died, from a paralytic seizure, often he murmured, "My soul hath a desire and longing to enter the courts of the Lord; my heart and my flesh rejoice in the living God." How full of pathos are the words used to describe the heart's desire for God! *Longeth* comes from a root meaning to *grow pale,* expressing one effect of strong emotion—*grows pale with longing.* This effect of passionate love is used by Shakespeare in the line—

Sicklied o'er with the pale cast of thought.

Fainteth signifies to be consumed with longing, a dying of love, one who so desires to obtain the loved object, that he wastes and pines away unless his wish is gratified. *Crieth* comes from a root meaning to shout, shrill, or cry out, as soldiers do at the beginning of a battle. The Hebrew word denotes a strong cry, or to cry as a child when it is sadly hungry, and when every part of the child cries—hands, feet, and face. The sole object of such vehement yearning is "The Living God."

The sparrow . . . the swallow, 84:3. The thought of the Psalmist here is that as birds delighted to nest in covered nooks in God's house, so he loved to dwell in same, knowing that he was of more worth than many sparrows. *Herodotus* speaks of Aristodicus making a circuit of the temple at Branchidae, and taking the nests of sparrows and other birds. In *Aelian* is the story of a man who was slain for harming a sparrow that sheltered in the temple of Aesculapius. Theologian Ewald has a reference to birds nesting in the Kaaba at Mecca. What confidence it should give us to know that "God fails not to find a house for the most *worthless,* and a nest for the most *restless* of birds." Among ancient nations, a custom persisted for generations that birds building their nests around temples should not be driven away, much less killed, but left alone in their secure and undisturbed abode. Thus the application is made that all those who love to dwell in God's House, praising Him, are richly blessed of Him.

Blessed is the man . . . in whose heart are thy ways, 84:5. The root meaning of the word *ways* is "to cast up," and implies a highway marked by heaps of stones piled up at the side (Isa. 57). Solomon uses highway, or footway, as a metaphor for *the way of peace and righteousness* (Prov. 12:28). The well-known and deeply loved route to the sacred shrine at Sion is in the minds, and their hearts set upon it, is the thought the Psalmist expresses. Chaucer echoed this sentiment in the old English tongue—

> So pricketh hem Nature in her corages (in their hearts)
> Than longen folk to go on pilgrimages.

In whose hearts are the ways of them, literally means, "the steeps are on their hearts"—that is, the steep ascents on which the Tabernacle stood. The natural heart of man is a pathless wilderness, full of cliffs and precipices. When the heart is renewed by God's Spirit, a road is made, *a highway prepared for God,* Isa. 40:3, 4.

They go from strength to strength, 84:7. The margin has it, "from company to company," which suggests a picture of the actual progress of the various bands composing a caravan on the pilgrimage to God's House, in which each difficulty surmounted on the way added fresh courage and vigor to the hearts of the pilgrims. Matthew Arnold has the verse

> And he who flagg'd not in the earthly strife,
> From strength to strength advancing, only he
> His soul well knit, and all his battles won,
> Mounts, and that hardly, to eternal life.

Jocelyn, in his life of Kentigern, tells of an interview between him and Columba, in 584, at a place called Mallindenor, later identified as a little stream by Glasgow Cathedral, used for the primitive mill nearby. It was here that they and their companies met one another singing Psalms. Those said to have been sung were on the side of Kentigern, Psalm 138:5; and on the side of Columba they sang with tuneful voices Psalm 84:7.

I had rather been a doorkeeper, 84:10. Ellicott comments that a better rendering is, "I had rather wait on the threshold," as one not worthy—Vulgate version reads, be rejected in scorn—to enter the precincts. Yet although the idea of a doorkeeper is not necessarily involved in the Hebrew word it is suggested in a Korahite Psalm like Psalm 84, since the Korahites were "keepers of the gates of the tabernacle, and keepers of the entry." A Greek poet puts into the mouth of his hero, who sweeps the threshold of Apollo's temple, the words—

> A pleasant task, O Phoebus, I discharge,
> Before thine house in reverence of thy seat
> Of prophecy, an honored task to me.

Sitting at the threshold of a place of worship was, to the Eastern mind, a situation and posture of deep humility. Poor, heathen devotees sat near the threshold of the temple. Beggars sat, or prostrated themselves at the threshold of the door, or gate until they received gifts.

The Lord God is a sun and shield . . . no good thing will he withhold from them that walk uprightly, 84:11. Dr. John Ker tells us that when Thomas Carlyle left his quiet mountain house at Craiginputtock for the untried tumult of London, in doubt and despondency, that he quoted this verse for the comfort of his brother Alexander and himself, but mingled it with Romans 8:28. "All things work together for good." Although he was not as burdened in Scripture knowledge as in his literary works, yet Carlyle's faith at its core was Christian. "I turned my thoughts heavenward, for it is in heaven only that I find any basis for our poor pilgrimage on earth. Surely as the blue dome of heaven encircles us all, so does the providence of the Lord of Heaven. *He will withold no good thing from those that love him!* This, as it was the Palmist's faith, let it likewise be ours. It is the Alpha and Omega, I reckon, of all possessions that belong to man."

The Lord God is a shield, 84:11. Do you remember that name of *Little Faith* in Bunyan's "Pilgrim's Progress"? It appears that *Hopeful* was greatly surprised that the robbers had not taken his jewels from him; but he was given to understand that *they* were not in his own keeping. Yes, *Christian,* HE shall be thy "shield" to cover thy hope when it appears to be giving up the ghost . . . Yes, and He will be a shield *to thy property.* "Hast thou not set a hedge about *all* that he hath?"

The Lord will give glory, 84:11. It has been said that "Man is the glory of the lower world; the soul is the glory of man; grace is the glory of the soul; and Heaven is the glory of Grace. Glory is grace matured and brought to infinite perfection." In Heaven we shall see the Face of Him through whose redeeming grace we reached there, and His name will be written in our foreheads, as we go forward to share His eternal reign.

Psalm 85

On September 16, 1656, Oliver Cromwell, after he had become Lord Protector, sat in the Palace of Whitehall, reading and pondering Psalm 85. The following day he rode in state from Whitehall to the Abbey Church of Westminster to open the second Parliament of the Protectorate. The service ended, Cromwell returned to Whitehall with the same pomp and ceremony, and, entering the Painted Chamber, delivered a speech to the newly assembled members, which in part was an exposition of Psalms 85 and 46. "Yesterday, I did read a Psalm, which truly may not unbecome both me to tell you of, and you to observe. It is the 85th Psalm; it is very instructive and intelligent though I do but a little touch upon it, I desire your perusal and pleasure." Then Cromwell expounded his vision of hope—God's will done on earth, and England an emblem of Heaven where God's will reigns supreme. This was the task to which he exhorted his Parliament to set their hearts.

As to the historical setting of the Psalm itself, its whole tone identifies it with the post-exile period in Israelite history. Punishment had fallen upon the nation because of its departure from God, and the glad return Israel experienced was a proof that God had forgiven her, and taken away her sin. But the bright prospect was quickly overclouded, and the troubles succeeding the nation's return to God, perplexed those who had come back, seeing they felt purified and forgiven. Hence the many pathetic cries of the Psalm, particularly the cry that arose from the dread of famine, which was always regarded as a judgment on national sin, 85:12. But as he utters his lament, the prophet—for the Psalm has a true prophetic ring, and is in the highest sense Messianic—sees the cloud break, and hails the promise of abundant harvest, as he watches the sunshine of prosperity and peace once more strike across the land.

To the foregoing summary of the Psalm in Israel's life and experience as given by Ellicott, we can add a sentence or two from Spurgeon's preface to his exposition of the Psalm. "It is a prayer of a patriot for his afflicted country, in which he pleads the Lord's former mercies, and by faith foresees brighter days. We believe that David wrote it, but many question that assertion . . . It is remarkable that, as a rule, the more sceptical a writer is, the more resolute is he to have done with David; while the purely evangelic annotators are for the most part content to leave the royal poet in the chair of authorship . . . Our belief is that David penned this national hymn when the land was oppressed by the Philistines, and in the spirit of prophecy he foretold the peaceful years of his own reign and the repose of the rule of Solomon, the Psalm having all along an inner sense of which Jesus and his salvation are the key. The presence of Jesus the Savior reconciles earth and heaven, and secures to us the golden age; the balmy days of universal peace."

Those, however, who believe the Psalm to be the production of some unknown poetic genius, touched, purified, and exalted by the fire of celestial inspiration, affirm that it is a relic of that golden age, when the Hebrew music was instinct with a spirit such as never breathed on Greece or Rome. Those who hold strictly to the anonymity of some of the Psalms bid us remember how largely the Church of God is indebted to nameless worthies who wrote for us hymns and spiritual songs, full of richer strains than ever were poured forth by the most illustrious of pagan names.

Forgiven . . . covered, 85:2. The Hebrew reads, "Thou hast borne, or carried away, the iniquity," the allusion being to the ceremony of the scapegoat. When God covers sin, He does so, not as one would cover a sore with a plaster, thereby merely hiding it only; but He covers it with a blood-plaster that effectually cures and removes the sore altogether.

Thou hast turned thyself from the fierceness of thine anger, 85:3. Israel's history is studded with illustrations of times when her judgments were severe, God in mercy stayed His hand. The Book of Judges is full of incidents of this nature. Personal experience testifies to judgment being stayed, and tenderness manifested. Fierce anger is to be feared and avoided, and the speaking of peace encouraged . . . 85:8. The dreariest period of one's spiritual life can be transformed into gladness, as the hymnist suggests in the lines—

> The Lord can clear the darkest skies,
> > Can give us day for night.
> Make drops of sacred sorrow rise
> > To rivers of delight.

Cause thine anger toward us to cease, 85:4. Literally this phrase reads, "Break thine anger toward us." The word for *cease* comes from a root meaning a *breaking* by means of *notches* and *gaps,* as when the *edge* of anything is broken by notches and gaps, and it is made utterly useless. *Indignation,* so long as it is vigorous and spreads its effects, has an *edge,* which smites and pierces; but it is considered blunt and broken when it ceases to exert itself, and produces evils no longer. This is affirmed of the righteous anger of God.

I will hearken what the Lord God will say concerning me, 85:8. Thomas à Kempis, who gave himself "to the interior life and devotion," wrote a spiritual classic, *De Imitatione Christi*—The Imitation of

Christ—which in thought, feeling, and language, is largely based on the Psalter. The keynote to the third book in *Imitation,* Psalm 85:8, supplies its keynote, and this section largely treats of internal consolation. What the Psalmist heard from the Lord was the word of *peace,* which comprehended all Israel sighed for—

> Peace,
> Dear nurse of arts, plenties, and joyful truth.

It was because of the higher meaning of Divine peace that the Church directed that this 85th Psalm should be read on Christmas Day. Bernard gives us this description of a good ear—"Which willingly hears what is taught, wisely understands what it heareth, and obediently practices what it understandeth." Well might we pray, "O Lord, give me such an ear to hear what Thou dost say, and I will hang on it jewels of gold, and ornaments of praise."

That glory may dwell in our land, 85:9. Robert Southwell, a Jesuit and Elizabethan poet, born in 1560, was one in whom the power of the Psalms was illustrated in fullest detail. To be a Jesuit in those days was to be counted as a wild beast and hunted down as vermin and destroyed. Southwell himself described some of his Catholic friends who suffered purgatory at the hands of those who hated those of this faith. The poet, knowing that fate might soon be his own, wrote, "But come what pleaseth God, we hope that we shall be able to bear all in him that strengthens us. In the meantime, we pray that they may be put to confusion that work iniquity; and that the Lord may speak peace to His people, that, as the royal prophet says, 'His glory may dwell in our land.'" When a gloriously devout worship is rendered to God continuously, a glorious measure of prosperity is enjoyed in consequence. Whenever Israel was faithful to God, true glory was hers.

Mercy and truth . . . Righteousness and peace, 85:10. This was the text, Dr. Thomas Goodwin, the great Independent divine, used at the opening of Parliament, January 27, 1659, when Richard Cromwell was installed as Protector. The sermon was a reasonable plea for liberty of conscience, and an exhortation to unity and peace—seed cast on stormy waters, not to be found till after many days. The coming together of Mercy and Truth, and the kissing of Righteousness and Peace are suggestive of an ideal love-match. Wrote George Horne—

> These four divine attributes parted at the fall of Adam, and met again at the birth of Christ. *Mercy* was ever inclined to save man, and *Peace* could not be his enemy; but *Truth* exacted the promise of God's threat—"The soul that sinneth, it shall die"; and *Righteousness* could not but give to every one his due, Jehovah was to be true in all his ways, and righteous in all his works. Through grace, union has been restored between the four attributes.

Bernard said of *Mercy* and *Peace,* which pair well, that they were "bed-follows," sleep together, and also that they "sucked one milk, one breast." Commentator Adam Clarke makes it that these four virtues were reconciled when Christ poured out His life at Calvary. *"Mercy* and *Peace* are on one side; *truth* and *righteousness* on the other. *Truth* requires *Righteousness; Mercy* calls for *Peace.* They meet together on the way; one going to make inquisition for sin, the other to plead for reconciliation. Having met, their differences on certain considerations are adjusted," and their mutual claims are blended together in one common interest, on which *Peace* and *Righteousness* immediately embrace. Thus, *Righteousness* is given to *Truth,* and *Peace* is given to *Mercy,* at the Cross.

Ellicott draws attention to the exquisite personification of verses 9-11, with their remarkable likeness to Isaiah's manner of presentation (Isa. 33:16; 45:8; 59:14). "It is an allegory of completed national happiness which though presented in language peculiar to Hebrew thought, is none the less universal in its application. Nor does it stop at material blessings, but lends itself to the expression of highest truths. The poet sees once more the *glory* which had so long deserted the land, come back—as its symbol, the Ark, once came back—and take up its abode there. He sees the covenant *favor* once more descend and meet the divine *faithfulness* of which, lately, perplexed minds were doubting, but which the return of prosperity have now proved sure. Righteousness and Peace, or prosperity, these inseparable brothers, kiss each other, and fall lovingly into each other's arms."

Truth shall spring out of the earth . . . righteousness shall look down from heaven, 85:11. This is a delicious scene! Earth yielding flowers of truth, and heaven shining with stars of holiness; the spheres echoing to each other, or being mirrors of each other's beauties. "Earth carpeted with truth and canopied with righteousness," shall be nether heaven. When God looks down in grace, man sends his heart upward in obedience.

The Lord shall give that which is good . . . our land shall yield her increase, 85:12. God alone can reclaim the world from its desolation caused by sin. But the Messianic promise is that—

> Freed from the curse, the grateful garden gives
> Its fruits in goodly revenue. Nor frost,
> Nor blight, nor mildew fall, nor cankerworm,
> Nor caterpillar, nor one ripening hope,
> The clouds drop fatness. The very elements
> Are subject to the prayerful will of those
> Whose pleasure is in unison with God's.

The material and moral blessings that often go together in personal and national experience, as the last two verses of the Psalm indicate, are emphasized for us in Wordsworth's *Ode to Duty*—

> Stern Lawgiver! Yet thou dost wear
>   The Godhead's most benignant grace,
> Nor know we anything so fair
>   As in the smile upon thy face.
> Flowers laugh before thee on their beds,
> And fragrance in thy footing treads;
> Thou dost preserve the stars from wrong,
> And the most ancient heavens through thee are fresh and strong.

Shall set us in the way of his steps, 85:13. From Bohemian History we learn that St. Wencelas, the king, one winter night going to his devotions, in a remote church, barefooted in the snow and sharpness of unequal and pointed ice, his servant Podavivious who waited upon his master's piety, and endeavored to imitate his affections, began to faint through the violence of the cold and snow; till the king commanded him to follow him, and set his feet in the same footsteps, which his feet should mark for him: the servant did so, and either fancied a cure, or found one; for he followed his prince, helped forward with shame and zeal to his imitation, and by the forming footsteps for him in the snow.

Is this not what our Lord urges us to do? He knows if our way is troublesome, obscure, full of objection and danger, apt to be mistaken, so He commands us to mark His footsteps, to tread where His feet have stood, and not only invites us forward by the argument of His example, but He has trodden down much of the difficulty and made the way easier and fit for our feet to follow.

Psalm 86

At the outset, we observed the position of this Psalm, which is an earnest appeal, standing between two others, which promise great things to the cause of God (Psalms 85, 87). This is one of the plaintive songs, edged with hope—"a cloud turning out its silver lining on the night"—with which the French Huguenots were accustomed to march to death. It would seem, as Ellicott suggests, that his Psalm is mainly composed of a number of sentences and verses from older compositions, arranged not without art, and, where it suited the adapter, so altered as to present forms of words peculiar to himself, as, for instance verse 5, the original of which is found in Exodus 20:6; 34:6-9; Numbers 14:18, 19; also verse 6, as marginal references show, taken from Exodus 15:11.

Its simple title, *A Prayer of David,* or, as the margin has it, "A Prayer, being a Psalm of David," and both its matter and wording were suitable to his varied circumstances and expressive of the different characteristics of his mind and so is rightly called *The Prayer of David;* even as Psalm 90 is entitled *The Prayer of Moses.* This is one of the 5 Psalms entitled *Tephillahs,* or "prayers," and bears a resemblance to Psalm 17, which has the same title, but in other aspects it is very different. "The prayers of a good man have a family likeness," says Spurgeon, "but they vary as much as they agree." Yet this 86th Psalm consists of praise as well as prayer but as it is directly addressed to God it is most fitly called a *Prayer.* "A prayer is none the less but all the more a prayer because veins of praise run through it."

Good, and ready to forgive . . . plenteous in mercy, 86:5. It would seem as if David had stood in the cleft of the Rock with Moses and to have heard the name of the Lord proclaimed even as the great lawgiver did, for in two places in this Psalm, David almost quotes *verbatim* the passage already mentioned, Exodus 34:8.

David I, the just and merciful ruler of Scotland, who died on May 24, 1153, spent his last hours of conscious existence in repeating verses from the Psalms. The confidence of faith expressed in verse 7 of Psalm 86 was precious to the ruler's heart, *In the time of my trouble I will call upon Thee, for Thou hearest me.* This Psalm was also conspicuous in the experience of the great scholar, Casaubon, who, with his wife, sailed in an open boat on the Seine to Charenton to worship there with the Huguenots. Psalm singing was constant during the sail, and when the two of them had just reached Psalm 92:7, a heavy barge struck the stern of the boat and threw the wife overboard. Casaubon saved her, after almost losing his own life in the effort. But, in doing so, he dropped into the river his Book of Psalms, given to him by his wife as a wedding present, and for 22 years the constant companion of his travels.

Finally, the two reached the Temple at Charenton, and when the chant of the Psalms began, Casaubon put his hand in his pocket for his book, and for the first time discovered his loss. He did not recover himself till the congregation had finished more than half the 86th Psalm. The verse at which he was able to join in singing was the end of the 13th. *Thou hast delivered my soul from the nethermost hell.* Says Casaubon in his *Journal:*

> I could not but remember that place of Ambrose where he says, "This is the peculiarity of the Psalter, that every one can use its words as if they were completely and individually his own."

But thou, O Lord, art a God full of compassion, and gracious, long-suffering, and plenteous in mercy and truth, 86:15. This sublime revelation of God was embodied in Tennyson's poem, *Rizpah*—

> Sin? O yes—we are sinners, I know—let all that be,
> And read me a Bible verse of the Lord's goodwill towards men—
> "Full of compassion and mercy, the Lord," let me hear it again;
> "Full of compassion and mercy—long-suffering." Yes, O yes!
> For the lawyer is born but to murder, the Savior lives but to bless.

Save the son of thine handmaid, 86:16. David recognized himself as a home-born servant of God. As the sons of slaves were their master's property by their birth, so the Psalmist gloried in being the son of a woman who herself belonged to the Lord. What others might think a degrading illustration he uses with delight to show how intensely he loved the Lord's service; and also as a reason why the Lord should interpose to rescue him, seeing that he was no newly purchased servant, but had been in the house from his very birth.

Show me a token for good, 86:17. God does nothing by halves. Those whom He helps He also consoles, and so makes them not merely safe, but satisfied and joyful. Weiss paraphrases this verse—"Make of me such a sign or monument of good works that all my enemies may be arrested by it, and be daunted at injuring a man so assisted by the Lord."

> Some token of thy favor show,
> > Some sign which all my foes may see;
> And fill'd with blank confusion know,
> > My comfort and my help in thee.

Psalm 87

It was while he was in prison in 1553, that Bishop John Hooper wrote an *Exposition* on this Psalm, as well as of three other Psalms. The Psalter was a constant source of consolation and strength until his execution in 1555. Brief, yet blessed, Psalm 87 is unique not only in the Psalter, but in Hebrew literature in that, as in no other place, its Jewish exclusiveness is spoken. The nameless poet who wrote it goes beyond the forceful submission of the Gentile world to anticipate the language of the Gospels and the spirit of Paul. Zion becomes in his song *the mother of us all*—Gentiles as well as Jews.

As to the historical setting of the Psalm, the mention of *Babylon* suggests a later date than David's reign. The general opinion is that it was written after Jerusalem and the Temple had been built, and had enjoyed a history of which glorious things could be spoken—and were. Among other marvels of God's love in its latter history, it had been untouched by Sennacherib when other cities of Israel and Judah had fallen victims to his cruelty. It was in Hezekiah's reign that Babylon became prominent, when the ambassadors came to congratulate the king concerning his recovery. At that time Tyre would be more famous than at any period in David's day. Bishop Bruno gave the Psalm the title, *The Voice of Prophecy Concerning the Heavenly Jerusalem,* that is, the Church of Christ. Historically, however, the immediate interpretation is associated with the ancient nations mentioned.

His foundation is in the holy mountains, 87:1. The motto of the University of Durham, England—*Fundamenta ejus*—is taken from this opening verse of the Psalm. Jerusalem is rightly named "The Mountain City" because of its remarkable elevation. From every side, the ascent to the city is perpetual, and once in it you breathe the mountain air. Such a capital has been described as the *mountain throne,* the *mountain sanctuary,* of God. Dean Stanley wrote of "the multiplicity of the eminences," the city spires, though in smaller compass, with Roman and Constantinople. *His foundation* is equivalent to *that which He hath founded,* and the *gates* is another way of describing the city itself.

> His foundation on the holy hill
> Loveth Jehovah, (even) Zion's gates.
> More than all Jacob's dwellings.

Spiritually, the holy mountains represent the eternal purpose of Jehovah—the purpose out of which the being of Israel, of the Church, and the whole dispensation of Divine love have sprung. We know that the Church is so firmly founded in Him, Who came as the Rock of Ages, sits so securely, that even the gates of Hell cannot prevail against her.

The Lord loveth the gates of Zion, 87:2. Gates of a walled city give access to it and power over it, and are therefore naturally put there for the whole. *Loving* implies constant and habitual attachment. Augustine chose for the motto of his work on *The City of God,* the words founded on this second verse. "Very excellent things are spoken of Thee, O City of God." This remarkable treatise written in the 4th century, in the glare of burning Rome, expresses with glowing eloquence Augustine's sense of the eternal destinites of the City of God.

The great festivals, when the crowds surrounded the temple gates of old, were fair in the Lord's eyes, and even such in "the general assembly and church of the first born," whose names are written in Heaven. Although it is written, "God loves the dwellings of Jacob," here we are told that "He loves the gates of Zion more than such dwellings." Nothing attracts His attention and captures His love like the people of God bound together in a spiritual capacity such as Zion represents.

Glorious things are spoken of thee, O city of God, 87:3. The most glorious things that can be spoken of all other excellencies in the world are but titular things, mere shadows alongside the blessedness to be found in God's habitation. The Shechinah, which appeared upon Sinai, and marshalled the army of the Israelites upon their journey through the wilderness, has now fixed its residence in the city of God. "The Lord is among them, as in Sinai, in the holy place," Psalm 68:17. The conspicuous *Selah* of the Psalms occurs in this short Psalm in even verses, twice over. Verses 4-6, in which Zion is *the birthplace* of the nations, is thrice mentioned, the section verses 4-7 are bounded by a *Selah* behind and before. The Jews of old interpreted this term as meaning "everlasting." As already indicated, to those who composed the music for many of the Psalms, *Selah* represented a pause in the music, a period in which to *think* and *thank.* Spurgeon's comment on the double use of *Selah* in this Psalm says, "With the prospect before him of a world converted, and the most implacable foes transformed into friends, it was meet that the Psalmist should pause. How could he sing the glories of new-born Tyre and Ethiopia, received with open arms into union with Zion, until he had taken breath and prepared both voice and heart for so divine a song."

I will make mention of Rahab, Babylon, Philistia. Tyre and Ethiopia were born there, 87:4. The superfluous word *man* inserted by the translators should be dropped, because not an individual person, but whole nations were born anew. Great rival nations forgot their old enmities, and became fellow-worshippers. What a wonder it is when whole nations are born unto God! Whether some were born in Egypt or came from Ethiopia, all were equally honored as home-born sons of the city of God. How matchless are His grace and power revealed in the miraculous translation of nations from darkness to light, and from the lowest degree of one to the highest degree of the other!

> The proud from *Egypt,* who for her haughtiness is called Rahab—
> The worldly from Babylon, the city of confusion—
> The wrathful from Philistia—long the enemies of Israel—
> The covetous from Tyre, the rich city of the traders.

The slaves of ignorance from Cush, and from the land of Ham, are brought under the regenerating, transforming power of the Spirit of God. When the Lord come to write up His people, there will be multitudes from these, and all other countries down the ages, who will find their names inscribed upon the pages of the Divine register-book.

Attention has been drawn to the phrase, *"This and that man* was born in *her,"* 87:5. Two things are signified in this expression, as branches of their honor; the one is the *quality* of the persons; and the other is the *number* of them. For the *quality* of them, *this;* for the *number* of them, *this and that.* To have both of these born in Zion, persons of *note and eminency;* and a *multitude and plurality* of such persons; this is a part of that dignity and renown which belongs unto it. *This man* in the Hebrew implies an *honorable* man, eminent in many ways. The Chaldee paraphrase of the text reads, *"This King* was born there," thought by many to be Solomon.

The Lord shall count, when he writeth up his people, 87:6. It was deemed to be a great honor to have one's name written in the golden book of the Republic of Venice. Kings and princes paid dearly for the honor. But a perishable honor-book is not worthy to be compared to the Book of Life with the far rarer dignity of those whose names are eternally recorded therein. God's census of His born-again ones will differ so much from the registers of earth, for He will count many whom men would have disowned, and omit many whom society would have reckoned. And His registration will be infallible and irreversible. As for ourselves, our names will not be found written in the Lamb's Book of Life, unless, by adoption and regeneration, we have found a place among the heaven-born.

The singers as the players on instruments shall be there, 87:7. There— Where? Among the heaven-born. Because their names are inscribed on the Divine scroll, they will praise with perfect voices. The Hebrews may have surpassed all the nations mentioned in this Psalm in the skill of poetry and music, but those included in Zion's birth-register will experience a perfect harmony of voice never known on earth, because their eternal song will be of Him Who brought them into His eternal city.

All my springs are in thee, 87:7. The Greeks had their Pierian Springs, their fountain of Aganiffe dedicated to the Muses, but Jerusalem had more sacred springs, her fountains of inspiration, in a much higher degree. It is to these the holy land alludes in this verse, as John Milton does—

> Or if Zion's hill
> Delight thee more, or *Sion's fount that flowed*
> *Hard by the oracle of God,* I thence
> Invoke thine aid to my adventurous song.

Some there are who translate *springs* as *melodies* or *songs,* and thus the couplet—

> Whether songs or melodies
> In Thee are all my well-springs.

Yet others affirm that *springs* represent *hopes,* or *affections,* or *thoughts.* Of this we are confident—all the silver springs of grace, and the golden springs of glory are in Him, Who is the hidden source of calm repose, and Who, in want, is our plentiful supply.

Psalm 88

Because of its biographical nature, Dummelow, in his *One-Volume Bible Commentary,* suggests that, although nothing is known as to the identity of the author, or when he wrote, that this Psalm stands out as "the saddest and most despairing of all the Psalms; and that the writer was apparently the victim of some incurable disease like leprosy, with

which he had been afflicted from his youth, verse 15—
which cut him off from society of men, verses 8, 18—
that his life was already a living death, verses 3-6—
and beyond death he had no hope, verses 10-12—
that his trouble could be traced to God's displeasure, verses 7, 14, 16—
yet it is to God that he turned in pathetic appeal for relief, verses 1, 2, 9, 13."

Lord Bacon once wrote that "If you listen to David's harp you will hear as many hearse-like airs as carols," and Psalm 88 with its "hearse-like air," stands out among the Psalms of this nature, alone and peculiar, because of the sadness of its tone. From beginning to end, with the solitary exception of its opening approach, "O Lord God of my *salvation,*" there is nothing to relieve the monotony of grief and wail of sorrow so characteristic of the Psalm as a whole. It is doubted by some commentators whether the Psalm is a picture of individual sorrow and anguish, and not rather a figurative description of national trouble. The phrase "from my youth up," 88:15, is not against the reference in the Psalm to Israel as a nation, seeing this very phrase is used of her, Psalm 129:1.

Bishop John Hooper, mentioned often in this coverage of the historical associations of the Psalms and who was burned at the stake at Gloucester, 1555, during the reign of Queen Mary, spoke highly of this 88th Psalm to his wife, when writing to her from prison. "It contains," wrote the martyr, "the prayer of a man brought into extreme anguish and misery, and who, being vexed with adversaries and persecutions, saw nothing but death and hell. And although he felt in himself that he had not only man but also God, angry towards him, yet he by prayer humbly resorted unto God, and the only port of consolation in his desperate state of trouble. These Psalms be for the purpose of help, when the mind can have no understanding, nor the heart any joy of God's promises; and therefore were the 6th, 22nd, 30th, 31st, 38th, and 69th Psalms also made, from the which you shall learn both patience and consolation."

The title of the Psalm is suggestive in the light of its nature. It reads *A Song or Psalm*. But, as Spurgeon remarks, "This sad complaint reads very little like a *Song*, nor can we conceive how it could be called by a name which denotes a song of praise or triumph; yet perhaps it was intentionally so called to show how faith glories in *tribulation also*. Assuredly, if ever there was a song of sorrow, and a psalm of sadness, this is one. *The Sons of Korah* who had often united in chanting jubilant odes, are now bidden to take charge of this mournful dirge-like hymn."

The phrase, *Upon Mahalath Leannoth,* means "Upon the sickness of distress," or upon a sickening distress, and indicates the mental malady which occasioned this plaintive song. This title may have been the name of a tune, or the first words of a hymn associated with music suitable to this melancholy effusion. It is also another *Maschil* Psalm, or instructive ode, and reminds us that the sorrows of one saint can be lessons to others, and that experimental teaching is exceedingly valuable. Whether any poet by the name of *Heman* (see 1 Chron. 15:19) wrote this poem is of little consequence. Whoever the writer was he must have been a man of deep experience, who had done business on the great waters of soul trouble.

My life draweth high unto the grave, 88:3. This phrase brings into prominence the idea, expressed elsewhere in the Psalms, that the thought of death severs covenant relations with God, and so presents an irresistible reason why prayer should be heard now before it is too late. In his most helpful work, *Reflections on the Psalms,* C. S. Lewis has a chapter on "Death in the Psalms," in which he contrasts the dim light of Old Testament saints on death and the after life with that of the clearer and final revelation of the New Testament. Thus, of old *Death* was "the land," where, not only worldly things, but all things "are forgotten, 88:12, and that once in the grave, the dead are not remembered by God anymore, 88:3-5." The dead are "clean forgotten, out of mind," even to God, and that His helping hand stretched out to living men, does not reach to the grave.

Like the slain, 88:5. The moaner felt as if he were as utterly forgotten as those whose carcases are left to rot on the battlefield. As when a soldier, mortally wounded, bleeds unheeded amid the heaps of slain, and remains to his last expiring groan, unpitied and unsuccoured. It is sorrowful how low the spirits of good and brave men can sometimes sink, and we should never ridicule the nervous and hypochondriacal, their pain is real; though much of the evil lies in the imagination, it is not imaginary.

Thou hast laid me in the lowest pit, 88:6. Here the writer compares himself to a captive who has been cast into a deep, foul, dark, and slimy pit, where he is shut up and plunged in filth and darkness, having not a remnant of hope and life—something akin to Jeremiah's sufferings, chapter 37. By the use of such a simile, the Psalmist meant that he was in the greatest anxieties and sorrows of mind, destitute of every hope and sense of consolation, and that the terrors of death continually increased and augmented. On the Cross, Jesus could have said with the writer, *Thy wrath lieth, Lord, upon me,* and as He endured Divine wrath because of sin, there was wrung from His heart that doleful outcry, *My God, My God, Why hast Thou forsaken Me?*

Thou hast put mine acquaintance far from me . . . My lovers and friends Thou hast put away from me, and hid mine acquaintance out of my sight, 88:7-10. These were the words attendants heard Henry of Navarre sing as he lay in bed, ill, feverish, and depressed. After the massacre of St. Bartholomew in 1572, Henry found himself a prisoner of Catherine de Medici, who sought to corrupt his spirit through sensual indulgence, as she had done with her own son. But the brave Reformer never lost his conscience, and as his servant, Agrippa d'Aubigné heard him sighing to himself the above words from this Psalm, he said to Henry—

> Sire, is it not true that the Spirit of God is still dwelling and working in you? While your friends are fighting against your enemies, you fail them. Your friends fear only God, and you, a woman before whom you crouch when they stand erect like men.

One could go on and enumerate incidents down through the whole of history strangely linked together by the wail of this Psalm, which, alas! Henry of Navarre did not lay enough to heart.

Selah! 88:7. After the groanings of a gracious heart toward Jehovah, the God of Salvation, presented in the first seven verses of the Psalm, there was certainly need for a rest! This exclamation is also found at verse 10, where the complainer sits down at the mouth of a tomb to meditate, before returning to his doleful theme. Says Spurgeon, "Above the breakers this swimmer lifts his head and looks around him, breathing for a moment, until the next wave come. Even lamentation must have its pauses. Nights are broken up into watches, and even so mourning has its intervals. Such sorrowful music is a great strain both on voices and instruments, and it is well to give the singers the relief of silence for a while."

I am shut up, and I cannot come forth, 88:8. The distressed writer felt like a prisoner in his cell, or like a leper in the lazarette, or as a condemned criminal, as in forced confinement he awaits death. The mind also was bound with fetters of iron, and he felt no liberty of hope. When God shuts friends out, and shuts us in to pine away alone, is it any wonder if we water our couch with tears?

Mine eye mourneth . . . I have called, 88:9. Sobs and supplications are united, prayers and tears go together. "I have heard thy prayers, and seen thy tears." The first clause in this verse literally means the soreness and dimness of sight caused by excessive weeping, as illustrated by the Latin poet, Catullus, in the lines—

> Nor my sad eyes to pine with constant tears
> Could cease.

Shall thy lovingkindness be declared in the grave? 88:11. The beauty and pathos of this poem are most expressive in its Scottish Version—

> A solemn voice
> Of several voices in one solemn sound,
> Was heard ascending: mournful, deep, and slow,
> The cadence as of Psalms—a funeral dirge!
> We listened, looking down upon the hut,
> But seeing no one: meanwhile, from below,
> The stain continued, spiritual as before;
> And now distinctly could I recognize
> These words:—*Shall in the grave thy love be known,*
> *In death thy faithfulness?*

Destruction . . . darkness . . . forgetfulness, 88:11, 12. Here we have three prominent features of the Hebrew conception of the underworld. It is a place of "destruction" (see Job 26:6, 28:22), of "darkness" (Psalm 88:6), and of "forgetfulness," which may imply not only that the dead are forgotten, both of God and men (Psalm 31:5, 12), but that they themselves have, to borrow the heathen figure, drunk of the water of Lethe (see Eccles. 9:5-10). How privileged we are to have the full revelation of life, death and the vast Eternity, the New Testament presents!

I am afflicted and ready to die from my youth up, 88:15. There are those who suffer far more than others. William S. Plumer, Bible expositor of the 18th century, wrote: "I have seen a child, who at the age of 20 months had probably suffered more bodily pain than the whole congregation of 1,000 souls, where its parents worshipped. Asaph seems to have been of a sad heart. Jeremiah lived and died lamenting. Heman, the writer of this Psalm, seems to have been of the same lot and of the same turn of mind."

Thy fierce wrath goeth over me, 88:16. The Hebrew has it, *"Thy hot wraths."* This is something akin to a sea of liquid fire (Ps. 42:7). *Thy terrors have cut me off.* Gregory Nazianzen in his first oration concerning *Peace,* called Grief—*the prison of the heart.* "Cut me off," means to shut up and press into some narrow place, in order that one may not breathe or escape. *Like water* signifies, not merely because it drowns, but because it searches every crevice, goes to the very bottom, and makes its way on all sides, when once it obtains an entrance, thus fitly denoting the penetrating force of temptation and trouble.

Lover and friend hast thou put far from me, 88:18. It is not difficult to apply some of the phrases of this Psalm to Him Who knows what lonely sorrow was. During His passion, the Lord Jesus learned all about the wormwood and the gall. In dreadful loneliness He trod the wine-press, and all His garments were stained with the red blood of those sour grapes. It has been pointed out that the very rhythm of this last verse shows that the piece is not complete. The ear remains in suspense until the majestic Psalm 89 bursts forth upon it like a bright Resurrection-morning.

Mine acquaintance into darkness, is not correct, and should read, "My acquaintance is darkness," or "darkness is my friend," having taken the place of those removed. The feeling resembles Job 17:14, or we may illustrate it by Tennyson's lines—

> O sorrow, wilt thou live with me.
> No carnal mistress, but a wife.
> My bosom friend, and half my life?
> As I confess it needs must be.

Psalm 89

This long Psalm is like the Celestial City after the *Slough of Despond* of the previous Psalm. O what a change! Psalm 88 commences with a *sob*—Psalm 89, with a *song*. The former ends in darkness, the latter in a benediction and doxology. As Christopher Wordsworth expressed it, "The present Psalm makes a pair with the preceding one. It is a spiritual Allegro to that Ponseroso . . . Psalm 88 was a dirge of Passion-Tide, this Psalm is a carol of Christmas." What makes this Psalm doubly precious is its Messianic foregleams, because there are many passages in it that cannot clearly, pertinently, and appositely be applied to anyone else but to Him Who made Christmas possible.

Here we have another national and Historical Psalm, which was born in times of great national depression and trouble, and which celebrates Israel's victory over her enemies. The Captivity is past, and the nation is free again, and the poet can think only of the splendid promises of God to the race, and the paradox that while made by a God of truth and faithfulness, they have yet been broken. This is another *Maschil,* or instructive Psalm, and full of lessons regarding our Covenanting-keeping God, hence its worthy title of "The Majestic Covenant Psalm," which Spurgeon gives it.

As to its composer, the Psalm is said to have come from *Ethan the Ezrahite,* mentioned in 1 Kings 4:31; 1 Chronicles 2:6. "Perhaps this is the same person as Jedutha, who was a musician in David's reign; was noted for his wisdom in Solomon's reign, and probably survived until the troubles of Rehoboam's period. If this be the man, he must have written this Psalm in his old age, when troubles were coming thick and heavy upon the dynasty of David and the land of Judah; this is not at all improbable, and there is much in the Psalm which looks that way." While some scholars may not agree with Spurgeon's sketch of its author, the Psalm is the utterance of one whose faith was rooted in God, and who knew how, in the presence of great national disaster to plead with Him, and from Whom he expected help and deliverance because of His faithfulness. Ellicott says that the time of the persecution of Antiochus Epiphanes suits best of all the conditions presented by this Psalm whose poetical form is regular, and its parallelism well-marked.

I will sing of the mercies of the Lord forever, 89:1. Alas! the lyric soon loses itself in a dirge. In our coverage of the Psalm frequent mention is made of St. Francis de Sales, Bishop of Geneva, whose life and ministry were inspired by the Psalm. When he came to die in 1622, the Psalms were always on his lips, and among verses he quoted was this one—"My song shall be alway of the loving-kindness of the Lord," 89:1.

Saint Gregory the Great raised the question as to how perpetual singing *of the mercies of God* is compatible with unalloyed bliss in Heaven, inasmuch as the thought of mercy connotes the memory of sin and sorrow, which needed mercy, whereas Isaiah said that "the former troubles are fogotten," and "the former things shall not be remembered, nor come upon the heart," 65:15, 17. Then Gregory gives the explanation, "It will be like the memory of past sickness in time of health, without stain, without grief, and serving only to heighten the felicity of the redeemed, by the contrast with the past, and to increase their love and gratitude towards God." It would seem as if this was also the sentiment of saintly Bernard of Clairvaux, expressed in his verse—

> Their breasts are filled with gladness,
> > Their mouths are turned to praise,
> What time, now safe forever
> > On former sins they gaze:
> The fouler was the error,
> > The sadder was the fall,
> The ampler are the praises
> > Of Him Who pardoned all.

Mercy shall be built up forever: thy faithfulness shalt thou establish, 89:2. The two attributes, often combined in Scripture, expressed here, are commonly in the Psalms, the attitude of the Covenant God towards His people. The art of the poet is seen in the opening of the Psalm, in which he strikes so strongly this note of the inviolability of the Divine promise only to make the deprecation of present neglect on God's part presently more striking. Then the phrase *built up forever* is striking. Former mercies are fundamental to later ones. Mercies we enjoy today are founded and built upon the mercies of former days. As Richard Mant poetically describes it—

> For I have said, Thy mercies rise,
> A deathless structure to the skies:
> The heav'ns were planted by Thy hand,
> And, as the heav'ns, Thy truth shall stand.

The two attributes, then, are presented as an edifice for every rising or foundations laid in the heavens (see Psalm 119:89). *The heavens* are at once the emblems of God's own immutability, splendor, and height. Wordsworth could glorify Him as the One—

Who fixed immovably the frame
Of the round World, and built by laws as strong
The solid refuge for distress,
The towers of righteousness.

Thy seed . . . Thy throne . . . Selah! 89:4. Jesus, Who came as David's Greater Son, established forever the *seed* David himself rejoices to see. The dynasty of David never decays. On the contrary, it is evermore consolidated by the great Architect of heaven and earth. David's Son and Lord is King as well as progenitor, and His throne is ever being built up— His kingdom comes—His power extends. Well might we rest awhile at the bidding of this another *Selah,* and, lifting up our hearts, proceed with the sacred poet to echo forth the praises of the Lord.

The heavens shall praise thy wonders, 89:5. After the repetition of the Divine promise, the poet appeals to nature and history to confirm his conviction of the enduring character of the truth and grace of God. How wonderfully the heavens witness to same (see Psalm 1:4, 6; 97:6). *Wonders.* The original word is in the singular, and sums up all the covenant faithfulness of God as one great display of wonder. "The heaven" . . . "the congregation of saints"—the whole family in heaven and earth unite in admiring and praising the covenant God.

Who among the sons of the mighty can be likened unto the Lord, 89:6. This was the verse used by a French Huguenot in reply to a courtier who urged Henry IV to choose the strongest side.

God is greatly to be feared, 89:7. One translation of this phrase reads, "God is daunting terrible." The original Hebrew word for *feared* means, "he was broken, bruised, terrified." Says Bythner of this conception of the Almighty, "An epithet of God as breaking all things." Another has it, "God is to be vehemently feared," in opposition to any careless, trifling, vain spirit in worshipping Him.

God sublime in the council of the holy ones,
And terrible among those surrounding Him.

O Lord God of Hosts, who is a strong Lord like unto thee? 89:8. Jehovah is here presented as being robed with the garments of omnipotence and faithfulness. The Hebrew setting marches more grandly than our A.V.—

Jehovah, God of Hosts
Who as Thou is mighty, Jah?
And Thy faithfulness surrounds Thee.

Thou hast broken Rahab in pieces, 89:10. There is a twofold reason why *Egypt* is spoken of as *Rahab.* First of all, Rahab signifies "strength," and Egypt was a very strong nation, hence its Divine reproof for seeking the help of other nations, which to the Israelites were broken reeds. Secondly, *Rahab* means "pride," or "the proud." Usually the strong are proud of their strength, and Egypt being strong was also a very proud nation. Egypt was Israel's ancient foe, and its overthrow called for the most exulting songs. When our Rahab is broken, our sins overthrown, what else can we do but praise Him Who is our Deliverer?

The north and the south thou hast created them, 89:12. The Scottish saint, Robert Murray McCheyne, describing a visit to the Holy Land, wrote of "the position of Tabor and Hermon as being the *umbilicus terrae*—the central point of the land," and led me to infer that his is the true explanation of the manner in which they are referred to in Psalm 89:12. It is as if the Psalmist had said, North, South, and *all that is between,* or in other words, the whole land from "North to South, to its very center and throughout its very marrow—shall rejoice in thy name."

Another way of looking at this verse with its geographical content is that *North* and *South* are opposite poles, yet agree in this fact that Jehovah fashioned them. *Tabor* and *Hermon* represent east and west, but were equally created by the Lord, and praise Him, as Keble wrote—

> Both Hermon moist, and Tabor lone,
> They wait on Thee with glad acclaim.

Justice and judgment . . . Mercy and truth, 89:14. What a marvelous quartet of Divine attributes are here combined by the writer. The first two form the basis of Divine government, the sphere in which God's sovereignty moves. As for the latter two, they are the harbingers and heralds of the Lord, and in the person of Jesus they were His ambassadors. These four attributes are the robes God invests Himself with.

> *Justice* defends His subjects, and acts in a right way toward every one.
> *Judgment* restrains rebels, and preserves from injuries.
> *Mercy* shows compassion, pardons, supports the weak.
> *Truth* performs all that God has promised.

Pinder called *Truth* "the daughter of God." Epaminondas the Theban general cultivated truth so studiously, we are told, that he was never known to have spoken a falsehood even in jest. In the Courts of Kings this is a rare virtue. Jesus personified *Truth* when He declared, "I am . . . the Truth."

Thou art the glory of their strength, 89:17. A better word for "glory" is ornament, for the crown of a nation's strength, says Ellicott, is not the triumphs it wins, nor the prosperity it secures, but the spirit in which these are used. Humility, not pride, acknowledgment of God and not conceit in her wealth or power, was the ornament of Israel's strength, and made her greatness in her best days. As for the exaltation of the *horn,* the poet promises a man of lofty bearing is said to carry his horn very high. In the Orient, one proudly interfering with the affairs of another would say, "Where is your *komba*—horn?" "Here," the questioned one would reply, pointing to his possessions and influence. "Truly, my lord, you have a great horn." Two others sayings reveal the typical significance of the horn, "Chinnan has lost his money; ay, and his hornship too." "Alas! alas! I am like the deer whose horns are fallen off."

Spurgeon says that the horn was an eastern ornament, worn by men and women, and by the uplifting of this the wearer showed himself to be in good spirits, and in a confident frame of mind. As the children of God, we wear no such outward vanities, but our inward soul is adorned and bravely triumphant when His favor is felt by us.

The sea . . . the rivers, 89:25. It is suggested that we have a reference here, as in Psalms 72:8; 80:11, to the limits of the Solomonic kingdom, the Mediterranean and the Euphrates. For the figure, we may compare a saying attributed to Curtius to some Scythian ambassadors, who addressed Alexander in these terms—

> If the gods had given thee a body as great as thy mind, the whole world would not be able to contain thee. Thou wouldst reach with one hand to the east and with the other to the west.

Thou art my father, 89:26. As David, or any other poet or prophet in the Old Testament is spoken of as calling God—*Father,* the verse surely carries a Messianic significance, for when the True David appeared, He could say, "My Father and your Father, My God, and your God." *Father,* was Christ's favorite mode of address, and often He cried, "My Father." God had one Son without sin, but He never had a Son who lived without prayer.

My firstborn, 89:17. This position, formerly given to the nation, Exodus 4:22, is here assigned to its king. But do we not see Jesus in such a relationship? Who can rival Heaven's Firstborn, Who is higher than all the kings of earth, and Who is "established forever as the moon"? Whatever original application this verse may have had to the quality and perpetuity of David's kingdom, it will receive its perfect fulfillment in the eternal Kingdom of David's greater Son and Lord.

As a faithful witness in heaven, 89:37. Another translation reads, "As the rainbow's faithful sign." According to Greek mythology the *rainbow* was the daughter of *wonder—a sign to mortal men.* Therefore its appearance was regarded as a messenger of celestial deities. Homer with remarkable conformity to Scripture speaks of the *rainbow* which "Jove hast set in the clouds, in sign to men." But the parallelism of the verse makes *the moon* the faithful witness in the heavens. The *moon* to the

Jews, and ancients generally, was reckoned to be "the arbiter of festivals," and the festivals were signs of the covenant, consequently this luminary can be called "a witness in heaven."

Cast off and abhorred . . . Profaned his crown, 89:38, 39. For *abhorred* the R.V. gives us "rejected." Scholars are divided over whether *Thine anointed* refers to the Jewish nation as a whole, or to one of her kings. The crown of the king, as with that of the high priest, carried the inscription, "Holiness to the Lord," Exodus 28:36, and was therefore deemed a sacred possession and thus to cast it in the dust was to profane it.

The days of his youth hast thou shortened, 89:45. Several kings of Israel did not reign half their days, nor live out half their lives. The last *four* kings of Judea reigned but a short time, and either died by the sword or in captivity. Old Testament history records that—

> *Jehoahaz* reigned only *three* months, and died a captive in Egypt.
>
> *Jehoiakim* reigned only *eleven* years, was delivered to the Chaldeans who put him to death, and flung his body into a common sewer.
>
> *Jehoiachin* reigned *three months and ten days,* and became a captive in Babylon. Latterly released he was never invested with power.
>
> *Zedekiah* reigned only *eleven years,* when his eyes were put out, and loaded with chains, he was carried to Babylon.

Most of these kings, then, died a violent and *premature* death. *The days of their youth*—of their virility, power, dignity, and life—"were shortened, and they themselves, covered with shame." *Selah!* Truly this is something to pause and think about that kings were wrapped up in the winding-sheet of shame.

Thou hast also turned the edge of this sword, 89:43. A soldier's position is perilous when his sword is *broken,* or its *edge turned,* or his *gun misses fire.* The *Gauls,* when invaded by the Romans, had no method of *hardening* iron; at every blow their swords *bended,* so that they were obliged, before they could strike again, to put them under their foot, or over their knee, to straighten them; in most cases before this could be done, their better armed foe had taken away their life! The edge of their sword was turned, so that they could not stand in battle; and hence the *Gauls* were conquered by the Romans.

Wherefore hast thou made all men in vain? 89:47. Literally, "For what vanity hast thou created all men?" Says Matthew Henry, "If we think that God hath made man *in vain,* because so many have short lives, and long afflictions in this world, it is true that God *hath made* them so: but it is not true, that therefore they are *made in vain.*" How apt are the lines of Byron, the unhapppy Scottish poet—

> Count all the joys thine hours have seen,
>   Count all the days from anguish free,
> And know, whatever thou hast been
>   'Twere something better not to be.

What man is he that liveth, and shall not see death? 89:48. The word for *man* here means, *what hero,* or *champion,* or *great man.* The same word is used of a *king,* Isaiah 22:17; Jeremiah 22:30. None can doubt Shakespeare's familiarity with the Psalms. "Death, as the Psalmist saith, is certain to all: all shall die." So *Justices Shallow* to *Silence,* alluding to Psalm 89:48. "What man is he that liveth and shall not see death?"

Death spares no *rank,* no *condition* of men. We read that Julius Caesar bid the master of the ship wherein he was sailing, take courage notwithstanding the boisterous tempest, because he had Caesar and his fortunes embarked in the vessel, as much as to say, the element on which they then were could not prove fatal to an Emperor, so great a one as he was.

England's William, surnamed *Rufus,* once said that he never heard of a king that was drowned. Charles the 5th, at the Battle of Tunis, being advised to retire when the battle became fierce, told them that it was never known that an Emperor was slain with great shot, and so rushed into battle. But the fact of the matter is that no king or crowned head escaped the blow of death at last. The scepter cannot keep off "the arrows that fly by day and the sickness that wastes at noonday." Great tyrants have vaunted that they had power of life, and death, but yet were not able to guard against the shafts of their own death. To king and knave alike the King of Terrors comes.

> The boast of heraldry, the pomp of power,
>   And all that beauty, all that wealth e'er gave,
> Await alike the inevitable hour—
>   The paths of glory lead but to the grave.

The footsteps of thine anointed, 89:51. The experience depicted was the time when every step taken by Israel was the subject of reproach. Rabbinical writers connect this verse with the delay of the Messiah, since it brings reproach on those who wait for Him in vain.

Blessed be the Lord forever more, Amen, and Amen, 89:52. The Psalmist ends where he began; he has sailed round the world and reached port again. Perhaps he wrote this Psalm in his old age when troubles were coming thick and heavy upon the dynasty of David and the land of Judah, and thus left a text-book for the spiritual instructions for future generations. Victory begins to shine in this last verse, marking the end of the Third Book of Psalms. (See Pss. 41:13; 72:18, 19.)

BOOK FOUR • PSALMS 90 TO 106
Psalm 90

What a Psalm of deep solemnity and pathos this is, beginning, as it does, with a past Eternity, moving on to an eternal future, while it gathers into its bosom people with their sins and brief fading lives, and supplicates for them God's forgiving and tender mercy! The old Russian Church made its first four verses its burial song. At the funeral of the renowned John Hampden in the churchyard of Great Hampden, a detachment of his favorite troops mournfully chanted as they slowly marched along the dirge from this Psalm, "Lord thou hast been our dwelling-place in all generations. Thou turnest man to destruction." "Many generations of mourners have listened to this Psalm when standing around an open grave, and have been consoled thereby, even when they have not perceived its special application to Israel in the wilderness and have failed to remember the far higher ground upon which believers stand."

Psalm 90 appears to be the oldest of the Psalms, and stands between two Books of Psalms as a composition "unique in its grandeur, and alone in its sublime antiquity." This Fourth Book, covering Psalms 90-106, is distinguished by smaller groups or collections—

Psalms 93, 95-100 are known as Theocratic Psalms, seeing that they celebrate God as King, finding in the restoration of Israel from Babylon the evidences of His government of the World. These Psalms are probably to be dated soon after that event when it was still fresh in the people's minds.

Psalms 90, 91, 94, and 102, suggest times of national humiliation and sorrow Israel knew a great deal about.

Psalms 103 and 104 are twins, and more than likely were by the same writer.

Psalms 105 and 106 also form a pair, and like all the rest of the Psalms in this section, characteristically use the august, Divine name, *Jehovah*.

In the classification of the nature of these Psalms, divisions necessarily overlap one another—

Penitential Psalms—90, 91, 94, 102.
Thanksgiving Psalms—92, 93, 95-100.
National Psalms—94, 97, 99, 102, 105, 106.
Historical Psalms—105, 106.
Psalm 101 is described as *Gnomic*.

While Psalm 90 is ascribed to Moses, and Psalms 101 and 103 to David, most of them appear to be anonymous. The Septuagint Version *(LXX)* gives Psalms 91, 93-99, 101, 103, and 104 to David. Although Psalm 90 is stated to be *A Prayer of Moses The Man of God,* some scholars affirm that it must have been written long after the patriarch's day, seeing that the average length of life in his time was greater than the "three-score years and ten" mentioned in verse 10 (Deut. 34:7; Joshua 24:29).

For ourselves, however, we have no doubt that Psalm 90 is the composition of Moses and that he can be considered as the first composer of sacred hymns. It has a marked unlikeness to any of the Psalms of David, and almost every conservative Bible scholar from Jerome down has accepted it as *A Prayer of Moses The Man of God* whose name it has always carried. This oldest poem in the world has similarity of diction to the poetical portions of the Pentatauch without the slightest trace of imitation or quotation. Mighty in word and deed, Moses gives us in his Psalm one of his weighty utterances comparable to his glorious oration recorded in Deuteronomy.

Moses was worthy of the title given him for he was peculiarly a man of God and God's man—chosen of God, inspired by God, honored of God, and faithful to God in all his house and labors. As the first great leader of Israel, he was well-qualified to record the experiences of the nation in the wilderness as he pre-eminently illustrates in almost every verse of his *Prayer.* The internal evidence, therefore, with the turns, expressions, and words similar to many in the Pentateuch, favors its Mosaic origin. This, of course, was not the only prayer of Moses, for as a man of God he had "a correspondence fixed between earth and Heaven." It is a specimen of the way the Seer of Heaven communed with Heaven and interceded for Israel's salvation and sanctification.

Because Moses contrasted the Eternity of God with the transience of human life, verses 1-6 traced the brevity and troublesomeness of man's existence to God's displeasure with sin, 7-12 ended with a prayer for God's forgiveness and favor, 13-17 have been used for centuries as an appropriate Scripture at Burial Services. As for historical incidents connected with this Psalm, like other odes in the Psalter, its influence has been widely felt. For instance, Charles V, the champion of the Pope against the Protestants and avowed foe of Martin Luther, was yet one with the Reformer in love for the Psalms. In September 1558, as he lay on his deathbed, passages were read aloud to him from the Bible, especially his favorite Psalm 90. At his request, the Emperor received the Sacrament, but said, "It may not be necessary: yet it is good company on so long a journey." He died September 21, 1558.

Newman, in his *Dream of Gerontius,* has some striking passages which are echoes from the Psalms. As the Angel committed his charge to a temporary keeping of the Angels of Purgatory, the Souls within the golden prison break into a solemn chant, which is a parapharased part of Psalm 90—

1. Lord, Thou hast been our refuge in every generation;
2. Before the hills were born, and the world was, from age to age Thou art God.
3. Bring us not, Lord, very low, for Thou hast said, Come back again, ye sons of Adam.
4. A thousand years before Thine eyes are but as yesterday.

John Ruskin as soon as he was able to read learned many passages from the Psalms sitting at his mother's side, and among them was Psalm 90 which became precious to him. Admiral G. E. Belknap, of the U. S. Navy, who led the capture of the Barrier forts in China in 1856, and who was engaged in many Civil War battles, wrote—

> Among many noteworthy and suggestive chapters in the Bible, not omit-ting the magnificent epic of Job, *Psalm 90* is a great favorite with me. Its majestic phrasing and solid statement often sounds in my ears. It seems to declare and impress upon us the height and majesty, the omnipotence, the unchanging purposes and eternal grace of Almighty God more compre-hensively and profoundly than any other chapter of Holy Writ. It also sets forth the solemn fact of man's brief life and evanescent work in a way that even a fool in his sublimest folly can understand and take home to himself the ever-living truth that from the earth he sprang and that to the earth he must soon return, while God reigns from everlasting to everlasting and his testimonies are ever very sure.

Psalm 90 stands out as one of the most sublime of human composi-tions—the deepest feelings—the loftiest in theologic conception—the most magnificent in its imagery. Isaac Taylor goes on to say that it is true in its report of human life as troubled, transitory, and sinful. It is also true in its conception of the Eternal as the Sovereign and Judge and yet also the refuge and hope of all people, who, notwithstanding the most severe trials of their faith, lose not their confidence in Him, but in the firmness of faith, pray for, as if they were predicting, a near-at-hand season of refreshment.

If only Plato had known God as Moses did, this is the kind of Psalm he might have written. It belongs to no age, but to the sorrows and the hopes of all the successive generations, who, at the open grave have derived, and shall derive, consolation and faith. It is *The Funeral Hymn of the World.* The Russian Church used verses 1-4 of this Psalm as a burial song.

Lord, thou hast been our dwelling place, 90:1. Both the LXX and the Vulgate Versions have *refuge,* for "dwelling place," and the idea of God as our *continued abode* is the key-note of the Psalm. Martin Luther says that this is a remarkable expression, the like of which is found nowhere else in Scripture. In other places the opposite is used—men are called temples of God in whom He dwells. Says Paul, "The temple of God is holy, which temple ye are." Moses inverts this, and affirms we are the inhabitants of this house, and seeks to show that all our hopes are placed most securely in God. The Italian writer of the 14th century, Giovanni Pico wrote that, "God created the earth for beasts to inhabit, the sea for fishes, the air for fowls, and heaven for angels and stars so that men hath no place to dwell and abide in but God alone."

One generation goes, another comes, but the saints in each generation rest in the unchanging God Who rules over all human history; and, transient creatures as they are, they can be secure and at home in Him. As the first verse of the hymn of Francis Bacon on verses 1-6 expresses it—

> O Lord, thou art our Lord, to whom we fly,
>   And so hast always been, from age to age,
> Before the hills did intercept the eye,
>   Or that the frame was up on earthly stage.
>   One God thou wert, and art, and still shall be;
>   The line of time, it does not measure thee.

Even from everlasting to everlasting, thou art, O God, 90:2. The short duration of each succeeding generation of men on earth is contrasted with the Eternity of God Who was *when nothing else was.* He would be a most uncertain dwelling-place for His people, if He was not the Eternal One. If He was the God only of yesterday, He would not be a suitable refuge for mortal man. Thus in contrast to the brevity of human life, His eternal existence is exalted. *Mountains* are used as a frequent symbol of antiquity and of enduring strength, but God existed before the everlasting hills. He *was*—

> Before the mountains were born
> Or ever the earth and world were brought forth.

Thou turnest man to destruction (or dust), 90:3. One generation dies and another takes its place, and the continuance of the human life is due to Divine power. The frailty of man is here forcibly set forth. God created him out of the dust, and back to dust he goes at the word of his Creator. Man is not said to die because of the decree of fate, or the acton of inevitable law, but because of Divine edict—*Thou turnest.* Dealing with this verse, Augustine said, "We walk amid perils. If we were glass vases we might fear the dangers. What is there more fragile than a vase of glass? And yet it is preserved, and lasts for centuries: we therefore are more frail and infirm."

A thousand years in thy sight are but as yesterday when it is past, 90:4. In the history of the world, a thousand years is a very long stretch of time. Crowded into it are "the rise and fall of empires, the glory and obliteration of dynasties, the beginning and the end of elaborate systems of human philosophy, and countless events, all important to household and individual, which elude the pens of historians." Yet, if to God, a thousand years is as a single night-watch, what must be the lifetime of the Eternal? Stephen Charnock, an 18th century expositor, says that the Holy Spirit expresses truth according to the manner of men, and gives us a notion of an indefinite devotion by a resemblance suited to our capacity.

> If a 1000 years be but a day to the life of God, then, as a year is to the life of man, so are 365,000 years to the life of God; and as 70 years are to the life of man, as are 25 millions, 550,000 years to the life of God. Yet still, since there is no proportion between time and eternity, we must dart our thoughts beyond all these, for years and days measure only the duration of created things, and of those only that are material and corporeal, subject to the motion of the heavens, which makes days and years.

It is also most remarkable that to Him Who is from the infinite past to the infinite future, and Whose purpose runs through the ages, a thousand years pass as part of a night spent in sleep. As Francis Bacon puts it in poetical form—

> A thousand years, with Thee they are no more
> Than yesterday, which, ere it is, is spent.
> Or, as a watch by night, that course doth keep,
> And goes and comes, unawares to them that sleep.

It has been pointed out that in the East the people had no clocks, and several parts of the day and of the night, eight in all, were given notice of. In the Indies, the parts of the night were made known by instruments of music in cities, as by the rounds of a watchman, who cried, and played small drums to give sleepers notice that a fourth part of the night was past. As those cries awaked those who had slept all the quarters of the night, it appeared to them but a moment.

In this Psalm, Moses uses similitudes to show how frail the life of man is, particularly when contrasted with the undecaying strength of God.

> Death comes as a *Flood,* violently and suddenly—
> We are as a *Sleep*—
> We are as *Grass*—
> Our life is like a *Dream*—
> Our days are spent as *a Tale that is told.*

Thou carriest them away as with a flood, 90:3. Having the keys of life and death, *God* overrides in the swift passage of men. The most ancient mode of measuring small sections of time was by water flowing out of a vessel, the *clepsydra* of the Greeks and Romans; and Ovid has compared the lapse of time to the flowing of a river. The multitudes of Noah's day, because of their violence and corruption, experienced what it was to be carried away and drowned in the deluge overtaking them. *They are as a sleep.* What a difference there is between the rushing torrent and a peaceful sleep! It would seem as if the writer mixed his metaphors. But no, for before God men must appear as unreal as the dreams of the night, the phantoms of sleep. Not only are our plans and desires like a sleep, but we ourselves are such. "We are such stuff as dreams are made of."

In the morning they are like grass that groweth up, 90:5. The force of the figure used here is the same whether we think of the generations dropping away like withered grass, or cut down and dried like hay. *Like grass!* Is there anything upon earth more frail than grass? We are not massive oaks or cedars, but only poor grass, vigorous in the spring, but not lasting the summer through. Flourishing in the morning, at evening cut down. The history of man is as the history of grass—*Sown, Grown, Blown, Mown, Gone.*

We are consumed by thine anger, 90:7. It will be noticed that in all the similes Moses used, God is prominent as the Arbiter of Life and Death. *Thou* and *Thine* are conspicuous. The history of Israel in the wilderness provides an illustration of this verse, for their lives were cut short by Divine justice because of the nation's waywardness. Did Moses have in mind the mournful sight of seeing the whole nation melt away during the pilgrimage of 40 years, till none remained of all that came out of Egypt, when he penned this verse of men being terror-stricken at the sight of God's righteous indignation?

Thou hast set our iniquities . . . our secret sins in the light of thy countenance, 90:8. The last phrase, "the light of thy countenance," usually means *favor.* Here the word rendered *light* is not the usual one employed in that expression, but rather means a body of light: *the sun—or eye—of Thy countenance.* Southey, in *Curse of Kehama,* has the couplet—

> Then Seeva opened on the accursed one
> His eye of anger.

We spend our years as a tale that is told, 90:9. The margin gives *meditation* for "tale," and is sometimes rendered *thought.* Theognis wrote that "Gallant youth speeds by like a thought." Life passes as rapid and idle as a gossip's story. The Chaldean Version has it, "Life the breath of our mouth in winter." When Israel came out of Egypt, her time was perfectly trifled away and was not worthy to be the subject of a history, but only *as a tale that is told.* The rapid, speedy passing away of man is inevitable, but to spend what life is given in a trifling manner to little valuable purpose is fatal.

Life, at best, may be very brief, yet it may be as a story well told. Some of our years may be as a pleasant story, others as a tragical one; most mixed, but all short and transient; that which was long in the doing may be told in short time. It is not the *length* of life that counts, but the *quality* of it. Jesus lived for only 3 years, but what a life it was, and what a story it told! Whether our life-story is short or long, may all of it redound to the glory of God Who is the Length of our days.

Threescore years and ten . . . fourscore, 90:10. The writer of this age limit far exceeded it himself, for Moses was 120 years of age when he died, Deuteronomy 34:7. Yet, if one lives to be as old as Methuselah, who was 969 years when he died, what are the years of our life when contrasted with Eternity? As a result of Adam's sin, there came in a gradual abbreviation of man's life, particularly after the Flood, and when Moses appeared he sets the bounds as being 70 up to 80 years. At 80, mankind is subject to "labor and sorrow." Samuel Johnson's reflection on this verse reads—

> Unnumbered maladies his joints invade,
> Lay siege to life, and press the dire blockade.

Barzillai, you will recall, moaned to David, "I am this day fourscore years old, and can I discern between good and evil? Can thy servant taste what I eat or what I drink? Can I hear any more the voice of singing men and singing women?" 2 Samuel 19:35. Old age, they say, is a good guest, and should be made welcome. Alas! however, often he brings a troublesome troop with him. Often the aged have no reason to congratulate themselves on passing the ordinary limit of life as inmates of Old Folks' Homes can testify.

It is soon cut off, and we fly away, 90:10. Literally, this clause implies, "Thus passeth haste, and we fly away—as a bird—there comes a haste that we fly away." Even although one may pray for an extension of life, if granted, it brings with it such weariness that we long at last to escape—a fact sufficiently true to experience, as Shakespeare reminds us in the lines—

> Yet are these feet, whose strengthless day is numb,
> Unable to support this lump of clay,
> *Swift winged with desire to get a grave.*

Even according to thy fear, so is thy wrath, 90:11. Spurgeon says that, "Moses saw men dying all around him: he lived among funerals and was overwhelmed at the terrible results of the divine displeasure." He felt none could measure the might of the Lord's wrath against sin which results in death. Israel was urged to mark well the thousands of graves of lust left behind in the wilderness. Modern writers may rail at those like Milton and Dante, Bunyan and Baxter, for their terrible imagery of Hell; but the truth is that no vision of poet, or denunciation of holy seer, can ever fully describe the horrors of the blackness of darkness forever. How constant we should be in warning sinners to flee from the wrath to come.

So teach us to number our days, 90:12.

> We should—
> Improve Time in time, while Time doth last,
> For all Time is no time, when Time is past.

Samuel Johnson wrote of an Italian philosopher who expressed in his motto that *Time* was his estate; an estate, indeed, that will produce nothing with cultivation, but will always abundantly repay the labors of industry and satisfy the most extensive desires if no part of it be suffered to lie waste by negligence, to be overrun by noxious plants, or laid out for show rather than for use.

We cannot apply our hearts unto wisdom, as instructed by Moses, except we number every day as our possible last day. Too many refuse to leave the earth when the earth is about to take them. Sir Thomas Smith, secretary to Queen Elizabeth, some months before he died said, "It was a great pity men knew not to what end they were born into the world, until they were ready to go out of it." Of all arithmetical rules this is the hardest—*to number our days.* Men can number their herds and droves of oxen and of sheep, they can estimate the revenue of their businesses, manors, and farms, and count up the money they have, but commit the folly of never numbering their days and of neglecting to provide for Eternity.

Another historical incident regarding this Psalm in connection with Queen Elizabeth is when Bishop Rudd was requested to preach before Her Majesty by the Archbishop of Canterbury because Rudd was a special favorite with the Queen, and was, indeed, designed as the Archbishop's successor when he died. The Archbishop had said to Rudd, "The truth is, the Queen now is grown weary of the vanities of wit and eloquence, wherewith her youth was formerly affected, and plain sermons which come home to her heart please her best." Encouraged by this guidance, honest Bishop Rudd chose for his text, Psalm 90:12, and touched on the infirmities of age with a personal application to the Queen. But Her Majesty, to whom hearing about death was most ungrateful, was highly displeased, and Bishop Rudd lost both the refersion of the archbishopric and Her Majesty's favor. Rudd, however, justly retained the repute of a godly prelate and carried such an estimation of his character to the grave.

Let the beauty of the Lord our God be upon us, 90:17. What a beautiful benediction this is to such a grand Psalm! The phrase, *The work of our hands,* was a favorite one with Moses who used it 7 times in Deuteronomy. The word for *beauty* combines the ideas of both "beauty" and "favor." There is a twofold Rabbinical tradition respecting the last two verses of this Prayer-Psalm of Moses the Man of God, namely, that they were the original prayer recited by Moses as a blessing on the work of making the Tabernacle and its ornaments, and that subsequently he employed the verses in the usual benediction for any newly undertaken task, whenever God's *glorious Majesty* was to be consulted for an answer by Urim and Thummim. Martin Luther reckoned that in the word *beauty* employed here "there is something like a deluge of grace." May such a deluge be ours as we seek to live under the influence of this mighty Prayer of Moses!

Psalm 91

Theodore de Beza, 1519-1605, composer of the metrical version of Psalm 68 which became the battle-song of the Huguenots, in his later years became the colleague of John Calvin at Geneva. In his younger days Beza had a passion for culture and poetry, worldly success and fame, but found his earlier faith in Divine realities shadowed by doubt. A critical illness revived his former love for God and His Word, and when he took refuge at Geneva it was an escape from the bondage of Egypt as he called his former life. In 1548, when he attended for the first time the service of the Reformed Assembly, the congregation sang Psalm 91, and Beza never forgot the effect of the words, "I will say of the Lord, He is my refuge and my fortress: my God; in Him will I trust." His fears were conquered, and courage became his to meet any danger. When he came to die, he testified to those at his bedside that amid all the changes of life, he found the promises of God one by one fulfilled.

John Ruskin included Psalm 91 among those he learned by his mother's side. Whoever first breathed these words of trust in an unfailing God, thousands, like Ruskin, found them a source of strength and faith in the hour of trial and danger. Several years ago Stier mentioned an eminent physician in St. Petersburg who recommended this Psalm as the best preservative against *Cholera*. In the whole collection of the Psalms there is not a more cheering one than Psalm 91 with its elevated tone sustained throughout, and in which faith is at its best and speaks nobly. It is in truth heavenly medicine against any plague or pest, and they who live in its spirit will be fearless, "even if once again London should become a lazar house, and the grave be gorged with carcases."

Whether or not the imagery of the Psalm was in part drawn from the Passover Night when the Destroying Angel passed though Egypt while the faithful and obedient Israelites were sheltered by God, we cannot say. This we do know that the Psalm is one of the most excellent of this kind ever written. "It is impossible to imagine anything more sober, more beautiful, more profound, or more ornamental. Could the Latin or any modern language express thoroughly all the beauties and elegancies as well as of the *words* as of the *sentences,* it would not be difficult to persuade the reader that we have no poem, either in *Greek,* or *Latin,* comparable to this Hebrew ode."

As the Psalm is without a title, or name of author, or date of composition, we cannot with certainty assign it to a particular period or person. Whoever wrote it sometimes speaks in the first person, 91:1, 2, 9 and sometimes addresses his promises to the godly man, or to the nation, in the second person, 91:3-8, 9-13. Then God Himself is presented as the speaker, 91:14-16. Jewish scholars in later Old Testament days felt that when the author's name did not appear at the head of a Psalm that it could be assigned to the writer of the previous Psalm, which, in this case, would be Moses, The Man of God. In fact, many expressions used in Psalm 91 are similar to those Moses used in *Deuteronomy,* and the internal evidence, from the peculiar idioms, would point towards the Law-giver as its composer.

He that dwelleth . . . shall abide, 91:1. As the reader ponders this Psalm, he should note the different names for God the writer employed, which, by their accumulation makes the promise of assurance doubly sure. Then the variety of figures used indicates a general view of life and its possible perils, even in times when war and pestilence are raging. During the religious wars of the 17th century, the Psalms were precious to the Huguenots. Henri de Rohan, the soul of the Protestant cause in France, threatened with assassination, wrote to his mother, April 30th, 1628, "I have no fear. Whoso dwelleth under the defense of the Most High, shall abide under the shadow of the Almighty."

Secret place, 91:1. God, Who cares for His children has a place of refuge from the storms of the world under the secret of His providence. By the phrase, *Secret place of the Most High,* some ancient writers understood the castle of God's mighty defense to which His people run, being pursued by enemies, as the wild creature does to his hole or den for succour when the hunter has him in chase and the dogs are near. As for the phrases, *He that dwelleth . . . shall abide.* The word *dwelleth* implies that God's children do not come to His *secret place* as guests to an inn, but as inhabitants to a safe dwelling place where they can live securely. As for the words *shall abide,* the Hebrew signifies "he shall pass the night," and indicates a constant and continuous dwelling under the protection of God.

Under the shadow of the Almighty, 91:1, may have been suggested by the awful and mystic symbols of the historical Ark, the emblems of the Divine glory and presence the High Priest alone gazed on, once a year. It is an expression implying great nearness, for we must walk very near to a companion, if we would have his shadow fall upon us. In Solomon's beautiful allegory, "I sat down under His shadow with great delight," he prophesied of the privileged communion of the Church with her Lord. It is said that a stag roamed about in the greatest security by reason of its having a label on its neck inscribed with the words, *Touch me not, I belong to Caesar.* All who abide under the shadow of the Almighty are safe even among all wild creatures, and amid all raging elements for both alike know and reverence the shadow of God. What an impregnable refuge and fortress He is!

> God is rest, and where He dwells is stillness,
> And they who dwell in Him that rest shall share.

Surely he shall deliver thee from the noisome pestilence, 91:3. The story is told of Lord Craven who lived in London when the calamitous plague of the 15th century struck the city. His house was in the part known as Craven Buildings. In order to evade the spreading epidemic, his Lordship, to avoid danger, resolved to go to his country home and ordered his coach and baggage to be ready for the journey. As he was about to enter his carriage, he overheard his servant who cared for his horses say to another servant, "I suppose, by my Lord's quitting London to avoid the plague, that his God lives in the country, and not in town."

Although the servant uttered the statement in the simplicity of his heart, it gripped Lord Craven and made him say to himself, "My God lives everywhere, and can preserve me in town as well as in country. I will stay where I am." The ignorance of that servant had just now preached a very useful sermon. "Lord, pardon this unbelief, and that distrust of Thy providence, which made me think of running from Thy hand." He immediately ordered his coach to be put away, and continued to live in London, being remarkably used among the plague-stricken without catching the infection.

Pestilence is from a Hebrew word meaning, "to speak, and speak out," implying that a pestilence is a speaking thing, proclaiming the wrath of God among the people. *Piel,* a root, signifies "which is to decree," expressing that a pestilence is not casual, but decreed in Heaven. "I will smite them with the pestilence," Numbers 14:12. As for *noisome,* such a word is linked on to the infectious, contagious character of a pestilence.

Thou shalt not be afraid for the terror by night, nor for the arrow that flieth by day, 91:5. How remarkable is the variety of similes the Psalmist uses to illustrate the Divine protection promised! In these modern times with their violence and corruption, there are many terrors at night producing fear. But the shadow of the Almighty removes all gloom from the shadow of night. If covered by the Divine wing, we have nothing to fear from the winged terrors of darkness or from any night attack by an enemy, Proverbs 3:23-26. Milton reminds us "To bless the doors from nightly harm."

The arrow that flieth by day. There are those who see in this day-time danger an Oriental expression for the pestilence, since it is so called by Arabians. Spurgeon gives us the following quotation from Busbequin's *Travels.* "I desired to remove to a less contagious air. I received from Solyman the Emperor this message: that he wondered what I meant in desiring to remove my habitation. *Is not the pestilence God's arrow, which will always hit the mark?* For all those who have God as their refuge, no weapon formed against them can prosper."

The pestilence that walketh in darkness . . . destruction that wasteth at noonday, 91:6. In Oriental climates, night and noon are the most unwholesome, the former from exhalations, the latter from the fierce heat. The word *destruction* comes from a root meaning, "to cut off," and is parallel with "deadly sickness." Pestilence may walk in darkness, but the believer dwells in light. Destruction may waste at noonday, but for those under the Divine wing another sun has risen upon them affording preservation.

A thousand . . . ten thousand, 91:7. It was in 1576 that Cardinal Carlo Borromeo, Archbishop of Milan, the worthiest of all the successors of St. Ambrose, learned that the plague had smitten Lodi, and he went at once to the city. His Council of Clergy advised him to remain in some healthy part of his diocese till the sickness spent itself out, but he replied that it was a Bishop's duty to give his life for his sheep and not abandon them in time of peril. The Council owned that this was the higher course. "Well," said the Cardinal, "is it a Bishop's duty to choose the higher course?" In the midst of the deadly sickness, he led the people to repent, watched over them in their suffering, encouraged by his example his clergy to carry spiritual consolation to the dying. The plague lasted for four months, but the Cardinal's ministry was fearless and unwearied, and the remarkable feature of this experience was that of his whole household only two died, and these were those who had not been called to move among the plague-stricken.

A similar incident is associated with the plague in England, in the year 1666, when criers went through London with the call *Bring out your dead! Bring out your dead!* The Rector of Eyam in Derbyshire, the Rev. W. Mompesson, performed the functions of physician, legislator, and minister of the afflicted as he saw the town nearly depopulated by the plague. It was his exertions that prevented the spread of the disease to other districts. The Rector himself survived unharmed, and tradition still points to a cavern near Eyam, where the worthy pastor used to preach to his parishioners who had not been smitten by the plague.

Israel knew the full significance of the promise, "It shall not come nigh thee," for when disasters overtook her enemies, it seemed as if she lived a charmed life. Safe under Divine protection, she only saw the *effect* of perils that passed by her harmless. Was this not so at the Red Sea? And was it not so when Sennacherib's army perished, and God's people were safe?

> Our God his chosen people saves
> Amongst the dead, amidst the graves.

Only with her eyes did Israel behold the reward of the wicked, as the experience of Joshua and Caleb verified.

Because thou hast made the Lord . . . thy habitation . . . no evil shall befall thee, 91:9, 10. Spurgeon relates a personal experience in which these two precious verses soothed his heart. Here is his own biographical account of what took place. "In the year 1854, when I had scarcely been in London twelve months, the neighborhood in which I labored was visited by Asiatic cholera, and my congregation suffered from its inroads. Family after family summoned me to the bedside of the smitten, and almost every day I was called to visit the grave. I gave myself up with youthful ardor to the visitation of the sick, and was sent for from all corners of the district by persons of all ranks and religions.

"I became weary in body and sick at heart. My friends fell one by one, and I felt or fancied that I was sickening like those around me. A little more work and weeping would have laid me low among the rest; I felt that my burden was heavier than I could bear, and I was ready to sink under it. As God would have it, I was returning mournfully home from a funeral, when my curiosity led me to a notice in a shoemaker's window in Dover Road. It did not look like a trade announcement, nor was it, for it bore in a good bold handwriting these words—*Because thou hast made the Lord, which is my refuge, even the Most High, thy habitation; there shall no evil befall thee, neither shall any plague come nigh thy dwelling.*

"The effect upon my heart was immediate. Faith appropriated the passage as her own. I felt secure, refreshed, girt with immortality. I went on with my visitation of the dying in a calm and peaceful spirit; I felt no fear of evil, and I suffered no harm. The providence which moved the tradesman to put those verses in his window I gratefully acknowledge, and in the remembrance of its marvelous power I adore the Lord my God."

The Psalmist, who assured himself of Divine protection, likewise consoled all saints that the same preservation is afforded to all whose trust is in Him Who is our Refuge in time of storm. If the Most High is our habitation, then no plague will afflict our dwelling. The word used here for *dwelling* literally means "tent," and if Moses wrote this Psalm, then he knew all about the life of a tent-dweller. He proved that even such a frail covering was a sufficient shelter for one who had chosen God as his eternal refuge. "It matters little whether our abode be a gypsy's hut or a monarch's palace if the soul has made the Most High its habitation."

> For this no ill thy cause shall daunt,
> No scourge thy tabernacle haunt.

Austin, one of the Early Fathers, decided to visit a certain town to minister the Word to believers living there. But the day and place were known to his enemies who sent armed men to lie in wait for him on the road on which he was to travel and kill him. As God would have it, the guide who went with Austin to prevent him going out of the right way, mistakenly took a by-lane, but brought the preacher at last to his journey's end. When the people came to know how the enemies were foiled, they magnified God for His providence and gave thanks for Austin's deliverance.

He shall give his angels charge over thee, to keep thee in all thy ways, 91:11. Not one guardian angel is here promised, but a bodyguard of all the princes of the blood imperial of Heaven, commissioned by their Lord to watch carefully over the interests of the faithful. It is to be regretted that even the faithful do not meditate as they should upon the untiring ministry of their angelic bodyguard commissioned by the God Who created them to garrison every child of His. If *one* angel could destroy a hundred and fourscore thousands of the host of Assyria in a night, what must be the fearful power of a legion of angels invested with Divine authority? If we take the word *angel* in its literal meaning, as *messenger,* then we can look upon any agency God employs to strengthen, protect, and help us, as *His angel* to us.

The idea of a special guardian angel for each individual had its origin in heathen belief. As Menander put it—

> By every man, as he is born, there stands
> A spirit good, a holy guide of life.

Whether one, or many, of the bright angelic squadrons are sent to our aid is the decision of the Lord of angels. Edmund Spencer, spiritual poet of the 15th century, left us a wonderful poem on angelic ministry, the first verse of which we repeat—

> And is there care in Heaven, and is there love
> In heavenly spirits to these creatures base,
> That may compassion of their evils move?
> There is, else much more wretched were the race
> Of men than beasts. But oh, the exceeding grace
> Of highest God, that loves his creatures so,
> And all his words with mercy doth embrace,
> That blessed angels he sends to and fro,
> To serve us wicked men, to serve his wicked foe!

The Spaniards have a proverb when they would signify eminent favor and friendship. It goes, "They carry him upon the palms of their hands," which means they exceeding love him and diligently keep him. The angels bear us up in their hands, or carry us, lest we stumble and fall over stones. That which we carry in our hand we are sure to keep, and it is so with our heavenly guardians.

The lion and adder . . . young lion and the dragon, 91:13. These creatures of the animal world are here used as emblematic of the various obstacles, difficulties and dangers which threaten life. In the struggle between the Roman Church and the State, the Psalms illustrated many aspects of such a feud. Legend in the spirit of the conflict represented the Pope placing his foot on the neck of a kneeling emperor, repeating the words, "The young lion and the dragon shalt thou tread under thy feet."

Disillusioned by the lofty idealism of Plato, Augustine gave himself up to the study of the Bible, and came to use the language of the Psalms in telling fashion. Describing Platonic writings as being destitute of anyone singing in them, "Truly my soul waiteth upon God; from Him cometh my salvation: He only is my rock and my salvation," this student and friend of Ambrose wrote—

> It is one thing to see afar off, from some tree-clad height, the fatherland of peace, yet to find no path thither, and, struggling vainly towards it, to wander this way and that among wilds beset by the ambushments of lurking runagates, with their prince, the lion and the dragon (Psalm 91:13). It is another thing to tread securely on a highroad that leads directly thither, but by the Heavenly Emperor, whereupon no deserters from the celestial host lie in wait to rob the traveler, for they shun it as a torment.

It was this same Augustine who said that *the lion* represents "overt wrath" and *the dragon* "covert lurking." As for *the adder,* the Egyptian cobra, equally dreaded by travelers, it, too, can be trodden upon by God-protected feet. While, figuratively, these wild beasts may have represented Pharaoh as head of Egyptian power, and Nebuchadnezzar, head of the Chaldean monarchy, in the lives of saints, they stand for the victory of a Man Who was able to tread the lion and adder under His feet and Who makes His own sharers of such dominion. "The people of God are the real 'George and the Dragon,' the true lion-kings and serpent-tamers. The dominion over the powers of darkness makes them cry, *Lord, even the devils are subject unto us through Thy word!"*

He hath known my name, 91:14. Eternal safety is ours because of our trust in all God is in Himself, for *name* represents His nature, being, and glorious attributes. Knowing His name, then, means the recognition of and trust in Him as our Omniscient, Omnipresent, Holy, and All-Gracious Lord Who revealed Himself in His beloved Son, our Savior. Doubtless the express *name* implied here is that of JEHOVAH, the Sacred Name of God, the Jews were afraid to utter, and regarded it too holy to be pronounced by them in common use, and strove to keep it from being taken in vain by the heathen around. Thus, this august Name was known to them only, who not only knew it, but trusted in all that it was of Himself in His Word, Providence, and above all in His Son.

Dr. J. M. Thoburn, Missionary Bishop of the Methodist Church in India and Malaysia, 1888-1900, who wrote *Light in the East* and *Christless Nations,* said of his Bible meditation, "I have no permanent favorite among Scripture passages but nearly always have a verse or verses in mind, suited to the emergency of the hour or day. At present I am drawn to Psalm 91:14-16."

D. L. Moody, the American evangelist who rocked two continents nearer God, held Psalm 91 to be his favorite. When in November, 1892, he and his fellow passengers on the steamship *Spree* were threatened by a billowy grave, he preached to a most attentive audience from the words found in verses 14 to 16 of this Psalm. They called upon God and he answered them and delivered them.

With long life (Hebrew—length of days) will I satisfy him, and shew him my salvation, 91:16. Ellicott comments that "the promise of a long life, while in accordance with the general feeling of the Old Testament, is peculiarly appropriate at the close of this Psalm, which all through speaks of protection from danger that threatened life." The divinely protected person portrayed in the Psalm fills out the measure of his day by the grace of Him Who is the length of his days. Whether he dies young or old, he is quite satisfied with life and is content to leave it for a more blessed life beyond. Such a man rises from life's banquet as one who has had enough, and would not have more, even if he could.

Bryan W. Proctor's poem on this last verse is most apt, the opening stanza of which reads—

> They err who measure life by years,
>   With false or thoughtless tongue;
> Some hearts grow old before their time,
>   Others are always young.
> 'Tis not the number of the lines
>   Of life's fast filling page,
> 'Tis not the pulse's added throbs
>   Which constitute their age.

When God satisfies those who dwell in the secret place of the Most High with His fore-ordained length of days, then, when Time ends and Eternity begins, He will show them *His salvation.* Theirs will be the full revelation of His love, grace, and glory. *Now,* we only know in part. Horatius Bonar gave us this expressive poem on the phrase, *With long life—*

> He liveth long who liveth well!
>   All other life is short and vain;
> He liveth longest who can tell
>   Of living most for heavenly gain.
> He liveth long who liveth well!
>   All else is being flung away;
> He liveth longest who can tell
>   Of true things truly done each day.

Psalm 92

The title of this ode is most suggestive—*A Psalm to be sung on the Day of the Sabbath.* The Jews of old appropriated certain Psalms to particular days, and every day of the week had its allotted Psalms. The songs which the Levites formerly sang in the sanctuary are these—

On the *first* day, Psalm 24,
On the *second* day, Psalm 48,
On the *third* day, Psalm 82,
On the *fourth* day, Psalm 114,
On the *fifth* day, Psalm 81,
On the *sixth* day, Psalm 93,
On the *seventh* day, Psalm 92, based on its title.

The *Talmud* confirms this saying that Psalm 92 was sung on the morning of the Sabbath at the drink offering which followed the sacrifice of the first lamb (Num. 28:9).

Some ancient Rabbinical writers thought perhaps this last Psalm was composed by Adam as a tribute to the seventh day of Creation, but dismissing such a contention as *raving,* Spurgeon says, "Adam in Paradise had neither harp to play upon, nor wicked men to contend with." Although nameless, no one acquainted with David's style in the Psalms credited to him hesitates to ascribe to him the authorship of this Divine, Sabbath Hymn. A notable feature of this Psalm is the sevenfold name of JEHOVAH in Verses, 1, 4, 8, 9, 13, 15. Seven times is the Sabbatical number.

Here, again, we have an admirable combination and composition, *A Psalm or Song,* or a Psalm to be sung upon the day of rest. Full of equal measures of solemnity and joy, its subject is the praise of God for all His work, and the joyful occupation of hearts resting in the Divine Worker. If David wrote it, then the Holy Spirit certainly gave him utterance, for the style is worthy of the theme and of the day it is dedicated to. The general theme is set forth in the first four verses. Ellicott's introduction says, "In this Psalm we seem to have the Sabbath musings of one who had met the doubt born of the sight of successful wickedness, and struggled through it to a firm faith in *the Rock of Whom is no unrighteousness,* though sometimes on earth iniquity seems to flourish and prevail."

It is a good thing to give thanks unto the Lord, 92:1. The word *good* carries the ideas of honest—pleasant—profitable. If there is any difference between *thanks* and *praises,* we thank God for all His benefits, and praise Him for His perfections. When tempted to discouragement, Martin Luther would say, "Come, let us sing a Psalm, and drive away the devil." Devout gratitude and praise are never out of season, but especially suitable for the Lord's Day. "A Sabbath without thanksgiving is a Sabbath profaned." It is, indeed, a "good thing to give thanks unto the Lord"—

> Good ethically, for it is the Lord's right and request,
> Good emotionally, for it is pleasant to the redeemed heart,
> Good practically, for it leads others to render to God the same homage.

Lovingkindness in the morning . . . faithfulness every night, 92:2. The twin attributes of "lovingkindness" and "faithfulness" are most conspicuous in the revelation of God's covenant relation towards His redeemed people. As to the periods of the day allotted to the manifestation of these attributes, Ellicott's comment is most assuring, "The connection of *lovingkindness* or *grace* with the morning, and *faithfulness* or *truth* with the evening, is only a result of Hebrew poetic style; and yet there is a fitness in the association. Love breaks through the clouds of doubt as the morning light rises on the night; and thoughts of God's unerring and impartial justice best suit the evening—the trial time of the day."

As God's *grace* is the morning ray, scattering away darkness (see Psalm 30:5; 59:16), so *faithfulness* is His guardianship, assuring us against night peril. Rich blessings are ours if we observe the morning watch. The Brahmins rise 3 hours before the sun to pray. Indians esteemed it a great sin to eat in the morning before praying to their gods. The ancient Romans considered it impious if they did not resort to their prayer-chamber as a new day began. As we profess to have the true light, the zeal of the heathen should not surpass ours. God should be the Alpha and Omega of each of our days. Welcoming the morning with gladness, we should not be afraid of the night which, as the poet asks—

> This sacred shade and solitude, what is it?
> 'Tis the felt presence of the Deity.

Upon an instrument of ten strings . . . the psaltery . . . the harp, 92:3. One cannot read the Old Testament without realizing what an integral part instrumental music played in the worship of the people. The range of musical instruments used is impressive, *the harp,* David popularized, having the pre-eminence. It would be a harp of some kind made up of ten strings, the Psalmist refers to in the verse before us. We cannot say that we agree with Chrysostom that "Instrumental music was only permitted to the Jews, as sacrifice was, for the heaviness and grossness of their

souls. God condescended to their weakness, because they were lately
drawn off from idols; but now instead of organs, we may use our own
bodies to praise God withal."

Away back in the cradle of humanity we read of one *Jubal*—from
which we have the term "jubilant," that he was the father or originator of
all who handle the harp and organ (Genesis 4:21). Justin Martyr
expressly says "that the use of singing with instrumental music was not
received in the Christian churches as it was among the Jews in their infant
state, but only the use of plain song." The insistence of some writers is
that instrumental music was not in use in the church until about the fourth
century. Athanasius, Bishop of Alexandria, wrote of the inspiration he
received in congregational singing by "clear voices and appropriate
tunes." Isaac Watts would have us sing—

> Oh may my heart in tune be found,
> Like David's harp of solemn sound.

The Psalmist felt that every sweet-sounding instrument should be consecrated in God, as General Booth believed, when he introduced
band-music and tambourines to match his militant form of service and
worship for his "soldiers." The wise observation of Spurgeon on this matter is worthy of note, "It is much to be feared that attention to the mere
mechanism of music, noting keys and strings. Fine music without devotion, which is the soul and essence of praise, is but a splendid garment
upon a corpse."

> Strings and voices, hands and hearts,
> In the concert bear your parts:
> All that breathe, your God adore,
> Praise Him, praise Him, evermore.

Eusebius, prominent Biblical scholar of the 4th century, commenting
on Psalm 92 says, *"The psaltery of ten strings* is the worship of the Holy
Spirit performed by means of the *five* senses of the body, and the *five*
powers of the soul," and in confirmation of his application goes on to
quote 1 Corinthinas 14:15. Carrying this application further, all who are
the Lord's can look upon the human frame made up of two eyes, two ears,
two hands, two feet, one mouth and one heart—ten in all, as the instruments of ten strings with which to praise and magnify the Lord. This is
the truth embodied in Havergal's searching hymn—"Take my life and let
it be, consecrated Lord to Thee."

Thou hast made us glad through thy work, 92:4. Already we have
drawn attention to the use Dante made of the Psalms, directly or symbolically, and in his *Purgatorio* we have a further illustration of this use
when he describes the beautiful form of Matilda. Wondering at the bright-

ness of her smile, she tells him that she is gladdened by verse 4 of Psalm 92, beginning, *Delectasti,* "Thou, God, had made me glad through thy work." Is it not this delight in God's service, and labor in His cause, that make the perfect happiness of active life on earth? The Psalmist, of course, was referring to God's works in *history,* and not in *nature,* and expresses his gladness at God's wonders wrought for Israel (Psalm 90:15, 16). Succeeding poets, however, have been enraptured with the sight of God's handiwork in nature, and burst forth in adoring verse. John Milton in *Paradise Lost* commences Book Five with the line—

> These are thy glorious works, Parent of good, Almighty!

Thomson, in his *Seasons,* rises to a wonderful height in his ascription—

> These, as they change, Almighty Father, these
> Are but the varied God.

William Coleridge in *Hymn before Sunrise, the Vale of Chamouni,* equally well treads the high places of triumphant devotion, as he cries—

> Awake my soul! not only passing praise
> Thou owest! not alone these swelling tears,
> Mute thanks and secret ecstacy! Awake,
> Voice of sweet song! Awake, my heart, awake!
> Green vales and icy cliffs, all join my hymn.

The *brutish,* 92:6, or boorish man, sees nothing either in history or nature to praise God for. His foolish mind and unbelieving heart fail to see in ten thousand creations around him—*great works,* great because of their number, extent, design and glory—that magnify God's power in Creation, History, Redemption, and Providence. *Brutish* comes from a root meaning "to eat," and refers to the man of mere animal nature, who lives for his appetite and consequently has no desire for an appreciation of God's works. *Fool,* means "gross," "stupid." Thus, "in one case the moral sense has not come into play at all, in the other it is overgrown by sensuality, so that spiritual discernment, insight into the glories of the Divine mind, is impossible."

I shall be anointed with fresh oil, 92:10. Possibly there is an allusion here to the custom of *anointing* persons at their solemn installation in an important office, such as Hebrew Priests and Kings were, as, for example, when Samuel took a vial of oil, and poured it upon Saul's head. The literal meaning of *fresh* is "green," and so Ainsworth gives the rendering "I shall be anointed with *green* oil." This is because the original implies "precious fragrant oil," and that as it was poured out the perfume spread. As *Oil* is used as a type of the Holy Spirit, how tragic it is if we try to serve God, without His anointing which alone can keep us ever-green.

"Mine eye shall see *my desire . . . my desire,*" 92:11. Given in italics means that these words were supplied by the translators, and it would have been better had they not been used, for the Psalmist did not say what he should see concerning his enemies, he leaves that blank, and, as Spurgeon goes on to say, "we have no right to fill in the vacant space with words which look vindictive. The Psalmist would see that which would be for God's glory, and that which would be eminently right and just."

Like the palm tree . . . like a cedar, 92:12. As we have already mentioned, Casaubon, one of the most learned and devout scholars of the 16th century, took an open boat up the Seine to worship with the Huguenots at Charenton. Singing psalms made the sail pleasant. Alas! however, a large barge struck the stern of their boat, throwing Mrs. Casaubon in the river, but her husband dived in and saved her. After the experience the saint said, "On embarking, my wife, as her custom was, began to sing Psalms. We had finished Psalm 91 and had reached Psalm 92:12, when the boat sank. With difficulty we saved our lives, but the psalm-book, which had been a wedding gift to my wife twenty-two years before, was lost."

Typical use of the tree-world is common to Scripture. In the verse before us two noble and long-lived trees are chosen to illustrate spiritual truths, especially the ability of believers "to bring forth fruit in old age." Theirs is a permanency natural productions do not possess.

> The plants of grace shall ever live;
> Nature decays, but grace must thrive;
> Time, that doth all things else impair
> Still makes them flourish strong and fair.

Stately palm trees, standing out on the plain like military sentinels with feathery plumes nodding gracefully on their proud heads; and the cedar, waving its mighty branches in perpetual verdure on the summit of the mountain, have been emblematically expounded by many writers. Tristram's *Natural History of the Bible,* and Thomson's *Land and the Book* should be consulted as to the natural qualities and spiritual significance of the *Palm Tree* and the *Cedar,* as well as other trees of the East. In this twelfth verse we have the only place where the palm, because it is tall, slender, and erect, appears as an emblem of moral rectitude and beauty of character, yet aptness for such comparison has often been noticed.

As for the cedar, the moral use of this is more often made. Emblem of kingly might, it also became the type of the imperial grandeur of virtuous souls. Thus, "the contrast of the palm's perennial verdure, and the cedar's venerable age, an age measured not by years, but by centuries, with fleeting moments of the brief day of grass, to which the wicked are compared, (92:7), is very striking, as striking as that in Psalm 1, between the empty husk and the flourishing fruit-tree."

Those that he planted in the house of the Lord, 92:13. The last four verses of this Psalm describe the abiding prosperity and blessedness of the righteous, and are last seen as trees flourishing in the Temple courts. Because they are rooted in God, theirs is growth and prosperity. Many are found in the house of Divine worship, but they are not planted in the Lord, and thus cannot flourish in His courts. There cannot be fruit without root.

They shall bring forth in old age, 92:14. In the garden of grace, plants weak in themselves because of natural physical decay, are yet strong in the Lord and bear fruit acceptable to Him. Even if bedridden, they bear the fruit of patience. *Grinders* (teeth) may fail, but the bread of Heaven is to feed upon. The literal translation of this verse reads—"Still shall they sprout in hoary age, sappy and green shall they be," an allusion to the great fruitfulness of the date palm, and to the fact that to the very last this fruitfulness continues. The aged, fruitful believer is a letter of commendation of the immutable fidelity of Jehovah as the Rock and as the Righteous One. Journeying on to the end, the godly, well-stricken in years, daily prove that God's dispensations have no flaw in them, and can no more be moved than a rock can be dislodged from its age-long foundation. The Psalm, then, presents a *Divine climax,* that the venerable godly, far from declining, climb higher and higher as they travel on to life's last milestone.

Psalm 93

D r. H. B. Whipple became Episcopal Bishop of Minnesota in 1859, held this office for over 40 years when the State of Minnesota was almost a wilderness, and accomplished a remarkable work among the Indians there. He once wrote, "I believe that the Bible was written under the guidance and inspiration of God, and that all is good. The three texts which have come most often to me in the cares and burdens of over 40 years of my Episcopate are Psalms 93:1; 23:1; and John 14, last clause of the ninth verse."

As brilliant as it is brief, we have no indication from this titleless Psalm when or why it was written. It may have been inspired by some particular historical event such as the deliverance from Babylonian captivity and the return of Israel to their own land. What is evident is the writer's expression of an important truth, namely, that God is King and consequently all the rage and unrest of the world are impotent. "The angry tumult of men beats as vainly against the granite firmness of His righteous will as waves against the shore. The tempests of history subside and pass as the tempest of the sea, but His laws remain forever fixed and sure."

Psalm 93 is grouped along with Psalms 95-100 seeing that all of them celebrated the sovereignty of Jehovah over all forces. Spurgeon named the Psalm we are now considering *The Psalm of Omnipotent Sovereignty* because it reveals that, despite all opposition, God reigns supreme. It was, therefore, a sacred ode reminding an oppressed people that their Lord was still King, as its five verses clearly prove—

> His sovereignty, majesty, and strength, verse 1.
> The eternity and stedfastness of His royal throne, verse 2.
> His supremacy above the waves of the sea, verses 3, 4.
> The holiness of His Temple, verse 5.

> The Lowland fold are still justly proud of—"The tales
> Of persecution and the Covenant
> Whose echo rings through Scotland to this hour."

As we have frequently mentioned, Covenanters were greatly inspired by the Psalms. At one time, on "Clydeside, east of Glasgow," a shadowy throng of men and women seemed to gather round a tent in which a few of the faithful were gathered, but Psalm 93 was chanted with such celestial sweetness, Prothero says, that all who heard the strains stood motionless till the chanting ceased.

The Lord reigneth! 93:1. Such a magnificent opening of this Psalm seems to indicate a morning of calm repose after a night of raging storm, a day of tranquility after the tumult of battle. No matter what turmoil and rebellion there may be beneath the clouds, above them the eternal King sits enthroned in all supreme serenity, and clothed with majesty. His is not the semblance, but the reality of sovereignty, seeing He is clothed, not with the emblems of majesty, but with majesty *itself.* The Creation, Nature, History, and Redemption, He is infinite in majesty.

Clothed can be better expressed, "majesty He has put on," as the next phrase implies, "girded Himself with strength." As athletes gird up their loins for running, and laborers for working, so the Lord presents Himself as one preparing for action, girt with His omnipotence. The same language is used of Jehovah as a warrior arranging himself for battle, Isaiah 59:17; 63:1, or as a monarch robed in splendor, Psalm 104:1. Because He is thus clothed and girded, *the world is stablished,* for God's rule is the security of moral order in the world (see Psalms 75:3; 82:5).

Thy throne is established of old, 93:2. Science of the Middle Ages was more or less governed by the Psalms. Thus, medieval cosmologists argued that the earth could not be in motion or suspended in mid-air, but, like the Creator's throne, firmly fixed. "He hath made the round world so fast that it cannot be moved." It has been suggested that the phrase, "the world also is established, that it cannot be moved," would be better as a beginning to verse 3 or the Psalm. Says Ellicott, "That the earth should be solidly seated in its hidden foundation, is itself a marvel; but this wonder is mentioned only to bring into greater relief the next verse, that the throne of God, to which the earth is only a footstool, Isaiah 66:1, that its foundation firm and everlasting, free from the vicissitudes which beset earthly monarchies."

The Septuagint Version gives the title to this marvelous ode, "On the day before the Sabbath, when the earth was founded: A Psalm of thanksgiving to (or for) David." Such a title was also adopted by the Vulgate and Oriental Versions in general. *Established of old,* or as the Italian has it *from all Eternity,* comes from a Hebrew root signifying an Eternity without a beginning (Prov. 8:22). We read of ancient dynasties, but where are they today? Divine sovereignty is no upstart sovereignty, but an eternal one. Earthly monarchies and kingdoms are subject to varying vicissitudes, and thrones are shaken, if not by the death of their kings, then by ambitious revolutionists who marshall forces to overthrow their rule. But no one, and no thing can disturb the rule exercised by Him Who sits on His eternal throne, and because He reigns as the Lord God Omnipotent, His is the power to make the earth tremble.

The floods . . . the floods . . . the floods, 93:3. Here we have a poetic triad of the breaking of the waves of the sea on the shore (Psalm 24:20). Then there is the threefold repetition of *Lift up,* emphasizing the frequency of wicked assaults upon the government of God. *Floods* and *waves* are emblems of the heathen nations, but God is not moved by their fury. Whenever He utters His commanding voice, the earth melts. Virgil, adopting the simile of the Psalmist, describes the violence of the Grecian Army breaking into the Citadel of Priam—

> In rush the Greeks, and all apartments fill;
> Those few dependents whom they find, they kill.
> Not with so fierce a rage the foaming flood
> Roars, when he finds his rapid course withstood;
> Bear down the dams with unresisted sway,
> And sweeps the cattle and the cots away.

But often the *voice* of the floods is the voice *of* God, *from* God, and *for* God, as Eliza Cook suggests in the lines—

> God hath a voice that is ever heard,
> In the peal of the thunder, the chirp of the bird;
> It comes in the torrent, all rapid and strong,
> In the streamlet's soft gush, as it ripples along;
> In the waves of the ocean, the furrows of land.
> In the mountain of granite, the atom of sand;
> Turn where ye may, from sky to the sod,
> Where can you gaze, that you see not God.

The Lord on high is mightier than . . . noise of many waters . . . than mighty waves of the sea, 93:4. What a defiant Divine declaration this is! Whether the description given is of a raging sea or emblematic of war and its horrors has no difference for He Who is throned on high is mightier than the mightiest powers of earth. Is He not the Master of ocean, earth and sky? Jehovah, as the Self-existent and Omnipotent One, has a stronger voice than the noise of many waters and the mighty, angry waves of the sea. The waters of affliction may rise high, but He, Who is on high, is higher and mightier still, and therefore able to deliver.

> Loud the stormy billows spoke,
>   Loud the billows raised their cry;
> Fierce the stormy billows broke,
>   Sounding to the echoing sky.
> Strong the breakers tossing high,
>   Stronger is Jehovah's might.
> True thy words; and sanctify
>   Well becomes thy temple bright.

Thus, as the mariner in straits because of storms looks up to the stars for guidance, may we ever remember that He on high is able to direct and preserve us when the billows are tossing high. Our Sovereign Lord is all-powerful to restrain the haughtiness and rage of impious men and overrule their malice. Whether kings or angry mobs, emperors or savages, all are under His almighty hand which forbids hostile forces to touch a hair of the head of any of His saints.

Thy testimonies are very sure, 93:5. The twin truths of Scripture's reliability and Divine holiness making up this last verse must be linked back to the previous verse. The permanence and security of the Covenant, and of the outward signs attesting it, were to Israel proof of the superiority of Divine power over all the forces of nature. Extending the thought, we can say that the moral law is a truer evidence of God than the uniformity of natural laws. The *testimonies* and *holiness* are very sure and cannot change. The most beautiful tapestry for God's house, or to adorn His children, is *Holiness.*

History records that Solon, the renowned Athenian lawgiver, enacted that none should serve the gods *obiter* or "by and by," but that their sacrificers should purify themselves some days beforehand. Of old, the blind heathen were choice and devout in the service of dumb idols; they served them in white, the emblem of purity; they thought nothing too good for those false gods, for whom the worst was not bad enough. Are we so devout in our approach to the living and true God? Does not this precious Psalm teach us that we should be? Its first word is *Jehovah reigns,* and His sovereignty is the main theme of the Psalm, with holiness as its final result. "A due esteem for the great King will lead us to adopt a behaviour becoming His royal presence. Divine soveignty both confirms the promises are sure testimonies, and enforces the precepts as seemly and becoming in the presence of so great a Lord. The whole Psalm is most impressive, and is calculated to comfort the distressed, confirm the timorous, and assist the devout." Well might we pray with Spurgeon in the conclusion of his exposition of the Psalm—

> O Thou Who are so great and gracious a King, reign over us forever! We do not desire to question or restrain Thy power, such is Thy character that we rejoice to see thee exercise the rights of an absolute Monarch. All power is in Thine hands, and we rejoice to have it so. Hosannah!

> Hosanna!

Psalm 94

While this nameless Psalm was the expression of national sense of wrong and injustice as can be gathered from verses 5 and 14, and, by implication verse 10, yet the poet, whoever he was, must have experienced in his own person the bitterness of such trouble as the closing personal references indicate. Note the personal pronouns in verses 17-22. Historically, it would seem as if this was a national Psalm, written at a time when Israel was oppressed by foreign enemies. It may have been connected either with the days of Exile, or with some later period of national distress. As to the construction of the Psalm, Dummelow suggests this outline—

The opening appeal to God to show Himself a judge of the earth, 1, 2.

The misdeed of the oppressors are next described, 3-7.

The rebuke is addressed to certain Israelites who were tempted to give up their faith in God, 8-11.

The assurance of the blessings of adversity, 12, 13.

The certainty that God will not forsake His people, 14, 15.

The Psalmist's confession that God was his only refuge and comfort, 16-19.

The conviction that God will overthrow the wicked, 20-23.

If Psalm 93 and 94 came from the same composer, then we can appreciate the sense of Divine sovereignty he had been singing about in the former Psalm leading him to appeal to God, as the great Judge of the earth, with much vehemence and importunity, as he does in the present Psalm, which is another pathetic form of the age-long enigma—*Why do the wicked prosper?* It also offers another instance of a godly man, perplexed by the prosperity of the profligate, consoling his troubled heart by remembering that there is, after all, a King in Heaven with the power to overrule *all* things for good. Can He not make the wrath of man to praise Him?

O Lord God, to whom vengeance belongeth, 94:1. Dr. Samuel Johnson, referring to the lack of sufficient attention to the distinction existing between *revenge* and *vengeance* said, "Revenge is an act of passion, vengeance of justice; injuries are revenged, crimes avenged." Vengeance belongs to God, and not to man who, because of his feelings and propensities, would allow it to degenerate into revenge. "If the execution of justice be a right thing—and who can deny the fact?—then it must be a very proper thing to desire it; not out of private revenge, in which case a man would hardly dare to appeal to God, but out of sympathy with right and pity for those who are made wrongfully to suffer. Who can see a nation enslaved, or even an individual downtrodden, without crying to the Lord to arise and vindicate the righteous cause?"

God of vengeance, *shew thyself.* The original of this opening verse of the Psalm is far more striking in its conciseness. It reads—*God of retributions, Jehovah, God of retributions, shine forth.* The emphatic repetition of a phrase is characteristic of this Psalm. *Shew thyself—Shine forth!* The bare sight of a just God suffices to alarm tyrants into ceasing their oppressions. More than ever in these last evil days when the wicked triumph, the world needs a manifest display of God's power over the gathering forces of darkness.

Lift up thyself, thou judge of the earth, 94:2. History is replete with illustrations of the proud looking down upon the gracious poor and striking them from above as a giant might hurl down blows upon his adversary. It was in this way the Psalmist prayed to God to ascend His judgment-seat as the acknowledged Ruler of men and strike with all His might, as strong men do, and "return a recompense upon the proud." The Psalmist urged God to give measure for measure, a just retaliation, and so invoked the retributions of Divine justice in plain speech.

Lord, how long shall the wicked, how long shall the wicked triumph, 94:3. The repetition here not only emphasized the Psalmist's appeal for justice but, as old John Trapp expressed it, "Twice he saith it, because the wicked boast day after day, with such insolency and outrage, as if they were above control." The word *triumph* used here come from a Hebrew word meaning "to exalt," the implication being that the wicked give themselves vain applause on account of their prosperity and declare their success both with words and with the gestures of their body, like peacocks spreading their feathers. *How long? How long?* The record of the Inquisition reveals the innumerable times this bitter complaint—one of the saddest of all utterances in which misery bemoans itself—was heard in the dungeons, at the whipping-posts of slavery, and in prisons of oppression. But God is neither deaf nor dead, and in His time and way, armed with almighty power, crushes the ascendancy of evil.

How long shall they utter and speak hard things? 94:4. The term *utter* originally meant "they shall flow," "they shall cast forth," and suggests the metaphor taken from fountains springing out of the rock with a rush and abundance of water. The application is that "where the abundance of words is, note their rashness, their waste and profusion, their sound and eagerness, their continuance and the difficulty of obstructing them." Ellicott says it is better to omit the italics in this verse and render, *They speak out of utter impudence: all evil-doers boast.* Modern scholars connect the word rendered *boast* here with the Arabian title *Emir,* meaning "a commander." The wicked present themselves to be persons of distinction, or, perhaps, *lord it* over God's people. But for such *distinction,* His justice meets out *extinction.*

They break in pieces thy people, O Lord, and afflict thine heritage, 94:5. The word for *break* implies "to crush." Isaiah uses this word in parallelism with "grind the faces of the poor," 3:15. There are still far too many of these grinders in the world, and *totalitaranism* is one of them with its determination to beat both Jews and Christians to pieces. The Hebrew word for *break* is often used as a meaning to crush under foot—to trample on—to oppress. "To crush under his feet all the prisoners of the earth," Lamentations 3:34.

They slay the widow and the stranger, 94:6. Philip Judaeus, an ancient Jewish writer, pointed out how aptly the titles of *widow* and *orphan* befitted the Hebrew nation because it had no helper save God only, and was cut off from all other people by its peculiar rites and usages whereas the Gentiles, by the mutual alliances and intercourse, had, as it were, a multitude to help them in any strait. As for the *stranger* mentioned, also an object of murderous attack, he appeared to be one of the friendless and helpless, under the tyranny of the great, which seems to imply that domestic, and not foreign oppression, was the grievous experience (Exod. 22:21). The most evident objects of compassion were singled out not only for fraud but murder. But He Who is as a Husband to the widow and as a Father to the fatherless knows all about the tears of widows, groans of strangers, and of the blood of orphans poured forth, and will deal in justices with those who are guilty of such crimes.

Yet they say, the Lord shall not see, 94:7. As nothing is hid from the Lord, He is ever cognizant of all inhuman conduct. Brutish men, blindly wicked, dream of a blind God. The ungodly are guilty of arrogant and abominable blasphemy when they assert that God takes no notice of the actions of cruel men. The history of the Church reveals that He cares for His own by a thousand acts of grace. Ellicott reminds us that this professed carelessness of Heaven to injustice and crime which, in the mouth of the heathen—or, perhaps, of apostate Jews—appeared so monstrous to Hebrews, was a doctrine or philosophy of ancient times. This feeling was well expressed by Tennyson in *Lotus Eaters*—

> Let us swear an oath, and keep it with an equal mind,
> In the hollow Lotus-land to live and die reclined,
> On the hills like gods together, *careless of mankind.*

The Divine Names used here, *Jehovah* and *God of Jacob,* prove the absurdity of godless men who believed that He could not, or would not observe the cruel treatment of His own. John Milton's lines, based on the first seven verses of this Psalm, are most telling—

Avenge, O Lord, thy slaughter'd saints, whose bones
  Lie scatter'd on the Alpine mountains cold:
  Even them who kept thy truth so pure of old,
  When all our fathers worshipt stocks and stones,

Forget not: in thy book record their groans
  Who were thy sheep, and in their ancient fold
  Slain by the bloody Piedmontese that role'd
  Mothers with infants down the rocks. Their moans

The vales redoubled to the hills, and they
  To Heaven. Their martyr'd blood and ashes sow
  O'er Italian fields, where still doth sway

The triple tryant; that from these may grow
  A hundredfold, who, having learn'd the way,
  Early may fly the Babylonian woe.

Understand, ye brutish . . . ye fools, 94:8. The Psalmist describes those who held that God was blind, or indifferent, to inhuman treatment as *boarish,* or *swinish* men. The phrase, *among the people,* seems to indicate that those described, who were tempted to adopt the heathen point of view as to Heaven's neglect of the ill-treated, were apostate Israelites. The same were not only wicked, but *fools.* The proverb has it, "No fool like a learned fool." They thought themselves wise, but God calls them fools and asked, "*When* will ye be wise?"

He that planteth the ear . . . formed the eye, 94:9. Two parts of our physical make-up, *Ears* and *Eyes,* are used with great effect as symbols of spiritual truth. Jupiter of Crete was pictured without ears and thus could not be at leisure to listen to and attend upon small matters. But our God is all ears and all eyes and therefore, as the Creator of these senses, cannot Himself be deaf and blind. The Psalmist asserts that "God *planted* the ear," and the mechanism of the ear, like a root *planted* in the earth, is sunk deep into the head and concealed from view. Its deep-seated position and wonderful construction make it a remarkable organ of the body. Fixed in the most convenient position near to the brain, the ear works in harmony with it. The question is asked, "Having designed the marvelous ear, is the Divine Designer not able to hear?" We are assured by other sacred writers that God's ears are ever open to the cries and prayers of His own and to the groans of a lost world.

The second question asked is, *He that formed the eye shall he not see?* It has been pointed out that the term used of the creation of the *Eye* is not merely "made," as the Prayer Book version reads, but *formed,* a word directing our attention to the remarkable mechanism of the organ of sight, and thence to the marvelous skill of the Artificer Himself. *Formed* is sometimes used to describe a *potter,* and the application is that God so molded or formed the eye as the potter fashions the clay. And the more the eye, optic nerve, eyeball, and all its curious mechanism are studied, the more the mind is impressed with the perfect wisdom of God, and also of the utter absurdity of believing that although He thought of such a creation, that He Himself is unable to observe the doings of His creatures to whom He gave eyes. *The eyes of the Lord* is a profitable meditation for the Bible reader to pursue.

Neale, in his work in The Psalms, quotes the wise counsel of the Rabbins who affirmed that the three best safeguards against falling into sin are to remember, *first,* that there is an ear which hears everything; *secondly,* there is an eye which sees everything; *thirdly,* that there is a hand which writes everything in the Book of Knowledge which shall be opened at the Judgment.

He that chastiseth . . . he that teacheth man knowledge? 94:10. The argument set forth in the two previous questions is continued in the further two questions making up this verse. By *heathen,* nations are implied, and all history proves that the God Who reproves whole nations with national judgment likewise judges single persons. The next question regarding *knowledge* is equally full of force and asked with the same degree of warmth. And the premise is, Does not the Author and Revealer of all knowledge Himself know? We have no knowledge that is not derived from God, or from the external world—which is His creation. The idolater wants a God who is deaf, blind, and dumb, but such a god is not our Omnipotent God. Paul's teaching in Romans 1 is an expansion of the Psalmist's argument.

A summary of the questions asked in verses 8-10 is set forth most profitably by Ellicott's Commentary—

> The reality of a Divine Providence is proved both from nature and history—from the physical constitution of man and the moral government of the World. The Psalmist's questions are as powerful against modern atheism, under whatever philosophy it shelters itself, as against that of his day. Whatever the source of physical life or moral sense, their *existence* proves the prior existence of an original mind and will.

The questions asked in verses 9 and 10 made a strong impression on the mind of Sophia, the Electress of Hanover, a woman of decided mental power, and were adopted by the philosopher Leibnitz in his oppostion to *Atheism.* The principle on which he reasoned was, that as the stream cannot rise above its fountain, intelligence in man implies an intelligent source. Before such an argument advanced by Leibnitz, Descartes in his Meditations, III., formulated the same idea, and so wrote, "Now it is manifest by the light of nature that there must be as much reality in the efficient cause as in the effect; from whence could the effect draw its reality but from the cause? And how could the cause communicate power to it, if it had it not in itself? And from this follows, not only that nothing can be produced from nothing, but also that what is more perfect cannot be a result of, and dependent on, what is less perfect."

The Lord knoweth the thoughts of man, that they are vanity, 94:11. Paul must have lived much in this Psalm for he also quotes this verse, with modification, in 1 Corinthians 3:20, adding *wise men* for *men.* When we think of the millions of daily thoughts occupying the minds of men, whether wise or otherwise, how the Omniscience of God staggers us! The charge levelled against such thoughts is that many of them are *vain.* "Man *at his best estate* is altogether vanity." The Syriac Version reads, for they are a *vapor* (See James 4:14). "The literal rendering, *for they are breath,* refers not to the *thoughts,* but to man collectively, and gives equally good sense, and would, notwithstanding the order of the words, be natural, since the masculine pronoun is used."

Blessed is the man . . . thou chasteneth . . . and teachest, 94:12. What a vital connection there is between chastening and teaching! The two must go together, else chastening will be profitless. Afflictions are sanctified when they correct and teach us. It is by trials that God teaches. Trials, in themselves, can be severe schoolmasters, but the Divine Schoolmaster knows how to guide us into a deeper knowledge of all He is in Himself through them. As seeds, deepest covered with snow in winter flourish most in spring, so God knows that the sorrows of life can yield much fruit in our witness for Him.

That thou mayest give him rest. 94:13. Chastening teaches us to rest in the Lord. Final freedom from days of adversity will only come when we reach the end of life's pilgrimage. Meantime, grace is ours to abide quiet under all trying providences, knowing that *all* things work together for a beneficient end. Ours is the rest of a calm, self-possessed spirit, a quietness of mind and spirit no matter what cares beset us. As for the wicked, there is no rest for them. The pit of eternal despair has been dug for them, for Hell is a prepared place for a prepared people. Thus, as the days of grace ripen saints for glory, days of God-rejection hasten the days of unending grief for the wicked. Reviewing verses 12 and 13, Ellicott has the summary—

> A far higher note than one of mere complaint, or even of trust in God, is struck here. The beatitude of suffering could not be made altogether plain in the Old Testament, though in Job the spirit of it is nearly reached. Here the poet sees thus far, that he who is the victim of misfortunes may be congratulated if he may stand aside and calmly watch the course of Divine Providence involving evil men in punishment. What he has himself endured has chastened him, and caused *him to be quiet* all his days—that is, has calmed him in viewing evil circumstances.

For the Lord will not cast off his people, 94:14. Here, again, Paul dips into this Psalm, for in Romans 11:2, he quotes this first half of verse 14. Personal history testifies to the fact that although the Lord may suffer us to be cast down, He can never cast us off, seeing that through grace, we are His forever. We must never mistake our feelings for actualities. In times of severe persecutions, saints felt as if the Lord had forsaken them, but His promise is that He will never forsake His inheritance. As the poet reminds us—

> He may chasten and correct,
> But He never can neglect,
> May in faithfulness reprove,
> But He ne'er can cease to love.

But righteousness shall return unto righteousness, 94:15. Says Spurgeon, "A delightful hope is here expressed in poetic imagery of rare beauty . . . a gladsome procession follows the chariot of right drawn in triumph through our streets." The opening clause of the verse is a phrase of speech frequent in the Old Testament to signify retaliation, *like* for *like*. Martin Luther's fine paraphrase reads, "For Right must, whatever happens, remain Right." Israel was often encouraged to believe that seeming contradiction in her history would end; that God's righteousness would triumph over the injustice under which she groaned, that His providential dealings would be vindicated and that in the end she would acknowledge that "there is a reward for the righteous, as God Who judges in the earth," Psalm 58:11. *Shall follow it,* or "shall after it," is a phrase often used for expressing attachment and adherence to a party or cause, Exodus 23:2 etc., and here denotes the decision to adhere to Jehovah, 1 Samuel 12:14.

Who will rise up for me against the wicked? 94:16. History testifies that in succeeding ages men who neither feared God nor regarded men have combined together and formed confederacies or groups to carry out their works of darkness, thus showing themselves wise in their generation, for in unison they more effectively promoted the kingdom of their father the Devil, than otherwise, as individuals, they could have done. But every age testifies to the efforts of God's children to join together to oppose the works of darkness and to spread the knowledge of His saving power throughout the World, and in their unity of purpose found strength. Valiant men like Martin Luther and John Knox were champions of truth because of the faithful who surrounded them and encouraged them in their witness. The term *rise up* implies "stand up as champions," as Shammah did in his exploits, 2 Samuel 23:11, See Psalm 2:2. May grace be ours to stand up and be counted among the number witnessing against the working of iniquity!

Our souls—and lips—dwell in individual silence if the victorious Lord is not our help. The word *help* in verse 17 signifies "helpfulness" or "full help." In Him is a perfect sufficiency of help in our united witness for Him. Apart from such Divine assistance, we are guilty of remaining as silent as the grave.

In the multitude of my thoughts within me thy comforts delight my soul, 94:19. For *thoughts* the LXX and Vulgate Versions have "griefs." The word implies "perplexing" or "anxious thoughts" (see Job 4:13; 20:2). Tennyson has the couplet akin to the meaning of the word used here for *thoughts*—

> This way and that dividing his swift mind,
> In act to throw.

As for the term *delight,* the same literally means to *stroke* and *so soothe.* The Hebrew word is used of a mother quieting her child with the breast, Isaiah 66:11, and also of the cup of consolation given to mourners at funerals, Jeremiah 16:7. "*Thy* comforts"—God is the source of all happiness and satisfaction and rest. Xerxes offered great rewards to the person who could find out a new pleasure to experience. The comforts of God cannot be surpassed and ever recruit the heart. "There is as much difference between heavenly and earthly comforts, as between a banquet that is eaten and one that is painted on a wall."

The throne of iniquity . . . which frameth mischief by a law, 94:20. "The workers of iniquity," 94:4, have their *throne,* and what a travesty of reign it represents! Our reigning Lord cannot ally Himself to such a false throne—a fraud upon humanity and a blasphemy of Heaven. Lacking righteousness, evil holders of power must come to an end, and all their decrees be abandoned. Syndicates of violence and crime are set against the witness of the righteous and seek to condemn innocent blood, but *the* King, Who sits in the heaven, is the defense and rock-like refuge of the righteous, those whom united, evil forces would trample upon. The throne of iniquity will be destroyed by its own iniquity, 94:23. "Providence arranges retaliations as remarkable as they are just."

God shall bring upon them their own iniquity, 94:23. Thrones established in opposition to the Throne of God, iniquitous thrones trespassing on civil liberty and infringing religious equality, are deriving revenue from evil commerce and from crime, no matter what their pretensions are but by their nature are excluded from Divine fellowship, and will be *cut off,* or destroyed because between His holy throne and their unholy throne a great gulf is fixed. It is on this note that this great Psalm ends, with faith reading the present in light of the future, thus concluding her song without a trembling note.

Psalm 95

In the Crusades, representing a struggle between temporal and spiritual powers, the use of Psalms was prominent. Battlefields against the Saracens resounded with *Venite exultemus Domino*—"O come, let us sing unto the Lord." This 95th Psalm was the battle-cry of the Templars, the Knights of the Red Cross, when during the Crusades they entered into battle with the Saracens for the conquest of Jerusalem. From earliest times this Psalm has played the part of an invitatory Psalm in the Christian Church, as it does in the English morning service today. Its first seven verses are fitting as a call to worship, seeing they consist of a call to praise God as King, as the Creator of the World, and as the Shepherd of His people. The remainder of the Psalm is made up of a warning against unbelief, drawn from the fate of the rebellious in the wilderness, 95:8-11.

Naming this invitation to worship as *The Psalm of the Provocation,* Spurgeon wrote, "It has about it a ring like that of the church bells and like the bells it sounds both merrily and solemnly, at first ringing out a lively peal, and then dropping into a funeral knell as if tolling at the funeral which perished in the wilderness." Although the Psalm appears authorless in the A.V., the LXX prefixes a title ascribing it to David. Paul, who doubtless had much to do with the composition of the Epistle to the Hebrews, quotes the Psalm as being "in David," and we believe it to be a truly Hebrew song, directed both in its exhortation and warning to the Jewish people from the inspired pen of "the sweet psalmist of Israel." Paul, however, in quoting from the Psalm uses a passage as an appeal and entreaty as he deals with Gentile believers, Hebrews 4:7; Psalm 95:7, 8.

Further, there is nothing to indicate its date. The Psalm appears to be part of a group, Psalms 95-100, to which Psalm 93 is closely related, of songs composed for the celebration of the return of Israel from exile in Babylon. Thus, although composed for congregational use, from the contents of Psalm 95 it would seem as if its author sensed some danger to the nation's recognition of God, and so recalls the disobedience and perversity of the early history of the race as a warning.

O come, let us sing unto the Lord, 95:1. Other nations sang unto their gods, and so David invites the nation he ruled to sing unto Jehovah, and to make a joyful noise unto Him as its Rock of Salvation. The invitation to sing unto the Lord is general, and this exhortation to worship God is not with penitence, but with loud thanksgiving, which is the more remarkable considering the somber strain in which the latter part of the Psalm is written. The phrase *joyful noise* is an encouragement for those of us who cannot sing tunefully but make a *noise*. Yet if *joyful* as unto the Lord, He, Who loves the crows, as well as the nightingales, is pleased. The original means to make a loud sound of any sort, either with the voice or with instruments. "There is no one English expression for the full burst of instrumental and vocal music which is meant by the Hebrew word here applied to the Temple service."

The object of our song is Jehovah as the Rock of our Salvation. All praise should be directed towards the Lord Himself. It is to be feared that much of our religious singing in churches is not unto the Lord, but unto the ear of the congregation. Israel sang for joy when, in the wilderness, the smitten rock poured forth its cooling streams, and now she must make a joyful noise unto the Rock of her Salvation. History is woven into the first part of this hymn of David's, who had in his mind's eye, the Rock, The Tabernacle, The Red Sea, The Mountains of Sinai. What praise should be ours for Him Who became the smitten Rock at Calvary, even Jesus, Who opened a fountain for sin and uncleanness!

Let us come before his presence with thanksgiving, 95:2. The Hebrew for "before his presence" means *go to meet—be there with the first—prevent his face*. This English *prevent* has a different meaning in the original to that which we attach to it. It implies, "suddenly seized upon," and suggests *haste* in praising God. "Let us go speedily," Zechariah 8:21. There may be an historical reference in the phrase "before his presence" to a peculiar presence of God in the Holy of Holies above the mercy-seat, and also to the glory which shone forth out of the cloud which rested above the Tabernacle. The quality of joyfulness is twice insisted upon. Serious, as we should be in sanctuary singing, we should not present the aspect of misery, but remember that joy is as much a characteristic of true worship as solemnity itself.

For the Lord is a great God, and a great King, above all gods, 95:3. The plural, *gods,* does not refer to angelic beings but to the gods of surrounding nations, as more fully explained in the next Psalm—96:4, 5. These nations, whose idol gods were lifeless, imagined Israel's living God to be a mere local deity, the god of a small nation, and therefore one of the inferior deities, each of whom received a certain amount of respect. Grounds for praise are the titles given of the Lord Who is *a great God and a great King*. Pre-eminence and Power are His. The three names used of the Supreme Being in this verse could not apply to false gods—

> *El,* implying His perfect strength,
> *Jehovah*, His being and essence,
> *Elohim*, His covenant relation to mankind.

Israel had been guilty of falling into the sin of worshipping gods, destitute of life, and, therefore, of any sovereign power. David urges the people to recognize Jehovah's supremacy as the secret of their preservation as a religious nation. True worship revolves around the Being, greatness, and sovereign dominion of the Lord.

In his hand are the deep places of the earth, 95:4. It is interesting to find that *deep places* comes from a root meaning "to search," perhaps by digging, either in mines or from mineral wealth. *Strength,* used in this verse, is a rare word found only here and in Numbers 23:22; 24:8, "strength of a unicorn," and also in Job 22:25, margin, "silver of strength." Here, again, is the idea of labor in extracting precious metal from the earth. The implication is that the deepest and most retired parts of the earth are ever explorable by the eye of God. "Go where man may, with all his toil and searching in the heights or in the depths of the earth, he cannot find a place beyond the range of God's dominion."

The sea is his, and he made it, 95:5. Whenever God speaks in defense of His sovereignty, His chief arguments are usually drawn from His created works. (See Job 38). Having made the heavens and the earth, He is portrayed as "*Lord* of heaven and earth," Acts 17:24. When we think of the illimitable acreage of waters all over the world, we realize that they have no other lord but *God.* Whether it be the Atlantic, Pacific, Mediterranean, or Arctic oceans, no person can map out a part of same and claim, "This is mine!" God is their sole Proprietor and Monarch. *Neptune* is but a phantom, the Lord is God of the oceans, and as their Creator and Controller they obey His will. In like manner "the dry land" was fashioned by His power. No matter where we tread, we can look upon the earth beneath us and "count it all as the floor of a temple where the footprints of the present Deity are visible, before our eyes, if we but care to see."

He made it! John Milton gave us this description of God as the sole Creator of the Universe—

> The Earth was form'd, but in the womb as yet
> Of waters, embryon immature involv'd
> Appear'd not: over all the face of Earth
> Main ocean flow'd, not idle, but, with warm
> Prolifick humor softening all her globe,
> Fermented the great mother to conceive,
> Satiate with general moisture; when God said,
> Be gather'd now, ye waters under Heaven
> Into one place, and let dry land appear.
> Immediately the mountains huge appear
> Emergent, and their broad bare backs upheave
> Into the clouds; their tops ascend the sky:
> So high as heav'd the tumult hills, so low
> Down sunk a hollow bottom broad and deep,
> Capacious bed of waters.

Let us worship . . . let us kneel, 95:6. When, in 1792, William Carey arrived in India he found that Christian Friedrich Schwartz, 1726-97, had already inscribed over the portal of his Mission Church, at Tranquebar, the verse, "O come, let us worship and fall down, and kneel before the Lord our Maker." The text of the sermon preached at the service held to dedicate Carey to his great work was from a Psalm, "They that run after another god shall have great trouble," 16:4. *Worship*, in the verse before us, implies the prostration of oneself. *Kneeling*, which was Daniel's usual posture, 6:10, was the practice of kneeling low, as they still do in the East. First mentioned in 2 Chronicles 6:13, kneeling was only used in moments of deep humiliation.

Kimchi distinguishes the several gestures expressed by the different words the Psalmist uses in this verse. "The *first* we render 'worship,' and signifies, the prostration of the whole body on the ground, with hands and legs stretched out. The *second* a 'bowing' of the head, with part of the body; and the *third* a 'bending' of the knees on the ground." Posture, of course, is not everything. The very aged with crippled joints cannot kneel, and it is blessed to know that their prayers are heard although their knees cannot bend. To those, however, whose adoring hearts seek to worship the Lord, bended knees indicate their approach to One holier than themselves.

He is our God . . . we are the people . . . the sheep, 95:7. Some scholars affirm that this verse should be linked on to the first part of the next verse so that it should read, "For He is our God, and we are the people of his pastures. The sheep of his hand. Today would that ye would hearken to his voice." Doubtless there is an allusion here to the Oriental custom of leading flocks by the voice. See John 10:4, and note resemblance in 95:6, 7 to 100:3, 4.

Harden not your heart, as in the provocation . . . as in the day of temptation, 95:8. As the former shepherd, David recalls the guiding voice his sheep obeyed, and so presents God as addressing the sheep of His pasture, and in this verse begins the Divine warning regarding the peril of disobeying such a voice. For "provocation" the R. V. has *Meribah* (Num. 20:13), and for "temptation," *Massah,* Exodus 17:7. (The places were denominated by the names taken from the transactions that occurred in them; and the introduction of these names gives more liveliness to the allusion. It was in these places that the people tempted God and chided with Moses. See same effect in Psalm 81:7; where the Bible translation retains the proper name.) The importance of this passage is emphasized by the writer of *Hebrews* where in 3:7-11, verses 7-11 of Psalm 95 are quoted as being the inspired voice of the Holy Spirit, and again in 4:7, where David is named as being the human channel the Spirit used to record such a warning.

Your fathers tempted me . . . proved me . . . saw my work, 95:9. The
term *proved* is used of trying metals, and is employed to denote man's
attitude towards Providence, both in a good and bad sense, Malachi 3:10,
15. The Divine assertion, *saw my work,* implies that the people watched
Him in His dealings with ever the same readiness to murmur and repine,
and try Divine patience. They knew what He was able to do, yet wanted
to have proof of His presence and of His power to act even in an extraordinary manner. For forty years God suffered the treatment of His people,
and after *ten* temptations deprived them of their land. They had had abundant and conclusive evidence of His faithfulness, but ever provoked Him
to anger—

> They saw his wonders wrought,
>   And then his praise they sang;
> But soon his works of pow'r forgot,
>   And murmur'd with their tongue.

> Now they believe his word
>   While rocks with rivers flow;
> Now will their lusts provoke the Lord,
>   And he reduc'd them low.

Forty years was I grieved with this generation, 95:10. Quoting this
verse, Paul adds the word *Wherefore,* not found in the Psalm, to make the
connection more distinct. The Hebrew term for "grieved" is very
strong and reads, "I loathed a whole generation"—God was angry with
a privileged people because they took no knowledge of His ways both in
Providence and Discipline. Warnings were fruitless. "A people that do err"
literally means, *a people of wanderers in heart*—they were morally astray
through ignorance of God's ways. All mortals err, but here it is said that
the Israelites erred *in their heart.* They went astray not through ignorance,
but through corruption and perversity of heart, which was not right with
God. "Lust in the heart, like vapor in the stomach, soon affects the head,
and clouds the understanding." How patient and longsuffering God was
to allow His rebellious people 40 years in which to grieve Him! The
ancient Jews believed that "the days of the Messiah were to be 40 years."
Is it not remarkable that 40 years after Christ's Ascension, the whole
Jewish nation were cut off as equally as they fell in the wilderness?

I sware in my wrath that they should not enter into my rest, 95:11. As
Israel was guilty of an unbelieving heart, how could she enter into Divine
rest? If the Manna and Miracles of 40 years could not satisfy her, neither
would the promised land flowing with milk and honey. How solemn is the
fiat of Heaven, "They should not enter into my rest!" What an abrupt conclusion for this Psalm! There is no cheering prospect to relieve the
threatening. As the Psalm forms one of a group, perhaps it was meant to

stand alone, leaving a brighter outlook to companion Psalms to express.

As for the *Rest* God had prepared for His wayward people, it was the Promised Land. In New Testament quotations of verses 8-10 of the Psalm, a future rest for the redeemed of the Lord is in the mind of Paul, notably in his argument in Galatians 3:13-16. As those saved by Divine grace, we are urged to beware lest we fail to enter a promised, present rest, as well as the prospective rest remaining for us, Hebrews 4:1-11. Spurgeon reminds us in his conclusion to the exposition of this 95th Psalm that there is a lesson we must not forget—

> It is clear that there is a rest of God, and that some enter into it: but "they to whom it was first preached entered not in because of unbelief, there remaineth therefore a rest for the people of God." The unbelievers could not enter, but "we which have believed do enter into rest." Let us enjoy it, and praise the Lord for it forever. Ours is the true Sabbatic rest, it is ours to rest from our own work as God did for His. While we do so, let us "come into his presence with thanksgiving, and make a joyful noise unto him with Psalms."

Psalm 96

It was in 361 A.D., that Julian, nephew of Constantine, succeeded to the Roman Empire and renounced Christianity which had been established by his revered uncle, and devoted his brief but energetic reign of two years to the attempted restoration of Paganism. He made strong efforts to put a new spirit of philosophy into old forms, and, without returning its sanguinary persecution, he used measures of restriction on Christians which were more dangerous. Historians of that period recorded that the Psalm commonly sung by all who were true to the faith during the reign of Julian was the 96th, and read in this light, it must have been singularly appropriate with its declaration—"All the gods of the nations are idols."

William Law, who wrote his masterpiece of devotional literature, *Serious Call,* in 1729, invited Christians therein to practice what they professed, "to live more nearly as they prayed." Law stressed the use of the Psalms as an aid to devotion and at the end of one of the most eloquent chapters of his *Call* said: "Do but so live that your heart may truly rejoice in God, and then you will find that this state of your heart will neither want a voice, not ear to find a tune of a Psalm." Law's choice for a morning hymn was Psalm 145, but in his selection of Psalms best adapted for devotional use, he quoted Psalm 96, along with Psalms 103, 111, 146, 147, stating that these wonderfully set forth "the glory of God, and, therefore, you may keep to any one of them at any particular hour as you like: or you may take the finest parts of any of the Psalms, and so, adding them together, may make them fitter for your own devotion."

Although the Psalm appears authorless, it is ascribed to David in the LXX Version, inconsistently so, affirms Ellicott. Whoever the author was he evidently took it from the sacred song composed by David when "the ark of God was set in the midst of the tent which David prepared for it, and they offered burnt-offerings and peace-offerings before God," 1 Chronicles 16. The former part of that song was probably omitted in Psalm 96 "because it referred to Israel, and the design of the Holy Spirit in this Psalm was to give forth a song for the Gentiles, a triumphant hymn wherewith to celebrate the conversion of the nations to Gospel times. It is therefore a grand *Missionary Hymn,* and follows fitly upon the last Psalm, which describes the obstinacy of Israel, and the consequent taking of the Gospel from them that it might be preached among the nations who would receive it, and in due time be fully won to Christ by its power."

In his original Psalm in 1 Chronicles 16, large-hearted David rejoiced before the Ark, as he saw in vision all the earth turning from idols to the one living and true God, a time when the earth would be filled with the glory of the Lord. Psalm 96, the substance of which is taken from Chronicles, can be rightly called a *Millennial Anthem.* As to any historical association of the Psalm, "its tone is closely akin to that of Isaiah 40-66, and was in all likelihood inspired by the deliverance from Exile." The existence of the second Temple will then be implied in verses 6, 8. While attempts have been made at a division of Psalm 96, Spurgeon says, "We will make none, for the song is one and indivisible, a garment of praise without seam, woven from the top throughout."

O sing unto the Lord a new song, 96:1. It would seem as if this "new song," breathing aspirations and hopes, was a kind of national and religious *lyric cry* after the Restoration (See Isa. 42:10). Yet the song in universal use awaits a complete fulfillment (Rev. 5:9; 14:3). Although the term may have marked the revival of national psalmody after the Captivity, *the redeemed* out of all nations will alone sing the new song in all its full significance as they gather around the throne of God in Eternity.

The wider range of singing is stated in the last part of the verse, "Sing unto the Lord, *all* the earth." This proves that the song was not for Israel alone, but envisages a time when national jealousies will be dead, and Jews and Gentiles will lift up one common psalm with one heart and voice unto Jehovah alone. "The multitudinous languages of the sons of Adam, who were scattered at Babel, will blend in the same song when the people are gathered at Zion. All the earth Jehovah made, must sing unto Him." Well might we pray, "Lord, hasten such a glorious advent!" In the first two verses of the Psalm the name *Lord* is thrice repeated and not without meaning. Is it not unto the Three-One Lord "that the enlightened nations will sing? The sacred fire of adoration only burns with vehement flame where the Trinity is believed in and beloved." Unknown before then, this *new* song awaits the chorus voices of all the whole earth.

Declare his glory among the heathen . . . among all people, 96:3. What was called *salvation* is now named *glory,* then *wonders!* By *heathen* we understand "nations," or "all people." Here we have the missionary application of the Psalm which forms part of the commission of Jesus to His Church to go into *all* the world and preach His Gospel to every creature. The tragedy is that there are millions all over the earth who have not heard of Him who died to save a lost world.

All the gods of the nations are idols, 96:5. Says Paul, "an *idol* is *nothing,*" 1 Corinthians 8:4, and idols fashioned by men are *nothing,* or nonentities. Mere images of wood and stones are destitute of life, and therefore, of creative power, *"but* the Lord made the heaven." Hence the argument for His universal praise and adoration. "The reality of His Godhead," says Spurgeon, "is proved by His works, and foremost among these the psalmist mentions that matchless piece of architecture which casts its arch over every man's head, whose lamps are the light of all mankind, whose rains and dews fall upon the fields of every people, and whence the Lord's voice of thunder is heard speaking to every creature."

Throne and majesty . . . strength and beauty, 96:6. This quartet of attributes reach their perfection in Him in whom are combined all that is mighty and lovely, powerful and resplendent. These four virtues are also His constant attendants in His sanctuary where they were typical of the costly splendor of the sanctuary in Israel and its rites. Said Apollinaris, "Pureness and stately glory fit His shrine."

> Oh, if so much of beauty doth reveal
> Itself in every vein of life and nature,
> How beautiful must be the Source itself,
> The ever-Bright One!

When we reach Heaven, His eternal sanctuary, then all the Lord is of Himself will be more peculiarly manifest.

Give unto the Lord . . . give unto the Lord, 96:7. Giving Him glory is the honor *due* unto His name, and *due* implies "debt," and a debt, in equity, must be paid. Are we paying our due? It will be noticed that the first six verses commence with an exhortation to sing, three times repeated, with the name of Jehovah thrice mentioned; here we meet with the expression "Give unto the Lord," used in the same triple manner in verses 7 and 9. Poets, whose flaming sonnets have won the ear and heart of people, are those who know how to reiterate choice words and phrases till they penetrate the soul and fire the heart.

What can poor mortals among the kindreds of earth *give* unto God Who giveth to all men liberally? They can give Him *glory and strength,* meaning that they recognize these virtues of His and ascribe them to Him in song. They can give Him *the glory due unto His name.* But who among them can do this to the full? If we feel we cannot bring in the full revenue God justly claims, we must not fail from want of honest endeavor to give Him the best. *Give—Bring.* We are not to appear before Him empty. He must receive, not only the praise and gratitude of our lips for all He is in Himself, but our gifts for the maintenance and extension of His cause.

O worship the Lord in the beauty of holiness, 96:9. The motto of one of the London City Companies is *All worship be to God only*—a motto each of us should make our own, for as Massillion expressed it, "God alone is great." For *the beauty of holiness* the margin gives us "in array." What God delights in where His people gather to worship is not beauty of architecture and apparel, but in the moral and spiritual beauty of the worshippers. "Purity is the white linen of the Lord's choristers, righteousness is the comely garment of His priests, and holiness the royal apparel of His servitors." Would that we could see *all the earth* fear before Him! The word "fear" in the original means *tremble* and expresses the profoundest awe, just as "worship" is more accurately translated as *bow down.* It was the sight of the King in all His beauty that made John in Patmos fall at His feet as dead. Do we worship Him with the same prostrate awe and sacred fear? *Fear before Him* can be more literally translated, "Let all the earth be moved before His face."

While this 96th Psalm is without an author's name, Psalm 29 is *A Psalm of David*, and the first two verses of same are repeated in Psalm 96:7-9, in which, in accordance with the world of new ideas and feelings in which Israel lived after her Captivity, a message, truly Messianic in character, is addressed to all the people of the world.

Say among the nations that the Lord reigneth, 96:10. The watchword of the Restoration of Israel, "Jehovah has become King," is an Evangel, not only for Jerusalem, but for the world at large. The prophetic strain found in Israel's poets looks beyond time and the world (See Rev. 19:6). The stability of the world, *it shall not be moved,* is an emblem of the stability and justice of Divine Government. History makes it clear that a settled government is essential to national prosperity, and when Jesus comes to reign in truth and righteousness, universal prosperity will be of the highest degree. Not a few modern nations prove that iniquity makes the dynasties of tyrants to fall; equity, however, has ever, and will ever, characterize Divine rule under which there are never any victims of a despot's arbitrary rule.

It would seem as if this 10th verse is the basic point of this theocratic and missionary Psalm. Occupying practically the center of the Psalm, it is full of deep, spiritual truth. Our English Version ends with "the Lord reigneth," but an old Latin Version reads, *The Lord reigneth from the tree.* Justin Martyr accused the Jews of erasing the word "from the tree" from the original because of their intense hatred of Christ, Who is foreseen in the Psalm as Messiah-King. Through centuries the Latin quotation was cherished as a prediction of the Cross, but was rejected by the Jews of the first two or three centuries. Thus all crucifixes before the eleventh century portray Christ with a robe and crown.

Jesus was born *King,* and the throne from which He reigns is not a gilded one as thrones of earth, but the gory cross of Calvary. As an old Latin hymn expresses it—

> Fulfilled is all that David told
> In this prophetic song of old.
> "Amid the nations God," saith he,
> "Hath reigned and triumphed from the tree."

The last cry, "It is finished," was declared of the King Who had triumphed over Hell's forces and secured a perfect salvation for a sinning race. In the realm of Grace, He still reigns from His cross, and the tree will ever remain His throne, even when we see him as the Lamb slain from the foundation of the world.

> The truth that David learned to sing
> Its deep fulfillment here attains;
> Tell all the earth the Lord is King!
> Lo, from the cross a King He reigns.

John Ellerton's lines suggest a similar thought,

> Thron'd upon the awful tree
> King of grief, I watch with Thee.

Let the heavens . . . let the earth . . . let the sea . . . let the field . . . let all the trees, 96:11, 12. All above and below are to join in the paean of joy because of the Lord's dominion over all the earth. Angels, seas, fields, and all trees are to waft the story of Him Who reigns, and Who will judge the earth with righteousness. John Keble must have thought that the Psalmist included *birds* with rejoicing trees, and thus versified the passage—

> Fields exalt and meadow fair,
> With each bud and blossom there,
> In the lonely woodlands now
> Chants aloud each rustling bough.

John Milton expresses Nature's homage to her Maker in the lines—

> His praise, ye winds that from four quarters blow,
> Breathe soft or loud, and wave your tops ye pines,
> With every plant in sign of worship wave.

For he cometh, for he cometh, 96:13. Here we have another instance of striking repetitions in Scripture—repetition signifying Divine emphasis. In this concluding verse of the Psalm, the repetition has the natural expression of gladness over God's righteous judgment, which is welcomed and not feared, seeing it means a deliverance of His people and the final overthrow of their enemies.

The concluding verses, 11-13, reveal "the magnificent progress of the Divine Judge through all His realm. There is only one thought, that of the inauguration of a righteous sway of all nations, at its advent, as in Isaiah's glorious vision (see Isa. 35:1, 2; 42:10; 44:23; 55:12), all nature seems to join the chorus of gladness." If the whole universe is to be clothed with smiles, should we not be glad and rejoice? As John Howe, devout expositor of a past age expressed it—

"Shall we not partake in this common dutiful joy, and fall into concert with the adoring chorus? Will we cut ourselves off from this gladsome obsequious throng? And what should put a pleasant face and aspect upon the whole world shall it only leave our faces covered with clouds, and a mournful sadness?"

> Jesus shall reign wher'er the sun,
> Doth its successive journeys run:
> His Kingdom stretch from shore to shore,
> Till moons shall wax and wane no more.

Psalm 97

S trange though it may seem, this further theocratic Psalm has an historical association with Julian the Apostate Roman Emperor, 361-363, and with the Christians of the East at that time. We know from The Acts that the Gospel gained an early hold of the important city of Antioch (Acts 11:26), and, although in the time of godless Julian, was weakened by impurity, it still retained great influences among the masses. One of the Bishops of the Church was Babylas who had suffered martyrdom a century before and had to be buried in the grove of Daphne, sacred to Apollo, on the banks of the famed Orontes.

When Julian came to power he decreed the grove to be restored to the worship of *the god of day* and ordered the body of godly Babylas to be removed, which the Christians of the city did, and carried it in solemn procession to another resting place, chanting the 97th Psalm along the way. This spot was visited during a survey of Palestine by Captain Conder who wrote of it as being "bright with the red blossoms of the oleander, which here rise to the dignity of trees. This plant must have been the true *Daphane*—the *Dahane* or *Dawn*—sacred to Apollo, as there is no flower in the East whose delicate rosy flush could be so well used as the emblem of the opening morning."

There is a lofty confidence running through this 97th Psalm, and the Church historian of the third century refers particularly to the 7th verse, doubtless having godless Julian in mind—"Confounded be all they that serve graven images, that boast themselves of idols: worship Him, all ye gods," 97:7. Whether the funeral singers meant it or not, when they reburied Babylas, there are words in the Psalm that had a fitting reference to the occasion, "Light is sown for the righteous, and gladness for the upright in heart," 97:11.

Although this Psalm is another lacking a named author, and modern critics affirm that David could not have possibly composed it, yet being one of the group of theocratic Psalms, with the LXX Version ascribing one of them to David, namely, Psalm 95, we are of the opinion that Psalm 97, and the rest in the group, are of the same author. While, in a very great measure the Psalm is a compilation from his other Psalms, by more than one fine touch it proves itself the product not only of a thoughtful, but of a truly poetic mind such as the sweet psalmist of Israel possessed.

It would seem as if the 97th Psalm is a continuation of Psalm 96, seeing it begins with a phrase from the former. "The Lord reigneth, let the earth rejoice." Extension of thought can be seen in that while Psalm 96 sings the praises of the Lord in connection with the proclamation of the Divine message among *all* men, irrespective of nationality, Psalm 97 seems to foreshadow the mighty working of the Holy Spirit in subduing the colossal systems of error and the casting down of idol gods. Psalm 97, in language sufficiently explicit, describes the completion of the great event, *The Lord reigneth.*

As to the historical implications of this Psalm, God takes vengeance on His enemies in a way to which all nations respond.

> Across the sea to maritime regions a voice cries for rejoicing over the Divine rule, verse 1.
>
> The clouds and darkness, and saved fire manifest themselves as agents of Divine judgment, verses 2-3.
>
> Lightnings and intense heat illustrate the beneficial aspects of the revelation of Divine sovereignty. All nations bathe in the glory of the Lord, verses 4-6.
>
> Idols and their worshippers are denounced, the false gods being confounded, God's people rejoicing, and God Himself exalted, verses 7-9.
>
> God calls His people to hate evil and to share the gladness which ought to be their portion. There is an exhortation to holy steadfastness when persecution comes with the assurance of a glorious reward, verses 10-12.

Thus the Psalm seems to divide itself into four sections, each containing three verses, and has been described as a *mosaic* of phrases from other Scriptures. Like the preceding Psalm, this one may have been associated with the end of Israel's exile.

The Lord reigneth, 97:1. The thought and imagery here occur in the foregoing Psalm, 96:10-11, and in other Psalms and Scriptures. The challenging phrase, *Jehovah reigns!* is the watchword of the Psalm and is the reason why the earth should rejoice in a Divine government which is legislative, providential, mediatorial, and judicial. Then the present tense used here must not be overlooked, "The Lord *reigneth.*" Certainly, He has yet to be seen reigning "wher'er the sun doth its successive journeys run," but He is on His throne *now.* "The Lord God omnipotent *reigneth!*" Amid all the chaos, sin, violence, corruption, and bloodshed characterizing the nations today, it would seem as if Divine rule is inoperative, but in spite of godless and changing kingdoms, God is working out His just purposes with inexorable justice.

I had a friend who paraded the streets with an open umbrella upon which was written *God Reigns!* Upon fine days, with no visibility of rain, people would stop him and say, "Why have you got the umbrella up, it's not raining?" Then he would lower it and point to what was painted on it and say, "No, but He is!" The Psalmist calls upon "the multitudes of the isles" to rejoice over the glorious fact that *God reigns.*

Here the reference is to the coastlands beyond Palestine and is an expression of the great Gentile world beyond. This wide glance to the westward embracing the isles and coasts of the Mediterranean (See Psalm 72:10), possibly even more distant ones, still is characteristic of the literature of post-exile times (See Isa. 42:10, 11; 51:15). He, Who died for the world, deserves to be the Lord of the Isles, and now that all lands can be reached by ship and airship, we should constantly intercede for the extension of His reign in grace.

A delightful, historical incident illustrating the ever-present sovereignty of Jehovah concerns Bulstrode Whitelock who embarked as Oliver Cromwell's envoy to Sweden in 1653. Resting at Harwich overnight, he was very much disturbed in mind as he thought upon the distracted state of the nation, with very stormy weather only adding to his anxiety. Whitelock's confidential servant had a bed in the same cabin, and when he saw his master could not sleep, ventured to say—

> "Pray, sir, will you give me leave to ask you a question?"
> "Certainly."
> "Pray, sir, do you think God governed the world very well before you came into it?"
> "Undoubtedly," replied Whitelock.
> "And pray, sir, do you think that He will govern it quite as well when you are gone out of it?"
> "Certainly."
> "Then pray, sir, do you not think that you may trust Him to govern it quite as well as long as you live?"

Whitelock made no reply to this last question; but turning about in his bed was soon fast asleep till he was summoned to journey on.

Clouds and darkness . . . righteousness and judgment, 97:2. Israel knew from past history that God surrounded His essential Deity, lest His excessive glory should destroy them. "It is the glory of God to conceal a thing," and in the poetical and historical books of the Old Testament, the appearances of God to the saints and patriarchs were all accompanied with the clouds and darkness of our text, particularly at Sinai. *Clouds* are emblems of *obscurity, darkness, of distress,* and God's government is often obscure and productive of distress to mankind, though righteousness and judgment are the habitation of His throne. To finite minds all operations of the power and wisdom of the Infinite One are always shrouded with mystery. Ellicott remarks that the immediate effect on the Hebrew mind, of the awful manifestation of the Divine power in nature, is not fear, but a sublime sense of safety in the established right and truth of God.

They knew that it is one and the same power—a truth Tennyson in his *In Memoriam* poetically describes—

> Which makes the darkness and the light,
> And dwells not in the light alone.
> But in the darkness and the cloud,
> As over Sinai's peaks of old,
> While Israel make them gods of gold,
> Although the trumpet blew so loud.

The reigning Lord has a throne fixed upon the rock of eternal holiness, thus He never departs from straight justice. *"Righteousness* is His immutable attribute, and *Judgment* marks His every act." Blessed to know that absolute power is in the hands of Him Who is not a despot but Who, in His rule, cannot err, or act unrighteously (Ps. 89:14). By *habitation* we can understand "foundation," or "pillars" of the throne, the two attributes being the pillars.

A fire goeth before him, and burneth up his enemies round about, 97:3. Scripture may offer historical instances of Divine judgment by fire— Sodom and Gomorrah for example (Pss. 18:8, 50:3; Hab. 3:3, 5, etc.). *Fire,* like an advance guard, clears the way, as it did at Sinai. The very Being of God is power consuming all that is alien and hostile to His holy will and purpose. "Fire is the sign both of grace and wrath (Exod. 3:2; Ps. 18:9). Majesty marches forth in both displays of Deity." Tongues of fire attended the advent of the Holy Spirit at Pentecost, who ever burns His own way, irresistibly destroying falsehood, sin, superstition, and hardness of heart.

His lightnings enlightened the world: the earth saw, and trembled, 97:4. Evidently this graphic description of the Almighty's power was taken from Psalm 77:17, 18. Zechariah has the prediction, "His arrow shall go forth as the lightning," 9:14. Historically, this is characteristic of the Gospel which sped through all the world like lightning as the records of *The Acts* prove. In the atmospheric realms, in times of tempest the whole of the heavens is lighted up with a lurid glare, that even the light of the sun itself seems dim compared with the blaze of lightning. In apostolic times the truth of Christ's redeeming Gospel flashed with the force and speed of a thunderbolt, and priests and philosophers trembled before a power they were not able to restrain. "Faith even now sets the world on fire, and rocks the nations to and fro."

The hills melted like wax at the presence of the Lord, 97:5. Already we have mentioned that this Psalm is a *mosaic* of phrases from other parts of the Bible, and away back in the Book of Judges we have the original of the symbol before us. "The mountains melted from before the Lord, even that Sinai from before the God of Israel" 5:5. See also 68:8; Micah 1:4.

History eloquently testifies that States and Kingdoms, standing out in the world like mountains, are utterly dissolved when God decrees their end. Systems as ancient and firmly rooted as the hills pass away when the Creator, inanimate nature knows and worships after its own fashion, looks upon them. In our spiritual experience, the Holy Spirit, reigning within our hearts, is the Fire consuming our lusts and melting our wills into loving obedience.

Further, this wonderful effect of the presence of the Lord is felt throughout "the whole earth." Abraham declared Him to be "the Judge of the whole earth," Genesis 18:25. Thus, although to surrounding nations with their tribal gods Jehovah was a tribal God of Israel, yet here is the reminder that He is a God with universal dominion and power.

The heavens declare . . . all the people see his glory, 97:6. The Psalmist did not say that the heavens exercise righteousness, but only *declare* it. Then the phrase is not, *God declares,* but, the heavens declare His righteousness. The creature is the revealer and servant of Divine righteousness. Further, it is not *our* righteousness the heavens declare but *His.* All our righteousness is but as a filthy rag in His holy eyes. What a great day that will be when the whole earth sees His glory! All the splendors of the storm witness to His eternal righteousness (Psalm 89:6).

Worship him, all gods, 97:7. The word *confounded,* describing those serving graven images, means "ashamed" (See Isa. 42:17; Jerm. 10:14). The same idea is conveyed by the very word *idols* in Hebrew—empty, worthless things, *shaming* those who worship them. As for the phrase, *all ye gods,* it is directly intended to include among superhuman beings the agencies worshipped by heathen nations as deities. The quotation in Hebrews 1:6 is taken from the LXX Version of Deuteronomy 32:43. "A man who worships an image is but the image of a man, his senses must have left him. He who boasts of an idol makes an idle boast."

Zion heard, and was glad . . . the daughters of Judah rejoiced, 97:8. *Zion* represents Jerusalem, and *Daughters,* the other cities of the land (See Psalm 48:11). The Greeks thought only of the men who made Athens strong, but the Hebrew traces all national blessings back to God. The rejoicing daughters may be an allusion to a custom in Judea of forming choral bands of maidens after a victory or some happy circumstance. Miriam, sister of Aaron, took a timbrel, and all the women followed her with timbrels and dancing. When David returned from the slaughter of Goliath, the women came out of all the cities of Israel, singing, dancing, and playing instruments of music. Jehovah was not only high over Judea, but all the earth, nor is He exalted over men only, but over everything that can be called good. Thus we render unto the Lord the Glory and Praise due to Him alone (97:9. See 83:18).

He preserveth . . . he delivereth, 97:10. This wonderful verse reveals the Psalmist more a true poet than a compiler of gathered phrases (See Psalm 34:10-20; 37:28). If we are among the number who love the Lord, then we cannot truly love Him without hating all He hates. The more we love the Lord, the more shall we be found hating evil. A heathen writer used the striking illustration of Philosophy holding a dialogue with Lucian, and being made to say, "To love and to hate, they say, spring from the same source." To which he replied, "That, O Philosophy, should be best known to you. My business is to hate the bad, and to love and commend the good, and that I stick to."

For all the saints who mirror Divine hatred for all that is evil there is the twin provision of *preservation* and *deliverance.* Preservation is keeping lest we should be imperilled—Deliverance has reference to those already involved in perils. The saints, then, who love the Lord and hate evil are the safe ones. The grace that saved them keeps them saved and secure.

Light is sown for the righteous, 97:11. The metaphor used here is an obvious and common one. Milton, with this Psalm in mind, enriched the metaphor in the lines—

> Now words, her rosy step in the Eastern clime
> Advancing, sow'd the earth with orient pearl.

Light—Gladness! Is there not a vital connection between the two? Only the right-hearted are glad-hearted. "Right leads to light. In the furrows of integrity lie the seeds of happiness, which shall develop into a harvest of bliss. God has lightning for sinners and light for saints."

Rejoice . . . give thanks, 97:12. Unless we know what it is to rejoice *in* the Lord, we cannot worthily give Him thanks for His unflecked holiness. The R.V. gives us "to his holy name" for *holiness.* "To remember that Jehovah is holy is becoming in those who dwell in His courts, to give thanks of that remembrance is the sure index of their fitness to abide in His presence." "The Lord reigneth"—"Rejoice in the Lord." What a sublime beginning and ending of a Psalm this is!

Psalm 98

We heartily agree with Spurgeon that "this song is worthy to rank among the most devout and soul-stirring of sacred lyrics." It bears the plain, brief title A Psalm, in Hebrew, a single word, Psalm, the only one in the collection of royal Psalms to be thus named. The R.V. heads it, A Melody, and what a melodious ode it is, so vibrant with vocal, instrumental and universal joyful singing and playing! Beginning and ending in the same way as Psalm 96, it is closely akin to it, and belongs to that circle of literature produced by the joy of the Restoration. Joyful occurs three times in the Psalm, just as we have triple Sing.

Historically, the Psalm celebrates a victory God had wrought for Israel in the sight of the whole earth, 1-3; summons all men, 4-6, and all nature to praise Him as King, and as the One Who is coming to judge the world 7-9. Thus we have three stanzas of three verses each. The first triad *why,* second triad *how,* third triad, *who* are to praise Jehovah. This singularly bold and lively song continues the theme of the previous Psalm, for if Psalm 97 declares the publication of the Divine message and the setting up of the Divine kingdom, Psalm 98 officially proclaims the Lord as the conquering Monarch over the nations with singing and joyful noises, blasting of trumpets, playing of harps, clapping of hands in celebration of a glorious triumph. It can be named A Coronation Hymn.

O sing unto the Lord a new song, 98:11. We had a *new* song in Psalm 96, proclaiming the advent of the Lord, but this *new* song celebrates the accomplished fact of his advent and of all He achieved by His right arm. He is praised for marvelous things—He created a marvelous universe—established a marvelous government—inspired a marvelous Book—bestowed upon the World the gift of His marvelous Son Who lived a marvelous life on earth, died a marvelous death, experienced a marvelous resurrection, ascended marvelously into Heaven, and by His Spirit produces a marvelous transformation in the lives of those who turn to Him in penitence and faith.

The victories of the Lord are not brought about by physical but by moral power—through the energy of love, goodness, justice and truth, all of which are associated with His *holy* arm. All praise is due to Him Who never stoops to use policy or brute force in pursuit of victory. Glory be to this Conqueror for His unsullied perfection in the security of a complete victory over all powers of evil. And so—

358

Victor alike in love and arms,
  Myriads before him bend;
Such are the Conqueror's matchless charms,
  Each foe becomes a friend.

His salvation . . . His righteousness, 98:2. Myriads in Heaven and on earth praise God for having made known His *salvation* which His beloved Son accomplished for a lost world. As we know, the kindred word *righteousness* was the favorite expression of Paul, Apostle to the Gentiles, who loved to dwell on God's methods of making lost men righteous, and vindicating His justice by the atoning blood. This redeeming Gospel had been proclaimed among the nations for well-nigh two millenniums in response to the Redeemer's commission to go into *all* the world and preach such a Gospel.

The house of Israel . . . all the ends of the earth, 98:3. The Lord came to be a Light unto the Gentiles and the Glory of His people Israel, and multitudes of Jews and Gentiles form His Church in which there is neither Jew nor Gentile, but all are one in Him. Emphasis is on the phrase, *hath seen,* implying not a nominal faith but an actual faith, born of the Spirit and united with knowledge and experience of God's saving power. *His mercy and his truth*—mercy constraining Him to *promise* Salvation—truth, engaging Him to *perform* it, have been declared over the whole globe for there is no nation that has not received the Gospel although there are millions in many nations who have not *seen His salvation.*

Make a joyful noise, 98:4. The Argives, when delivered by the Romans from the tyranny of the Macedonians and Spartans, expressed great joy and loud outcries rent the air. The very birds, it is said, that flew over them, fell to the ground, astonished at their noises. The crier at the Nemean Games was forced to pronounce the word *Liberty!* The exhortation to make a joyful noise actually means *break out into songs and music.* John Wesley used to say to his followers, "Sing lustily, and with a good courage. Beware of singing as if you were half dead or asleep; but lift up your voice with strength. Be no more afraid of your voice now, nor more ashamed of its being heard, than when you sung the songs of Satan." His brother, Charles, left us hundreds of joyful songs to sing gladly. The Psalmist, like the Salvation Army today, wanted every kind of music pressed into the service of magnifying the God of our Salvation.

Sing unto the Lord with the harp, 98:5. The repetition here is emphatical and implies that men must make the most ardent attempts to celebrate and proclaim the great work of the world's redemption. David loved his harp—a sweet instrument of music—and none could rival him in the skilful use of it in the singing of his Psalms. He believed that skill in music should not be desecrated to the World's evil mirth, but should aid the private devotions and public praise of the saints. George Herbert could sing—

> My God, My God,
> My music shall find thee,
> And every string
> Shall have his attribute to sing.

Accompanying the music of the lovely harp was *the voice of a Psalm,* or with a *musical voice,* as distinguished from common speech. The human voice had many modulations—of complaint—of sorrow—of pleading—of command, and there is a Psalm to match the mood and modulation. What history revolves around the singing of Psalms!

> Jehoshaphat and Hezekiah celebrated their victories with Psalms.
>
> Israel returned from exile in Babylon singing Psalms.
>
> Maccabees gained courage and strength in their brave struggles to achieve their country's independence by singing Psalms.
>
> Jesus, the night before He died, sang Psalms with His Apostles.
>
> Paul and Silas sang Psalms at midnight and inspired their fellow-prisoners by so doing.
>
> Jerome tells us that in his day the Psalms were heard in the fields and vineyards of Palestine.
>
> Sidonius Apollinaris made his boatmen, as they took their heavily laden barge upstream, to sing Psalms till the river banks echoed with Hallelujahs.

D. Israel, in his *Curiosities of Literature,* tells of a very curious piece of Psalm-singing, in which he mentions the spread of Psalm-singing in France, which first started among the Romanists by the version of Clement Marot, the favored bard of Francis the First. D. Israel then goes on to say, somewhat sneeringly, that in the time of the Commonwealth, "Psalms were now sung at Lord Mayor's dinners and City feats; soldiers and them on their march and at parade; and a few houses which had windows fronting the streets, had their evening Psalms."

With trumpets and sound of cornet, make a joyful noise, before the Lord, your King, 98:6. We may have a reference here to the public rejoicing commonly manifested at the Coronation of Kings or the celebration of undertakings for public safety. Such an idea is not foreign to this passage, since Jehovah is represented, and rejoiced in, as King and Savior of the people. The trumpet was mainly used for convening a public assembly for worship or for assembling the hosts for battle. Trumpets and cornets will symbolize the power which should be put forth in the praise of Jehovah, the King, Who is worthy of the best melody voices and instruments can render. These particular instruments were in constant use among Jews, and a spiritual signification has been attached to each instrument. Cardinal virtues supposed to be represented are—The harp, speaking of *Prudence;* The Psaltery, *Justice;* The Trumpet, *Fortitude;* The Cornet, *Temperance.*

Origen called the writings of the Apostles—*Trumpets,* at whose blast all the structures of idolatory and the dogmas of the philosophers were utterly overthrown. This Early Father also taught that by the sound of the *Trumpets* is prefigured the trumpet of universal judgment, at which the world shall fall in ruin, and whose sound shall be joy to the just and lamentations to the unjust. What must be underlined is the fact that all vocal and instrumental music must be *before the Lord* and not for the mere satisfaction of an audience.

Let the sea roar . . . Let the floods clap their hands; Let the hills be joyful, 98:7-8. What exuberance Nature displays in her adoration of her Creator and Sustainer! She recognizes Him as

> Creator of the rolling spheres,
> Ineffably sublime

These verses akin to Psalm 96:11, 12, must have been in the mind of that remarkable poet of Nature, William Wordsworth, when he wrote—

> Listen! the mighty Being is awake
> And doth with His eternal motion make
> A sound like thunder everlastingly.

The Psalmist makes it clear that man is not denied a place in the grand orchestra of Nature. He must be in harmony with the roaring sea, happy floods, and joyful hills—*The World, and they that dwell therein.* The clapping of hands is said to be a token of delight and approbation, and the striking or dashing of the water in a river being, for the noise of it, a resemblance of that, the *rivers* are here said to *clap their hands.* As men greet their Sovereigns and Rulers with acclamation, so rolling rivers, tidal estuaries, roaring cataracts, mighty mountains, in concert with man, burst forth into a sublime uproariousness of mirth such as the sad poet, Byron, depicts in *Childe Harold—*

> Far long
> From peak to peak, the rattling crags among,
> Leaps like his thunder! Not from one lone cloud,
> But every mountain now hath found a tongue,
> And Jura answers, through her misty shroud,
> Back to the joyous Alps, who call to her aloud.

James Thomson adopts a similar strain in his lines—

> And thou, majestic main!
> A secret world of wonders in thyself,
> Sound his stupendous praise, whose greater voice
> Or bids you roar, or bids your roarings fall.

Before the Lord: for he cometh to judge the earth, 98:9. The R.V. gives *peoples,* not "people" (See Psalm 96:13). The coming complete rule of the King, praised and extolled by man and nature in this Psalm, will be a reign of *Holiness*—the proper and distinctive nature of His dominion—a reign of Justice, to all on the earth. *Righteousness* and *Equity* will be prominent in His rule for His government will be like the Judge Himself, flawless in character. What else can we do but join in Keble's song based upon the last four verses of this Psalm.

> Ring out, with horn and trumpet ring,
> In shouts before the Lord and King:
> Let ocean with his fulness swing
>   In restless unison:
>
> Earth's round and all the dwellers there,
> The mighty floods the burden bear,
> And clap the hands: in choral air
>   Join every mountain lone.
>
> Tell out before the Lord, that he
> Is come, the Judge of earth to be,
> To judge the world with equity,
>   Do right to realm and throne.

Psalm 99

This further Psalm, included in the section of Psalms composed to celebrate the Return of Israel from Exile (95-100), is taken up with renewed worship and nationality which made it possible for the poet to compare his age with that of the greatest saints and heroes of old such as Moses, Aaron, and Samuel. Belonging to the same period as precious Psalms in this group, Psalm 99 continues the prominence given to God's Kingship the preceding ones manifest. On the Psalms as a whole, Spurgeon says that "it is a hymn most fitting for saints who dwell in Zion, the holy city, and especially worthy to be reverently sung by all who, like David the King, Moses the Lawgiver, Aaron the Priest, or Samuel the Seer, are honored to lead the Church of God, and plead for her with the Lord." Bengel wrote of this Psalm that it has three parts in which the Lord is celebrated as He Who is to come, as He Who is, and as He Who was.

The Lord reigneth, 99:1. Writers and poets have favorite words and phrases they like to ring the changes on, and ever and anon the repetition of them appear in their works. This is the third Psalm in the group exalting God for His sovereignty in which this phrase occurs, Psalms 93, 97, and 99, and as Paul ascribed Psalm 95 to David (Heb. 4:7), it would seem that the triple declaration, "The Lord reigneth," was a favorite expression of his. How he loved to magnify and extol the universal dominion of Jehovah.

This is one of the most joyful utterances which ever leaped from mortal life and ever left pen in a human hand. No wonder the phrase occurs three times, for conquest over evil, and the reign of Jehovah as goodness, justice, and truth are worthy to be sung over and over again, not only by the cherubim surrounding the throne, but by all the earth. The tragedy is that people today do not tremble nor manifest any solemn awe at the thought of God's majesty as the Sovereign Lord. Failing in reverence for Him, there is no fear of His autocratic power.

God's position is beautifully described as *He that sitteth between the cherubim,* those representatives of the angelic world who incline their faces one toward the other, touch one another with their wings (Exod. 25:18), and covered or overshadowed the *Mercy-Seat* with their wings. It was from this *Seat* God spoke to Moses, Exodus 25:20, 22; Numbers 7:8, 9. In the grandeur of sublime glory, yet in the nearness of mediatorial condescension, Jehovah revealed Himself. Reigning from such a

throne of grace should excite the emotion and adoring gaze of not only
"the people" but the whole earth. Thus, the pomp of Heaven surrounds
Him Who sits as universal Monarch, symbolized by the outstretched
wings of adoring cherubs. "Let not the earth be less moved to adoration,
rather let all the tribes bow before his infinite majesty, yea, let the solid
earth itself with reverent tremor acknowledge His presence."

The Lord is great in Zion . . . high above all people, 99:2. The Temple
at Jerusalem was God's dwelling place and the seat of His rule and worship of Him as the great King. The sacred hill was the place where His
grandeur was most clearly beheld. Now His true Church is His favored
palace in and through which His glory is displayed, acknowledged and
adored. *Great!* Yes, He is great, not only in Zion, but in Himself, great in
all His attributes and great in all His works. It is because He is *Great* that
"He is high above all the people." The metaphor used here was likely
taken from great, high objects such as palaces and towers, which were
more valued because of their height, and which symbolized greater
strength than smaller buildings. God, however, towers above man's loftiest conceptions. "If Israel delighted in Saul because he was head and
shoulders above the people, how much more should we exalt in our god
and King, Who is as high above us as the heavens are above the earth.
The highest are not high to Him, yet, blessed be His name, the lowliest are
not despised by Him."

Let them praise thy great and terrible name; for it is holy, 99:3.
Hebrew commentators saw here the mystic "tetragrammation," whose true
pronunciation was kept a profound secret by the Rabbis, owing to a feeling of aweful reverence. The Greeks, however, were precise in bidding us
take of that name, which is *terrible* to God's enemies, *holy* to His friends,
and *great* to both—the name of JESUS. Further, the Trinity is seen as the
triple description of the august Name. The *Father's* name is *great,* for He
is the Source, the Creator of all; the *Son's* name is *terrible,* for He is to be
our Judge; and the name of the *Holy Spirit* is *holy,* for He it is Who
bestows sanctification. But these three adjectives, *great, terrible,* and *holy,*
portray different aspects of the Divine character, whether terrible or tender, pardoning or punishing.

It is because God is perfection itself that He is *holy* in all His words,
thoughts and acts. At the conclusion of the three main divisions of this
Psalm we have the triple, *It is holy* or *Holy is He,* 99:3, 5, 9. Wholly
excellent, without flaw or fault, excess or deficiency, error or iniquity, He
is indeed the thrice-Holy One. Truly, no attribute is sounded out so lofti-
ly, with such solemnity, and so frequently by angels standing before His
throne as His perfect holiness. Then, the Psalmist declares that He is to
be praised by us as we meditate upon all the facets of His nature, for by
name, we understand all that God is in Himself. Do we praise Him as we

ought for all He is to us as the *Great* and *Holy* One, and all He is to arrogant sinners as *Terrible* One?

The king's strength . . . judgment . . . equity . . . righteousness, 99:4. Here are further portrayals of the Divine Being and Character, the *King* being *Jehovah* of the opening verse. It has been said that the previous verse and this one should be joined closely so as to read—"The great and terrible name saying, Holy is He, and mighty, a king that loveth justice." We are reminded that God Himself is our *Strength,* but His own strength is never exerted unjustly or tyrannically, even although He is the Sovereign One and absolute in His government. He *loveth* judgment because He delights in what is right and just. Perfect justice is ever tempered with perfect mercy. Often men set up kingdoms, inequitable in character, such as Adolph Hitler tried to do, but who saw his kingdom fall in ruin and himself driven to a suicide's grave. But God establishes, not a court of *equity* merely, but equity itself which is as stable as His throne from which He executes the immaculate purity of His justice. As for His *righteousness,* He is ever right in all His ways. Historical annals reveal that many human governments have been written in the tears of the downtrodden and the curses of the oppressed, but God's Kingdom is of another sort for He ever reigns in righteousness.

Exalt . . . worship . . . He is holy, 99:5. Bishop Horsley gives us this rendering of the verse—

> Exalt ye Jehovah our God,
> And make prostration before his footstool;

It is holy. Although, by virtue of all He is in Himself and in His works, yet He would have us exalt Him by lip and life. "Infinite condescension makes Him stoop to be called *our* God, and truth and faithfulness bind Him to maintain that covenant relationship; and surely we, to whom by grace He so lovingly gives Himself, should exalt Him with all our hearts." Then the Psalmist calls us to worship or prostrate ourselves at *His footstool.* The earth is called the *footstool* of God (Isa. 66:1; Matt. 5:35); and in other Scriptures the expression is used of the Sanctuary, and also of the Ark (1 Chron. 28:2; Psalm 132:7. See Isa. 60:13; Lam. 3:1). The more we exalt Him, the lower we prostrate ourselves before Him.

Then, for the second time the note rings out—*He is holy.* It was from the Ark, the Divine footstool, that the cherubim among whom the Lord sitteth, pealed forth their anthem, *Holy, Holy, Holy, Lord God of Sabaoth!* Isaiah took up the strain and cried, *Holy, Holy, Holy, is the Lord of Hosts;* and the four living creatures John speaks of never rest day or night in the same paean of praise for the conspicuous tribute of Holiness, *Holy, holy, holy, Lord God of Almighty.* Everything about Him is holy—His name, His justice, His wisdom, His promise. There appears to be great propriety and beauty in the construction of this poem into three parts with praise for Divine holiness ending each section. "Of these," says Richard Mant, "the first terminates with ascribing 'holiness' to the *name* of Jehovah; the second, with ascribing the same property to His *abode;* and then, at the conclusion of the hymn, *holiness,* essential holiness, is ascribed to Jehovah *Himself.*"

Moses and Aaron . . . and Samuel, 99:6. The historical reference here is instructive, for the poet was enhancing the sacred character of his own day by likening the priest and minister of the Temple to the sacred heroes of the past, as we might distinguish a period of great scientific achievement by saying, "We have a Newton or a Bacon among us." Summarizing verses 6-8, Dummelow says—

> These verses may be taken as an illustration from the past of the principle on which God still deals with His people, or they may be translated by present tenses, as referring to the intercessors in Israel whose prayers God has answered in the deliverance from captivity, and who are figuratively called *A Moses . . . An Aaron . . . A Samuel.*

Thus, a better translation of this sixth verse is given us, "A Moses and an Aaron among His friends, and a Samuel among them that call upon His name, calling upon the Lord, and He answers them, in the pillar of cloud He speaks to them." The word used here for *priest* means, "to plead a cause," an intercessor, mediator, or advocate and the three worthies mentioned in the verse all functioned in this way. "All three stood in His courts and saw His holiness each after his own order—

> Moses saw the Lord in flaming fire revealing His perfect law—
> Aaron full often watched the sacred fire devour the sin-offering—
> Samuel witnessed the judgment of the Lord on Eli's house because of the error of his way.

These each one stood in the gap when the wrath of God broke forth, because His holiness had been insulted; and, acting as intercessors, "they screened the nation from the great and terrible God, who otherwise would in a dreadful manner execute judgment in Jacob." Then intercessions were not in vain for *they called upon the Lord, and He answered them,* in staying great plagues and turning away fiery wrath as the merciful and prayer-hearing God. *His priests.* Blessed to know that all who have an inward connection with God, free access to the throne of grace, and the passion for intercessory prayer are included in God's *kingdom of priests,* Exodus 19:6. Through grace, the saved have been made "priests unto God," Revelation 1:6; 5:10; 20:6.

He spake . . . They kept his testimonies, 99:7. The fiery cloudy pillar was a visible token of the presence of God in the midst of Israel, and responses came to both Moses and Aaron out of that glorious overshadowing cloud. To Samuel came the mystic voice thundering forth from that Divine canopy. God spoke to them, and they obeyed His will and went forth to *keep His testimonies,* and likewise *the ordinances He gave them.* Divine instruction, as well as practical precept, were observed. Loving Him, they keep His words. Well might we pray—

> Lord, teach us like Moses to hold up our hands in prayer and conquer Amalek,
> like Aaron to wave the censer between the living and the dead till the plague is stayed,
> like Samuel to say to a guilty people, "God forbid that I should sin against the Lord in ceasing to pray for you."
> If Thou make me mighty with Thee in prayer, we shall also be kept faithful before Thee in the service which Thou hast laid upon us, Amen!

Answereth them . . . forgivest them . . . tookest vengeance, 99:8. The triple truth proclaimed in this verse proves that both in the past and in the Psalmist's time, God manifested at once His hatred of sin and His forgiving love to His erring people. He heard the prayers of Moses, Aaron, and Samuel on behalf of the people and answered them. Generously, He granted them their supplications, and on the basis of same, forgave the sins of those prayed for. Yet He took vengeance on their inventions, or fruit of their sins. God ever speaks to destroy that which He hates in the lives of His own.

There is a difference among commentators as to whether the Psalmist had in mind Moses, Aaron and Samuel when he uttered the words of this verse. Certainly all three saints, eminent for their piety, were also conspicuous for having the Divine displeasure on account of their failings. Moses was not allowed to enter the promised Land— Aaron would have been destroyed had it not been for the intercession of Moses—Samuel's heart was brought down in sorrow to the grave because his sons knew not the Lord.

Yet it would seem as if the declaration was addressed to the people at large rather than to the personages mentioned. The train of thought and inference to be drawn from the verse is something like this, "There are great saints among us, as in olden time, but, as then, their prayers while often procuring forgiveness, could not altogether avert punishment for sin; so the present community must expect retribution when sinful, in spite of the mediation of the better part of the nation."

Exalt the Lord our God, and worship at his holy hill, for the Lord our God is holy, 99:9. Twice over in this Psalm we are exhorted to exalt and worship Him. Three times over He is described as *the Lord our* God, indicating that the Psalm is Trinitarian in structure. "In each of His sacred persons the Lord is God of His people; *The Father* is ours, *The Son* is ours, *The Holy Spirit* is ours: let us exalt them with all our powers." Because of the offices of each of the Holy Three, they should have our unceasing worship and adoration in their hearts and home and in the holy hill of the Church.

The Psalm ends with the devout description, thrice repeated, *He is holy.* What a fitting climax to such a Song of Sovereignty! It is because of the triple tribute to God's Holiness, the harmony of His crown, that Spurgeon suggests that we should call the Psalm *The Sanctus,* or, *The Holy, Holy, Holy Psalm,* seeing its subject is the holiness of Divine government and the sanctity of the Lord's mediatorial reign. "His power is not His choicest jewel, nor His sovereignty, but His holiness." What else can we do then but worship and adore Him, "whose character is unsullied purity, unswerving justice, unbending truth, unbounded love, in a word, *perfect holiness"?*

Psalm 100

How rich is this brief Psalm in its historical associations and uses! The magnificent version of the Hundredth, set to Martin Luther's majestic tune, not only wedded Lutherans and Calvinists to eternity but has girdled the earth with its sweet melody and praise. The metrical version of the Psalm provided the people of North Britain with a practical substitute for the papist *Te Deums* which they abhorred. This version, commencing with *All people that on earth do dwell*, was composed by a Scottish divine and friend of John Knox, William Kethe, in 1560-61 to fit the tune in the Genevan Psalter by Louis Bourgeois, now known as *The Old Hundredth*. Words and tune have survived all the changes of thought and fashion that the progress of over four centuries has witnessed.

Psalm 100 is one of the few Psalms to which Shakespeare makes reference in his Plays. In *The Merry Wives of Windsor,* Mrs. Ford imagined that the 100th Psalm would not agree with the tune of *Green Sleeves.* The poet Longfellow, in *Courtship of Miles Standish,* refers to the New England settlers, "Singing the Hundredth Psalm, that grand old Puritan anthem." When Philip Melancthon, close friend of Martin Luther, was mourning the death of his son in Dresden, July 12, 1559, not long before his own death, he drew comfort from the words, "It is he that hath made us, and not we ourselves; we are his people, and the sheep of his pasture," 100:3.

The Scottish Version of this Psalm, with the accompaniment of Luther's melody, has girdled the earth, being the great Psalm of praise sung in all lands for centuries. After Commodore Matthew Galbraith Perry rode the U.S.S. Mississippi to anchor in the harbor of Urages on July 10, 1853, he spread out the Stars and Stripes over the capstan, and using it as a pulpit read the 100th Psalm, and in his message called upon Japan, with all other lands, to "make a joyful noise unto the Lord." But the world was hardly cognizant of the wondrous change which was to take place in Japan as it opened to the Gospel with many coming to sing this grand Psalm in their own tongue.

This Psalm, so universally known and loved, composed of four verses (verses 1 and 2, being one) containing triplets of truth in each verse, even when it was sung in the Temple in the composer's day amid the exclusive notes of Judaism, its opening words must have inspired something of that catholic spirit and sentiment which pervades a congregation today when singing what we know as the *Old Hundredth.* The Greeks of old affirmed that the Psalm was written by David, who in it invites all the world to join with the Israelites in the service of God whose Divine sovereignty he here recognizes.

It is the only Psalm entitled *A Psalm of Praise* because it is peculiarly adapted, if not designed, to be sung when *the sacrifice of thanksgiving* was offered. See Leviticus 7:12. In this Divine lyric, bearing the exclusive, precise inscription, the poet was ablaze with grateful adoration, and thus gave the world a song that has remained a great favorite with congregations ever since it was written. Spurgeon declared that "nothing can be more sublime this side of Heaven than the singing of this noble Psalm by a vast audience." Watts' paraphrase, beginning, "Before Jehovah's awful throne," and the Scotch, "All people that on earth do dwell," are both noble versions; and even Tate and Brady rise beyond themselves when they sing—

> With one consent let all the earth,
> To God their cheerful voices raise.

Especially adapted for the particular ceremony of *The Thankoffering,* the title can be given as A Psalm of Thanksgiving, or possibly for the Thankoffering. What is evident is the fact that this formula of Praise was meant to be sung with gladness as the congregation thought of the creating power and goodness of the Lord, the people also trembling as they adored His holiness.

Make a joyful noise unto the Lord, all ye lands, 100:1. Here is another instance of a writer known by his favorite words or phrases, for this opening *Jubilate* is found in Psalms 95:1; 98:4, 6. *All ye lands* implies "all the earth." The original word for *joyful noise* signifies "a glad shout," such as loyal subjects give when their sovereign appears among them. The term *blessed* means "happy," so when God is spoken of as "the blessed God," we can translate it *the happy God,* and as such He should be worshipped by a happy people. We are to serve Him with a gladsome mind. The happy, cheerful spirit in our songs and life is in harmony with God's nature and acts. What a different earth this would be if only in every land, there was one unanimous shout to the only God for all His goodness!

Serve the Lord with gladness . . . with singing, 100:2. The Psalmist is not inviting us to a funeral ceremony, but to a marriage feast. The first half of this verse is from Psalm 2:11, only that instead of *with fear,* there, where he had to do with fierce rebels, there is the substitution of *with gladness* because such is a sign that the oil of grace has been poured into the heart. How we need a constant anointing with "the oil of gladness" to serve the Lord aright! Further, we can only sing acceptably to Him as we come into

His presence, if our heart has been made glad through His regenerating power. Such glad singing is a fit anticipation of the worship of Heaven.

> Let those refuse to sing
> Who never knew our God;
> But favorites of the heavenly King
> Must speak His praise abroad.

Know ye . . . he hath made us and not we ourselves, 100:3. Edward Fitzgerald, English poet and writer of the 18th century, was born with an original mind and character and made his life his own peculiar creation, yet the text he chose for his tomb was, "it is He that hath made us and not we ourselves." Fitzgerald loved and enjoyed leisure, lived remote from bustle and publicity and admitted into his paradise of music and books nothing that did not "breathe content and virtue." To many, the choice of the above text for his grave was the defense for a career that seemed wasted which perhaps was a feeling Fitzgerald felt at some moments in his life. Tennyson, however, gave him generous praise for his—

> . . . golden Eastern lay,
> That which I know no version done
> In English more divinely well.

"Know ye"—the *ye* here refers to the nations, "all ye lands" of verse 1, but *us* refers specially to Israel. "Man, know thyself," is a wise aphorism, but to know God as *our* God is truer wisdom for man cannot know himself aright until he knows God as his Savior. *The Lord he is God—The Lord is good,* 100:3, 5. Is He not a God celebrated for and intelligently worshipped for His goodness and grace?

This Jehovah is also our *Maker* for He made us, and so we are *His.* When a potter makes an earthenware vessel, if the clay be not his own which he makes it of, he is not the full owner of the vessel, though he formed it: "the form is his, the matter is another's." But with the Divine Potter it is different for both the *matter* and the *molding* are His. We did not make ourselves or contribute anything towards our composition. The Lord made all of nothing, or of such matter—as dust—as Himself made, all is wholly His, matter and form, all entirely. Our Creator is our Owner. *He made us . . . we are His.* Consequently we are "His people, and the sheep of His pasture."

The French Emperor, Henry, while out hunting on the Lord's Day called *Quinquagesima,* meaning the Sunday before Lent, came unattended to a certain church, and feigning himself to be a soldier, simply requested a mass of the priest who was a man of notable piety but so deformed in body that it made him conspicuous and pitied. As the Emperor watched him he began to wonder why God, from whom all beauty proceeds, should permit so deformed a man to administer the sacrament. But presently, when the Mass commenced, and they came to the passage, *Know ye that the Lord he is God,* which was chanted by a choir-boy, the priest rebuked the boy for singing negligently, and said with a loud voice the verse omitted, *It is he that hath made us, and not we ourselves.* Struck by these words and believing the priest to be a prophet, the Emperor raised him, much against the deformed man's will, to the Archbishopric of Cologne which *See* he adorned by his devotion and excellent virtues.

Know ye. This call means to consider and apply such a Divine subject of knowledge, then we will be more close and constant, more inward and serious in the worship of Him as our Maker. Such an ever-increasing knowledge will enable us to be true amid superstition, hopeful in contrition, persistent in supplication, unwearied in exertion, calm in affliction, firm in temptation, bold in persecution, and happy in death. The last part of this third verse is an echo of Psalm 95:7. Who are His people? All who are twice born, separated from the world, and who constantly experience the safety and provision of Him Who is their Shepherd.

With thanksgiving . . . be thankful . . . bless His name, 100:4. It is more than likely that the twofold mention of *thanks* in this verse gave the Psalm its title. Can we say that we abound in thanksgiving? The sacrifice of Gratitude is never out of date. "So long as we are receivers of mercy we must be givers of thanks." Into whatever court of the Lord we enter, praise should be in our hearts and on our lips. We should ever be ready to bless His name for all His attributes and acts. His benefits, He daily loads us with, should never be forgotten. It has been suggested that the former part of this Psalm may have been chanted by the Precentor when the Peace-Offering was brought to the altar—and this verse used as the response, sung by the whole company of singers at the moment when fire was applied to the offering.

The Lord is good, his mercy is everlasting; and his truth endureth forever, 100:5. What a wonderful triad of attributes closes this famous Psalm! What a unique summary of the Divine character it presents! God is good, and His goodness faileth never. His mercy is like Himself, everlasting, and will be ours world without end. As for His truth, it will never be revoked. Amid a changing world we would be in perpetual fear of shipwreck, but we have a God Whose word has never been broken. Everything about Him is everlastingly unchangeable, and such should call forth thanksgiving unwearied from hearts that never faint.

Psalm 101

At the head of the list of authors of the Psalms stands David, the poet-king and prophet (Acts 2:29-31). Naturally most gifted, possessed in a very high degree of that rarest of endowments, a poetic genius, he was a man who acted under the inspiration of the Holy Spirit (2 Sam. 23:2). Beside all this, David stood in a peculiar relation to God for he was a man after His own heart (1 Sam. 13:14). It may not be easy at times to see how his character comports with this remarkable commendation; but in the Psalms we put our finger on his heart-pulse and feel the very throbbings and movements of his soul. Pre-eminently he was the friend of God as this 101st Psalm reflects. And what a Psalm this is! It has gathered around itself many historical associations in the biographies of outstanding individuals and has been viewed in so many different ways. Appropriately, it has been called: The Householder's Psalm. What domestic happiness and contentment there is when families regulate their households by the rules of the conscientious Psalmist who outlined the regulations of a royal court as well as his household.

The Magistrates' Mirror. How apt is this designation given to the Psalm by some of the old expositors. If every capital in the world would become a "City of the Lord," the magistrates must perform the functions of their responsible office in the light of the administration of justice as indicated in this Psalm.

The Princes' Mirror. David was a King when he wrote this grand Psalm (101:6, 7), and so propounded a rule to himself for the choice of his courtiers. Kings and Rulers reveal their wisdom when they seek to reign as David did. When Sir George Villiers became the favorite and prime minister of King James, Lord Bacon, in a beautiful *Letter of Advice,* counselled him to take Psalm 101 for his guide in the promotion of those within the royal courts—

> In those the choice had need be of honest and faithful servants, as well as of comely outsider who can bow the knee and kiss the hand. King David propounded a rule for himself in the choice of courtiers. He was a wise and good king; and a wise and good king shall do well to follow such a good example; and if he find any to be faulty, which perhaps cannot suddenly be discovered, let him take on him this resolution as King David did, "There shall no deceitful person dwell in my house."

It would have been well both for the Philosopher and the Favorite if they had been careful to walk by this rule. Eyring, in his Life of *Earnest the Pious*—Duke of Saxe-Gotha, records that he sent an unfaithful minister a copy of the 101st Psalm, and that it became a proverb in the country when an official had done anything wrong; "He will certainly soon receive the Prince's Psalm to read."

The noblest of Russian Princes was Vladimir Monoachos who greatly loved this Psalm, as did Nicholas Ridley, one of the gentlest of English Reformers. But, as Stanley in his erudite study, *Jewish Church*, points out, "Psalm 101 by its first leap into life found itself carried far into the future. It is full of stern exclusiveness, of a noble intolerance, not insubordination, but against the proud heart, the high look, the secret slanderer, the deceitful worker, the tellers of lies. These are the outlaws from King David's court; these are the rebels and heretics whom he would not suffer to dwell in his house or tarry in his sight."

When Monica, mother of Augustine, was struck down by fever and died when she was only 56, it was in this Psalm that her famous son found comfort in his grief. When the first gush of his weeping was over, his friend, Melancthon, took up the Psalter and began to sing, the whole household joining him in the chanting of Psalm 101.

An ancient record of Columba, the famous Irish missionary who, for more than thirty years, labored among the Picts and Scots, says that when he knew only how to read the alphabet, he was able to learn the Psalms by heart. The priest, Cruithnechan, who baptized Columba, was called upon at an ecclesiastical festival to recite Psalm 101, but memory and voice failed him. In the place of his guardian, Columba the child repeated the Psalm, and thus, "the names of God and of Columba were magnified by the miracle."

It is also said that Bishop Ridley often read and expounded this Psalm to his household, hiring them with money to learn it by heart. As it is a Psalm of *wills* and *shalls*—of 9 wills and 5 shalls, it is worthy of being learned by heart, seeing that, as a whole, it teaches us that resolutions should be made with *deliberation*—"shall," and yet with *reservation*—"if the Lord will." Further, as Edersheim suggests, "Such a hymn of praise as the grand doxology of Psalm 99, could not die away without an echo." Accordingly Psalm 100 may be regarded as forming the chorus of the Church, and Psalm 101, as taking up and applying that part of the doxology which celebrated the *present* manifestation of "the King in his beauty." After Songs of Praise, a Psalm of Practice not only makes variety, but comes in most fittingly. The Psalm before us teaches us that we never praise the Lord better than when we do those things which are pleasing in His sight.

As to the authorship of the Psalm, its contents indicate that it was written at some remarkable period in David's life. Although several different times have been given for the historical basis of the Psalm, its second verse seems to suggest that it is associated with the occasion when David removed the Ark from the house of Obededom to Zion and lodged it in the vicinity of his own abode (2 Sam. 6:6-19). Spurgeon says, "The Psalm is David all over, straightforward, resolute, devout; there is no trace of policy or vacillation—The Lord has appointed him to be king, and he knows it, therefore he purposes in all things to behave as becomes a monarch whom the Lord Himself has chosen."

In the two general divisions of the Psalm, David first utters his resolves as to his personal life and conduct, verses 1-4. Then he announces his purpose of choosing his servants only from among the upright, and of discouraging and exterminating all forms of wickedness, verses 5-8. For these reasons we can call his vows—*The Psalm of Pious Resolutions.*

I will sing . . . unto thee, O Lord will I sing, 101:1. Some scholars feel that this opening verse was inserted as suited to the "sweet singer," and also as giving the vow more of the character of a hymn. "That it did not form part of the original composition seems sufficiently certain from the unpoetical character of the Psalm, which only in its parallelism preserves any features of poetry."

David vowed that mercy and judgment—love and severity—would temper his administration as monarch because he had adoringly perceived them in the dispensation of Jehovah, worthy of all praise. As the badge of the ship Paul sailed in was *Castor* and *Pollux,* twin brothers, so the badge of this practical Psalm is *Mercy* and *Judgment,* inseparable companions. What is said of Saul and Jonathan is equally true of these two attributes. "They were lovely and pleasant in their lives, and in their deaths they were not divided." Solomon set up two goodly pillars in the porch of the Temple, the one he called *Jachin,* the other *Boaz*—which names signify "stability" and "strength." The pillars of any nation should be *Mercy* and *Judgment.*

God's throne is "established by justice," and "upheld by mercy," Proverbs 16:12; 20:28. Thus David sings of both for as justice is the bones and sinews in the body politic, mercy is the veins and arteries. An 18th century expositor says that, "This song of Israel is peculiar to earth; they do not sing of *Judgment* in Heaven, for there is no sin there; they do not sing of *Mercy* in Hell, for there is no propitiation for sin there." Some scholars cite *grace* and *right* instead of mercy and judgment, and both are especially requisite attributes of a good monarch or of magistrates generally. Almost all commentators reckon these twin virtues are to be first regarded ideally as attributes of the Divine King whom David loved so dearly.

> And earthly power doth then show likest God's
> When mercy seasons justice.

I will behave myself . . . I will walk . . . with a perfect heart, 101:2. Ernest the Pious—Duke of Saxe-Gotha—to whom references have been made, was the bosom friend of Gustavus Adolphus, and after his fall on the field of Lutzen, the Duke brought up the reserve which turned the tide and secured victory. When peace returned to Germany after the terrible *Thirty Years' War,* the Duke set himself to repair its ravages, and many of the institutions remain which were founded by him. He was one of the first since the Reformation to interest himself in foreign mission work and sent Embassies to Egypt and Abyssinia for that end. He took for his own guide this second verse of Psalm 101, "I will behave myself in a perfect way . . . I will walk within my house with a perfect heart." Himself the son of a pious mother, he superintended the religious instruction of his own children, in the midst of his public duties, so thoroughly that they could repeat by heart the greater part of the Bible.

The interjected phrase, *When wilt thou come unto me?* may refer to David's longing for the presence of God, as symbolized by the Ark, in his capital. As for his resolve to behave himself as becometh a king and a father, excellent though it was, his practice did not always tally with it. Although it was well he had it in his heart, he was not always as wise and perfect as he should have been. Perhaps his cry, "O when wilt thou come unto me? expressed his longing to be more closely conformed to the Divine image. More literally, the resolution of David means, "I will look to a guileless way." Behaving circumspectly carries the idea of caution and then wisdom arises from that of looking. The English idiom, *Look to your ways,* illustrates the Hebrew here.

I will walk within my house with a perfect heart. Ellicott says that "this vow of an *Eastern* monarch should be read with the thought of the palace of a caliph at Bagdad, or a sultan at Constantinople, before the mind. But it is a reflection of universal application, that piety should begin at home, and religion should show itself in the household as much as at church." What hypocrisy it is for a person to pose as a saint at church, yet act as a devil at home! What we are at home, that we are indeed. "He cannot be a good king whose palace is the haunt of vice, nor he a true saint whose habitation is a scene of strife, nor he a faithful minister whose household dreads his appearance at the fireside."

More figuratively than actually, the Psalms make much of *walking.* The three natural acts of walking are—*motion, progress,* and *moderation. Motion* is opposite to lying, standing, or sitting. *Progress in motion* is opposed to jumping or capering up and down in the same place. *Moderation* is a progressive motion, is the opposite to violent running, and these acts can be spiritually applied to all who seek to walk even as Jesus walked. In a home parental conduct is a great aid in the development of character in children. Guy Rivers, speaking in later life of his mother said, "She told me not to lie, and set me the example herself by frequently deceiving my father, and teaching me to disobey and deceive him." What a despicable conduct it is when a parent says to his child, "Do as I bid you, not as I do." Example should ever accompany precept.

I will set no wicked thing before mine eyes, 101:3. By *wicked thing,* we understand "thing, or word of Belial." The phrase *an evil disease* in Psalm 41:8, is given in the margin as "thing of Belial" and implies "a moral evil." Not only did David vow to have no desire for any form of evil, but also to hate the doing of false things. Such conduct of those who walked on a crooked road would not be condoned by the Psalmist. He was expressing the same thought of the dying statesman who said, "Corruption wins not more than honesty." *It shall not cleave unto me,* or such conduct will not be mine. I will ever disown such. The word *cleave* implies that a wicked plan or purpose is represented as having a tendency to fasten itself on a man, or to *stick to him*—as pitch, or wax, or a *burr* does.

A froward heart shall depart from me. I will not know a wicked person, 101:4. The word "froward" means *twisted* or *perverse,* and applied to character implies "twisted around," or a line of conduct which is crooked as opposed to being straight. We can say that "froward" indicates *from ward,* as opposite to *toward,* and thus signifies a disposition turned away from good. "David refers both to himself, and to those round about him; he would neither be crooked in heart himself, nor employ persons of evil character in his house; if he found such in his court he would chase them away. He would disown all around him who disowned righteousness."

Whoso privily slandereth . . . hath a high look . . . a proud heart, 101:5. What a trinity of Christless possessions this verse presents! During the life and reign of David, he knew by experience the misery caused by slander and resolved to have no one around him guilty of stabbing another in the back. Informers and haughty favorites were not unknown characters in an Oriental court, but David was determined to have none of them around him. From a goodly tree of his nation he was determined to lop off all such superfluous boughs as slanderers, high looks, and proud hearts. A slanderer is a dangerous viper, proud hearts are hard, and those of high looks provoke enmity and discontent, and all wreck the stability of the throne, and, therefore, are not to be suffered as holders of office.

The faithful . . . he that walketh in a perfect way, 101:6. Bacon, whose genius was one of the glories of the Elizabethan Age, studied and quoted the Psalms and proved himself to be a versifier of them by his work published in 1624 which he dedicated to George Villiers, *Certain Psalms Written in Sickness.* It was on Psalm 101, known as the *Mirror for Magistrates,* that Bacon founded his advice to George Villiers, Duke of Buckingham.

Mine eyes are upon the faithful. There is an eye of *search* and an eye of *favor;* the one is for seeking and finding out the faithful, that they serve the King; the other for countenancing their persons, and rewarding their service. And what a reward they have—*Shall dwell with me—Shall serve me.* The Lord has many faithful in the land, and theirs is the privilege of dwelling with Him and of serving Him. David, in his banishment before he came to the throne as king, knew something of the evil of a disordered home and resolved what he would do when God made him the head of a royal family. David saw in Saul's court the mischief of having wicked and ungodly servants compassing him about and vowed to have a court after God's own heart. If we are to walk in a perfect way, verse 6, we must have the perfect heart, verse 2.

He that worketh deceit . . . he that telleth lies, 101:7. Although Orientals had the reputations of reckoning deceit to be a virtue, David, having power to choose his courtiers, was determined to set his face against any who were guilty of cunning devices. He wanted his house and his palace to be free of any who plotted mischief. The same resolve applied to liars. "Grace makes men truthful, and creates in them an utter horror of everything approaching to falsehood." The phrase, "not tarry in my sight," can be rendered, "not be established before mine eyes," and implies any liar would not be allowed to function as a courtier in the royal presence. Homer expressed the feeling of David in the lines—

> Hateful to me as gates of hell is he
> Who hides one thing within his mind and speaks another.

I will early destroy all the wicked . . . I may cut off all wicked doers, 101:8. The R.V. has "morning by morning" for *early.* David vowed that there would be a daily purging of all worthless servants while he governed as King. It was the Oriental custom to hold courts of law in the early morning, Jeremiah 21:12; Luke 22:26. Thus, like a righteous magistrate, he would not "bear the sword in vain." The Psalmist knew from his experience in Saul's court that "to favor sin is to discourage virtue; and that under leniency to the bad is unkindness to the good." As for wicked doers being cut off from "the city of the Lord," being *The Holy City,* all within it must bear out its name in character, Psalms 46:4; 48:2, 8. For those of us who believe in the Return of the Lord, is it not blessed to know that a bright and glorious morning will dawn when all filthiness will be purged away, that true purity may everlastingly shine forth?

Spurgeon's opening comments on this Psalm make a fitting conclusion to this discussion:

> This is just such a Psalm as the man after God's own heart would compose when he was about to become a king in Israel. It is David all over, straight-forward, resolute, devout; there is no trace of policy or vacillation—

the Lord has appointed him to be king, and he knows it; therefore he purposes in all things to behave as becomes a monarch whom the Lord Himself has chosen.

If we call this "The Psalm of Pious Resolutions," we shall perhaps remember it all the more readily. After songs of praise a Psalm of practice not only makes variety but comes in most fittingly. We never praise the Lord better than when we do those things which are pleasing in His sight.

Psalm 102

The remarkable prayer forming this heart-moving Psalm has been woven into the experiences of the saints of God down the ages since it was first offered to God by David. A remarkable piece of spiritual biography is Jonathan Edwards' account of the life of David Brainerd whose one object in life was the strenuous concentrated effort to attain nearness to God. After five years of missionary work among the Indians of Delaware and Pennsylvania, anxiety, exposure, and privation brought death to Brainerd's sickly overwrought frame. He was only 30 years of age when he died of consumption, but as he died, the words of Psalm 102, sung at his bedside by friends, were ringing in his ears as he was being taken away to Glory after shortened days, 102:23.

The version of this Psalm in the oldest Scottish Psalter, a remarkably fine one, was written by John Craig, colleague of John Knox, when he was at St. Giles, Edinburgh, and whose own experience colored the version of the Psalm he composed. When a Dominican monk at Rome, Craig embraced the principles of the Reformation, was cast into prison by the Inquisition, and was about to die at the stake. The very night before he should have been martyred, however, the Pope died and insurrection broke out; prisons were thrown open, and Craig escaped through a series of remarkable deliverances to become God's agent in the work of reform in his native Scotland.

Further, the poignant suffering raising its voice to Heaven as found in this Psalm was the keynote to Mrs. Browning's *De Profundis*—Out of the Depths—which was composed in the anguish of bereavement during which the gifted poetess drew hope from the thought of an unchanging God—

> By anguish which made pale the sun,
> I hear him charge his saints that none
> Among the creatures anywhere
> Blaspheme against him with despair,
> However darkly days go on.
> And having in thy life—depth thrown
> Being and suffering—which are one—
> As a child drops some pebble small
> Down some deep well, and hears it fall,
> Smiling ... So I! THY DAYS GO ON!

380

But what gives intrinsic value to this expressive Psalm is the fact that it is used by Paul as a forecast shadow of Christ Himself to Whom it is applied, and who, after passing through the depths of anguish, rises to His throne and says to His brethren, "Because I live, ye shall live also," Hebrews 1:10-12; Psalm 102:26, 27. Prominent among the *Seven Penitential Psalms,* Psalm 102 gives us "the picture of a man who has sunk to the deepest abyss of trial, crushed in body, broken in spirit, surrounded by what seems the utter wreck of the cause of God; and then rising to confidence and gladness when he remembers the power and faithfulness of Him who is everlasting." None has ever reached the depths of anguish like the Man Christ Jesus Who became, "A Man of Sorrows," but emerged from a brutal death to become the Lord of Glory.

As to the historical setting of this somber Psalm, many writers feel that it belongs to the closing days of the Exile and utters hope of Israel's Restoration (verses 13-22). Spurgeon, however, says that "it is in vain to enquire into the precise point of Israel's history which thus stirred a patriot's zeal, for many a time was the land oppressed, and at any of her sad seasons this song and prayer would have been a most natural and appropriate utterance." The Psalmist not only speaks in the name of his nation, but describes his own personal distress caused by the captivity and humiliation of his people. We find him speaking of his fellow-countrymen in the plural, and then going on to express his own shrinking from premature death (verses 11, 23, 24). Further distinctly personal notes are in his wasting away with lonely sorrow (verses 1-7, 9) and in his consciousness of being mocked by enemies and suffering affliction as a token of God's displeasure (verses 8, 10). Yet the eternity and changelessness of God are the ground of hope both for himself and for the whole of God's people (verses 12, 24-28).

Naming the Psalm, THE PATRIOT'S PLAINT, Spurgeon reminds us that "this is a patriot's lament over his country's distress. He arrays himself in the griefs of his nation as in a garment of sackcloth, and casts her dust and ashes upon his head as the ensigns and causes of his sorrow. He has his own private woes and personal enemies, he is moreover sore afflicted in body by sickness, but the miseries of his people cause him a far more bitter anguish, and this he pours out in an earnest, pathetic lamentation. Not, however, without hope does the patriot mourn; he has faith in God, and looks for the resurrection of the nation through the omnipotent favor of the Lord; this causes him to walk among the ruins of Jerusalem, and to say with hopeful spirit, 'No, Zion, thou shalt never perish. Thy sun is not set forever; brighter days are in store for thee.'"

The title of this Psalm of *The Afflicted One* makes it one of the most remarkable of all the Psalms. John Keble, with the long title of the Psalm in mind, wrote—

This is the mourner's prayer when he is faint,
And to the Eternal Father breathes his plaint.

A Prayer of the Afflicted. As the majority of us are afflicted at some time or another and in one way or other, this is a prayer each saint can make his or her own. Historically, it bears the marks of the sufferer who composed such a Prayer. It is recorded of Jabez that "his mother bore him with sorrow," so may we say of this Psalm; yet as Rachel's Benoni, or child of sorrow, was also her Benjamin, or son of her right hand, so is this Psalm as eminently expressive of consolation as of desolation. While we have referred to it as one of the Penitential Psalms, Psalm 102 is rather that of suffering than sinning. While it has its own bitterness, it is not over iniquity as in Psalm 51. Here the afflicted one suffers in heart more for others than for himself, more for the City and House of the Lord than for his own house.

When he is overwhelmed. Sorrow and fear came upon him like a flood causing him to be anxious, troubled and depressed for the best of men are only men at the best, and are not always able to stem the torrent of sorrow overtaking them, as it did Job. "Even when Jesus is on board, the vessel may fill with water, and begin to sink."

Poureth out his complaint before the Lord. The word for complaint used here does not imply fault-finding or refining, but should be rendered "moaning"—the expression of pain, not of rebellion. And as the One acquainted with our grief, the Lord is the ever-sympathetic Friend into whose ear we can pour our complaint. It is only the heart renewed by Divine grace that can appreciate that the Lord's ear is ever open to its cry.

Hear my prayer . . . my cry, 102:1. The repetition of the personal pronoun of the first two verses of this Psalm prove the prayer to be not one he composed for others but for himself. The cry came out of his own heart and unfeigned lips and was dictated and inwrought by the Holy Spirit. Somehow we can detect the feeling of exhaustion by the one crying to God as if he could cry no more. Thus David sent his prayer as a sacred ambassador to God, and the requisites for a prosperous embassy are that the ambasssador must be regarded with a favorable eye; he must be heard with a ready ear; he must speedily return when his demands are conceded. As a suppliant asks these requisites from God his King and so prayed in verse 2.

Hide not thy face . . . incline thine ear . . . answer me speedily, 102:2. In these opening verses the Psalmist gathers up a variety of expressions all to the same effect, namely, "in all of them he entreats an audience and answer of the Lord, and the whole may be regarded as a sort of Preface to the Prayer which follows." While the Lord graciously permits us to present our cry and cause, we have no right to dictate to Him when and how He should answer. Immediacy or delay are according to His wise will.

My days are consumed like smoke . . . my bones are burned as an hearth, 102:3. *Like smoke* is given in the R.V. as "in smoke." *Pass* away *as in smoke,* as if disappearing in smoke and ashes. The same expression is used by David of "the enemies of the Lord"—"They shall consume as smoke" Psalms 37:20; 68:2. *Burned as an hearth* is better as "burned as a faggot," the sentiment in both illustrations being "My days go away to nothing, turn to no account, are lost." David, moved to overwhelming grief by a view of national calamities, felt as if his spirit had dried up and his life was ready to expire. "His soul was ready to be blown away as smoke, and his body seemed likely to remain as the bare hearth when the last comforting ember is quenched." No nation can die while there are true hearts ready to be put out like a puff of vapor for its salvation.

My heart is smitten . . . I forget to eat my bread, 102:4. Are you not amazed at the variety of metaphors David uses in this notable Psalm? Here he is describing his patriotic heart being like a plant parched by the fierce heat of a tropical sun and dries up when once the scythe has laid it low. "I forget to eat my bread," is better rendered, "because I forget to eat my bread." Grief destroyed his appetite for food, and such a neglect only produced a deeper sinking of despair. The burden of affliction had driven everything else into the background. Israel knew what it was to be smitten with the judgments of God and then withered under the fire of the *Chaldeans.* But the nation came to experience that mourning and fasting are natural companions. Daniel 10:3.

My bones cleave to my skin, 102:5. An eye-witness relates of Cardinal Wolsey that when he heard that his master's favor was turned from him, he was wrung with such an agony of grief, which continued a whole night, that in the morning his face was dwindled away into half its usual dimensions. The patriot, weighted down by suffering for his nation, found himself emaciated with sorrow. Actually, he had groaned himself down to a living skeleton until in bodily appearance he was more like the smoke-dried, withered, burnt up thing he had compared himself to. The patriots of any nation and the members of churches are very few and far between to be wasted down to skin and bone for the spiritual welfare of nation or church.

I am like a pelican . . . I am like an owl, 102:6. Here are two further instances of the art of illustration as the Psalmist goes to the bird world for similes of truth and likens himself to two birds which were commonly used as emblems of gloom and wretchedness. The *pelican* is a mournful and even hideous object, the very image of desolation; and *the owl,* loving solitude, moping among ruins, and hooting discordantly—and David feels himself to be as desolate and lonely as these two birds as he sat among the

fallen palaces and prostrate temples of his native land. Thomas Gray, poet
of the 17th century, wrote thus of the owl of the desert—

> Save that from yonder ivy-mantled tower,
> The moping owl does to the moon complain
> Of such as, wand'ring near her secret bow'r,
> Midst her ancient solitary reign.

In this Psalm David compares himself to an *owl,* and in the next Psalm
to an *eagle,* and no two birds are of a more different kind. The *owl*—
scorn; the *eagle*—sovereign. The first, *slowest;* second, *swiftest.* The first,
dim-eyed of all birds, the eagle the most sharp-sighted. Lonely in his grief
as an owl, David came to experience what it was to fly high with comfort.
It is interesting to observe that in Christian Art, the *Pelican,* as a symbol
of Christ, is guided by the comparison to the pelican in the wilderness of
Psalm 102:7.

How heart-moving is this further metaphor of the Psalmist's desolation.
When a common sparrow loses its mate, it will sit on the house-top alone
and long lament its loss. Like a sad, solitary little bird, David sat alone and
kept silent (Lam. 3:28) as inwardly he grieved over what his beloved
nation had lost. The power of the Psalms in fullest detail is illustrated in
the history of Robert Southwell, a Jesuit and Elizabethan poet who was
born in 1560. It was during his lonely misery in a filthy dungeon in the
Tower, London, awaiting his cruel martyrdom that he compared himself
like David to the sparrow and the pelican in verses 6 and 7 of this
Psalm—

> In eaves sole sparrowe sitts not more alone
> Nor mourning pelican in desert wilde,
> Than sely I, that solitary mone,
> From highest hopes to hardest happ exil'd;
> Sometyme, O blisfull tyme! was Vertue's meede
> Ayme to my thoughtees, guide to my word and deede.
> But feares are now my pheares (companion of bed-fellows), griefe
> My teares my drinke, my famisht my delight,
> Day full of dumpes, thoughtes my bredd; nurse of unrest the nighte
> My garmentes gives (fetters), a bloody fielde my bedd;
> My sleepe is rather death than deathe's allye,
> Yet kill'd with murd'ring pangues I cannot dye.

Mine enemies reproach me . . . they that are made against me, 102:8.
When reproach cuts like a razor and is continued from day to day, it
makes life itself unbearable. David's patriotism and his griefs were made
sport of by his enemies whose rage was unrelenting and unceasing. Those
who vented themselves in taunts and insults bound themselves by an oath

to destroy the patriot whose name had become a synonym of abhorrence and contempt. So, what with inward sorrows and outward persecutions, he was in dire straits. Plutarch wrote that "men are more touched with reproaches than with other injuries; affliction, too, gives a keener edge to calumny, for the afflicted are more fitting objects of pity than of mockery."

I have eaten ashes like bread, and mingled my drink with weeping, 102:9. There is nothing in nature so unfit a thing to eat as ashes; it is worse than Nebuchadnezzar's *grass.* If the Psalmist's food tasted bad, his drink was worse when mingled with tears. What are tears but brinish and salt-humus, and surely brine is not a fit liquor to quench one's thirst. It would be better to endure thirst than to quench it with such drink. What is meant by this metaphorical language is that all-saturating and all-embittering sadness can be the portion of the best of men, not through any fault of their own, but for the love that they have for the Lord and His cause.

Because of thy . . . wrath . . . thou hast lifted me up and cast me down, 102:10. By this assertion, the Psalmist was conscious that his affliction was a token of God's displeasure. It would also seem as if he accused God not of cruelty but of bewailing his own misery. Spurgeon, Prince of Commentators, says that our translation of this verse "gives the idea of a vessel uplifted in order that it may be dashed to the earth with all the greater violence and the more completely broken in pieces; or to change the figure, it reminds us of a wrestler whom his opponent catches up that he may give him a more dispersate fall. The first interpretation, however, is more fully in accordance with the original, and sets forth the utter helplessness which the writer felt, and the sense of overpowering terror which bore him along in a rush of tumultuous grief which he could not withstand."

My days are like a shadow . . . withered like grass, 102:11. Sun-dials all over the world bear texts from the Psalms to enforce the solemn passage of time. *My days are gone like a shadow* can be found traced on sun-dials in Arbroath, Scotland, and at St. Hilda's, Whitby, as well as on some European dials. Two illustrations of the brevity of life are here used by the writer. First, a passing shadow. A shadow is unsubstantial enough, how feeble a thing must a declining shadow be? The thought intended is that the term of a writer's life was as the lengthening shade of evening that shows the near approach of night.

As for the next simile, "I am withered like grass," the *and I* in the Hebrew stands in designed contrast to "But *thou,*" verse 12. Man is like grass, blasted by a parching wind or cut down with a scythe and then left to be dried up by the burning heat of the sun, but withering can never affect Him Who is the ever-living One. Like David, many saints have experienced that heart-break has a tragic withering influence over the entire human system until the flesh is but as grass. When it is wounded with sharp sorrows, beauty fades, and the flesh becomes shrivelled, dried, and uncomely.

But thou, O Lord, shalt endure forever—thy remembrance to all generations, 102:12. For "endure" the original has *sit* and thus reads, "Thou, Jehovah, to eternity shall sit," implying that, in contrast to decaying and dying man, He ever reigns whatever happens, and therefore all is well. Men and Nations may wither away as grass, but God remains forever unchanged. Man may forget man, but God's own are ever mindful of Him from age to age. Over all that declines, is cast down, withers like grass, is the one Eternal, Immutable Light Who shines on and will continue to until all the shadows have declined into nothingness.

Arise, have mercy upon Zion, the time to favor her . . . is come, 102:13. Bishop John Fisher, to whom reference has been made in this *Odyssey,* and who was martyred in 1535, preached before the Countess of Richmond on this particular verse and described that the Church was first built upon the soft slipper earth in which the foundation was set and hardened into stone by the fire of Love. Peter, who denied his Master, became a rock. Thus the Church had become supported by strong and mighty pillars and was able to endure the very worst for God's glory. David knew that Zion, chosen of old by God and wonderfully preserved by Him, would, in the memory of past wonderful mercies, have mercy shown toward her.

Once a Divine decree goes forth, no one and nothing can hinder its fulfillment when the set time comes. We know from history that there was an appointed time for the Jews in Babylon, and that once the weeks of imprisonment were fulfilled, no bolts nor bars could further hold the ransomed of the Lord. In His own appointed season He arises and carries out His will and purpose. As we look around at the spiritual impoverishment of the Church, we pray that the set time to favor her with a mighty quickening of the Holy Spirit may be imminent.

For thy servants take pleasure in her stones, 102:14. A melancholy yet pleasing spectacle, even today, is the assembling of Jews every Friday at the site called *The Wailing Wall.* There is reason to believe that a considerable portion of the *lower part* of the walls which enclose the present Mosque of Omar, which occupies the site of the ancient Jewish temple, are the same as those of Solomon's Temple. One part where the remains of this old wall are the most considerable and of the most massive character—where two courses of masonry composed of massive blocks of stone rise to the height of 30 feet—is where the Jews assemble to pray and bewail the desolations of their holy places and sometimes weep. Taking pleasure in the stones, they indicate that they do not forget the past Jerusalem.

When the Lord shall build up Zion, he shall appear in his glory, 102:16. Appearing in His glorious apparel, He will adorn Zion which is as the apple of His eye to Him. History proves that kings loved to display their skill and wealth in the creation of their capitals to which they often give their names. The Lord also will reveal the splendor of His attributes in the restoration of Zion and in the translation of the redeemed at His appearing.

We will regard the prayer of the destitute, 102:17. God ever listens to the cry of greatest need. When great kings build their palaces they never think of turning aside to listen to beggars who plead for help. But when the King of Kings appears in His robes of glory to build Zion, He will not treat the pleas of the poor with contempt but incline His ear to every request of the needy. The destitute will be assured of Divine regard. Commander Gardiner, whose passion to devote himself to missionary work after he retired from the Royal Navy in 1826 ended in hardship, failure and death, recorded his gratitude to God, for killing five ducks with his almost last grain of powder, in his Diary—"16th June—He will regard the prayer of the destitute, and not despise their prayer."

This shall be written . . . the people . . . shall praise the Lord, 102:18. How enriched our literature is with the histories of nations—their changes of rulers, their wars, national upheavals, famines and catastrophes! How more thrilling are the registers of Divine grace and goodness generation after generation have the privilege and joy of meditating upon! The decision, "Shall be written," reveals how fallible our memories are and how that God, lest His gifts should fail to be remembered, had the bestowal of them committed to writing. Calvin's comment of this verse is apt—

> The Psalmist intimates that this will be a memorable work of God, the praise of which shall be handed down to succeeding ages. Many things are worthy of praise which are soon forgotten; but the prophet distinguishes between the salvation of the Church, for which he makes supplication, and common benefits. By the word *register* he means that the history of the world be worthy of having a place in public records, that the remembrance of it might be transmitted to future generations.

How grateful we should be that we are included among the great number no man can number, created anew by the regenerating work of the Holy Spirit, who praise the Lord for His matchless grace!

He looked down . . . hearing the groaning . . . to loose those, 102:19-20. Dear Matthew Henry says that "God takes notice not only of the prayers of His afflicted people, which are *the language of grace;* but even of their groans, which are *the language of nature.*" From their historical past, the Jews thought of the time when, during their captivity, they were appointed to death by Haman, but God, looking down from the height of

His sanctuary, heard their groans and mercifully loosed them from a cruel fate. In memorial of same, they joyfully kept the Feast of Purim. As God looks down from the battlements of Heaven, He sees and hears all, even the bondage of those suffering for Him or who are bound with the chains of sin, and seeks to make them the recipients of His glorious liberty.

The people . . . the kingdoms to serve the Lord, 102:22. Dr. John Ker affirms that there is no grander missionary hymn than verses 13-22 of this Psalm, forming a fitting companion to Isaiah 60, taking up, to use the word of John Milton, "The whole passion of pity on the one side, and joy on the other . . . like that of our Savior Christ suffering to the lowest bent of weakness in the flesh, and presently triumphing to the highest pitch of glory in the spirit, which drew up His body also till we in both be united to Him in the revelation of His kingdom."

> Thou shalt arise, and mercy yet
> Thou to Mount Zion shall extend:
> Her time to favor which was set,
> Behold, is now come to an end.
> Thy saints take pleasure in her stones,
> Her very dust to them is dear.
> All heathen lands and kingly thrones
> On earth Thy glorious name shall fear.

What a blissful era for earth that will be when all the nations unite in the sole worship of Jehovah, and the histories of olden times are read and pondered over with adoring wonder, and His ever-bountiful hand rests upon the sacramental host of the Elect! What praise will ascend to Him for hearing the sighing of the prisoner and loosing him from his captivity!

My strength . . . my days . . . my days, 102:23, 24. Many have proved to their disappointment that the omission of one word in a will shattered their hopes of participation in a relative's or friend's estate. The want of one Word in these verses means the sinner's loss of Heaven and will act as a dagger piercing his heart with anguish forever. It is the pronoun *MY*—as much worth to the soul as a boundless eternal heritage. This pronoun of personal possession is the door at which the King enters into the heart with His whole train of spiritual benefits. All we need is locked up in a private cabinet of which *"MY* God" is the key.

The phrase *take me not away* actually means "take me not *up,*" and may have a possible historical reference to Elijah who was "taken up." As for the repeated phrase, "My days" implies that the Psalmist wanted to cover the usual course of life. *To ascend* means the same as to be *cut off*—death "cuts off" the saint from this world but he "ascends" to a better. The writer mournfully complained that he had bright hopes for Jerusalem, but that if he is a short-lived man, his vision would not become a reality.

The importance of verses 25-27 of this Psalm is seen in Paul's application to the Son of God in the section describing Him as being better than angels, Hebrews 1:10-12. The changelessness of God is a guarantee that His kingdom will endure among men. "Because I live, ye shall also live." How magnificently He is portrayed both as Creator and Redeemer. He laid the foundations of the earth, fashioned the heavens above which, in spite of their splendor as the garment of the invisible Architect, will be put aside as worn out clothes as He robes Himself with a new Heaven and a new Earth wherein dwelleth righteousness, with the saints being clad with their eternal glory. His children are to be established forever. The symbols used here of incessant change and visible decay, and then of endurance and perpetuity, may have supplied Goethe with the thought in his expressive lines—

> Tis thus at the roaming loom of time I ply,
> And weave for God the garment thou seest Him by!

Carlyle, too, in his *Philosophy of Clothes,* doubtless had the imagery of these verses in mind when he wrote, "Why multiply instances? It is written, the heavens and the earth shall fade away like a vesture, which, indeed they are—the time vesture of the Eternal." As *Grace* is not hereditary, it is incumbent upon us to discover whether we are truly His children through the regenerating work of the Spirit and therefore certain of a glorious perpetuity.

Psalm 103

How true is the ascription of praise that "there is too much in this Psalm for a thousand pens to write, it is one of those all-comprehending Scriptures which is a Bible in itself, and it might alone suffice for the hymn-book of the church!" The way in which it is bound up with the history and biography of many saints is evidence of its unceasing influence in life and character. Beza, an ancient writer, said that David when he wrote the Psalm was "carried out of himself as far as Heaven"; and without doubt, it is heavy with the fragrance of the heavenly abode where seraphs dwell.

Israel Zangwill, celebrated, self-educated, man of letters, and author of *Dreamers of the Ghetto* and other renowned works, once wrote, "I think that people might do worse than study Psalms 103 and 104, and I like 1 Corinthians 13 verse 7." We can add that there is nothing better for all the people in the world to do than live in the atmosphere of these Psalms, particularly the one before us which Robert Sanderson, Bishop of Lincoln who left his mark on the history of the *Common Prayer Book,* repeated daily before his death in 1662. William Law, in *Serious Call,* named Psalm 103 as one that wonderfully set forth "the glory of God, and, therefore, you can use it at any particular hour as you like." This was also one the Psalms John Ruskin learned by heart in his childhood. H.C. Morrison, one-time Bishop of the Methodist Church South, and Pastor for 12 years in the largest Methodist Churches in Louisville, Kentucky, said that "The 103rd Psalm had been a favorite with me from my boyhood."

Andrew Bonar, the notable Presbyterian Minister D.L. Moody loved to hear preach, tells a story of this Psalm saints in Scotland used to sing when they celebrated the *Lord's Supper.* The story is connected with a remarkable case in the days of John Knox—Elizabeth Adamson, a woman who attended Knox's preaching, "because he more fully opened the fountain of God's mercies than others did," was led to Christ and to rest, on hearing Psalm 103, after enduring such agony of soul she said, concerning the racking pains of body. "A thousand years of this torment, and then times more joined, are not to be compared to a quarter of an hour of my soul trouble." She asked for this Psalm again before departing: "It was in receiving it that my troubled soul first tasted God's mercy, which is now sweeter to me than if all the kingdoms of the earth were given me to possess."

A well-known German version of Psalm 103 was composed by John Graumann at the request of Albert I, Duke of Prussia, so that he could sing in verse the words of it he highly prized. When on his last sick-bed, the Duke had the same frequently sung to him, and he would join in adding his own thoughts. The Psalm was also the death-song of Christian III of Denmark who expired as the verse was reached, "Like as a father pitieth his children, so the Lord pitieth them that fear him!" Then when Gustavus Adolphus entered Augsburg, the city of the Protestant Confession, after his great victory at Leipzig which struck the decisive blow for religious freedom in Germany, he went straight to his Church of St. Ann and caused this 103rd Psalm to be sung in the German version.

Conspicuous during the *Killing Times* among the Cameronians in Scotland during the 16th century was James Renwick, the last sufferer in the long 28 years of persecution. Charged with denying the authority of King James VII, young Renwick was sentenced to death and was executed at the Grassmarket in Edinburgh, February 17, 1688. Although his words were drowned by the drums, he sang part of Psalm 103 which was always chanted by "The Saints" at the celebration of the Sacrament. People around caught up the words Renwick tried to sing and encouraged the martyr as he died on "the most joyful day he had ever seen." Psalm 103 was read over, once every day, in the family of John Angell James of Birmingham who, when his wife died, was asked if it should be read. "Yes," he said, "it is as full of comfort as of thanksgiving." As we journey through the Psalm further historical associations of it will appear. Regarding any exposition of the Psalm, Spurgeon wrote, "Our attempt of exposition is commenced under an impressive sense of the utter impossibility of doing justice to so sublime a composition; we will call upon our soul and all within us to aid in the pleasurable task; but, alas, our soul is finite, and all of mental faculty far too little for the enterprise."

In respect to the time of the writing of the Psalm, soon after the return of Israel from Exile has been suggested, but there is nothing in the Psalm to indicate when David wrote it. The title *A Psalm of David* agrees with passages of the Psalm, the independence of which cannot be mistaken seeing they bear a striking resemblance to the other Psalms of David, and also by its connection with Psalm 102. In Psalm 103, David teaches his posterity to *render thanks*, but in Psalm 102, he taught them to *pray.* There are no supplications or cries whatever in Psalm 103. The deliverance from deep distress which forms the subject of prayer in the previous Psalm, forms here the subject of thanksgiving. As the hope of Psalm 102 has been fulfilled, sorrow gives place to song in Psalm 103. After the cloud comes the sunshine which also describes the checkered experience of the child of God. In Romans 7 Paul cries and groans, but in Romans 8, he rejoices and leaps for joy. "Though weeping may endure for a night, joy cometh in the morning."

Appraisals of the beauty and blessedness of Psalm 103 abound. Ellicott says of it, "This Psalm has been compared to a stream and volume till its waves of praise swell like those of the sea. The poet begins by invoking his own soul to show its gratitude for the Divine favor, and, by a highly artistic touch, makes the Psalm, after rising to sublime heights, end with the same appeal to personal experiences. But national mercies fill much the larger space in his thought, and he speaks throughout as much in the person of the community as his own."

John Stevenson, in his *Exposition of the Hundred and Third Psalm*, written in 1856, says that, "The Psalm bears the character of quiet tenderness. It is a still clear brook, of the praise of God. In accordance with this we find that the verses are of equal length as to structure and consist regularly of two members. It is only at the conclusion, where the tone rises, that the verses become longer: the vessel is too small for the feeling. David touches every cord of his harp and of his heart together, and pours forth a spontaneous melody of sweetest sound and purest praise. No petition occurs throughout the entire compass of its twenty-two verses."

But of all ascriptions of praise regarding the marvel of this Psalm that of Spurgeon stands out as *par excellence*—

> The Psalm is David's own style when at its best, and we should attribute it to his later years when he had a higher sense of the preciousness of pardon, because a keener sense of sin than in his younger days. His clear sense of the frailty of life indicates his weaker years, as also does the very fullness of his praiseful gratitude. As in the lofty Alps some peaks rise above all others, so among even the inspired Psalms there are heights of song which overtop the rest. This 103rd Psalm has ever seemed to us to be the *Monte Rosa* of the divine chain of mountains of praise, glowing with a ruddier light than any of the rest. It is as the apple tree among the trees of the wood, and its golden fruit has a flavor such as no other fruit ever bears unless it has been ripened in the full sunshine of mercy. It is man's reply to the benedictions of his God, his Song of the Mount answering to his Redeemer's Sermon on the Mount. Nebuchadnezzar adored his idol with flute, harp, sacbut, psaltery, dulcimer and all kinds of music; and David, in far nobler style, awakens all the melodies of heaven and earth in honor of the one only living and true God.

Bless the Lord . . . bless his holy name, 103:1. It was in October, 1871, when Stanley found David Livingstone at Ujiji, almost a living skeleton through starvation. At last, Stanley was able to secure men and stores for the remarkable missionary-explorer, and he records his joy in the Diary he kept. "August 9, 1872—I do most devoutly thank the Lord for His goodness in bringing my men near to this. Three came today, and how thankful I am I cannot express. It is well—the men who were with Mr. Stanley came again to me. *Bless the Lord, O my soul, and all that is within me bless His holy name,* Amen" (Psalm 103:1).

In the threefold *bless* of the first two opening verses of the Psalm, David strikes its prominent key-note and, stirring up all within him to praise the Lord, proves that "soul music is the very soul of music." Others might blame the Lord and murmur against him but as for David, he aroused his own heart to bless the Lord, "O *my* soul." And, not only with his lips was he determined to bless God and His holy name, but he called upon *all* within him to adore Jehovah. All his faculties, affections, thoughts, emotions, and capacities—God gave them all, and all must join in the chorus of His praise. By *his holy name* is represented His revealed character, all He is in Himself.

Bless the Lord, o my soul, and forget not all his benefits, 103:2. While the word "benefits" literally means *actions,* whether good or bad— Judges 9:16; Proverbs 12:14—yet there is tremendous significance in the restricted meaning of the English term "benefits," for all God's *acts* are all *benefits*—beneficial in character. The application here is to the Divine dealings to what God had *done* for David, that he found a reason for blessing His name. What these *dealings* were he specifies in the following verses. *Forget not!* Forgetfulness is the secret spring of so much ingratitude in the world. The good Lord, Who never forgets His own, deliver us from want of re-collection and remembrance of all His mercies. David called upon *all* within his soul to remember *all* the Lord's benefits. How we should give heed to the warning that, "memory is very treacherous about the best things; by a strange perversity, engendered by the Fall, it treasures up the refuse of the past and permits priceless treasures to lie neglected, it is tenacious of grievances and holds benefits all too loosely. It needs spurring to its duty, though that duty ought to be its delight."

Who forgiveth all thine iniquites; who healeth all thy diseases, 103:3. Augustine said of this verse that it implies a quick moral sense: "God's benefits will not be before our eyes unless our sins are also before our eyes." This is the first and most important of all God's benefits for all those who aim at the higher life through Divine readiness to forgive and renew. What comprehensiveness is packed into the *alls* David loved to multiply! *All* within me—*All* his benefits—*All* iniquities—*All* diseases. God's *all* covers *all* our need. Iniquities means in-equities, suggesting that this is nothing just or right in us. The whole of life is made up of in-equity towards God, towards our neighbors—towards ourselves. But the glory of grace is that God is ready to forgive not *some* or *many* of our iniquities, but *all*. Further, the promise is in the present tense—*forgiveth*—implying that this Divine benefit is continual. "Who keeps on forgiving our iniquities."

As for *diseases* God heals, this term being parallel with *iniquities* proves that it is to be understood in a moral sense. Physical diseases and sicknesses came into the world by sin, and even these God is able to heal. Often, however, when the *cause* is removed the *effect* remains, as many a grossly sinful person, saved by Divine power, can testify. *Healeth* also indicates a continuous benefit. No disease of the soul can baffle God's skill, and as each malady arises the Divine Surgeon is present to heal.

Who redeemeth . . . Who crowneth thee, 103:4. "Destruction" means *pit* or *grave* as seen in Psalm 16:10. "He will not suffer us to see corruption." Christ has delivered us from going down into the pit by giving Himself as our ransom, and His redeeming grace will ever constitute and continue as one of the most blessed benefits to praise Him for. By His blood and His power He redeemed us from *spiritual death* and from *eternal death* which would have been its consequence. The word *redeemed* implies "redemption of life by the kinsman," and thus is a prophecy of Him Who became partaker of our flesh and blood that He might have the right to redeem us from death by dying in our stead.

As David wrote this verse, past history must have passed before him for, from earliest days, he had been the child of Providence. What hairbreadth escapes and wonderful deliverances had been his! The jaw of the lion, the paw of the bear, the sword of Goliath, the men of Keilal, the Philistine lords, and the unnatural rebellion of his own son, testified to the way his Almighty Friend covered his head in the day of battle. But how bountiful was this Friend for not only had he been cleansed, healed, redeemed, the forgiven sinner must be crowned as a king. The metaphor *crowneth* is drawn from the common custom of wearing wreaths and garlands on festive occasions. See Psalm 8:5.

The double crown of *lovingkindness* and *tender mercies* is a crown decked with jewels of mercy but made soft for the head to wear by a lining of tenderness. Those thus crowned do not earn their crown for "it is of *mercy* not merit," and as they feel their own unworthiness of such a coronet of love and compassion, His mercy is cushioned by tenderness just as His kindness towards them is wrapped up in love.

Who satisfieth thy mouth with good things, 103:5. This further blessing in the bundle of benefits actually means, "filling with good thy soul." The Redeemer not only saves but satisfies to the full, and soul-satisfaction loudly calls for soul-praise for "all good things around us sent from Heaven above." David did not say that the Lord satisfied us with *rich* things, or *many* things, or for *everything* we ask for, but *good* things, that is, all mercies in harmony with His goodness—things good or beneficial for our souls. The next phrase, *Thy youth is renewed like the eagle's*, is an evidence of God's goodness:

> Who satisfieth thine age with good, so that
> Thy youth renews itself like the eagle.

According to an ancient Rabbinical story the eagle is able to renew its youth when very old, and the Psalmist has a poetical allusion to the fresh and vigorous appearance of the bird with its new plumage. Doubtless the idea of the eagle renewing its youth was founded on its great longevity and its power, like other birds, to moult plumage periodically thereby increasing its strength and activity. Vigor and activity constantly renewed, and not *renovation,* is implied both by David and Isaiah—see 40:31. All who are the redeemed of the Lord are blessed with eternal youth. So—

> He who sat moping with the owl in Psalm 102, here flies high with the eagle. The Lord works marvelous changes in us, and we learn by such experience to bless His holy name. To grow from a sparrow to an eagle, and leave the wilderness of the pelican to mount among the stars, is enough to make any man cry, *Bless the Lord, O my soul!*

The Lord executeth righteousness and judgment for all that are oppressed, 103:6. Here David passes from individual to *national* mercies, and goes back in history to the memorable manifestations of Divine favor vouchsafed to Israel and the nation's leader, Moses. The R.V. gives "righteous acts, and judgments," that is, deliverances. The Psalmist knew that when God's people were in Egypt, He heard their cries and executed judgment for those who were oppressed by overthrowing Pharaoh and his host in the Red Sea. Because "He is known by the judgments which He executeth, man's injustice towards His saints and martyrs will receive retribution at His hands. Vengeance is His, and He will repay. He cares so kindly and gloriously for those who suffer cruel wrongs from oppressors."

The next verse reveals how Moses and Israel were made to see and experience the manner in which He deals with those who strive to injure those who are within the covenant of grace. God was the Instructor of Moses for, "*He* made known his ways." The law-giver was not left to discover the Divine method himself. Does He not have a way of manifesting Himself unto His own as He does not to the world?

The Lord is merciful and gracious, 103:8. The original confession at the time of national deliverance, Exodus 34:6, became a formula of national faith. It is profitable to compare marginal references at this verse with Psalm 145:8 and Joel 2:13. The Hebrew for "plenteous in mercy" reads *great, mighty in mercy.* God's chief glory is the attribute of mercy as herewith emphasized, and teaches us how to estimate and praise true greatness. Altogether in this verse we are given four glimpses of the Divine character. God is *merciful* and therefore any sinner can hope for pardon. He is also *gracious* which gives a sinner further hope to expect to receive what God deems best to give. He is *slow to anger.* The Bible expresses slowness to anger, and hastiness to anger, by the different frame of the nostrils; as, namely, when the Lord is said to be "slow to anger," the Hebrew has it, *long of nostrils,* which is a forceful simile of God's patience. Last of all, He is not only compassionate but *full of compassion.* As the Good and Perfect Samaritan, God not only binds up our wounds but cares for us all through.

He will not always chide; neither will he keep his anger forever, 103:9. God has no love of chiding any of His children and seeks to get rid of it as soon as He can. Neither can He keep His anger on account of injuries done to Him but strives to be reconciled to all who offend. Does God not set a grand example to His people not to harbor resentments in their hearts? Grudges against others are like babies—the longer they are nursed the bigger they grow.

He hath not dealt with us . . . nor rewarded us according to our iniquities, 103:10. This is among the most precious verses in the Bible. Had God rewarded Israel long ago and ourselves in this modern age according to our sins, all would have been consigned to the lowest Hell. So, while we praise Him for all He has done for us, the negative side also deserves our adoring gratitude. He has not dealt with us nor rewarded us according to our deserts. Is not the primary reason why God has not dealt with us after our sins, the fact that He dealt with Another after our sins? "Christ died for our sins"? Our sins and iniquities deserved eternal death, but the accursed load was laid on Him. Now mercy is offered to sinners, and the next verse declares the superabundance of this virtue towards us who seek the Lord.

As far as . . . so far, 103:12. The truth of the two previous verses is geographically illustrated in this arrestive verse in which is described the glorious message of the Gospel that once a sinner is pardoned, the guilt of his sin can no more return than east can become west, or west become east. An ancient commentator says that the distance for the *east to west* is used because "these two quarters of the world are of greatest extent, being all known and inhabited. From whence it is that geographers reckon that way their longitudes, as north to south their latitudes." The miracle of Divine love is that if the distance between east and west is incalculable, then imagination fails to grasp the distance God has placed between the sin by repentant, believing sinners and themselves. Jesus our Scapegoat bore their sins away!

Like a father . . . the Lord pitieth them that fear him, 103:13. Psalmist and Prophet alike anticipated Christ's revelation of the paternal heart of God. The story is told of a Chaplain to seamen at an American port who was called upon to visit a sailor who appeared to be near death. The Chaplain spoke kindly to the man about the state of his soul and urged him to cast himself on the Savior, but with an oath the sick man told the Chaplain to go. The man of God, however, replied that he had to be faithful in warning him that if he died impenitent, he would be lost forever. But the sailor, sullen and silent, pretended to fall asleep. Repeated visits brought similar ill success. At length, during a further call, the Chaplain suspecting that the sailor was a Scotsman repeated a verse of the old version of this Psalm.

> Such pity as a father had
>   Unto his children dear,
> Like pity shows the Lord to such
>   As worship him in fear.

As he listened to these words, tears filled his eyes, and when the Chaplain asked him if he had a godly mother, he replied that she had taught him this Psalm and prayed for him, and that often the memory of her faith and love moved his heart. The ministry of the Chaplain was blessed by the Spirit of God for the sailor's life was spared, and he lived to prove the reality of his conversion.

The kind of mercy David attributes to God is not that of a man, say a rich man pitying a poor man, or a freeman, a captive, but as a *Father.* Then seeing He is the "Father of all mercies," His pity is abundant. We have a saying that "it is better to be envied, than pitied," but with us it is not so, seeing it is far more blessed to be pitied of God than to be envied of men.

He knoweth our frame; he remembereth that we are dust, 103:14. John S. Huyler, one-time philanthropist and manufacturer and deeply interested in a mission in New York, recorded that he had many texts for special times and occasions, but the most prominent one for general use was, "He knoweth our frame; he remembereth that we are dust." The word for *frame* implies "fashioning," and may refer to the creative act of God when He made man a living soul (Gen. 2:7), or to the common simile in the Prophets of the potter's vessel. The Duke of Wellington, victor over Napoleon, is often referred to as *The Iron Duke*, but those described as having *iron* constitution were dissolved long ago. At the grave, the appropriate requiem is, *Dust to dust.* God knows all about our fragile frame for He fashioned it and thus is very gentle towards us. May we ever remember, as Henry Vaughan poetically reminds us, that we are but dust—

> O how in this Thy quire of souls I stand,
> —Profit by Thy hand—
> A heap of sand!
> Which busie thoughts—like winds—would gather quite,
> And put to flight
> But for Thy might;
> Thy hand alone doth tame
> Those blasts, and knit my frame.

As grass . . . as the flower of the field, 103:15. The insignificance of man as *dust* is further emphasized in the twin metaphors of withering grass and fading flowers. Spurgeon exhorts us to read this verse over and over again, seeing it contains the history of man, "who lives on grass and lives like grass. Corn is but educated grass, and man, who feeds on it, partakes of its nature. The grass lives, grows, falls beneath the scythe, dries up, and is removed from the field. He lives out his little day, is cut down at last, and it is far more likely that he will wither before he comes to maturity, or be plucked away on a sudden, long before he has fulfilled his time."

Further, God has appointed and determined the several growths and decays of flowers and fruits with the same laws that are applied to man. As a flower preserved beyond its bloom, drops and perishes upon the stalk, so is it with the saint of God. Blessed to know, however, that we have within us "an incorruptible seed which liveth and abideth forever!" James Beattie, poet of the 17th century, left us the lines on the metaphor, *As a flower of the field*—

> What is life! like a flower, with the bane in its bosom,
> Today full of promise—tomorrow it dies!—
> And health-like the dew-drop that hangs in its blossom,
> Survives but a night, and exhales to the skies!
>
> How oft 'neath the bud that is brightest and fairest,
> The seeds of the canker in embryo lurk!
> How oft at the root of the flower that is rarest—
> Secure in its ambush the worm is at work.

The wind passeth over it, and it is gone, 103:16. The wind referred to here is not a blasting whirlwind so destructive in its course, but a breath of air or a *gentle wind* as the Hebrew suggests. The whispering breeze, passing over him, takes him away. This is different from the hot, scorching blast Isaiah mentions, Isaiah 40:7. The pestilential winds of the East, bringing heat like an oven, immediately destroy every green thing. In a more humid climate—

> If one sharp wind sweep o'er the field,
> It withers in an hour.

Is there not something pathetic in the phrase, "the place thereof shall know it no more," whether the flower withered at the gentlest touch or was removed by a tempest? The figure of speech declares that man vanishes away without leaving a trace behind, the pathos of which has been well expressed in the well-known lines of Grey—

> One morn I missed him on the accustomed hill,
> Along the heath, and near his favorite tree:
> Another came, not yet beside the rill,
> Nor up the lawn, nor at the wood was he.

But although there may be only a mound of earth to remember us by, is it not wonderful to know that there is "an existence of another kind coeval with Eternity, but this belongs, not to our flesh, which is but grass, but to a higher life, in which we rise to close fellowship with the Eternal."

The mercy of the Lord is from everlasting to everlasting, 103:17. David is here expressing the same assurance of the undecaying character of the Redeemer and the Redeemed as found in his previous Psalm—102:23-25. History records that human benevolence is never perpetually the same; apparently kind men today may be transformed into killers tomorrow, examples of which can be found in the life of Nero. A supreme benefit, however, to bless God for is His unchangableness. Like His mercy He, too, is ever the same. Yesterday, today and forever, His grace knows no decay. The gaze of paternal love is never removed from us and from our children's children if they are His, and never will be, world without end. The same perpetual mercy is the possession of all who remember His commandments to do them. Such commands are to be remembered in order to fulfill them in our daily life.

The Lord hath prepared his throne, 103:19. The word *prepared* is better translated as *established,* as given in the R.V. No hasty resolve marked such an establishment of the universal rule. As the Eternal One, God is the sole cause of His own kingdom whether it be in the heavens, as "Creator of the rolling spheres," or Lord over all time, places, and creatures. When Philip Melanchton was extremely solicitious about the affairs of the Church in his days, his dear friend, Martin Luther, would admonish him in the exhortation—

> Let not Philip make himself any longer governor of the world.

Is it not comforting to know that God's sceptre is over the whole universe; that matchless sovereignty is His, that His government has no surprises to be met or unexpected catastrophes to be warded off; that He is no delegated sovereign but an Autocrat whose dominion arises from Himself and is sustained by His own innate power? To us, the whole world appears to be rent with anarchy, atheism, crime, violence, murder, and war, but as the blessed and only Potentate, King of Kings, and Lord of Lords, His throne is forever fixed and immovable.

> He sits on his precarious throne,
> Nor borrows leave to be.

"Thus has the sweet singer hymned the various attributes of the Lord as seen in nature, grace, and providence, and now he gathers up all his energies for one final outburst of adoration, in which he would have all unite, since all are subjects of the Great King."

Bless the Lord . . . Bless the Lord . . . Bless the Lord, Bless the Lord, 103:20-22. What exultant verses these are! What jubilance as the angels and works of God wait in adoration to Him for His universal dominion! The Psalm, opening with a trinity of *bless,* closes with a quartet of such a turn of praise. In verses 20 and 21, angels are prominent in their chorus of gratitude for "just as in the highest, revelation made by angels in Heaven rejoices over the repentant sinner, so in David's view the mercy of Jehovah to His faithful people is cause for high acclaim among the hosts around the throne." Dealing with these last three verses as a whole, the Psalmist speaks of three grades of beings associated in the hierarchy of praise. *All His hosts,* namely, Angels mighty in strength and constantly obedient to the voice of their Lord. Next to these high angels around the throne, are all *His hosts,* sun, moon, stars, winds, and lightnings, specially commissioned to carry out His behests. Like the angels they do "His pleasure," Psalms 19:1; 104:4. What planets do unconsciously, the angels do consciously and with instinctive love, "hearken unto the voice of His Word." Both together constitute the Lord's hosts.

The weight of offering praise unto God is too heavy for men alone to lift; and as for the host of angels, it takes all their mighty strength and their best ability to magnify Him aright. That they wonderfully succeed is evident from all we learn about the ministry of angels in Scripture. Not only do they mightily execute the Divine commands they are also ready to catch the slightest intimation of the Divine will and obey it—whether its execution be pleasing or painful as when they smote Balaam for his coventousness, David for his vainglory, Sennacherib for his blasphemy, Sodom for its rottenness, and Herod for his pride.

By *His words* we understand not only angelic hosts, the heavens and their hosts, but "Earth with her thousand voices praises God." It is interesting to compare the repeated blessing in these concluding verses with the Mosaic formula of Numbers 6:24-26. David ends his most unique Psalm on the same personal note as he began it, "Bless the Lord, O *my* soul." Let all His words in all places of His wide dominion unite in the universal chorus of praise and blessing extolling Jehovah, the One supremely great, supremely good, but David has his personal responsibility to his own heart, and so the Psalm turns back into itself and assumes the form of a converging circle, "Bless the Lord, O *my* soul," verses 1 and 22. May we make the repeated self-dedication with which he began and ended his Psalm our very own. May all within you and me magnify the Lord!

Psalm 104

This lyrical poem of the whole universe—the heavens and the earth—rightly called an inspired Oratorio of Creation, instructs us how to admire with one eye the works of God, and with the other, God Himself their Creator and Preserver. Such a solemn and exalted poetic portrayal of the Cosmos in brief compass yet comprehensive and sublime has never been surpassed. Within it we have David the poet setting forth his version of Genesis' record of God's creative ability. The Psalm is composed of "one of the loftiest and longest-sustained flights of inspired muse, with an interpretation of the many voices of nature, and sings sweetly of both Creation and Providence. The poem contains a complete Cosmos; sea and land—cloud and sunlight—plant and animal—light and darkness—life and death are all proved to be expressive of the presence of the Lord."

Alexander von Humboldt, who died in 1859, recognized the Psalm as an epitome of scientific progress, a summary of the laws which govern the universe. "A single Psalm, the 104th" he wrote, "may be said to present a picture of the entire Cosmos . . . We are astonished to see, within the compass of a poem of such small dimension, the Universe—the heavens and the earth—thus drawn with a few grand strokes." John Ruskin said of Psalm 104 that it "anticipated every triumph of natural science." C. S. Lewis says that the Psalms in their doctrine of Creation leave Nature full of manifestations revealing the presence of God, any created energies which serve Him. Thus in "Psalm 104, the light is His garment, the thing we partially see Him through, verse 2—the eruption of a volcano comes in answer to His touch, verse 32. The world is full of His emissaries and executors. He makes winds His messengers and flames His servants, verse 4."

Of all the glowing estimation of this unique Psalm, none is comparable to that which is found in the preface Ellicott's *Commentary* gives. Here is this superb appraisal in full—

> This Psalm touches the highest point of religious poetry. It is the most perfect hymn the world has ever produced. Even as a lyric it has scarcely been surpassed; while as a lyric inspired by religion, not only was all ancient literature, except that of the Hebrews, powerless to create anything like it, but even Christian poetry has never succeeded in approaching it. Milton has told the story of Creation, taking as the Psalmist does, the account of Genesis as his model; but the seventh book of *Paradise Lost*, even when we make all

the difference between the narrative and lyrics styles, in tone and prolix—
seems to want animation and fire—by the side of this hymn.

At the opening we feel the magic of a master inspiration. The world is
not, as in Genesis, created by a Divine decree. It springs into life and motion,
into order and use, at the touch of the Divine Presence. Indeed, the pervading
feeling of the hymn is the sense of God's close and abiding relation to all
that He made; the conviction that He not only originated the universe, but
dwells in it and sustains it; and this feeling fastens upon us at the outset as
we see the light enfolding the Creator as His robe and the canopy of Heaven
rising over Him as a tent. It is not a lifeless world that springs into being.
There is no void, no chaos; even the winds and clouds are not for this poet
without denizens, or they themselves start into life and people the universe
of his satisfaction. He cannot conceive of a world at any time without life
and order. Nor has any poet, even of our modern age, displayed a finer feeling for nature, and that not in her tempestuous and wrathful moods—usually
the source of Hebrew inspiration—but in her calm, everyday temper. He is
the Wordsworth of the ancients, penetrated with a love for nature, and gifted with the insight that springs from love.

This Psalm of Nature, celebrating God's majesty and power as seen in
His works both inanimate and animate, follows to some extent the order
of the creation-poem of Genesis 1, and may be compared also with
Job 38. As Spurgeon reminds us, "Traces of the six days of creation are
very evident, and though the creation of man, which was the crowning
work of the sixth day, is not mentioned, this is accounted for from the fact
that man himself is the singer: some have even discerned marks of the
Divine rest upon the earth in verse 31 . . . Nor is it alone the present condition of the earth which is here the subject of song, but a hint is given of
those holier times when we shall see, 'a new earth wherein dwelleth righteousness,' out of which the sinner will be consumed, verse 35. The spirit
of ardent praise to God runs through the whole, and with it a distinct realization of the divine Being as a personal existence, loved and trusted as
well as adored."

As to the authorship of this majestic hymn, although in the Hebrew it
is anonymous, the LXX Version ascribed it to David. That Psalm 104 has
a close connection with Psalm 103 is seen in the unique feature that both
Psalms begin and end in the same way, the inference being that he who
wrote the one Psalm, penned the other. So as David is given as the author
of Psalm 103, we conclude him to be, as a great lover of Nature, the composer of Psalm 104. But whoever "the human penman may have been the
exceeding glory and perfection of the Holy Spirit's own divine authorship
are plain to every spiritual mind." It is a beneficial exercise to go through
the Psalm and count the numerous pronouns, *Who, Thou,* and *He* used.

Coming to an examination of the most expressive metaphorical lan-

404 Psalms: *A Devotional Commentary*

guage used throughout the Psalm, one is amazed at its descriptive variety—a variety of rhythm. The first four verses, for instance, instead of describing the *creation* of light during the first and second days of Creation, "The poet makes a sublime approach to his theme by treating it as a symbol of the Divine majesty. It is the vesture of God, the tremendous curtain of His tent, whose supporting beams are based not on earth, but on those cloud-masses which form an upper ocean. This curtain is then, as it were, drawn aside for the exit of the Monarch attended by His throng of winged messengers."

Bless the Lord . . . thou art very great; thou art clothed with honor and majesty, 104:1. "My soul"—"My God." At the outset the Psalmist expresses his own personal faith in and adoration for the infinite Jehovah he calls "*my* God." Prostrate with wonder and awe at His almightiness, David cried out in utter astonishment, not, "Thy universe is very great," but "*Thou* art very great." The honor and majesty of his great God overwhelmed his soul and found expression in praise. Although God is not seen, His works are called His robes or garments, and as garments both conceal and reveal a man, so do the works of God act in this double way. He is worthy of *honor* for the skill seen in His creations, and of *majesty* for He ever fashions His works according to His sovereignty. He asks no man's permission for all He desires to accomplish. The clothing oneself or girding oneself is used to represent Jehovah as a *warrior* arraying Himself for battle, Isa. 59:17; 68:1. Here, in the opening verse of the Psalm, He is before us as a *monarch* robed in splendor, or "pavilioned in splendor."

Who coverest thyself with light as with a garment, 104:2. The present tense used in *coverest* and *stretchest* indicates that the poet did not think of these works as a single past act, but as a continued glorious operation of Divine power and glory. As Sir R. Grant expresses it in his well-loved hymn of worship—

> Whose robe *is* the light
> Whose canopy space—

Light is not as the modern poet puts it—

> Nature's resplendent robe,
> Without whose vesting beauty as were rapt.
> In unessential gloom

but it is the dress of Divinity, "the ethereal woof" that God Himself is forever wearing for His own wear. Although He dwells in light inaccessible, He yet irradiates the whole earth with light. As for the beautiful phrase of *stretching out the heavens like a curtain*, it is usual in the East, not only in the summer season, but upon all occasions when a large company is drawn together, to have the court of the house sheltered from the heat or rain by a curtain or veil, expanded upon ropes from one side of the parapet wall to another, which can be folded or unfolded at pleasure. Thus as a man spreads out a tent-curtain, God spreads out the heavens as a tent to dwell in. See Isa. 40:22.

If "the *robe* is essential light, to which suns and moons owe their brightness, the *curtain* is the azure sky studded with stars for gems." Different explanations have been given of the figure of the *tremulous movement* of the folds of the curtain, as the Hebrew expresses it. Some writers see in the "curtain" an allusion to the curtains of the Tabernacle, or to the rich folds of the curtain of the Holy of Holies within same, all of which were dear to a religious Hebrew (Exod. 26:27). Thus a modern poet writes of—

> The arras-folds, that variegate
> The earth, God's anti-chamber.

Others see in the image a survival of the nomadic instinct of pitching and striking of tents. But there is no need to limit the application of a metaphor so natural and suggestive which can be used of palace, temple, and tent, as suggested by Shelley in his *Ode to Heaven*—

> Palace roof of cloudless night!
> Paradise of golden lights!
>   Deep immeasurable vast,
> Which art now, and which wert then;
>   Of the present and the past
> Of the Eternal where and when,
>   Presence-chamber, temple, home.
>   Ever-canopying dome
> Of acts and ages yet to come.

Who layeth . . . who maketh . . . who walked, 104:3. These triple, continuous acts of the Almighty add to His greatness and glory. *Layeth* literally means, "maketh to meet," which *chambers* implies upper stories, Jerem. 22:13,14. *Waters* are those above the firmament which are the source of rain, verse 13. As we consider the figures used here it is simple absurdity to interpret literally, language so poetical. The upper rooms of God's great house, the palatial chambers in which He resides, are based upon the flood forming the upper ocean. People in the East used to retire to the upper chamber whenever they sought solitude. Beams have to be substantial, strong, and even to sustain the weight of an ordinary house, but the remarkable astonishing fact is that God makes the waters the foundation of His heavenly palace.

The pavilion, then, God rears for His abode appears to rest on a floor of rain-clouds, like a tent spread on a flat eastern roof, Psalm 18:11; Amos 9:6,7. Southey's description of the Palace of Indra in his *Curse of Kehama* aids our imagination at this point—

> Built on the lake, the waters were its floor;
> And here its walls were water arched with fire,
> And here were fire and water vaulted o'er;
> > And spires and pinnacles of fire
> > Round watery cupolas aspire,
> And domes of rainbow rest on fiery towers.

Making *clouds His chariots* is a figure found in Psalm 18:10 where *cherub* takes the place of "chariot." The Targum has it "upon the swift clouds, like the wings of an eagle." There was a heathen motion that Jupiter was carried in a chariot through the air when it thunders and lightnings. Of this we are certain, that Jehovah's chariot of mercy drops plenty as it traverses the celestial road. Grant's hymn has the lines—

> His chariots of wrath
> > The deep thunder-clouds form,
> And dark is His path
> > On the wings of the storm.

As for the metaphor of *walking upon the ways of the wind*, doubtless same is related to the clouds, which, in a windswept sky, float along like "the drifted wings of many companies of angels." This third figure is a direct parallelism with that of the *cloud* chariot. Shakespeare's familiarity with the Psalms characterizes his works. For instance, in the address of Romeo to Juliet he had this fourth verse in mind when he compared Juliet to "a winged messenger of Heaven"—

> When he bestrides the lazy-pacing clouds
> And sails upon the bosom of the air.

Other poets have used the same figure of the *wings*. John Milton in *Lycidas* has the couplet—

> Every gust of rugged *wings*
> That blows from off each beaked promontory.

Tennyson in his *In Memoriam* has the phrase—

> No *wing of wind* the region swept

Surely there is no more sublime idea of Deity than that found here of God "serenely walking on an element of inconceivable swiftness, an uncontrollable impetuosity." And what unequalled elegance this is in the Divine motion—not *fleeth*, or *runneth*, but *walketh* on the most turbulent element raised into the utmost rage, and sweeping along with incredible rapidity. How appealing is Spurgeon's summary of this phrase—

> What a stately car is that which is fashioned out of the flying clouds, whose gorgeous colors Solomon in all his glory could not rival; and what a Godlike progress is that in which spirit wings and breath of winds bear up the moving throne—*O Lord, my God, Thou art very great.*

Who maketh his angels spirits, his ministers, a flaming fire, 104:4. The God Who is able to make His angels to be as the wind, can also make winds to be His angels, as they are constantly so in the economy of nature. *His angels spirits* can read either, *His angels winds,* or, as in the R.V. "winds his messengers." Dummelow observes "the former rendering holy love." See Isa. 6:6.

Who laid the foundations of the earth that it should not be removed forever, 104:5. How apt is the poetic description of this sublime fact by Sir R. Grant—

> The earth, with its store
>   Of wonders untold,
> Almighty. Thy power
>   Hath founded of old;
> Hath 'stablished it fast
>   By a changeless decree,
> And round it hath cast,
>   Like a mantle, the sea.

In a summary of verses 5 to 18, Ellicott says they present the work of the third day of Creation in its two great divisions—

1. The separation of the land and water, verses 5-9.
2. The clothing of the earth with grass, herbs, and trees, verses 10-18.

The poet, however, ranges beyond the Mosaic account, and already peoples the earth with the living creatures of the fifth day. Perowne says of this same section, "It is not a picture of still life like that of *Genesis*, but a living, moving, animated scene."

The science of the Middle Ages was governed to a great extent by the Psalms. Medieval cosmogonists argued that the earth cannot be in motion, or suspended in mid-air, but was firmly fixed, for "He laid the foundations of the earth that it never should move at any time." Historical interest attaches to this verse seeing it supplied the Inquisition with an argument against Galileo, who was the first man to use the telescope to study the skies and amassed evidence proving that the earth revolves around the sun and was not the center of the universe as had been believed. For this radical departure from accepted thought, Galileo was tried by the Inquisition in Rome and ordered to recant and forced to spend the last eight years of his life under house arrest.

As the being and existence of earth is of God, so is its stability. While earthquakes may have moved parts of the earth, the whole body of the earth has never removed so much as one hair's breadth out of its place since God laid its foundations. Archimedes, the great mathematician said, "If you will give me a place to set my engine on, I will remove the earth." But such a brag was hollow, since the One Who can make the earth is the only One Who can quake and shake it. But God has declared of His creation, "it shall not be removed forever." Laplace has demonstrated that the earth has not varied the one hundredth of a second during the last two thousand years or more. See Job 38:4-6; Prov. 8:29.

Some Bible lovers may be troubled about the statement, "He laid the earth upon nothing," Job 26:7, which seems to be inconsistent with God fixing the earth on foundations, but in both cases the treatment and language are poetical, not scientific. *Foundations* implies stability and endurance as in Shakespeare's time, "The frame and huge foundation of the earth." The reference in Psalm 82:5, "All the foundations of the earth are out of course," is a description of the very existence of society on the earth being threatened when the source of justice is corrupt.

Thou coverest it with the deep as with a garment, 104:6. Round the earth, God has cast "like a mantle, the sea." Geologists announce as a discovery that in the first ages, before man appeared, the proud waters ruled the whole earth, vapor as from a steaming cauldron covered all. But the Holy Spirit, Co-Creator, revealed the fact long, long before that "the new-born earth was wrapt in aqueous swaddling clothes." In the passage before us, the Psalmist presents the Creator as commencing His work, laying the foundation for future order and beauty. The water-world, covering the mountain-tops, had risen beyond its right, and at the Divine rebuke is forced to retire within narrower limits. "It is noticeable that the idea of a chaos finds no place in the poetic conception of the world's genesis. The primitive world is not formless, but has its mountains and valleys already existing, though merged beneath the sea."

Verses 7-10 are parallel with Genesis 1:9, 10 and present God's commands to the waters as having been uttered in thunder, verse 7. And, as Milton describes it—

> Immediately the mountains huge appear
> Emergent—

The obedience of the mighty waters to the laws of their God is most noticeable, not only in Creation, but in the experience of Jesus when storm-tossed in a boat on the Galilean waters. The Divine Word can work the greatest miracle. Waterfloods of trouble and the raging billows of sin, as well as the boisterous rapids, are rebuked at the thunder of Jehovah's voice.

He sendeth the springs into the valleys, 104:10-12. These three verses are eloquent with "the beautiful part of the Lord's arrangement of the subject waters: they find vents through which they leap into liberty where their presence will be beneficial in the highest decree." An Oriental poet thinks first of the springs and rivers on which fertility and life depend. And such is his sympathy with nature that in disregard of the original record he hastens at once to people his world with creatures to share the Creator's joy in its beauty and goodness. But first in order are the valley-springs flowing between the hills—then water for every beast of the field, seeing that the cattle upon a thousand hills are His. Even asses, and wild ones at that, are not beyond the heavenly Father's care. If He did not water them, who would? The pronoun HE is prominent in verses 10, 13, 14, reminding us of the lines of Lord Byron—

> All things are here of *HIM*; from the black pines,
> Which are his shade on high, and the loud roar
> Of torrents where he listeneth, to the vines
> Which slope his green path downward to the shore,
> Where the bow'd waters meet him, and adore,
> Kissing his feet with murmurs.

The birds, also, in their nests among the branches are able to pour forth their melodious notes as the result of the God-directed valley-springs. Singing among the branches should inspire us to sing where we dwell— even if it be like Paul and Silas in a prison cell. John Wesley wrote that, "the music of birds was the first song of thanksgiving which was offered from the earth, before man was formed." Said Izaak Walton, great lover of birds, especially the nightingale, "Lord, what music hast thou provided for the saints in heaven, when thou affordest bad men such music on earth?"

The earth is satisfied with the fruit of thy works, 104:13. "He watereth the hills from his chambers" refers to the fertilizing rain causing the earth to bring forth fruit—grass for the cattle—herb for the service of man—wine to make glad the heart—oil to make his face shine—bread for his daily nourishment, verses 14, 15. Nothing and nobody on the earth is left unsupplied when God opens His stores of refreshment. The bounties of God's kindness satisfy all birds and beasts, every species of vegetation, and the desires of man. All have "their veins with general moisture fed," by no other than his fostering hand.

The trees . . . where birds make their nests . . . house . . . refuge, 104:16-18. The trees are His—He made them, and the poet's transition from men to trees indicates that if God so nourishes men created in His own image, He will not grudge to extend His cares to trees so beneficial to birds. While the Psalmist mentions *cedars*, because it is the tree *par excellence* of the Bible, all the trees display the power and wisdom of God. *Full of sap*. The Romans believed that the gum exuding from the cedar had the power of rendering whatever was steeped in it incorruptible; and we are told that the books of Numa, the early king of Rome, which were found uninjured in his tomb 500 years after his death had been steeped in oil of cedar. "The trees of the Lord are full of sap" is better translated *Jehovah's trees are satisfied*. The cedar was the grandest and fairest tree known to the Hebrew, and thus, like lightning and the tropical rain, is honored by the epithet most expressive of grandeur—*which He planted*. The poet felt that such a tree must have been planted by the Divine hand itself—man could grow herbs, but not cedars—a proof of the lavish provision made by the Creator for the fertility of the earth he states that even these monarchs of the forest have enough.

How great is the God we adore to make such suitable homes for birds and beasts! The great marvel is that Jesus is in Heaven preparing a home for those redeemed by His blood, John 14:1-3. We cannot read the above verses, and walk among the trees, and fail to hear the voice of the Lord God. The Psalmist gives us a picture of all the earth full of happy life, with every place having its appropriate inhabitant. Goats, storks, conies, and sparrows "each contribute a verse to the Psalm of Nature; have we not also our canticles to sing unto the Lord?"

The moon . . . the sun . . . Darkness . . . Night, 104:19, 20. Verses 19-24 of this Psalm formed the Evensong of the Russian Church. In a previous Psalm the moon is described as a perpetual and faithful witness in Heaven. To the Jews, and to the ancients generally, the moon was reckoned to be "the arbiter of festivals," and festivals were signs of the Covenant, and thus the inferior luminary is mentioned first in verse 19, partly due to its importance in fixing the calendar, and partly also to the diurnal reckoning—the evening and the morning, as making the day. See 81:3; 89:37. In the Jewish day the night leads the way. The waxing and waning of the moon by which the year is divided is the result of Divine appointment. The lamp of night provides service for man.

The Psalmist uses the same poetic imagery of the sun as it retires from sight and sinks beyond the horizon. To him, the sun was no mere mechanical timepiece, but a conscious servant of God. "How beautifully this mention of sunset prepares the way for the exquisite picture of the nocturnal landscape, as the sunrise in verse 22 does for the landscape of the day." How men should praise the Lord for the sun and moon, these great lights as chronometers to keep our world in order and to suffer no confusion to distract us! The Divine *He* is the directing cause. *He* appointed the moon for seasons—God knoweth the going down of the sun—Thou makest darkness.

Augustine observed that in Genesis it is said that *light was made*, but not that *darkness was made*, because darkness is nothing, it is mere non-existence. But the gifted poet of Israel says that God makes darkness, and He, Himself, claims to be the *Maker of light and the Creator of Darkness*. Night is the time when the beasts trample on through the forest, the darkness aiding their stealthy motion when on the track of their prey. Compare verse 25 with Job 37:8; 38:40. "Darkness is fitter for beasts than men; and those men are most brutish who love darkness rather than light." With the rising of the sun—greatest of miracles, and the most amazing of blessings—animals retire to their quiet quarters, out of man's way, for rest.

Man goeth forth unto his work and to his labor until the evening, 104:23. These words were written long before man fought for shorter working hours, larger wages, and longer holidays. The curse of labor on which *Genesis* dwells had given way to "the poetry of labor," when after a day's healthy toil, the evening brought happy rest. It may sound strange to say that the lions seek their meat from God, when in darkness and with craft they catch their prey, but their *roar*, it is said, can be interpreted, *asking their meat of* God. All creatures are fed and nourished by a general Providence, even man, for God grants him health and strength to work so that he can earn the money to eat and live. No wonder the poet exclaims in adoration, "O Lord, how manifold are thy works! In wisdom thou hast made them all (the luminaries, beasts, and man): the earth is full of thy riches." For *riches* the LXX Version gives, "creation." Ellicott comments that—

> There is something as fine in art as true in religion in this sudden burst of praise—the *evening voluntary* of grateful adoration—into which the poet bursts at the mention of the day's close. Weariness leaves the soul, as it is lifted from contemplation of man's toil to that of God. Athanasius remarked on the sense of rest and refreshment produced by this change of strain.

Thy riches, or *Thy possessions*, is a phrase implying that God? is the Creator and Owner of all He has, yet the glory of His grace is seen that He does not keep His riches to Himself, but blesses all His creatures with them. We hear and read a great deal about "the wealth of nations," but what have the nations they did not receive from our bountiful God? Every table would be bare if He withheld His hand.

This great and wide sea . . . There go the ships, 104:25, 26. The R.V. has it "yonder is the sea, great and wide." For "things creeping," or "things moving," see Genesis 1:21; and for *leviathan*, or sea-monster, see Job 41, where the crocodile is referred to. There is a Rabbinical tradition that *Leviathan* is God's plaything. As for *ships*, the Psalmist

412   Psalms: A Devotional Commentary

writes like one who had witnessed the navies of Phoenicia. Here "for once we seem to catch a breath of enthusiasm for the sea—so rare a feeling in a Jew." In the Middle Ages the explanation was given for the motions of the Leviathan that when his tail is scorched by the sun, he seeks to seize it, and labors so powerfully that the earth is shaken by his efforts.

Among the immense number and variety of Jehovah's works are the sea with its minute forms, as well as the fish and gigantic mammals and all humans who sail in ships. Did not Noah's Ark, the original ship, owe its plan of formation to God Himself? As for things innumerable in the mighty seas of the world, they sport and play in the element in which they can live joyfully and blessedly. John Milton's lines on verses 25 and 26 are worthy of repetition—

> The sounds and seas, each creek and bay,
> With fry innumerable swarm, and shoals
> Of fish that with their fins and shining scales
> Glide under the green wave, in shoals that oft
> Bank the mid sea; part single, or with mate,
> Graze the sea-weed their pasture, and through groves
> Of coral stray; or sporting with quick glance,
> Show to the sun their wav'd coats drop't with gold;
> Or, in their pearly shells at ease, attend
> Moist nutriment; or under rock their food
> In jointed armour watch: on smooth to seal
> And bended dolphins play; part huge of bulk
> Wallowing unwieldy, enormous in their gait,
> Tempest the ocean: their leviathan,
> Hugest of the living creatures, on the deep
> Stretch'd like a promontory sleep or swims,
> And seems a moving land; and at his gills
> Draws in, and at his trunk spouts out, a sea.

Thou mayest give them their meat . . . That thou givest them they gather, 104:27, 28. These verses describe *The Commissariat of Creation.* When we think of the countless millions of living things in the creeping and swimming things of the sea, the armies of birds filling the air, the vast hordes of animals and insects peopling dry land, and the 3,000 million or more humans on the earth, what a stupendous task it is to provide the necessary food for all! The great *THOU* used three times here solves the problem, and the task is easy for Him to accomplish because He is Infinite. John Burton has given us three stanzas on verses 27-32, the first of which poetically describes verses 27 and 28 of this Psalm—

These, Lord, all wait on thee, that thou their food
   may'st give them;
   Thou to their wants attendest;
   They gather what thou sendest;
Thine hand thou openest, all their need supplying
O'erlookest not the least, the greatest satisfying.

Gathering what is Divinely given may be an allusion to the history of the Manna (Exod. 16:1-16), which, although provided from Heaven had to be daily gathered by the Israelites. The Lord ever provides, but both man and beast must exert themselves and gather what He bestows. God opens His hand and satisfies the desire of every living thing, Ps. 145:16, but we have to open our hand and appropriate what He so bountifully gives. "When we see the chickens picking up the corn which the housewife scatters from her lap we have an apt illustration of the manner in which the Lord supplies the needs of all living things— He gives and they gather." How grateful we should be for our ever open-handed Provider!

Thou hidest . . . Thou takest . . . Thou sendest . . . Thou renewest, 104:29,30. What a wonderful quartet of *THOU'S* these verses present! All living things are dependent upon God's smile and favor. If he hides his face, what anguish follows. Often, hiding of the face is the figure of displeasure, but here it implies withdrawal of providential care. Then as the little sparrows cannot fall to the ground without our Father in Heaven knowing, so all life is dependent upon the will of the Eternal. The Psalmist declares that death is caused by the act of God—*Thou takest away*. Yet He is able to begin life as well as end it. "They are created." At the Flood, the world was stripped of all life apart from the occupants of the Ark, but God renewed the face of the earth. Winter brings desolation and death, but the Lord awakens the earth with the voice of spring and robes it anew with the beauty of youth. *Providence is creation continued.* Spiritually, these verses are applicable to the Holy Spirit's work within the soul.

Lady Jane Dudley, a trumpeter proclaimed as *Lady Jane, Queen of England*, who was martyred at the Stake for her Protestant faith, spent her last hours before her execution on Feb. 12, 1554, writing letters to her dear father and to friends. To "Master Harding," formerly Chaplain to the Duke of Suffolk, "but not fallen from the truth of God's most Holy Word," she wrote an appeal, couched in vehement language of reproach for his apostasy. She urged him to lay to heart "the saying of David, in the 104th Psalm, verses 29,30, where he says: 'When Thou takest away Thy Spirit, O Lord, from men, they die, and are turned again to dust; but when Thou lettest Thy breath go forth, they shall be made, and Thou shalt renew the face of the earth.' Fight manfully, come life, come death: the quarrel is God's, and undoubtedly the victory is ours." To her sister, Lady

Katharine, she sent her New Testament, urging her to "desire with David to understand the law of the Lord God."

Thou sendest forth thy spirit . . . thou renewest the face of the earth, 104:30. Wilfrid, one of those conspicuous in the establishment of the Benedictine Rule of England, committed the Psalter to memory in the version of Jerome. Although he suffered exile and imprisonment, his spiritual purpose never wavered. Visiting Northamptonshire he was seized with a fatal illness, and round the dying man gathered the whole community, chanting the Psalms which he had loved so well. As they reached the 30th verse of Psalm 104, "When Thou lettest Thy breath go forth, they shall be made," Wilfrid's breathing ceased, and his stormy life of 65 years ended in 709.

The works of the Lord are majestically simple, says Spurgeon, and are performed with royal ease—a breath creates, and its withdrawal destroys. At a Flood the World was stripped of almost all life, yet how soon the power of God refilled the desolate places. The same applies to the earth, when, after winter, the voice of Spring calls the earth to put on anew the beauty of her youth.

The glory of the Lord shall endure for ever: The Lord shall rejoice in His work, 104:31. God is looking on His finished work with delight. Where no human foot had yet trod, the Creator rejoices in the fertility of His inventiveness. Although nothing is said of a Sabbath in this Psalm, it is possible that the thought of the Sabbath hymn of praise led the writer to join man with the Divine Being in celebrating the glory and perfection of His manifold works; while he may pass away, His glory will ever remain.

When it came to the creation of man, God also rejoiced over such a masterpiece, but He came "to repent that He had made man on the earth," Genesis 6:6. When He looks down and sees His supreme work polluted by corruption, He ceases to take delight in what His power produced. May we never give Him any cause to lose His delight in us!

He looketh . . . the earth . . . trembleth: He touched the hills, and they smoke, 104: 32. The double physical action, *look* and *touch*, describes the dreadful visible judgment when it comes. When God's finger touched the mountain, it *burned with fire,* Heb. 12:18. Scientists may spend their labors investigating the natural causes of earthquakes and volcanoes, but the power of Jehovah ever remains their true and ultimate cause. Nothing in creation can withstand His looks and touches. When Henry II came to Canterbury to make expiation for the murder of Thomas 'a Becket, he kissed the stone where Becket had fallen, recited the penitential Psalm against wrath, Psalm 6, prostrated himself before the tomb of the Archbishop and then, placing his head and shoulders upon it, was scourged by the bishops, monks, and abbots who were present. The king's humiliation was so profound that the chroniclers appealed to the language of the Psalm to describe the impression it produced—"The mountain trembled at the presence of the Lord," 104:32, and left the records, "The mountain of Canterbury smoked before Him who touches the hills and they smoke." As God's creations are dependent on His will for their existence, a glance, a touch is sufficient to shake them to their foundations and consume them.

I will sing . . . I will sing praise . . . while I have my being, 104:33. The latter phrase "while I have my being," can be expressed as "in my eternity," suggesting endless progression and praise. The original reads, "I will sing unto the Lord with my *lives*"—the life that I *now* have, and the *life* that I *shall have* hereafter. Praise will be intensified and perfect when the redeemed see their Creator-Redeemer.

My meditation of him shall be sweet, 104:34. The last words ever written of the saintly Henry Martyn, dying among Mohammedans in Persia, was, "I sat in the orchard and thought with sweet comfort and peace of God, in solitude my company, my Friend and Comforter." Ancient writers point out that the first clause here can read "My meditation shall be sweet unto Him"—not only *of* but *to* Him. Certainly this agrees with a similar statement, "Let the meditation of my heart be always acceptable in thy sight," Psalm 19:14, or as the Chaldee Version has it *before Him*. God, who rejoices in His works, delights in gladness when it is mutual and reciprocal, *I will be glad in the Lord.*

Let sinners be consumed out of the earth—let the wicked be no more, 104:35.

> Sinners are the only blot upon God's fair creation in which—
> Every prospect pleases,
> And only man is vile.

While the Psalmist in holy indignation expressed the desire for God to rid the world of sinners, through the advent and death of Christ for "world of sinners lost and ruined by the Fall," the redeemed now pray that by grace sinners may be transformed into saints, and rebels fashioned into kings and priests.

This imprecation, concluding an otherwise Psalm of praise and adoration, has been variously excused. Dummelow, for instance, says that the point of the Psalmist's prayer is that evil may be banished from the world, though he identifies sin with sinners, and seems to include their destruction in his wish. But Ellicott suggests that the poet touches even a profounder truth that, in reality, the power of sin interferes with God's pleasure in His universe—an undercurrent of thought pervading Psalm 103, as well as Psalm 104. "In the former it is implied that forgiveness and restoration are requisite before the harmony of the universe can become

audible (103:20-22). These two Psalms are also closely related in
form. The harmony of Creation was soon broken by sin, and the harmony
of the song of Creation would hardly be complete, or rather would be
false and unreal, did not a discord make itself heard."

The form such a suggestion would take was conditioned by the nationality of the poet; the spirit of it brings this ancient hymn to its close into
accord with the feeling of modern literature, as reflected by Wordsworth's
well known *Verses Written in Early Spring*—

> I heard a thousand blended notes,
> While in a grove I lay reclined,
> In that sweet mood when pleasant thoughts
> Bring sad thoughts to my mind.
> To her fair works did Nature link
> The human soul that through me ran
> And much it grieved my heart to think
> What Man has made of Man.

Bless thou the Lord, O my soul. Praise ye the Lord. What a magnificent
way to conclude such a marvelous Psalm! As *Praise ye the Lord* means
HALLELUJAH, here we have its first use in the Psalter, outside of which
it is never found. Such a heavenly word closes the Psalm: for what more
remains to be said or written—HALLELUJAH! Thus, this delightful and
instructive Psalm, a lyrical poem of God's manifold works, begins as it
ends, and reminds the saints that beginning in the spirit, they should end
in the same way and not seek to be perfect in the flesh.

Psalm 105

This historical Psalm brings us to a consideration of the Longest Psalms in the Psalter. Many among those we have dealt with are comparatively short odes. But "these varying lengths of the sacred poems should teach us not to lay down any law either of brevity or prolixity in either prayer or praise. Short petitions and single verses of hymns are often the best for public occasions, but there are seasons when a whole night of wrestling or an entire day of Psalm singing will be none too long. The Spirit is ever free in His operations, and not confined within the rules of conventional propriety. The wind bloweth where it listeth, and at one time rushes in short and rapid sweeps, while at another it continues to refresh the earth hour after hour with its reviving breath."

Further, Psalm 105 is the first of a series of Confitemini Domino—"O give thanks unto the Lord," Psalms. See also Psalms 106:1; 107:1; 108:1, and Psalm 136:1. Psalm 105 and the following one forms a closely connected pair and may be looked on as by the same author. Both of these Psalms are partly wrought into the composite poem in 1 Chronicles 16, indicating that they were composed for liturgical use soon after the re-establishment of Israel in their country after the Captivity; and the hearts of God's people were specially directed to that faithfulness which could not fail, and must keep for them all that it had promised (Psalm 89:33). It was only natural, then, to recapitulate the past as an argument for a similar interposition again on their behalf or that God would be so mindful of them again. This song of David—and he wrote it (1 Chron. 16:7)—was suitable for the historic occasion for it wonderfully describes the movements of the Lord's people and His guardian care over them in every place, and all this on account of the Covenant of which the Ark, then removed, was a symbol. Psalm 104 sang the opening chapters of Genesis—Psalm 105 takes up its closing chapters and conducts us through Exodus and Numbers.

The close affinity of these two Psalms is seen not only in the fact that both begin and end in the same Hallelujah! way, but also in their continuing narrative of the history of Israel. In Psalm 105 we have God's providence and care of His people, the performance of the Covenant on His part and of His sovereign grace that ruleth over all. But in Psalm 106 we have the breaking of the Divine Covenant, and the sad story of Israel's rebellions, yet of God's over-ruling mercy. Both Psalms dwell on the predestinating will of God, and that no matter how human sin may oppose that will, it cannot make it void. Long ago God chose Israel, that she might be the object of grace, and her land the theatre of its display. When He returns to Israel, as the day of His kingdom of glory dawns, she shall have a full share—the very fullest and richest—in His blessings temporal and spiritual.

It is because of the clear and concise, and continuing history of Israel related in these two Psalms, in which the events recorded speak for themselves, we are not treating them verse by verse but simply using stories of the influence of the Psalms down the ages, and citing poetic settings of some of the historic events these kindred Psalms relate. Preachers might find the following outline of Psalm 105 serviceable as a starting point for an exposition of it—

1.   The extolling of Jehovah in joyful praise, 1-7.
2.   The Divine care of Israel during her infancy as a nation, 8-15.
3.   The journey of Jacob and his family into Egypt, 16-23.
4.   The putting forth of the Lord's arm in great wonders, 24-38.
5.   The marvelous journey through the wilderness into Canaan, 39-45.

Verse 1. Richard Baxter, eloquent preacher and voluminous theological writer, was one of the first and greatest of Nonconformist divines. By his personal holiness, patience during lifelong pains of disease and of almost incessant persecution because of his adherence to the faith, he so transformed Kidderminster, where he died in 1692, that "on the Lord's Day there was no disorder to be seen in the streets; but you might hear a hundred families singing Psalms and repeating sermons as you passed by the people." The Psalms were Baxter's daily support, and inscribed upon the pulpit he once occupied are the words, "Call upon his name, and declare his works among the people," 105:1. This verse, which is found word for word in Isaiah 12:4, is apparently one of the recognized doxologies of the Hebrew Church. "Call upon His name," implies call with, or glory in, His name, 105:3. The name by which He loves to be called is Jehovah, and He desires His people to proclaim all His titles and fill the world with His renown.

Verse 2. Sing . . . Talk. In the first five verses of the Psalm we have a series of holy exercises: "Give thanks"—"Call upon His name"—"Make known"—"Sing"—"Talk"—"Glory"—"Rejoice"—"Seek"—"Remember." Men love to speak of marvels, and no one would be blamed as a *Mr. Talkative* if his constant theme was the catalogue of God's amazing works. *Sing—Talk.* Music and conversation are two things that can produce much good or a great deal of harm. But when we *sing to God* and *talk to God,* we enjoy a heaven upon earth. Is He our constant Table Talk?

Verse 3. "Glory . . . Rejoice." Idolaters may well be ashamed of the actions attributed to their fancied deities, their names are foul with lust and red with blood, says Spurgeon, but Jehovah is wholly glorious; every deed of His will bear the strictest scrutiny, His name is holy, His character is holy. This is why our hearts rejoice as we seek Him. What worldly songs are fuller of real mirth than what the world slightingly calls *Psalm-singing*? What glory and joy are in His holy name! Is this not why we sing?—

> And those who find Thee find a bliss,
> Nor tongue nor pen can show:
> The love of Jesus what it is,
> None but His loved ones know.

Remember, 105:5. It was Sir James Barrie who used the sentence in a Rectoral address, "God gave us memory that we might have roses in December." The famous Gipsy Smith once wrote in an autograph book of mine, "Remembrance is a Paradise from which we need not be driven." Memory is never better employed than when it recollects all the marvelous work God has accomplished, and such remembrance strengthens faith, generates gratitude, and makes love intense.

The word which he commanded to a thousand generations, 105:8. Here the Divine promise is said to be commanded or vested with all the authority of a law. This was a proclamation from a Sovereign, the decree of an Emperor, whose laws shall stand fast in every jot and tittle though heaven and earth shall pass away.

When they were but a few men in number; yea, very few, 105:11,12. God is not always on the side of big battalions. One with Him is ever in the majority. The smallness of a church and the poverty of its members are no barriers to the possession of Divine resources. The Apostles were few and feeble as they went out to preach the Gospel of redeeming grace, yet by God's power they turned the world upside down.

He reproved kings for their sakes, 105:14. The greatest kings the world has known have been slow to recognize that they are very second-rate persons with God in comparison with His chosen servants. Thus Pharaoh and Abimelech were both made to respect the singular strangers who had come to sojourn in their land. The mightiest ruler must wait his permission before he can place a finger on a child of God. In Him, all are secure, for they cannot be touched without Divine sufferance. Thomas Goodwin in his *Works*, writing on verses 14 and 15 of this Psalm, condenses the history of the world to show that those nations which have persecuted and afflicted the people of God have invariably been broken in pieces.

He was laid in iron, 105:18. The Prayer Book Version has it, "The iron entered into his soul," a translation that has established itself so firmly among expressive proverbial sayings. Symachus expressed it, "His soul came into iron," and the LXX Version has, "His soul passed through iron." The Vulgate Version follows the Targum by giving us, "The iron passed through his soul." Certainly, Joseph was imprisoned in irons, and imprisonment is one of the most severe trials of the soul which suffers more than the body. But the iron fetters of Joseph prepared him to wear chains of gold, and made his feet ready to stand in high places. He did not sink under his sufferings but came out of his prison to a palace.

The word of the Lord tried him, 105:19. God often allows His promises to try us, that He may accomplish His own purposes of discipline. Men of genius often stand in the front of their age with thoughts and schemes the world cannot understand; and such items are dreams until suffering and scorn try these men, and they are awakened into effort to realize such dreams. The great idea of an undiscovered land across the wastes of the Atlantic Ocean smote the soul of Columbus; but it remained a dreamy faith until by opposition and ridicule he was tempted to regard it as a dream. Then came the heroic endeavor, and the New World was found.

Egypt . . . the land of Ham, 105:23. Students of ancient history have clearly established that the Egyptians were a branch of the race of Ham, thereby confirming the statements of the Book of Genesis. These people came from Asia through the desert of Syria to settle in the valley of the Nile.

He sent darkness, and made it dark, 105:28. One translator, by a very slight change, makes this verse to read, "He sent darkness, and darkened them, that they might not discern his tokens." Thus the plague of darkness, by such a change, is made to symbolize the moral blindness displayed by the Egyptians. That there was an awful significance in this plague of darkness is proven by the fact that a leading object of devotion among Egyptians was the sun, given the name *Osiris*. The very name Pharaoh means, not *king*, but also *sun*, characterizing the king himself as the representative of the sun and entitled in a way to divine honors. When the light of the sun was withheld, Egyptian sun-worship was covered with shame and confusion.

He turned their waters into blood, 105:29. By this miraculous change of water into blood, God rebuked, in a most practical way, the superstitions of the Egyptians who deemed the Nile a sacred and beautiful river, birthplace of their gods, center of their devotion and benefactor and preserver of their country. According to Pliny, "the Nile was the only source from whence the Egyptians obtained water for drinking." To witness this sweet and refreshing water turned to blood must have turned their love of the water into an abomination. "Slew their fish." The quantity of fish in Egypt was a great boon to the poor classes, and when the Nile overflowed the inhabitants of the inland villages benefitted by the annual gift of fish from the river, as did the land by the fertilizing mud deposited upon it.

Brought forth frogs in abundance, 105:30. At the very commencement of the mythology of ancient Egypt, we have mention of the creation of a goddess, *Ranipula*, meaning, "Driver away of frogs." It is difficult for us in the Western World to form a tolerable idea of this most loathsome plague of frogs finding their way into "the houses, bed-chambers, beds, and kneading-troughs" of the Egyptians. In an ordinary rainy season, myriads send forth their constant croak in every direction, causing inhabitants much irritation, and ready to exclaim—

> Croak, croak! Indeed I shall choke
> If you pester and bore my ears any more
> With your croak, croak, croak!

What must a plague of them have been like when the God of Nature availed to Himself to vindicate His power before Pharaoh and before Egypt? The Lord smote all the land, even the palace as well as the hovel of the poor with such a disaster, to prove that kings are no more than other men with God. Pharaoh was a heartless king, and if his palace had been spared the plague, the plight of his people would not have disturbed him very much.

Many sorts of flies, 105:31. The term used here serves to denote a kind of insect that alights on the skin or leaves of plants, by its bite inflicting pain in the one case, and causing destruction in the other. Long ago, Philo described the dog-fly or gad-fly as a grievous pest of Egypt. Travelers tell us that the swarms of flies in Egypt are usually numerous, and excessively annoying, producing much pain when they alight on the moist part of the eyelids and nostrils. Gnats and mosquitos are also abundant and virulent in Egypt, and a plague of them, such as God alone was to send, must have caused immense suffering and desolation.

He gave them hail for rain, 105:32. What a disastrous substitute this must have proved for the people and their land! Ordinarily, Egypt never receives the amount of rain that the people in Europe are used to. Thus, those heavy, destructive hailstones, accompanied by hurricanes and thunderstorms must have been as awesome as destructive. In general history books there are extraordinary reports of the magnitude of hailstones. For instance, there is the mention of a hailstorm during the reign of Charlemagne, in which hailstones fell which measured 15 feet in length by 6 feet in breadth, and 11 feet in thickness. This may sound like a fable, but several countries have historical accounts of hailstones having occurred in which stones from half to three-quarters of a pound have fallen. As *God* smote Egypt with hail, it must have been of the most destructive kind to break every tree of the field.

Locusts . . . Caterpillars . . . without number, 105:34,35. What a lover of variety God is! After the devastating hail from Heaven, there came the unnumbered hosts of locusts and caterpillars from earth as a further evidence of His judicial power. Matthew Henry comments "that God did not bring the same plague twice, but where there was occasion for another, it was still a new one; for He has many arrows in His quiver." Some idea of this horrible plague of locusts can be gathered from Major Moore's description of a swarm of these pests he witnessed in India in 1825. "The column occupied a space of 40 English square miles, contained at least 40 millions of locusts in one line, and cast a long shadow on the earth. The column they composed extended many miles, and were so compact when it was on wing, that like an eclipse, it completely hid the sun, so that no shadow was cast by any object." Robert Southey, religious poet of the early 18th century, gave us this lyrical portrayal of an advance of the numberless host of locusts upon Egypt—

> Onward they came a dark continuous cloud
>   Of congregated myriads numberless;
> The rushing of whose wings was as the sound
>   Of some broad river, headlong in its course,
> Plunged from a mountain summit; or the roar
>   Of a wild ocean in the autumnal storm,
>   Shattering its billows on a shore of rocks,
> Onward they came, the winds impelled them on.

He spread a cloud . . . fire to give light, 105:39. It is said that in the army of Alexander the Great, marches were begun by a great beacon being set up on a pole as a signal from headquarters, so that "the fire was seen at night, the smoke in the daytime"; and this plan was continued for many years among the caravans of Arabia. It is probable enough in that unchanging land that such may have been the custom at the time of the Exodus, and that God taught the people by parable in this wise, as well as by the fact that He was their true leader and Heaven the general pavilion, whence the order of the march was enjoined. All of us are familiar with Sir Walter Scott's wonderful poem on this 39th verse which we quote in full—

> When Israel of the Lord, beloved,
>   Out of the land of bondage came,
> Her father's God before her moved,
>   An awful guide in smoke and flame.
>
> By day, along the astonished lands,
>   The cloudy pillar glided slow;
> By night, Arabia's crimson sands
>   Returned the fiery column's glow.
>
> Then rose the choral hymn of praise,
>   And trump and timbrel answered keen,

> And Zion's daughters poured their lays,
>> With priest's and warrior voice between
>
> But present still, though now unseen,
>> When brightly shines the prosperous clay,
> Be thoughts of Thee a cloudy screen
>> To temper the deceitful ray.
>
> And oh, when stoop on Judah's path,
>> In shoal and storm, the frequent night,
> Be Thou—long-suffering, slow to wrath—
>> A burning and a shining light.

He brought forth quails . . . He . . . He . . . He, 105:40-45. These concluding verses express the bountiful provision of God for His people. Meat, Bread, and Water were abundantly bestowed upon His own He brought forth with joy out of their bondage. The term *quail* is from a Hebrew root signifying "to be fat," and is descriptive of the round, plump form and fat flesh of the quail which the Israelites caught and "spread out" or dried in the sun. Sir Philip Sidney, poet of the 15th century, gave the world the following stanza on verses 40-52 of this inspiring Psalm—

> Brought from his store, at sute of Israel,
>> Quailes, in whole heavies each remove pursue;
> Himself from skies their hunger to repell.
>> Candies the grasse, with sweet congealed dew.
> His woundes the rock, the rock doth wounded, swell;
>> Swelling affordes new streames to channells new,
> All for God's mindful will can not be dryven,
>> From sacred word once to his Abraham given.

He brought forth not only quails, but "His people with joy." All benefits mentioned in this Psalm as being bestowed on Israel are shadows of spiritual blessings for the Church today. Redeemer—enriched—restored—satisfied with heavenly bread—drinking of the spiritual rock—made to sit in heavenly places. What can we desire more? May grace be ours not to rebel against such a bountiful Provider.

Psalm 106

This further Hallelujah! Psalm is actually a continuation of the previous historical record of Israel, the difference being that in Psalm 105 we have the revelation of God's providence and care of His people, whereas in this Psalm we have the reminder of Israel's rebellions and also of God's mercy. The previous Psalm is a history of Divine provision—Psalm 106, a history of human provocation with its main character being the humble confession of same. Dr. F. B. Meyer observes that "if, as is supposed, Psalm 106 dates from the Captivity, it is in harmony with the confessions of Daniel & Nehemiah; and it tends to show that the sharp discipline had done its work, and that God was about to restore His people to the land of their fathers." Agreeing with this sentiment, Dummelow remarks that, "as Psalm 105 gives thanks for God's goodness, so Psalm 106 confesses Israel's sin and acknowledges God's mercy, both being illustrated in a historical retrospect from the deliverance from Egypt down to the return from Captivity—see Psalm 78, Ezekiel 20."

The first of the series of Hallelujah! Psalms, the first verse begins with a Hallelujah! and the last verse ends with a Hallelujah! Psalm 106 is closely related to these long liturgical confessions of national sins which are distinctly enjoined in Deut. 26, where the type form of them is given, and of which the completest specimen is retained in Nehemiah 9. A sinning people had to manifest sincere penitence from which alone a deep reformation and restoration of the nation could be expected. Spurgeon says that we can entitle this Psalm, *A National Confession*, seeing that Israel's history is here written with the view of showing human sin, even as the preceding Psalm was composed to magnify Divine goodness. "Psalm 106 includes an acknowledgement of the transgressions of Israel in Egypt, in the Wilderness, and in Canaan, with devout petitions for forgiveness such as rendered the Psalm suitable for use in all succeeding generations, and especially in times of national captivity."

As the language of this Psalm speaks for itself, we shall confine our survey of it, as we did in the previous Psalm, to ancient, historical associations and poetic presentations of some of its verses. For those wishing to expound the Psalm in pulpit or Bible-class, the following outline may serve as a guide:

1. An introduction of inimitable sweetness, in which praise and prayer are blended together, 1-5.

424

2. A confession covering the sins of Israel—
   * In Egypt, 6-12.
   * In the Wilderness, 13-33.
   * In Canaan, 34-43.
3. A merciful task to gather Israel from among the nations, 44-46.
4. Closing prayer and doxology, 47, 48.

Verses 1-5. These introductory thanksgivings and supplications, though occurring first in the Psalm, were doubtless the result of the contemplations succeeding them, and may thus be viewed not only as the *preface*, but also as the *moral* of the whole sacred song. These verses also make it evident that while the writer spoke as one of a community, and for the community, he still felt his *personal* relation to Jehovah—"Remember *me*, O Lord . . . that *I* . . . that *I* . . . that *I*."

Verse 1. This formula of praise, the first appearance of which cannot be fully ascertained, was used as a choral refrain in the Jewish Church and occupies a similar position to *Gloria Patri* in Christian worship. It was used at the dedication of the second Temple, Ezra 3:11, and was more generally used after the Captivity. It was also in use during the Maccabaean Period, 1 Macc. 4:24.

Verse 3. It was by a Psalm that St. Louis of France regulated his life. Before taking the seat of judgment he was wont to repeat the words: "Blessed are they that always keep judgment, and do righteousness." If, through inadvertency, he had granted an unjust suit, corrected by the Psalmist's words, he had better thoughts and gave judgment quite contrary.

O visit me with thy salvation, 106: 4. Hugo took this *visit* of God as that of a physician of whom healing of the eyes is sought, because it is immediately added, "That I may see." There is an ancient Jewish interpretation which is noteworthy, namely that the petition of this verse is for a share in the resurrection in the days of the Messiah in order to see His wonderful restoration of His suffering people.

Sinned . . . committed iniquity . . . done wickedly, 106: 5. The Rabbis of old said that there are three kinds and degrees of sin, here set down in an ascending scale; *against one's self—against one's neighbor—against God*; or sins of ignorance, sins of conscious deliberation, sins of pride and wickedness.

We . . . we . . . we, 106:6. Ellicott says that "regard must be paid to the fact that the confession includes the speaker and his generation, as well as the ancestors of the race. The Psalm proceeds from the period of the Captivity, when the national conscience, or at all events that of the nobler part of the nation, was thoroughly alive to the sinfulness of idolatry."

*At the sea, even at the Red Se*a, 106:7. This sea was only *called* Red, but the sins of Israel were scarlet in reality; it was also known as the "sea of weeds," but far worse weeds grew in the hearts of God's people. Pliny states that it is called the Red Sea from King Erythras, or from the reflection of a red color by the sun, or from the sand and its ground, or from the nature of the water. Provocation cannot shut men out of the love. There is ever a *Nevertheless*, Neh. 9:31; Ps. 73:23; 89:33. We have another *Nevertheless* in verse 44 of this Psalm.

He rebuked the Red Sea also, and it was dried up, 106:9. This is a poetical expression signifying that the Sea retired at God's command, just as a slave would fly from his master's presence on being severely rebuked. The sea sweetly obeyed its Creator's will.

They believed . . . They sang, 106:12. But though Israel "sang His praise" they soon "forgot His works." Between Israel's singing and sinning there was scarcely a step. Their song was good while it lasted, but it was no sooner begun than over. This verse is an epitome of Exod. 14:31 and 15.

Verses 13-33. This portion covers the desert wanderings, beginning with the discontented spirit mentioned in Exod. 15:23.

Verses 16-18. When the poet composed these verses he must have had Numbers 16 and 17 in his mind. What a sad and tragic story these chapters record! Joseph Hall wrote that "there are two sorts of traitors; the earth swallowed the one, and the fire the other. All the elements agree to serve the vengeance of their Maker. Nadab and Abihu brought fit persons, but unfit fire, to God; these Levites bring the right fire, but unwarranted persons, before Him: fire from God consumes them both. It is a dangerous thing to usurp sacred functions. The ministry will not grace the man; he may disgrace the ministry." God has more than one arrow in His quiver, the fire can consume those whom the earthquake spares.

They made a calf, 106:19. Bishop Thomas Westfield of Bristow in the 16th century, writing on this verse said: "He that would take heed of idolatry, let him take heed of Egypt; the very air of Egypt is infectious in this kind. Israel had seen the worship of a young bullock in Egypt, and they must have a bullock . . . The local seat of Antichrist is called by three names—*Egypt*, in regard to *idolatry*, Rev. 2:8—*Sodom*, in regard to her *filthiness*, Rev. 2:8—*Babylon*, in several places, in regard to her cruelty."

As an ox that eateth grass, 106:20. The Egyptians, when they consulted *APIS*, presented a bottle of hay or grass, and if the Ox received it, they expected prosperity.

Before him in the breach, 106:23. The metaphor used here to describe how Moses stood in the gap and diverted the wrath of God is taken from a city which is besieged, and in the walls of which the enemy have made a *breach* and is just entering it, to destroy it, unless he is driven back by some valiant warrior. It was thus that Moses stood "in the breach," and averted Divine judgment upon the Israelites. See Exod. 32.

They believed not his word, 106:24. This was Israel's key sin—the key which turned the lock against them. "They could not enter in because of unbelief." We know from Bunyan's *Pilgrim's Progress* that "when pilgrims to the Celestial City began to doubt the Lord of the way, they soon came to think little of the rest of the journey's end, and this is the surest way to make them bad travellers. Israel's unbelief demanded spies to see the land; the report of those spies was of a mingled character, and so a fresh crop of unbelief sprang up, with consequences most deplorable." Illustrating the phrase, "They despised the pleasant land," old Thomas Watson recorded reading of certain Spaniards in his day that lived near a place where there was a great store of fish, yet they were so lazy that they would not put themselves about to catch them, preferring to buy the fish of their neighbors. "Such a sinful stupidity and sloth," says Watson, "is upon the most, though Christ be near them, though salvation is offered in the Gospel, yet they will not work out salvation."

Verses 24-27. In this section we have a report of the rebellion that followed the observation the spies brought back.

They ate the sacrifices of the dead, 106:28. That is, the sacrifices of a *dead* divinity. The word used in the Hebrew signifies *dead men*; for the idols of the heathen were generally *men*—warriors, kings or lawgivers—who had been deified after death; though many of them had been execrated during their life. Virgil's lines on eating the sacrifices of the dead are most expressive—

> His obsequies to Polydorus paying
> A tomb we raise, and altars to the dead
> With dark blue fillets and black cypress bind
> Our dames with hair dishevell'd stand to mourn;
> Warm frothy bowls of milk and sacred blood
> We offer in his grave the spirit lay,
> Call him aloud, and bid our last farewell.

Verses 32, 33. Marginal references indicate these verses are related to the insurrection against Moses and Aaron at Meribah Kadesh, entailing on the Lawgiver the forfeiture for himself of entering into Canaan.

They provoked his spirit, 106:33. This historical reference is capable of a double interpretation. The LXX and Vulgate Versions have "they embittered his (Moses) spirit," and this would be the natural interpretation of the phrase. Yet it could be used to refer the temper of the people towards God, "they rebelled against His Spirit."

Verse 34-39. In this portion of the Psalm we have the sad account of Israel's national sin following her settlement in Canaan, namely, identification with the idolatry and idolatrous practices of the land of promise. "They served their idols." But fascinated by the charms of Canaanitish idolatry, Israel came to experience the misery it brought upon its votaries. Sin is like birdlime, to touch it is to be taken by it. Samson laid his head in the Philistine woman's lap, but ere long he woke up shorn of his strength.

They shed innocent blood, 106:38. Human sacrifice, and especially that of *children*, was a Canaanite practice. It seems to have been inherent in Phoenician custom, for Carthage was, two centuries after Christ, notorious for the same foul deed. The tragedy was that Israel sank so low as to sacrifice the blood of her sons and daughters.

Many times did he deliver them, 106:43. These deliverances occupy the historical accounts found in the Books of Judges and the Kings. In fact, the section, verses 40-43, "having made review of the sinful past the poet briefly but impressively describes the punishment which once and again had fallen upon the nation. But as his purpose is to make the generation look on the Captivity as a supreme instance of this punishment, and to seek for deliverance by repentance, he mentions only the judgments inflicted by foreign foes."

Verses 40, 41. Spurgeon says of these verses that the feeling described in them is like to that of a husband who still loves his guilty wife, and yet when he thinks of her lewdness feels his whole nature rising in righteous anger at her so that the very sight of her afflicts his soul. How far the divine wrath can burn against those whom he yet loves in his heart it is hard to say, but certainly Israel pushed the experiment to the extreme.

He made them also to be pitied, 106:46. This phrase literally means, "Gave them for companions," and is also found in Solomon's prayer, 1 Kings 8:50. See also Dan. 1:9. Evidently this verse implies the return from the Captivity, although it would seem from the closing verses of this Psalm written after the first return from exile had taken place, that many Israelites were still scattered among the nations. See particularly verse 47.

Blessed be the Lord . . . Amen. Hallelujah, 106:48. What a wonderful ending to such a sad story of Israel's rebellions. Such a doxology is almost identical with that found in 1 Chron. 16:36—a passage proving that the direction to guide the people in their worship was carried out. The God we raise our Hallelujahs to is the Eternal One, "the Lord God of Israel from everlasting to everlasting." With this magnificent ascription the Fourth Book of Psalms is closed. As already hinted, this Psalm begins and ends with a *Hallelujah!* and as Spurgeon points out "the space in between these two descriptions of praise is filled up with the mournful details of Israel's sin, and the extraordinary patience of God; and truly we do well to bless the Lord both at the beginning and the end of our meditations when sin and grace are the themes." As the first and last two verses are to be found in that sacred song which David delivered to Asaph when he brought up the Ark of the Lord, the probability is that the sweet Psalmist was the composer of this 106th Psalm, extolling the infinite patience of the Most High with His sinning people.

Psalm 107

This highly poetical Psalm, if viewed merely as a gifted poet's composition, would be hard to find its superior among human productions. The Bards of the Bible hold no second place among the sons of song. The Psalm begins with the goodness of the Lord and ends with His lovingkindness, and in between magnifies God's manifold providence. The main theme of the Psalm is *Thanksgiving* and the motives for it. Temporal favors are but types and shadows of spiritual blessings. Dr. George Smith, in his biography of the life of the distinguished missionary Dr. Alexander Duff, records that on his first voyage to India, in 1836, the vessel was wrecked amid breakers off the coast of South Africa. Miraculously, the passengers reached a small island, with nothing left to them but life. A sailor, walking along the beach, noticed an object cast ashore. Going up to it, he found it was a quarto copy of Bagster's Bible, and a Scottish Psalm Book, badly shattered, but with Dr. Duff's name on both. Taking his find to the hovel where the passengers had sought shelter, the sailor presented the Bible and Book to the owner. Receiving them, the stranded company knelt down, and spreading the Books on the white bleached sand, Dr. Duff read Psalm 107. After reading the four deliverances among them of the sailors in the storm, the spared travelers thanked God and took courage. Of the 800 volumes Dr. Duff had taken with him to found a library in India, only his Bible and Psalm Book remained.

From the exhortation about exalting God in the congregation, and praising Him in the assembling of the elders, verse 32, it would seem as if this Psalm was composed to be sung at religious services in which joy was the keynote. As for the phrase, "sacrifice the sacrifices of thanksgiving," verse 22, some would suggest that the Psalm was also connected with the offering of sacrifices and thank-offerings. While it is felt that it was written for the first celebration of the Feast of Tabernacles after Israel's return from Exile, when the people gathered as one man at Jerusalem, and sacrifices were offered, Ezra 3:1-3, yet there are passages that appear to present a general picture or group of pictures of the vicissitudes of human life and the interposition of Divine Providence. Vivid pictures, notably the sea-piece (23-32), are not directly historical. Perhaps the Psalm lies intermediate between the historical and general, or appropriate to the whole Church, and to each child of God, after experiencing some marked Divine interposition or deliverance. As Ellicott summarizes the question—

> While, therefore, the Psalm may properly be regarded as a lyric embodiment of the lessons of the Captivity, it applies these lessons to the human lot generally, and travels over the whole experience of human life for the pictures under which it presents them. The fortunes of his own race were uppermost in the Psalmist's mind, but the perils depicted are typical of the straits into which men of all lands and all times are driven; and he had learnt that the goodness and wisdom which at the cry of prayer came to extricate and save are not confined to one race, but are universal and continuous.

Without doubt, this is a choice song for the redeemed of the Lord in any age, and all ages to honor and glorify Him with. It will be noted that with Psalm 107, we have Book 5 of the Psalter, covering the remaining Psalms 107 to 150, and that, in the main the contents of these last Psalms are a surer guide to the period to which they belong than is the case in the previous 4 Books, seeing many of them give either direct references or unmistakable hints regarding experiences of the Exile or the Return. This last Book with its 43 Psalms is liturgical in character, many of them having been prepared for public use, e.g. Psalm 115:9-18; 116:12-19. Fifteen of these Psalms bear the title—OF DAVID, and emphasize the choice of *Jehovah* as the Divine name, which occurs 236 times, with *Elohim* appearing only 7 times.

Here, as in the two previous Psalms, the language is so clear and expressive that it speaks for itself and we are again confining our survey of Psalm 107 to historical, biographical, or poetical associations of some of its verses. As for an outline of the Psalm with its illustrations of the lovingkindness of the Lord, the following features are clearly evident—

1. The people are exhorted to praise God for all His works, 1-3.
2. The people in their wilderness caravans, 4-9.
3. The people in their prison-captivity, 10-16.
4. The people in their sickness, 17-22.
5. The people in the vicissitudes of sea-going, 23-32.
6. The people received and restored, 33-42.

The Psalm has *four cries* in *fourfold trouble*, 6, 13, 19, 28, and the *Oh!* refrain at intervals, 8, 15, 21, 31. In each of these sections we have a similarity of expression—first of all trouble—cry for help—gracious deliverance—exhortation to declare gratitude for a token of lovingkindness and goodness referenced.

Verses 1, 2. After opening with the oft-repeated choral refrain, which was used as a formula of praise in the Jewish church, the writer voices the

necessity of the redeemed of the Lord to *say so*. While this second verse
has a particular reference to Israel redeemed from the Egyptian bondage,
all the *redeemed* by the precious blood of Jesus should be members of this
choral *Say so* choir. Already the people had before them in the Law
Moses had given them, a clear and full idea of what they were to understand by the word *Gal*, rendered "Redeemed." Same as any person either
sold as a slave or carried away as a captive, then his kinsman who was
nearest to him in blood-relationship, had the right and equity of redemption. But no other person could redeem, or buy back, the captive, and such
a kinsman was called "the redeemer," after he had paid the price for which
his relation was sold to be a slave, or paid the ransom for which he was
led captive. The central message of the Gospel is that Jesus gave His life
as a ransom to deliver sin-bound souls from satanic captivity, and from
the power of the archenemy of God and man. For those who are redeemed
it is not enough to think of His mercy, but to *say so*.

He gathered them out of the lands, 107:3. Evidently this is a direct
reference to Israel's return from Captivity, see Isa. 43:5, 6; 56:8.
Mention of the *West* directs our thoughts to Egypt, and to the remembrance of the bondage and labors of ancestors of the present Israelites
in Egypt. *Gathered* is the usual prophetic word for Israel's Restoration,
see margin, also Isa. 49:12. The same word is used of the saints of God
who are to be *gathered* unto the Redeemer when He returns to gather
His own out of every quarter of the world (Rev. 7:1; 14:6; Matt. 24:31;
25:32).

In a solitary way, 107:4. Historically, this verse may refer to wanderings on the way to Egypt, but the reference to a "city of habitation,"
verse 7, points rather to the return from Babylon to Jerusalem. "Solitary
way," is better given as in "a desert track" of which Shelley's lines are certainly true—

> Boundless and bare
> The lone and level sands stretch far away.

But whether the verse represents an historical fact, or merely draws an
imaginary picture, the description of the dangers of Eastern travel is equally clear and distinct. Not only Israel, but travelers down the ages have
proved that the loneliness of a desert has a most depressing influence upon
them if lost in the waste, "boundless and bare" with solitude becoming a
great intensifier of misery. Of course, Israel had no city to dwell in for the
simple reason there was no city around in burning sand of the wilderness.

In their solitary way through the world, believers are spiritual travelers, finding no settlement, rest, joy, and comfort but in Christ through
whom they have a continuing city yet to come, Heb. 13:14. As they journey over the path of trial here below, God's children may often feel lonely,

yet they are never alone for He has promised never to leave them until they reach the Celestial City.

Then they cried unto the Lord in their trouble, 107:6. Hungry and thirsty, with their soul fainting within them, as they painfully traveled over the desert track, the people were indeed in trouble and distress. All they could do was to cry as they did four times, to the only One Who could help them—*to the Lord*. It is only in extremity that some are forced to cry. Happy are those who have learned how to pray *always*. The moment the cries reached the ear of God, help was given and the people found themselves delivered out of their distresses. They cried, not *before* or *after* their trouble but *in* the midst of it. When their sore trouble was wrapped around their head, as the weeds were wrapped around the head of Jonah, then they looked up to Heaven, and found themselves miraculously saved.

Verses 8, 15, 21, 31. This repeated exclamation has often escaped the hearts of those experiencing some form of Divine deliverance. During his fight at Nazeby, Oliver Cromwell had seen "the enemy draw up and march in gallant order towards us, and we, a company of poor, ignorant men at pains to order our battle." Yet, "he smiled out to God in praises, in assurance of victory, because God would, by things that are not, bring to naught things that are. Of which I have great assurance; and God did it. Oh that men would therefore praise the Lord, and declare the wonders that He doeth for the children of men!" Psalm 107:8.

Such as sit in darkness and in the shadow of death, 107:10. The prophets use *darkness* as a common synonym for a "dungeon." See Isa. 42:7; 49:9; Micah 7:8. Ellicott informs us that this description is applicable to prisons in all ages but the most modern being specially suitable for those of the ancients, who admitted no light at all, as, for instance, the Mamertine Prison at Rome. The LXX Version gives us, "in poverty and in iron," for "affliction and iron." Only those who have been doubly fettered in heart and body know the pain of such affliction. Perhaps those of us who live in a free society would value our liberty more if we knew by experience what manacles and fetters mean. Are we not bidden to remember those who are in bonds as being bound with them?

He brought down . . . they fell down, 107:12. *Brought down* literally means, "made them bend," and *fell down*, "stumbled." The root of these phrases describes a process of *weakening* by *compressing the wings* or shrinking the fingers, and is properly applied to *birds*, which, when their wings are compressed are obliged to fall to the ground, or to men, who by shrivelling up with their fingers lose the power of working—when the same is transferred to *oppressions* or *depressions* of any kind. "The whole verse presents a picture of men staggering under forced labor which was the usual fate of captives under the great Oriental monarchies." See 2 Thess. 3:2.

God weakened and curbed those towering passions by which the people vainly vaunted themselves above the law and worship of God, until they bowed and submitted themselves to Him Who knows how to bring the mighty, in their own estimation, down from their high seat, and cause them to cast themselves prostrate at His feet. It is only then, when they realize they are nothing and have nothing apart from Him Who alone is their Helper, "Then they cried unto the Lord," verse 13—it is only when their hearts are brought low, and hopes were dead that they sought the Lord, Who speedily relieved them.

He hath broken the gates of brass, and cut the bars of iron in sunder, 107:16. In his unconverted days when fears disquieted him, John Bunyan, who had a heart aflame to be converted, yet found that his unbelief set its shoulder to the door to keep out his Lord. Then, with many a bitter sigh, he would cry, "Good Lord, break it open: Lord, break these gates of brass and cut these bars of iron asunder," Psalm 107:16. Ere long, Bunyan came to experience that he was not beyond the pale of Divine mercy.

Verses 17-22. While this section of verses—10-16—is taken up with the plight, pain, and plea of the prisoners, verses 17-22 are given over to the sick—physically and spiritually—and to their Divine healing.

He sent . . . healed . . . delivered, 107:20. As in *history*, Psalm 105:19—in the natural world, Psalm 147:18, God's Word is His messenger, so here the same Word healed and delivered those who drew near to the gates of death. See Isa. 55:10, 11. *Destructions* is better expressed as "pits," and is a metaphorical allusion to the *depths* of suffering, or literally, of the *graves* of sufferers. One of the Divine names is *Jehovah-rophi*—"The Lord that healeth thee," Exod. 15:26.

While he was preaching in Kyle, word was brought to George Wishart, the renowned Scottish Reformer, of the plague of pestilence that had broken out in Dundee. Hastening to the plague-swept city, Wishart took up his position at West Port, where those that were whole sat or stood within, and the sick and suspected were without the Port. Standing, as it were, between life and death, Wishart preached to the people from this verse, "He sent His Word, and healed them." Such was the effect of his message that the people judged them more happy that should depart as the result of the plague, than such as should remain behind. Dundee became one of the foremost towns in the Cause of the Reformation. Not long after his Dundee visit, Wishart suffered at the stake in St. Andrews.

They that go down to the sea in ships, 107:23. In this sea-section, verses 22-32, the Psalmist gives us a most vivid description of a storm at sea. "The great waters" was the way the Mediterranean appeared to David and his countrymen, and they viewed those who had business upon it, enduring its storms as brave men and worthy of admiration. These were the men who witnessed God's wonders in the deep. Their voyages were looked on as descending into an abyss *"going down* to the sea in ships." Now, our more fearless sailors speak of "the high seas." As navigation was little practiced among the Israelites, mariners were invested with a high degree of mystery, with their craft being thought singularly daring and perilous.

When the waves were whipped up into fury by some hidden force and leapt toward the sky, and those in ships could not keep their feet, but staggered like drunken men, were at their wits' end after using every expedient then known to navigation to keep afloat, in their last resort they cried unto the Lord. Prayer is always good in a storm. Though at their wits' end, verse 27,—The R.V. margin has it "all their wisdom is swallowed up"—those storm-tossed sailors had wit enough to pray—their heart was melted, but it ran out in cries for Divine help, and there came the Almighty fiat, as at Creation, "He spake and it was done." God spoke, and the turbulent waves became tranquil.

In this portion of the Psalm, we have the very soul of poetry, with the utmost simplicity of diction being employed to convey the grandest thoughts. No language is more sublime than that the poet used in this Psalm to describe a storm at sea. Luiz de Cameous, poet of the 15th century, left us the following portrayal of a storm in *The Lusiad*—

> While thus our keels still onward boldly strayed—
> Now tossed by tempest, now by calms delayed;
> To tell the terrors of the deep untried,
> What toils we suffered, and what storms defied;
> What rattling deluges the black clouds poured,
> What dreary weeks of solid darkness low'red;
> What mountain surges mountain surges lashed,
> What sudden hurricanes the canvas dashed:
> What bursting lightnings, with incessant flare,
> Kindled in one wide flame the burning air;
> What roaring thunders bellowed o'er our head,
> And seemed to shake the reeling ocean's bed:
> To tell each horror in the deep revealed,
> Would ask an iron throat with tenfold vigour steeled.
> Those dreadful wonders of the deep I saw,
> Which fill the sailor's breast with sacred awe;
> And what the sages, of their learning vain,
> Esteemed the phantoms of a dreamful brain.

Perhaps the verse of Virgil, the Roman poet, was colored by the Psalmist's portrayal of the waves mounting up to heaven—

> To larboard all their oars and canvas bend;
> We on a ridge of waters to the sky

>Are lifted, down to Erebus again
>Sink with the falling wave; thrice howl'd the rocks
>Within their stony caverns, thrice we saw
>The splash'd-up foam upon the lights of heaven.

Then they cry unto the Lord, 107:28. Emphasis here is on *then*. Afflicted, the distressed at sea *cry*, and if not then, then never. Hence the proverb, "He that cannot pray, let him go to sea and learn." Ovid, Roman poet, around the time of Christ, left us the prayer—"Gods of the sea and skies—for what resource have I but prayer—abstain from rendering asunder the joints of our shattered bark." The familiar poem of Joseph Addison, founded on verses 25-31 of this Psalm, commencing with the following lines, is well-known—

>Think, O my soul, devoutedly think
>   How with affrighted eyes
>Thou saw'st the wide, extended deep
>   In all its horrors rise.

Oh that men would praise the Lord for His goodness, 107:31. The exclamation *Oh!* expresses surprise, grief, or a wish. Although only a little word with two letters, no word that ever man utters with his tongue comes with that force and affection from the heart than this word of the highest expression—a word when a man can say no more. Used four times in this Psalm *Oh*, such an interpretation usually starts out of the heart upon a sudden from some unexpected conception, or admiration, as it did here with God's immediate calming of the troubled sea.

He turneth a wilderness into a standing water, 107:33. The change in character and style of the Psalm from this point on has led some scholars to suggest an addition by another hand. Six times over we have the personal *He*. Not only is the previous artistic form dropped, and the series of vivid pictures each closed by a refrain, succeeded by changed aspects of thought, but the language becomes harsher. The poet, if the same, suddenly proclaims that he has exhausted his imagination. The concluding verses describe that *He* accomplishes His works on a grand scale. By a word *He* can transform a sandy waste into a deep lake.

A fruitful land unto barrenness for the wickedness, 107:34. Wrote Joseph Hall, preacher of the 18th century, "When I meet with a querulous husbandman, he tells me of a churlish soil, of a wet seed-time, of a green winter, of an unkindly spring, of a lukewarm summer, of a blustering autumn; but I tell him of a displeased God, who will be sure to contrive and fetch all seasons and elements, to his own wise drifts and purposes." Richard Baxter, preaching in the 16th century during a plague of disease and famine, said, "Sicknesses run apace from house to house, and sweep away the poor unprepared inhabitants, because we seep not out the sin that breedeth them." As—

    'Tis God who lifts our comforts high,

Or sinks them in the grave—it is incumbent upon us to walk before Him with reverential gratitude, and so to live that it will not be imperative for Him to afflict us.

Again they are diminished . . . through oppression, 107:39. The ups and downs of Israel were direct consequences of her constant sins and repentances. "Nations and churches soon diminish in number when they are diminished in grace. If we are low in love to God, it is small wonder that He brings us low in other respects. God can reverse the order of our prosperity, and give us a *diminuendo* where we had a *crescendo*; therefore let us walk before Him with great tenderness of spirit, conscious of our dependence upon His smile."

He poureth contempts upon princes, 107:40. No part of the world has probably witnessed so many and great reverses of this kind as the regions and countries of the East. History is laden with the stories of mighty potentates, once the terror and dread among nations, but who, when once denuded of their dignity and power, became the sport even of their own dependents. We think of Napoleon, and in our own time of Hitler and Mussolini.

Who is wise and will observe these things?, 107:43. Dr. Alexander Duff, high in the role of dedicated missionaries, when he sailed for India in 1829, the ship *Lady Holland* ran into rough weather, struck a reef and had to be abandoned. Refuge for the stranded passengers was found on Dessen Island. One of the sailors who went out in search of food and fuel, found a Bible, and a Psalm-book bearing Duff's autograph. To the shipwrecked party, as we have already noted, these precious Books seemed a message from God, and led by Duff, the people knelt down on the sand while he read to them this Psalm, and stressed its conclusion, "Whoso is wise, will ponder these things." From the various dispensations of Divine providence, Duff came to understand the lovingkindness of the Lord.

This Psalm ends in the style, and almost in the very words of Hosea— see 14:9—which present the best observation and the noblest understanding, and prompt us to ask God for this true wisdom and spiritual insight enabling us to see those indications of Divine mercy, and then treasure them in our hearts for our comfort and assurances, and as sources of praise.

Psalm 108

Kruger, past President of South Africa, made frequent appeals to the Psalms in his struggle with the British Empire of his day. In his appeal in a final dispatch to his officers from Machadodorp, Kruger wrote, "See the promise of the Lord in Psalm 108, where He says, they who fight through God shall do so valiantly, and the Lord will deliver them, and tread down their enemies. Keep courage, therefore, you God-fearing band; the Lord will display His strength to your weakness. ... Dear brothers, through God's Word I am sure of this, that the victory is ours." Kruger found much satisfaction in interpreting the promises of the Psalm in favor of the Boers. In his speech to the Volksraads, on Oct. 2nd 1899, he said, "Read Psalm 108 attentively and associate your prayers with it, then will the Lord guide us; and when He is with us, who shall be against us?"

God—Elohim—is prominent in this Psalm in which David adores his God, and strengthened his heart by, as he entered upon the conflicts of another day. An old Prussian officer was in the habit in prayer to invoke the aid of *His Majesty's August Ally*, so David appealed to his God to set up his banner in His name. This Psalm then, can be named *The Warrior's Morning Song*, for, in the final verse the warrior hears the war-trumpet summoning him to join battle immediately, and march out into his fellow soldiers to join the fray. As a whole, the Psalm was meant to express, on behalf of the people of God in all ages, their firm confidence that He would contain them in the conflict against evil forces, and ultimately make them victorious over all their enemies.

As to the composition, or style of the Psalm, several writers speak of it as a composite or patchwork Psalm, with sections borrowed from other Psalms, with slight alterations, and then pieced together by David. For instance, verses 1-5 are the replica of Psalm 57:7-11, and verses 10-13 of Psalm 60:7-14. Those who deal with this Psalm, used with others for *Ascension Day,* affirm that the two fragments were brought together in a separate collection from Book 2, and subsequent perhaps to the formation of that Book. Spurgeon, however, while agreeing that the two portions of this Psalm to be sung jubilantly was a national hymn, or solemnly as a sacred Psalm, are almost identical with verses from two previous Psalms, says that the words would not have been repeated if there had not been an object for doing so. "We are not so presumptuous as to dispute the wisdom of those who speak of verses being borrowed from other Psalms; but we hold for ourselves that the words would not have been repeated in case hearers said, *Ah, we had that before, and therefore we need not meditate upon it again.* The Holy Spirit is not so short of expressions that He needs to repeat Himself, and the repetition cannot be meant merely to fill the book: there must be some intention in the arrangement of the former divine utterances in a new connection; whether we can discover that intent is another matter. It is at least ours to endeavor to do so, and we may expect divine assistance therein." *Repetition* is here sanctioned by inspiration, just as the *rearrangement* is.

Verses 1-5. As already indicated, these opening verses of Psalm 108 are found, almost verbatim, in Psalm 57:7-11 the only important alteration being the use of the august name of JEHOVAH in verse 3 instead of ADONAI, in 57:9. While there are slight differences, the chief point of difference lies in *the position* of the verses. The notes of praise in Psalm 57 follow prayer and grow out of it, but in Psalm 108, David begins at once to sing and give praise, and afterwards prays in a remarkably confident manner. In Psalm 57, the words are a song in "the cave of Adullam, and are the result of faith, which is beginning its battles amid domestic enemies of the most malicious kind; but in Psalm 108, the portion expresses the continued resolve and praise of a man who has already weathered many a campaign, has overcome all home conflicts, and is looking forward to conquests far and wide. . . . It may be that our heavenly Father would here teach us that if we are unable to find a great variety of suitable expressions in devotion, we need not, in the slightest degree, distress ourselves, but may either pray or praise, *using the same words."*

O God, my heart is fixed, I will sing, 108:1. David had the assurance that nothing could disturb his settled mind. Outwardly, he might be tossed to and fro by wars and cares, but his was a fixity of heart toward God nothing could move. Therefore his was a singing heart because it was a stable one. In the Hebrew the word *fixed* signifies, first, *ready*, or *prepared*—secondly, *fixed*. An unprepared heart is *mixed*, not fixed. An old translation has it, "O God, my heart is ready," and when prepared firmly, it is ready to sing and praise. *With my glory* appears in the Prayer-Book Version as "with the best members I have." The tongue, being considered the "best member" (Psalm 30:12), can be taken as the *glory* of man, and with such a member directed by an established heart, God is magnified.

Awake . . . I myself will awake early, 108:2. David loved his well-tuned harp as an accompaniment in his songs of praise. It seemed to be in sympathy and incorporated with the sweet psalmist's soul. "Only when a thoroughly enraptured soul speaks in the instrument can music be

acceptable unto God: as mere musical sound the Lord can have no pleasure therein, He is only pleased with the thought and feeling which are
thus expressed. When a man has a musical gift, he should regard it as too
lovely a power to be enlisted in the cause of sin." Charles Wesley, who
had an enormous gift of praising God with music and verse, prayed—

> Thine own musician, Lord, inspire,
> And let my consecrated lyre
>   Repeat the Psalmist's part,
> His Son and Thine reveal in me,
> And fill with sacred melody
>   The fibers of my heart.

I will myself awake early. The margin has it, "I will awake the dawn."
Rashi observed, "The dawn awakes the other kings; but I, said David, will
awake the dawn." On this verse the *Talmud* has the note—"A cithern used
to hang above David's bed; and when midnight came the north wind blew
among the strings, so that they sounded of themselves, and forthwith he
arose and busied himself with the Tora until the pillar of dawn ascended."
The best and brightest hours of the day should find us heartily aroused to
bless the Lord. "*Early* will I seek thee." It was Henry Vaughan of the 16th
century who left us the lines—

> Yet never sleep the sun up; prayer should
> Dawn with the day, there are set the awful hours
> 'Twixt heaven and us, the manna was not good
> After sun-rising, for day sullies flowers.

I will praise thee, O Lord, among the people, 108:3. David's heart-felt
praises were not only for his personal joy and satisfaction, but for the pleasure and benefit of others. One wonders whether David was inspired to
foresee that his treasury of Psalms would be sung in every land and
tongue from "Greenland's icy mountains" to "India's coral strands"?
Having made his choice to be the Lord's musician, "he retains his office
as the Poet Laureate of the Kingdom of Heaven, and shall retain it till the
crack of doom."

Above the heavens . . . above all the earth, 108:5. Truly this was a missionary prayer David offered the day he sang this Psalm! His was not the
exclusiveness found among some professed believers today. He wanted the
whole earth to be filled with the praises of Jehovah. What an hour of rapture that will be when heaven and earth are full of Divine praise and glory!

That thy beloved may be delivered . . . answer me, 108:6. The *me* is
changed to *us* in the R.V. The saint never prays alone; the voice of Jesus
and of the universal Church blends with his in petition for the *beloved* is
the BELOVED, Eph. 1:6. David poured out his soul in his urgent prayer

for the deliverance of needy saints as their intercessory representative. The world in general, and the Church in particular, has no conception of what they owe to the Lord's band of intercessors, who pray without ceasing.

Gilead is mine, Manasseh is mine . . . Ephraim also . . . Judah is my lawgiver, 108:7. Gilead and Manasseh on the east of Jordan, and Ephraim and Judah on the west, are employed to denote the whole dominion as the Lord's territory. Israel knew that He Who had given Gilead and Manasseh into their hands would not fail to give them the rest of the promised land. *Ephraim* is referred to as "the strength of mine hand," probably because it was the most populous of all the tribes. This was the tribe that furnished David with more than 20,000 "mighty men of valor, famous throughout the house of their fathers." So God regarded the tribe as His *strength*, His helmet of state and the guard of His royal crown. As for *Judah*, this tribe is called by God, *My lawgiver*. The term *lawgiver* comes from a Hebrew verb meaning to *cut* or *engrave*, and is, as here applied to the lawmaker himself or to the *staff or scepter* which was the emblem of the law, Gen. 49:10; Num. 21:18; Deut. 33:21. No tribe could lawfully govern but Judah: till Shiloh came the divine decree fixed the legal power of that state. To us there is no lawgiver but our Lord Who sprang out of Judah.

Moab . . . Edom . . . Philistia, 108:9-10. How appropriate is the metaphorical language, describing God's treatment of these three further nations. *Moab is my washpot*. The figure used here, probably a footbath, expresses great contempt illustrated for us by the story of Amasis and the golden footpan, which he had broken to pieces and made into an image of one of the gods—from base use made divine—an allegory of his own transformation from a private person to a king. An explanation of the simile is that it is associated with an Arabic proverb, that the conqueror would as it were nail his face, that is, acquire renown in Moab. Or "possibly the comparison of Moab to a bath was suggested by its proximity to the Dead Sea, which might be said to be at the foot of Israel." That David treated his detested rival with contempt is seen in the fact that the Moabites became his servants, 2 Sam. 8:27.

Over Edom will I cast my shoe. This was another proud nation David subjugated, and threw his slipper at. Although its capital was high, David cast his sandal over it. "The most natural explanation of this figure," says Ellicott, "is that Edom is disgraced to the character of a slave to whom the conqueror tosses his sandals that they might be cleaned, Matt. 3:11. The symbolic action of Ruth had a different meaning, namely, the transfer of a right of ownership, 4:7, and so cannot be employed in illustration."

Of the *shoe*, as a figure of what is vilest and most common, Dr. J. G. Wetzstein quotes many Arabic proverbs. A covering for the feet would naturally draw to it such associations. Compare the use of the footstool repeatedly in the Psalms, and Shakespeare's use of foot—

"Wash my foot, my tutor!"

"But the custom which Israel brought from Egypt, Exod. 3:3, of dropping the sandals outside the door of a temple, and even of an ordinary house, must have served still more to fasten on that article of dress, ideas of vileness and profanation."

Over Philistia will I triumph. In Psalm 60:8, this phrase reads, "Philistia, triumph thou because of me," and the marginal note has it, "triumph thou over me" (by an irony). The verse should read, "Philistia is my triumph." The LXX Version and Vulgate translate the proper name—"the foreigners have been subdued by me." David had smitten and subdued the Philistines, even as he had defeated Edom and filled it with his garrisons, 2 Sam. 8:1. Through Christ victory is ours over all satanic foes.

> Thy right hand shall my people aid;
> Thy faithful promises makes us strong;
> We will Philistia's land invade,
> And over Edom chant the song.

There came the practical question after Edom had been defeated, *Who shall lead me into Edom?* 108:9-10. David knew that *Selah* or *Petra*, the capital of Edom, was strong and hard to enter, and that he could not possess it by his own power. With only two possible approaches to the city, each a long, narrow, tortuous defile, and that the place itself was so buried in its ravines that it could not be seen from any spot in its neighborhood, far or near, prompted David to pray, "Who will lead me into Edom? Wilt not thou, O God?" Most of us have an *Edom* before us, in the form of some difficulty or temptation; but if we are abiding by faith in God, ours will be the secret of entering, even the city of *rock*—which Petra means, seeing it was a city cut in the rock—more than conquerors. "If God calls David to take Petra, he shall take Petra," and our God will give us help even to overcome rocklike trouble. The help of man may be vain, but we never find it vain to call upon God to deliver us from the stronghold of trouble.

Through God we shall do valiantly, for he shall tread down our enemies, 108:13. "Vanity of vanities" is written on all human aid, and on our resolutions and endeavors, but when we allow God to lead the way, He treads down all our foes. *Through God,* is the secret source of our courage, wisdom, strength, and victory. All foes become prostrate before Him to march over, and His conquest is ours to appropriate by faith.

> Through Thee we shall most valiant prove,
> And tread the foe beneath our feet;
> Through Thee our faith shall hills remove,
> And small as chaff the mountains beat.

Psalm 109

In the pocket Bible of a devout and popular writer of two generations ago, one word was found written opposite this Psalm after his death. It was the word *Mysterious*, which represents the utter perplexity with which this solemn Psalm is generally regarded. Yet although it is one of the most prominent of the imprecatory Psalms, there is no reason whatever for us to deem it unworthy of inclusion in Holy Writ. As its inscription shows it was actually, if not primarily composed for public use in the sanctuary, which immediately divests the Psalm of any personal character, and whatever its origin, and whoever the original object of the curses was, this fact is certain that it became public, ecclesiastical and national. When David said, "The Spirit spake by me," Psalm 109, with all its imprecations, is included with Psalm 23, and all its tender services of the Shepherd. Both—yes, all the Psalms—were Divinely inspired.

In his *Reflections on the Psalms*, C. S. Lewis has a most interesting chapter on "The Cursings," in which he says that "in some of the Psalms the spirit of hatred which strikes us in the face is like the heat from a furnace mouth . . . examples of which can be found all over the Psalter, but perhaps the worst is in Psalm 109." Rejecting the premise that these terrible Psalms should be left alone, Lewis goes on to say that "if we still believe that all Scripture is *written for our learning* or that the age-long use of the Psalms in Christian worship was not entirely contrary to the will of God, and if we remember that our Lord's mind and language were clearly steeped in the Psalter, we shall prefer, if possible to make some use of them."

Then, in his own unique way Lewis goes on to elaborate on ways by which these imprecatory Psalms can be viewed and used, and concludes the chapter by saying, "Against all this the ferocious parts of the Psalms serve as a reminder that there is in the world such a thing as wickedness and that it (if not its perpetrators) is hateful to God. In that way, however dangerous to human distortion it may be, His word sounds through these passages too." As to the origin of the cursings in this extraordinary Psalm, Ellicott suggests that "it is quite possible that from the first the writer spoke in the name of the persecuted nation against some oppressive prince, such as Antiochus Epiphanes. Certainly, when sung by the congregation it expressed not an individual longing for revenge, but all the pent-up feeling—religious abhorrence, patriotic hatred, moral detestation—of the suffering community." It will be recalled that Shakespeare puts curses equally fierce and terrible into Timon's mouth—

> Piety and fear,
> Religion to the gods, peace, justice, truth,
> Domestic awe, night-rest, and neighborhood,
> Instruction, manners, mysterious, and trades,
> Degrees, observances, customs, and laws,
> Decline to your confounding contraries,
> And let confusion live!

John Calvin noted the awful use of this Psalm by certain monks of his time, who hired themselves out to recite it against private enemies. But this Psalm does not contain "a pitiless hate, a refined insatiable malignity," to be poured out on one's enemy. The man who wrote it was not of a malicious, vindictive spirit, but a man after God's own heart. Certainly the Psalm is one of the hard places of Scripture, one making the soul to tremble when read, yet it is a Psalm unto God, and given by inspiration; and, therefore, it is not ours to sit in judgment upon it, or ignore it but to bow our ear to what God the Lord would speak to our heart through its verses. Dr. F. B. Meyer has the most gracious approach to the Psalm we have encountered, and with which one is in full agreement. After showing that the internal evidence agrees with the inscription in ascribing it to David, and that along with other Psalms of a similar character, Psalm 109 dates probably from the time of Saul's persecution, Dr. Meyer goes on to say that—

> It is full of appeals for the Divine vindication of persecuted saints. These old sacred writers had very clear, strong views of the enormity of wrong-doing, and did not scruple to invoke the Divine justice against those who perpetrated it, Psalm 28:4. Here are sentences which exhibit a like spirit in the New Testament, Acts 23:2; I Tim. 1:20; 2 Tim. 4:4, but on the whole we are taught by the Gospel to speak more leniently of those who oppress us, Matt. 5:44; Luke 23:34; Acts 7:20. We cannot forget the quotation made from this Psalm (verse 8) by the Apostle Peter with reference to Judas Iscariot the betrayer, Acts. 1:20, and thus we are led to question whether these strong imprecations may not be a foreshadowing of that useful fate which must overtake such as knowingly and wilfully sin against God's children and causes.

We readily concede that it is Christlike to pray for the conversion of the worst enemy we might have, as David himself likewise did, but when we think of the cruel foes of law and order, the doers of iniquity, the cold-blooded murders of innocent people, the horrible barbarities and atrocious hooliganism and vandalism, crafty plots for ruining the innocent and other forms of crime, characteristic of our own professed, enlightened age, do we not blaze with righteous indignation against the inhuman wretches trampling upon laws of protection, and setting at nought every good dictate of humanity? God is just, and His arm will bear itself for the wielding of the naked sword of justice, and when as Judge of all the earth He threatens to punish tyrannical cruelty and false-hearted treachery, virtue gives her assent and consent, and every just man in his inward soul says, *Amen!*

Hold not thy peace, O God of my praise, 109:1. Knowing that the mouth of the wicked and deceitful would have plenty to say against, David begins his Psalm by calling upon God not to be silent, but to speak on his behalf, and silence those about to slander him. As God had been his constant Object of praise and honor, the Psalmist now entrusts to God the vindicating of his innocence as the calumnies of his foes are hurled at him. If we honor Him, we have His assurances that He will honor us. "The Psalmist prays that Jehovah's silence may not make his confident glorifying in the covenant promises vain."

The wicked . . . the deceitful . . . have spoken against me with living tongue, 109:2. The tongue, a power for good or evil, is here employed to wickedly misrepresent the character of the Psalmist. "A blow with a word strikes deeper than a blow with a sword." Bad tongues not only vilify bad men, but the most gracious and innocent of saints. How hard it is to be assailed with slander—

> Whose edge is sharper than the sword, whose tongue
> Outvenoms all the worms of Nile.

In verses 1 to 5 the Psalmist prays that deliverance will be his from his remorseless and false-hearted enemies. Robert Pollock has a most expressive poem on verses 2 to 5, in which he exposes those who "early rose, and made most hellish meals of good men's names." Here are some lines from his work—

> . . . Rumor was the messenger
> Of defamation, and so swift that none
> Could be the first to tell an evil tale.

> 'Twas Slander filled her mouth with lying words;
> Slander, the foulest whelp of Sin. The man
> In whom this spirit entered was undone
> His tongue was set on fire of Hell; his heart
> Was black as death, his legs were faint with haste
> To propagate the lie his tongue had framed.

Words of hatred . . . without a cause, 109:3. The writer found himself hedged in with falsehood, misrepresentation, accusation and scorn, all born of hatred. Every word uttered was as full of venom as an egg is full of meat, and the worst feature of all their open charges was the fact that they were without cause. This made the injured one feel more acutely the wrongs done to him.

My love . . . my adversaries . . . I give myself unto prayer, 109:4, 5. One of our poets says of the Lord Jesus that He was "found guilty of Excess of love." Truly, He was hated without a cause! The Psalmist loved his adversaries but they returned him "evil for good, and hatred for my love." Good for evil is God-like, but Evil for good is devil-like. How did David regard those guilty of such a hellish exchange? Why, he tells us that he gave himself unto prayer. In the face of all the taunts and reproaches of his maligners he simply and naturally had recourse to prayer. The three words in this verse *give myself unto* are in italics which, if omitted, leaves us a beautiful thought, *But I—prayer*; as if the one response made by the Psalmist was PRAYER; and so much so, that his existence for the time was summed up in this word. He not only prayed, he, himself, was a *Prayer*. In the allegory of the ancients, "*Hope* was left at the bottom of the basket, as the sweetener of human life, but God in far richer mercy gives prayer as the balm of human trial."

A wicked man over him . . . Satan at his right hand, 109:6. Who does not admire the justice of God when he reads of fierce Romans ruled by Tiberius and Nero? "Those who are righteous find the rule of the wicked a sore bondage, but those who are full of resentful passions, and haughty aspirations, are slaves indeed when men of their own class have the whip hand of them." And as like draws like, Satan, "the father of lies," and also "the adversary," ever stands near his own children in their wicked treatment of God's people. Peter Vega, the Spanish theologian of the 18th century, in his work *The Penitential Psalms*, writing of the first six verses of Psalm 109, said "there cannot be anything worse than that of a man who diligently and of set purpose inspires others by speaking deceitfully, by surrounding with speeches of hatred, by attacking without cause, by slandering, by returning evil for good, hatred for love; therefore, in this place it is desired that a wicked man may be set over such a one, and the devil at his right hand; as if he should be doomed to take the lowest place because he is the worst."

With this sixth verse commences the curses pronounced on those who serve Satan, and who, at last, must share his doom. Some writers hold that this imprecatory section from verse 6 to 15, is a quotation of what was desired by the Psalmist's foes; but it is better to consider them not as imprecations but as predictions, the imperative mood being put for the future tense, agreeably to the custom of the Hebrew. C. S. Lewis dealing with this section says, "let his prayer be turned into sin," verse 6, "this means, I think, not his prayers to God, but his supplications to a human judge, which are to make things all the hotter for him—double the sentence because he begged it to be halved. May his days be few, and his job given to someone else, verse 7. When he is dead may his orphans be beggars, verse 9. May he look in vain for anyone in the world to pity him, verse 11. Let God always remember against him the sins of his parents, verse 13."

In the mental history of John Bunyan, the power of the Psalms is strongly marked. The thought of the misery that might overtake his family, and especially his blind child, made him shrink from imprisonment. But, with the Psalm as his source of direction and comfort Bunyan's irresolution was momentary, and he wrote—

> If I should venture all for God, I engaged God to take care of my concernments; but if I forsook Him and His ways, for fear of any trouble that should come to me or mine, then I should not only falsify my profession, but should count also that my concernments were not so sure, if left at God's feet while I stood to and for His name, as they would be under my own tuition, though with the denial of the way of God. This was a smarting consideration, and was as spurs unto my flesh. That Scripture—Psalm 109:6-20—also greatly helped me to fasten the more upon me, where Christ prays against Judas, that God would disappoint him in his selfish thoughts, which moved him to sell his Master; pray read it soberly, Psalm 109, verses 6, 7, 8.

The terrible curses of these verses, the Holy Spirit dictated, form an abiding prophecy or prediction of the deserved punishments awaiting all who fight against the Kingdom of Christ.

Let his prayer become sin, 109:7.   Kimchi in his *Annotations* explains this phrase thus, "Let it be without effect, so that he does not get what he asks for; let him not hit the mark at which he aims; for *sin* sometimes has the meaning to *miss*." Jerome, dealing with this same verse said that "Judas's prayer was turned into sin, by reason of his want of hope when he prayed: and thus it was in that despair he hanged himself." As the clamors of a condemned malefactor not only find no acceptance, but are looked upon as an affront to the court, so the prayers of the wicked become sin, because soured with the leaven of hypocrisy and malice. On the horribleness of this curse see Proverbs 15:8.

Let another take his office, 109:8.   Mark the application of this phrase to Judas Iscariot by Peter, Acts 1:20. To the Early Fathers Psalm 109 was known as *Psalmus Iscarioticus*. No one would desire a betrayer like Judas to live long. The shortening of the life of tyrants means the lengthening of the world's tranquility. "A bad man does not make an office bad: another may use with benefit that which he perverted to ill uses"—as Matthias did who succeeded Judas on the oversight of the Early Church.

Let his children be fatherless, and his wife a widow, 109:9.   On the sur-

Psalms: *A Devotional Commentary*

face it would appear that this curse was somewhat heartless in that the resentment of the imprecator cannot satisfy itself or the *person* of his foe, but fastens also on his innocent descendants. The pronouncement of the speedy death of the wicked man does not content the Psalmist; he must feast his anger with the thought of the fatherless children and desolate widow, and greatly pleased when he sees them homeless and wandering about as vagabonds.

But what must be remembered is that David, speaking as a king and judge, was pronouncing these terrible maledictions over the enemies of God and thus saw in the plight of those left of those who deserved death, the result of their death. Pity was due to the orphans and widows, but a father's atrocious actions may dry up the springs of pity. "Who mourned that cruel Pharaoh's children lost their father, or that Sennacherib's wife became a widow. As Agag's sword had made women childless none wept when Samuel's weapon made his mother childless among women."

Continually vagabonds . . . let them seek bread, 109:10. For "desolate places," we have *ruins,* and the figure is of the fatherless creeping out of the ruins of their houses to beg. The Vulgate and LXX Versions express it, "let them be driven out of their homes." Apt are the lines of Seneca—

> Worse evil yet I pray for on my spouse;
> Let him still live, through strange towns roam in want,
> Exiled, suspected, cowering, with no home.

Spurgeon confesses that as he read many of these curse-verses that he had need of all faith and reverence to accept them as the voice of inspiration. "The exercise is good for the soul, for it educates our sense of ignorance, and tests our teachableness. Yes, Divine Spirit, we can and do believe that even these dread words from which to shrink have a meaning consistent with the attributes of the Judge of all the earth, though His name is LOVE. How this may be we shall know hereafter." Of verses 7 to 19, John Le Clerc wrote—

> These and the following verses, although they contain terrible imprecations, will become less dreadful if we understand them as spoken concerning men pertinaciously cleaving to their vices, against whom only has God threatened punishments; not against those who repent with all their heart, and become thoroughly changed in life.

Let the extortioner catch all that he hath, 109:11. A better reading has it, "Let the usurer lay trap to catch all that he hath." So Timon—

> Let prisons swallow them,
> Debts wither them to nothing.

The word *catch* refers to the obligations between creditors and debtors, and he calls them "snares," by which, as it were, the insolvent debtors are caught, and at last come to servitude. The Romans, that they might deter the citizens from usury, placed a statue of Marayas in the Forum or lawcourt, by which they signified that those who came into the hands of usurers would be skinned alive; and to show that usurers, as the most unjust litigant, deserved hanging, they placed a rope in the hand of the figure.

Let his posterity be cut off. . . let their name be blotted out, 109:13. This may seem a harsh curse, but is it not better when an evil, vile brood vanish from memory and existence? "It would be undesirable that the sons of the utterly villainous and bloodthirsty should rise to honor, and if they did they would only revive the memory of their father's sins." Evidently the Hebrew theory of the Divine government was that if ruin did not overtake the sinner himself, it would fall on his posterity; his name would be forgotten, and his race extinct. Those who are of an effeminate benevolence may deem a curse like this far too stern, but is it not wiser to agree with God's curses than with the devil's blessings? When our heart kicks against the terrors of the Lord we should see our need of greater humbling before Him, and seek to live more in harmony with His thoughts and less in sympathy with evil.

Let the iniquity of his fathers be remembered . . . let not the sin of his mother be blotted out, 109:14. Although one cannot fully explain the righteousness of this curse, we yet fully believe in it. Often a man's sins were learned from evil parents, and he procures punishment upon the parents' sins which he made his own. A bad child brings to mind its parents' bad points of character. Ellicott's comment is enlightening—"The sweet of vengeance lies in its completeness. The curse must strike backwards as well as forwards, and the root as well as the branch be destroyed. Undoubtedly the Mosaic Law, which proclaimed that 'the iniquity of the fathers should be visited on the children,' suggested the form of this imprecation."

Apart from the necessity of parallelism was there some definite occasion in the poet's thought to account for his mention of the *mother*? Those who claim that this portion of the Psalm, 6-20, a quotation of curses really uttered by Shimei against David, find an historical allusion to a Moabitish descent on the mother's side.

He remembered not . . . persecuted . . . even slay, 109:16. Those who remembered not to show mercy to the poor and needy, have their memory cut off from the earth. Unreasonably merciless in their treatment of others, the fearful punishment of such sinners is that they are always under the eye of a just God. The story is told of Lafayette, the friend and ally of George Washington who, in his youth was confined in a French dungeon.

In the door of his cell was cut a small hole, just big enough for a man's eye; at that hole a sentinel was placed, whose duty it was to watch, moment by moment, till he was relieved by a change of guard. All Lafayette saw was the winking eye, but the eye was always there; look when he would, it met his gaze. In his dreams it was staring at him. "Oh," he wrote after his release, "it was horrible, there was no escape; when I laid down and when I rose up, and ate and read, that eye searched me."

Thus the merciless are before the eye of the Lord continually. Why, what is their crime? They remembered not to show mercy, but persecuted the poor, and sought to slay even the broken in heart. What a long vial full of the plagues of God is poured out upon the unmerciful man!

The section, verses 17 to 20, contains the most heavy curse of God upon those who loved cursing others. Such a divine curse consists in the deprivation of all good and in being swallowed up of all the most fearful miseries a holy and just and eternal God can righteously inflict, or lay upon the soul of the sinner who has no delight in any blessing from the Lord. Such a doomed one proves that his "curses, like chickens, come home to roost." Verses 17 and 18 express facts, and the imprecation comes in verse 19. *Let*, is a fateful word in this Psalm, in which it occurs 27 times and implies the handing over of the wicked to their just punishment. They are judged by their own rule. They receive what they loved. Retaliation as a measure of public justice was what the Psalmist demands.

It was but common justice that the malicious should receive a return for his malice, and receive it in kind, too. An illustration of the principle propounded in this section is found in the fabled shirt of Messus, which ate into the mighty arm of Hercules. In a good sense the same figure was a favorite one with the Jews—see Isa. 11:5. Throughout the four verses forming this imprecation our attention has been fixed upon those who maliciously assailed the inoffensive man of God. "David, himself, was a man of gentle mould, and remarkably free from the spirit of revenge, and therefore we may here conceive him to be speaking as a judge or as a representative man, in whose person great principles needed to be vindicated and great injuries redressed."

In the remaining portion, verses 21-31, we breathe a different and more welcome air for in it the writer turns from his enemies to God. David sets the great *THOU* over against all his adversaries, and his heart is at rest. *Do thou for me!* Wisely he leaves everything to God to settle, and thus opened his final plea with an exquisite prayer, *For thy name's sake.* Because God's *mercy* is *good*, it is far better to let Him act for us than act ourselves. See Psalm 119:124; Jerem. 14:7. It is almost impossible in English to retain the emphasis of appeal in verse 21, made still more emphatic by the sudden change from imprecation on an enemy to prayer for mercy toward self.

I am gone like the shadow . . . as the locust, 109:23. Two figures of speech are here used to describe David's feeling of helpfulness. Bishop Horsley renders the first figure—"I am just gone, like the shadow stretched to its utmost length," and remarks—"The state of the shadows of terrestrial objects at sunset, lengthening every instant, and growing faint as they lengthen; and in that instant that they shoot to the immeasurable length disappearing." The implication is that the suffering thus vanish, but not into darkness if they are the Lord's. As for the tossing up and down of the locust, such a timid insect is the sport of the winds, and must go where the breeze carries it. While locusts have sufficient strength of flight to remain on the wing for a considerable time, they have little or no command over the winds which whirl them round and round by their ever-carrying currents. In his distress, David felt as powerless, and thus pled for Divine pity.

Help me . . . save me . . . Lord, thou hast done it, 109:26, 27. "Help me, O Lord!" is another of these sweet exclamatory petitions, of which we should each carry a quiverful for daily use. Note the two pronouns, *me* and *my*. Poor and needy, and weak through fasting, with his flesh dwindling away, David utters a very rich, appropriating word *my*. Thus he lays hold on Jehovah for strength to rise superior to his heavy load, and thereby reveal to the ungodly that his deliverance was all of Him—*Thou hast done it*. There could have been no mistaking the Author of so thorough a vindication, so complete a turning of tables.

Coming to the closing portion of the Psalm, verses 28-31, it is impossible not to note the anti-climax reached in it, if they were spoken by the same person as verses 16-20, and directed against the same enemies, of whom the one there singled out is the prominent figure. *He—He*. Now there is a change to the plural number, *Them*, yet the same imprecations are repeated in a diluted and modified form. *Let them curse, but bless thou*, or "they will curse, but thou dost bless." It is well to be persecuted, if with every curse of man we can detect the silver tones of the Divine benediction, saying, "Blessed are ye," Matt. 5:11. Matthew Henry reminds us that "men's curses are impotent, God's blessings are omnipotent." Adversaries are covered with a mantle of confession, but the saint who is the object of their curses is mantled with God's merciful blessings. He ever stands at the right hand of those who look to Him alone for help, to save them who set out to condemn them. There He stands, in any time, or kind of trouble, as the Friend, Surety and Deliverer. How brave is the accused if he enters the court leaning on the arm of the noblest in the land. How futile is it to condemn when the Judge of all stands beside to justify! "Who shall lay anything to the charge of God's elect? Shall God that justifieth?" Romans 8:33. Should it not console our heart to know that Jehovah is the poor man's advocate, just as an adversary was the wicked man's accuser? Let us ever remember that our Great King is in court, to turn sentences against our false accusers. What else can we do but close our meditation on this Psalm with the prayer Spurgeon offers at the end of his commentary upon it—

> O Lord, save us from the severe trial of slander: deal in Thy righteousness with all those who spitefully assail the characters of holy men, and cause all who are smarting under calumny and reproach to come forth unsullied from the affliction, even as did Thine only begotten Son. Amen.

Psalm 110

A s we seek to enter upon a meditation of this short yet sacred Psalm, we share the feeling of Moses when, as he turned to gaze upon the burning bush, God's voice called to him out of the midst of the bush, saying, "Put off thy shoes from off thy feet, for the place whereon thou standest is holy ground." We are, indeed, on most holy ground in Psalm 110, well designated as the crown of all the Psalms, and one of which Martin Luther said that it was worthy to be overlaid with precious jewels. Edward Reynolds, theologian of the early 16th century left us this appraisal—

> This Psalm is one of the fullest and most compendious prophecies of the Person and Offices of Christ in the whole Old Testament, and so full of fundamental truth, that I shall not shun to call it *Symbolum Davidicum*, or "The Prophet David's Creed." And indeed they are very few, if any, of the articles of that Creed which we all generally profess, which are not either plainly expressed, or by most evident implication couched in this little model.

Already we have dealt with Martin Luther's love of the Psalms. Psalm 110 was one of his chief favorites and so he wrote of it, "The 110th Psalm is very fine. It describes the Kingdom and Priesthood of Jesus Christ, and declares Him to be the King of all things and the Intercessor for all men; to Whom all things have been remitted by His Father and Who has compassion on us all. 'Tis a noble Psalm; if I was well, I would endeavor to make a commentary upon it."

It was the Psalm we are now considering that Oliver Cromwell had in mind when, in July 1650, he embarked upon war with Scotland. He professes his readiness to sacrifice his life in the service of the people, declaring that he desired nothing better than a "free and equal Commonwealth." Speaking at great length before he left Whitehall, on "the great providences of God now upon the earth," Cromwell discoursed "at least an hour in the exposition of 110th Psalm," saying that he looked upon the design of the Lord in that day to be the freeing of His people from every burden, and that he himself was the chosen instrument for the accomplishment of the events foretold in that Psalm. Then Cromwell set out assured, as he had read, that the Lord would make His enemies His footstool, that "in the day of His wrath He would wound even kings," and that He would "judge among the heathen," and "fill the plain with dead

453

bodies." Some three years later when Cromwell constituted his *Barebones* Parliament, his speech to the strange assembly was loaded with references from Psalm 110 and Psalm 68.

As to the historical setting of the Psalm it was evidently composed by David when the Seat of Government and the Ark of the Covenant were already on Mount Zion. David himself had already received the grand promise of 2 Samuel 7 that his house, and kingdom and throne should be established forever; and there rings through this Psalm an eager anticipation of victory over all his foes. But any remote reference to David fades into comparative insignificance as we read into the words of the Psalm the prophecy and conception of the glory, perpetuity, and ultimate victory of David's greater Son, the wonderful King-Priest.

The title ascribes the Psalm to David, and Jesus Himself declared in the days of His flesh that it was written by David in the Holy Spirit, Matt. 22:41-46. There are those critics who dare to contradict Jesus as to His witness to the Davidic authorship of the Psalm, affirming that it was not so much written *by* him as *of* him. But the man after God's own heart saw beyond himself in his marvelous Psalm, when he prophesied of the ultimate victory of the One he called "my Lord." No other portion of the Old Testament is more frequently quoted in the New. In addition to Matthew 22:41; Mark 12:36; Luke 20:42; Acts 2:34, see 1 Cor. 15:25; Heb. 1:3, 13; 5:6, 10; 7:17, 21. Of this highly Messianic Psalm Luther said that it was "the true, high, main Psalm of our beloved Lord, Jesus Christ."

C. S. Lewis remarks that when Christ asked the Pharisee how He could be both David's son and David's Lord, He clearly identified *Christ*, and therefore Himself with the "my Lord" of Psalm 110—and in such a question hinted at the mystery of the Incarnation by pointing out a difficulty which only it could solve. Professor Lewis, still dealing with Psalm 110 as referring to the Messiah, the regal and anointed deliverer Who would subject the world to Himself, goes on to say that "probably all instructed Jews in the first century saw references to the Messiah in most of those passages where our Lord saw them; what was controversial was His identification of the Messianic King with another Old Testament figure and of both with Himself. Two figures meet us in the Psalms, that of the *Sufferer*, and of the conqueror and liberating *King* . . . our Lord identified Himself with both these characters." This Ode of Victory to a Priest-King will find its fulfillment in the continuous and final triumphs of Christ.

For the true believer, the authorship and purpose of the Psalm are beyond all conjectures by the way in which our Lord made use, in a most emphatic manner, of its first verse as the Divinely inspired utterance of David. As already indicated, early Jews recognized in Jesus the prophesied Messiah of Psalm 110, but this was not only a current belief, for He himself declared that He was the One predicted by David.

Because of this we cannot agree with Ellicott that "the application Jesus made of current opinions and beliefs does not necessarily stamp them with the seal of Divine authorization." Unequivocally, He set His seal upon this short but sacred Psalm in the Spirit's portrayal of Himself as God's King-Priest.

The Lord said unto my Lord, 110:1. David did not use the usual prophetic phrase, "Thus saith the Lord," but an expression marking an immediate inspiration. As to Divine titles found in verses 1, 2 and 4, the Hebrew word *Jehovah* is rendered *Lord*: where the second mention of the word "Lord" occurs in verse 1, and also in verse 5, the Hebrew word is *Adonai,* meaning, Master, Ruler, Lord. "My Lord," was an address of honor to those more noble than the speaker, or superior in rank—

> to a father, Genesis 31:35.
> to a brother, Num. 12:11.
> to a royal consort, 1 Kings 1:17, 18.
> to a prince, 1 Kings 3:17

with the addition of the royal title, "My Lord, O King," 2 Sam. 14:19. As to the person David had in mind when he used the personal pronoun, "*my* Lord," it is ridiculous to apply the title to anybody else save the Messiah, of whom David spoke with a prophetic consciousness of His Deity, and of His superiority as a Prince over all other princes. The verse as a whole expresses co-partnership in the throne, with the seat at the King's right hand being a mark of extreme honor. See 1 Kings 2:15; Psalm 45:9. Jehovah called upon His Son to sit at His right hand until *He* makes the Son's enemies His footstool, or a *stool for thy foot*. Such imagery is akin to the custom mentioned in Joshua 10:24. As a footstool bears the whole weight of the body, so the enemies of the Lord are to bear the weight of His heavy and everlasting wrath upon their souls if they die unrepentant. The One sharing a glorious throne also has a footstool.

When we think of this opening verse presenting Christ's Person, Wars, and Victory, what else can we say of it, or of the Psalm as a whole, but what Tully said of Brutus in his laconical epistle—*How much is a little!* Of the application of the phrase "Sit Thou at My right hand!" F. B. Meyer says, "This was the welcome of the Ascension Day—the word with which the Father greeted Jesus. And all through the ages He has been engaged in making the foes of Christ the footstool of His feet. This is not accomplished yet, but it is sure." We feel that we cannot conclude our meditation of this remarkable initial verse without quoting Spurgeon's final words in his comment on it.

> How condescending on Jehovah's part to permit a mortal ear to hear, and a human pen to record His sacred converse with His co-equal Son! How greatly should we prize the revelation of His private and solemn discourse

with the Son, herein made public for the refreshing of His people! Lord, what is man that Thou shouldest thus impart Thy secrets unto him!

The rod of thy strength . . . rule thou, 110:2. The word for *send* is rendered *stretch* in other passages. "Abraham stretched forth his hand" Genesis 22:10, and here, as frequently, it implies the stretching out of the hand with hostile intent. In the verse before us David, speaking in his own person, addresses the King, to whom the oracle has just been announced. As for the phrase, *the rod of thy strength*, it is better given as, "the scepter of thy majesty," that is of "Thy kingly majesty," as in Jerem. 48:17—the scepter being the emblem of royal power and dominion. This symbol of kingly rule is prominent in Scripture, Psalm 45:6. By his rod, Moses smote the Egyptians, and wrought wonders for Israel. By his rod Aaron proved his power as the Divinely-ordained high priest.

Out of Zion implies out of Judaism, the seat of which was Zion—from the narrowest nation under Heaven—that the Word has gone forth with its message to the entire race and with power to enclose the whole world in its embrace. When the Messiah appeared among men He commanded them, "Go and make disciples of all nations," and out they went with a rod more powerful than those of Moses which divided rivers. But, with the scepter of the Gospel, the Apostles, beginning at Jerusalem, went forth and broke in pieces the ungodliness of the world. The rod of the Cross, which to men seemed the very emblem of shame and weakness, was, in truth, the power of God unto salvation. By the Cross. Christ rules in the midst of His enemies, making rebels willingly submissive and disposing the antagonistic to obey Him. He makes "the rebel a priest and a king."

Thy people . . . Thy power . . . Thy youth, 110:3. As cast in the A.V. this is not an easy verse to understand. Literally, it runs, "Thy people willingnesses—or, willing offerings—in the day of thy force in holy attire, from the womb of morning dew of thy youth." The first part probably means, "Thy people offer themselves in the day of thy mustering," that is, of the army for battle. In Judges 5:9, the noun *willingnesses* expresses the alacrity with which the northern clans mustered for battle, and applied to Him Who is to rule indicates the willingness of people to rally on His musterday, as He goes forth to conquer. They will be eager to enlist under the banner of the Priest-King, responding to His call as spontaneously, even as the dew comes forth in the morning.

"In the beauties of holiness." Several scholars translate this phrase, "on the mountain of holiness," or "on the holy mountain," and give the picture of the people mustering for battle in glittering battle-dress on the mountains around Zion, under the eye of Jehovah Himself, and in obedience to the outstretched scepter. Spurgeon's application reads—

As Jesus is a Priest-King, so we His people are priests and kings, and the beauties of holiness are their priestly dress, their garments for glory and for beauty; of these priests unto God that shall be an unbroken succession.

The beauties of holiness is a frequent phrase for the sacerdotal garments, the holy festal attire of the priests of the Lord. The conquering King presented in the Psalm is heralded as a *Priest for ever*, and followed by an army of priests, and clad, not in heavy mail, but in priestly robes and using weapons that are not carnal, even as those who compassed Jericho had the Ark as their standard, and trumpets as their weapons.

"From the womb of the morning—thou hast the dew of thy youth"—which is taken as a description of the vigor and freshness of the person addressed—"Thine is the morning dew of youth," meaning, "thy young men gather to Thy standard like the dew for its fresh energy." The dew comes out of the womb of the morning—"The meek ey'd morn appears, *mother of dews*." The young men as a band of youthful warriors in the fresh strength and countless numbers and gleaming beauty like the glittering morning dew rally to the banner of the King.

The image of the *dew* was familiar to Israel as an emblem at once of *multitude* (2 Sam. 17:11, 12), and of *freshness* and *vigor* (Psalm 133:3; Hosea 14:5). Used here with "the additional idea of brightness we have a picture of an array of young warriors, in their bright attire, recalling the multitudinous glancing of the ground on a dewy morning—*Thy young warriors come to Thee thick and bright as the morning dew*." It will be recalled that John Milton used the same figure for the innumerable host of angel warriors—

> An host
> Innumerable as the stars of night
> Or stars of morning, dewdrop, which the sun
> Impearls on every leaf and every flower.

Then we have the expressive lines of N. Brady and N. Tate—

> Then, in thy power's triumphant day,
>   The willing nations shall obey;
> And, when thy rising beams they view,
>   Shall all (redeem'd from error's night)
> Appear as numberless and bright
>   As crystal drops of morning dew.

But as the Lord Jesus is prominent in this Psalm we find it fascinating to apply the phrase, "Thou hast the dew of Thy youth," as expressive of His eternal agelessness. Was it not true of Him in the days of His flesh? When Isaac Watts originally wrote his well-known and much-loved Calvary hymn, the opening lines read—

> When I survey the wondrous Cross,
> On which the *young* Prince of Glory died.

Jesus was only 30 years of age when He entered His public ministry, and about 33 when He was crucified. He died for our sins when the dew of youth was still His—

> Not one golden hair was gray,
> On His crucifixion day.

When he ascended on high a few weeks after His 33rd year as the *Man* Christ Jesus, He entered Heaven the youthful Warrior, and when we see Him, in His eternal youthfulness, we shall be like Him—33 some day! As I write these lines in 1974, an old man of well over 88 years, I shall welcome the return of a youthfulness that never fades. "Jesus Christ has the dew of His youth personally, doctrinally, and mystically, being surrounded by new converts, who are as the early dew."

Thou art a Priest for ever after the order of Melchizedek, 110:4. This prominent Messianic verse brings us to the dominant truth of the Psalm, namely, the *formal* union in one person of the royal dignity and the priesthood. While some of Israel's kings at times assumed priestly functions, only in one instance in Scripture can the dual offices of king and priest be said to have been *formally* combined—in the person of Joshua son of Josedech, Zech. 11:12, 13. In this Psalm we have One whom Jehovah has declared by solemn oath a priest—One in whom the priesthood was indubitably and firmly fixed, and Who is exalted at Jehovah's right hand as a King, and, as a Warrior, rides on with Jehovah to triumph.

The Priesthood of the Messiah, however, is not after the model of Aaron, Israel's renowned high priest, but according to that of Melchizedek, the more ancient, actual and formal priesthood combined in the same person, with kingly rank, Gen. 14:18. This recognized sanction of the union of king and priest is emphasized in Heb. 5, 6, and 7, and forms, not only the heart of the Psalm, but the very center and soul of our Christian faith. Jesus "glorified not Himself to be made an high priest," but by the ancient oath of Jehovah was thus ordained. "*Thou art* a priest for ever," meaning, Thou was and art and art to come, in all ages a Priestly King. At present, He is at the right hand of God, making intercession for His people. *Thou art* is a "constituting word," and declaration of God's eternal decree.

After the *order*, or manner, of Melchizedek, means that like him, Jesus combined Priesthood and Kingship in one Person. As Melchizedek had no successor, Jesus can have no successor in His priesthood, God confirmed by an oath as "a priest for ever." Having sworn thus, *He will not repent*, meaning that the priesthood of Jesus is not like that of Aaron, which was after a time to expire, and is now actually, under grace, with all the ceremonial law abolished, but is a priesthood never to be altered, changed, or terminated. Thus, "our Lord Jesus, like Melchizedek, stands forth before us as a priest of divine ordaining; not made a priest by fleshy birth, as the sons of Aaron; he mentions father, mother, nor descent as his right to the sacred office; he stands upon his personal merits, by himself alone; as no man came before him in his work, so none can follow after; his order begins and ends in his own person, and in himself it is eternal, *having neither beginning of days nor end of years.*" Then Spurgeon in his exposition makes the application—

> The King-Priest has been here and left His blessing upon the believing seed, and now He sits in glory in His complete character, atoning for us by the merit of His blood, and exercising all power on our behalf.

> O may we ever hear Thy voice
> In mercy to us speak,
> And in our Priest we will rejoice,
> Thou great Melchizedek.

Well might we pray, "O King-Priest, we who are, in a minor degree, king-priests too, are full of gladness because Thou reignest even now, and wilt come ere long to vindicate Thy cause and establish Thine empire for ever. Even so, come quickly. Amen!"

The Lord at thy right hand shall strike through kings, 110:5. The last three verses of the Psalm have a triumphant ring about them. Here we see the Priest-King leaving His sitting posture at the Father's right hand, and entering into war with godless rulers. Leading the final charge in person, His own right hand and His holy arm secure a complete victory. Triumph is assured because of the omnipotence of the King. Having bruised the serpent's head by His death and resurrection, the Messiah will ultimately destroy Satan and his kingdom. As for "the day of His wrath," when swift and overwhelming ruin is to overtake His foes, John enlightens as to the occasion when he describes the Lord leaving His throne to smite the nations and tread the winepress of the fierceness and wrath of Almighty God, Rev. 19:11-16.

Then, as Edersheim puts it, "On His stirrup is engraven, *I will make thine enemies thy footstool*, and upon His diadem, Thou art a priest for ever." To "strike through" implies a perfect victory, full confusion to the enemy, and a wound, so incurable, that they stagger and fall to rise up no more. See 1 Sam. 26:8; Nahum 1:9. N. Brady and N. Tate have this poetic description of such a calamitous yet victorious day—

> The sentenc'd heathen he shall slay,
> And fill with carcasses his way,
> Till he hath struck earth's tyrants dead;

> But in the high-way brooks shall first
> Like a poor pilgrim slake his thirst,
> And then in triumph raise his head.

We do not accept for one moment the suggestion that both David and John give us a "poetical description of the overthrow of all rebellious powers and the defeat of all unholy principles." Real kings and nations are meant, and terrible things in righteousness will happen to them when the King of kings wounds the heads of godless rulers "over many countries," or as we can read the phrase, "He has smitten the head over the whole earth." Jesus must, and shall reign, where'er the sun doth its successive journeys run, but He cannot reign until His enemies are smitten, as they will be over a wide area. The picture this Psalm and Rev. 19 give us is that of a vast battlefield with heaps of slain.

He shall drink of the brook . . . shall lift up the head, 110:7. We find ourselves in disagreement with Ellicott in the assertion that this is an "abrupt ending of this short Psalm which has led many critics to regard it as a fragment." We believe it to be a complete Psalm, divinely inspired, and that its last verse is by no means *abrupt*, but most apt and beautiful, as it pictures the victorious King, pausing at the stream crossing His path, and refreshed, continues His pursuit of the enemy with head uplifted. This is not a portrayal of a thirsty warrior unworthy of Jehovah, and does not, by any means, suggest timidity, Isa. 63:1-6. It is simply a detail true to life, as seen when Jonathan took of the honey and was refreshed, 1 Sam. 14:27. Our last glimpse of the Priest-King is that of One with head lifted high in victory, to end His struggle of long-suffering love, and to usher in His reign of universal righteousness. "He shall not fail nor be discouraged till he has set judgment in the earth."

We can, of course, think of "the brook in the way" as a type. F. B. Meyer's spiritual application is, "Our Lord drinks of the love and devotion of His people, and goes forward without discouragement to the victory which awaits Him. Have you been a brook from which He has drunk? Is Jesus refreshed by you?" Jesus, Himself, used "water" as a symbol of the quickening ministry of the Holy Spirit, and He was the *Divine Brook*, Jesus drank from during His earthly ministry. When He said, *I, by the Spirit of God*, He was not confining Himself to the aid of the Spirit in casting out demons, but to the whole phase of his labors. The life-giving Brook was ever in His way, as His constant Source of strength and refreshment. Ere He left His own, Jesus bequeathed this heavenly Brook to His own—*I will send Him unto you*, and the dramatic story of The Acts reveals how the Apostles drank deeply of the Brook because, as the result of a constant draught of "the rivers of living waters," they were empowered to turn the world upside down for their victorious Lord.

Psalm 111

In his *Serious Call*, William Law included Psalm 111, with other Psalms, as wonderfully setting forth the glory of God, and therefore fitting to keep to it at any particular hour we like, and to use it to feed our devotion. Actually, this Psalm should be studied as a companion of the next Psalm, for the two make a lovely pair. Both Psalm 111 and 112 are titleless, begin with a *Hallelujah!*, are alphabetical, have the same number of verses, and clauses of each verse. Then Psalm 112 coincides with its predecessor in many of its words and phrases which means that the reader should carefully read the two Psalms line by line. While the structure of these Psalms is identical, such a resemblance calls attention to something deeper and more important. The subject of the one is the exact counterpart of the subject of its companion. Psalm 111 celebrates the character and works of God—Psalm 112, the character and felicity of the godly.

This *Psalm of God's Works*, as we can name it, becomes more precious seeing it is supposed to have been among the Psalms usually sung at the eating of the Paschal Lamb, and used as a hymn by Jesus and His disciples before they went out into the Garden of Gethsemane, Matt. 26:30. The word *Works* is the keynote of the Psalm, and occurs five times, as does the word *ever*. Thus, when tempted to lose heart, because of present trials and difficulties, let us go back on the former deeds of the right hand of our eternal Lord. The theme, then, of Psalm 111 is the refrain of Psalm 107, "Oh that men would praise the Lord for his goodness, and for his wonderful works to the children of men." What God has accomplished should be known by His people, and such knowledge should be, not only a certain cause of unfailing adoration, but an aid to practical piety.

As to the historical setting of the Psalm, probably it was written after the return of Israel from Captivity. "The circumstances of the new colony were poor and depressing. And the aim of the religious leaders of the people was to get them to look up to God, and expect from Him a gracious repetition of the marvelous works of the past." All He *was*, He *is*, and will *ever* be.

Praise ye the Lord. I will praise the Lord, 111:1. The writer did not reserve his *Hallelujah!* for the end of his recital of God's works, which would have been fitting, but as he introduced his adoration of such marvelous works. And what a grand start it is, not only for a Psalm, but for every fresh opportunity of meditating upon all God is in Himself, and all His acts. But while the Psalmist calls upon *all* the saints to praise the Lord, he wanted to make it clear that whether the rest called upon their hearts, and all that was within them to praise Him, he was determined to have his *own* heart all on flame. "*I* will praise the Lord with *my* whole heart." He believed that the best way to enforce his exhortation was to set an example. Thus he practiced what he preached. His attitude was not, "Do as I say," but "Do as I do." *I will praise . . . Praise ye.*

Three realms from which praise and adoration ascend to God are emphasized in this initial verse. First, we have the personal realm, "*I* will praise thee with *my* whole heart." Too many are particular about public church worship and attendance, but sadly neglect their inner spiritual shrine. No amount of congregational worship can make up for one's own personal communion with God. The private chamber of the heart must ever be fragrant with the reverent approach to the Mercy Seat. Then come "the assembly," originally applied to the redeemed who gathered to celebrate the Passover; and "the congregation" representing the public worship connected with the Feast. The R.V. gives us "council" for *assembly* which term is sometimes used of a "secret gathering." Whether for our heart and home, the choicest society of the saved, or the large, communal meeting place, the praise of the Lord is most suitable; and at the very least the true heart should sing *Hallelujah!* in any circumstance and every place.

The works of the Lord are great, sought out, 111:2. As it is "the glory of God to conceal a thing," His marvelous works, particularly in nature, have to be searched out, with telescope or microscope, on Alpine solitude, by mountain stream, or in the great world of human life. We must seek, if we desire to trace God's footsteps. "The works of Jehovah are great, enquired into by all who take delight in them." Doubtless this enquiry after Jehovah was related in the Psalmist's mind to historical proofs of His goodness to the chosen race, but his words are capable of a far wider range. John Ruskin, who loved to think God's thoughts after Him, warned us against the danger of insensibility to natural beauty. No matter where we try to seek the Lord, if sincere, we shall find Him. Delitzsch reads the above passage, "Worthy of being sought after in all their purposes," which is true, for the design and end God has in all He creates or does is equally admirable with His works themselves.

In the Hebrew, the word *great* has so extensive a range of meaning, that in the English there is no single substitute expressive enough to take its place. As used by the Psalmist the word implies *greatly magnified or augmented*, in respect to the influence of Divine works on the minds of those who search them out, and also a greatness because of their number, variety, character, beauty, and utility. "Great and marvelous are thy works,

Lord God Almighty!" May ours be the ever increasing pleasure in spying out the Word and the Works of the Lord, and the consequent experience of an ever-deepening love and gratitude to Him as He rewards our search in the further revelation of Himself!

His work . . . His righteousness, 111:3. It will be noted that the writer passes from the *plural*—"works," to the singular, "work." All God's "Works" are the *Work*, emanating from one source, tending to one result—

> One law; one plan;
> One far-off Divine event.

From contemplation of the great works of the Lord in general, the Psalmist was irresistibly drawn away to the meditation of a particular work, honorable and glorious in its nature. What was *this* work that eclipsed all God's other works? As the verse goes on to speak of His eternal *righteousness*, can it be that this was the most marvelous special work distinguished from His many other manifestations of power and wisdom? Apart from His righteousness, with its perfect justice, provision of salvation and sanctification, and final overthrow of all sin and Satan making up one glorious whole, what other single works of His fathers found itself such honor and glory? In no single deed of God can unrighteousness be found, because of the whole plan of Divine righteousness is perfect, even as its Creator is perfect, and also like Him eternal in nature.

He hath made his wonderful works to be remembered, 111:4. Because the Lord Himself is "gracious and full of compassion," like Himself, His works should never be forgotten. Literally, the first part of the verse should read—"He hath made a memorial for His wonderful works." See Josh. 4:7. Says Wm. S. Plumer, theologian of the 18th century, "The most amazing perverseness of man is proven by the fact that he does not remember what God has so arranged that it would seem impossible that it should be forgotten." How wise and blest we are, if, with John Milton we can say—

> For wonderful indeed are all his works,
> Pleasant to know and worthiest to be all
> Had in remembrance always with delight.

Israel of old was constantly urged not to forget Divine benefits but remember them and with a grateful heart bless God for them. By the ordinances of the Mosaic Law, the deliverance from Egypt, the sojourn in the wilderness, and other memorabilia of her history were continuously brought before the mind of the people with the exhortation to magnify Him for all He had wrought. All the sweet spices of Divine works had to be beaten to powder by meditation, and then laid up in the cabinet of memory. While two outstanding Feasts called for remembrance—The Paschal Lamb under the Old Testament—The Lord's Supper in the New Testament, whatever recalls the Divine works to the memory, is worthy of the highest reverence.

Dunstan, ecclesiastic and statesman, who became Archbishop of Canterbury, whose last public act was the coronation of Ethelred in 978, at Kingston, spent his retired years in Canterbury, delighting himself in the practice of handicrafts, in prayer, in the service of the Church and in the singing of Psalms. He died in May 988. As he died he was heard giving thanks in the words, "The merciful and gracious Lord hath so done His marvelous works, that they ought to be held in remembrance. He hath given meat to them that fear Him." 111:4, 5.

He gave food unto them . . . He will ever be mindful, 111:5. Often the word *meat* means "prey," from its being torn as by a wild beast, but it is also used in the simple sense of *food*. See Prov. 31:15; Mal. 3:10. The unceasing supply of manna and quails for Israel's physical needs throughout the wilderness journey testified to God's ability to feed His people. Was He not forever by His providence supplying the necessities of His redeemed children? In times of scarcity there was always food convenient for them. This was a part of His covenant, God was ever mindful of. "Lacked ye anything?" As our heavenly Father, He knows what we have need of, and has promised that our food and raiment are assured. Did not Jesus teach us to pray, "Give us day by day our daily bread?"

It is because of the blood-covenant God has with us that we know all we need, His bountiful hand will supply for our body. Then there is the spiritual meat He has plentifully furnished us with to feed our soul. There is Jesus Himself, and we are urged to eat and drink of Him—the royal dainty of His Word, in which we have the finest of the wheat. Every time, then, as we cut our daily bread, or feed upon the Word, let us praise the Giver of All that through His covenant of grace, He will care for us until we reach Heaven, where the saints hunger no more. As we journey through the wilderness of this world, there will be times when need is not immediately met, but we must not judge the Lord by His delays; but by His covenant-promises. Often "He *waits* that He may be gracious."

He hath shewed . . . That he may give, 111:6. The phrase "He hath shewed," actually means, "He placed before their eyes," *the power of His works*. The reason for this specified revelation was the unbelief of the Jews who murmured against God in the desert, as if He would not enable them to enter the promised land, and possess it, because the cities were walled, the inhabitants strong, and giants to deal with. But He shewed His people what He was able to do, and under Joshua, they entered the land, and He gave them the Canaanites as their heritage. The Church today is slow to learn that the millions of heathen have been bequeathed to her, and that she must take possession of them as an inheritance. Did not Jesus, when He commissioned His own to go into all the nations and make disciples, assure them that His own divinely bestowed power would be theirs for the security of such a spiritual heritage?

The works of his hands . . . All his commandments, 111:7, 8. What wonderful twins this great verse presents. First, the works of God's hands are never imperfect, shoddy, or contrary to His good and perfect character. There is harmony between all He is in Himself, and all that He does. His works are ever the essence of truth and justice. He always acts His own truths. They are always "Yea and Amen in Christ," 2 Cor. 1:20. The decrees of our King are not fickle but *sure*, and will remain forever—

> Whatever the mighty Lord decrees,
>   Shall stand forever sure,
> The settled purpose of His heart
>   To ages shall endure.

The Psalmist goes on to say that God's commands, purposes, courses of action, are not swayed by transient motives, or moved by the circumstances of the hour, but are the immutable principles by which He rules within His courts, and which abide forever. Springing from *truth and uprightness*, His works and commandments are never revoked, but remain eternally the same. The term *stand fast* has the implication of being *propped up, buttressed forever*. His works and words can never fail, for His power supports them, and His providence preserves the record of all He has said and done. All His works are nothing else but the making good of His Word, and not one jot or tittle shall pass from the law of His mouth, till all be fulfilled.

He sent redemption . . . He hath commanded . . . Holy and reverend is his name, 111:9. A characteristic feature both of this Psalm and the next, is the number of verses containing either twin, or triple truths. The verse before us presents a triad of facts concerning Jehovah. *First*, "He sent redemption to his people," which God did when He brought His people out of Egypt. Through Christ a greater redemption is ours, seeing we represent a people purchased by His own precious blood. *Second*, "He hath commanded his covenant for ever." God's decree made the covenant of His grace a settled and eternal institution; redemption by blood proves that the covenant cannot be altered, for it ratifies and establishes it beyond all recall. It is sealed by blood, which should arouse us to an ecstacy of gratitude to the Lamb Who was slain. *Third*, "Holy and reverend is His name"—which therefore we should not presume on a sudden to blurt out, says old John Trapp. The Jews would not pronounce the name. The Grecians, when they would swear by their Jupiter, forbore to mention him. This should act as a check to the profaneness common among us. Let those who would have their *name revered*, labor to be *holy* as God is holy. The term *reverend* occurs only here in Scripture, and is used of God, as an evidence of profound homage. Spurgeon, who always called himself, *Pastor*, wrote that "the foolish custom" of men calling themselves *reverend* should "fall into disuse. How good men can endure to be called *reverend* we know not. Being unable to discover any reason why our fellow-men should reverence *us*, if we half suspect that in other men there is not very much which can entitle them to be called *reverend, very reverend*, and *right reverend*, and so on."

The fear of the Lord . . . his commandments . . . his praise, 111:10. Here is another triplet of truth—a threefold cord we cannot break—the X, Y, Z, of this alphabet Psalm, others of the same nature being Psalms 9, 10, 34, 37, and 112. It is singular that not only are Psalms 111 and 112 perfectly regular, in contrast to the other alphabetical Psalms, but furthermore, that not one various reading of note or importance occurs in either of these Psalms. The following alphabetical translation of Psalm 111 is taken from *The Psalms Chronologically Arranged*, published almost a hundred years ago—

                                                                                                                        verse
*A*ll my heart shall praise Jehovah 1
        *B*efore the *c*ongregation of the righteous;
*D*eeds of goodness are the deeds of Jehovah,....................................2
        *E*arnestly desired of all them have pleasure therein;
*F*or his righteousness endureth for ever, ...3
        *G*lorious and honorable is his work;
*H*e hath made his wonderful works to be remembered, ...4
        *I*n Jehovah is compassion and goodness;
*J*ehovah hath given meat to them that fear him,................................5
        *K*eeping his covenant for ever,
*L*earning his people the power of his works,.....................................6
        *M*aking them to possess the heritage of the heathen;
*N*ought save truth and equity are the works of his hands,.................7
        *O*rdered and sure are his commands,
*P*lanted fast for ever and ever,..8
        *R*ighteous and true are his testimonies;
*S*alvation hath he sent unto his people,..9
        *T*heir covenant hath he made fast for ever;
*U*pright and holy is his name,..10
        *V*erily, the fear of the Lord is the beginning of wisdom,
*Y*ea, a good understanding have all they that do thereafter;
        *Z*ealously shall he be praised for ever.

The dungeons in the Tower, London, still bear record of the power of the Psalms to soothe the "sorrowing sighing" of Roman Catholics who suffered for their faith. For example, Charles Bailly inscribed on the walls of his cell in the Cobham Tower, "*The fear of the Lord is the beginning of wisdom. Be frend to one. Be ennemye to none. Anno D. 1571, Sept 10.*" The *Fear* mentioned is the first line of the trinity of assertions in this verse, is a fear compatible with perfect love, and not the kind of fear suggesting dread, such as one experiences in meeting a cruel person, or an impending evil. "The fear of the Lord" is a childlike fear which is afraid to offend Him, a reverential trust and confidence in Him at all times, and which alone results in the wisdom, enabling us to enter into God's secrets, read their meaning, and understand all He is in Himself. See Prov. 1:7; 9:10. Holy reverence of God is at once the first element of wisdom, and its chief fruit.

The fear of the Lord implies all the graces of virtues of Christianity, and all that holiness of heart and life so necessary to the possession of eternal happiness. Such *fear* is not only the beginning of wisdom, but the middle and the end. "It is indeed the Alpha and Omega, the essence, the body and soul, the sum and substance. . . . The principle whence wisdom springs, and the fountain from which it flows." See Job 28:28.

The second truth is the triad this verse presents, emphasizes the fruit of *Obedience*. "A good understanding have all they that do his commandments." Speaking, or writing about these commandments does not produce a "good understanding," or "good success," as some render it, but only obeying them. "If we *do* these things, we shall *know*." If the fear of the Lord rules in the heart, there will follow a constant conscientious desire and effort to keep His Word. "A good estimation have all they that do them," says Ellicott. "Not only is piety the beginning of wisdom, but righteousness wins good esteem." The standpoint, then, from which we view things is of the utmost importance to our right understanding of them. The best proof of spiritual intelligence is found in actually doing the will of the One we fear.

The final line of the Psalm agrees with its first line, "Praise ye the Lord"—"His praise endured for ever." By *His praise*, we understand the praise of those who fear and obey the Lord. Because His works never cease, the recipients of them never cease to praise Him from whom all blessings flow. May we ever be found among those of whom it is said, "Blessed are they that dwell in thy house: they will still be praising thee," Psalm 84:41. May all our days commence and end as this precious Psalm does, with praise to Jehovah!

Psalm 112

A mong the Psalms John Ruskin learned by heart, as soon as he was able to read, was Psalm 112, which he came to make most personally his own. As soon as we enter the door of this Psalm, we notice the last thoughts of the previous Psalm provide the first of this Psalm. Not only does it begin with a *Hallelujah!* as Psalm 111, but *praise, fear, commandments,* are terms ending the one Psalm and commencing the other. Such repetition means Divine emphasis. In our introduction to Psalm 111 we pointed out that it should be studied with Psalm 112, seeing that the one is a pendant of the other. In addition to what we have already said regarding the similarity of these two Psalms, in their close relation exhibited in their subject, "Psalm 111 exhibits Jehovah in covenant with man; Psalm 112, man in covenant with Jehovah. The one sings the Divine praise in view of the kindness of God shown to Israel; in the second, the feeling of the just man, that is, the Israelite faithful to the covenant, is the subject. In both we discover the strength of these religious convictions, which, in spite of the contradictions experienced in actual life, persist in maintaining the grand principle of Divine justice, and declaring that the cause of virtue will triumph, and success and wealth never fail the faithful."

Features common to both Psalms have already been pointed out. A further evidence of the close relation of the two is marked by the echo in the second, of phrases applied in the first to Jehovah—"Righteousness endureth for ever," 111:3; 112:3, 9—"The Lord is gracious and full of compassion," 111:4; 112:4, 6. In the first Psalm the praises of God are directly celebrated, and in the second one, the same praises are indirectly declared by those gifts which are conspicuous in the lives of those who fear the Lord. The subject of the poem in Psalm 112 is "The blessedness of the righteous man," and so bears the same relation to the preceding Psalm which the moon does to the sun; for, while the first declares the glory of God, the second speaks of the reflection of the Divine brightness in men born from above. In Psalm 112, God is praised for the manifestation of His glory as seen in His people, just as in Psalm 111, He is magnified for His own personal acts. The opening *Hallelujah!* closely relates the Psalm to its previous companion and also the following Psalms. Evidently these Praise Psalms were composed about the same time, and more than likely by the same author, and belong manifestly to the era of return from the Captivity in Egypt. Such an exhortation—Praise ye the Lord—is not given too often, for the Lord always deserves praise, and we ought always to be ready to render it.

Blessed is the man that feareth . . . that delighteth, 112:1. The subject clearly stated here is enlarged upon under several heads through the succeeding verses, with a contrast between the eternal destiny of the righteous and the ungodly concluding the Psalm. As we saw in the previous Psalm, its last verse declared that "the fear of the Lord is the beginning of wisdom," and the man before us in this first verse of Psalm 112 has begun to be wise, and his wisdom brought him present joy, and secured for him eternal felicity. As indicated before, the *fear* expressed in these verses is not slavish fear associated with bondage, but a godly fear or reverence sweetening into filial love. Fear, by itself, produces misery and wretchedness, and results in being in fear where no fear is. What the Psalmist extols is "the fear of *the Lord*," a fear of which He is the author, Jerem. 32:39, 40, which restrains from sin, Prov. 3:7, and inspires well-doing, Eccles. 12:13. Because the man described fears *the Lord*, he is not afraid of *evil tidings*, 112:7, 8. Further, this praising, God-fearing man has great delight in meditating upon Divine precepts, and obeying them. To him, it is not drudgery to study Scripture, but a *delight*, and his cheerful obedience to the commandments is the only acceptable obedience to God. In fact, such a man comes to see that the only way of delighting in God's dictates is to do them Rev. 22:14. The Hebrew word for *delighteth* is somewhat emphatic, says John Calvin, and means to *take his pleasure* or *to delight himself.* Thus the Psalmist, "makes a distinction between a willing and prompt endeavour to keep the law, and that which consists in mere servile and constrained obedience."

His seed . . . the generation of the righteous, 112:2. The word for *mighty* implies the sense of being *wealthy,* see Ruth 2:1. "Wealth and riches are in his house," verse 3. The message of this verse is clear, namely that successive generations of those who fear the Lord are influential in society. The true seed of the righteous are those who follow them in their virtues, and are in sympathy with their values, just as believers are said to be "of the seed of Abraham," because they imitate his faith. While there is ample warrant for believing that though godliness is not hereditary and grace does not run in the blood, yet the godliness of Christian parents has the strongest possible influence on children and is also a blessing communicated to after generations. See Psalm 103:17; Isa. 59:12.

The accumulating of wealth, and the willing of it to others, by no means implies that we leave behind us a flourishing posterity. Doubtless Lot thought of enriching his family when he chose the fertile plains of Sodom, yet it was not so. Abraham "feared the Lord, and delighted greatly in his commandments," and it was he and his descendants who became "mighty upon earth." Generally, it is thus in every age when the posterity imitate the father of the faithful.

Wealth and riches . . . and his righteousness, 112:3. Here we have a combination of things material and spiritual. It is because of the *righteousness* of the God-fearing man that he is none the worse for any wealth that may come to him, and is not drawn aside by the deceitfulness of riches. If financial prosperity is not ours, the Bible declares that true spiritual riches are stored up for those who may be poor, both in silver and in spirit, for says Paul, "As poor, yet making many rich; as having nothing, and yet possessing all things," 2 Cor. 6:10. Who can be richer than he who is the heir of God and joint heir with His Son, Jesus Christ? Spurgeon has the comment on this verse—

> What wealth can equal that of the love of God? What riches can rival a contented heart? It matters nothing that the roof is thatched, and the floor is of cold stone; the heart which is cheered with the favor of Heaven is "rich to all intents of Bliss."

The Psalmist goes on to say about the blessed man that if gold comes in, grace does not go out, for "his righteousness endureth for ever." Prosperity did not destroy his purity of life. The same clause is repeated from Psalm 111:3, and used again in the 9th verse of the Psalm before us, and the word for *righteousness* seems to require for it the limited sense which the Talmud gives it, namely, *liberality* or *beneficence*. See also LXX Version, and Daniel 4:27. Yet the declaration is true in its widest sense. "There is nothing, no, nothing, innocent or good, that dies or is forgotten; let us hold to that faith, or none." Although our Christian dispensation is one of spiritual, rather of temporal, blessing—it is nevertheless true that "Godliness is profitable unto all things, having promise of the life that now is, and of that which is to come," 1 Tim. 4:8.

The upright . . . he is gracious, and full of compassion, and righteousness, 112:4. What a great verse this is with its promise for those who fear the Lord, and who reflect His character! How richly the first clause of it has blessed saints and martyrs of the past! "Unto the upright there ariseth light in the darkness." James Melville, the renowned Scottish covenantor, found in the Psalms the expression of his sorrow, his gratitude, his triumph, and in the hour of death, his strength and courage. As he came to enter the valley of the shadow, he requested that "the candell behind his back be brought before him, that he might sie to die. Be occasionne quhairof that pairt of the Scripture was rememberit."

Light arises to the righteous in the midst of darkness, 112:4. In the religious history of Scotland, Thomas Chalmers was the leading spirit in the Reformation in 1843. To secure spiritual independence from civil control, Chalmers and 470 ministers resigned their livings and joined the *Free*

Church and with this memorable description the Psalms were associated. It was from the words, "Unto the godly there ariseth up light in the darkness," that Chalmers preached a sermon in Edinburgh, on Nov. 17, 1841 which greatly inspired those who dreaded the unknown future. Dr. Buchanan, writing of the effect of that sermon said, "Never was the truth—*A word spoken in season, how good is it,* more vividly realized when the preacher gave out his text. Every man looked at his neighbor, and exchanged the silent but strong expression of conscious comfort and encouragement which the very utterance of these words at such a moment called forth."

The Hebrew verb for *ariseth* is commonly used of the sunrise. Psalm 97:11; Isa. 58:8. Its message here for those who are upright is that the darkest night of trouble and sorrow will have a dawn of hope. They may not always see the light, but it is behind the cloud, waiting God's signal, Isa. 50:11. The sunrise, one of the most beneficent natural phenomena is a daily victory over darkness which is likewise true in the spiritual world. "Unto the upright there ariseth light in the darkness." The gifted expositor, George Horne, said that we on earth are subject to a threefold *darkness*—"the darkness of error, the darkness of sorrow, the darkness of death. To dispel these, God visiteth us, by His Word, with a threefold *light*—the light of truth, the light of comfort, and the light of life."

He is gracious, and full of compassion, and righteous. These three attributes, usually applied to God, are here used to describe the upright ones for whom light arose to banish their darkness. As God's children we know from the Word and from experience that "He is gracious, full of compassion, and righteous," and that ours should be the instinctive imitation of Him toward others, Matt. 5:45, 48; Eph. 5:8. This trinity of excellencies in their union, form a perfect character when they are well balanced in daily life. Can we say that we are copies of the Great Original in this threefold way?

> *Gracious*—full of kindness, never sour or churlish, but courteous to all, kind to the needy, forgiving, and sincere for the good of all.

> *Full of Compassion*—not compassionate when we feel like it, but so full of it that we cannot suppress being willing to pity, and care for sorrowing hearts in trouble. The gracious man is brimful of humanity, running over with sympathy for the needy.

> *Righteous*—Being "upright" means that such a person is always the right side *up*, always obeying the dictates of his Spirit-enlightened conscience in all his transactions with others. His justice or uprightness, however, are always tempered with compassion, and seasoned with graciousness.

A good man sheweth favor . . . He will guide his affairs with discretion,

112:5. How varied are the descriptions of the person exalted in this Psalm! He is a *blessed* man, *upright, righteous, good, unafraid, established,* and *exalted.* The first part of this verse carries a premonition of our Lord's words in Matt. 5:42. The *gracious* man is a *good* man, or as we can translate the phrase, "Happy is the man who gives and lends"—*good* being here not used in a moral sense, but meaning *prosperous.* The R.V. puts it, "Well is it with the man that," etc. Providence has made such a man able to lend, and grace makes him willing to lend. Wisely, he uses the talents instructed to him, and exercises great care and discretion in the choice of the objects of his benevolence, and also in the management of all his affairs. "True religion is sanctified common sense." Are we not told that the man diligent and honest in business is fit to stand before kings? "It is required as stewards that a man be found faithful."

A story illustrating the virtue of *Discretion* concerns some of the ancient Fathers who came to St. Anthony, enquiring of him, what virtue did by a direct line lead to perfection, that so a man might shun the snares of Satan. Anthony asked every one of the enquirers to state his own opinion. One said, watching and sobriety; another, fasting and discipline; yet another said humble prayer; while others said poverty and obedience, or piety and works of mercy. After the Fathers had spoken their mind, Anthony's reply was that all these were excellent graces indeed, but *discretion* was the chief of them all. Without such a guide of all our actions, and the moderator and orderer of all our affections, virtues can become vices. It is wisely said, "that an ounce of discretion is worth a pound of learning."

He shall not be moved . . . shall be in everlasting remembrance, 112:6. All who emulate the foregoing virtues and graces shall never be moved, Psalm 15:5, and his name will never rot, Proverbs 10:7. Those who are blessed of the Lord, and who honor Him in all their ways are rooted and established by Him, and their influence and memory abide with God Himself taking charge of their memorials. Away back in 1790, godly John Dun wrote, "The stately and durable Pyramids of Egypt have not transmitted to posterity even the names of those buried in them. And what has even embalming done, but tossed them about, and exposed them to the world as spectacles to the curious, of meanness, or horror. But the piety of Abraham, of Jacob, of David, of Samuel, and others, is celebrated to this very day. So when the Pyramids shall sink, and seas cease to roll, when sun and moon and stars shall be no more, *the righteous shall be an everlasting remembrance.*"

He shall not be afraid . . . his heart is fixed, 112:7. Trust in the Lord produces fearlessness, and fixity of heart. The best illustration of this verse is the record of Job when the messengers of trial and tragedy succeeded one another so fast, and he met the prophets of doom with the triumphant assertion, "Though He slay me, yet will I trust Him." It has been said that "A good conscience before God is the best armor against fate." In Shakespeare's *Measure for Measure* we have the line—

"Virtue is bold, and goodness never fearful."

Faith and Fear can never exist together, for trust is expulsive of terror. The heart that is firmly and trustingly fixed on God is not afraid, because it knows that no tidings can reach it save through the Father's permission; and that all tidings must be of His appointment. The verse does not say that evil tidings will not reach us, but that when they do, they cannot move us from our trust in God, seeing it is fixed on Him. If we dread evil tidings coming some morning, we must not look along the road by which the postman comes, but upward and Godward. Distressful tidings may force us to change our plans, but not the purpose of our soul. Job was not afraid at the evil tidings brought him, for his heart was kept in an equal poise. "The Lord gave, and the Lord hath taken away; blessed be the name of the Lord."

The Bible and history provide us with many inspiring examples of those whose heart was established fearlessly. Moses when he was before the Egyptians, and then before the Red Sea. How bold were the three youths in prospect of Nebuchadnezzar's fiery furnace! How fearless and defiant was Stephen before the Council! Basilius could say in answer to the cruel threats of Caesar Valens, "such bug-bears should be set before children." Then there was the taunt of Athanasius over the effort of Julian, his persecutor, to get rid of him, "He is a mist that will soon disappear." A good outline for the preacher on this 7th verse is the following:

1. *The Waves*—"Evil tidings."
2. *The Steady Ship*—"He shall not be afraid."
3. *The Anchor*—"His heart is fixed, trusting."
4. *The Anchorage*—"In the Lord."

His heart is established . . . his desire upon his enemies, 112:8. The first part of this verse is the repetition of the previous verse, while the verse as a whole emphasizes heart establishment—the confidence flowing from it—and the sight seen by all who possess such security and tranquility. The courage of the man who fears God has a firm foundation, being supported by Omnipotence. He is no rolling stone, but firmly settled by experience, and confirmed by years. Consequently, along with his holy heart, he has a brave face. He has no fear what men or demons may do. After his victory over them who tried to make him afraid, he desires his enemies' good. The original of "until he sees his desire upon his enemies," reads, "until he looks upon his oppressors," that is, till he beholds them securely, and, as we say, confidently *looks in their faces*; as being

Psalms: *A Devotional Commentary*

no longer under their power, but freed from their tyranny and oppression. A further comment on this last clause reads—

> His faith will not fail, nor shrink, nor change, while one by one his enemies are brought to the knowledge of the truth and love of Christ, and he shall see his heart's desire fulfilled upon them, even that they may be saved.

He hath dispersed . . . given to the poor . . . his righteousness . . . his horn, 112:9. Here we have a threefold portrayal of the blessings of the man who fears God and delights in His commandments. As a whole, the verse exalts *benevolence*—its exercise is almsgiving, its preserving influence upon character, and the honor it wins. What the unafraid saint received, he distributed. He was God's reservoir from which flowed streams of liberality to relieve the needy. And the mark of such a God-fearing man is that the more he gives, the more he receives—

> There was a man, some thought him mad,
> The more he gave, the more he had.

There is never any difficulty in relieving the poor, materially, once we have come to appropriate our unsearchable riches in Christ, and to be convinced that our "righteousness endured for ever." Twice over in the Psalm this remarkable sentence is applied to the man who fears God, and whose liberality salts his righteousness, proves its reality, and secures its perpetuity. "The character of a righteous man is not spasmodic, he is not generous by fits and starts, nor upright in a few points only; his life is the result of principle, his actions flow from settled convictions, and therefore his integrity is maintained when others fail."

His horn shall be exalted with honor. The horn is the symbol of *strength* and *power*—it is the beast's strength, offensive and defensive—of *plenty*, for it has within it a capacity to contain what is put into it—of *sanctity*, for in it was put the holy oil, with which kings were consecrated—of *dignity*, both in consequence, namely, expressing might, influence, and sacredness associated with sovereign dignity. The horn also graces the creature possessing it with *beauty*. The phrase before us, then, can imply an high, holy, firm, and solid honor, as a reward for the godly who are bountiful, to the worthy and unworthy alike.

The wicked shall see . . . the wicked shall perish, 112:10. What a striking contrast the first and last verses of this heart-warming Psalm present! It begins with the blessedness of the saint and ends with the doom of the sinner. Then, how marked is the difference between the ending of Psalm 111, and of this, its twin Psalm. Each end with a triad, but they are so adverse in truth. What sight is it that grieves the wicked as he sees it? Can it be that he is vexed, partly because he is aware that the God-fearing man possesses that of which he is destitute, and because his own schemes melt away before his eyes, as wreaths of smoke? Do not the ungodly witness the life and honor of saints to their own condemnation, and will not their eternal misery increase as they dwell upon the eternal peace and joy of the godly? But once the wicked have crossed the bar, no amount of grief can alter their eternal woe.

The Jewish *Mishna* says that the word for *wicked* is used emphatically by the Jews, to denote him who neither gives to the poor himself, nor can endure to see other people give; while he who deserves but one part of this character is only said to have *an evil eye in regard to other people's substance.* How lamentable is the phrase, "the wicked shall see it!" It is more than likely that Cowper had this verse before his eyes when he penned his poetic commentary on the truth it presents—

> . . . The same word, that like the polished share
> Ploughs up the roots of a believer's care,
> Kills, too, the flow'ry weeds where'er they grow,
> That bind the sinner's Bacchanalian brow.
> Oh that unwelcome voice of heavenly love,
> Sad messenger of mercy from above,
> How does it grate upon his thankless ear,
> Crippling his pleasures with the cramp of fear!
> His will and judgment at continual strife
> That civil war embitters all his life;
> In vain he points his pow'rs against the skies,
> In vain he closes or averts his eye
> Truth will invade.

The symbolism of the wicked gnashing with his teeth, this melting away, is most expressive. An angry man snaps his teeth together, as if about to bite the object of his anger. Thus in the book of *Ramyanum*, the giant Ravanan is described as in his fury gnashing together his *thirty-two teeth.* Of angry men, with temper at high pitch, it is often said, "Look at them, gnashing their teeth," and others are afraid to approach them. The *melting away* bespeaks the effect of hatred and envy, as the envious are consumed. It has been said that, "Envy is most hateful, but has good in it, for it makes the eyes and the heart of the envious to pine away." Spurgeon's comment on *melt away* reads, "How horrible must be that life which like the snail melts as it proceeds, leaving a slimy trail behind. Those who are grieved at goodness deserve to be worn away by such an abominable sorrow."

There is no more solemn, poignant phrase in the whole of Scripture than the one that closes this further alphabetical Psalm. *The desire of the wicked shall perish.* Jesus declared that all who believe in Him as the Divinely given Savior, *shall not perish.* For the man fearing God, delighting in His Word, and reflecting the image of his Lord, there is a memory which shall be always green. But for the wicked, their name shall rot. Do we really grasp how wide and deep the gulf, separating the righteous from the wicked, actually is, and how eternally different their end is? If we did, we should find ourselves more deeply grateful to God for saving us from sin and eternal condemnation, and strive more faithfully to "rescue the perishing, and care for the dying," telling them of the One mighty to save, and able to deliver them from the peril of dying in their wickedness.

> Stir me, Oh! stir me, Lord, till all my heart
> Is filled with strong compassion for lost souls;
> Till Thy compelling word drives me to pray;
> Till Thy constraining love reach to the poles
> Far north and south, in burning deep desire,
> Till east and west are caught in love's great fire.

Psalm 113

To John Calvin belongs the honor of editing the first printed edition of metrical Psalms for Church worship. It was in 1539, when he became Pastor of the French Protestant Church at Strasburg that he had printed one Psalm in prose—*Psalm 113*—and seventeen others in verse, set to music. But this praiseful Psalm has a more sacred, historical association, for it is thought to have been the Hymn or Psalm sung by our Lord and His disciples after the celebration of the Lord's Supper, Matt. 26:30. This Psalm, and the five following Psalms, constitute the *Hallel* Psalms, or Hymns of Praise, from *Hallel*, meaning "to praise." Psalm 113 is sometimes referred to as *The Great Hallel*, though such an estimation is more properly confined to Psalm 136, recited at the great Jewish Feasts.

Psalms 113 and 114 were sung before the second cup at the Passover Feast, and Psalms 115-118, after the fourth cup. Psalm 113 has been called *The Magnificat of the Old Testament*. Tradition shows, says Dr. Andrew Bonar, that the ancient Jews perceived in these six Psalms some link of close connection, for they all sing of God the Redeemer, in some aspect of His redeeming character. This being so, while they suited the Paschal Feast, they were most appropriate on the lips of the Redeemer, in His Upper Room.

Psalm 113, sings praise to Him Who redeems from the lowest depth.

Psalm 114, sings praise to Him Who once redeemed Israel, and shall redeem her again.

Psalm 115, utters a song—over earth's fallen idols—to Him Who blesses Israel and the world.

Psalm 116, sings His resurrection-song of thanksgiving by anticipation.

Psalm 117, the song of praise comes from the great congregation.

Psalm 118, sung before leaving the Upper Room for Gethsemane, pours forth the story of His suffering, conflict, triumph, and glorification.

Psalm 113 has a further historical connection in that its opening verses began the Evening Hymn of the Apostolic Institutions—"From the rising of the sun to the going down of the same, the Lord's name be praised." The gifted Biblical scholar, Edersheim, informs us that the Talmud dwells upon the peculiar suitableness of the *Hallel* to the Passover, "since it not only recorded the goodness of God towards Israel, but especially their deliverance from Egypt, and therefore appropriately

opened with, *Praise ye Jehovah, ye servants of Jehovah*—and not servants
of Pharaoh."

Praise . . . Praise . . . Praise, 113:1. Such a rousing call to "praise,"
which is the frankincense, as "prayer" is the myrrh, constrains us to name
the Psalm, *The Herald of the Hallel*. The Psalm, as a whole, is ruled by
the number "three"—three strophes of three verses each. In this first verse
we are exhorted three times to *praise* the Lord—although the term appears
five times in the Psalm. Also it is the *name* of the Lord we are urged three
times over to praise—*name* representing all He is in Himself. Edersheim
tells us that responses were common in the Temple service, that after
every line of the Psalm repeated by the Levites, the people would respond
by repeating, *Hallelu JAH*. Such a liturgical introduction and response
must have been impressive. By "servants of the Lord," we are to understand *Israel*. See Psalm 69:36.

The repetition of *praise* is not without significance. We are too slow,
or forgetful of praising God from Whom all blessings flow, and thus need
such stimuli. Such repetition also signifies assiduity and perseverance in
echoing forth the praises of God. How fitting are the lines of Richard
Mant—

> Hallelujah, praise the Lord!
> Praise, ye servants, praise His name!
> Be Jehovah's praise ador'd,
> Now and evermore the same!
> Where the orient sun-beams gleam,
> Where they sink in ocean's stream,
> Through the circuit of his rays,
> Be your theme Jehovah's praise.

Blessed be the name of the Lord from this time and for evermore,
113:2. Because His name is excellent in all heaven, and earth, it is worthy of being magnified by the redeemed in both spheres. We can imagine
how the disciples that sat at the table with Jesus would repeat with mingled feelings of thanksgiving and sadness this ascription of
praise—"Blessed be the name of the Lord from this time forth and for
evermore." In our own hearts as well as publicly, we are to praise Him,
and pray for the triumph of His cause and truth. By *the name* the Psalmist
would have us bless the Most High for each of His attributes, "which are
as it were the letters of His name." No new name is to be invented, for the
variety of His designations in Scripture is sufficient.

The point of time set for blessing the Lord is interesting to observe—
"From *this* time forth." A commentator asks, "What Israelite in all the
Paschal Chambers at Jerusalem on that night, as he sang the *Hallel* or
hymn, or which of the disciples at the sorrowing board of Jesus, could

have understood or entered into the full meaning of the expression, 'From this time forth'? From *what time*?" John gave us a clue to the very hour and moment of which the Psalmist, perhaps unconsciously, spake. He tells us that when the traitor Judas received the sop, he immediately went out; and when he left to clinch and ratify his treacherous purpose, Jesus said, "*Now* is the Son of Man glorified, and God is glorified in Him." . . . "A few more hours and the covenant will be sealed in My own blood; the compact ratified, when I hang upon that cross."

It is always time to bless the Lord, but for those who have not commenced to do so, now is the time to start at once to praise Him. At the beginning of every year, or at the opening of every day, for that matter, we should hear the Lord saying, "From this time will I bless thee," and our reply should be, "Blessed be the name of the Lord *from this time* forth." Then the Psalmist goes on to say that such is not only during our time on earth, but when time shall be no more. *For evermore* which means eternally. Endless duration is to be ours, and not until we see the Lord shall we bless Him as we ought. As His servants, we are to sing His praises to the world's end, and then in Heaven, world without end. This phrase *for evermore* proceeds on the supposition that our God will forever continue to develop and unfold His glorious nature, so that there will be always some new occasion to bless and adore Him for. "If the praise begun on earth be continued in Heaven, *we* must be in Heaven to continue the praise."

From the rising of the sun unto the going down of the same, the Lord's name is to be praised, 113:3. This is an extension of the *time* element of the previous verse. As Jesus uttered this prediction, how His heart must have rejoiced that when mid-day would be turned into mid-night at Calvary, His sufferings would be over. The language in this most expressive verse, implies everywhere, from east to west—*west* being used in the Hebrew for sunset, or the sun's going down. From sunrise to sunset the ceaseless praise should rise to Jehovah's throne, and from east to west over the whole round earth pure worship should be rendered unto His glory. But alas! it is not so, for millions do not know Him sufficiently to bless and magnify His name.

Is not this third verse a prediction yet to be realized when the Sun of Righteousness arises with healing in His wings, Psalm 72:11; Mal. 1:11; Rev. 15:3, 4? Then the sun's course as it awakens the successive populations of the globe shall be tracked by songs of praise. May we endeavor to sanctify every day as it commences, continues, and concludes with praise! "At early dawn let us emulate the opening flowers and the singing birds"—

> Chanting every day their lauds,
> While the grove their song applauds;
> Wake from shame my sluggish heart,
> Wake and gladly sing thy part.

The Lord is high above all nations—His glory above the heavens,
113:4. God has set His glory "above the heavens," Psalm 8:1. Yet even
"the heaven of heavens cannot contain him," 1 Kings 8:27. He is high
above all nations here below where His glory is displayed in His *name,*
but His *real* glory is above the heavens. God is so high that He surmounts
all created capacity to comprehend Him. See Job 11:7-9. While He is far
beyond the pomp and might of the rulers of the nations, it is to be doubted whether *any* nation today recognizes His pre-eminence and superiority.
"Like the great arch of the firmament, the presence of the Lord spans all
the lands where dwell the varied tribes of men, for His providence is universal: this may well excite our confidence and praise." But when Jesus
reigns "wher'er the sun doth its successive journeys run," then universal
homage and praise will be His.

It is because God dwells on high, that His glory is higher than the
heavens—heavens, being the loftiest part of Creation; the clouds are the
dust of His feet, and sun, moon, and stars twinkle far below His throne.
Above the heavens, is Heaven, His eternal dwelling place, and from here
He rules the nations and the heavens, as the infinite, omnipotent God.
Thus, above all, let us adore Him Who is above all. The next verse
emphasizes the uniqueness of Him Who dwells on high. None is like Him
among the monarchs of earth, and the angels of Heaven. None can be
compared to Him when we think of the perfection of His nature, acts, and
attributes. "The Lord most high" is the Omnipotent, Omniscient, and
Omnipresent One and there is none among men, like unto Him. All created beings with all their excellencies are but nothing and vanity in
comparison with Him who is "an infinite ocean of perfection, without
either brink or bottom."

> Eternal Power! whose high abode
> Becomes the grandeur of a God:
> Infinite lengths beyond the bounds
> Where stars revolve, their little rounds.
>
> The lowest step around thy seat
> Rises too high for Gabriel's feet;
> In vain the tall archangel tries
> To reach thine height with wond'ring eyes.
>
> Lord, what shall earth and ashes do?
> We would adore our Maker too;
> From sin and dust to thee we cry,
> The Great, the Holy, and the High.

Who humbleth himself to behold . . . heaven . . . earth, 113:6. Literally,
this revealing verse reads, "Who stoopeth down to look in heaven and on

earth." We should be found living in the depths of humility, with this action of the Most High stooping so low to save such unworthy recipients of His loving humiliation. In His incarnation, Jesus stooped through the immense distance between heaven and earth to become man, Phil. 2:6-8. The two propositions human reason will never be able to unite are *Who dwelleth on high*, but *He humbleth Himself*, yet the two are in perfect harmony in the greatest text in the Bible, "God so loved the world that He gave His only begotten Son that whosoever believeth in him should not perish, but have everlasting life." Wrote Valentine Nalson, of the early 17th century—

> To see the great King of heaven stooping from his height, and condescending himself to offer terms of reconciliation to his rebellious creatures—
>
> To see offended majesty courting the offenders to accept of pardon—
>
> To see God persuading, entreating, and beseeching men to return to him with such earnestness and importunity, as if his very life were bound up in them, and his own happiness depended on theirs—
>
> To see the adorable Spirit of God, with infinite long-suffering and gentleness, submitting to the contempt and insults of such miserable, despicable wretches as sinful mortals are—Is not this amazing?

It certainly is.

Heathen philosophers of old found it impossible to believe that the great God was observant of the small events of human history, and of a person's own life. Their conception of Him was of One abiding in serene indifference, or ignorance of the wants and woes of His creatures. But Scripture ever extols the high and lofty One condescending to dwell in those of a contrite and humble spirit. Ever regarding the low estate of His own, for their own sakes although rich He became poor.

He raised up the poor . . . and lifteth up the needy, 113:7. How precious is this demonstration of God's gracious stoop of love! How gifted He is at repairing Satan's broken earthenware, of taking the lowest of mankind out of all their filth and degradation and bringing them into positions of power and honor. Looked upon as worthless refuse, corrupt and loathsome, sinners are marvelously transformed by the condescending Savior into new creatures. "Out of the dust . . . out of the dunghill," are almost word for word from Hannah, 1 Sam. 2:8.

By *dunghill* we can understand a heap of rubbish, a place where the household would heap up sweepings of their stalls in the market. It was on such a heap warmed and made to smell by the sun, that Job sat, for such was an emblem of poverty and desertion. Both in Syria and Palestine, a man shut out from society would lie upon the *magbele*, or dunghill, or heap of ashes, by day calling upon passersby for alms, and by night hiding himself in the heap that had been warmed by the sun. Yet the compassionate eye of God is ever open on the lowest of the low, and is ever ready to grace and exalt those of low degree. "His blood can make the vilest clean." He knew that we could never raise ourselves out of the dust, and dunghill, and out of the sepulchre, in which we were spiritually dead, and so His arms brought salvation. What else can those do who have been taken out of the miry clay and placed securely upon a rock, but praise and magnify Him for His transforming power?

Set with princes . . . with princes of his people, 113:8. Actually, this is the other half of the previous verse, and indicates that God is not content until He honors those raised from the dust, to become peers of His kingdom. By His Spirit, He is ever striving to make rebels, kings and priests unto Himself, that they might reign with Him forever. He took John Bunyan, the swearing tinker of Bedford, and made him a prince among princes by giving him a *Dream* that almost rivals the vision of a previous John in his Apocalypse. Truly the distinctions and accolades bestowed upon men by a government are tawdry alongside the exalted position granted to those saved by grace. In Britain, the highest honor to be coveted is elevation to *The House of Lords*, but how such an exaltation fades into nothingness alongside of being made to sit among the princes of God's people. How blest we are if among those elevated to the Peerage of Heaven, we live forever in the House of the Lord of lords!

The barren woman . . . to be a joyful mother of children, Hallelujah! 113:9. Anything thought exceeding valuable earned this description: "This is as precious as the son of the long reputed barren woman." The verse concluding this Psalm is an echo of Hannah's song, 1 Sam. 2:1-10, and reveals that barrenness was a grievous sorrow to a Jewish wife. The condition indicated may perhaps typify the Jewish Church in her low, fruitless estate, or even the Gentile Church, Isa. 54:1-3; but when God wills, and in answer to believing prayer, her spiritual children are multiplied. The margin gives us the Hebrew, "to dwell in a house," alongside "to keep house," and Ellicott follows with this notation—

> Motherhood alone assured the wife of a fixed and dignified position in her husband's house. The quotation from Hannah's song suggested the allusion to her story. We are no doubt right in taking this joyful mother as emblematic of the nation itself restored to prosperity and joy.

Historical illustrations of the miraculous power of God in literally fulfilling the concluding statement of the Psalmist can be found in Bible women like Sarah, Rachel, Manoah's wife, Hannah and Elizabeth whose childlessness was banished by Him whose offspring we are, and who lifted up their voices in praise, saying with Hannah, "There is none holy as the Lord's for there is none beside thee, neither is there any rock

like our God." Several expositors remind us that it was the strong desire
of wives in the East to have children, and that the birth of a child was
hailed as the choicest of favors, while barrenness was considered a curse.
Thus, it would seem as if this verse is placed last as if to crown the whole,
and to serve as a fitting climax to the story of God's condescending grace
and mercy. So the music of the Psalm concludes upon its key-note
Hallelujah!

This Psalm is a glorious circle, ending where it began, *Praise ye the
Lord*! From its first syllable to its last, praise abounds for God's condescension in human affairs, as well as for all He is in Himself as the One
high over all; and also for the pity and love He came to bless the domestic circle with. As the reader has already gathered from this *ODYSSEY, I*
revel in Spurgeon's unrivalled expositions of the Psalms, and without a
blush give you his masterly conclusion to this psalmodic *Magnificat*—

> May our life-psalm partake of the same character, and never know a
> break or a conclusion. In an endless circle let us bless the Lord, whose mer-
> cies never cease. Let us praise him in youth, and all along our years of
> strength; and when we bow in the ripeness of abundant age, let us still praise
> Him, who doth not cast off his old servants. Let us not only praise God our-
> selves, but exhort others to do it; and if we meet with any of the needy who
> have been enriched, and with the barren who have been made fruitful, let us
> join with them in extolling the name of him whose mercy endured for ever.
> Having been lifted ourselves from spiritual beggary and barrenness, let us
> never forget our former estate or the grace which has visited us, but world
> without end let us praise the Lord. Hallelujah!

Psalm114

This highly symbolic Psalm, which has earned the reputation of being "one of the finest lyrics in literature," has many interesting historical connections. It was with the words of this Psalm, "When Israel came out of Egypt," that men like Francis Borgia, Duke of Gandia, 1510-72, turned their backs on wealth and worldly honors to enter religious societies. Dante, in *Purgatorio*, sees in a light bark, without oars or sails, driven swiftly to land by the wings of the angel, a hundred spirits or more, who sing with one voice together Psalm 114. The passage from the song of the spirits in Purgatory reads—

> Upon the storm stood the celestial Pilot; Beatitude seemed written in his face, And more than a hundred spirits sat within.
> *In Exita Israel de Egypto*
> They changed all together in one voice,
> With whatso in that psalm is after written.

This Psalm of deliverance from bondage was that with which one of the Huguenot martyrs, Ayman de la Voya, marched to death by fire with noble constancy in 1552.

Then in 1568 there was the experience of Huguenot leaders and their families and followers, when pursued by their enemies, they were forced to leave the refuge at Rochelle, and make for the Loire, near Sancerre. They waded at great peril through the rising river, and placed a barrier between themselves and their pursuers. Reaching the farther bank, they fell on their knees and gave thanks, singing this 114th Psalm, "What ailed thee, O thou sea?" In 1762, Francis Rochette, the last martyred minister in France, ascended the scaffold singing this Psalm in Marot's version. The Psalms, as we have already seen, threw their spell over John Milton in early life. At the age of 15, already an undergraduate at Christ's College, Cambridge, he translated into verse Psalm 114, as well as Psalm 136—which see.

To all who are truly Christian this short, superb Psalm will ever remain precious seeing it was part of the hymn sung by Christ and His disciples just before His death. Tributes to its excellence abound. For example, it is said to be among the most artistic Psalms in the whole of the Psalter. "While its versification is regular, and the stanzas are complete and finished as in a modern hymn, consisting each of four lines, and presenting each a perfect example of parallelism, yet a higher art displays itself here. The reserve with which the Divine name is withheld, till everything is prepared for its utterance, and the vivid manner in which each feature of the rapid scene is flashed upon us by a single word so that a whole history is accurately presented in a few graphic touches, achieve a dramatic and a lyric triumph of the most remarkable kind."

Isaac Watts also extolled this 114th Psalm as "an admirable ode," and recorded how impressed he was with the omission of any Divine Name until, "with a very agreeable turn of thought, God is introduced at once in all His Majesty." So inspired was Watts with the nature and language of the Psalm that he sought to preserve the spirit of the sacred author in a six-verse poem of his own, commencing with the lines—

> When Israel, freed from Pharaoh's hand,
> Left the proud tyrant and his land,
> The tribes with cheerful homage own
> Their King, and Judah was his throne.

As for Spurgeon, he wrote that "this sublime *Song of the Exodus* is one and indivisible. True poetry has here reached its climax: no human mind has ever been equal, much less to excel, the grandeur of this Psalm. God is spoken of as leading forth his people from Egypt to Canaan, and causing the whole earth to be moved at his coming. Things inanimate are presented as imitating the actions of living creatures when the Lord passes by. They are apostrophized and questioned with marvelous force of language, till one seems to look upon the actual scene. The God of Jacob is exalted as having command over river, sea, and mountain, and causing all nature to pay homage and tribute before his glorious majesty." What a marvelous tribute to the greatness of the Psalm this is!

As to the historical connection of the Psalm, it clearly belongs to the period of return from the Captivity, and under the figure of the old exodus from Egypt, the writer, who is nameless, changes the return from Babylon, seeking, thereby, to comfort the people under much discouragement, in the recollection of their blessed and glorious past. In all ages of the Church this Psalm has been used to celebrate the release from the bondage of sin, hence its suitability as a hymn for Easter night.

When Israel went out of Egypt . . . from a people of strange language, 114:1. How dramatically this stirring Psalm commences! It begins with "a burst as if the poetic fury could not be restrained, but over-leaped all bounds. The soul elevated and filled with a sense of divine glory cannot wait to fashion a preface, but springs at once into the middle of its theme." It would seem as if the words tumbled out of the writer's mouth, before he could put a shirt on them. Out of the midst, or the bowels of the Egyptians, the Jews were delivered by a high, stretched-out arm, mightier than all the power of Egypt. For *went out* the LXX Version has, "In the Exodus of Egypt."

The two names of the patriarch occur in this opening verse—the family-given name, Jacob, and Israel, the Divinely bestowed name. As Israel, he never forgot that he was once Jacob. Through Divine grace all Jacobs may become Israels. Then the phrase "house of Jacob" is an interesting description in this connection. When the people went down into Egypt at Joseph's request and arrangement, it was as a single family and though they had multiplied greatly, they were still united and regarded by God as a single unit. "Unanimity is a pleasing token of the divine presence, and one of its sweetest fruits."

Then Israel's deliverance was from "a people of strange language," that is, of unintelligible speech or foreign tongue. The LXX Version has "a barbarous people," seeing the Hebrew word for "strange" implies a certain scorn or ridicule, which ancient races generally had for those speaking another language. One suggestion is that Egyptians were described as people of a *strange tongue* because they could not *speak of God* as Israel could. They were not of *pure life*, Zeph. 3:9, or, the lip that calls on the name of the Lord. What is evident is the fact that Israel was not at home in Egypt among tyrannical people. "The language of foreign taskmasters is never musical in an exile's ear." The truth we learn from this initial verse is that we all have our Egypts and our people of strange tongue; but when the lesson of our bondage is learned, our God brings us out.

Judah was his sanctuary, and Israel his dominion, 114:2. The first impressive features of this verse is the art with which the name of God is reserved, and the simple pronoun, *His*, is twice used. See Exod. 19:6. The poet, so full of the miracle performed, forgot to mention who the august person was, just as the spouse in the Song of Solomon began her plea, "Let *him* kiss me," or Mary Magdalene, when she cried, "Tell me where thou hast laid *him*?" A more practical suggestion is offered for the mission of a divine name, by the gifted expositors Ewald and Perowne—

> It is more satisfactory to regard the missions of the Holy Name in this part of the Psalm as a practical artifice to heighten the effect of the answer to the sudden apostrophe of verses five and six. There would be nothing marvelous in the agitation of the sea, and the river, and mountains in the presence of God, but it may well appear wonderful till that potent cause is revealed, as it is most forcibly in the dignified words of the seventh verse.

Then the double name and the double divine association under the double pronoun *his*, calls for attention. *Judah* and *Israel* are only poetically distinct: by this time there was no Israel except Judah, and there was the implication that the Northern Kingdom never had the Divine sanction since the only recognized sanctuary is in Judah. This one verse expounds and exemplifies two prime petitions of the Lord's Prayer, "Hallowed be thy name, thy kingdom come." *Judah* was God's sanctuary, because *hallowing his name*; and *Israel* his dominion, as desiring *his kingdom to come.*

Judah, meaning not the tribe of Judah only, though they in many things had the pre-eminence. Says John Gill, "The kingdom belonged to it, the chief ruler being out it, especially the Messiah; its standard was pitched and moved first; it offered first service to the Lord; and the Jews have a tradition that this tribe with its prince at the head of it went into the Red Sea first; the others fearing, but afterwards followed, encouraged by their example. In this place all the tribes are meant, the whole body of the people."

No division of the people into two sections, Judah and Israel, is to be inferred, then, in their separate mention here, seeing the poet speaks of the marvelous escape from Egypt as *the house of Jacob*—a united people—experiencing such a deliverance. Of old the common parlance was "Go number Israel and Judah," Judah being mentioned singly because she was the Lord's *holy thing*, or set apart for His special use. Thus, the delivered people as a whole formed the shrine of Deity, the entire nation being Jehovah's dominion, a Theocracy in which He alone was King. How condescending it is for the Eternal to find His home in the midst of His people! Can you say that your heart is His sanctuary and dominion? Deut. 33:12; 2 Cor. 6:16; Rev. 21:3.

The sea saw, and fled, 114:3. Verses 3 to 6 give us a poetical description of the passage through the Red Sea, and of Jordan; also of the giving of the Law. See Psalm 68:16. The phrase, *the sea saw*, implies the observance of the Divine Presence in the dividing of the Sea, and of Jordan, the opening and closing events of the deliverance from Egypt. "Awestruck nature recognized and obeyed its Master's will," and immediately there was "a great calm." Beholding Jehovah leading His people, the sea *fled*, not divided, as generally supposed, but rolled backwards.

The sea saw and fled, was a bold figure to use, because the poet did not sing of the suspension of natural laws, or of a singular phenomenon, as being responsible for dry land to pass over. It was the Creator's work who brought the Sea into being. What else could it do but flee, as it did, of whom it is said, "The sea is his, he made it!" Abraham Cowley of the 16th century left us this poetic description of the miracle—

> The waves on either side
> Unloose their close embrace, and divide,
> And backwards press, as in some solemn show
> The crowding people do,
> (Though just before no space was seen,)
> To let the admired triumph pass between.

> The wondering army saw on either hand,
> The no less wondering waves like rocks of crystal stand.
> They marched betwixt, and boldly trod
> The secret paths of God.

Mountains skipped like rams . . . little hills like lambs, 114:4, 6. Theodosius, in his *De Situ Terrae Sanetae,* tells how the "little hills" had walked exulting before the Lord, when He descended to baptism, even as David had said, "The mountains skipped like rams, and the little hills like young sheep," and how, to the pious eye of the traveler, even to this day they seem to be in the act of jumping." The word for *skipped* is translated *dance* in Eccles. 3:4 (See Psalm 18:7). While Exod. 19:18 may have been in the poet's mind, the leaping of hills formed part of every Theophany. In the miracle before us the sudden agitation of the rams and lambs, as poetically described, implies the concussion caused by the thunder and lightning accompanying the Divine presence. They sprang, frightened, from their places at the manifestation of the terrible majesty of Jehovah. John Keble has given us the lines of these two verses—

> What ails thee, sea, to part,
> This Jordan, back to start?
> Ye mountains, like to rams to leap,
> Ye little hills, like sheep?

John Calvin's comment on the double verse is helpful—

> The figure drawn from the *lambs* and *rams* would appear to be inferior to the magnitude of the subject. But it was the prophet's intention to express in the homeliest way the incredible manner in which God, on these occasions, displayed his power. The stability of the earth being, as it was, founded on the mountains, what connection can they have the rams and lambs, that they should be agitated, skipping hither and thither? In speaking in this homely style, he does not mean to detract from the greatness of the miracle, but more forcibly to engrave these extraordinary tokens of God's power on the illiterate.

Tremble, thou earth, at the presence of the Lord . . . the God of Jacob, 114:7. The Hebrew for *tremble* means "to be in pain," as a travailing woman—

> At the presence of the Lord be in pangs, O earth.

All the earth might well writhe in agony at the approach of its Maker. The answer to the poet's question in the previous verse, "What ailed thee, O thou sea?" is answered with consummate art. Well may the mountains tremble, when it is the Lord, the God of Jacob, Who is present. It will be noted that till now the mention of Divine power which wrought the deliverance was kept in suspense. Now the secret is out, it was *The Lord, The God of Jacob*, and these Divine titles carry their significance. *Lord* is "Adonai," the Sovereign Ruler, and most fitly does the Psalm call upon all nature to feel a holy awe because its Ruler is in the midst—

> Quake when Jehovah walks abroad,
> Quake earth, at sight of Israel's God.

As for *God of Jacob*, is it not surprising that it does not say the *God of Moses*, for he was the human channel of the miracle, the ruler of God's people who defied proud Pharaoh, led the people out, and through the Red Sea, and on to the borders of Canaan? But it is not *Moses* but *Jacob*, God identified Himself with, perhaps to remind us that He often condescends to use a faulty person, as Jacob was, to accomplish His glorious purpose. The convulsions of Nature, then, which accompanied the Exodus, were not only the birth-pangs of the Israelite people, as a people born anew in a day, but the revelation of Him by whose power alone human nature can be regenerated.

Under Grace, the Divine Presence is always with us, Matt. 28:20, though so often we are insensible to its majestic glory. If the earth, so long ago, should tremble before Him, much more should we—not with the fear of slaves, but with the godly fear which dares not grieve His Holy Spirit. "Awe is not cast out by faith, but rather it becomes deeper and more profound. The Lord is most reverenced where He is most loved."

Turned the rock into a standing water, and flint into a fountain of waters, 114:8. The last verse of the poem on this Psalm by Isaac Watts, referred under the first verse, reads—

> He thunders—and all nature mourns;
> The rocks to standing pools he turns;
> Flints spring with fountains at his word,
> And fires and seas confess their Lord.

Wonderful is it not, that the same almighty power turning waters into a rock to be a wall for Israel, Exod. 14:22, now turns the rock into waters to be a refreshing well to Israel?

> From stone and solid rock he brings,
> The spreading lake, the gushing springs.

For the two wilderness incidents here spoken of see Psalm 78: 12, also Isa. 41:18. As for the *flint* being made to produce *a fountain of waters*, the gushing forth of such from rock of flint is a practical proof of unlimited omnipotence. It seemed impossible for a flinty rock to become a fountain, but He speaks, and it is done. By the same power the hard and flinty hearts of men can be softened and miraculously transformed. He is still the God of miracles, causing the most unlikely things to yield the streams, quenching our thirst and satisfying our souls. Well might we pray, "Work such miracles, blessed God, on the rocks and flints which glaciers of trouble have brought into our lives! Amen." As all our spiritual necessities are all met by the water and the blood which flowed of old from the riven rock, Christ Jesus, may we be found magnifying Him for all He is as the smitten Rock, and also as the Rock of Ages.

Psalm 115

A further evidence of the continuous influence through the centuries of the Psalms is the experience of men and nations, can be found in the prominence Psalm 115 enjoys in the history and biography of outstanding rulers, leaders and saints. As an Englishman, born in Greater London, this Psalm has a historic interest for me. Henry IV gave his son as a motto when he called him to share in the government of his kingdom, the Psalm before us that reminded the young Henry of a life-long ambition to be victorious over his father's enemies. Thus, after the Battle of Agincourt in 1415, the English army fresh from battle, chanted on bended knees by the order of Henry V, the opening verse of the Psalm "Not unto us, O Lord, not unto us, but unto Thy Name give the praise."

The war-shout of John Sobieski, king of Poland, when, on Sept. 12, 1683, he marched down from the heights of Kulenberg to defeat the vast army of Turks besieging Vienna was Psalm 115. Such was a turning point in history for it meant the end of final invasion of the East that had thundered at the gate of Europe. Historians relate the indescribable enthusiasm as Sobieski's victorious men sang the battle-song. "Wherefore should the heathen say, Where is now our God? But our God is in the heavens: he hath done whatsoever he hath pleased," Psalm 115:2, 3.

The final stage of the struggle of Alphonso the Valiant, first King of Castile, to drive back the Moors from Toledo was reached in 1510, when Cardinal Ximenes in full pontificals led the Spanish troop against the Moors at Oran. The town was captured, and the victorious Cardinal rode through the streets singing Psalm 115. "Not unto us, O Lord, not unto us, but unto thy name give the praise."

As to features of the Psalm itself, the appeal of the first verses seems to indicate that the nation was passing through a period of suffering. Whatever the unknown emergency was, Jehovah's help was sought, for He alone is the true God, and He alone therefore to be trusted and worshipped. The LXX and other ancient Versions make Psalms 114 and 115 one, but the style and contents differ so much that these two Psalms must originally have been quite distinct. The prominence given to priests in Psalm 115, and its silence regarding king and prophets, prove that the Psalm was composed after the Captivity Era.

Evidently it was composed for temple use, to be sung antiphonally—the first eight and the last three verses to be sung by the congregation, and verses 9, 10, 11, responses by the choir. For instance, a Levite would sing, "O Israel, trust thou in the Lord," with the choir responding, "He is their help and their shield." Although the Psalm may celebrate some martial success, it is very much priestly in character. As the Psalm was sung at the Passover, it may bear some relationship to the Divine deliverance from Egypt.

Preachers will have no difficulty in tracing an expository outline of the Psalm—

1. Prayer to Jehovah for help since the humiliation of His people is His own humiliation, 1-3.
2. The gods of the heathen are helpless, and therefore are useless to trust, 4-8.
3. Israel is exhorted to seek refuge in Jehovah who can and does deliver, 9-11.
4. Assurance that Jehovah has blessed and will continue to bless Israel, 12-15—Resolution, 16-18.

There does not seem to be any evidence as Hitzig contended that Psalm 115-119 form a kind of poetical dream in which the incidents into Galilee, Psalm 115, to his triumphant return to the Jerusalem Temple, Psalm 118. See 1 Macc. 11.

Not unto us, O Lord . . . but unto thy name give glory, 115:1. Since its original composition centuries upon centuries ago, this verse has found a very wide and varied use. As we have already noticed King Henry the Fifth sang his *Non nobis Domine!* in thanksgiving for his Agincourt victory, using his paraphrase—

> O God, Thy arm was here;
> And not to us, but to Thy arm alone
> Ascribe we all. . . .

What is known as *Palissy Ware*—the lustrous glaze and life-like reproductions of nature objects, was the invention of Bernard Palissy, the Huguenot potter, who beggared himself and family to perfect and produce his art. Amid bitter reproach he found consolation in the Psalms, and when he learned to imitate with marvelous skill the beauty and variety of nature, he compared the infinite power and goodness of God with his own petty cares and trials, and fell on his face crying—

> Not unto us, O Lord, not unto us, but to Thy name give praise.

William Wilberforce was a loving and diligent student of the Psalms, and it was in their language and spirit that his reflections on his political successes were expressed. Often he meditated upon the opening verse of Psalm 115, and gave God praise for the carrying of his Parliament Bill for the Abolition of the Slave Trade.

Actually, however, this first verse is not in the form of thanksgiving for deliverance from adversaries, or a doxology for the establishment of any personal interest or success, but as a *prayer*, in which praise and glory are ascribed to God. The repetition of the phrase, *Not unto us*, emphasizes the very sincere desire to disclaim any self-glory in the supplication, and to have grace at any cost to the suppliants to magnify His own name. Israel had been reviled by idolatrous foreigners, so the people appeal to God to vindicate His honor. We could re-phrase the prayer in the following form, matching a similar prayer in Daniel 9:18—

> We seek Thy aid not that glory may come to us by the resulting victory, but that Thy lovingkindness (not *mercy*) and faithfulness (not *truth*) to Thy own may be displayed. Thus will Thy name, Thy character be revealed.

The rejection of all self-praise voiced in this prayer, is implied in all Hebrew poetry. As to the two attributes mentioned, they are indissoluble. What would the heathen think of Jehovah as a merciful and faithful God if He gave His people over to the adversaries? Such glorious virtues would be in jeopardy, and God Himself dishonored. God's glory is exhibited when He shows mercy to His people, and fulfills the truth of His promises on their behalf. How it would eliminate from success and praise their power to harm us, if we would, from the heart, give utterance to these noble words, "Not unto us, Lord, not unto us, but unto thy name give glory."

Wherefore should the heathen say, Where is now their God? 115:2. Both of the covenanted blessings of "mercy" and "truth" were assailed by this heathen taunt, "Where is now their God?"—a question often asked, see Exod. 32:12; Num. 14:13; Psalms 42:3, 10; 74:10; Joel 2:17; Micah 7:10. The Hebrew word for *now* is different from the adverb of time. "It is the rhetorical *now*: 'Where, prithee, is that God of theirs?' This particle is absent from Psalm 79:10, which otherwise agrees exactly with Psalm 115:2." Dealing with the subject of this Psalm, Spurgeon says that "in the previous Psalm the past wonders which God had wrought were recounted to his honor, and in the present Psalm he is entreated to glorify himself again, because the heathen were presuming upon the absence of miracles, were altogether denying the miracles of former ages and insulting the people of God with the question, 'Where is now their God?,' or, more literally, 'Where, pray is their God?' It grieved the heart of the godly that Jehovah should be thus dishonored, and treating their own condition of reproach as unworthy of notice, they beseech the Lord at least to vindicate his own name."

The question asked in this verse is, of course, answered in the next verse, as we shall find, but with verse 2 and 3 in mind, we can point out how those accustomed to some visible embodiment of God are always amazed at spiritual worship, set forth by Jesus in John 4:24. We are told that Pompey was very much surprised to find nothing in the most Holy Place when he visited it. An agnostic teacher wrote on the blackboard—*God is nowhere*. A Christian girl in the class, however, asked leave to write the same phrase, which she did, but what a difference, for she printed in capitals *GOD IS NOW HERE!*

> What if Thy form we cannot see,
> We know and feel that Thou art here.

But our God is in the heavens: he hath done whatsoever he hath pleased, 115:3. It may be difficult for us "to reproduce in imagination the apparent triumph of the idolater, who could point to *his* deity, felt that he had it over the worshipper of the invisible God, when outward events seemed to be going against the latter. But we may estimate the strength of the conviction, which even under the apparent withdrawal of Divine favor, could point to the heavens as the abode of the Invisible, and to misfortune itself as a proof of the existence and power of One who could in everything do what pleased Him."

Thus, the assertion, "Our God is in the heavens," implies the spirituality of Jehovah, the One Who is not material, visible, tangible. If the phrase had meant only, "He lives in heaven," or is "confined to heaven," that would have been also a low view of deity. But He is in heaven, and the God of heaven, and therefore able to save His people, and also to exercise His sovereign right to do what He pleases. God is in the heavens, where He should be, seeing He is their Creator and Possessor, and the idolaters of earth must learn that He is supreme above all opposing forces and reigns upon His throne high and lifted up, far above all mortals' sneers and scorn.

Amid all the sin and strife characteristic of the nations today we might well repeat the jeering question, "Where is now their God?" But amid all the godlessness of our time we rest confident in the belief that His providence is undisturbed, His throne unshaken, and His purposes unchanged; that He ever doeth according to His will among the inhabitants of earth whatsoever is pleasing to His own loving, beneficial heart. God's good pleasure is never arbitrary, but always conditioned to the highest welfare of His creatures.

We now approach the section of the Psalm, verses 4-8, in which the helpfulness of the gods of the heathen is vividly described. These supposed Gods had an external form, or outward embodiment that could be seen—a supposed advantage over the Jew who worshipped a God who had no visible form for man to see. In his *Heroes and Hero Worship*, Thomas Carlyle, argued, "An idol . . . is not God, but a symbol of God; and perhaps one may question whether any, the more benighted, mortal ever took it for more than a symbol." But to the idolaters, the Psalmist describes an idol as being more than a symbol, otherwise they would not have cried day and night unto it for help. *Idol* is the English form of the Greek word used in the LXX Version as "something seen."

Isaiah has a passage in which, with magnificent irony he unmasks the folly of idolatry, 44:9-20, and although the description of such as given by the psalmist both in the section before us and also in Psalm 135:15-18, can compare with Isaiah's bitter contempt, yet there is still a noticeable vein of sarcasm running through these Psalms, visible more in the original than in the English. Theodoret tells us of Saint Publia, the aged abbess of a company of nuns at Antioch, who used to chant Psalm 115:4-8, as Julian went by in idolatrous procession, and narrates how the angry Emperor caused his soldiers to buffet Publia till she bled, because of his inability to endure the sting of the old Hebrew song declaring the uselessness of idols fashioned by men. It was also with this section of the Psalm that Christians defied the imperial order to sacrifice to Caesar.

Their idols . . . work of man's hands . . . They that make them are like them, 115:4-8. How sarcastic is the coverage in this section of the utter helplessness of material idols in time of need! These idols in question were not made of silver and gold but covered over with these metals, as they usually were. What a waste of precious substance this was! Further, the value represented by the silver and gold did not in any way increase the power of the idols to meet the need of the idolaters. Says Matthew Henry, "Silver and gold are proper things to make money of but not to make gods of." Then, what irony underlines the statement, "Idols . . . the work of men's hands." How monstrous it is of man to think that he can make a god to which to pray! Is not the maker always greater than the article he has made?

In the verses 5-7, in which the writer portrays idols as being blind, deaf, dumb, senseless, motionless and impotent, they are represented as having apparently every bodily organ, but are unable to perform any of the corresponding functions. The emphasis is on the term *cannot*, implying lack of life within to use such organs.

Mouths, but they speak not. The noblest function of the mouth is to speak, but these idols are dumb—and those who made them were just as dumb.

Eyes . . . but they see not. Being blind, they could not see their worshippers or what they offered. There are certain idols having most costly jewels as eyes, but although the gems are worth a king's ransom they leave the idol just as sightless. Who, in his right senses, and has sight, wants to blind deity? How blind the man must be who worships a blind god!

Ears . . . they hear not. The Cretians pictured their Jupiter without ears, so little hearing or help they hoped for from him. As for Socrates, such was his contempt of heathen gods, that he would sooner swear by an oak, a goat, or a dog; as holding same as better gods than lifeless objects. Gold and silver cannot hear, although we say that "money speaks." Heathen deities were often disfigured by monstrous ears, but although as large as those of the bad wolf in *Little Red Riding Hood*, they were unable to hear the cries shouted by a million voices.

Noses . . . but they smell not. In sacred scorn, the Psalmist mocks at those who make gods unable to perceive the perfume of the burning sweet spices in the temple. What's the use of a nose if it cannot function? So the finger of contempt is pointed to every part of the countenance of the image, as the poet heaps together sentences heavy with the grim sardonic spirit of Elijah when he said, "Cry aloud; for he is a god; either he is talking, or he is pursuing, or he is on a journey, or peradventure he sleepeth, and must be awaked."

Hands . . . but they handle not. What folly to create a god unable to receive gifts handed to it, or to grasp the scepter of power, or to distribute gifts to the needy! As Augustine expressed it—

> Even their artist therefore surpasseth them, since he had the faculty of molding them by the motion and functions of his limbs; though thou wouldest be ashamed to worship that artist. Even thou surpassest them, though thou hast not made these things since thou doest what they cannot do.

In the Hebrew *handle* means "to touch"—"to feel one's way"—as in the dark. Idols were not able to face their own way but had to be lifted to and fastened in the shrines they occupied. Having dead hands, the idols could not come to the rescue of those seeking their aid.

Feet . . . but they walk not. Why the meanest insect on earth had more power of locomotion than the greatest of the heathen gods, the Psalmist condemns!

Neither speak they with their throats. The original implies not only the want of articulate speech, but of any utterance at all. In verse 5, speaking is referred to in connection with the mouth, but here we have inarticulate sounds in the throat, which have not reached the stage of speech. The idols were incapable of even a guttural sound, the lowest beasts are capable of. They were unable in any way to voice a response to the requests of worshippers. Crafty ways were taken to make them believe that on special occasions these dumb idols would utter hollow sounds. And so surveying the idol from head to foot, the Psalmist wrote it down as being utterly contemptible.

They that make them shall become like them, 115:8. During October, 1645, Oliver Cromwell engaged in the battle at Basing, and issued the command that no mercy must be shown to defenders who were too few to resist Cromwell's forces, and were wiped out, and the place left a heap of blackened ashes. Lieutenant-General Cromwell, Hugh Peter tells us, "had spent much time with God in prayer the night before the battle; and seldom fights without some text of Scripture to support him. This time he rested upon the blessed Word of God, written in Psalm 115—They that make them are like unto them; so is everyone that trusteth in them, which, with some verses going before, was now accomplished."

The consistent testimony of Scripture is that those who worship helpless idols shall become helpless themselves. See 2 Kings 17:15; Isa. 44:9; Jerem. 2:5; Rom. 1:21-23.

> Who molds in gold or stone a sacred face
> Makes not the god; but he who asks his grace.

Like unto them, meaning as hollow and as unprofitable. Matthew Henry's comment on this verse is apt—"They that make them *images*, show their ingenuity, and doubtless are sensible men; but they that make them *gods* show their stupidity, and are as blockish things as the idols themselves." Such a censure is not severe for those who sink so low as to be capable of confiding in idols have reached the extreme of folly, and are worthy of the contempt heaped upon their detestable deities. There is, of course, a striking thought in this 8th verse for our own hearts. "We resemble our ideals; we become like what we worship. And though we may not be now tempted to prostrate ourselves before the idols of the heathen, yet there are idols which may fascinate us. See 1 Cor. 10:4; Col. 3:5; 1 John 5:21; We must not trust gold, or success, or any earthly thing, but God in Christ, till we become like Him. 2 Cor. 3:18."

We have now reached the section in the Psalm in which Israel is urged, not to be like the surrounding heathen who trust in lifeless gods of their own creation, but to seek refuge in the all-helping Jehovah, verses 9-11. Here we have a triple appeal for trust, addressed to the congregation, the priests, and perhaps the proselytes. See Ruth 2:12. The highest cannot do without God, and the lowest may appropriate Him. The three classes addressed are, *Israel* (verse 9), *House of Aaron*, and *Ye that fear the Lord*. Almost the same triple division is found in Psalms 118:2-4 and 135:19. By the first class we are to understand Israel as the whole, by the second the Priests of the Lord, and by the third proselytes, that is those who, though not of Abraham's seed, had his faith and inherited the promises made to him. See 1 Kings 8:41; Isa. 56:6; Acts 10:2, 22.

O Israel . . . O house of Aaron . . . Ye that fear the Lord, he is their help and their shield, 115:9-11. Here is consummate art in this sudden change of address from idols to living beings. It is like some pointed application in a sermon. It must have been impressive when priests and people sang their song of scorn of surrounding dominant idolatry by the repetition of the threefold, *Trust in Jehovah. Trust* in taking what God gives. As for the threefold *Help* and *Shield,* together they make a very assuring combination for those whose trust is only in the Lord. *Help,* means that God is our succor in every time of need; and *Shield,* that He is our defense at all times. *Priests* of the house of Aaron were the leaders, teachers, and exemplars of the people, and therefore above *all* others who should place their unreserved reliance upon Israel's God so that it might become evident, *Like priests, like people.*

The last section of the Psalm, verses 12-18, is eloquent of the truth that having blessed Israel, Jehovah will continue to bless her. The threefold repetition of the word *bless* adds great effect to the passage. It was God's triple answer to the triple appeal. God had been mindful of His people, and would continue to bless them. The LXX Version translates the 12th verse as "Jehovah having remembered us will bless us." The same today as yesterday, all He has been and done, that will He be and do. Are we not all at liberty to argue from the past to the future, and believe in our unchanging, and unchangeable Jehovah? All we have experienced we may expect.

He will bless . . . both small and great, 115:13. Covering the proselytes, this phase of the beatitude implies whatever their rank and position, God's richest blessings would be theirs. For this method of expressing totality, see 2 Kings 18:24. So long as a man feared the Lord it made no difference whether he was a prince or a peasant, patriarch or pauper, none would be forgotten by Him Who delights in placing the least before the greatest, because their need is often greatest.

The Lord shall increase you, more and more, you and your children, 115:14. A more literal rendering reads—

> Jehovah shall heap blessings on you,
> On you and your children.

The bountiful God here presented is the One daily loading godly homes with His benefits. The wish expressed here refers to the whole nation, and was very appropriate after the return from Babylon with its impoverishment. It is a prayer the Church can offer for increased light and knowledge; for gifts and graces, for faith and utterance, for expansion in numbers. The blessings of God are *ever-flowing*—"more and more"; and *over-flowing*—"you and your children"—more signally blessed for their parents' sake. While in Egypt, God multiplied the people exceedingly, and thus is it with His spiritual seed. The first blessing upon mankind has never been abrogated, "Be fruitful, and multiply, and replenish the earth."

Ye are blessed of the Lord, which made heaven and earth, 115:15. Prospective blessings for us and ours are assuring, but here the Psalmist reminds the people that manifold, present blessings from the Omnipotent One were their portion. The creative character of Jehovah is mentioned to declare both His ability and willingness to bless His people. His description as "Maker of heaven and earth," is used in contrast to inert idols, themselves made by men's hands. Heaven and earth are separated as the above respectively of God and man. See verse 3. The affirmation expressed in this 15th verse is an extension of the blessing of Melchizedek, "Blessed be Ahran of the Most High God, possessor of heaven and earth"—a blessing resting upon every child of His. Because He is the Maker of heaven and earth, and remains our Portion until we arrive in His palace above. While below, the lot of God's children may seem hard and arduous at times; but it is ever a blessed one, having Him as our peace and rest.

The heavens are the Lord's . . . the earth . . . given to the children of men, 115:16. Lord Burghley, greatest statesman during the reign of Queen Elizabeth, was a diligent student of the Psalms all his life. His will, dated October 20th 1579, disposed of his lands and goods in a manner that he hoped "shall not offend God, the giver of them all to me; considering, as it is in the Psalm, 'All the whole heavens are the Lord's; the earth hath he given to the children of men, Psalm 115, verse 16.'" Heaven is Jehovah's wherein He dwells, but He gave to man the earth as a dwelling place, and it is for the meek to inherit it.

As Heaven, and the heavens form God's possession, He has every resource in Himself, and is dependent upon no one. Man, however, has been given to the earth rather than the earth to him, and it is his responsibility to subdue it for Him Who is coming to reign over it. Has He not given us the heathen for our inheritance, and the uttermost parts of the earth for our possession?

The dead praise not the Lord, neither any that go down into silence, 115:17. Ellicott reckons that the connection of the last two verses with the rest of the Psalm is far from plain. "Why the Psalmist should suddenly be struck with the dreadful thought that death broke the covenant-relationship, and silenced prayer and praise, is not easy to see. Was the Psalm first chanted after some victory? and was this suggested by the sight of the slain, who, though they had helped to win the triumph, could yet have no share in the praises that were ascending to Jehovah?"

But we see no problem whatever in the somewhat dramatic change from the living, blessed of the Lord, to the silent dead. The connection is clearly evident, namely, the reason for praising Jehovah now, is the fact that our bodies shall soon be in the silent land of the grave so let us praise Him now while we have life. Corpses cannot unite in the Psalms and Hymns and Spiritual Songs with which living saints adore their Lord. The best of preachers cannot magnify His Lord from a coffin. Songs of Praise are never heard in sepulchers. Then, there is the further solemn truth that unrepentant souls passing out into the silence of eternal death, cannot praise Jehovah, having never learned to do so while in the land of the living.

But for those trusting in the Lord, and blessed of Him, although their mortal tongue will be silent in the grave, do not die; if theirs was also eternal death, the praise of God would die with them, and this is impossible. Praising Him in this life they praise Him for evermore. Going down into silence means the tomb that sends forth no voice. But the saints, absent from the body, are present with the Lord, swelling the harmonies of Heaven above. Certainly the view of the *Hereafter* was partial to Old Testament saints, 2 Tim. 1:10, yet Job knew that beyond death he would see God.

But we will bless the Lord from this time forth and for evermore, 115:18. Here we have praises to God *before* the grave, "from this time forth"; and praises *beyond* the grave, "for evermore," and Eternity cannot exhaust the reasons why God should be glorified. Not until we are with Him shall we praise Him as we ought. "As those who were dead and gone could no longer sing Psalms unto the Lord among the sons of men, the Psalmist exhorts the faithful who were then living to take care that God is not robbed of His praise, and then he closes with an exulting Hallelujah. Should not living men extol the living God?"

Praise the Lord, or HALLELUJAH! Although the LXX Version places this at the beginning of the next Psalm, several modern critics affirming that it belongs there, we prefer to leave it where it is in the A.V., as a fitting conclusion to a Psalm so full of praise and blessing. The songless dead cannot praise God, and the careless here, and the wicked in Hell will not, yet as those redeemed by the blood of His Son, we will shout our *Hallelujah* for ever and ever.

Psalm 116

A journey through this impressive Psalm strikes one immediately with its highly individualistic character, in which the poet tells out his personal experiences and feelings. What an abundance of personal pronouns it holds! In its 19 verses, *I* occurs 19 times, *MY*, 11 times and *ME*, four times, leading us to name it, *The Pronoun Psalm*. This peculiar feature provides us with the occasion to discuss the significance of the more than half the Psalms in the Psalter which were uttered in part or wholly in the person singular, and which in Germany were called the *I Psalms*.

Throughout half-a-century or more, much has been written by outstanding theologians of various nationalities as to whether this *I* stands for the poet himself, or for the personified nation or religious community. Occasionally in the Old Testament, nations are personified and addressed in the singular. See Num. 20:18; 21:22; Deut. 2:27-29; Judges 1:3; 9:19; Zech. 7:3; 8:2. But in these instances the personification is manifest, and quite in keeping with ordinary usage. But it is a different matter altogether to say of some 80 Psalms, crammed with personal deep feeling and spontaneity, that the *I* was not the writer himself, but some kind of impersonal society either political or religious.

The position generally held both among Jews and Christians is that the *I* is the individual Psalmist, his personal song being appropriated for congregational use because the experience of the author was typical, and the sentiments he expressed general. Dr. T. Witton Davies, whose erudite article in *The Century Bible* on *"The Speaker in the I Psalms,"* we are largely quoting from, cites the modern illustrations of Cowper and Charles Wesley who were, in the first instance, with but few exceptions, prompted by what their authors thought and felt. Their poems and songs, however, became incorporated in congregational hymn books because these Christian poets had an experience that is representative. Dr. Davies also quotes Tennyson who wrote in his *In Memoriam*, "I is not always the author speaking of himself, but the voice of the human race speaking through him." Yet in this same remarkable poem, Tennyson expressed what he himself believed and felt, though he happened at the same time to be voicing the beliefs and emotions of the race.

The principle to recognize, then, is that every *I* Psalm is to be interpreted as individual unless exegesis makes this impossible, which is rare.

In the majority of these Psalms no other interpretation can be given, apart from the personal one. How else can be explained passages like?—

> "Behold I was shapen in iniquity," 51:5.
> "I am become a stranger to my brethren," 69:8.
> "At midnight I will arise and give thanks unto thee," 119:62.

Or take the Calvary Psalm; how could the congregation or the nation make vows, and in what way was it possible for it to praise God in the midst of itself, Psalm 22:22, 25? We, therefore, are one with Dr. Davies in his conclusion that these *I* Psalms have such spontaneity and intensity of feeling as to make it almost certain that they are the genuine outcome of individual experience. If we reduce the writer to the level of mere spokesman, hired to put into singable form the prevailing sentiments, we rob the Psalms in question of reality and force. It is the individual character of the Psalms which has been, in all ages, their charm, and which makes them an unfailing source of comfort and encouragement to men struggling with sin, sickness, or outward foes. The God who was the refuge and strength of these ancient saints is still that, and, in Jesus Christ, even more, to tried and tempted ones in our own time.

It is with these sentiments of Dr. Davies in mind that we approach Psalm 116, with its gripping, bald, and bold opening, "*I* love Jehovah!" As we proceed with our meditation it will become more evident that to empty this Psalm of its individual character is to take from it its chief religious element; and that we are dead set against those who seek to practically expunge from it the constant strain of a personal relationship with God. A soldier-saint who made this Psalm was *Quaker* Wallace of the 93rd regiment who, at the Relief of Lucknow, India, in 1857, went into the Secundrabagh, according to an eye witness, "like one of the Furies, if there be any male Furies, plainly seeking death, but not meeting it," and quoting the 116th Psalm, Scottish version in meter—

> I love the Lord, because my voice
>   And prayers He did hear,
> I, while I live, will call on Him,
>   Who bowed to me His ear.

This fighting Quaker who not only braved death, but courted it, plunged into the struggle, quoting a line at every shot fired from his rifle, and at each thrust given by his bayonet—

> I'll of salvation take the cup,
>   On God's name will I call;
> I'll pay my vows now to the Lord
>   Before His people all.

Another illustration of the personal influence of this personal Psalm can be found in the experience of Burkard Waldis, a monk who became a noted evangelist in Germany. After embracing the doctrines of the Reformation, he was seized by night, and kept in severe imprisonment till rescued by his two brothers, John and Bernhard, at cost of great danger and travail. While in prison he read and re-read Psalm 116, and made it the foundation of his remarkable hymn of thanksgiving, which he dedicated to his brothers, and to his companions in captivity. Waldis said that he wrote the hymn this Psalm inspired, "To drive away the sad and weary thoughts and Satanic temptations with which he was assailed." It is also interesting to note that Psalm 116 was a burial song of the Early Church, looking through death to life, and in this way a companion of Psalm 16.

The recurring theme of this Psalm, baring as it does, the Psalmist's inner and outer experiences, is that of thanksgiving and vows for deliverances out of great distress, and severe sickness, and has been used by individual believers all down the ages to express spiritual as well as temporal Divine aid. There is also evidence that it was a song of gratitude, composed to accompany the offerings and vows after some kind of victory. As we have already indicated in the coverage of this *I* Psalm, its strong personal feeling would not exclude it being adapted to express the sentiments of Israel as a whole. Forming part of the Paschal Hallel, the Psalm contains an underlying reference to the escape from Egypt, and also to deliverance from the captivity in Babylon, but predominantly it expresses the writer's own sweet personal experiences of redeeming mercy, and his own song of thankfulness to *Jehovah*, which name occurs 15 times, and *JAH* once. Various stages of these experiences are discernible, namely, Suffering, verse 3—Prayer, 4 and 5—Deliverances, 6-9—Public Thanksgiving, 12-19.

Because Psalms 115-118 were probably the hymns sung by our Lord and His disciples as He faced Calvary, deep and solemn significance is attached to Psalm 115, thus "we can hardly err in seeing here words to which He could set His seal,—words in a measure descriptive of His own experience; the Psalm has thus been understood of those who love to find their Lord in every line." Broadly speaking the Psalm falls into two sections—

1. Personal acknowledgment of Jehovah's goodness and mercy in delivering the Psalmist out of some severe illness, or from some other situation of danger, verses 1-6.

2. Personal vows and promises of thanksgiving for all Jehovah had accomplished, 7-19. The LXX Version divides it slightly different—verses 1-9; verses 10-19, but begins each division with a *Hallelujah!*

I love the Lord . . . because! 116:1. *Loving* is the present, the poet is *singing* of the past—"Hath heard"—*vowing* for the future—"I will," verse 2. What a captivating way to begin, not only a Psalm, but our approach to God. This short, abrupt expression of the writer's affection, *I love*, is but one word in the original and expresses as a full and entire sentence in itself. "I love because the Lord hath heard," etc. The concise clause *I love*, declares a more entire and ardent affection than a more full and round phrase would do. "Great is the force of true love, so that it cannot be sufficiently expressed." *Love begets love.* Said John, Apostle of Love, "We love Him, because He first loved us." Can we, *personally*, confess, "Thou knowest all things, thou knowest that I love thee"? Such love is the sweetest of all graces and the surest of all evidences that we are the Lord's. Spurgeon says—

> Personal love fostered by a personal experience of redemption is the theme of this Psalm, and in it we see the redeemed answered in their God, walking at large, sensible of their obligations, conscious that they are not their own but bought with a price, and joining with all the ransomed company to sing Hallelujahs unto God.

The superabundant reason the Psalmist gives for loving the Lord is *"because* he heard *my voice*, and my *supplications.*" If David wrote this Psalm, and we feel he did, then his reason for his love *for* the Lord, was the love *of* the Lord in hearing his prayers, "uttered or unexpressed." Here he used his *voice*, and in private devotion it is most helpful to pray aloud without being overheard. The prayers he voiced are called *supplications*, composed and orderly forms of prayer. We are told that both verbs in this verse may be translated in the present, thus it runs, "I love because Jehovah *hears* my voice, my supplications." So, "continual love flows out of daily answers to prayer."

He hath inclined his ear unto me . . . I will call upon him as long as I live, 116:2. This is an echo of a previous Psalm of David's, Psalm 18:3, and is a proof that sentences from other Psalms are woven into the one before us. It is a waste of energy to use our voice, if the ears of the one we try to speak to are closed, or the person is stone deaf. But God's ears are not heavy that He cannot hear, and we have the assurance that His ears are ever open to hear our cries. Thus, the Psalmist gives us another *because*, another reason for loving the Lord, "He hath inclined his ear unto me." If we are very feeble, and can scarcely hear our own voice when we pray, our petition is audible to God who bows down from His grandeur with a listening ear. The figure used here "seems to be that of a tender physician or loving friend leaning over a sick man whose voice is faint and scarcely audible, so as to catch every accent and whisper."

Prayer heard and answered may well incite to renewed love; but we must not love Him less, if delay to our prayers is experienced. Perhaps the delay or withholding is a greater proof of love than giving would be. See

John 11:3-15. David, however, who had his supplications granted, vows to call upon the Lord for the rest of his life. "As long as I live," can be expressed as *in my days*—every day the Ancient of days would hear his call. Said godly Ambrose, "Not on some few days, but every day of my life; for to pray on certain days, and not on all, is the mark of one who loathes and not of one who loves." Behind the *I will*, this was a determined decision. Not the other "I wills" of the Psalms in verses 9, 13, 14, and 17.

The sorrows of death . . . pains of hell . . . trouble and sorrow, 116:3. What a heavy load of suffering the Psalmist was carrying at the time when he called upon the Lord! Enduring so much grief and anguish, praying was the best thing he could do. As Dr. F. B. Meyer's paragraph on this verse expresses it, "Many who are reading this Psalm may be in a similar position. And excessive grief is sometimes apt to check prayer. The soul is too sore and hurt even to cry out. Yet it is well worth our while, when we are in such circumstances, to break through all restraints and call out to God, Who is very merciful."

The sorrows of death compassed me. For *sorrows*, "cords" can be read, as found in the margin of Psalm 18:4, 5. "The cords of death compassed me"—"The cords of hell compassed me about." The figure of the hunter used in the latter verse—*snares*—corresponds to "cords." "As hunters surrounded a stag with dogs and men, so that no way of escape is left, so was David enclosed in a ring of deadly griefs." Another commentator suggests that the metaphor is taken from—

> Cruel creditors, who would be sure to tie their debtors fast, as with cords, so that they could not loose themselves. It is also used of the mast of a ship fast fixed, and tied on every side with cords. Thus such a word expresses a most lamentable and inextricable condition.

So the Psalmist was bound around with the cords of sorrow, weakness and terror with which death is accustomed to bind men ere they are dragged away to their long captivity. Only One can snap these fetters, even Jesus Who came to set men free.

The pains of hell gat hold upon me. Here we have an extension of the previous expression of bondage. The words "gat hold upon me" are given in the margin as "found me." *Pains* corresponds to *Cords*. In the original the word translated as *pains* is one for sacks fast bound together, and flint stones, and fierce enemies, and hard straits; so that this word suggests aggravated misery. As an officer of the law finds a person wanted for arrest, and handcuffs him, so the pains of hell found the Psalmist and took him into custody. One word in the original for *gat hold* expresses the double act of finding, and taking hold of what is taken. The writer's horrors seized him and held him as a prisoner. The term *hell* is also given as

Sheol, meaning, "the pit," and to be saved from such means simply to be preserved in the upper world, where fellowship with God is eternal, and where He can be praised. The thought conveyed here is that the sufferer endured those pangs belonging to death, and the terrors connected with the grave. The margin of the R.V. gives the "grave," and the Psalmist felt that he was at the gates of death.

I found trouble and sorrow. Double grief was felt what with trouble around, and sorrow within. *Trouble* has a near affinity with *pain* and indicates great misery which is aggravated by the next word, *Sorrow*, implying a calamity causing deep grief causing others to pity such as those enduring it. Taken together, *Trouble* and *Sorrow* speak of a very perplexed and distressed condition of heart. The writer was not looking for them, but he found them, or they found him, as the elegancy in the original Hebrew suggests.

I called . . . I beseech thee, deliver my soul, 116:4. For double distress there was double relief in prayer and deliverance. In his extremity, David called upon the *name* of the Lord. As "the name" represents all that Jehovah is in Himself, he earnestly invoked all the attributes of the Most High on his behalf. *I called*, in the original reads, "I continued to call," that is, he prayed with importunity. His prayer, "I beseech thee deliver me," may seem a very short one for such a great need, but Heaven does not hear us for our much speaking. Assiduous prayer brings effectual relief from distressing agonies. We should pray, not only when things are at their worst, but at their best. Still, in special times of trial, *then* as we storm Heaven, deliverance is given. The prayer of faith is generally short, and always to the point, taking the soul and placing it before God in its real state and true character. May we be found relying upon the promise, "Call upon Me in the day of trouble, *I will deliver thee.*"

Gracious is the Lord, and righteous . . . merciful, 116:5. What a blessed trinity of Divine virtues this verse presents—Graciousness, Righteousness, and Mercy, these three, and the greatest of these is *Mercy*, which is God's beloved attribute. The whole of Scripture proclaims Him as a merciful God, and the writer of this Psalm joined in the adulation, as seen in the Divine titles he used. *The Lord*—Jehovah—sets forth His excellency, His greatness and goodness is His grace and justice, but *Our God* is a title manifesting a peculiar relation between Him and those who love Him and believe in Him, and who, through His mercy came to know Him as the Deliverer.

As for the order of these three attributes it has been suggested that *righteousness* is very significantly placed between the *grace* and the *mercy*, for it is necessary that evil should be thoroughly dealt with. Grace lays, as it were the foundation for salvation, and mercy perfects the work; but not till righteousness has finished its intermediary work. God is "gracious" in *hearing*, "righteous" in *judging*, and "merciful" in *pardoning*. "The attribute of righteousness seems to stand between two guards of love: Gracious, *righteous*, merciful. The sword of justice is scabbarded in a jewelled sheath of grace."

The Lord preserved the simple . . . saved me, 116:6. At the very outset let us dispose of the modern idea of a person being *simple*, as one a little *dotty*, not mentally bright, but slow to comprehend matters—a simpleton. Both the LXX and the Vulgate Versions give *babes* for "simple." Widely used in the Book of Proverbs this term denotes those who have a character opposed to craftiness, underhandedness, scheming. See 14:15, 18; 22:3; 27:12. *Simple* equals the New Testament virtue of *Simplicity*, which implies a pure mind toward God, free from all dissimulation, expecting salvation and help from no quarter, save Heaven alone. Those who have a great deal of wit may take care of themselves, but for those with no worldly craft or graft or guile, simple trust in the Lord brings heavenly wisdom.

The Psalmist applies the description of a simple soul being Divinely preserved to himself, "I was brought low, and he helped me." Simple though I was, reduced in circumstances, distressed in spirit, sick in body, the all-wise God did not pass me by. *He* helped *me*, even me in all my simple-mindedness—such was his compassion. How encouraged we are to know that those of us who are simple in a good sense, simple in our own eyes, yes, and simple in a wrong sense in the world's account, are yet cared for by God. We may be poor and needy, but He thinks of us. *Brought low* literally means to hang down, to be pendulous, to dangle, to swing to and fro, and also to be feeble and weak. Used here, it may refer to prostration of strength by disease or suffering. See Psalm 30. But help came—He restored me. God helped him to bear the worst, and hope for the best.

Return unto thy rest . . . the Lord hath dealt bountifully with thee, 116:7. This was the verse with which Babylas of Antioch comforted his heart in prospect of his martyrdom under the Emperor Decius. The historian of the time wrote of the choice of this verse by Babylus, "From this we learn that our soul comes to rest when it is removed by death from this restless world." The soliloquizing of this verse can be translated, "Turn away, O my soul, from the things which disturb and distract to Him Who is thy rest." The repose the writer sought was not the worldling's presumed serenity nor the sensualist's security, but the repose of the quiet conscience and the trusting heart.

Two words here call for attention, namely, *Return, Rest*. The word used here for *Return* is the same term the angel employed in his appeal to Hagar who had fled from her mistress, Genesis 16:9. As Hagar through her mistress' rough dealing with her fled from her, so the heart of the

Psalmist by reason of his sore afflictions fell from its former quiet confidence in God. As the angel bade Hagar "return to her mistress," so the Psalmist called upon his soul to return to its rest, even to God Who had dealt so bountifully with him.

As for the word *Rest*, in the Hebrew it is put in the plural, denoting perfect, complete, entire rest, at all times, and under all circumstances—*the plural of intensity*—coming to those whose outward conditions make for restfulness, or prosperity and safety. See 84:4. No wonder Spurgeon says, "What a text is this! and what an exposition of it is furnished by the biography of every believing man and woman!" We *may* return to our rest for we are invited to, "Come unto Me . . . and I will give you rest." We *must* return if peace is to be ours instead of soul-agitation. The wonder is that we ever leave such rest, and wander from our home in God. Yet his love ever invites us back. Romans 2:4. And there is no *rest* so warm and safe for the heart, as in the love and care of our bountiful God.

As for any historical association of this verse, "It is the continuation of the Paschal Hallel, and there must in some measure be interpreted in connection with the coming out of Egypt. The Psalm as a whole has all the appearance of being a personal soul in which the believing soul, reminded by the Passover of its own bondage and deliverance, speaks thereof with gratitude, and praises the Lord accordingly. We can conceive of the Israelite with a staff in his hand singing, 'Return unto thy rest, O my soul,' as he remembered the going back of the house of Jacob to the land of their fathers."

Thou hast delivered my soul . . . mine eyes . . . my feet, 116:8. What a blessed *trinity* of deliverances the Triune God can provide! The three particulars of this verse can be distinguished in this way—

> "He hath delivered my soul from death"—by giving me a *good* conscience.
> "Mine eyes from tears"—by giving me a *quiet* conscience.
> "My feet from falling"—by giving me an *enlightened* conscience.

Paul reminds us of a threefold deliverance—Past, Present, and Prospective, 2 Cor. 1:10, and also of the great Deliverer Himself, Who by His death saves from the *penalty* of sin—by His resurrection, saves us from the *power* of sin and Who at His coming, will save us from the entire *presence* of sin. David too emphasizes the triad of blessings under the covenant of grace, in the verse before us, namely, Salvation—Solace—Sanctification.

Speaking in the past tense, the Psalmist magnifies his bountiful God for the threefold escape—Death was vanquished, Tears were dried, and Fears were banished. If we have been delivered from the prospect of eternal death, as well as the dread of physical death, then why should we weep?

What reason for sorrow remains? If tears are ours, is it not comforting to know that a Divine hand waits to dry them? If our trembling feet have been steadied, then let us not be content until with firm feet we can pursue the path of the upright, escaping thereby all snares and stumbling blocks in the way.

> Take my feet, and let them be,
> Swift and beautiful for Thee.

I will walk before the Lord in the land of the living, 116:9. Having experienced deliverance from stumbling, the Psalmist makes the resolution to walk, with a firm and resolute step before the Lord, as he continues to live out his daily life before those wherever he may live in the land. The sense of the latter end of the verse is—"In the land where living people are," as opposed to Sheol—*the land of shades*. "Now that Jehovah has kept me in this world alive, I will walk so as to please Him." Some writers suggest that not this present world, or habitable earth is meant, but the *heavenly land*, the region of living saints, alive for evermore. According to the original, *land* is of the plural number—"lands"—and implies that no matter what land he found himself in the writer would walk as in God's presence, and live under the influence of His all-observing eye. The sense of living and walking before the Lord develops faith, holy fear, and true holiness.

I believed . . . I was greatly afflicted, 116:10. The reading from the original Hebrew Bible has the translation, "I believed in Jehovah even when I had to say, I am much afflicted." This verse became proverbial, and Paul, writing of "the Spirit of faith" uses it to great effect. 2 Cor. 4:13. The only speech convincing men is that having in it the accent of the speaker's personal conviction and spiritual experience. We should never say more than we believe. Many try to speak of the Lord who have never known what it is to exercise a saving faith in Him. When it comes to the things of God, no man should speak unless he has a relationship with Him. The outstanding men of faith in Church History have been those who could say, *"I have believed*, therefore have I spoken." Believing is an act of the heart for it is with the heart that man believes, and the tongue should be in harmony with the heart. "The tongue should always be the heart's interpreter, and the heart should always be the tongue's suggester; what is spoken with the tongue should be first stamped upon the heart and wrought from it." Greatly afflicted, the Psalmist had not ceased to believe: his faith had been tried and strengthened, not destroyed by his sufferings.

I said in my haste, All men are liars, 116:11. There was no need to make such a declaration in *haste* for since Adam, all men have been guilty of telling or acting a lie, being prompted by him who is "the father of lies." The only man who never told a lie was not George Washington, as history would have us believe, but the Man Christ Jesus. The rebuke we learn from this verse is that hasty speaking lies at the root of so much misery to ourselves and others. How we need to pray daily for a holy collectedness of spirit and for a Divine watch upon our lips! Said an eminent director of souls, "I shall have good hopes of you when you can speak and move slowly."

The margin of the R.V. gives us "in my alarm," for *in my haste*. Then the original expresses the affirmation of the verse as *All men are a lie*, or *All men are lying*, meaning "break their word, or are treacherous." The LXX Version puts it, "In an ecstasy of despair I said, *The whole race of mankind is a delusion*." Thus although the Psalmist confessed his hasty speech, there was much truth in what he said. His error lay in passing judgment on some of his fellowmen whose truthfulness and conscientiousness he did not know. Doubtless, with his repentance for being hasty, he learned to bridle his tongue.

> If you would keep your lips from slips,
> Five things observe with care—
> Of whom you speak, and what you speak,
> And when, and how, and where.

What shall I render . . . for all his benefits? 116:12. Turning from his fretting about man's falsehood, David directs his sole attention to Him Who is the Perfect One, and to how he can honor Him for all His grace and goodness. The Lord had rendered so much mercy to him, and now he desired to acknowledge all His bestowments in every possible fitting way. From the teaching of Jesus, Who rendered to God His all, we learn that true loyalty in rendering to Caesar the things that are Caesar's but that true piety is giving to God the things that are God's, Matt. 22:21. Are we exercised as to by what things, and by what means we can repay Him Who is so abundantly munificent in His daily benefits? If it be true as the poet puts it that—

> Man's ingratitude makes countless mourn—

what must man's ingratitude to God do to His loving and bounteous heart?

I will take the cup of salvation, and call upon the name of the Lord, 116:13. Here we have one of the paradoxes of our Christian faith, for *render* and *take* are opposite actions. Yet the Psalmist's answer to his own question, "What shall I render"—"I will take"—more from Him appears to be a contradiction of terms. Yet it was the wisest reply that could possibly be given.

> The best return for one like me,
>   So wretched and so poor,
> Is from his gifts to draw a plea,
>   And ask him still for more.

The further benefit he took from the Lord was "the cup of salvation," which in itself was an act of worship, and was accompanied with a form of adoration, "I will call upon the name of the Lord." Various interpretations are given as to the nature of *the cup* in question. Perhaps it was the drink offering or oblation accompanying festival celebrations, Num. 29:19. "I will take," literally means "I will lift up," and the figure may be obtained from the pouring out, and lifting up libations as a sacrifice to deity. Thus the Psalmist desired to make an offering in acknowledgment of the deliverance accorded by God, solemnly raising the cup to Him in gratitude. Others think that it was the Passover Cup mentioned by our Lord when this Psalm as part of the Hallel was sung, Matt. 26:27. Still others take the figurative meaning of the cup, as portion, or lot, as in Psalm 16:5 or in Psalm 23, "My cup floweth over."

Whatever the identity of *the cup*, it was one brimful of God's blessing, and such a cup is ours only because our dear Lord drank a cup brimming with bitter sorrow for our salvation, John 18:11. "Upon the table of infinite love stands the cup full of blessing; it is ours by faith to take it in our hand, make it our own, and partake of it, and then with joyful hearts to laud and magnify the gracious One Who has filled it for our sakes that we may drink and be refreshed. We can do this figuratively at the sacramental table." It is interesting to note that verses 13-19 of this Psalm in meter has been the Communion Song of many Presbyterian worshippers through the centuries.

I will pay my vows unto the Lord now in the presence of all his people, 116:14, 18. The repetition emphasizes the Psalmist's determination to carry out his resolution, and here commences to perform his desire to render unto the Lord all that was due to His holy name. By rejecting his declaration he indicated his earnestness to fulfill his vows, not in some secret place but in public before all God's people. Although the Divine mercies came to him privately and personally, his praise for same would be spread abroad. Probably the vows in question embraced sacrifices and gifts of money for the Temple. Similar vows of this kind are still often made in some churches. The sense of these verses says Dr. Witton Davies seems to be, "What I have vowed to Jehovah in the event of my being rescued from so great danger I will now pay."

What we appreciate is the Psalmist's resolve for present, immediate action in respect to the payment of his vows—*now*. "Good resolutions cannot be carried out too speedily; vows become debts, and should be promptly paid." Foxe, in his heart-stirring volume, *The History of Martyrs*, relates the story of one of those who died for the faith, John Philpot. Says Foxe, "He went with the sheriffs to the place of execution, and when he was entering Smithfield the way was foul, and two officers took him up to bear him to the stake. Then he said merrily, What will ye make me a pope? I am content to go to my journey's end on foot. But first coming into Smithfield, he kneeled down there, saying these words, I will pay my *vows in thee, O Smithfield."* This brave martyr was another who paid his vows in the presence of the people.

Precious in the sight of the Lord is the death of his saints, 116:15. During his Crusade, St. Bernard made special use of the Psalms in his preaching, and he had great preference for this verse, "Right dear in the sight of the Lord is the death of His saints." The word *precious* implies of such consequence to God that He will require penalties for it. It is a word indicating what is rare, and therefore much thought of. "Jehovah does not regard the death of His favored ones as a thing of no importance, as trivial, as cheap: it is much thought of, and will not be allowed unless strong reasons call for it." This is why He often raises a saint from the very borders of the grave, as He did Hezekiah of old. Balaam's wish to die was not granted because it went forth from feigned lips, Num. 23:10.

Many saints did not have God to make their bed in sickness for the simple reason that they were not allowed to die in a comfortable bed. Thomas à Becket, for example, was slain on the altar steps. For a valiant army, the cold, damp floor of a dungeon was their last resting place. Yet God was with them, baring His bosom for their spirits, as He made their dying bed, rough and cruel though it was "as soft as downy pillows are."

> The chamber where the good man meets his fate
> Is privileged beyond the common walk of life.

We might ask why the Psalmist intrudes upon his theme of paying vows and offering sacrifices of thanksgiving with the thought of *death*. But twice over he had referred to the grim side of man's last enemy— "Sorrows of death"—"Delivered my soul from death," but now views it from God's viewpoint. "Each saintly death-bed is the scene of minute care on the part of God our Father, since it is there that He puts the finishing touch on a perfected character." It must be borne in mind that only the death of *saints* is "right dear" in the sight of the Lord. Who and what is a saint, as far as Scripture is concerned? In the Roman Catholic Church a conspicuous member of its community must be dead for years before being worthy to be canonized as a *Saint*.

But all God's saints are living ones. Paul speaks of all believers, or born-anew men and women as being "saints in Christ Jesus." Thus, all true Christians are saints, although, withal, some are more saintly than others. Further, no child of God dies prematurely, although we may think so, if he or she dies in youth. Every saint is immortal until his work is done, and when death comes, whether early or late in life, it is precious in God's sight, for the one dying was redeemed by the precious blood of

His precious Son—Whose death was more precious in the Father's sight than all other sacrificial deaths.

I am thy servant . . . Thou hast loosed my bonds, 116:16. As the word for *servant* here means "slave," what a marvelous avowal the Psalmist repeats, in the phrase "I am thy servant," although some theologians affirm that the second same avowal is repeated by a copyist's mistake, or, simply used as poetic variety. David's mother was evidently a gracious, God-fearing woman, a handmaid of His, and as her son he felt he was altogether God's by claims arising out of his birth in a godly home. David knew that not only himself but his family were in the covenant, and, as very commonly in the East, the mother is selected for mention instead of the father.

Loosed from his bonds of sorrow and trouble and threatened death, the Psalmist wishes to be bound to the service of God. *I am thy slave.* Had he known George Matheson's appealing hymn, "Make me a captive, Lord," he would have sung it joyfully, for through his slavery he found freedom. To be the slave of the Master Who was sold for the price of a slave is to taste the sweets of liberty. Those who became God's slaves are loosed by Him from all other bonds, John 8:31-36.

I will offer to thee the sacrifice of thanksgiving . . . Praise ye the Lord, 116:17, 19. These verses illustrate the way David paid his vows in the presence of God's people, for his sacrificial praise was offered in the courts of the Lord's house—the house itself being entered by priests only. God's praise is not to be confined to some secret place, or whispered in holes and corners, as if we were afraid that others should hear us, but in the thick of the throng, and in the very center of assemblies—in the Lord's house, and in the midst of Jerusalem. Four times over in the Psalm, the writer expresses his fondness for calling upon the name of the Lord. "Good feelings and actions bear repeating; the more of hearty callings upon God the better."

Are you not held by the word *sacrifice*—a blood-red word—in connection with praise? Do we think of thanksgiving, and calling upon the name of the Lord, as exercises costing us dearly? Mere lip-praise may not be sacrificial, but thanksgiving of the heart is, for it means that with our song is the surrender of ourselves to Him from whom all blessings flow. What costs us nothing cannot be of much value to us. The Psalm closes with a *Hallelujah!* which provided a very fit conclusion to a song sung by all the people gathered together at Jerusalem to keep the Feast. It is a song also every saint today should learn to sing.

> When all the heart is pure, each warm desire
> Sublimed by holy love's ethereal fire,
> On winged words our breathing thought may rise,
> And soar to Heaven, a grateful sacrifice.

Psalm 117

What a mighty midget of a Psalm this is! The *Tom Thumb* of the Psalter, it enjoys the reputation of being the shortest chapter in the Bible, and the central portion of the Bible as a whole. We have a saying that "Little is much if God is in it," which is certainly true of this Psalm, little in its letter, but exceedingly large in its spirit. What it lacks in quantity, is made up by its excellent quality. A worthy title of this short but sweet Psalm would be *Multum in parvo*, or "much in little." Paul and History testify to the importance and value of this two-versed Psalm, which has been described thus, "It is a dew-drop reflecting a universe." When the Apostle Paul came to unfold the glorious truth that Jewish and Gentile converts are one in salvation, he quoted this Psalm in defense of his argument, Romans 15:10, 11. Thus in this Psalm, and in Isaiah 11:10, and elsewhere, the spirit of Judaism forgets its natural exclusiveness, and reaches out its hands to the world.

As for historical association of the Psalm, as Hampton's troopers carried him to his last resting place among the Chiltern Hills, to the sublime strains of the 90th Psalm, so Oliver Cromwell sang with his soldiers the 117th Psalm on the battlefield of Dunbar, during a brief respite. Practical in his religion as in all else, Cromwell chose the shortest Psalm in the Bible to voice his triumph over the Scottish troop on Sept. 3, 1650. Afterwards by the Puritans this Psalm became known as the *Dunbar* Psalm.

Then it was the custom of Philip Henry to sing the 117th Psalm every Sabbath after the first sermon, as the fullest expression of thanksgiving. This ruler used to say that the more singing of the Psalm there is in our families and congregations on Sabbath, the more like they are to Heaven; and he preferred singing whole Psalms to pieces of them. What ever would he think of the doggerel hymns of today?

As to the authorship, and nature of the Psalm's composition, we credit David with it, seeing it fits in with the adoring, catholic spirit of the sweet Psalmist of Israel. We do not accept that it is a fragment or appendage of another Psalm, but as the spirit of praise gripped his soul he gave vent to this briefest of Psalms, as love's extra for his Lord. His feeling must have been that of S. T. Francis, a far later poet who wrote—

> Then these lips, sure, a tribute shall bring,
> Though unworthy the praises must be;

> Shall all nature be vocal and sing,
> And no psalm of rejoicing from me?

Spurgeon felt that "in all probability it was frequently used as a brief hymn suitable for almost every occasion, and especially when the time for worship was short. Perhaps it was also sung at the commencement or at the close of other Psalms, just as we now use the doxology. It would have served either to open a service or conclude it. The same divine Spirit which expatiates the 119th Psalm, here condenses his utterances into two short verses, but yet the same infinite fullness is present and perceptible."

The evident fact is that the Psalm is a doxology calling upon Jews and Gentiles to praise Jehovah. *All* people are invited to magnify His name, and the two verses give the reasons for such a universal summons, namely, Jehovah's covenant kindness and the fulfillment of His promises to Israel.

Praise the Lord, all ye nations . . . all ye people, 117:1. While there are three Hallelujahs in the two verses, the middle word for *praise* is different from the other two occasions. Here it means *laud*, or perhaps, to *soothe*. If the former, then it means the celebration of the praises of God with a high voice. If the latter, the suggestion is that the nations are calmed and ready to make peace with Israel's God after seeing His display of power for their sakes, and also to join in praising Him as the great Jehovah. The term *nations* consistently implies Gentile nations. Moses prophesied, "Rejoice, O ye nations, his people," Deut. 32:43, and Jesus came as "a light to lighten the Gentiles," and when He returns to reign Gentile dominion will be His, and Israel will be His glory. Then a universal song will ascend to Him as Lord of *all*, Who is infinitely deserving of the love and homage of all mankind.

His mercy . . . the truth of the Lord, 117:2. The themes of universal praise are the greatness of Jehovah's love and the permanence of His Word. In the original the term "mercy" implies *lovingkindness*. As for the phrase "great towards us," same means, "higher than we deserve." Mercy and Truth are often joined together in Scripture to prove that the Lord reveals Himself to His people not only in mercy but truth also. His mercy is bounded by His truth, so that none may either presume Him more merciful than His truth or word declare, and also that none may despair because of their great sins that His mercy is not *gratis*, according to the truth of His promise. Mercy ever flows towards the multiplied race of Jews and Gentiles.

Then how consoling to know that in spite of the efforts of men to destroy the continual worth of Scripture, that as Divine truth it has a permanency none can obliterate. Truth became personified in Him Who called Himself *The Truth*, and both the Living Word and Written Word are to endure forever. Not one promise of Jehovah can fail, nor ever will. His amazing grace and eternal Word are the causes of constant and grateful praise, wherefore this wee Psalm concludes as it commences with a joyous *Hallelujah!* Because God is ever the same in mercy and truth let us render to Him here and now, our gladsome praise.

Psalm 118

Prominent in history, this is a Psalm which might have a history to itself, sounding the depths of trial, rising to the loftiest heights of triumph, and looking far forward to Him Who measured them both in His rejection and His final victory—beginning and closing with thanksgiving for everlasting mercy. As we shall later see, this Psalm found an echo in persecuted scattered groups on the moorlands and in the hearts of dying men on the scaffold.

Basil, chief organizer of the monastic community in Eastern Christendom, in the 3rd century, opened a temporary retreat in Pontus, and introduced devotional exercises which the monks practiced during the night. Psalms were sung, divided by two and two, the monks answering each other, one leading the chant, the rest following. Then, as morning broke, they all in common, with one mouth and from one heart, lifted to the Lord the Psalm of Confession, Psalm 118. As the day began, so it ended.

Martin Luther began his public career as a teacher at Wittenberg in 1512, where he lectured on the Psalms. Clinging to the "old and ragged" Psalter as a tried and trusty friend, he wrote his renowned commentary on *The Seven Penitential Psalms*. It was during his solitude at Coburg that he wrote his exposition of Psalm 118, and paid it a most glowing tribute in the dedication of his translation—

> This is my psalm, my chosen psalm. I love them all; I love all Holy Scripture, which is my consolation and my life. But this Psalm is nearest my heart, and I have a familiar right to call my own. It has saved me from many a pressing danger, from which nor emperor, nor kings, nor sages, nor saints could have saved me. It is my friend; dearer to me than all the honors and power of the earth.

The Diet of Worms, of 1521, by which Martin Luther was condemned and placed under the ban of the Empire, was opened by Charles V, the champion of the Pope against the Protestants. Yet, in the love of the Psalms, Emperor and Reformer were not divided. Charles presented Marot with 200 gold doublons for his metrical version of 30 Psalms, and asked him to translate his own special favorite, Psalm 118.

The massacres of the Huguenots provoked the Wars of Religion, and once the sword was drawn, the Psalms became the war-songs of the

Huguenots. On the battlefields of Coligny or Henry of Navarre could be heard the stirring chanting of Psalm 118, and other Psalms. They sang this 118th Psalm on bended knee at Coutras, when some of the courtiers in grand dress cried, "See, the cowards are already begging mercy." "No," said an officer, who knew their way, "you may expect a stern fight from the men who sing psalms and pray." After the victory the Huguenots sang the 124th Psalm.

As to the historical setting of this Psalm, while there is agreement among commentators that it was called forth by some outstanding event, there is divergence of opinion as to what the event was. That it was a Temple song of thanksgiving is stamped on every line of it. Possibly it was sung in turn by a full choir, the congregation and the priests. In Ezra's account of the laying of the foundation of the Temple, the first and last verses of Psalm 118 are mentioned in such an account, which indicates that this sublime song was chanted then, after "the ordinance of David king of Israel," who, doubtless was also the composer of the Psalm. As it follows Psalm 117, both Psalms, though each is a distinct portion in itself, Psalm 117 is an exordium of the Psalm 118. The Conqueror and His attendants sing the former Psalm as an introductory hymn, inviting all Jews and Gentiles to share in God's merciful kindness and to sing His praises, and in the latter Psalm we have the song congregation and priests sang to the praise of Jehovah.

As to the subject of the Psalm, as it is one of the *I Psalms*—the pronoun occurring 15 times—whoever he was, while he had much to say about himself, he may not have strictly adhered to details of his own personal experience. We have no doubt that the heroic personage was David. "The elect champion who found himself rejected by his friends and countrymen and at the same time violently opposed by his enemies. In faith in God he battles for his appointed place, and in due time he obtains it in such a way as greatly to display the power and goodness of the Lord. He then goes up to the house of the Lord to offer sacrifice, and to express his gratitude for Divine interposition, all the people blessing him and wishing him abundant prosperity." Who else could this have been but David, who became the illustrious King of Israel?

But a Greater than David is here, even though the Psalm was called forth by the circumstances of the time, and expressed the gratitude, joy and faith of the writer, and other pious Israelites. David's Greater Son, the Lord Jesus, applied verse 22 of this Psalm to Himself, Matt. 21:42, and Peter applied the same words to his Lord, Acts 4:11; 1 Peter 2:11. It is believed that Jesus and His Disciples sang this Psalm before He went into the Garden, Matt. 26:30; Mark 14:26. As Psalm 118 is the last of the Hallel Psalms 113-118, and was used after the Paschal meal, it is very impressive to read into this Psalm some of those thoughts which must have filled the heart of our Savior as with it on His lips, He stood on the margin of the cold river.

But though David had been given a prophetic view of the coming Messiah it must not be held that every particular line and sentence in his Psalm should be read in reference to the Messiah. We must not hunt for parallels in all the minutae of David's struggles and prayers. Within the Psalm we have the prophetic expression of that exultant strain of antic-ipative triumph when Christ, and the rejected Stone, becomes the Chief Corner Stone of His own Temple.

O give thanks unto the Lord, 118:1. While David has prominence in the Psalm, he gives his Lord the pre-eminent place for in the original, *Jehovah* occurs 22 times, corresponding with the number of letters in the Hebrew alphabet; *Jah*, contraction of "Jehovah," occurs 5 times. The first and last verses are exactly the same. When, on Nov. 5, 1688, William of Orange cast anchor at Torbay, pledged to support the Protestant faith, and his troop disembarked, William asked William Carstares to conduct a divine service on the shore. After praying, Carstares asked for Psalm 118 to be sung, and standing along the beach the soldiers sang, "O give thanks unto the Lord, for He is gracious; because His mercy endured for ever." The historian said that "this act of devotion produced a sensible effect." Ultimately Carstares became the chief instrument in bringing about the settlement of the Church of Scotland in 1688, and died during his Moderatorship of the General Assembly for the fourth time in 1715, and was buried in the historic churchyard of Greyfriars, Edinburgh.

In the first four verses of the Psalm we have a general invitation for all to give thanks to Jehovah, and later on, three classes are specially men-tioned to express their gratitude. See Psalm 115:9-13, for a similar choral arrangement. The whole nation of Israel was concerned in David's tri-umphant accession and therefore it was only right that all should unite in his adoring song of praise. All praise must go, not to David, but to the *Lord*. Two reasons are stated for such universal thanksgiving, namely, His *goodness* and *mercy*.

God is *good*! In spite of all appearance to the contrary we must hold fast to this virtue of Him "Whose goodness faileth never." His dispen-sations may vary and not seem good to us, but His nature and acts are always the same—*Good*! The skies may be dark with clouds, but behind them is His kind face, for goodness is His essence, and must therefore be praised.

God is *merciful*! Mercy is an integral part of His goodness, and the virtue concerning us more than any other, seeing we are sinners and in need of His mercy. "God be merciful to me a sinner!" In the verse, David singles out the endurance of such divine mercy as a special subject of song. The last Psalm closed with "His truth endured for ever," now it is

His mercy—sister of truth—endless mercy, mercy to Eternity, we are to bless the Lord for. Because He is the One Who said, "I change not," there can never be any change in His matchless mercy.

Let Israel . . . Let the house of Aaron . . . them that fear the Lord, 118:2-3. In each of the three exhortations there is the repetition of the subject of praise by the three classes mentioned, namely, "His mercy endured for ever." All had to unite in the exaltation of Jehovah as the Merciful One.

Israel. If this nation, with whom God had made a covenant of mercy and love, but who became guilty of so many transgressions yet was forgiven, does not sing of mercy, who can? If Israel had not sung when David came to her throne as King, the very stones would have cried out.

House of Aaron. Not only "the house of Israel," but "the house of Aaron," the elite of the nation, those set apart to come nearest to God, they, too, must magnify the everlasting mercy of the Most High. If this Psalm 118 is an echo of David's experiences, then the priests had a special reason for gratitude as he came to the throne, for Saul had made a great slaughter among them, and often intruded into their sacred office.

Them that fear the Lord. By this class we understand those who were not of "the house of Israel," nor of "the house of Aaron," that is, native Jews, but proselytes who adopted the Jewish religion and came to fear Israel's God. These are likewise called upon to unite with all the rest in thanksgiving, not only for David's exaltation to the throne, but also for the everlasting mercy of Jehovah. Common to all three exhortations is the little word *now.* "There is no time like time present for telling out the praises of God. *Now* with us should mean always. When would it be out of season to cease from praising God, whose rich mercy never ceases?"

The fourfold testimonies to the everlasting mercy of God is the first four verses of the Psalm, are before us like four evangelists, "each one declaring the very pith and marrow of the Gospel; and they stand like four angels at the four corners of the earth holding the winds in their hands, restraining the plagues of the latter days that the mercy and long-suffering of God may endure towards the sons of men." Here are four cords to bind the sacrifice to the four horns of the altar and four trumpets with which to proclaim the year of jubilee to every quarter of the world. For ourselves, *now*—

> Let us with a gladsome mind
> Praise the Lord, for he is kind;
> For his mercies shall endure
> Ever faithful, ever sure.

I called . . . the Lord answered me, 118:5. Sin-stricken and sorrowful souls can hardly do better than take David's prescription. If it healed him,

why should he not avail for us? See Psalm 34:6. Is not his experience of
Jehovah's deliverance an encouragement to our faith? By the word *distress*, we can understand "in a strait place," or "in my straightness," or
"when I was hemmed in, perplexed," as David often was when pursued
by Saul. But he did not sit down and moan over his lot, as if there was no
way out of his distressing situations with all the tears they caused. David
said, "I called upon the Lord," and his sad situation soon changed.

The Psalmist was answered with boundless freedom, which must have
been a great relief after his straightness when, for instance, he was forced
to hide in the cramped condition of a small cave and, as Shakespeare
expresses it in Macbeth, he found himself

> . . . cabin'd, cribb'd, confin'd, bound in
> To saucy doubts and fears.

Prayer was answered and the Lord "set me in a large place"—the last
clause literally meaning, *with room*, or with "the freedom of Jehovah."
The implication is that roominess described by Shakespeare in *King John*,
"Now my soul has elbow-room." See Psalm 18:19. "The Lord answered
me largely," is one translation of the phrase. David was brought out of a
narrow and confined condition into a place of liberty, where he could
move and roam at large. The figure of "a large place" represents a state
of ease and comfort, the opposite is conveyed by the phrase "in a strait,
narrow place." The principal Hebrew word for "salvation" means
enlargement, and the name "Jesus" means strictly *The Enlarger*, or "He
who sets at large." He is also ever with us taking our part, never leaving
us to fight any foe alone.

Such a marvelous deliverance was a striking evidence that the Lord
was on the side of His servant. "The Lord is for me," is a translation of the
first part of verse 6, and David feared no foe "with Him at hand to bless."
Further suffering might come his way but he would not dread of what his
foes might try to do. He knew that they could not go any further than
Divine permission. See Psalm 56:11. The writer of the *Hebrews*
expressed his assurance of Divine help and protection in the same language, Heb. 13:6. When Herod was highly displeased with the armies of
Tyre and Sidon, they did not care to approach him until they had made
Blastus the king's chamberlain, their friend. If such and such a person be
on their side, men think that all must go well. But who is so safe-guard-
ed and sure of assistance as he who says, *The Lord is on my side*?

In his sermon to the garrison in Londonderry, prepared to hold the city
against the forces of King James, in 1689, Rev. George Walker sought to
encourage the defenders when food and ammunition were very low with
the words of this 118th Psalm. "There is nothing too hard for the Lord,
when He designs to bring about His purpose . . . . The Lord is on my side.

I will not fear what man can do unto me." "Let us take courage, then, and faint not, but acquit yourselves like men." Sunday, July 28, 1689, was a memorable day—"a day to be remembered with thanksgiving by the besieged of Derry as long as they live, for on this day we were delivered from famine and slavery." God took them out of straitened circumstances into the large place of freedom.

Prothero tells us that it was this Psalm that William Cowper, a timid, delicate, sensitive child in Dr. Pitman's School in Hertfordshire, nerved himself to endure the torture inflicted by an elder boy. In after years Cowper wrote—

> I well remember being afraid to lift my eyes upon him higher than his knees; and I knew him better by his shoe-buckles than by another part of his dress.

Yet, as he sat on a bench in the schoolroom, fearing the immediate coming of his tormentor, he found in the text, *I will not fear what men doeth unto me*, "a degree of trust and confidence in God that would have been no disgrace to a much more experienced Christian."

If we would have God on our side, we must take care to be on His side. When one a poor, needy saint and God are on the same side, deliverance and victory are certain, as both David and Paul were assured of, Rom. 8:33; Heb. 13:6.

It is better to trust in the Lord than man . . . than princes, 118:8, 9. To *trust* implies to take refuge in, and the Lord is our best and most secure hiding place. Martin Luther said of these verses that trust is the art of arts, that he had well studied and learned not to put confidence in man. Seeing there are some 31,174 verses making up our Bible, then the middle verse would be this 8th verse, the 15,587th. The dual "it is better" literally means, "Good is it to trust in Jehovah," and is the Hebrew form of comparison. It is better in every way to trust in the Lord, because it is wiser, seeing He is more able to help us than the best of men, who are only frail men at the best. It is also safer to have Him as the Object of confidence, because we are always secure in His hands. Trust in man can never produce a sacred calm of spirit, and sanctity of the soul, as the Lord can in the hearts of those who trust in Him.

Even if men are princes, the same arguments apply, for princes although noble, true and chivalrous are but men. Old John Trapp left us the saying that, "Great men's words are like dead men's shoes; he may go barefoot that waited for them." All who trust in the Lord are better provided for than minions of princes. "In Eternity a prince's smile goes for nothing; heaven and hell pay no homage to royal authority. The favor of princes is proverbially fickle, the testimonies of worldlings to this effect are abundant." Shakespeare, the world's greatest poet, put into the lips of the dying Wolsey, the power of the truth of Psalm 118:8-9.

> O how wretched
> Is that poor man that hangs on princes' favors!
> There is, betwixt that smile we would aspire to,
> That sweet aspect of princes, and their ruin,
> More pangs and fears than wars or women have:
> And when he falls, he falls like Lucifer,
> Never to hope again.

The Lord will destroy . . . The Lord will destroy . . . The Lord will destroy, 118:10-12. These verses give us some of the triads of the Psalm. How David loved triplets of truth! A threefold encompassment was his, but a threefold destruction of those who had hemmed him in is in each of his three pleas, he used "the name of the Lord." The adversaries surrounding the Psalmist, so that he could scarcely find a loophole of escape out of the ring about him, were *all nations*. If David is the hero of this Psalm, and we believe that he is, then we know that when he came to reign he was surrounded with innumerable enemies and was forced to make war with them.

It was Napoleon who said that God was always on the side of the biggest battalion—a dictum he lived to regret. David the warrior, however, knew that although he was a solitary champion, the Lord of Hosts was on his side, and that he would emerge from the circle of his enemies, more than a conqueror. Further, he did not speak of merely escaping from them as a bird out of the snare of the fowler, but that destruction would be theirs that there should be no further fear of repeated hostility.

In a vivid fashion, David describes his foes as a swarm of *bees*, attacking him at every point. Like the plague of flies in Egypt, the Psalmist found those who encompassed him as numerous, audacious, as nimble flying bees, attacking and stinging then flying off. The lines of Homer are apt at this point, although he wrote of *wasps*. Bees, although they produce painful stings, yet provide honey, as David's much-loved friend, Jonathan, proved—

> As wasps, provoked by children in their play,
> Pour from their mansions by the broad highway,
> In swarms the guiltless traveller engage,
> Whet all their stings, and call forth all their rage,
> All rise in arms, and with a general cry,
> Assert their waxen domes, and buzzing progeny;
> Thus from the tents the fervent legion swarms,
> So loud their clamors, and so keen their arms.

The destruction meted out upon the fervent legion upon David's bee-like enemies was that they might be quenched by the fire of thorns. Three times over he said, "In the name of the Lord will I destroy them," and the nations that had surrounded him came to an inglorious end. He had no need to crush such bees, for like crackling thorns they died of themselves. Fire of thorns quickly kindles into a blaze, and the flame is soon gone. Foes are compared to bees, Deut. 1:44; Isa. 7:18. The LXX Version has it, "They burnt out like a fire as thorns." One wonders whether Shakespeare had this verse in mind when, in *King Henry IV*, he wrote—

> Shallow jesters and rash bavin (brushwood) wit,
> Soon kindled and soon burnt.

Too often we go forth to the conflict in our own name and might, thinking that by our own arm we can gain victory over our enemies. What folly it is not to arm ourselves with the impenetrable armor—*In the name of the Lord.* Is it not better to trust His name, "high over all, in hell, or earth, or sky," than to war and work in the flesh?

The Lord helped me . . . my strength and song . . . my salvation, 118:13, 14. Still dwelling upon his persistent adversaries, David tells us how they concentrated all their thrusting power upon him to bring him down, with the thought changing to the scene of the encounter. "Thrusting, thou hast thrust at me." Says Ellicott, "This sudden change of person and challenge of the foes themselves is very dramatic." The wounds given and received smarted, and were exceeding sore, and put David in great danger. Because of his trust, however, victory was his over those sorely afflicting him.

"But the Lord helped me." Here we have one of those blessed *Buts* of Scripture. The Lord came to the hero's aid, and rescued him from the cruel assaults of surrounding foes. "The Lord helped *me*." Cannot many of us join the Psalmist in this declaration of personal, Divine aid? Because of such conquest we have another triad. "The Lord is my strength and song . . . my salvation." See Exod. 15:2; Psalms 27:1; 62:6.

My strength. Not only was Jehovah David's strength when arrayed against strong, cruel enemies, giving him a strength not his own, over them, but remained his *strength*. Jehovah *is* my strength. "God is our . . . strength," Psalm 46:1. For the saint, satanic forces never cease their attack, and thus he needs daily strength to resist and overcome.

My song. Because of his many miraculous deliverances, David had a great deal to sing about, and sing he did, as the songs he wrote prove. The song sung after the passage of the Red Sea, is here sung by David, and shall be sung to the end of the world by the saints of the Most High redeemed by His precious blood. It will be noted that it was not his exploits that formed his song but *The Lord*.

My salvation. Primarily, the Psalmist here extols Jehovah as his *Savior* from visible nations surrounding him, and seeking his overthrow. But he was saved from assaults, and here says that as the result of such a physical salvation, "He is *become* my salvation." From now on, his song would be "Salvation is of the Lord," and how his prolific pen became in magnifying God as the Savior from sin's penalty and power.

Donald Cargill, fearless preacher among the Scottish Covenanters became a marked man, because of his public denunciation of the King, and many nobles. A large reward was offered for this "most seditious preacher, villainous and fanatical conspirator," and his many escapes were narrow. One of his close friends told him that when his danger was sorest, that he preached and prayed the best. He replied by saying, "The Lord is my strength and song, and is become my salvation." But on July 11, 1681, he was captured and over two weeks later was executed at the Cross of Edinburgh. As he died he sang this Psalm 118 from the 16th verse to the end.

William Law in his *Serious Call* urged Christians to practice what they professed, to "live more nearly as they prayed." He invited the saints to imagine themselves "with Moses when he was led through the Red Sea," and went on to ask, "Do you think that you should then have wanted a voice or an ear to have sung with Moses, *The Lord is my strength and my song, and He is become my salvation?*"

William Cowper, to whom reference has just been made, suffered much from despondency and at one time was placed in Cotton's Asylum at St. Albans. But he recovered, and his joy, like his previous despair, was clothed in the language of the Psalms. On leaving the Asylum he declared, "The Lord is my strength and my song, and is become my salvation—I shall not die but live," Psalm 118:14, 17-19. It was his ambition to become the Poet of Christianity, and his efforts remain in wonderful hymns such as

> "GOD MOVES IN A MYSTERIOUS WAY"
> "HARK, MY SOUL, IT IS THE LORD"
> "O FOR A CLOSER WALK WITH GOD."

The right hand . . . the right hand . . . the right hand, 118:15, 16. The personal song of praise of the previous verse must become the public voice of rejoicing and salvation in the tabernacles of the righteous. By *tabernacles* we are to understand "tents" or poetically for "dwellings," and the "rejoicing" implies those shouts of joy such as celebrate a victory. These two verses tell us what the "voice" echoed forth. David, the conquering hero, desired all the families of his kingdom to rejoice with him over the victory Jehovah had granted. He was not content with his own individual praise, his people in their households must not be silent. *All* among the righteous should have the rooms of their dwelling resounding with the voice of hymns and sacred songs. The 15th verse of this Psalm used to be quoted by Philip Henry in commendation of family worship, with the remark that "it is a way to hold forth godliness, like Rahab's thread, to such as pass by our windows."

What impresses us about the two verses before us is the thrice celebration of God's right hand, and what a blessed triad the Psalmist gives us. Some see in it a prophetic reference to the Sacred Trinity; that in it he is jubilant with praise as he dwells upon the Triune God. The threefold mention of the *right hand* invites us to consider what Scripture actually means by such a position. We are not to suppose that God has *hands*, whether left or right, or that anyone sits in any particular position about God. The phrase is taken from our manner of speaking, and implies that one is exalted to power and honor in the heavens. As it was esteemed the place of *highest* honor to be seated at the right hand of God, means only, in the case of the Lord Jesus, that God has exalted Him to the highest honor in the universe, Mark 16:19.

Among the Hebrews, the *right hand* was used to denote *power*, thus "being by the right hand of God exalted" Eph. 1:20-22, emphasizes the power of God in raising His Son from the dead and exalting Him on high. The phrase, as the symbol of *power*, is common to Scripture. "Thine own right hand can save me," Job 40:14. See Psalms 17:7; 18:35; 20:6; 21:8, etc. Our Redeemer and Mediator is said to sit at God's right hand, which illustrates the position of activity and might He holds for us, therefore He must prevail for us, Psalm 110:1; Rom. 8:34; Heb. 1:3.

In verses 15-18 of Psalm 118, Jehovah is to be loudly praised for His goodness to the nation. His *right hand* is exalted, the attitude of a warrior, the hand that struck down David's enemies, is lifted up to defend again. Such a hand lifts up all who trust in God, and casts down all who resist Him. The LXX Version reads, "The right hand of the Lord exalts me." The double *valiantly*, emphasizes God's power to accomplish valiant things as the previous verses of the Psalm indicate. The same was true of Donald Cargill, leader of the Covenanters after the death of Richard Cameron, who, as he suffered martyrdom sang part of this 118th Psalm which was his favorite Psalm. When ascending the ladder to be executed, he said, "The Lord knows I go on this ladder with less fear and perturbation of mind than I have sometimes entered the pulpit to preach." Silenced by the beating of the drums, he could only quote three verses 16-18, which he had often used during life—

> The right hand of the mighty Lord
>   Exalted is on high;
> The right hand of the mighty Lord
>   Doth ever valiantly.
> I shall not die, but live, and shall
>   The works of God discover,
> The Lord hath me chastised sore,
>   But not to death given o'er.

I shall not die . . . He hath not given me over to death, 118:17, 18.
Threatened with death by those who had compassed him about like bees,
the Psalmist felt that the danger of dying was now past. So we have another of those blessed *buts*—"But he hath not given me over to death." There
is always a *but* of merciful reservation of God's dealings with us, Isa.
38:17. Because David escaped death, so did the nation he came to reign
over. Thus, in a sense, Israel, and not an individual claims a continuance
of life for the display of God's glory. We often find that "hope is so
expressed to suit not only the community for whom the Psalm was composed and sung, but each member of it individually."

The Psalmist was cheerfully assured that no arrow could carry death
beneath the joints of his harness and no weapon of any sort could end his
earthly sojourn. The time of his departure had not yet come, and he felt
immortality beating within his bosom. Is this not true of all who have been
made kings and priests unto God? They stand unharmed till their last sacrifice has been presented to Him. "No bullet will find its billet in our
hearts till we have finished our allotted period of activity."

> Plagues and death around me fly,
>   Till he please I cannot die;
> Not a single shift can hit,
>   Till the God of love sees fit.

Seeing he had been preserved of the Lord, David resolved to devote
himself to His cause, and bear witness to His faithfulness, which he does
in this Psalm. "Declare the works of the Lord." Evidently Martin Luther
had the same purpose in life for it is said that he had this verse written on
his study wall. Because Christ rose from the grave, "we shall not die, but
live," implying that although we may die physically, we cannot die eternally but like our Lord be "alive for evermore," and in Glory declare the
works of the Lord as we cannot do on earth.

There are those who do great violence to Holy Writ when they take the
words, "I shall not die, but live," and use them to bolster the *swoon theory* in which they affirm that Jesus did not actually die but swooned away,
or passed out, under the strain of anguish, and came to while in
Joseph's tomb. Such teaching is absolutely contrary to the unmistakable
revelation of Scripture, that it was His glory that He should come as a
Man, die a man's death, but rise again triumphant o'er the grave, providing thereby a perfect salvation for a race of doomed and dying sinners.

John Wyclif, of the 13th century, who translated the Bible into the
tongue of the people, and whose passion was to erect an ecclesiastical fabric differing from the old in doctrine and also in organization, lay dying
on St. Sylvester's Day, in 1834, at Lutterworth. The Friars of the Abbey,
it is said, crowded around him, urging him to confess the wrong that he

had done to their Order. Wyclif had denounced Papacy, as the Antichrist. But the indomitable old man caused his servant to raise him from his pillow, and, gathering all his remaining strength, exclaimed with a loud voice, "I shall not die, but live; and declare—the evil deeds of the Friars"—who immediately rushed from the death chamber.

Open to me the gates . . . this gate . . . my salvation, 118:19-21. Praise to Jehovah unites these three verses as one. While the gates in question are capable of endless spiritual applications, in their context they refer to "this gate of the Lord," that is, the gate of the Temple which Israel, righteous before Jehovah, alone entered. At the back of the figure, we can visualize a procession chanting the triumphal song as in Psalm 24, and summoning the gates to open on its approach. It was because of Divine righteousness that the victory came, David celebrates in his Psalm. See Psalm 112:3. Among explanations of the gates, there are these two—

1. Gates through which the righteous alone should go. See Psalm 124.
2. Gates leading to the abode of the God of righteousness. See Psalm 20:2; Jerem. 21:23.

The plural *gates* refers to the three main gates, and *the gate*, the main entrance, before which the procession stood. The 20th verse gives us the reply of the Levites within the gate. Now, through grace, the Lord has many gates, through which the righteous pass, into the inner chamber of His presence, Rev. 21:12, 25. Spurgeon says that the phrase "the *gate* is sometimes used to signify power or empire. For instance, *The Sublime Porte* was used of the seat of the Empire of Turkey; the entrance to the Temple was the true *Sublime Porte*, and what is better, it was the *Porta Justitiae*, the gate of righteousness, the palace of the great King, Who is in all things just."

Entrance through the gate was asked for in set form, and the reason given for admission to the hallowed shrine—*I will praise the Lord*. The righteous are a rejoicing people, and thus entered the Temple for the best of purposes, namely, to praise Jehovah for Himself and His mighty works. "Public praise for public mercies is every way most appropriate, most acceptable to God, and most profitable to others . . . Under another aspect our Lord Himself is *the* gate, and through Him, as the new and living Way, all the righteous delight to approach unto the Lord to express their personal praise to Him for His great salvation."

Historically, if verses 19-23 imply the completion of the Temple, it is natural to fix on the first complete celebration of the Feast of Tabernacles after the Return, Neh. 8:14.

The stone . . . the head stone . . . we will rejoice . . . Save now, 118:22-25. The text from which Ebenezer Erskine preached before the Synod of

Perth and Stirling, Oct. 10, 1732, was, "The stone which the builders refused is become the head stone of the corner." This historic meeting led to the formation of the Secession Church, and began a new movement in Scotland's religious history. One of the most eloquent preachers of the Secession Church in later years was Dr. Alexander Smellie, whom I heard so often during my years in Scotland, and from whose writings I have gained so much. His perfect English, expressed in his written works, is a model for all preachers to follow.

Primarily, *the stone* was Israel, and *the builders* rejecting it, the surrounding nations, David refers to previously, "All nations compassed me about," verse 10. In verses 21-28, we have the procession entering the gate singing these words of praise and thanksgiving to Jehovah Who has so signally preserved and blessed the nation. They extolled Him as the One Who had become their *Salvation*, or as their Deliverer, Exod. 15:2. The nations had rejected Israel as being of no political account in the shaping of the destinies of Eastern nations at their own pleasure. But, as the proverb expresses it, "Man proposes, God disposes," and in His purpose, Israel was destined to have a chief place in the building up of history.

David could see a reflection of his own experiences in his message of the glorious end of the rejected stone. Had he not been rejected by those in authority, fit only to be thrust out, but did not God preserve him and place him in the position of the highest honor and the greatest usefulness when He made him the chief corner-stone of the nation—King of Israel? Is not history full of striking illustrations of men, rejected even by Church builders, who became chief cornerstones? The late Dr. G. Campbell Morgan was rejected by the Methodist Church when he decided to become a Minister of the Gospel, but what a marvelous cornerstone of a Biblical expositor he became!

What is exactly meant by "the head stone of the corner"? It has been suggested that the Temple builders found difficulty in fitting a certain stone into it, and put it on one side, though it afterwards occupied a very important position in the completed structure. Tradition has it that at the building of the second Temple there was a particular *stone* of which the description given by the Psalmist was literally true, and which became an object of reverential interest. But what of the *corner*? Same was the place where two walls met, and coupled the sides of the walls together. It was requisite that the corners should form the main strength of a building, sustaining thereby the whole weight of the edifice. The Jewish builders of religion rejected Jesus for the *head*-place, because they could endure *no corner*. They wanted to stand alone upon their own single wall.

"The expression, *Head of the corner*, occurs nowhere else in the Old Testament," observes Dr. Witton Davies, "but wherever elsewhere the word *corner* is used of a part of the building it refers to the foundation, the corner stone at the basis of the building and not one at the top, Isa. 28:16; Jerem. 51:26. What is here meant is that large stone in the lowest layer of stones which binds two rows at right angles. We have perhaps in this verse a proverbial saying, but in any case the general sense is clear enough. The nation—or the individual—once despised has come to great honor and glory."

The natural, ultimate, and prophetic application of this symbol is associated with the Lord Jesus, seeing the Messianic hope is poured into it. Such an aspect is seen in the fact that Jesus, after quoting the 22nd verse of the Psalm, took the rejected and exalted stone as being illustrative of Himself, Matt. 21:42; Luke 20:17. Then, under the inspiration of the Holy Spirit, Peter, in his address to the Sanhedrin, adopted the same symbol and applied it directly to Jesus. "This (Jesus of Nazareth) is the stone which was set at nought of *you* builders," Acts. 4:10-11. Thereafter the Apostle, with Isaiah's references to the same figure, 8:14; 28:16, enlarged upon it, when he came to write of Jesus as "the living Stone," at once the foundation of God's spiritual house and a stone of stumbling to all rejecting Him, 1 Peter 2:4, 8. See Eph. 2:20. Although His own received Him not, He has become to myriads "the chiefest among ten thousands" and the "altogether lovely one."

> Higher yet and ever higher, passeth he those ranks above,
> Where the seraphs are enkindled with the flame of endless love;
> Passeth them, for not e'en seraphs ever loved so well as he
> Who hath borne for his beloved, stripes, and thorns and shameful tree;
> Ever further, ever onward, where no angel's foot may tread
> Where the four-and-twenty elders prostrate fall in mystic dread;
> Where the four strange living creatures sing their hymn before the
>   throne,
> The Despised One and rejected passeth, in his might alone;
> Passeth through the dazzling rainbow, till upon the Father's right
> He is seated, his co-equal, God of God, and Light of Light.

Can we wonder at the confession following such a wonderful change—*This is the Lord's doing, it is marvelous in our eyes?* Historically, the change of destiny which made Israel of sudden political importance, is ascribed to none but Jehovah Himself. It is always His *doing* when those, despised and rejected for His sake, become highly honored. The verse can read, "Through Jehovah this has come about." The feeling expressed being "We are indebted for it all to Him, not to our courage and skill." See Neh. 6:16. In the Hebrew, "marvelously in our eyes" reads, "it is wonderfully done," which was true, not only in respect to Israel, but to Him Who came as her "Glory." His exaltation after rejection was so wonderfully done, that only an omnipotent God could have done it.

On the death of Queen Mary, rival of Queen Elizabeth in the struggle between Protestantism and Roman Catholicism, the latter was relieved from constant dread of execution, and expressed her gratitude in the words, "This is the Lord's doing: and it is marvelous in our eyes," which text in Latin was the stamp of her gold. Oliver Cromwell's appeal to the Kirk Commissioners that their cause was unrighteous and that he would resist them, was backed with his confident assertion that "before it be long, the Lord will manifest His good pleasure so that all shall see Him, and His people shall say, 'This is the Lord's work, and it is marvelous in our eyes; this is the day that the Lord hath made, we will rejoice and be glad.'" But as history records such victory cost Cromwell dearly.

What triumph rings in the exaltation, "*This* is the day!" And what an historic day it was when David himself the one-time fugitive became the King of Israel, and when Israel herself, no longer rejected, became politically important among the nations. Such a day of triumph, won by Jehovah, became immortalized in this great Psalm of David. "We will rejoice and be glad *in it*"—these last two words remind us that it was not the *day* they rejoiced in, but the remarkable event they joyfully commemorated on that day, as they magnified Jehovah for all He had accomplished. Israel celebrated such a victory with a day of feasting, music and song.

This verse, however, has been applied in other ways, the most popular being *The Lord's Day*, ordained of Him for worship. The Jews called the Sabbath, "The Queen of Days," which is certainly true of the Christian Sabbath, of which, when its light breaks upon the world, we sing—

> This is the day the Lord hath made,
>   He calls the hours his own;
> Let heaven rejoice, and earth be glad,
>   And praise surround the throne.

The quaint George Herbert says of the Lord's Day, the hours of which should be clad in royal apparel of delight—

> Thou art a day of mirth,
>   And where the week-days trail on ground,
> Thy flight is higher as thy birth.

Then we must not forget the lines, that—

> A Sabbath well-spent, brings a week of content,
>   And health for the toils of the morrow.
> But a Sabbath profaned, what'er may be gained,
>   Is a certain forerunner of sorrow.

Then the day Jesus was exalted to be the Head Corner-Stone, and His

Church came into being, was surely the most momentous of days for the earth—and Heaven! What rejoicing is ours when we think of Him leading captivity captive! There are a few most interesting historical uses of verses 24, 25. For instance, at the battle of Courtes, Oct. 20, 1587, before their fight began, the Huguenots knelt in prayer and chanted them, and were assured of deliverance.

Louis Rang, a Protestant minister, was arrested at Livron, and condemned to die, March 2, 1745. Freedom was offered him if he would but abjure his faith, but he rejected such relief. His sentence was that he should be hung in the market square at Die, and that his head should be severed from his body and exposed on a gibbet where he had lived. On his way to the scaffold, he sang, "This is the day the Lord hath made; we will rejoice and be glad in it." Thus he met his death, joyfully, for his Lord.

A few weeks later, another Protestant Pastor, Jacques Roger, a venerable man of 70 years of age, 40 of which had been spent in the ministry, during which he was often tracked like a wild beast because of his rejection of Catholicism, suffered the same fate as Louis Rang, and like him quoted this same 24th verse on the scaffold. Then we have the terrible record of the massacre of St. Bartholomew's Day, in 1760, when Francois Rochette, who had the charge of 25 Reformed Churches, and was a marked man because of his Protestant beliefs and works, was committed to prison. Petitions on his behalf were presented to Duc de Richelieu, and to Marie Adelaide, Princess of France, the daughter of Louis XV, who had shown herself inclined to mercy, but all was in vain. Rochette was found guilty and condemned to death. Refusing the offer of release if only he would deny his faith, he was executed on Feb. 20, 1762, and became the last Protestant martyr. It was fitting, therefore, as he mounted the scaffold with a firm step, that he could be heard singing, "This is the day the Lord hath made: we will rejoice and be glad in it."

Save now, I beseech thee, O Lord . . . send now prosperity, 118:25. This is not the adverb of time. *Now*, should be omitted, and the opening clause rendered, *Save, we pray.* See Matt. 21:9. The words of this verse were sung on one of the days of the Feast of Tabernacles, and were known as the *Great Hosanna*, and became a liturgical formula. The Hebrew for "Save now" is *Hosteea na amme*, from which we have *Hosanna*. What Hosannas must have ascended when David became King, and God granted the nation much prosperity under his reign. How the Church should raise her Hosanna to David's Greater Son for all He has accomplished, and incessantly plead for her spiritual prosperity from above!

The last four verses of Psalm 118 are in the form of a Benediction, and provide the Psalm with a most fitting climax.

Blessed be he . . . we have blessed you, 118:26. When Charlemagne reached the portal of St. Peter's, Rome, April 2, 774, Pope Hadrian took him in his arms, and then together they entered the basilica hand in hand, and then prostrated themselves before the high altar, while the multitude thronging the building chanted, "Blessed be he that cometh in the Name of the Lord." The next day Charlemagne was hailed by the Pope as his champion and by the people as their deliverer.

Historically, the verse formed words of welcome probably spoken by the Levite in charge, to the procession approaching the gates. According to Rabbinical writings, pilgrim caravans were thus welcomed on their arrival at Jerusalem. It is more than likely that this verse was sung in chorus by the multitudes who attended Christ's triumphant entry into Jerusalem, Matt. 21:9. Probably the same verse will be on the nation's lips when Zechariah 14 is fulfilled. Compare Isa. 25:9 with Matt. 23:39.

The object of Divine blessing is enriched because he came in *the name of the Lord.* Everyone who entered the Temple courts was blessed through Jehovah's name, or through Jehovah Himself. See Num. 6:27; 2 Sam. 1:18. This double benediction was directly associated with David who had defeated his foes, risen to the throne, and paid his vows "in the name of the Lord." It was through Jehovah alone that he came forth as the King of His people. Then those within, as well as those without, "the house of the Lord," blessed David in Jehovah's name. The priests whose office it was to bless the people, also blessed their deliverer and champion whom the Lord had chosen to be their sovereign. This benediction can likewise be applied to the first advent of David's Greater Son, of whom many chanted as He appears as the Messiah, "Blessed is He that cometh." Then what will it be at His second advent to receive His redeemed Church to Himself? Why, myriads of voices will echo the precious benediction, "Blessed is He that cometh according to His promise to return."

It is most likely that the remaining three verses were sung by the choir at the head of the procession as it entered the Temple gates, and approached the altar. The verses present both a public and personal recognition of God as Jehovah and a recognition of the truth that new light demands more devoted service.

Light . . . the sacrifice, 118:27. The R.V. reads "God is Jehovah who hath given us light." In *light* we have something received, and in *sacrifice*, something returned. God blesses us, and in response we bless Him. Ellicott thinks that it is difficult to determine whether the first clause is to be taken literally or figuratively. If *literal* it may be a repetition of verse 24, or if there is a particular reference in this Psalm to the Feast of Tabernacles which connects the light with the pillar of cloud and fire, of which the Feast was very probably specially commemorative, is most worthy of notice, Exod. 13:21. *Figuratively* the words would, of course, mean "the light of salvation and hope" so frequently mentioned in the

Psalms. It is also possible there may be an allusion to the priestly benediction where the verb is the same, Num. 6:25.

Without doubt, David himself had light from heaven enabling him to
prophetically describe the Messiah as the rejected yet exalted Stone, and
he magnified his Jehovah God for the enlightenment received and closes his Psalm confessing his personal faith in the Father of light. The
perfect fulfillment of the light from Heaven is found in the Messiah, Who
came as a light to lighten the Gentiles, and proclaimed Himself to be "The
Light of the World." Our solemn obligation is to daily walk in the light
even as He is in the light.

Along with the revealed and received light, we have the binding of "the
sacrifice with cords." The language of this latter clause does not mean,
"tie the victim to the horns of the altar." The word *cords* literally means
"what is twisted," and authorities are fairly agreed that "the word here
denotes those bundles of twigs from palm, willow, and myrtle trees which
the Jews, from time immemorial call *lulabs.* They were branded about the
altar as they are in modern times about the bema during the festivals
Tabernacles and Kanukah. Then, this part of the verse can be rendered, Set
a-going the sacred dance with your lulabs in your hand, even up to the
altar edge."

A more logical explanation of the phrase is that sometimes restive bul-
locks were bound to the altar before they were slain, hence the poet's
setting of the verse—

> He, Jehovah, is our Lord:
> He, our God, on us hath shined:
> Bind the sacrifice with cord,
> To the horned altar bind.

The American Board of Missions, New York, has as its seal an ox, with
an altar on one side, and a plough on the other, and the motto, *Ready for
either*—ready to live and labor, or ready to suffer and die. What
Jehovah desires of all who are His is full consecration to Himself and to
His redemptive purpose. The brave Huguenots did most of the singing at
night as they gathered round the ruins of their churches which cruel foes
had demolished. The sound of Psalms would rend the air—"A song in the
night as of a holy solemnity." Most frequently the words they lovingly
sung were, *God is Jehovah, which hath shewed us light.*

My God . . . my God . . . He is good, 118:28, 29. At the end of verse
28, the LXX Version repeats verse 21. See Exod. 15:2. The repeated pronouns reveal the Psalmist's heartfelt personal gratitude to his mighty God
who had done great things for him whereof he was glad. God was all His
prize, and alone worthy of exaltation. It was true that God could and did
exalt Himself, but David knew it was his undoubted duty and privilege to

exalt Him. The original word for *God* lends weight to David's personal aim. "Thou art my *El*—the mighty One; therefore will I praise thee; my *Eloah* (a varied form with substantially the same sense), and I will extol thee"—lift thee high in honor and glory. The great end of sincere praise of God should be to His exaltation.

In the concluding verse of the Psalm, which is a repetition of its opening verse, making a complete circle of joyful adoration, David invites all around him in a public tribute of gratitude to God for all the works, *O give thanks unto the Lord* and we can imagine how the people sang more joyfully this great verse the second time, having all in between the first and last verses in mind. Thus, as Spurgeon concludes his unique coverage of the Psalm—

> To the sound of trumpet and harp, Israel, the house of Israel, and all that feared the Lord, forgetting their distinctions, joined in one common hymn, testifying again to their deep gratitude to the Lord's goodness, and to the mercy which is unto Eternity. What better close could there be to this right royal song? The Psalmist would have risen to something higher, so as to end with a climax, but nothing loftier remained. He reached the height of his grandest argument and there he paused. The music ceased, the song was suspended, the great *Hallel* was all chanted, and the people went every one to his own house, quietly and happily musing upon the goodness of the Lord, whose mercy fills Eternity.

Psalm 119

Historical connections of this, the longest and most noble of the Psalms, and to which the LXX Version gives the title *Hallelujah,* are most numerous which prove its abiding influence through the ages. Augustine, of the 3rd century, gave himself to a lifelong study of the Psalms. In one his works on the Psalter he had a vision of Psalm 119 rising like a Tree of Life in Paradise. Thomas à Kempis added to the devotional literature of his time by his remarkable Rule Book for the brotherhood of the Canons Regular. He called it, *Little Alphabet of the Monks in the School of Christ,* which he modeled on the acrostic Psalm 119, the initial letters of his precepts running consecutively through the alphabet, the first and last letters of which we cite as illustrative of his plan—

> Aspire to be unknown, and to be accounted nothing: for this is more healthful and profitable for thee than the praise of men.
>
> Zaccheus, my brother, come down from the tree-top of knowledge.
>
> Come thou and learn in the school of God the way of humility, of meekness, and of patience; so, by the teaching of Christ, wilt thou at length be able to attain to the glory of eternal blessedness.

Wilberforce was an avid lover of the Psalms and in his Diary is an entry revealing the secret of his serenity of mind in the troubled year of 1819—"Walked from Hyde Park corner, repeating the 119th Psalm, a great comfort." Among the Psalms, John Ruskin, as a child read and studied this Psalm 119, of which in after life, he wrote, "It is strange, that of all the pieces of the Bible which my mother then taught me, and which cost me most to learn, and which was, to my child's mind, chiefly repulsive—the 119th Psalm—has now become of all the most precious to me, in its overflowing and glorious passion of love for the law of God."

In his most revealing *Journal,* Henry Martyn, missionary extraordinary, tells us that his heart was soothed and encouraged in seasons of great stress by learning portions of the Psalms by heart. In this way he committed to memory Psalm 119, and quickened his devotional feelings thereby. In his Diary are frequent references to this Psalm, such as the following—

> "found some devotion in learning a part of Psalm 119." "In the evening grew better by reading the 119th Psalm, which generally brings me

into a spiritual frame of mind." "Again in a fretful frame; it was not till I learned some of Psalm 119, that I could return to a proper spirit."

Then there is the record of another intrepid missionary, David Livingstone, who, as a boy of nine, won a New Testament from his Sunday school teacher for repeating by heart Psalm 119.

William Edwards, a prominent magistrate during the Indian Mutiny, in 1857, faced terrible experiences during the massacre of natives. His wife and children were elsewhere in India, and a native promised to carry a note to them. But all Edward had was half the fly-leaf of *Bridges on the 119th Psalm*. On this he wrote his message of assurance that he was safe, then dipped the pencilled note in milk to make the writing indelible, and set it out to dry. Hardly had he done so, when a crow pounced on it and carried it off. But fortunately his native servant had seen what had happened, followed the bird, and recovered the note. On August 24, he wrote in his Diary, "Finished today, for the second time, that excellent work, *Bridges on the 119th Psalm*; the sole book in my hands, except my Bible, for the past two months; and fortunate have I been to have had these sources of consolation."

Then there is the story of one of our most popular hymns, *We speak of the realms of the blest*, written a few weeks before her death, by Mrs. Elizabeth Mills, who died in 1839 at the age of 24. The hymn had its origin in Psalm 119, and was written after Mrs. Mills had studied *Bridges on the 119th Psalm*.

That fearless defender of the faith, George Wishart, Bishop of Edinburgh, would have been martyred had it not been for a most singular expedient. When upon the scaffold, he availed himself of the time, which permitted the condemned to choose a Psalm to be sung. Wishart selected the 119th Psalm, and before two-thirds of it had been sung, a pardon arrived, and his life was preserved. Doubtless the length of this Psalm was sagaciously employed as a means of gaining time, and, happily, the expedient succeeded. In the course of our coverage of this Psalm further historical references will be given.

Eulogies as to the value of this Psalm are as numerous as the 176 verses composing it. It is highly praised as showing, and shining itself, among the other 149 Psalms.

> Like the moon, the feebler fires among
> Conspicuous shines.

It is a star in the firmament of the Psalms, of the first and greatest magnitude, because of its elegant and exultant matter. The German version gives it the most appropriate inscription, *The Christian's Golden A.B.C. of Praise, Love, Power, and Use of the Word of God*. Those who accept the Davidic authorship of the Psalm extol it. *David's Pocket Book* or *This is David's Spoil.* Then it has been praised as *The Alphabet of Divine Love, The Paradise of All Doctrines—The Storehouse of the Holy Spirit—The School of Truth—The Deep Mystery of the Scriptures—The Perfection of Teaching and Instruction—An All-Containing Medicine for the Various Spiritual Diseases of Men.* Spurgeon's eulogy is superb—

> This sacred ode is a little Bible, the Scripture condensed, a mass of Bibline, Holy Writ rewritten in holy emotions and actions. Blessed are they who can read and understand these saintly aphorisms; they shall find golden apples in this true Hesperides, and come to reckon that this Psalm, like the whole Scripture which it praises, is a pearl island, or better still, a garden of sweet flowers.

Matthew Henry, the renowned expositor, in his biography of his father, *Account of the Life and Death of Philip Henry*, has the sentence, "Once, pressing the study of the Scriptures, he advised us to take a verse of Psalm 119 every morning to meditate upon, and so go over the Psalm twice in a year; and that, he said, will bring you to be in love with all the rest of the Scriptures. He often said, *All grace grows as love to the Word of God grows.*"

Opinion differs as to the authorship and historical occasion of the Psalm. There are those who think it to be post-exile. Bible literature and religious duties neglected by Israel while in the Exile in Babylon are here strongly emphasized. After the Exile, devoted meditation on the Law was a feature of Judaism. Other scholars contend that because of the prominence given to the Divine Word during the period known as *Scribism*, a system concentrating on the preservation, interpretation and studying of the Law than to its observance, the Psalm came into being about the *Maccabean,* when zeal for the Law of God caused a revolt. Whoever the writer was, the record of his experience must have been hard to bear— trouble, sorrow, hostility of powerful foes, and even captivity. Further, he not only records his own trials but sometimes the experiences of the pious remnant of Israel.

Conservative scholars, such as Matthew Henry, believed the Psalm to be "a collection of David's pious and devout ejaculations, the short and sudden breathings of his soul to God, which he wrote down as they occurred, and towards the latter end of his time gathered them out of his day-book, where they lay scattered, added to them many like words, and digested them into this Psalm, in which there is seldom any coherence between the verses; but like Solomon's *Proverbs*, it is a chest of gold rings, not a chain of gold links."

Then, that fearless defender of the Faith, C. H. Spurgeon, without hesitation or apology wrote, "We believe that David wrote this Psalm. It is Davidic in tone and expression, and it tallies with David's reference in many interesting points. After long reading an author, one gets to know his style, and a measurement of discernment is acquired by which his composition is detected even if his name is concealed; we feel a kind of critical certainty that the hand of David is in this thing, that it is altogether his own . . . Like Martin Luther, David had shaken every fruit-tree in God's garden, and gathered golden fruit therefrom." Needless to say, I heartily agree that in this Psalm we have David's royal diary written at various times throughout a long life.

Regarding the conspicuous theme of the Psalm, namely, the preciousness of Jehovah's revelation through His word, "the writer never repeats himself; for if the same sentiment occurs it is placed in a fresh connection, and so exhibits another interesting shade of meaning. . . . It contains no idle word; the grapes of this cluster are almost bursting full with new wine of the kingdom." The dominant theme of the Word of the Lord is treated in many ways, and with different expressions. Out of the 176 verses of the Psalm, only three verses—84, 121 and 122—omit any mention of the Word. In the other 173 verses David heartily pursues his much loved theme, and left us a poem, or collection of poems, as the Psalm actually is, saturated with the truths of the other books of Scripture he possessed. No wonder it has been called "the holy man's soliloquy before an open Bible."

Certainly, it is of great length, and deserves the title *The Longest Psalm*, seeing it equals in bulk 22 Psalms of the average length of the Songs of Degree, we shall shortly think about. But not only has it *length*, but equally excels in *breadth* of thought, *depth* of meaning, and *height* of fervor, in the exaltation of God's infallible Word. The Psalm resembles "the city which lieth four square, the height and breadth of which are equal." Loaded, then, with holy sense in the unfolding of the inspiration and influence of the Word, and of the happiness resulting from its study, the Psalm is as weighty as it is bulky.

Outstanding, of course, is the absence of any logical connection between the string of short sayings, yet the fact that the 176 verses are held together by the external bond of the letters of the Hebrew alphabet, each letter having eight verses given to it, the key-letter beginning each of the eight verses. It is thus the most remarkable of all the *Acrostic* Psalms, and makes it easier to commit to memory, seeing its contents are broken into 22 short divisions or sections, with all the verses in each section beginning with the same letter of the Hebrew alphabet. This system is conducive to the realization of the great help and comfort resulting from studying continually the Law of the Lord.

One of the Early Fathers, Origen, said that the Psalm is alphabetical because it contains the elements or principles of all knowledge and wisdom; and that it repeats each letter eight times, because eight is the number of *perfection*. Nathanael Hardy of the 16th century observed that Psalm 119 is disposed according to the letters of the Hebrew alphabet, perhaps to intimate that children, when they begin to learn their alphabet, should learn this Psalm. As for Andrew Bonar, he draws attention to one of Christ's names, *The Alpha and Omega*—equivalent to declaring Him all that every letter of the alphabet could express. Is not such a thought suggestive seeing that He was, and came to earth as, *The Word of God*, and *The Word Who was God?* From *The Psalms Chronologically Arranged*, we take this specimen upon the first section of the Psalm—*Alegh:*

> *A* blessing is on them that are undefiled in the way and
>   walk in the law of Jehovah.
> *A* blessing is on them that keep his testimonies,
>   and seek him with their whole heart;
> *A*lso on them that do no wickedness,
>   but walk in his ways.
> *A* law hast thou given unto us, that we should
>   diligently keep thy commandments.
> *A*h! Lord, that my ways were made so direct
>   that I might keep thy statutes!
> *A*nd then shall I not be confounded, while I have
>   respect unto all thy commandments.
> *A*s for me, I will thank thee with an unfeigned heart,
>   when I shall have learned thy righteous judgments.
> *A*n eye will I have unto thy ceremonies,
>   O forsake me not utterly.

A further peculiarity of this Psalm is the regular recurrence of characteristic terms, or designations of the Divine Law. Examining these in order we have—

1. *Law.* The Hebrew is *Torah*, meaning instruction. See Psalm 78:1. This term comes from a verb meaning to direct, guide, to aim, to shoot forwards, and implies a rule of conduct. It is called *God's Law*, because it is enacted by Him as the Sovereign One. The *Law* can represent the universal rule called "the law of nature," or that which was revealed to Moses, and which was perfected by Christ.

2. *Way.* Although this word only occurs twice in the Psalm, it is as characteristic as any, seeing that Jesus, *The Word*, could say of Himself, *I am the Way.* By the designation we are to understand the rule both of Divine providence and of our obedience. Saul, before he became Paul, was on his way to imprison those who were "of this *Way*," or "that were of the Way," namely Christ. John 14:6.

3. *Testimonies.* Derived from a word signifying to bear witness, to testify, the Ark, Two Tables of Stone, The Tabernacle are called by this term

because they were witnesses of God's habitation among His people. These testimonies are particularly God's revealed law, solemnly declared to the world, and attested beyond contradiction. They are confirmation of His promises or affirmation of His will, and the earnest of our future salvation.

4. *Commandments* (See Psalm 81:4). Here, the word signifies, *lodged with us in trust*. At the root, it means to command or ordain, a word given with authority, such as God gave to Adam about the tree, and to Noah about the Ark. The term can also cover the *Ten Commandments* God gave to Moses.

5. *Precepts*. This designation, found nowhere outside the Psalter, is sometimes thought of as a synonym for "command." It means something entrusted to man—"that is committed to thee." These "precepts" are prescribed to us, and not left indifferent. As appointments of God, they have to do with conscience, man, as an intelligent being, must meet.

6. *Word*. The Greek form of the Hebrew word is *LOGOS*, as used in John 1:1, of Jesus Who came as The Word, or Logos of God. Words are the clothing of the thoughts of our mind. Jesus came as the revelation of the mind or thought of God. The term, *Word* is rendered "saying," and often has the sense of "promise." God's Word is the declaration of His mind, the revelation of His will, the announcement of His purpose.

7. *Judgments*. By these, we understand the judicial pronouncements of the Law. From a word signifying to govern, to judge, to determine, judicial ordinances, legal sanctions are implied. God's judgments are framed in infinite wisdom, and by them man must judge, and be judged.

8. *Righteousness*. All Divine judgments are righteous, and the Divine Word, is all holy, just and good, and provides the only authentic rule and standard of righteousness for man.

9. *Statutes*. Literally this term meant, "what is engraved," then "a law carved on stone or on metal," and ultimately "statute," and is applied to Joseph's law about the portion of the priests in Egypt, and to the Law of the Passover. In this Psalm, however, it has a more internal significance, namely, that moral law of God engraven on the fleshy tables of the heart—the inmost and spiritual apprehension of His will. Then statutes are fixed and determined, and of perpetual obligation.

10. *Faithfulness*. As a noun, this designation is the equivalent of *Truth*, which is but another way of describing the *WORD*. The principles upon which Divine law is built are eternal truths. Jesus declared Himself to be *The Truth*, John 14:6, or the manifestation of God's unchanging faithfulness.

Readers will find it a most pleasant and profitable exercise to take up "the *key-words* of this Psalm, which occur throughout its texture, and to dwell on them in all the varying lights flashed thereon by the context in each several case." These favorite words of the Psalmist are too numerous to set forth. An illustration can be found in the word *Quicken*, and its associations, 119:25, 37, 40, 88, 140, 156, 159. Then we have the repetition of certain phrases affording a helpful Bible study. For instance, several times we have the clause, *with my whole heart*, and the precise nature of a *whole* heart, can be found in the other descriptions David gives such as the *clean* heart, etc. It will also be observed that the name JEHOVAH (LORD) occurs exactly 22 times, corresponding to the 22 letters of the alphabet. This could hardly have been without intention, but is the change rung of the terms denoting the *Law*.

The double Divine benediction of verses 1 and 2, contain the seed growing into the tree of life throughout the rest of the Psalm. Note man's benediction Godward in verse 12. As we approach a more extensive coverage of this Psalm it is not our intention to stop and meditate on all its 176 verses. Same would take a large volume in itself, as the 400 pages Spurgeon devotes to them in his unmatched *Treasury of David*, prove. Our endeavor will be to summarize each of the 22 sections—dwell upon a verse or two in each section of special import—then note some of the historical incidents in connection with many of the verses.

Because of its alphabetical construction, no other outline of the Psalm is possible. The following captions have been given to its divisions—

Verses	1–8—	The Undefiled, and the Blessedness.
"	9–16—	The Sanctifying Influence of the Word.
"	17–24—	The Longings of the holy Soul.
"	25–32—	A Cry for Quickening
"	33–40—	Faithfulness, the Result of the Divine Inworking.
"	41–48—	Mercies, and their Effect.
"	49–56—	Hope in Affliction.
"	57–64—	God our Portion.
"	65–72—	A Review of the Divine Dealings.
"	73- 80—	The Creature's Appeal to the Creator.
"	81- 88—	Hope in Depression.
"	89- 96—	The Inimitable Word of God.
"	97-104—	The Benefits of Pious Musing
"	105-112—	Light for a Dark Landing
"	113-120—	Human Thoughts contrasted with God's Law.
"	121-128—	The Plea of the Oppressed.
"	129-136—	Thirst for the Living God.
"	137-144—	God's Righteousness.
"	145-152—	The Paragraph of the *Cry*.
"	153-160—	An Appeal for Consideration.
"	161-168—	The Believer's Eulogy on God's Word.
"	169-176—	A Closing Appeal.

ALEPH. Verses 1-8. Every line of this section commences with this first letter of the Hebrew alphabet. The Jews ascribed the meaning of *an ox*, the beast of useful service, and thus of many blessings, to *Aleph.* Is this not apt, seeing that the key-thought of the initial section of the Psalm is, "O the blessings!"? Here we have the declaration of the blessedness of walking in the way of God's Word. The lessons we learn from these *Aleph* verses are true piety in sincere, consistent, practical, hearty, intelligent, earnest, active, stirring, diligent, humble, distrustful of self, systematical, guileless, unspotted from the world, self-renouncing, confidence in God, delighting in thankfulness, fully purposed to keep the law, ready to confess helplessness apart from Divine grace, and fear of sin of not believing God's Word.

His Way, 119:1. We have the same use of the term *way* without a qualifying epithet in Psalm 2:12. "Ye perish from the way." There was only one way of safety and peace for an Israelite, here by the parallelism defined as "the law of Jehovah," verse 2. Heathen ethics bore witness to the same truth.

Then shall I not be ashamed, when I have respect, 119:6. The word *respect,* literally means, *to look upon* or *into,* as in a mirror. See James 1:23. The Divine Word is as a mirror, showing man his defects; the faithful, in looking in it, have no cause to blush. Shame is not theirs seeing they seek to obey God's commandments, and can subscribe to the sentiment expressed by Joanna Baillie, who died in 1851—

> I can bear scorpion's stings, tread fields of fire,
> In frozen gulfs of cold eternal lie;
> Be toss'd aloft through tracts of endless void,
> But cannot live in shame.

I will keep thy statutes: O forsake me not utterly, 119:8. Trace the *I wills* in the Psalm. Caesar was wont to say, "Princes must not way, *Ite* = go ye, without me; but *Venite* = come ye, along with me." Centuries before him Gideon uttered a similar thought, "As ye see me do, so do ye," Judges 5:17. In the verse before us David sets a personal example of obedience and holiness. If, as the King of Israel, he keeps God's statutes, then the people of Israel will be ashamed to neglect them. God will never forsake those who are bent on obeying His word. There may be periods of severe trial when we feel deserted of Him, but we must never mistake *feelings* for *actualities.* "He hath said, I will never leave thee, nor forsake thee."

BETH. Verses 9-16. In the original every verse in this section begins with this second letter of the alphabet, and it means *a house.* The thought of the division is that of making our heart a home for the Word of God, which alone can cleanse the heart, and keep it pure. Holiness through obedience to the Word is pronounced to be the only safeguard of the young against sin. Thus a prominent place in this Psalm of 22 parts is assigned to young men, and it is fitting that it should be so, for they need to know the secret of victory. God's holy Word is the *mirror*, revealing all spiritual deformity, and also the *water* cleansing from same. The Bible teaches the young the best way to live, the noblest way to suffer, and the most blessed way to die.

The age of Aristotle, the ancient dictator in Philosophy, was light and foolish, yet headstrong and intractable, causing him to despair of achieving so great an enterprise as the rendering of a young man capable of "his grave and severe lectures of morality." I wonder what he would say about our modern age with all the youth is capable of today. Youthful lusts are all too prevalent. Let it be proclaimed from the housetops that our godless young can only find victory and a noble purpose in life by taking heed to God's Word.

There is no inconsistency in the fact that David writes of the young in verses 9, 99, 100, and then of those of a mature, if not advanced age, in passages like 33, 52, and 96. He did not write his Psalm in "life's fair morning," but was like the one Browning depicts in Rabbi ben Ezra, while seeking how best to spend old age, looks back on youth, not so much with remonstrance at its follies, but with the satisfaction that even then he aimed at the best he knew as verse 9 implies.

> Go thou in life's fair morning, go in the bloom of youth,
> And buy for thy adorning, the precious pearl of truth.
> Secure this heavenly treasure, and bind it on thy heart,
> And let not earthly treasure ere cause it to depart.

Henry Scougal, author of *The Life of God in the Soul of Man*, when a youth, opened his Bible and lighted by peradventure upon this 9th verse, "Wherewithal shall a young man cleanse his way?" It went to his heart and led him to surrender himself to God, and into the Christian ministry. He became Professor of Theology, King's College, Aberdeen, and died in 1678, at the early age of 28, but left behind a great fragrance in his name.

With my whole heart, 119:10. What a joy it is to have the young speak to the Searcher of hearts in this way! God alone sees the heart—the heart alone sees God.

Thy Word have I hid in my heart, 119:11. Here is another trait of the young who strive to be godly in life. One old commentator says of this Psalm that it is *A holy alphabet for Zion's scholars*, and was evidently constructed to help ancient believers to carry out this principle of hiding God's Word in the heart as a preventative against sin. Dr. Maltbie

Davenport Babcock, of Baltimore, who succeeded Henry VanDyke in New York, wrote, "I believe profoundly in the custom of committing texts, or rather Psalms, to memory. *Thy word have I hid in my heart* is sufficient incentive."

Saint Bernard observed that "bodily bread in the cupboard may be eaten of mice, molder and waste: but when it is taken down into the body, it is free from danger. If God enable thee to take thy soul-food into thine heart, it is free from all hazards." This verse, proving that Scripture is ever profitable when remembered, approved, and delighted in, can be given this sermonic outline—

> The Best Possession—"Thy Word"
> The Best Plan—"Have I hid"
> The Best Place—"In my heart"
> The Best Purpose—"That I might not sin against thee"

I will delight . . . I will not forget, 119:16. Here are two further *wills* of the Psalmist and the one explains the other for the person whose constant delight is in the reading and study of the Word, is not likely to forget it. *Forget*—who ever heard of a covetous man forgetting where he had buried his treasure?

GIMEL. Verses 17-24. The benefit of truth to those whose eyes the Lord opens by His Holy Spirit is the dominant theme of this third section. It also expresses a pious resolve to cleave to the Word in spite of sneers. As in the preceding 8 verses the Psalmist prayed as youth newly come into the spiritual world, so here he pleads as a servant and a pilgrim, who growingly finds himself to be a stranger in an enemy's country. Thus his appeal is to God alone, and his prayer is direct and personal, speaking with Him as a man speaks with his friend.

Open thou mine eyes that I may behold, 119:18. Emphasis is upon the phrase "*out of* thy law," that is, brought out to view from a place of concealment. The wondrous truths we should see are there all the time, but we need our eyes open to see where the buried treasure is. Such a prayer as this verse contains implies "a conscious darkness, a dimness of spiritual vision, a powerlessness to remove that defect, and a full assurance that God can remove it." To the poor, longing one the gracious question of Jesus was, "What wilt thou that I shall do unto thee?" The answer was instant and expressive, "Lord! that I may receive my sight." The same compassionate One waits to draw the veil from our eyes that we may see glimpses of truth He has for us to appropriate for our edification, as well as our enlightenment. The Hebrew has it, "unveil my eyes," and this implies a double work, negative and positive, namely, the removal of the veil, and then an infusion of light. See Acts 9:18.

I was a stranger in the earth, 119:19. By "stranger" we are to understand, sojourner, or passenger, with but a short time to know and do God's will. A comparison of this verse with Genesis 47:9 and Psalm 39:12, reveals the general transitory condition of life is meant and not any particular circumstances of David's history is in view. "Human intelligence does not suffice to fathom the will of God. The mortal is a stranger on the earth; both time and strength are wanting to attain to knowledge which only Divine wisdom can teach."

My soul breaketh . . . at all times, 119:20. Thomas Chalmers once said that though "he could not speak of the raptures of Christian enjoyment, he thought he could enter into the feeling of the Psalmist, My soul breaketh for the longing that it hath unto thy judgments at all times." No preacher of the early 18th century produced so strong and irresistible an effect as this leading spirit in the secession of the Free Church ministers during the Reformation in Scotland's religious history. What do we know of the pressing desire to experience the judgments of God, until we are ready to break in pieces in such a longing? Is our passion to know and do the will of God as intense as David's—a passion felt in the straining of the mind, as if ready to snap with the heavenly pull? Must we not regret our lack of such a longing for the Word? It is to be feared that our handling of it is very superficial and destitute of any loving desire to delve into its secrets.

The Psalmist's painful, intense longing was for God's judgments which here mean, not those pronounced upon transgressors, but His commands, called *judgments* because by them right is judged and discerned from wrong. If men delight in these judgments, then those of condemnation will not overtake them. The Word of God is a code of justice from which there is no appeal. As Isaac Watts puts it—

> There is the Judge which ends the strife
> Where wit and reason fail;
> Our guide through devious paths of life,
> Our shield when doubts assail.

Further this ardent desire was not fitful, spasmodic, but constant *At all times*—a steady, habitual state of his soul on the subject. David yearned for a fuller revelation of God's command—

> In the time of adversity to comfort him—
> In the time of prosperity to humble him—
> In the time of affliction to be his cordial—

such, he felt, would keep him from pride and despair, being his antidote against all spiritual ills.

Thou hast rebuked the oppressed that are cursed, 119:21. One of the Early Fathers said that "Humility makes men angels, pride makes angels like devils," and he might have added that it makes devils of men.

Menander the heathen poet wrote that "Never soul escaped the revenge of pride." God ever makes good His own word, "A man's pride shall bring him low," for "The proud man is an abomination to the Lord." If the proud escape rebuke now, as sometimes they seem to do, in Eternity condemnation will assuredly be theirs. Proud-like Herod took the name of God, and was honored of all but the *worms*, which showed that he was not a god, but a man whose flesh made good food, Acts 12:21.

DALETH. Verses 25-32. The alphabetical letter for this section is *D*, which Spurgeon says "sings of *D*epression, in the spirit of *D*evotion, *D*etermination, and *D*ependence." In these eight verses we have the expression of longing for the consolation of God's Word to fortify good resolutions. David bewails the bondage to earthly things, his soul cleaved to the dust, melted for heaviness, and cried for enlargement from its spiritual prison. The Word of God, however, is the source of happiness to those whose heart God renews and enlarges. Such a quickening Word arouses prayer, verses 25-29, confirms choice, 30, and inspires renewed resolve.

My soul cleaveth . . . quicken thou me, 119:25. This was the expression Emperor Theodosius used when he was received into Church again by Ambrose at Milan, after acknowledging his sin in the massacre at Thessalonica. Prostrate on the floor of the Cathedral of Milan, the penitent Emperor, with tears and lamentations, prayed in the words of this verse and found peace of heart. Dante made great use of the Psalms in his *Divine Commedia*. Thus in one part he described those who had sinned from avarice and prodigality, prostrate with their faces downward, prone on the ground, weeping sore—

> "My soul have cleaved to the dust," I heard, with
> sighs so deep, they well-nigh choked the words.

During those dark years 441-51, when Atilla's hordes swept over Europe, leaving in the track a heap of corpses, and a blackened, desolate waste, even priests were not always spared. Nilasius, eleventh Bishop of Rheims, was cut down by a Vandal in 407, as he stood on the threshold of his church, chanting the words, "Quicken thou me, according to Thy word."

Cleaving to the dust is the same figure used of *death*, Psalm 22:29, and of deep degradation and dishonor in Psalm 44:25. The prayer "quicken thou me" or "make me live," suggests that the dust of death was meant by David, as in Tennyson's phrase, "Thou wilt leave us in the dust." Or if we think of the dryness of summer dust as a type of despondency and spiritual depression, then the lines of Coleridge are apt—

> A wicked whisper came, and made
> My heart as dry as dust.

This reiterated prayer for Divine quickening (see verses 40, 88, 107, 145, 154, 156), with its varied appeal to the Divine truth, lovingkindness, constancy, must certainly be regarded as the petition of Israel for revived covenant glory, though, at the same time, it offers a wide and rich field of application to individual needs.

My soul melteth for heaviness, 119:28. Maine de Biram, who died in 1824, was reckoned to be one of the greatest of French metaphysicians. Through his study of Fenelon's spiritual works he became a believer in Christianity. A great change in his life took place about 1818, and in his *Pensees* he commented on this 28th verse, "The Word that can make me live, will not come from me nor from my will, nor yet from anything that I hear or collect from without."

For "strengthen me," Gesenius has the translation, "Keep me alive," and was an entreaty that the waste of life through tears might be restored by the lifegiving Word.

The way of lying, 119:29. Lying was a sin that David, through diffidence, fell into frequently, as we gather from the lies he told in 1 Sam. 21:2, 8; 27:8, 10, and in this verse he seeks Divine deliverance from it. The whole life of sin is a *lie* from beginning to end. Hunt up the 8 times *lying* is mentioned in this Psalm.

I have stuck unto thy testimonies, 119:31. Says Matthew Henry, "the choosing Christian is likely to be the sticking Christian." In verse 25, David confessed, "My soul *cleaveth* to the dust." Here he testifies, "I have *cleaved* unto thy testimonies," for in the original *cleave* and *stuck* are the same. There is no contradiction between these two verses. Both are compatible in the experience of the believer. Within there is the body of indwelling sin, and also within there is the undying principle of Divine grace, as Paul makes clear Gal. 5:17 and Rom. 7:24. *Stuck*—true godliness evermore wears upon her head the garland of perseverance, as William Cowper put it.

HE. Verses 33-40. What a prayer-laden section this is! Its characteristic feature, not found in the other 21 sections is that, in every several verses there are several prayers, and the burden of these prayers is that the intercessor himself may learn how God's Word promotes unselfishness and Godly fear. A sense of dependence and a consciousness of extreme need pervade this prayer-portion, with its succession of pleas. In the previous sections we have *Gimel* beginning with a prayer for life, that David might keep God's Word, verse 17—*Daleth*, cries out for more life, according to this Word, verse 25—*He* opens with a prayer for Divine teaching of the Word, and commencing with supplication, the Psalmist continues, and concludes as a suppliant at the throne. Conspicuous among the entreaties of this division are these four in which David prays that the inspired, infallible Word of Jehovah might ever be before his Eyes, his

Mind, his Feet, and his Heart, the key-phrase being, "Set up before thy servant thy Word," verse 38.

The Word before the eyes, 119:33. In this initial prayer, the Psalmist prays for direction in its more superficial form. There were several paths leading down to death, but one path was before him, leading to life and so he besought Jehovah to show him His way, and he vowed that once seeing it he would follow it to the end. The phrase, *teach me*, literally means, "point out," or "indicate to me," and hence "to show." So light was desired for the eyes to identify the way Divinely indicated. Saint Bernard said that "He who is his own pupil, has a fool for his master." Wisely, David sought Divine instruction, and as the Indian pursues his trail with unerring eye and unfaltering step, on the alert, thereby for any deviation that might lead him to stray, David prays that he might pursue the only way leading to life.

The phrase, "I shall keep it unto the end," deserves a comment. It can be rendered, "So that I may attend to it as a reward," implying that the result of Jehovah's teaching is obedience, and this obedience is a reward from Him. The Hebrew for "unto the end" is "to the heel" or "quite through," and the force of the phrase seems to be, "Quite through, from head to foot." In the original, "unto the end" is one word, and is also translated "reward" in Psalm 19:11, where the reward is something following obedience, but in this 33rd verse it is obedience itself. Having prayed for the Word to be set before his eyes, David later asked that his eyes may pass from seeing vanity, verse 37. Having prayed for what he wanted to see, he now prays for the hiding of what he would not see.

The Word before the mind, 119:34. "Give me understanding . . . I shall observe it." This is an enlargement of the previous prayer. Having been shown the way of truth, the Psalmist seeks the gift of understanding it, in order that he might apply it to every phase of his life. Spiritual discernment is a spiritual endowment. The word used here for *understanding* means, mental comprehension, as distinguished from the mere direction of the previous verse. This prayer actually implies, "Make me to discern," or "Cause me to perceive," that is, with the understanding. With his outer senses, David saw the way, and he now intercedes that his mind fully understands it, so that his heart can follow it in faith and love. The repeated phrase *whole heart* stresses the importance of undivided obedience and love to all God reveals through His Word. "The heart is never one with God till it is one within itself."

The Word before the feet. What a wonderful prayer to offer—"Make me to go in the path of thy commandments, for therein do I delight." In the previous verse it was "Make me to understand," now we read "Make me to go." First the eyes and mind, then the feet. A clear understanding is necessary for practical action. There can be no effective *going* with the *knowing.* By the *path*, we have a word from the root "to tread," or "the trodden way," implying an accustomed trail, plain with the track of all the pious pilgrims' feet of past times. The particular word used here is not the broad open way employed in verse 33, but a term that never denotes a public and royal road, such as was raised up and formed by art, but always a footpath. Adam Clarke says, "It is a *path*, not a public road; a path where no *beast* goes, and *men* seldom. The Hindus call *path* or *way*, the line of doctrine of any sect followed, in order to attain to *mutsti*, or deliverance from sin."

Having received visual and mental perception of the way, David now seeks power to walk in this Divine path, which is equivalent to *the narrow way* Jesus spoke of as leading to life. Wrote William Cowper, "Not any new way, but the old and pathed way wherein we the servants of God have walked before him. . . . But howsoever this may be pathed, by the walking and treading of many in it, yet he acknowledged it is but one, yea, and narrow and difficult path to keep, and therefore seeks he to be guided into it." And David affirmed that as he trod this narrow way it would not be a drudgery but a *delight*.

The Word set before the heart. Blaise Pascal, in his *Thoughts*, impregnated as they are with quotations from the Psalms, and which he wrote on loose fragments of paper during his brief respites from the agony of mortal sickness, wrote on one slip of paper, "Feel no surprise that plain, unlettered men believe the Christian faith without exercising their reason. They are inspired of God with love of holiness and the hatred of themselves. God inclines their hearts to faith. If God does not so incline the heart, no man will believe with a true, effectual faith. But if the heart be so inclined by God, none can refuse belief. Of this truth David was well aware when he wrote, 'Incline my heart unto Thy testimonies,' Psalm 119:36."

Knowing the waywardness of his own heart, David prayed, "Incline my heart," and thus confessed his weakness, rather than defend his own strength. He knew that if Divinely inclined, he would not decline into covetousness, or any gain unjustly acquired. Ambrose said that "Covetousness is the loss of the soul." Clemens Alexandrinus wrote of this sin as "the citadel of vices." As it is with the heart man believeth unto righteousness, it is useless for the eyes to see, the mind to understand, and the feet ready to go the way of truth, if the heart be not inclined thereunto also. The proverb has it, "If wrong our hearts, our heads are right in vain."

Thus, then, appears to be the sense of these four methodical prayers we have considered—Make me to see, Make me to understand, Make me to go, and, Make me to love to go in, the beaten and narrow path of Thy testimonies. Martin Luther, in his exposition of this Psalm translates the opening words of verses 33, 34, 35, and 36, by terms signifying respectively—

> Point out to me,
> Explain to me,
> Lead me,
> Incline, or bend me, or my heart.
> *Quicken me in thy righteousness,* 119:40.

Previously David had prayed, "Quicken thou me in thy way," verse 37, now he pleads, "Quicken me in thy righteousness," and the two are one for *the way*, or *word*, of God is the righteousness of God; in which is set down the will of righteousness. "It is the *quick* who cry 'Quicken me'; it is those who have living desires who pray of it more life in the way of righteousness." *Quicken*, is an old English word meaning "to bring to life," thus "to revive one who is depressed and desponding," the latter being the implication in this 40th verse. Revival comes through the Word, through conformity to the Divine Law, 119:25, 50, 93.

David prayed that the sense of God's eternal justice would give him vigor and life; that he might experience the invigorating influence of a complete surrender to a righteous law. Wordsworth, in his *Ode to Duty* expresses a similar sentiment—

> I must commend
> Unto thy guidance from this hour.
> Oh let my weakness have an end!
> Give unto me, made lowly, wise
> The spirit of self-sacrifice.
> The confidence of reason give,
> And in the light of truth thy bondsman let me live.

Having a longing after the precepts of God, David prays for more life because God had promised to hear prayer when offered according to His righteous law. Thus he wanted the life he already possessed to reveal itself by longing for more. So the past fruits of grace were made the plea for further blessing, and "onward" in the heavenly life is the cry of this last verse under *He*. May we be found making the cry our own!

VAU. Verses 41-48. In this further portion of the alphabetical Psalm, although each verse begins with the letter *Vau*, or *V*, actually "there are almost no words in Hebrew that begin with this letter, which is properly a conjunction, and hence in each of the verses in this section the beginning of the verse is in the original conjunction." As a whole, this division of eight verses gives us Prayers and Promises—Prayers in verses 41 and 43, Promises in the other verses. Our promises should be always prayerfully made—and kept! The general theme of this portion is the desire for the strengthening of faith, and for the full revelation of the mercy and salvation of Jehovah.

Conspicuous in the section is the personal pronoun *I*, which occurs 12 times in its 8 verses. This longest Psalm is indeed the most prominent *I* Psalm in the Psalter. In the octave before us David personally expresses his firm trust and intense delight in God's Word, and an earnest desire to experience its full accomplishment in, and through, his life. Holy fear is apparent, and likewise a continual pleading for God's abiding grace in his soul.

Thy mercies . . . Thy word, 119:41. In the previous verse David prayed for quickening, and the mercies of God ever follow the man whom God quickens. Here the Psalmist unites the mercy of God with His Word, for these were to Him, and to every saint, the two strongest pillars of hope. Apart from the Word we have no evidence of His saving and eternal mercy, from which all His mercies spring.

I have wherewith to answer Him . . . I trust in thy word, 119:42. The LXX Version reads, "I shall answer my reviler a word, for I trust in thy word." The Psalmist's premise is that when reproached it will be enough to pronounce God's promise. The particular reproach consisted in the faith in a false God, but the Psalmist's vindication would be seen in Jehovah's deliverance—something a false god was not capable of. "If the reproaches are faithless Israelites, that deliverance would be a vindication of the claims of the orthodox Jewish party." Those who are assured of God's salvation have ready answers for those who sneer at the blessings of faith. Such answers may be short, but they are always true.

Hugo Cardinalis said that there are three sorts of blasphemers of the godly—Devils, Heretics, and Slanderers. *The devil* must be answered by the internal word of humility—*The heretic* by the external word of wisdom—*The slanderer* by the active word of a good life.

Take not the word of truth out of my mouth, 119:43. The word David trusted in was "the word of truth," and "thy judgments," and David prayed never to be deprived of the opportunity and power to testify of God's truthfulness and justice. Certain that the word had been hid in his heart, he wanted to be ready with his mouth to confess his Lord. Alas! too often we are dumb, and afraid to testify for the Master when a good opportunity for witness presents itself.

I shall observe thy law continually, for ever and ever, 119:44. It will be seen that verses 44-46 are made up of sentences expressing purpose or result. If the word was taken out of his mouth, David said that he would keep it continually or always, that is, as long as he lived. But when he went on to say "For ever and ever," he meant not only from age to age, but throughout Eternity. Perfect obedience, such as we cannot render here, will constitute a large proportion of heavenly happiness to all Eternity.

I will walk at liberty, 119:45.   The margin gives us "a large place" for "liberty." See verse 32, Prov. 4:12. The remarkable *Journal* of David Brainerd, who died in 1747, at the early age of 29, is permeated with the power of the Psalms on which are based, "five distinguishing marks of a *true Christian*." The fifth of these marks, wrote Brainerd, was having the laws of God as his delight in which he said, "The strict observance of them is not his bondage, but his greatest liberty. *I will walk at liberty; for I seek thy commandments*." How expressive is George Matheson's hymn on the paradox of spiritual bondage and yet liberty—

> Make me a captive, Lord,
> And then I shall be free.
> Force me to render up my sword,
> And I shall conqueror be.

He only is a free man, whom the truth sets free, and all are slaves beside. It is only as we, like David, observe God's law in the heart, in the mind, and in the actions, that we not only walk in the narrow way of fear, but in the large place of love and liberty. If we sincerely seek God's precepts, we are not free to do as *we* like, but only as He likes. We cannot freely move, until He has wrought our chains. If we would reach the monarch's throne, we must our crown resign.

I will speak of thy testimonies before kings, 119:46. This was the motto prefixed to the Augsberg Confession—the Charter of the German Lutheran Church. Kings in general are meant, and we have noble examples of fearlessness in the presence of royalty in Daniel, in the Maccabean heroes, and in John Knox. See Psalms 138; Matt. 10:18; Acts 26:1. Martin Luther was doubtless inspired by David's determination to witness before kings, for he was not only a man of great belief, but also great boldness in standing out against the highest in the land. When the Emperor sent for Luther at Worms, and his friends tried hard to prevent him going, he said, "Go, I will surely go, since I am sent for, in the name of our Lord Jesus Christ; yea, though I knew that there were as many devils in Worms to resist me as there be tiles to cover the houses, yet I would go."

Latimer was another clothed with holy boldness, and amid the spiritual darkness and profaneness of the age in which he lived, displayed much courage in the rebuke of evil. For instance, he presented to King Henry the Eighth, for a New Year's gift, a New Testament, wrapped up in a napkin, with this posie or motto around it—*Whoremongers and adulterers God will judge*. How this must have stung the conscience of such a licentious king! Can it be that we are ashamed to confess our Lord, if brought into high places? "The fear of man bringeth a snare"—of silence.

My hands also will lift up . . . I will meditate, 119:48. Delighting ourselves in, and loving God's commandments, greatly aids us in prayer and meditation. See Psalms 28:2; 63:5; 134:2; 141:2. We may have here the first hint at that worship of the written Word, the Law, which in later Judaism became so common. Perhaps we should read for *hands*—"lift up my *heart*," seeing the two words in Hebrew—"hands" and "hearts" are easily confounded. The Syrian Version has the addition to this last verse, and "*I will glory in thy faithfulness*," which was a blessed way to end the section, for great is His faithfulness.

ZAIN. Verses 49-56. How apt is the portion for an age like ours, seeing its message is the awakening of the comfort of hope in God, and in His Word, in evil days! Spurgeon's summary of these eight verses is very good—

> This octrain deals with the comfort of the Word. It begins by seeking the main conclusion, namely, the Lord's fulfillment of his promise, and then it shows how the word sustains us under affliction, and makes us so impervious to ridicule that we are moved by the harsh conduct of the wicked rather to horror of their behaviour than to any submission to their temptations. We are then shown how the Scripture furnishes songs for pilgrims, and memories for night-watchers; and the Psalm concludes by the general statement that the whole of this happiness and comfort arises out of keeping the statutes of the Lord.

Remember the word unto thy servant, upon which thou hast caused me to hope, 119:89. Occurring three times in the section, the term *remember* forms its key-word, as seen from the following repeated alternation—

> *Remember . . . Thou*, 49.
> Statement as to consequences, 50, 51.
> *I remembered*, 52.
> Statement as to consequences, 53, 54.
> *I have remembered*, 55.
> Statement as to consequences, 56.

David remembered the Lord, and calls upon Him to remember him as His servant. Already, he had the Divine promise, "Yet will I not forget thee," for Swinburne's couplet is so true of Jehovah—

> I shall remember while the light lives yet,
> And in the night-time I shall not forget.

God cannot forget promises given, and cannot therefore, disappoint any expectation which He Himself has raised.—"Upon which thou hast caused me to hope." As David remembered the judgments of God and was comforted, and remembered His name in the night, so in the opening verse of this division he beseeches God to remember him. Precept, it will be noticed, is before promise. "They have right to the promises, and may justly lay hold upon them, who are God's servants, they would apply themselves to obey His precepts, those only can rightly apply His promises to themselves." *Word*, in the verse, is given in other versions as "thy promise." The margin of the R.V. on the word *because* has the notation "upon which." "Hast made," is better as "makest," thus giving the thought, "Thou causest us by thy promise to have hope in thee; forget not the promise lest we be disappointed."

My comfort . . . Thy word, 119:50. Another rendering of the passage expresses it—"This is my consolation in my affliction—That thy word revives me." The only other use of the word given here for comfort is in Job 6:10. "I yet have comfort." What a blessed connection there is between the phrases, *Thy comfort . . . Thy word*! No comfort in trials and afflictions is comparable to that we are able to find in Scripture. The original for the word is "Nechamah" from which we have *Nehemiah*, whose name means "consolation." The Hebrew verb, however, signifies, first, to repent, and then, to comfort; and as Thomas Brooks expressed it, "Certainly the sweetest joy is from the surest tears. Tears are the breeders of spiritual joy. When Hannah had wept, she went away, and wept and was no more sad. The bee gathers the best honey from the bitterest herbs. Christ made the best wine out of water." The truth David learned was that the Word is a reviving comfort quickening the soul.

In verse 40, the Psalmist prayed that he might be quickened by the Word, and here, prayer is answered and fresh hope and courage were imparted. It made him lively. All coldness and indifference were banished, for God had sent His Word and healed him. But the same Word, a savor of life, to those who are the Lord's, is a dead letter to the ungodly who sees no treasure in it that they should desire it.

The proud have had me greatly in derision, 119:51. *Law*, appearing thrice in this strophe, implies "commandments," or "admonitions." Because of the infusion of life and vigor, David had experienced through the Word, he did not decline from it even when the proud worked iniquitously together to deride him. "It does not hurt the Christian to have the dogs bark at him." Joseph was nicknamed a "dreamer," Paul was a "babbler," Christ, was a "Samaritan," with intent of disgrace, a carpenter. The derision of the godly has continued through the ages, and we must expect the same from those to whom piety has no relish, but is distasteful to their palates.

I remember thy judgments . . . comforteth myself, 119:52. Another proof of the consolations of Scripture. Jerome wrote of that most godly lady, Paula, that she learned most of the Bible by heart, and because it dwelt in her, Col. 3:16, she ever remembered it and found consolation from it during her varied experiences. She could not forget the *jewel* hidden in the casket of her heart. "Can a maid forget her ornaments?" Jerem. 2:32. There is a disease called *lienteria*, in which food comes up as fast as eaten, robbing the eater, thereby, of necessary nourishment. If the Word stays not in the memory, much spiritual nourishment is lost. "Some can better remember a piece of news than a line of Scripture: their memories are like those ponds, where frogs live, but fish die."

Horror hath taken hold upon me because of the wicked, 119:53. While the *wicked* referred to may have been Jews who had turned their back upon the faith of their fathers to win the smiles and escape the smitings of Syrian, or Greek oppressors, we can apply the term to the wicked, the Bible says, are to be turned into Hell. What a fearful word *horror* is! Translations of it vary, "violent indignation," "a storm overtaking one," "a burning horror hath seized me," "a pestilential burning wind," "most horrid mental distress." The LXX Version has the reading, "faintness and dejection of mind hath possessed me." All of these explanations of the Word imply great trouble of mind, a vehement commotion, causing David to tremble.

Such deep agitation and distress was caused by the peril of those forsaking God's law. David was deeply moved by the dreadful misery and fate of those who turn from God and His Word. Does horror fill our heart as we try to imagine the terrible condition of those who die lost for evermore? See Psalm 11:6. David Brainerd, who literally wore himself out warning the wicked to flee from the wrath to come, was greatly moved by this verse, and wrote in his *Journal*—

> I have had clear views of Eternity; have seen the blessedness of the *godly*, in some measure; and have longed to share their happy state, as well as have comfortably satisfied that through grace I shall do so, but, oh, what anguish is raised in my mind to think of an *Eternity* for those who are *Christless*, for those who are mistaken, and who bring their false hopes to the grave with them. The sight was so dreadful I could by no means bear it: my thought recoiled, and I said—under a more affecting sense than ever before—"Who can dwell with everlasting burnings?"

Thy statutes have been my songs, 119:54. The precious Word of God became the theme of all the songs of the sweet psalmist of Israel. "Melodies have thy statutes been to me in the house of my pilgrimage." By *pilgrimage*, we can understand the transitoriness of human life, See Psalm 137:4, 9. It is said that in the early ages it was customary to versify the laws, and set them to music, that the people might learn them by heart, and sing them. What a mighty influence in Scottish history has the metrical version of the Psalms exerted! As one laboring in Scotland for many

years I can testify to the thrill of hearing a Scottish audience sing many
of the statutes as songs, especially the one a Scot knows by heart—"The
Lord's my Shepherd, I'll not want."

Of the Lord's people it is said, "They shall sing in the ways of the
Lord. The redeemed shall return, and come to Zion with songs." To
David, God's statutes when fashioned into songs gave him spiritual
refreshment, sweetened by hardships of his pilgrimage, and hastened his
steps with zest. Of this musical form of Scripture, H. W. Longfellow, who
died in 1882, wrote—

> Such songs have power to quiet
>   The restless pulse of care,
> And come like the benediction
>   That follows after prayer.
> And the night shall be filled with music,
>   And the cares that infest the day
> Shall fold their tents like the Arabs,
>   And as silently steal away.

I have remembered thy name, O Lord, in the night, 119:55. Could it be
that David had Job's wonderful question in mind when he wrote this
verse—"Where is God thy maker, who giveth songs in the night?" Job
35:10. The primary sense of "I have remembered" is "I think about." It
was because the Psalmist had kept the law during the day, that he was able
to muse over it during the silent hours of the night. "When other men are
sleeping, God occurs to my thoughts during my sleep." What he particularly thought about as darkness shrouded the earth was God's *name*,
representing as it does His revealed character, all He is in His Being,
Attributes and Actions, and in manifestations of His holiness, wisdom,
goodness and truth.

Not only in the darkness of midnight, however, is it comforting to
dwell upon all that God is in Himself, but also in the darkness of mental
depression, in the darkness of outward providence. No matter what kind
of night we may think of, God is able to turn these statutes of His into
songs. Thomas Fuller, in his *David's Heartie Repentance* has the verse in
old English—

> For sundry duties he did dayes devide,
> Making exchange of worke his recreation;
> For prayer he set the precious morne aside,
> The mid-day he bequeathed to meditation:
>   Sweete sacred stories he reserved for night,
>   To reade of Moses' meekness, Samson's might:
>   These were his joy, these only his delight.

This I had, because I had kept thy precepts, 119:56. What an apt conclusion to this section of the Psalm! David began by praying, "Remember thy word unto thy servant; upon which thou caused me to hope," and the sweet singer knowing that he had kept God's precepts, pleads with the Lord to fulfill His promises. "This I had," or, more literally, "This was to me," and implies "I had the comfort of keeping thy law *because* I kept it." "God's work is its own wages." The Rabbins have the saying, "The reward of a precept is a precept," or "A precept draws a precept," the meaning of which is, that he who keeps one precept, to him God grants, as if by way of reward, the ability to keep another and more difficult precept. Contrariwise, the Rabbins say, "the reward of a sin is a sin," or *Transgression draws transgression*. Thus the division ends, as Ellicott fittingly puts it—

> This consoling recollection of the mercies of God, of His covenant grace, was to him, happened, or came to him, in consequence of his habitual obedience. Virtue is indeed then, its own reward, in times of quiet reflection, like the night, when to the guilty came remorse and apprehension, but to the good man *calm thoughts regular as infant's breath.*

CHETH. Verses 57-64. Actually, this eighth section of the Psalm is an expansion of the last clause of the previous one. "This I had because I kept thy precepts"—"I have said that I would keep thy words." Thus David looks back with comfort upon what he had said, and in the threefold repetition of the term *keep* in the octave before us, verses 51, 60, 63, affirms his determination to continue in obedience to God's revealed will through His Word. He proclaims his fidelity to Jehovah's law even when persecuted by the wicked. As a whole, these eight verses express the joy which is inspired by the consciousness that God is his portion, and by fellowship with those who also love His Word, and by a persuasion that all things work together for good, to all who love God. The alteration is clearly evident:

Jehovah my portion, 57-60.
　　Statement *re* the work of the lawless, 61.
Jehovah my praise, 62, 63
　　Statement *re* the favor of Jehovah, 64.

Thou art my portion . . . I would keep thy words, 119:57. This verse is better paraphrased—

> I have said, "Jehovah is my portion,
> That I might keep Thy Word."

David the poet, lost in wonder as he meditates upon the greatness and goodness of God, expressed in a broken sentence his recognition of Him as his secret source of every precious thing. *My portion, Jehovah*! See Lam. 3:24. Martin Luther counseled all the Lord's people to answer all temptations with the brief saying *Christianus sum*—"I am a Christian." It is more effective to meet all temptations, sufferings, decisions, and needs with *The Lord is my portion*! He is all-sufficient in any circumstance that may arise, having infinite wisdom to direct, infinite grace to sustain, infinite power to protect, and infinite love to care and comfort. See Psalms 16:5; 73:26! "I have said," implies, inwardly, "I say to myself." May ours be the habit of saying to ourselves when any need appears, this adaptation of a well-known hymn—

> Thou art my portion, O my God,
>   I will give thanks and sing.
> My heart is at the secret source
>   Of ev'ry precious thing.

I intreated thy favor . . . be merciful unto me, 119:58. The impressive phrase, "Intreat thy favor," is also found in Psalm 15:12, and literally means, *to stroke thy face*. See Job 11:19; Prov. 19:6. Since the root-idea is one of *polishing* or *making bright*, we can render the clause, "Makes thy face bright or joyful," that is, with pleasure at God's mercy and goodness. To Hebrews of old, to seek God's face meant to come into His presence, and expressed familiar interchange with Him when they made known their requests face to face with God. David proves that God was his sole Portion by seeking Him face to face, and by his affirmation that he would keep His words. Seeking God with his whole heart, he resolves to make God's Word the rule of his life, confident that He, in turn, would ever be merciful, or gracious towards His child who had made His Word the ground of his confidence. God is made our voluntary debtor by His promises—"According to thy word."

I thought . . . turned . . . I made haste, 119:59-60. Pascal had a profound admiration for Psalm 119. His sister, Madam Perier, says that he often spoke with such feeling about it, "that he seemed transported." He used to say that "with the deep study of life, it contained the sum of all the Christian virtues." He singled out as giving the turning point of man's character and destiny: "I thought on my ways, and turned my feet unto thy testimonies," Psalm 119:59.

As well as a most gifted poet, David was a brave soldier, and there is something of a military air around the phrase, "I thought"—Stop! "I turned my feet"—Right about turn! "I made haste, and delayed not"—Quick march! The word used for "thought" implies repeated and frequent meditation. The past-tenses used in verses 59-61 should be in the present-tense, "I think"—"I turn"—"I make haste." Made conscious of his own words and works, and discovering how they were not according to the Divine rule, David immediately turned in heart and life to the Divine testimonies. The first two actions are characteristic of a sinner when he is converted. The Holy Spirit turns him to the Word, and conscious of his sin, he turns to the Lord. A good explanation of this 59th verse is that it tells us that no itinerary to the heavenly city is simpler or fuller than the ready answer made by an English prelate to a scoffer who asked him the way to Heaven: "First turn to the right, and keep straight on."

Often it is said that "second thoughts are best." But David did not think so for once he discovered where he was going, and should go, he brooked no delay. "Duty discovered should instantly be discharged." The phrase "delayed not," is very elegant in the original meaning, "I disputed not," or "I argued not with God," or "I was determined." The Hebrew implies, "I'll not stand *what—what—whating*, or, as we express the same sentiment, 'shilly-shallying' with myself". Faith asks no questions but yields immediate assent and humbly says *Amen* to every command of God. Delay in following who He reveals is next to disobedience, and generally springs out of it, or issues in it. "God commanded me to make haste," 2 Chron. 35:21.

The bands of the wicked have robbed me, 119:61. Who, exactly, were the wicked, David found himself entrapped by? Perhaps he had in mind his treacherous betrayal to Syrian or Greek rulers, yet held fast to his faith in God. For "bands" we can read, "cords of the wicked surrounded me," or "snares of wicked men surround me." What the Psalmist meant was that those who hated him sought by their plots to entrap him, as they would try to ensnare a wild heart for its destruction. But nothing could bind the Psalmist's free mind, for he was still at liberty in spirit not to forget God's law. Men might rob him of material possessions, but not his inner faith in God. As those who profess to be the Lord's, it is imperative for us to bear in mind that unknown spiritual adversaries are ever watching to make us their prey. Let us pray that we may never succumb as their *prey*.

At midnight I will rise to give thanks, 119:62. Prothero reminds us that abbeys and churches were built as shrines for the Psalter, and that to the chanting of a Psalm (84) their chosen sites were sprinkled with holy water. "Praise the Lord with harp," sanctioned the use of the organ in Divine service. By verses of the Psalms—"In the evening and morning, and at noonday will I pray," Psalm 55:8—"Seven times a day do I praise Thee," 119:164—"At midnight will I rise to give thanks unto Thee," 119:62, the canonical hours were regulated.

In the previous section, David confessed, "I have remembered thy name, O Lord, in the night," verse 55. It was at midnight in a prison cell that Paul and Silas sang praises unto God. It was because David praised God at midday, that he was willing to lose sleep and praise Him at *midnight* also. A bad conscience, sin, cares of the world, keep many ungodly men from sleeping, but if he was awake at midnight, or sleeping then, he arose to bless God for His righteous judgments or ordinances. How many of us are willing to interrupt our rest to praise the Lord for all He is in Himself, and for all His Word reveals of His purposes?

I am a companion of all them that fear thee, 119:63. David shunned the company of the wicked who sought his downfall, but ever identified himself with fellow-lovers of the Lord and of His Word. He knew from experience that—

> The fellowship of kindred minds,
> Is like to that above.

At the outset of the section David expressed his gratitude of having God as his portion, now he declares all saints to be his companions, and these two go together, namely, the love of God, and the love of His saints. It is a contradiction if one professes to love God, yet hates his brother. "Can two walk together except they be agreed?" Our companions, or fellow-believers must be those who like us fear God, and keep His precepts. Birds of such feathers will flock together. Wonderful, is it not, that Jesus condescended to call us His *fellows*? "Thy God hath anointed thee with the oil of gladness above thy fellows." It made no difference to David that he was King, and some of his companions were the humblest in his Kingdom. The poorest, if they feared God, were his companions.

The earth, O Lord, is full of thy mercy; teach me thy statutes, 119:64. David, a lover of nature, believed that the world, as well as the Word, revealed the power and goodness of God. All the earth shines forth in the rich expression of God's paternal benignity and mercy to those who inhabit it. Do we see the mercy of God in all good things around us, sent from Heaven above, in the glorious sunshine, in flowers and fruits, in the air we breathe, in the food we eat, in the clothes we wear, in the money we spend, in the homes we possess? Poet Thomas Davis, who died in 1864, left us three verses on this first clause, "The earth, O Lord, is full of thy mercy," the first verse of which reads—

> Why bursts such melody from tree and bush,
>   The overflowing of each songster's heart,
> So filling mine that it can scarcely hush
>   Awhile to listen, but would take its part?
> 'Tis but one song I hear where'er I rove,
> Though countless be the notes, that God is Love.

David goes back to the Word, from the world around, by concluding this octave with the prayer, twice repeated in the next section, verses 66,

68, "Teach me thy statutes." The mercies of God in nature were wonderful to him; but the *beau-ideal* of mercy was to be taught of God in the truths of His Word. Thus, the first verse of this division is fragrant with full assurance and strong resolve, and this last verse overflows with a sense of Divine fullness, and personal dependence upon the Divine Teacher.

TETH. Verses 65-72. In this ninth section all eight verses begin with the Hebrew letter *Teth.* Spurgeon observes that "in the original each stanza begins with *T*, and in our own version it is so in all verses but 67 and 70, which can easily be made to do so by reading, '*T*ill I was afflicted,' and '*T*is good for me that I have been afflicted.' The first verse of the section is the text, and the remaining seven verses the sermon, in which the blessed effects of affliction are preached. The term 'afflicted' occurs twice, and its end is instructive and chastening, in that it weans the soul from the world, and draws it nearer God. Even in his afflictions, David knew that God had dealt with him."

The terrible persecution of Protestants in the 15th century began while Francis I was engaged in war with Charles V, or detained as a prisoner in Spain, and while Louise of Savoy was Regent or France. Taken captive at the Battle of Pavia in 1525, Francis was brought under guard to the Church of the Certosa. As he entered the building, the monks were singing, Psalm 119:65-70, and when they came to verse 71, the king recovered himself sufficiently to join in the words, "It is good for me that I have been in trouble, that I might learn thy statutes." On his deathbed Francis ordered Marot's version of some of the Psalms to be read aloud for his consolation. He died March 31, 1547.

Thou hast dealt well with thy servant, O Lord, 119:65. The phrase "dealt well," implies, "Showest kindness to," and is equivalent to the expression, "dealt bountifully with," Psalm 116:7. Passing from the testimony of the universal goodness of God in the last verse of the previous section, David now confesses the verdict of his own heart regarding all God has done for him. "Thou hast dealt well with thy servant, O Lord," is not only the summary of the Psalmist's life, but of yours and mine as privileged servants of Jehovah, whose kind and gracious dealings are ever in harmony with His Word.

Even in affliction, whatever God may do or permit is for our good. As a saint of old put it, "If the children of God did but know what was best for them, they would perceive that God did that which was best for them." That warrior of the faith of a past generation, Rev. J. Brown, Haddington, Scotland wrote—

> No doubt I have met with trials as well as others; yet so kind has God been to me, that I think if he were to give me as many years as I have already lived in the world, I should not desire one single circumstance in my

lot changed, except that I wish I had less sin. It might be written on my coffin, *Here lies one of the cares of Providence, who early wanted both father and mother, and yet never missed them.*

Teach me good judgment and knowledge, 119:66. God is not only good in His providential dealings, but likewise *good* in His justice and wisdom. "Good judgment," actually means, "goodness of discernment," or the power of accurately discerning all the Word teaches. As for "knowledge," it has the force of "being able," or skill in applying all the Word reveals to the life of every day. "Good judgment" can also mean "good taste," in a moral, not aesthetic sense. Tact or delicate moral perception represents what the phrase implies.

David discovered, and developed, a *holy taste* for the Word, and recommended it to others, Psalms 19:10; 34:8. And, as we are discovering from our coverage of the Psalms, he had an ever-increasing relish for Divine truth, and for the holiness of life it pointed to. The original word for *judgment* used here is often applied to those objects of sense which are distinguished by the palate, but used in this verse in a metaphorical way, as the corresponding term frequently is in our own language, "Doth not the ear try words, and the mouth taste meat?" Job 12:11. We apply the term *taste* to many objects of mental decision, for instance, when we say that a person has not *good taste*, in respect to the clothes he wears. But a literal translation of David's prayer in verse 66, reads, *Teach me good taste*—in all that concerns Thy word.

If any distinction is to be made between "good judgment" and "knowledge," these two parts of our intellectual furniture have a more important connection and dependence upon each other—*Knowledge*, being the speculative perception of general truth, and *Judgment*, to practical application of same to the heart and conduct. *Knowledge*—of the Lord, of His Word, of ourselves—and *Good judgment* to direct and apply this knowledge to beneficial ends.

Before I was afflicted I went astray, 119:67. Although Ellicott feels there can be little doubt that there is an historical allusion here to the Babylonian exile, and its moral and religious effect upon the nation, the whole tenor of the section is an expression of the writer's personal experience. The first part of the verse reflects the prevalent belief among Jews of the close connection between sin and suffering, borne out by the contentions of Job's three friends and also in the Lord's time, John 9:1. Thus the idea in David's confession is "My sin brought on my suffering." Suffering can result in a change of life, but that is not the implication here.

Both the LXX and Vulgate Versions translate the clause, "Before I was humbled," seeing that the Hebrew has the general sense of being afflicted, and may refer to any kind of trial. The word for *astray* is used of erring through ignorance, Lev. 5:18. David elsewhere denies that he wilfully, wickedly and contemptuously departed from his God, Psalm 18:21. What happened was that through the weakness of the flesh, he left the right way and wandered from it before he was well aware. Trial, however, compelled him to retrace his steps, and he became obedient to the Divine Word. "By affliction God separates the sin which He hates from the soul which He loves." In David's case, the trial resulting from his wandering was medicine producing the restoration of spiritual health.

But—the pivotal point in the change—
Now—an immediate change—
Have I—an inward change—
Kept Thy Word—a Godward change.

Thomas Washbourne, who died in 1687 based a poem on this verse he named—*Affliction Brings Men Home*, the last verse of which reads—

Though for the present strifes do grieve me sore,
    At last they profit more,
And make me to observe thy Word, which I
    Neglected formerly;
Let me come home rather by weeping cross
    Than still be as a loss.
For health I'd rather take a bitter pill,
    Than eating sweet-meats to be always ill.

Thou art good, and doest good; teach me thy statutes, 119:68. The double "good" is often given as "kind," thus "doest good" can be given as "actest in a kind way." Because of all God is, and does, David desired a deeper knowledge of His ordinances. A characteristic feature of this marvelous Psalm is that the higher the conception of the Divine nature, the more earnest becomes the prayer for knowledge of His will in relation to life and conduct. Philo said, "The first Being must needs be the first good," and God is good of Himself, and in Himself, and both the pattern and the fountain of all the good in His creatures.

The proud have forged a lie against me, 119:69. In the octaves of this Psalm, David usually refers to his adversaries in one way or another. In this last section they were the wicked who robbed him. Here they are depicted as forging lies about him. These conceited men gave him a character that was not his own. "They cover me over with falsehoods." The Hebrew for "forged" means "to besmear" or "to cover over." The verb occurs twice in Job 13:4; 14:17, and carries the idea to "patch up." Shakespeare, in *Anthony and Cleopatra,* has the line—"You praise yourself by laying defects of judgment on me; but you patched up your excuses." But although David's foes trimmed up lies about him, he remained true to God despite the falsehoods the proud tried to hide his true fidelity. So long as his character was in harmony with God's precepts he had ever sought with his whole heart, he had no need to worry himself about the reputation his foes gave him.

Their heart is as fat as grease; I delight in thy law, 119:70. The Psalmist made no bones about his description of the lies patched up by his enemies. *Fat as grease* occurs nowhere else in Scripture and signifies not only "to make fat," but also "to make stupid and doltish." The proud, fixed in their resolve to do evil, became almost insensible as fat pigs are when pricked with a needle which cannot reach the flesh to hurt because of the excess of fat. Spiritually, *fatness* means "grossness of heart," Psalm 73:7. "Their heart is gross, as with fat." Thus we have in this verse an emblem of pride and insensibility, Psalm 17:10; Isa. 6:10. But the senseless, sensual, and voluptuous ways of the proud had no influence on David. He delighted in God's law which made him "fat and flourishing," in the right sense.

It is good of me that I have been afflicted . . . learn thy statutes, 119:71. This is the companion of verse 67, and both verses proclaim, "the sweet uses of adversity"—a truism of moralists down the ages.

> Who guideth mortals to wisdom maketh them grasp lore
> Firmly through their pain.

It is interesting to bring these two phrases together, "Thou hast dealt well with thy servant, O Lord" and "It is good for me that I have been afflicted." The affliction was hard for flesh and blood to bear, but it was indeed "well," and in harmony with God, Who is ever good, and can do nothing else but good, seeing that it accomplished most blessed results in the afflicted one. Trial led into more extension of tuition in the Divine statutes. Many things are good but not pleasant, such as sorrow. David's trials perfected his disposition, gave brightness to his piety, and created a deeper desire for the knowledge of God's will. Hugh Macmillan has expressed this sweet use of adversity in his lines—

> Amidst my list of blessings infinite
> Stands this foremost, that my heart has bled;
> For *all* I bless thee, most for the severe.

The sense of the passage before us, then, is—"The affliction brought on by my sin, turned out for my good, for thereby learned I thy law."

The godly wife of Martin Luther, writing on the result of trial "That I might learn thy statutes" said—

> I had never known what such and such things meant, in such and such Psalms, such complaints and workings of spirit, I had never understood the practices of Christian duties, had not God brought me under some affliction.

Our consolation is that it is those whom God loves, He chastens, and scourges, in order that their tears might become their telescope bringing to them a more glorious vision of His holiness and majesty.

> Ill that He blesses is our good,
> And unblest good is ill.
> All is most right that seems most wrong,
> If it be His blessed will.

The law of thy mouth better . . . than thousands of gold and silver, 119:72. The largest Bible in the world, which is in the Vatican, Rome, furnishes an actual comment on this verse. It is in Hebrew manuscript and weighs 320 pounds. Long ago Italian Jews obtained a view of the precious volume and told their friends in Venice about it. The result was that a syndicate of Russian Jews tried to purchase it, offering the Pope the weight of the book in gold as the price. Pope Julius the Second, however, refused the offer. At the present price of gold the offer would amount to an enormous figure. Thousands of gold and silver pieces are nothing in comparison with the inestimably precious Word of God.

Gold and silver are not current in the heavenly country in which we are urged to lay up treasures. Worldly riches secured with labor, kept with care, and often lost with grief, are false friends. Peter was so destitute of money that he did not have a coin to give the cripple, yet he gave him a blessing thousands of silver and gold pieces could not buy. Did not David declare that he desired the statutes of the Lord more "than gold, yea, than much fine gold" Psalm 19:10; 119:127? Is ours the same absorbing love for God's treasure-chest of priceless riches of truth?

It was reported of Nepotiamus, a young gentleman of Rome, that by long and assiduous meditation of Scripture his breast became the library of Christ. It was said of King Alfonus that he read the Bible over 14 times; and that Cranmer learned the New Testament by heart in his journey to Rome, and that his companion, Ridley, did the same thing during his walks in Cambridge. As for Thomas à Kempis, it is recorded of him that he found rest nowhere, but in a corner with the best of books in his hand. Then there is the achievement of Beza who, when he was over 80 years of age, could perfectly repeat any Greek chapter in Paul's Epistles. How those saints loved the Lord, and His law above anything else!

JOD. Verses 73-80. In this tenth section of the Psalm each verse begins with the Hebrew letter *Jod* or i, the smallest letter in the Hebrew alphabet, and called, by our Lord, in Matt. 5:18 *jot*—"one jot or tittle shall in no wise pass from the law." The eight verses before us, however, do not treat of jots and tittles and other trifles, but present a heart-felt prayer for instruction and deliverance. The octave is an anxious yet hopeful cry of one who is heavily afflicted by cruel adversaries and therefore makes his appeal to God as his only Friend and Helper. It also represents the example of the resignation and piety of the faithful, especially in affliction, as gently drawing others to God, Whose Word begets a fellowship in the fear of His name.

Thy hands have made me and fashioned me, 119:73. "Fashioned" carries the idea of something "fixed" or "established." God it was who made us, and not we ourselves. As our Maker Who by His skill and power molded us, He is able to move upon our minds enabling us to understand and learn His statutes. "The great Potter will complete His work and give us the finishing touch to it by imparting to it sacred knowledge and holy practice." With this verse before her Queen Elizabeth prayed, "Oh, look upon the *wounds* of thine hands, and forget the *work* of thine hands."

Hugo ingeniously noticed in the different verbs of this verse the particular vices to be shunned by those who delight in the Word—

> *Ingratitude*—"Thou hast made me"
> *Pride*—"And fashioned me"
> *Confidence in personal judgment*—"Given me understanding"
> *Prying inquisitiveness*—"That I may learn thy statutes."

When God created us He gave us "Understanding," but we need it opened to *learn* His commandments, to know the sense and meaning of them, and to experience their purity and spirituality. Jesus not only opened the Scriptures to His disciples, but also their *understanding* to grasp the relationship to Him, Luke 24.

> Open my mind that I may read
> More of Thy love in word and deed;
> What shall I fear while yet Thou dost lead?
> Only for light from Thee I plead.

They that fear thee will be glad when they see me, 119:74. What a contrast in the pronouns *Thee—Me*! When God makes our life the platform upon which to display His grace and power, others rejoice over such a manifestation. The verse can be rendered, "May those who fear thee, see me and be glad," or "When they see me may they have cause for joy in the faith which I have in thy law." "The great truth of spiritual communion, and the mutual help and consolation derived from it, is latent here. In its primary sense, that the preservation and deliverances of the righteous, who are victims of persecution, afford comfort and joy to all truly good, the verse has been amply confirmed by history." Such a faith springs from the understanding opened by God so that the Psalmist could catch glimpses of truth for his own heart. When our light shines, others glorify God, Matt. 5:16, for they see in us a notable example of the fruit of His holiness. Some of the ancient Hebrew writers gave the sense of the passage as being—"Because then I shall be able to instruct them in those statutes, when they shall see me, their king, study the law of God." The Vulgate Version gives for the last clause, "I have over-hoped in thy word."

Thou in faithfulness hast afflicted me, 119:75. This verse is a summary of verses 67-71, dealing with comfort in affliction. This was one result, those who feared the Lord were glad to see in David, who said *I know*. What did he know as the result of the Divine gift of understanding? Why, two tremendous truths, namely, that Jehovah's judgments are right and that because of His faithfulness He afflicted him. David did not say, "I think," or "may be," or "I hope," that His judgments are right, but *I know*—a statement addressed to God clearly declaring that his knowledge was a matter of faith, not of sight.

Judgments apply to God's dealing of every kind, especially of His afflictive dealings—which were Divine gifts clad in the garb of sorrow. The untoward experiences overtaking David were not wrong, but right. All that may seem wrong to us in God's providential dealings is always *right* and *faithful* in His sight, for He alone can see the beneficial blessings of affliction. Did Cardinal J. H. Newman have the Psalmist's thoughts on sanctified tribulation before him when he composed the poem?

> Yet, Lord, in memory's fondest place
>   I shrine those seasons sad,
> When, looking up, I saw thy face
>   In kind austereness clad.
> I would not miss one sigh or tear,
>   Heart pang, or throbbing brow;
> Sweet was the chastisement severe,
>   And sweet its memory now.
> Yes! let fragrant scars abide,
>   Love-token in thy stead,
> Faint shadows of the spear-pierced side,
>   And thorn-encompassed Head.
> And such thy tender force be still,
>   When self would swerve or stray,
> Shaping to truth the froward will
>   Along the narrow way.

Let, I pray thee, thy merciful kindness be for my comfort, 119:76, 77. In this prayer David does not ask for the removal of his affliction, but earnestly begs for comfort under it, according as God had promised was according to the mind of God seeing it was according to the Word of God. Strange, was it not, that the Psalmist should seek comfort at the hand of the One chastening him? But he knew that He Who wounded, would bind up the wounds, so pleads for the consolation mingled with *merciful kindness*. The sense here is, "Show me thy lovingkindness so that I may thereby be comforted," and so goes on to pray for the phase of mercy amending his life, "Let thy tender mercies come unto me, that I may live." Having delight in God's law, David desired to live by that law, and to experience its quickening influences in the hour of deep need. His delight in the law of God was the ground of his prayer. The claim to personal integrity and faith in God's Word pervades the whole of this Psalm.

Let the proud be ashamed for they have dealt perversely with me without a cause, 119:78. Yet once again David unmasks his cruel treatment by the wicked. In the previous section we saw how they forged a lie against him, how they deal perversely with him, wronged him, and so he prays that they might be *foiled* or *frustrated* in their falsehoods which is what the word "ashamed" means. "They have wronged me (at law) by making false accusations against me." *Overthrown* is used of diverting, or twisting justice, Job 8:5; Psalm 34:12. Ainsworth has the reading, "With falsehood they have depraved me." Caesarius said, "When any of you is singing the verse of the Psalms where it is said, 'Let the proud be put *to shame*, let him be earnest to avoid pride, that he may escape everlasting shame.' David was wise in not trying to combat his adverse, perverse treatment with carnal weapons of warfare. For him, the Word of God, he had made his constant meditation, was sharper than any two-edged sword, and thus well able to defeat his foes.

Let those that fear thee, O Lord, turn unto thee, 119:79, 80. In the previous section David declared that he was a companion of all who feared the Lord, and now prays that those who feared Him, and knew His testimonies, might turn to the Lord, for a deeper experience of His grace and mercy. As for himself, his closing prayer in this octave is that although he had asked God to make his proud foes *ashamed* of their treatment, that he himself would not be ashamed because of being unsound in God's statutes.

The LXX Version has it, "Let my heart be without spot and blemish." The prayer of a heathen was, "A sound mind is a sound body." But David desired more than this; he wanted a heart, sound to the very core, in the acceptance of the Word, as *God's* Word, and, therefore, infallible. Too many are not *sound*, or orthodox, as far as Scripture is, in these days of modernistic tendencies. All who discredit the Divine inspiration and perfection of Scripture have every reason to be ashamed of themselves. The reason why the ministry of such is so powerless, is because victory is not to be achieved by holding a blunt or damaged sword. Spiritual success ever crowns the witness of those who are sound in their acknowledgment and appreciation of the Word as God's infallible revelation of Himself, and of His purposes concerning mankind.

CAPH. Verses 81-88. This eleventh letter signifies the *hollowed*, or *curved hand*, and implies that the hand is hollowed either in order to retain something actually lying in it, or to receive something about to be placed in it by another. When small objects are offered us we instinctively cup our hand to hold them. Several expositors have pointed out that the hand may be God's, as the Giver of bounty, or man's, as the receiver of it. The whole scope of the section before us is a prayer for speedy help, with David holding out his hand as a beggar, supplicating the mercy of God.

In this octave we see David in the dumps, brought to the lowest condition of anguish and depression because of persistent persecution of the wicked. The eight verses before us are the midnight of the lengthy Psalm as a whole, and the situation was very dark and black. The Psalmist, however, is faithful to the Word, and trustful in his God. the last verse is the star-giving promise of the dawn. The section is an expression of intense desire for the coming of God's kingdom and subjugation of all things to Him, according to His Word. Thus, although in deep distress, David holds fast to God's commands and seeks His protection. The Word he hoped in begets a longing for the full peace of God's salvation.

My soul fainteth . . . but I hope in thy word, 119:81. In sore straits, David wanted no deliverance, save that which came from God. Weary with waiting, faint with watching, he believed that God would keep His promise and come as his *Salvation.* Faint, he yet pursued, believing God would fulfil His Word. *Fainting* is usually applied to the body, but here it is ascribed to the soul. Did not Paul warn, "Lest ye be wearied, and faint in your minds," Heb. 12:3? It is the same word given as *faileth* in Psalm 73:26, "My flesh and my heart faileth." Because of his intense desire for the display of God's salvation, David became weak, prostrate as the result of his strong emotion.

Here we have another blessed *but*—"But I hope," even although God's chariot seemed long in coming. Said William Burnall, "David knew where he moored his ship. Hope without a promise is like an anchor without ground to hold by, but David's hope fixed itself upon the Divine Word." His trust was ever in God's promises and precepts. The first clause understood in a higher sense can be applied to the saints today who lovingly long for the coming of the Savior as their Salvation from a sinning World.

Mine eyes fail . . . when wilt thou comfort me? 119:82. The word *fail* used here is the same verb translated *fainteth* in the previous verse. *Soul* and *eyes* have the force of strong personal pronouns, and are here to imply the thought of an exhaustion due to hope deferred. The *failing* of the eyes from sickness and grief, so frequently met with in the Psalms, see 6:7, is not meant here. The emblem is evidently to be understood of the effort of straining to catch or keep sight of a distant object—an application Shakespeare in *Cymbeline* makes—

> I would have broke my eye-strings, cracked them, but
> To look upon him.

Continuously lifting up his eyes to Heaven for help from God, his sight became dim. His eyes were asking the same question as his heart, "When wilt thou comfort me?" David did not complain *of* God, as help tarried, but *to* God, and, consequently came to prove that His delays are not denials. Thomas Hooker tells the story of a poor woman who had long questioned the slowness of God to meet her need, and came to doubt his salvation. As she sought spiritual guidance from her minister he said to her, "The Lord will not always give His children a cordial, but He has it ready for them when they are fainting." God is never before His time, and never behind.

I am become like a bottle in the smoke, 119:83. What a striking metaphor for a poet, a master in Israel, a King, a man after God's own heart to use of himself! With a character smoked with slander, and a mind parched with persecution, he had become in form and feature, like a wizened, old worn-out skin bottle. The Psalmist complains that he shrivelled up, black and useless by suffering, as a skin bottle fashioned out of the untanned hide of an animal is, in an Eastern house without windows, hung above a wood fire with no chimney outlet. As the smoke is thus contained it affects articles in the house very much. Thus this striking emblem, not only descriptive of Israel in her Captivity, but of David in the midst of his trouble, is the image of the abject misery he was brought to by his foes. He became, "As a wineskin in the smoke my heart is sere and dried," and became a companion of Job who moaned, "My skin is black upon me, and my bones are burned with fire," 30:30.

Another application of the emblem is that some of the ancients exposed their skin-bottles to the smoke in order to mellow the wine they contained by the gradual ascent of the heat and smoke from the fire over which they were suspended. We are thus taught the uses of affliction in ripening and improving the soul. What is evident is the difference in David's experience between the beauty and strength of the body and of the soul. Physically, he might have become like a bottle shrivelled and shrunk as the result of his fiery trials, but we read, "Yet do I not forget thy statutes." Remembrance of God's comforting promises was a Paradise from which David's foes could not drive him. The beauty of his soul was enhanced because of its holy frame. Outer attractiveness might have shrunk, but, inner grace had become more beautiful through the Word.

How many are the days of thy servant, 119:84. In that heart-stirring record of Scottish martyrs, *Cloud of Witnesses*, we have the voice of two of them coming as a cry from beneath the altar of testimony, who "at twilight of the evening were put to death at the Gallows—between Edinburgh and Leith, for the adherence to the Covenant," but who bravely died singing this verse of the Psalm in the Scottish metre.

> How many are thy servants' days?
>> When wilt thou execute
> Just judgment on these wicked men
>> That do me persecute?

We have already indicated that this 84th verse, along with verses 121, 122, 132, are the only verses out of the 176 forming the Psalm that carry none of the ten words used in reference to God's law. But one wonders whether the phase of judgment David desired God to execute upon his enemies is not one of them. It would seem that "judgment" must be understood in the sense which the word has throughout the Psalm, namely, "ordinance," or "injustice." So, "to execute judgment," as David prayed, meant "to carry out the principles of justice ordained by Jehovah, and forming an integral part of the law."

As for the phrase, *How many are the days*? the expression means "few at the most." Thus a rendering of the verse is given, "Seeing that my life is at best but short, let justice be done me soon, or it may be too late." David had no doubt that his adversaries would be judged and punished. What he wanted to know was—*When*? Impatience of delay, or, consciousness of the brevity of life did not impair his confidence of future deliverance. We might ask, How many are our days? The only answer is, "God is the length of our days."

The proud have digged pits for me, 119:85. Yet another contrivance of the wicked to try and get rid of one whose adherence to God and His Word troubled their conscience. "Those who do not conform to the law, the arrogant, have digged pits for me," is given in the LXX Version as "Transgressors have related to me frivolous tales, but not as thy law, O Lord." Of old, prisoners were sometimes shut up in pits and left without water, died the dreadful death of Christ. Planning pit-falls for saints is a devilish occupation, and God's Word testifies against such wickedness. But those who dig pits for others should beware, lest they themselves fall into the ditches they make, Psalm 7:15, 16. The gallows Haman raised for Mordecai provided his own execution. It is altogether against God's law for the wicked to delight in cruel practices to injure His saints. Often, in His righteous judgments, the wicked are snared in the work of their own hands, while His persecuted ones go free.

They persecute me wrongfully . . . almost consumed me . . . help thou me, 119:86, 87. Here we have a heartfelt wail of woe as foes press heavy and sore upon David, yet he encloses such a cry by a twofold confession as to the support he gained from God's Word. "All thy commandments are faithful"—"I forsook not thy precepts." In verse 83, he did not *forget* them—here, he did not *forsake* them in the hour of peril. *Consumed* means "made an end of," so we can render, "They had come near killing me." As for persecuting David wrongfully, they had prefaced their intention to get rid of him by destroying his character, "They utter false words in order to incriminate me." Probably the wicked lied against David because he had asserted that God's Word is *faithful*, or, as the Hebrew expresses it, "faithfulness," that is true, sure, and infallible. *Help thou me!*—a brief yet an excellent and comprehensive prayer. It is to be regretted that *God help me!* is so often used lightly, thoughtlessly, and as a by-word. Divine help is only promised to those who forsake not God's precepts.

Thy lovingkindness . . . Thy mouth, 119:88.   Here, again, is one of the key-words of the Psalm. *Quicken*, which the Psalmist used often because he had experienced that quickened by God he was able to bear affliction, baffle his cunning and cruel foes, and conquer sin within his own heart. Previously he had prayed to be quickened according to God's righteousness, now it is "after thy lovingkindness," and thus quickened, he would ever keep the testimony of God's mouth, and use his own mouth to testify to the power of the Word in his own life. May our every confession come directly from "the mouth of God," John 6:63!

LAMED. Verses 89-96.   Joseph F. Thrupp, Biblical expositor of the 18th century, wrote that with this section "the climax of the delineation of the supplicant's pilgrimage is reached." We have arrived at the middle of the Psalm, and the thread of the connection is purposely broken off. The substance of the *first eleven strophes* has evidently been: "Hitherto hath the Lord brought me: shall it be that I now perish?" To this the *eleven succeeding strophes* make answer, "The Lord's Word changeth not; in spite of all evil forebodings, the Lord will perfect concerning me the work He hath already begun."

Love perfecteth what it begins.   The atmosphere changes with the octave, for David, after tossing about on a sea of trouble leaps to shore and stands upon the rock of Jehovah's immovable Word. In the previous section David's soul fainted but now he looks away from self and perceives that the Lord fainteth not, neither is weary, neither has uttered a word that has failed. His Word abides because He, Himself, is faithful. The thesis of these eight verses, then, is that the Word is certain, immutable, everlasting, and infinite in perfection, a type of the Living Word Who "abideth for ever," John 12:34.

Forever, O Lord, thy word is settled in heaven, 119:89.   Is this not one of the most outstanding statements in Scripture? As we gaze upon the uncertain, shifting scene of this life, does not the thought of God's unchanging promises fill our hearts with joy? Men may have unsettled thoughts about the immutability and eternity of God's Word—a characteristic so evident in those who are modernistic in their appraisal of Scripture—but God's covenants and precepts are all settled in His own mind and like Himself, cannot change. If the Word is not settled in man's heart, bless God it is settled in Heaven. Grace, then, should be ours to settle in our own minds, the faith of Jehovah in His own Word. "Forever, O Jehovah, is thy Word: It is firmly fixed in heaven"—beyond the reach of earthly changes. See Psalms 72:5; 89:2.

It has been pointed out that while the words of this verse are usually rendered as making but one proposition, the accent *athnab* reveals there are two branches to be noted—

1. The Eternity of God Himself—"For ever—art thou—O Lord."
2. The Eternity of God's Word—"Thy word is settled in heaven."

Constancy and permanency of God's Word also marks God's Work. "Thou hast established the earth, and it abideth."

Thy faithfulness . . . Thou hast established the earth, 119:90, 91. God is not affected by the lapse of ages, or changing times, "He abides faithful." A simple hymn expresses it—

> Man may change, but Jesus never,
> Glory to His name.

Some of the promises God made go back to the first man He created, but they are not worn out by millenniums of use, for Divine faithfulness in the fulfillment of promises endured forever. Then in the verse David travels from Heaven to earth, to prove that God's immutability is related, not only to His Word, but to His Work. "Thou hast established the earth, and it abideth." Such an analogy is very impressive. As His Word is fixed in Heaven, so Nature below is governed by fixed laws, and keeps its abiding order by Divine command. If the globe displayed erratic movements, life would be impossible. See Jerem. 31:35, 36.

The heavens and the earth obey their Sovereign, and move according to the laws He imprinted upon them. Thus the sea contains itself in its bounds—the sun does not remove from its sphere—the stars march in their order, because "all are thy servants." The whole totality of things in Nature is as stable as the stability of Scripture. If, of course, God orders things contrary to the primitive nature of His created servants, they obey Him. They were created by His Word—"He spake, and it was done," and when He speaks to them, they immediately carry out His command, as the ravenous nature of half-starved lions was suspended when Daniel was

thrown among them. What a good morsel he would have been seeing he
was all muscle! In Joshua's time the sun which had been in perpetual
motion since God set it in the heavens, obeyed God's writ of ease and
stood still to aid Joshua's victory.

> Say not, my soul, "From whence
>   Can God relieve my care?"
> Remember that Omnipotence
>   Has servants everywhere.

The Word abides, so does the World—*It abideth.* Says William
Cowper, "Creation is as the mother, and Providence the nurse which preserveth all the works of God. God is not like man; for man, when he hath
made a work, cannot maintain it: he buildeth a ship, and cannot save it
from shipwreck; he builds a house, but cannot keep it from ultimate
decay. It is otherwise with God Who is Conserver, as well as Creator."

Unless thy law had been my delights, 119:92, 93. The words of verse
92 are written on Martin Luther's Bible by his own hand. The date is
1542, and the Bible is preserved at the Brandenburg Mark Museum,
Berlin. David declares how grateful he was for finding his study of God's
law delightful, seeing he was indebted to it for preservation during his
affliction. Philip Melancthon, friend of Luther, said that the handmaid
Heme told him at Dresden that it would have been impossible for him to
bear up under the manifold miseries of so long an imprisonment, had it
not been for the comfort of the Scriptures in his heart.

Delights! Do you not love the plural used here? Sorrows had crowded the life of David, but against them all he found as many comforts and
delectations in God's Word. For every feeling of depression, there was a
morsel of delight to counteract it. Alexander Wallace wrote a most
enlightening book on *The Bible and the Working Classes*, during the 18th
century. Among the incidents he recorded is the following experience—
"I happened to be in a grocer's shop one day in a large town in the West
of Scotland, when a poor, old, frail widow came in to make a few pur-
chases. At that time the town was in deep distress. Nearly every loom was
stopped. Respectable tradesmen were obliged to subsist on public
charity. A small amount of money was allowed for the really poor and
deserving. The destitute widow had received her daily pittance and was
now in the grocer's to spend it to the best advantage. A few coins were in
her hand, and carefully she made to buy a pennyworth of this and that
necessity of life, then she came to her last penny, and with a singular
expression on her heroic countenance and cheerful resignation on her
wrinkled face she said—'Now I must buy oil with this, that I might see
to read my Bible during these long dark nights, for it is my only comfort
when every other comfort has gone.'"

This lonely widow, like Daniel, would have perished in affliction had the Word not been her delight. The precepts of God were not forgotten in spite of poverty and old age. David testified to their quickening power—a power resilient in God. "With them *THOU* hast quickened me." All spiritual quickening comes through the Word, and the particular aspect of such a quickening for the Psalmist was comfort and support in his affliction. The precepts were to him spirit and life.

I am thine, save me; for I have sought thy precepts, 119:94. The first clause in this verse appears to state a contradiction. As David was already the Lord's, made His by matchless grace, then why did he pray to be saved? Having sought God's precepts was proof enough that he had found in Him his salvation. *Save*, here, was used in the sense of preservation from the wicked waiting to destroy him, and Salvation is ever a good plea for Preservation when beset by evil. Literally, *save* implies, "put me in a large place," or, "set me at large, give me a wide berth," Psalm 107:6. The root of the verb here used is that found in *Jesus* and *Joshua,* namely, "one that sets at large." Being the Lord's was a powerful motive to draw help from Him in time of trouble.

Cowper has the two phrases in this verse—"I am thine because I sought nothing but that which is thine, and that I might please thee" and—"In the observance of thy precepts in all my patrimony." There is a sense in which every Christian who can say, "I am thine, O Lord!" should pray, "Save me!" When saved from the *penalty* of sin, they became the Lord's, but being saved from its guilt, they need to be daily saved from sin's power and government, which means their sanctification ever reaching the life through the Truth.

The wicked have waited to destroy me, but I will consider thy testimonies, 119:95. Yet another condemnation of the Psalmist's enemies, who manifested *diligence* in that they waited for occasions to do him evil, and also *cruelty without mercy*, for it was their purpose to destroy him. But even as his life was being sought for David considered the promises of God without which he might have yielded to despair. Wisely, he considered God and His Word, rather than those seeking his life. He could not be drawn away from the testimony of Divine preservation.

I have seen an end of all perfection: but thy commandment is exceeding broad, 119:96. This concluding verse of the octave was the favorite one of Dean Stanley—a choice characteristic alike of the man and his work. The gist of the passage seems to be, "the most earthly things are finite and limited; but God's law is for all needs and all times." The term *perfection* means, "the farthest limit," or "the remotest point in space." See Job 11:7; 26:11. Thus the sense of the verse seems to be, "The horizon bounds my vision of space: my farthest visible point is bounded: but God's commandment is *exceeding broad*," that is, without end. The same adjective *broad* is used of God's perfection, Job 11:9. The Chaldee Version puts it, "I have seen an end of all things about which I employed my care; but thy commandment is very large."

Matthew Henry remarks that, "Poor perfection which one sees an end of! Yet such are all those things in this world which pass for perfections. David in his time had seen Goliath, the strongest, overcome; Asahel, the swiftest, overtaken; Ahithophel, the wisest, befooled; Absalom, the fairest, deformed. David's natural eye had seen the end of all human perfections, but his heart rejoiced in God's commandments as being broader, or having a Divine perfection without end. The exact thought of the Psalmist, of course, offers such a wide application, embracing so many truths of experience, that possibly he had more than one meaning in mind." Ellicott goes on to say, "Keeping as close to the context as possible, the meaning will be: *To all perfection (or apparent perfection) a limit is visible, but the Divine Law is boundless alike in its scope and its requirements*. This, translated into the language of modern ideas, merely says that the actual never corresponds with the ideal"—

> Who keeps a spirit wholly true
> To that ideal which he bears?

Perhaps the Anglican Prayer Book version, "I have seen the end of all settled things" mirrors David's thought as indicating the difference between mere change and progress. Tennyson in *Morte d'Arthur* expresses such a thought in the lines—

> The old order changeth, yielding place to new,
> And God fulfills Himself in many ways,
> Lest one good custom should corrupt the world.

In theological circles today, the term *broad* is of frequent occurrence, and is one modernistic and rationalistic theologians proudly apply to themselves in respect to their attitude towards God's perfect Word. Those who, of the evangelical faith, adhere to the infallibility of Scripture are deemed *narrow* or *bigoted* by those who try to chop up the Word, rejecting what they deem to be irrelevant or useless. Theirs, they affirm, is the *broad* outlook, and being broad, they are all *abroad* when it comes to the lover's acceptance of Scripture that it is of great breadth for his duty and delight. The only true *Broadchurchman* is the one accepting the Bible as "the perfect law of liberty," he who, in proportion to the strength of his faith, increases with the increase of God, and seeks to be filled with all the fullness of God. It is only the mind which apprehends God's Statutes from God's standpoint, that is the home of mental liberty. "Ye shall know the truth, and the truth shall make you free."

MEM. Verses 97-104. The renowned missionary, Henry Martyn, wrote, "I experienced a solemn gladness in learning this part *Mem* of the 119th Psalm." May ours be the same solemn gladness as we seek to examine what the octave teaches! Having turned away from all boasted perfection, David now turns in unto the law he dearly loved, growing wiser and holier thereby. To him, God's Word commanded the approval of the heart, seeing it was the only treasure-house of true wisdom, which the introversion and alternations of the section reveal—

> The Word of Jehovah, Precious, 97.
> > The source of Understanding and Reason, 98-100.
> > Wiser than mine enemies—Reason, 98.
> > Wiser than the aged—Reason, 100.
>
> The Word of Jehovah, Precious, 103.
> > The source of Understanding and Consequences, 104.

O how love I thy law! It is my meditation all the day, 119:97. Among the "five distinguishing marks of the *true Christian*," David Brainerd set forth was, "The *laws* of God are his delight. *Lord, what love have I unto Thy law, all the day long is my study in it*, Psalm 119:97." How arrestive is the opening of this further octave! The Psalmist began Psalm 116 with the old exclamation, "I love the Lord." Here he begins by confessing, "I love thy law," and the one aspect of love is wrapped up in the other. If we do not truly love the Lord, we shall not have much love for His Word; and if we not only reverence and obey His law, but deeply love it as to have it as our meditation all the day, same will evidence our love for Him Who gave us His Word. David's constant meditation of it was both the effect of his love, and the cause of it. Love for the Word is the measure of our love for the One it magnifies. In every one of the verses of this section Scripture is spoken of as the Lord's.

We are not to imagine by the phrase, *all the day,* that David did nothing else through its hours but study the only part of Scripture extant at that time. As King, he would have many other matters to think about, and responsibilities claiming a good deal of his time. What is implied is the way in which he made God's law his chief and principle set study; that he took every available opportunity of turning to it, never wearying when occasion to meditate arose, to drink deeply of the inexhaustible truths of Scripture.

Wiser than thine enemies . . . all my teacher . . . the ancients, 119:98-100. In these three verses David mentions three classes of men he outstripped in wisdom. *Enemies*, whose malice sharpens their wits, and makes them excel in policy—*Teachers*, who are furnished with learning because of their office, and who excel in doctrine—*Ancients*, who grow wise by experience and become safe in counsel. Yet David, by the Word, was made wiser than all these, and excelled them in wisdom.

Another rendering for verse 98 reads, "Thy commandment makes me wiser than my enemies, for it is my possession for ever." The same correspondence of wisdom, loyal obedience to the law, is found in the Book of Proverbs.

They are ever with me, referring, of course, not to his enemies, but God's commandments. The meaning of this clause is not merely "it is ever with me," but "it is for ever to me," implying mine, my inalienable, indefeasible possession. God, through His Word, enabled David to outwit his enemies in the art of opposition. "He who is taught of God has a practical wisdom such as malice cannot supply to the crafty; while harmless as a dove he also exhibits more than a serpent's wisdom."

We can imagine present day teachers raising their eyebrows if told that their pupils were beyond them in understanding and discernment. But "the superior wisdom David claimed had to do exclusively, with the Divine law as a guide of life: and of this the pupil might well have known more than his teachers, who were probably Greeks appointed by the Syrian government to instruct the Jews in the religion and philosophy of the dominant power. The teaching of the Law, and even of Hebrew, was suppressed by the Syrians." But David was Divinely taught Divine wisdom. The comment of Matthew Henry on this 99th verse would have us remember that "it is no reflection upon my teachers, but rather an honor to them, for me to improve so as to excel them, and no longer need them. By *meditation* we preach to ourselves, and so we come to *understand more than our teachers*, for we come to understand our hearts, which they cannot."

Augustine was first illuminated and converted by Ambrose, yet he came to excel his spiritual father and teacher, both in knowledge and spiritual grace. Because Augustine made God's testimonies his constant meditation, he came to acquire a fuller understanding of truth than Ambrose. We may sit under the wisest teachers and yet remain fools. If, however, we love the Word, and seek to live in it, and by it, wisdom will become ours—a wisdom outweighing the teachings of men if they were all gathered into one vast library. Thus, "it behoves us to follow closely the chart of the Word of God, that we may be able to save the vessel when even the pilot errs."

But David not only outstripped his foes and surpassed his tutors in wisdom, but outshone his elders, or old men because of the daily instruction he received from the Word. We prize antiquity and the *ancients* were held in high respect. We say, "The old is better," but the oldest of all is the best of all, and what is that but the inerrant Word of Him Who is the Ancient of days. Understanding gained by knowing and obeying God's commands is far better than wisdom secured by long, laborious learning. Although brought up as a shepherd, David became far wiser than his foes, instructors, and elders, because he was taught of God.

The key-word in this section is *understanding*, used 3 times. "Understand . . . keep." Obedience sprang from spiritual knowledge. David, the holier and more youthful learner excelled all others in understanding, because his wisdom was from above. Innocent of any self-consciousness, the Psalmist is not boasting of his own understanding, but of that which came to him as he observed in heart and life the precepts of the Lord. His was the superior knowledge of the Law becoming his because he obeyed such a Law. *Then kept* is better translated, *I keep*, for his was a constant obedience coming as the result of constant meditation upon the Divine statutes.

I have refrained . . . I have not turned aside, 119:101, 102. The qualifying phrase in these verses describing David's unswerving acknowledgment of God's judgment is, *For thou hast taught me!* Here was the secret of his I.Q. Jehovah was his real Teacher in the Law. How? Through His Law. The meaning of this apparent paradox is that it was through His Law Jehovah taught the Psalmist to keep it. David did not ascribe his higher wisdom to himself, but gave God all the glory for His instruction through His Word. Previously he had prayed, "Teach me thy way, O Lord, I will walk in thy truth," Psalm 86:11. The Divine Word is its own interpreter. Consequently he "refrained" or held back, from evil conduct of every kind, even of a religious kind after the sense of Acts 9:2; 19:2, 23; 24:14. He never departed, or swerved from following the Divine revelation. Contrast the two clauses *I have . . . I have not*, presenting as they do the positive and negative ideas of the Psalmist's holiness of life.

I have refrained. Sin avoided, that obedience may be perfected is the essence of this verse. As the last verse expresses it, "Through thy precepts I get understanding: therefore I hate every false way." Apart from grace, our feet naturally lead into the path of every sin. But once we are God's we are kept by His power through His word. So the Hebrew verb here given as *refrained* is much stronger in meaning, and denotes, "I *fettered* or *imprisoned* my feet," and implies David's recognition of his inability to keep his feet from straying.

I have not. "Departed not," declares both exactness and constancy on the part of David—*Exactness*, in that he did not go a hair's-breadth from the Divinely set course. See Deut. 5:32—*Constancy*. Had he departed from God and His law, he would have fallen from Him in judgment and practice. See Jerem. 32:40. All are well taught when God teaches, for what we learn from Him we never forget, and such tuition also has the practical effect of keeping us in the way of holiness.

How sweet are thy words . . . I get understanding, 119:103, 104. What an effective emblem of Scripture David uses—*Honey!* Those who despise endearing terms when it comes to the Lord and His word, may balk at David's expression of the sweetness of the words of Scripture—a sweet-

ness, the degree of which he cannot express but only cry *How sweet*! As
he fed on the Word he found it sweet, and bearing witness to it, it became
sweeter still. To the regenerated is given a new, supernatural sense, a certain Divine, spiritual taste for Scripture. The phrase "unto my taste"—"to
my mouth" are metaphorical and imply the pleasure David had in meditating upon the Word, and then talking, conferring with others about it, just
as the physical mouth loves honey, or finds it agreeable. See Psalm 19:10.

David's son, Solomon, tells us that while honey is good for us, to eat too
much of it upsets the digestive organs—"lest thou vomit it," Prov. 24:12;
25:16, 27. Well, it may be unwise to eat too much natural honey, but we
can never have enough of the honey of the Word. If we are to take the
sweet *words* as including God's *judgments* in the previous verse, one may
ask, How can His judgments be as sweet as His promises? Judgments are
so fearful and grievous, therefore, distasteful. The answer is that the godly
have no greater joy than when they feel either the mercies of God accomplished towards them that fear Him, or His just treatment meted out to
those who blatantly reject His overtures of love and grace.

It was through all aspects of the Word that David found understanding,
as well as agreeableness of taste. Obedience to the Divine will begets for
him wisdom of mind and action. It was because of this spiritual understanding that he came to hate every false way. One of the precepts of St.
Gregory was, "Whosoever therefore will understand, let him first make
haste to do what he heareth." For the Psalmist this meant hating every
false way. Those who get understanding by the Word are not only guarded against evil—they come to hate it. Evil is avoided because of the
spiritual profit received form the Holy Word.

NUN. Verses 105-112.   What a precious section this is, exalting
Jehovah's Word as it does as the source of light and joy! Such a heritage
is the only beacon-light amid the darkness and storms of the world.
Wherever the Bible is not found gross darkness prevails. The opening
verse of this octave was the text prefixed to a small book called *The
Lantern of Light*, which was the favorite reading of the Lollards before the
Reformation. These Lollards of England and Scotland, prominent some
70 years before the time of John Knox, were charged with reading the
Bible in their mother tongue, and with esteeming it above any instruction
they received from the priests! In 1494 many of them were tried and punished. As the close of a prayer in the Preface of the above book they loved
to read reveals the principles of those children of the dawn—

> When thou, O Lord, didst die upon the Cross, Thou didst breathe into
> Thy word the spirit of life, and didst give it power to quicken us through
> Thine own precious blood, as Thou Thyself hast said, *The words that I speak
> unto you, they are spirit and they are life.*

Shakespeare, too, must have had the language of this section, particularly the first verse, in mind for in the speech from the Second Part of "King Henry the Sixth," addressed by the king to Humphrey, Duke of Gloster, we have the lines—

> . . . God shall be my hope,
> My stay, my guide, and lantern to my feet;
> And go in peace, Humphrey,—

Wordsworth, it will be recalled, calls "Duty"—*A Light to guide*. The Bible, however, is a safer and more perfect guide to follow. We cannot read the eight verses before us without being impressed with them as David's desire to have his whole being illuminated and sanctified by the Word, as references to "my feet," "my path," "my mouth," "my soul," and "my heart" reveal. He wanted the Lord, through His Word, to hold over his entire life, absolute sway.

My feet . . . my path . . . I have sworn . . . perform . . . keep, 119:105, 106. King Solomon must have had his royal father's unique use of the emblem of light, in respect to Scripture in mind when he came to write, "For the commandment is a lamp; and the law is light," Prov. 6:23. Many attempts have been made to distinguish between the *lamp* and the *light*, the *feet* and the *path*, but same are integral parts of the figure of speech employed. The thought of these two passages is that God's Word gives guidance at all times. In the night it is as a lamp, in the day as the light of the sun; and that it is our responsibility to confirm, or ratify it to others, as well observe it ourselves.

A delight at all times, Scripture is *light*-giving, as well as *life*-giving, guiding our footsteps with perfect direction. This truth must be held firmly in our mind, and our confirmation of it solemnly declared before God. Having the light in our souls, as well as in Scripture, we must daily walk in such light. Basil the Great, interpreting the *Word* as God's will revealed in Scripture, observed that in the Old Testament, and in particular the Law, was only a *lantern*—lamp or candle—because an artificial light, imperfectly illumining the darkness, whereas the Gospel given by the Lord Jesus Himself, is a *Light* of the Sun of Righteousness, giving brightness to all things. To David, however, the Law which was about all he had to meditate upon, was not artificial light, but *the* light to lighten his pathway through life. And he could have sung Cardinal Newman's favorite hymn had it been in circulation then—

> Lead, kindly light, amid the encircling gloom
>   Lead thou me on.
> The night is dark, and I am afar from home,
>   Lead thou me on.
> Keep thou my feet; I do not ask to see
> The distant scene; one step enough for me.

With this revelation of the Word as the source and channel of illumination, David solemnly vowed both to live out, or perform, and hid God's judgments in his heart. Theodoricus, Archbishop of Cologne, when the Emperor Sigismunc demanded of him the directest and most compendious way how to attain true happiness, made this brief answer, "Perform when thou art well what thou promisedst when thou wast sick." David did so; he made vows in war, and paid them in peace; "I will perform and keep Thy Word." He was not like the evil one, of whom the epigram reads—

> The devil was sick, the devil a monk would be;
> The devil was well, the devil a monk was he.

David loved and honored the Word because it judged most righteously between right and wrong, truth and error.

I am afflicted very much . . . teach me thy judgments, 119:107, 108. After being sworn in as a soldier of the Lord, and ratifying his allegiance to Him, David is called to suffer hardness in such a capacity. "I am afflicted," suggests present trials, from which Jehovah did not screen, but was his quickening power during his affliction. Although he had but few promises to rest on, in comparison with the large number we have in the Bible as a whole, yet what he did have, he constantly pleaded, and proved them to be a sufficient antidote to the heaviest trial. Quickened by the precepts of God, verse 93, he confirms that he will never forget them but live according to them.

With his mouth David made confession of desire, and in the freewill offerings of his mouth, the sacrifice of prayer and praise would be spontaneously presented to God for the instruction received through His commandments. See Psalms 50:14; 51:19; Heb. 12:15. The Psalmist asked for acceptance of the witness of his lips—the word *accept*, literally meaning, "to be pleased with," or "accept as satisfactory." Under Levitical law, a "freewill offering" was one offered to God in gratitude for some particular blessing received, or for deliverance form danger. Such an offering was willingly, cheerfully and freely made.

I forget not thy law . . . I erred not from thy precepts, 119:109, 110. The phrase, "My soul is continually in my hand," is often used as an idiom for great danger, "I am in danger of losing my life," Judges 12:3; I Sm. 19:5; 28:21; Job 13:4. Such a danger lay in the snarls the wicked set in his path. But the threat, even of death, when David had to fight for existence, did not cause him to forget the Word he had received life and light from, or to err from the paths of virtue and piety. Although he lived with his life in his hand, he himself was in God's hand, so all was well. And, he never swerved from God's precepts, but kept to the King's highway of holiness. Paul testified, "I die daily," yet could say, "I live, yet not I, Christ liveth in me."

The rejoicing of my heart . . . I have inclined my heart, 119:111, 112. In the previous octave, the Psalmist spoke of the Word as being sweet to his taste, and the same sweetness is described in this 111th verse as the delight of his heart. Head-knowledge and heart-experience of the testimonies of the Lord had brought David so much joy, but he was determined to have them as his estate forever, or as a storehouse of celestial treasure. What an inheritance Scripture is for the saints to live on, and by.

Having prayed, "I have inclined my heart to perform," he now prays, "Incline my heart," and appears to be asking God to do something for him, he himself has already promised to do. Yet these are not contrary one to the other. "Man inclines by striving: God inclines by effecting. Neither in that which man attempts, nor that which he by striving achieves good-wards, from the man, but from God, Who gives *both to will* and to *do of His good pleasure.*"

Having taken the Divine admonitions as his heritage forever, David ends by prompting his heart to live out these statutes in his daily life, even to the end of his pilgrimage—"even unto the end." The phrases, "for ever," and "the end," can be thought of "as an eternal reward." See 119:32. "The mention of an inheritance in the law naturally suggests the thought of an eternal reward, the reward consisting of obedience to the law." David vowed to obey God's Word not for a time, but always, and unto the end of life, which he knew would be the beginning of glory, where he would see Him whom he loved, and whose Word had been the rejoicing of his heart throughout his earthly pilgrimage.

SAMECH. Verses 113-120. This fifteenth letter of the Hebrew alphabet, signifies a *prop* or *pillar*, and is in harmony with the subject matter of this octave, in which God is twice implored to uphold, or pillar up, His servant—"Hold thou me up"—"Uphold me." David was compassed about by those who faced destruction for making light of God's law, or who had encouraged skepticism regarding it, suffering thereby the same fate of the Philistine lords, on whom Samson brought down the roof of the house where they were making merry, by overthrowing the pillars which supported the roof. But David knew that the pillars supporting him in his effort not to swerve from the Word of God would sustain him.

All hateful and skeptical attempts to undermine the Psalmist's faith in God's statutes would recoil in confusion upon those who made them, and would result in them being cast away as dross; but for the Psalmist there was the security Jehovah's law provided. Thus the strophe is laden with his most ardent affirmations—

I love thy law—
I hope in thy word—
I will keep the commandments of God—

I will have respect unto thy statutes continually—
I love thy testimonies—
I am afraid of thy judgments.

With God's Word written upon his heart, David prayed that he might be enabled to write out His precepts in his life, hence, the difference between this octave and the last. The present one is thoughtful, just as the previous one was practical. Having attended to his *feet*, he now thinks of his *heart*. "The emotions of the soul are as important as the acts of life, for they are the fountain and spring from which the actions proceed. When we love the law it becomes a law of love, and we cling to it with our whole heart."

I hate . . . I love, 119:113, 114. David was as good a hater—in a good sense—as he was a lover. He commenced the 13th octave by declaring, "O how I love thy law." Here he begins by stoutly declaring his hatred against those spurning and breaking that law—"I hate men who halt between two opinions." See 1 Kings 18:21. Ellicott thinks that there may be a probable reference here "to those among the Jews who were for political reasons favorably inclined towards foreign customs and ideas, and who would not throw in their lot frankly and courageously with the national party." *Thoughts* here, imply divided or doubting thoughts, or them that are of double mind. See James 1:8. The Hebrew word signifies boughs or branches, which shoot up perplexedly or confusedly in a tree, and as used here implies perplexed or skeptical doubts.

Whether any vain thoughts ever entered David's mind we are not told, if they did, he hated them. He did not glory in his thoughts but God's. Men's thoughts—even what is known in theological circles as *modern thought*—are vain; but God's thoughts are verity. Further, the Psalmist does not say that he's *fully kept the law, but he* loved it even when he failed of exact obedience to it, and because of such a love his faith rested in the promise that God was his hiding place and shield from all thoughts tempting him not to hope in God's Word.

My hiding place and my shield . . . I hope . . . I will keep, 119:114, 115. David often used the two figures of speech he here employs to express his faith in God's protective care. In Him, he found a *hiding place*, to run to for shelter from vain thoughts, and from the vain men who made them vocal. From their tormenting intrusions, in the solemn silence of the soul he found God to be his covert, Psalms 27:5; 32:7; 84:9; 91:1. The thought here is safety because in hiding he would not be seen. *Hiding* means properly a secret, or a secret place.

God was also David's shield, that is, his protection against those approaching him with their wicked, divisive, and empty thoughts. God ever beats back the enemies of his people. "Bring them down, O Lord, our shield," Psalm 59:11. See Genesis 15:1. Jehovah's Messiah became our faith's shield, Eph. 6:16. Having God as his security and defense, the Psalmist affirms his hope in His Word, seeing he had tried and proved it. Promises of protection and preservation had been wonderfully faithful. Amid all fret and worry, the hope God's Word contains is an effectual quietus.

From speaking to himself, and then to God, David now addresses himself to those whose evil thoughts and action he could not tolerate. Now that he was safe and secure, they could depart. It may be that this edict was uttered to the parasites in the palace, David could harbor no longer under his roof, and so sent them out bag and baggage, for henceforth he was going to keep the commandments of God Who had become his hiding place and shield—something he could not do while in the company of evil counselors. "Come out from among them, and be ye separate, saith the Lord." Pagans of old deemed it a curse to go along with those who kept evil company. To inhabit, or to travel with an impious man, and one not beloved of the gods, was held by them to be unlucky and unfortunate. As Horace put it—

> They who mysteries reveal
> Beneath my roof never live,
> Shall never hoist with me the doubtful sail.

David had departed from them who had departed from his God. The beautiful epithet he uses here, *"My* God," occurs only in this one place in all of this long Psalm. The personal pronoun reveals a double grip, namely his grip upon God, and God's grip of him. Philip Doddridge has the stanza on this personal affirmation—

> *My God*! how charming is the sound!
>   How pleasant to repeat:
> Well may that heart with pleasure bound,
>   Where God hath fixed his seat.

In the marching orders David gave to evil thinkers and doers there is an anticipation of the dreadful sentence David's Greater Son will pronounce at the last day, "Depart from me, ye workers of iniquity." See Psalm 6:8.

Uphold me . . . Hold thou me up, 119:116, 117. The ancient Benedict Rule, largely made up of the Psalms, was introduced into England with the landing of Augustine. Under this Order when a novice's period of preparation was ended, and he was ready to become attached to the monastery for life, with outstretched arms, he sang three times the verse which was the *Open Sesame* of the monastic life, "O stablish me according to Thy Word, that I may live; and let me not be disappointed of my hope." Three times the community repeated the words, and added the *Gloria Patri.*

We join these two verses together seeing they express the same thought of being continually sustained by God: Uphold me from enemies about and without—Uphold me from enemies beneath and within. And David prayed that he would never be ashamed of, or be disappointed in the gracious upholding promised. Evil men would cast him down, but God was more than able to hold his servant up. Should this not be our daily prayer, "Hold Thou me up and I shall be safe"? Our foes are powerful, and our dangers many, and we are liable to fall. "There is no elevation like the elevation of abasement."

> Weaker than a bruised reed,
> Help I every moment need.

God will not disappoint our hope if it is reinforced with a continued respect for His statutes. His ear is ever open, His heart is ever tender, and His arm ever strong to lift us up, and keep us up. "I shall be safe" can be rendered, "so that I may be set in a free—unrestrained—place." Instead of *respect* ancient versions read, "then shall I *delight* myself in thy statutes continually." The LXX Version has it "shall meditate." Spurgeon summarizes the happiness of those who realize these verses in their lives—

> Upheld through their whole life in a course of unswerving integrity, they become safe and trusted servants, maintaining a sacred delicacy of conscience unknown to others. They feel a tender respect for the statutes of the Lord, which keep them clear of inconsistencies and conformity to the world that are so common among others, and hence become pillars in the house of the Lord.

Thou hast trodden down all . . . Thou puttest away all the wicked, 119:118, 119. *Trodden down* implies a drastic and humiliating defeat. Both the LXX and Vulgate Versions have "thou despised." Aquila put it, "Thou hast impaled," and Symmachus, "Thou hast convicted." Literally the word "trodden" seems to mean to *weigh* or *value*, but, from the habit of the buyer beating down the price by depreciating, comes to have a sense of this kind. See Prov. 20:14. Others suggest that the term implies "rejected," or "cast away." Sooner or later God sets His foot on those who turn their foot from His ways.

Because their "deceit is falsehood," God condemned them, brought them to nothing. The true sense of this phrase is, "for their cunning hath been fallacious," they deceived themselves and brought on their ruin. A paraphrase of the Hebrew reads, "for their wits are as fruitless as they are deceitful." All their craft was in vain, for the self-deception was a lie. The deception referred to was not that of others, but self-deceit.

Thou puttest away all the wicked like dross, is another emblem describing the punishment overtaking the wicked. The Hebrew for "puttest" is

causest to cease, and is a common figure of Scripture, Jerem. 6:28-30;
Ezek. 22:18-20. Where apparently vice succeeds and prospers it is really marked out for expulsion, as John Milton emphasizes in the lines—

> To those who
> All reassures and all gain esteem as dross;
> And dignities and powers all but the Highest.

As David's references to his adversaries are most frequent in his Psalms, and described in various denunciating ways, they must have been numerous and persistent in their efforts to destroy him. Wisely, however, he left their deserved judgment in the hands of the Judge of all the earth whose decisions are always right and just. Here, for instance, he prays that his relentless foes might be discarded as refuse. The LXX Version reads, "I have counted all the wicked of the earth as dross." God judged them to be the scum of the earth, and treated them accordingly by getting rid of them. As the Refiner and Purifier of silver, He will not have dross associated with His precious metal.

Cowper reminds us that, "the men of this world esteem God's children as the offscourings of the earth, so Paul—a chosen vessel unto God—was dis-esteemed of men; but ye see here what the wicked are, in God's account, but dross indeed, which is the refuse of gold or silver. Let this confirm the godly against the contempt of man: only the Lord hath in his own hand the balance which weigheth men according as they are." But the Psalmist amid all departure from God's statutes, deceit, and wickedness, and His judgment upon such re-affirms his own love for the Divine testimonies. The severities of God against the wicked, intensified his love for Him and His Word. Had He allowed men to sin with impunity, then His precepts would not have been fit objects of loving admiration. It is because God is glorious in holiness that He rids His Kingdom of rebels, and His temple of all who defile it, and His saints love Him all the more because of judgment of the ungodly.

My flesh trembleth . . . I am afraid, 119:120. David had just spoken of *love*, now he expresses *fear*, yet the one is consistent with the other. Fear which hath torment is cast out, but not the filial fear which leads to reverence and obedience. So David stands in solemn awe at the righteous judgments of God, which will make him afraid. The original for the first clause is far stronger, "The hair of my flesh stands up." See Job 4:15. "My flesh creeps," at the dispensation of punishment upon the wicked. Instead of exulting over his foes who fall under God's displeasure, David humbled himself, and stood in awe of Him before Whom the wicked cannot stand.

Henry Martyn, in his missionary *Journal,* made the following confession. "In prayer, in the evening I had such new and terrific views of

God's judgments upon sinners in Hell, that my flesh trembled for fear of them . . . I flew trembling to Jesus Christ as if the flames were taking hold of me! Oh! Christ will indeed save me or else I perish." These were the feelings of David whose faith consisted of a mixture of *fear* of God, and of *hope* in His mercy. "When we see the Great Refiner separating the precious from the vile, we may well feel a godly fear, lest we should be put away by Him, and left to be trodden under His feet."

AIN. Verses 121-128. We have now reached the sixteenth octave in this great Psalm, indicated by the Hebrew letter *AIN*—"a letter," says Barnes the commentator, "which cannot well be represented in the English alphabet, as there is, in fact, no letter in our language exactly corresponding to it. It would be best represented probably by what are called *breathings* in the Greek." This suggestion expresses the sentiment of the octave which is but the outbreathing for a stedfastness and soundness of heart and mind amid all the impiety and unbelief of a godless world, and the longing of the soul to have Jehovah stand by His Word—adherence to which warranted a plea of innocence.

I have done judgment and justice . . . Be surety for thy servant, 119:121, 122. A double reward was sought for the personal manifestation of Divine virtues, namely, deliverance from proud oppressors, and God as Surety for ever. Contemporary with Vladimir Monomachus and with Abelard, was David I, the just and merciful ruler of Scotland, who died May 24, 1153. As Aibred of Rievaulx tells the story of his death, the king received the *Viaticum*—venerated the famous black cross—and spent his last hours of conscious existence repeating verses from the Psalms, including 119:121. "I deal with the thing that is lawful and right. O give me not over unto mine oppressors."

These two verses are sometimes quoted as being conspicuous for the exclusion of any of the terms used to describe the Word in all other verses of the Psalm. But what we said on verse 84 applies to verse 121 where *judgment* appears, which is the same word given as *righteousness* in verse 123. *Judgment* and *Justice* are often paired together in Scripture, and when connected thus, the latter is as an epithet of the former, "I have done judgment justly exactly to a hair." In his judicial capacity David dealt out evenhanded justice. Many rulers of his time gave neither judgment or justice, others gave judgment without justice, but David gave both and saw to it that his sentences were executed.

> Do right and be a king,
> Be this thy brazen bulwark of defence,
> Still to preserve thy conscious innocence,
> Nor e'er turn pale with guilt.

As, however, the just judgment David executed was but the application of the judgments, or ordinances of God to the injustice of those oppressing him. This, then, would exclude this 121st verse being reckoned as without any mention of an epithet for God's Word. Twice he prays that God will effectively deal with oppressors. Having lived for what was right, he pleads for deliverance from those who would do him wrong. He had never oppressed others, and so appeals for protection against the injustice of others.

The Psalmist's prayer is enforced by the request, *Be surety for good.* See Prov. 11:15. David wanted God to be for him, what Christ is for all His redeemed ones, A Surety, Heb. 7:22. While verse 122 does not contain any reference to the Divine precepts whatever, it is yet most precious in its presentation of God as Surety for His servants. As Christ, our Surety, is the Living Word, then, perhaps, we do have a term in this verse of God's law. Having administered just judgment against those who had oppressed him, David, as the servant of God, asks not to be left to die by their Law. "Take up my interests and weave them into Thine own, and stand for me. As my Master, undertake Thy servant's cause, and represent me before the faces of the haughty men till they see what an august ally I have in the Lord my God." Thus, the first clause can be rendered, "Pledge Thy word as surety for my well-being." On the plea for God as Surety, Ellicott comments—

> Just as Judah became surety for the safety of Benjamin, Genesis 43:9, so the Psalmist asks God to be answerable for the servant who had been faithful to the covenant and stand between him and the attacks of the proud. So Hezekiah asks God to *undertake* for him against the threat of death, Isa. 38:14. There is also no doubt the further thought that the Divine protection would vindicate the profession which the loyal servant makes of his obedience, as in Job 17:3, where God is summoned as the only possible guarantee of the sufferer's innocence.

Mine eyes fail for thy salvation . . . Deal with thy servant, 119:123, 124, 125. The verdict of righteousness, given by the Judge on the proud oppressors, seemed to be long in coming. David wept, waited and watched for God's delivering hand, but relief tarried. He had looked to God alone, and looked long until his eyes ached, but God does not fail, nor do *His* eyes fail. He may not pay at the end of the week, but at last He pays, and utters the word of condemnation silencing all oppressors. One translation gives it, "I am dying for Thy deliverance." See verse 82. In times when the heart is burdened with care, the eyes express with amazing accuracy the distressed and anguished emotions of the soul.

David tells his Surety that the passing of sentence upon those oppressing him would be to the word of promised salvation, which the Lord has given in righteousness. Having meted out justice, he prays for "the word of justice" to be administered to his foes which would be the equivalent of the salvation desires. As God's servant, he had brought his service before Him only upon the ground of mercy, and seeks to be taught, still further, His statutes. Paul preached to Lydia, but God opened her heart, and this was what the servant sought from his Master, namely, to have his heart opened to receive His orders, and among the mercies David sought, this was the choicest. Three times over in this octave he calls himself, *Thy servant*, and as such he wanted God to speak for his ears were open to hear, about the spiritual understanding enabling him to know more fully the Divine testimonies. David desired every grace enabling him to serve his Master more fully. Said one of old, "That thou art *the servant of God*, thou shouldest regard as thy chiefest glory and blessedness."

It is time for thee, Lord, to work: for they made void thy law, 119:126. Those seeking to abolish the law were the proud oppressors of David. What he as King had done, he held Jehovah should do. As a servant it was always his time to work, and without delay he engaged in justice required upon offenders. Now he appeals to God to recognize that it was the time for Him to work against the workers, and the working of evil. The Psalmist felt that the extremity was God's opportunity, and reminded Him that it was time to declare that there was still a God of Righteousness in Israel.

To work is the Hebrew verb used absolutely for "to execute judgment," or "to administer justice by punishing the wicked." See Jerem. 28:23; Ezek. 31:11. Man had made void the law by utterly disregarding and scorning the authority of the Lawgiver Himself, and David pleads for the just punishment of such. It has been pointed out that the Hebrew word for *time* expresses emphatically *the proper time* for the Lord to do His own work; as if the Psalmist had said—

> It is not for us to prescribe the time and occasion for God to exercise His power, and to vindicate the authority of His own law; He does everything at the proper time, and He will at the proper season punish those *who made void His law*, and who have become notorious for their impiety and wickedness.

What must not be forgotten is the fact that God is always at work dealing with evil men and forces. Did not Jesus say, "My Father worketh hitherto, and I work," John 5:17? When He deems fit there are special manifestations of His power against those who make void and repeal His holy acts. It was a notion of ancient Jews that Messiah's coming would be when there was a time of great wickedness in the earth. See Mal. 3:1-3; 4:1-3. We live in an age when things are waxing worse and worse, and fast ripening for the scythe of God. May He, in mercy, grant a mighty spiritual upheaval ere the Savior returns to gather His redeemed ones out of the gross wickedness of earth.

I love . . . I hate, 119:127, 128. In these last two verses David returns to the love-hate expression he used at the opening of the previous octave, verse 113. If it was God's time to work, so it was David's time to love— to express a more vehement love for the law when evil men were slighting it, and to declare his sympathy with God in His hatred of everything false. The determined efforts of proud and impudent men to nullify God's Word and reject His claims, forced the Psalmist to express himself as he did. What they were despising became more dear to his heart.

> The dearer, for their rage,
> > Thy words I love and own,
> A wealthier heritage
> > Than gold and precious stones.

"Therefore I love," can be rendered, "Above everything I love thy commandments. Above gold and fine gold." Here David repeats the inestimable value of the Word he loved so sincerely, see verse 72, also Psalm 19:11. "As the wicked are hurt by the best things, so the godly are bettered by the worst. Saints sail with every wind." The most eminent saints in the Early Church were those of Caesar's household, who kept God's name where they lived where Satan's throne was, Phil. 4:22; Rev. 2:13.

The term *esteem* means "to walk in a straight way" and so the final verse can read, "Therefore I have walked in a straight way, according to thy precepts. Every false way (= faith) I hate." The LXX Version has it, "Therefore to all Thy commandments I was being directed. Every unjust path I hated." There was no compromising testimony to the integrity and value of Jehovah's precepts, even though some of them appeared to be distasteful. Note the twofold "Therefore," and the twofold "All," in these concluding verses. *ALL* is but a little word, but of large extent, and reveals David's high estimation of God's Word. The best of such love of truth was the contrary—hatred of sin and impiety. "Ye that love the Lord, hate evil." Loving the good with infinite intensity we must hate evil with the same intensity. "So far from any incompatibility between this love and hatred, they are the counterparts of each other—opposite poles of the same moral emotion."

PE. Verses 129-136. In the previous octave David prayed, "Give me understanding, that I may know thy testimonies," verse 125, and now confesses how wonderful they are both in their nature and effects. All the verses of this section begin with the 17th letter of the Hebrew alphabet, *P*, but each verse with a different word. With *P* in mind, Spurgeon says of these eight verses that they are Precious, Practical, Profitable, Power—Peculiarly so! The Word is peculiarly precious, seeing it is a testimony to God's character and will. This octave is heavy with the truth that such assurance brings its own light and comfort with it, to those who earnestly pray for them, and fills the heart with compassion for those who despise the words of His mouth.

Thy testimonies . . . Thy words . . . Thy commandments, 119:129-131. At the outset of our meditation on this Psalm, we indicated the particular nature of these different terms used of the same Divine Word. In addition to the triad in these verses other descriptions in the section are "Thy Name," "Thy Word," "Thy Precepts," "Thy Statutes," "Thy Law."

> *Thy Testimonies* demand Obedience.
> *Thy Words* prove Guidance and Wisdom.
> *Thy Commandments* satisfy inward longing.
> *Thy Word* offers direction and purity.
> *Thy Precepts* result in deliverance of man.
> *Thy Statutes* bring a benediction.
> *Thy Law* begets compassion for the lost.

Thy Testimonies, 119:129. "As His name is, so is He." God's name is *Wonderful*, Isa. 9:6, and His testimonies bear His character. Only those who know them, verse 125, deem them to be wonderful, and are so impressed by their marvel as to keep them in memory, and have their wonderful excellence charm the heart, and influence the life. "My soul doth keep them," as a greater treasure than gold or silver. The Bible itself is an astonishing and standing miracle both in its preparation and preservation, and like its Author, it is perfect. Psalm 19:7. St. Gregory called it, "The heart and soul of God."

The Book is a product of Divine knowledge, containing in it the *Credenda*—"the things which we are to believe," and the *Agenda*—"the things which we are to practice." It is both the breeder and feeder of grace. Martin Luther said of the two-edged sword which wounds the old Serpent, "Take away the word, and you deprive us of the sun." King Edward the Sixth, on the day of his coronation, was presented with three swords, signifying that he was monarch of three kingdoms. But the king said, there was one sword missing, and being asked by his counselors what it was, he answered, "The Holy Bible, which is the sword of the Spirit, and is to be preferred before these ensigns of royalty."

Another sovereign who highly esteemed God's testimonies, and kept them, was Robert, King of Sicily, who so prized them that he said to his friend, Petracha, "I protest, the Scriptures are dearer to me than my kingdom; and if I must be deprived of one of them, I had rather lose my diadem than the Scriptures."

David declared that he obeyed with his *soul*. Not only with head and hand did he keep the testimonies, but with his soul, his truest and most real self, held fast to them, and thus they became part and parcel of his life.

Thy Words, 119:130. In verse 133, the singular is used, here it is the plural—words of God in, and from, *The Word*. Henry Martyn, after he had translated Scripture into the language of people in India he labored among, confessed, "What do I not owe to the Lord for permitting me to take a part in the translation of His Word? Never did I see such wonders, and wisdom, and love, in the blessed Book, as since I have been obliged to study every expression, and it is a delightful reflection that death cannot deprive us of the pleasure of studying its mysteries."

The word *opening*, is, in the Hebrew, "door," "doorway." In Palestine, houses are mostly windowless, the light entering through the doorway. So light comes through God's Word as the sun's light through an Eastern door. "The first cause does not refer to the mechanical opening of the Book by the reader, but to the spiritual opening of its true sense by Divine illumination, to the mind which naturally cannot discern it." *Entrance*, then, means, an opening, unfolding, unveiling. Both *light* and *understanding* come through such an unveiling. Light manifests itself, and all things else. How do we see the sun, but by the sun, its own light? The same is true of Scripture. we see light in its light. Then it gives Understanding also—not merely knowledge, but the mental eye to appreciate the light.

The Divine Word, entering the chambers of the heart, is for the *simple*, or simple-hearted ones. In the Hebrew, *doorway* and *simple* are very much alike, and perhaps a word play is intended, corresponding to the proverb, "The *door* gives light to the *dull*." But *simple* does not describe those of the Simple Simon type, but those who are characterized by simplicity, who have a character opposed to all craftiness, underhandedness, and scheming. See Prov. 14:15, 18. How grateful we are that God gives understanding not to the wise, prudent, and skilled in letters, but to those who as children are willing to go into the Spirit's school to be taught, and learn that what is incomprehensible to the carnal mind, is adapted to every grade of enlightened intelligence.

Thy Commandments, 119:131. The wide open mouth implies an attitude of expectancy, see Job 29:23; Psalm 81:10. As for *panted*, same is a figure for "eagerly desired." The term *longed* is an Aramaic word found nowhere else in the Old Testament. All of these expressions reflect the inclination of David's soul after God's Word. *The opened mouth*, Ambrose said, was "the mouth of the inward man, which in effect is the heart." *Panted* is a metaphor taken from men scorched and sweltered with heat or from those who have run themselves out of breath in following something or someone they would overtake. Thus, if the former metaphor expresses the vehemency of David's love, this one indicates the earnestness of his pursuit: he was like a man gasping for breath, and sucking in the air, as he pursued his study of the Word.

Longed for. What yearning and desire are implied by the term. There was a day when, smitten with thirst, David longed for a drink of the well at Bethlehem, 1 Chron. 11:17. But his was a greater thirst for the water of the Word. Do we share David's estimation of Scripture, and is ours the same burning desire to know and obey all we read?

Look thou upon me . . . Order my steps . . . Deliver me, 119:132, 133, 134. This triple intercession carries with it the vehemence and intensity of soul so apparent in the three affirmations just considered. *Look,* implies "turn unto me," as if God had turned away from his servant because of sin, and he was therefore in need of His forgiving grace and mercy. The term "as thou usest to do," should read "according to the right of." The pardoning smile of God was David's not by custom but by right of God's ordained principles. There is always life in the Divine look. Wounded with sins, his own and others, and stripped by thieves of his virtues, the Psalmist pleads with God to turn to him in compassion, as He had promised to do when His children turn to Him. God had only one Son without sin, but He never had one without sorrow because of sin, and who, consequently had need for God to turn to them in mercy.

As can be seen, this 132nd verse is another of the very few in the Psalm that does not use one of the 10 terms, the Psalmist employs to describe Scripture. Yet note the phrase "love thy name." By *name* we understand the Being of God—all that He is in His attributes and actions, His Word and Work, and as such are only fully revealed through His Word, then, in a way, Scripture is implied in His august *Name* the saints love, as well as in verse 122.

As for David's second plea, "Order my steps in thy word," *order* means "direct" or "guide," and the Hebrew for "steps" is *feet* and is so rendered in 74:3 and 140:5. Both our *steps* and our *stops* are directed of the Lord according to His Word. In the next verse, David prays that he might be delivered from his oppressors who would have mastery over him. Here, in verse 133, he pleads that his own iniquity may not lord it over him. We often sing, "I dare not take one step without Thine aid"— and the God-directed life is ever a God-glorifying one. How blessed to know that He has promised to keep the feet of His saints.

The original has the thought of a *firm* step, in contrast to walking with a halting or unsteady step. May ours ever be steps butted and bounded by a Divine rule! It is only thus that we can be kept free from sin's dominion. The observation of Chrysostom as to such dominion is, "He does not say let it not tyrannize over me, but, let it not reign over you; that is, when you suffer it to have a quiet reign on your heart."

The third plea for deliverance from oppressors had already been made several times, but the particular request here was for *redemption* from them, so that David could keep God's precepts, seeing their oppression was a hindrance to his obedience. Two Hebrew words are used for *redeem*, the one meaning to set free by paying a ransom or by providing a substitute; the other word primarily applies to the setting free of slaves. Perhaps the latter sense is to be understood in this 134th verse, where David intercedes that he might not be left in the bonds of his haughty tyrants, but be kept free to obey the Divine statutes.

Make thy face to shine . . . Rivers of waters run down mine eyes, 119:135, 136. In these two concluding verses of the octave we have two faces, namely, the benign glorious face of God, and the tear-stained face of His servant caused by the rejection of God's law by the wicked. David wanted to walk in the light of His countenance and thus be further taught the royal statutes. Oppressors darkened and saddened the Psalmist's life, and so he prays for the shining face of God to banish the gloom, and affirms that the favor of God's smile will be experienced in a fuller revelation of Himself through His Word. This request for God to make His face to shine is implied in the previous desire, "Look thou upon me." Richard Alleine, devotional writer who died in 1681, said in his volume *Heaven Opened*—

> God hath many ways of teaching; he teaches by book, he teaches by His fingers, He teaches by His rod; but His most comfortable and effectual teaching is by the light of His eye—*O send out Thy light, and Thy truth, let them lead me!*

But the gracious smile of Jehovah did not prevent David's face from registering his deep pain and compassion because of those who disobeyed and rejected the Divine law. See Prov. 21:1; Lam. 3:48. How deep was the poet's concern over those who failed to keep God's commands! We often sing most heartily the Gospel hymn—

> Rescue the perishing, care for the dying,
> Weep o'er the erring one

—but how many tears have we shed over the perishing, and wept over the erring ones in our own family or over those at home and abroad who have not experienced that Jesus is mighty to save? If our Evangelism was not so dry-eyed, there would be fewer who are perishing in their sin. The English idiom for "rivers of waters," is *floods of tears*, and in his torrents of woe, David was a forerunner of his Greater Son, "Who beheld the city and wept." We are indeed journeying on with the Man of Sorrows when we come to sorrow over the sins of others.

David's tears were those of sympathy, and pity—Sympathy with God as he saw His holy law despised and broken; Pity for those thus drawing upon themselves the wrath of God because of their rejection of His Word. Matthew Henry says that "the sins of sinners are the sorrows of saints. We must mourn for that which we cannot mend." If we fail to grieve for the wicked, their sin may become ours. See Ezek. 9:8; 1 Cor. 5:2. May grace be ours to keep our hearts free from sin, but our eyes ever wet with tears of compassion over those whose hearts are not right with God!

> Lord, let me weep for nought by sin,
>   And after none but Thee,
> And then I would, O that I might!
>   A constant weeper be.

TSADDI. Verses 137-144. All verses in this octave begin with this 18th letter of the Hebrew alphabet, which is a term meaning *justice* or *righteousness.* That there is a play in the strophe of such a virtue is evidenced by the twofold use of *righteous,* and the threefold *righteousness.* The central theme of these eight verses is that the Word of God is a law of rectitude. Spurgeon notes that the initial with which each verse commences in the Hebrew is *P,* and the key-word is *Purity.* The whole scope of this section is eloquent with the truth that even the young and the inexperienced can stand strong and steadfast amid the troubles of the world, if theirs is a faith in the purity, truth, and righteousness of God's law. Here is unfolded for our learning the righteousness of Jehovah and the reminder of the struggles of a holy soul in reference to such righteousness.

Righteous art thou . . . Righteous and very faithful, 119:137, 138. As *upright* is but a form of righteous—the *right way up*—we have a righteous trial in these first two verses of the section, which provide the setting for the sermon that follows on the nature of righteousness. Gibbon gives us a most appealing historical association with verse 137 in the death of Emperor Maurice, who, by this Psalm, was encouraged to bow to the will of God. During the 20 years he ruled the Roman Empire, he had shown virtues, marking him out to succeed Tiberius II. But the army turned against him and in 602 he fled, with his wife and children, to Chalcedon, to escape the fury of the deformed and disfigured Phoeas.

But Maurice did not long remain in safety for by order of Phoeas, he and his 5 sons were seized and executed. He was the last to die. As, one by one, the boys were murdered before his eyes, the noble father cried aloud, with each stroke of the sword, "Righteous art Thou, O Lord, and true is Thy judgment." David, too, came to know by experience that the Lord is a righteous God; that He is impartial in His justice whether dealing with angels, saints or sinners. The poet who here extols God for His righteousness intermeddled with forbidden fruit, was driven from his palace, saw his concubines defiled, and his own son slain. Yet with these, and other calamities in mind, he could write, "Righteous art Thou, O Lord!"

The Psalmist recognized that God's will is the rule of justice, and that therefore as one who had been made the recipient of mercy, he did not cavil nor question His actions, but ascribed to God perfect righteousness. To him, God was always like His judgments, right, and actively right, or righteous. Coming from a righteous God, His judgments and testimonies reflect the virtues of their Author. What soul-comfort this truth imparts, especially in times of unjust treatment by others. See Rev. 16:5-7.

God's Word is His command, for all His precepts and promises are backed and inspired by His authority, and carry the imprint of royal omnipotence. The two qualifying terms, *righteous* and *very faithful*, are rich in their significance. The original of verse 138 is more forceful and can be rendered, "Thou hast commanded righteousness, thy testimonies are truth exceedingly." Some expositors have "faithfulness exceedingly" or "much faithfulness" here! The statutes God has commanded are "full of righteousness," just as they are "faithful to the uttermost." See Psalms 7:6; 119:144.

My zeal . . . Thy Word, 119:139, 140. In the last two verses David affirmed his faith in his righteous and faithful God and in His statutes bearing the Divine character, now he speaks of the vehement all-consuming flame in his heart because of those who had forgotten and forsaken God's words. Such zeal was the *esprit de corps* of the Kingdom of Heaven reflected in David's feelings over those dishonoring Jehovah by slighting His authoritative, pure words. See Psalm 69:6. The LXX Version has it *"Thy* zeal," meaning "zeal for thee," a pattern of Him of whom it is said, "The zeal of the Lord of Hosts hath eaten me up." *Consumed* has the sense of being "undone," "destroyed." David's zeal was not of the flesh, but similar to that the disciples experienced, when their hearts burned within them, Luke 24. The Psalmist's holy anger was drawn out as he saw the wicked denying and rejecting the rule of Scripture. His heart took fire by striking such cold flints. "Cold blasts make a fire to flame the higher, and burn the hotter."

David's zeal burned the fiercer as he thought of the absolute purity of the words men rejected. *Very pure* means "tried," "refined," "purified," like gold in the furnace. Through all human writings there runs the assertion that the Scriptures hands wrote are absolutely perfect, without dross of vanity and fallibility. The Word has been tried, and has stood the test. See Psalms 12:6; 18:30. Literally the clause means, "purged by trial," and, as Ellicott observes, "It is not only the evidence, but the *proved* excellence of the Divine Word, which is the object of love and adoration here."

No wonder David loved "the word of truth," which is without spot or blemish. He could not have been the servant of God had he not loved the

Word, without any mixture of error, others despised. But not only is it "very pure," free from all base admixture but the *purifier* of all who embrace it. The constant study of Scripture conveys something of its own inherent purity to the student. Said Jesus to His disciples, "Now are ye clean *through* the word I have spoken unto you." Thus David's heart made pure by the Word, was knitted to it, and sought to practice it, because it was pure to the very highest degree. Before he died in 1794, Sir William Jones wrote—

> Before I knew the Word of God in spirit and in truth, for it's great antiquity, its interesting narratives, its biography, its pure morality, its sublime poetry, in a word, for its wonderful and beautiful variety, I preferred it to all other books; but since I have entered into its spirit, like the Psalmist, *I love it above all things for its purity*; and desire, whatever else I read, it may tend to increase my knowledge of the Bible, and strengthen my affection for its divine and holy truths.

I am small and despised . . . Thy law is truth, 119:141, 142. Here David compares his own insignificance alongside of the mighty, eternally righteous law of God. *Small* does not denote "young" as the LXX Version translates the term, but of "no consequence," or "despised." Historically, he may have had in mind that "devotion to the Law more than counterbalances the drawback of belonging to a now unimportant and despised nation, struggling against great Eastern Powers." Still, the language David used was applicable to himself as an individual. His beginning was small, and his occupation as a young man was humble. He was never very *big* in his own esteem, and during his days with Saul, and after, he was held in high esteem by those who despised him. Being counted as the offscouring of all things has been the common lot of those who loved, and never forget, the precepts of God.

What we greatly admire about the Psalmist's piety is that, no matter how esteemed, he was calm, never carried away by flattery, nor overcome by shame. If despised, he was more in earnest about loving the despised commandments of God. The more poor and despicable his condition, the greater cause never to forget the consolations God's precepts provide. As he served a God Whose righteousness was everlasting in nature, he had no fear regarding what men thought or did. God's law was *truth*, and would prevail against the lies of men.

William Lawrence Merry, U.S.A. minister to Nicaragua, Salvador and Costa Rica, 1897-1900, and then for a number of years Commander of steamships on the Atlantic and Pacific Oceans, often quoted as his favorite text, "Thy righteousness is an everlasting righteousness, thy law is truth." Another translation has it, "Thy righteousness is right for ever and Thy law is truth." After ascribing righteousness to God in the opening verse of the octave, David now declares that, like Himself, God's righteousness is eternal, unchanging and unchangeable and enduring world without end. The expressions given are absolute for God's word is truth—the chief, only, pure, and the whole truth. Living, as we do, in a most unrighteous age, and surrounded by those who are unrighteous, may we be found living in the glorious truth of the perpetuity of God's righteousness.

Trouble and anguish has taken hold on me . . . I shall live, 119:143, 144. What, exactly, was the nature of the Psalmist's distress we are not told. Perhaps some affliction may have arisen "from his circumstance, or from the cruelty of his enemies, or from his own internal conflicts." What is evident is the double distress apprehending him—*trouble* without and anguish *within*, or as Paul put it, "Without were fightings and within were fears." The phrase, "take hold on me," is impressive, and in the original means, "have found me," as dogs track down a wild beast hiding or fleeing. The Psalmist had no need to find trouble and anguish—they found him.

Yet, is it not admirable that whatever his *distress* was, the commandments of God were his *delights*—note the plural? Aquinas said, "Men are good and bad, as the objects of their delights are: they are good who delight in good things, and they are evil who delight in evil things." Those who heaped trouble upon David delighted in their ignoble task, but he, himself, found refuge in delighting himself in the commands of Jehovah. In his distress they were his delight—in pain, his pleasure. Is it any wonder then that he reaches such a climax and a prayer?

> The righteousness of thy testimonies is everlasting
> Give me understanding, and I shall live.

The more David meditated upon the Word, the more detailed his description of it becomes. having affirmed that God's testimonies were righteous, then that they were everlasting he then went on to say that the *righteousness* of the said testimonies is everlasting. God's *moral law* enshrined in these *testimonies*, was not made for one people, or for one particular time: it is as imperishable, and of endless obligation. Hence the Psalmist's prayer for a deeper understanding of it, in order that he might live by it. "To live without understanding, is not to live the life of a man, but to be dead while we live." The understanding of God's testimonies is the only way to live, spiritually and eternally. *I shall live*, and by so living we are kept from those sins which deserve and bring death; and by living unto God as He reveals His will through His Word, we prepare ourselves for the fuller life in Glory.

KOPH. Verses 145-152. Actually, this octave and the following one are the same in nature in that both of them constitute an earnest prayer for the grace of faithfulness in distress and tribulation. In the eight verses before us David presents the time and manner of his devotions and how he interceded for deliverance in times of great need, believing that although answers seem to tarry, God would respond to his urgent call for help. Spurgeon suggests that this section shows—

1. How David prayed, 145.
2. What he prayed for, 146.
3. When he prayed, 147.
4. How long he prayed, 148.
5. What he pleaded, 149.
6. What happened, 156.
7. How he was rescued, 151.
8. How he witnessed to truth, 152.

I cried with my whole heart . . . I cried unto thee, 119:145, 146.   A distressed praying soul often expresses itself in warm, liquid pain—which tears are. The intense intercessions of Jesus were accompanied by "strong crying and tears." No wonder God heard Him! John Welch, of covenant times, went into his garden night after night as a covering, and cried as he prayed, "O God, give me Scotland, or I'll die!" Thus, vehement feeling will beget strong cries in prayer. But there are saints who cannot express themselves in this way. Alexander Peden, another Covenanter, was accustomed to pray, as if he had been engaged in calm conversation with a friend.

This brings us to say that the term *cried* used 3 times in the first 3 verses of the section do not imply that "rivers of water ran down the face," as David prayed. The word should be *call*, and so the R.V. gives us "I called," in each case. As he called with his "whole heart," and crying with the heart is of greater value than visible tears, for heart-cries, as of a creature in pain, are the essence of effectual prayer. Seeking with his whole heart to be obedient to God's statutes, he had confidence that God would hear his call. "He could not expect the Lord to hear him if he did not hear the Lord." So David backs up his importunate request, with a holy resolution.

In these two verses we have two petitions, which although brief, the whole compass of language could not make them more comprehensive. *Hear me—Save me.* David uses the title Jehovah, and desires to be heard in the name of such an all-prevailing Advocate. His whole heart is in the plea, "Hear me." Then, because Jehovah was also his Salvation, he called, "Save me," and he interceded thus knowing that He also could save, deliver, and comfort. These short utterances to a throne of grace were accompanied by the double vow to *keep*, or obey, the Word of God. If we hear Him in His precepts and obey His call, then ours is the assurance that He will hear us when we call upon His name.

The dawning of the morning . . . The night watches, 119:47, 148.   The

English word *prevent* used twice in these verses does not mean to hinder, or stop, as we now commonly employ it. The old English for the word, implied *anticipate*, or *forestall*, or *come to meet*. See Psalm 79:8. The sense of the first clause of verse 147 then, is "I was up before the morning and call." Because he hoped for some word from the Lord, David was up at twilight. Being able to rise at midnight to praise God for His goodness, verse 62, it was no hardship for him to rob himself of sleep in order to bow his knees as early morn dawned, to meet with God before he faced the agitating cares of the day. This early riser wanted to seek from God the gift to rightly understand His Word and then teach it to others.

David also spoke of himself as late taking rest, as well as rising early. Anticipating the regular division of the night he prepared to meditate in the Word. "My eyes forestall the night watches," meaning, " I am awake, meditating on Thy Word before the watchman announces by trumpet, a new watch, so much is my mind set on Thy law." A peaceful yet shining light of the Church was Robert Sanderson, Bishop of Lincoln, who died in 1662; and whose biography was written by Izaak Walton, and which was, perhaps, the most charming of his well-known biographies.

Walton describes how the Bishop loved the Psalter, "his treasury," as he called it, and made frequent use of the Psalms. "As the holy Psalmist said, that *his eyes should prevent the dawning of the day and the night watches*, by *meditating on God's Word*, so it was Dr. Sanderson's constant practice every morning to entertain his first waking thoughts with a repetition of those very Psalms that the Church had appointed to be constantly read in the daily morning service." Can we say that we prefer study to slumber; that we are to forego necessary sleep for necessary study? Such sacrificial meditation is often connected with fervent prayer: it is the fuel sustaining the flame.

Hear my voice . . . They are far . . . Thou art near, 119:149-152. David used his voice as he presented his earnest pleas for Divine help. Doubtless he had his seasons of quiet meditation when he was silent before the Lord. But here, he heard himself speak and he called upon God to hear what he was saying. The original is a little more emphatic and reads, *O do hear*! Then the double "according" is significant in verse 149. "According unto thy lovingkindness." Surely, *lovingkindness* is one of the sweetest words in our language. Had it not been for the possession of this precious virtue on God's part, prayer would have been impossible on our part. "According to thy judgment" is given in the Anglican Prayer Book as "According as Thou art wont," seeing that the Hebrew noun for *judgment* means "custom." It is ever God's custom to quicken those who call up Him.

Then it is profitable to combine and compare the phrases *They draw nigh—Thou art near*. "They, the wicked mischief makers, are *near* with their temptations to sin and their hindrance to virtue, and departure from the law. *Thou* art *near* with the aid and support of Thine established and true commandments." *They* were *nigh* to destroy—*Jehovah* was *nigh* to deliver from all malicious scheming. The ways of those wicked men were false—God's Word was true. *Thou art near!* May grace be ours to realize and rest in such blessed nearness!

Having vowed to be more obedient to the Divine statutes, to constantly hope and meditate in them, and to believe that they are as true as God Himself, is it any wonder that David ends this octave with the triumph of faith over all dangers and temptations? Concerning the revelation of God's will, and His counsels for His servants, he had known them from infancy having been like Timothy, brought up on the Scriptures in a godly home. He also knew them by the inspiration of the Holy Spirit, by his own experience, as well as that of others, and now rejoices anew in the fact that all the truths he had come to know were unalterable and eternal.

Thou hast founded them forever! "Founded" means that the Word of God is well grounded, settled and established, as immutable as the Divine Author Himself. David found of old that God has founded His testimonies of old, and that they would stand unmovable throughout the ages. It is most probable that the poet wrote this unique Psalm when he had grown gray and faced the sunset years of life, and valued more than ever the guidance and comfort of Scripture. Thus, as an established saint he praises God yet once again for His admonitions, He had eternally established. May we be found venturing every hope for eternity upon "The Impregnable Rock of Holy Scripture," as William Gladstone named the Bible!

RESH. Verses 153-160. The heart-cry for deliverance from affliction prominent in the section just considered is accentuated in this octave. In great distress David draws still nearer to Jehovah, and, stating his case, invokes His help with more boldness and expectation. He also affirms that the *Word*, an epithet he repeats 3 times, was his consolation in times of trial, desolation, and persecution. In 3 verses, he gives us 7 different descriptions of Scripture. Key-verses to note are *Quicken me*, used 3 times; *Deliver me*, twice; *Consider me*, twice. Throughout the section David pleads his intimate union with the Lord's cause as a reason why He should undertake for His loyal servant, who made such a cause his own.

Consider . . . Deliver . . . Plead . . . Quicken, 119:153, 154. The word *consider* means "reflect upon," or "behold." In afflictions it is a comfort to know that we have loved ones, friends who weep with us, when we weep. How more consoling it is to know that the merciful eye of our heavenly Friend, Who sticketh closer than a brother, beholds our need and with a powerful hand is ready to deliver. Those prayers of David are so penned with such heavenly wisdom that they are convenient for the state of each one of us to pray, "Behold *mine* affliction." See Psalm 9:13.

As for the term *deliver*, the particular word in verse 153 is different from that employed in the next verse. Here, the original means, "to rescue as with a gentle hand," for David is praying about his peculiar trial during which he never forgot God's law, or acted contrary to it. He asked, not for any hasty, dramatic rescue, but for a full consideration of his sorrow that would lead God to deliver him from in His own way and time. As he had not forgotten to meditate upon, love and obey God's Word, he knew that He would be faithful to His promise and not leave him long in his trouble.

The Psalmist then goes on to describe how God can vouchsafe His servant deliverance, namely, as an Advocate pleading his cause; by standing in his stead, and by making his fight His own. As one of the powerful Redeemer's clients, David pleads with respect to the misery of his condition. *Deliver*, in 154, is *Gaal*, meaning, to redeem, or to save by avenging. Thus we have God's double office, that of the *Advocate* able to defend David when arraigned before the tribunal of wicked men, then as the *Redeemer*, all-powerful to rescue him from all who falsely accuse him

Actually, there are three requests in this verse—"Plead my cause," or vindicate my innocence of the lies of the wicked.

> "Deliver me," as my near Kinsman.
> "Quicken me." This is the special aid he asks for because of his own weakness.

And the reason and ground of these three pleas is "According to Thy Word." David had rested upon the promises of God to help His own in time of need and distress, and now desires Him to act accordingly. What a mighty plea this was! No promise of His has failed, nor could possibly fail.

Wicked . . . Judgments . . . Persecute love . . . Transgressors, 119:155-158. In these bold verses David describes the nature and the crimes of his enemies. *Salvation*! What music sweeter than the music of a thousand worlds is in this word! But for the *wicked*, there can be nothing but condemnation all the time they fail to seek the Savior, the statutes reveal. The wicked are those who persevere in evil, and place themselves beyond the pale of hope. Yet God is ever merciful—great in tender mercies—and ready to forgive as soon as the wicked turn to Him in penitence and faith. When we think and speak of the damnable conditions of the wicked, let us remember that it is only because of God's grace that we are not as they.

Celerinus in Cyprian's Epistles acquaints a friend with his great grief for the apostasy of a woman through fear of persecution; which afflicted him so much, that at the Feast for Easter—Queen for Feasts in the primitive Church—he wept night and day, and resolved never to know a moment's delight, till through the mercy of God she should be recovered.

Those who actually assailed David, or secretly abhorred him, he counted as his persecutors, and enemies. These were the unscrupulous men who constantly hounded him, yet they failed to move him from his constancy and integrity. Although a man after God's own heart, he had those who hated him, even as his Greater Son Who was "born in the city of David" had. But in the teeth of cruel, persistent foes the Psalmist did not stray from God's testimonies for they were his shelter amid the malice surrounding him. The word for *enemies* means adversaries, or those who tried to hem David in. But they failed for he was a God-enclosed man.

Then because they were also transgressors, who failed to recognize and obey the testimonies as God's Word, David was *grieved*. The word *transgressors* means "traitors," or treacherous men. The term for *grieved* is a far stronger word in the Hebrew. It implies "was filled with loathing at, or sickened with disgust." As John Keble expresses it—

> The recreants I survey,
> And loathing turn away.

Perhaps David was sick and sorry, not only to see such sinners, spitting out their enmity not only upon him, but God's Word, but because he saw some tendencies in himself, over which, by grace, he had victory. See Job 42:6. This 158th verse can be rendered, "When I behold those who act treacherously I loathe, am disgusted and indignant with them."

"I beheld the transgressors, and I loathed them, abhorred them, contended with; but not so much because they were mine enemies, as because they were Thine." "They kept not Thy Word."

Philip Doddridge once preached on this verse which greatly influenced Colonel Gardner, whose sad end we have already described, as where *Life of Colonel Gardner* reveals the friendship between these two men. Doddridge wrote a hymn on verse 158, of which we cite two stanzas—

> Arise, my tenderest thoughts arise,
> To torrents melt my streaming eyes;
> And thou, my heart, with anguish feel
> Those evils which thou canst not heal.

> My God, I feel the mournful scene;
> My bowels yearn as the dying men,
> And fain my pity would reclaim,
> And snatch the firebrands from the flames.

Thy precepts . . . Thy lovingkindness . . . Thy righteous judgments, 119:159, 160. What glorious affirmations these final verses of the octave contain! Having called upon God to consider his affliction, David reminds God to consider how he loves His precepts, and loved them so much as to be grieved by those who failed to love them. He did not beg God to consider how he *performed* His precepts but how deeply he *loved* them.

"Thy law do I love," 119:113. And because he was grieved over the ways of the wicked, but loved God's ways himself, he prays for Jehovah to quicken him "according to thy lovingkindness," even as he had just prayed to be quickened, "according to thy word."

As the answer to the slanderous accusations of his enemies which were the great sting of his sorrow, David prayed that he might be quickened to outlive the animosity of his accusers, and he believed that because of His lovingkindness and tender mercy God would hear his prayer to keep the heavenly flame burning within his heart. As we have already seen the Psalmist often used this prayer for quickening grace and same was no *vain repetition* for each time it left his lips it was enlivened with ardent, abundant faith and with the vehemency of deep affection. See verses 25, 37, 40, 88, 107, 149, 154, 156, 159.

Thus quickened David ends this octave in the same vein as he did the last, namely by extolling the veracity of God's Word. "Thy word is true." He might be surrounded by liars, whose charges were false, but the truth of God has rung true since it was first uttered and written. It was true before even man was true to it. Some read the phrase as "Thy word is true from the head," that is, true all through from top to bottom. "Sum and substance, word and words." Scripture has been and will ever remain true and pure. Not only was the *beginning* of God's revelation faithful; it is *all* faithful, and, consequently, "All thy righteous ordinances are ever-enduring." Rotherham renders this last verse, "The sum of thy Word is truth, and age-abiding is every one of thy righteous regulations." Is it not comforting to know that God has never had to regret or to retract, amend or reverse any word of His, and that every word bearing the imprint of His character will outlive the stars?

SCHIN. Verses 161-168. In this 21st octave we have a prayer for deliverance from causeless persecution on the part of the powerful forces of this world, and a testimony to the peace and joy of those who thus maligned the love for God's Word imparts. All who keep Jehovah's law have an inner serenity even when surrounded by those seeking to destroy it. The verses, according to Bullinger, are made up of a repeated alternation—

Contrastive Statement, 161—Praise, "Thy" 162.
Contrastive Statement, 163—Praise, "Thy" 164.
Contrastive Statement, 165—Prayer, "Thy" 166-168.

Without a cause . . . standeth in awe, 119:161. David's persecutors, even though they were *princes*, did not cause him to tremble with fear. He only stood in awe of God's Word, and not of rulers in whom it was not safe to place any confidence, Psalm 118:9. Dr. Witton Davies says that by *princes* are "probably meant the King and Court of Syria, or perhaps

Israelitish nobles who had adopted the religion of the conqueror and had been appointed judges." An indication of the national character of this Psalm is seen in the way the whole community suffered from the intrigues and violence of princes.

As peers of the Realm they should have acted more nobly toward one of their own rank. If they fail to act justly when faced with the innocent, who is there then to defend the guiltless? It took the sting out of false accusations heaped upon David to know that he had in no way opposed the power and authority of the princes whose persecution of him were "without cause," or without any good reason for it. The clause can mean "to no purpose" and suggests the reading, "They gain nothing by it for I stand firm in my respect for the law." How admirable was the confession of Philip Doddridge, the renowned hymnist who wrote—

> I settle it as an established point with me that the more diligently and faithfully I serve Christ, the greater reproach and the more injury I must expect. I have drunk deep of the cup of slander and reproach of late, but I am in no way discouraged; no, nor by, what is much harder to bear, the unsuccessfulness of my endeavors to mend this bad world.

When Jesus came, He found Himself hated and persecuted *without a cause* by the religious princes of His day, and since Pentecost those who refused to obey the edicts of godless monarchies found themselves persecuted *without a cause*.

But there was no qualm of fear in David's heart seeing his heart was inflamed with love and reverence for God's Word. Such an *awe* killed any fear of crowns and scepters in the mind of one who perceived a more majestic royalty in the Divine King's commands. The term *awe* does not mean a slavish fear or dread, but a holy reverence or godly fear—a loving trembling of the heart which God ever respects. Archbishop Cranmer who, alas! was not as fearless of royalty as David, was, and suffered for his timidity, and in 1555 was martyred, yet had a profound reverence of the Word, he wrote much about. Speaking to students he said—

> I would advise you all, that come to the reading or hearing of this Book, which is the Word of God, the most precious jewel, and the most holy relic that remaineth upon earth, that you bring with you the fear of God, and that ye do it with all due reverence, and use your knowledge thereof, not the vain glory of frivolous disputation, but to the honor of God, increase of virtue and edification both of yourselves and others.

Thy word . . . thy law . . . thy righteous judgments, 119:162-164. The terms, "Thy word" and "Thy law" each occur twice in the section, as does "Thy testimonies." Such repetitions emphasize the nature of God's statutes. Although David trembled at the Word because of its Divine Author and authority, he yet rejoiced over it as a person finding great treasure. See Isa. 9:3. Discovery of fresh truth came as a glittering prize, which, miser-like, he could have kept to himself but shared all his discoveries of spiritual wealth with others, as his Psalms prove. To Martin Luther, all other books were as waste paper when compared to Scripture. But let us not forget the treasures here to be found. David did not find his great spoil on the surface, but had to dig prayerfully and persistently to find it. God's nuggets of gold are not usually found unexpectedly.

Different feelings, however, were the Psalmist's for that which was utterly detestable to him, and for which he used a double expression to describe his inexpressible loathing—*I hate* and *abhor lying*. While princes had lied against him, it was not so much falsehood in conversation, as perversity in faith and doctrine he had in mind. Not only did he *hate* it, nor simply *abhor* such form of lying, but *hate and abhor* it, thereby strengthening and increasing the sense, making it more vehement. *Sin* has its name from the Hebrew word *sana*, "to hate," which is the word David used here, because lying is the sin most of all to be hated.

The only security the poet had against falling into such a sin was faith in God, Who cannot lie, and in love for His Word which is true through and through. Twice over David declared his *love* for the Word—a love as ardent as the hate he felt toward those who would turn its Divine promises into a lie. "Thy law do I love"—"I love them exceedingly." He obeyed God's law, not by way of duty, but because of his deep, unutterable affection for it. "True men love truth, and hate lying." This *love* and *hate* combination was a favorite way with David in describing his opposite feelings toward truth and error, 119:127, 128. Both the *love* and *hate* in this 163rd verse are contagious, and when they are sanctified, to widen their influence the better.

Because the Word he dearly loved was so true from the beginning, with its judgments ever righteous, David found himself praising God for His law, seven times a day. Although monks came to observe canonical hours, and practiced the actual *seven* hours for praise and worship, it is to be doubted whether the Psalmist meant seven prescribed times to praise God. Seven in Scripture is a round number, Lev. 26:18, and was a number with sacred association for the Hebrews, Prov. 24:16; Matt. 18:21. Elsewhere we find *three* times as the stated occasions of prayer, Psalm 55:17.

It would seem that the number is to be thought of as meaning "often," "repeatedly." It is the number denoting spiritual perfection, and as used here can imply frequently, or without limit. A definite number is put for an indefinite exercise of heart. Whenever David found in the Word some precious gem of truth, he instinctively and immediately praised God for his find. Whenever a Scripture gripped his soul, a song leapt to his lips.

"Do we praise God seven times a day? Do we praise Him once in seven days?"

Thy law . . . Thy salvation . . . Thy commandments . . . Thy Testimonies . . . Thy precepts, 119:165-168. This last half of the octave is laden with the Psalmist's unfailing love for, and obedience to, the revealed will of God. Twice over he speaks of *loving* the Divine law, and thrice of keeping, or doing what it required. Where can we find a more charming comprehensive verse in Scripture than the 165th one? Think of these expressive terms: *Great peace; Love thy law; Nothing shall offend them.* What a wonderful triad of truth is compressed into these nine words!

Great peace. God is *great*, and greatly to be praised, and everything He supplies bears the seal of His greatness. In spite of his great persecution by the wicked, David experienced great peace, a treasure none could rob him of. It was a notable saying of St. Bernard that, "The pleasures of a good conscience are the Paradise of souls, the joy of angels, a garden of delights, a field of blessing, the temple of Solomon, the Court of God, the habitation of the Holy Spirit."

The precious Hebrew word for "peace"—*shalom*—signifies, not only peace of heart and conscience, but outward *felicity, prosperity, healthfulness, safety*, the *completion* and *consummation* of every good thing—all of which was in the mind of one Hebrew in his salutation to another—"Peace be with thee," or "May all things be prosperous with thee." Every blessing associated with fear was implied in the greeting, *Shalom lakha.*

Love Thy law. Here we have the secret and condition of God's bountiful peace. We must strive to keep a law because of the fear of a penalty in disobeying it. But when we keep God's law because we *love* it we indicate that it is already part of us, having entered into the moral texture of our being. It may sound strange to say, "*Love* thy law," yet this is the only way true divine life can become ours. As we have seen in verse 163, David expressed his own personal love for the law, as he often had done, verses 159, 167, etc.

Nothing shall offend them. What a tremendous claim to make! "It must needs be that offenses come, but then lovers of the law are peacemakers, and so neither give nor take offense." But the original for *offend* implies "stumbling block." When saints love the law, and walk in the light of it, stumbling blocks are seen and avoided. "There is none occasion of stumbling in him," 1 John 2:10. Both the Hebrew and Greek words for "offend" denote usually something which causes *others* to fall. Thus it is suggested that the sense of the verse is like this, "Those who love thy law have much happiness, and no fear, or distracting thoughts can disturb their inner joy."

Perhaps finding no hindrance because of a love for God's law may be more in the form of a wish, for is it not the fact that the faithful did *not*, and do not, stumble? This is why we like Rotherham's rendering of this sweet verse, "Blessings in abundance have lovers of thy law, and nothing to make them stumble."

The salvation . . . all my ways, 119:166-168. In these three verses David uses four terms to describe God's Word. He told Jehovah that he hoped for His salvation, seeing he had practiced His commandments. As a lover of the Lord, and of His law, he was already the Lord's, saved by His matchless grace. The first clause of verse 166 was likely borrowed from good old Jacob, see Genesis 49:18. The particular *hope* expressed here was perhaps deliverance and preservation from his foes, or personal severance from something in his life preventing fuller obedience to the word and will of God. Ours is "the blessed hope," a most vital and complete aspect of our salvation, for when Jesus comes we are to be delivered from the entire presence of sin within and around. *Done* and *Kept*—twice repeated indicate that those who are saved should be walking Bibles, having the written Word not only as a rule of knowledge, but a rule of obedience. And when we love the truth *exceedingly*, our soul delights to obey.

The last phrase of this octave is both solemn and comforting. Job could say, "Doth not God see my way, and count all my steps?" 31:4. Conscious of the truth, "Thou God seest me," we experience its sobering influence on heart and life. It is an aid to holiness to remember that "the very wounds shame would hide" are seen by the eye of God. Yet there is also consolation in the fact that He is the All-seeing God, and that all our ways are before Him Who knows the end from the beginning. Augustine said, "I may hide thee from my eye, but not myself from thine eye." We cannot read the future, but He knows the ways before us, and as we keep His precepts, He will guide us with His eye. When the captains of Alexander the Great met in counsel, if he was not present his empty chair was set before them, which remembered them to act as if he was present. We are ever before God to whom nothing is hid, but whether the ways before us are rough or smooth, He will be our constant Companion and Helper as we seek to acknowledge Him in all our ways. We may not know the way, but we have the Guide, so all will be well until the end of the journey is reached.

TAU. Verses 169-176. We have now reached the last division of this very long Psalm which is indicated by the last letter of the Hebrew alphabet—TAU—corresponding to our *t* or *th*. After reading so much about David's enemies in previous octaves of the Psalm, he has no mention of them in these final eight verses, in which he seems to be taken up exclusively with God. Here his lips are taken up with Prayers and Praises and—

> Prayers and Praises go in pairs,
> He hath Praises who hath Prayers.

Of this concluding section, William Cowper wrote, "Many prayers hath he made to God in this Psalm: now in the end he prays for his prayers, that the Lord would let them come before Him. Some men send out prayers, but God turns them into sin, and puts them away back from him: therefore David seeks favor to his prayers." Assured from the Word that answers would come in due time, he prayed earnestly for revival, for the bestowal of the gifts of understanding, assistance, favor, grace and safety from God. Owning his weakness and resting in Jehovah alone for support, the Psalmist's petitions gather force and fervency, and breaking into the inner circle of Divine fellowship are at the feet of the Almighty One whose help he implored, and to whom he uttered praise for Divine tuition and life.

Give me . . . Deliver me . . . Taught me, 119:169-172. In the first two verses, David prays for three things—that God would hear his prayer; give him understanding and deliverance. Witton Davies suggests the rendering of verse 169, "My cry (of anguish) comes near before thee, O Jehovah: Revive me according to thy word." Some writers indicate that probably the Psalmist had in mind the whole of this 119th Psalm, and meant something like this, "Let this whole preceding Psalm, and all the petitions therein contained, be highly accepted in Heaven."

David had prayed before for the illuminating of his mind by the Holy Spirit in order that he might have a spiritual insight into God's holy Word. "Give me understanding," verse 34—a prayer he frequently prayed, and here offers again. He sought, not the wisdom of the flesh, but enlightenment according to God's Word, or wisdom from above, and not judgment according to man. *Utter*, implying prayer and praise for favor, is a word meaning, "to pour forth," or "bubble over with," Prov. 15:2; 18:4, and expressed the Psalmist's desire to be forever rescued from his afflictions and his enemies. He recognized his need of heavenly understanding in order that he might be as wise as a serpent and as harmless as a dove in dealing with all adverse influences.

Praise is promised for answered prayer. Lips requesting favors become rejoicing lips. Preserving the metaphor of the Hebrew we have, "Let my lips pour forth or belch forth a stream of praise," Psalm 94:1. To praise God is the noblest employment of life, and one that glorifies Him. Not only did David praise God, as His Word was unfolded to him, but as verse 172 states it, his *tongue* spake of the same Statutes. He promises to sing and speak of God as he obtains practical instruction in the life of holiness. Both his lips and life must illustrate the Divine precepts. When we are daily taught the Statutes of Jehovah, our lips proclaim what our lives practice. T. H. Gill, in his book of Poems,

Breathings of a Better Life, published in 1881, included a brief ode on this 171st verse—

> O make me, Lord, thy statutes learn!
>   Keep in thy ways my feet,
> Then shall my lips divinely burn;
>   Then shall my songs be sweet.
>
> Each sin I cast away shall make
>   My soul more strong to soar;
> Each deed of holiness shall wake
>   A strain divine the more.
>
> My voice shall more delight thine ear,
>   The more I wait on thee;
> Thy service bring my song more near
>   The angelic harmony.

Emphasizing, yet once again, the righteousness and justice of God's commandments, or admonitions, the Psalmist declared that his tongue would be vocal with praise for them. The following suggested rendering of verse 172 shows this—"My tongue shall make response to Thy word, that all Thy commandments are true."

Thy hand . . . Thy precepts . . . Thy Salvation . . . Thy law . . . Thy judgments, 119:173-175. Twice over in these verses we have the phrase *Help me!*—a confession on David's part that he could do nothing, and was nothing of himself. His was both the direct and indirect appeal. First, he prayed directly, "Let thine hand—or power—help me!" Second, there was the indirect plea, "Let thy judgments help me!" Having chosen God's precepts to live by, and have them in his daily delight, his soul lived a new life, and his lips praised both God Himself and His Word, the twin sources of assistance in every time of need. See Ps. 119:20. The love of the Psalms Pope Gregory the Great had was illustrated by the picture of his mother Silvia, visible for centuries after her death, which he caused to be painted on the walls of what is now the Church of St. Gregory at Rome. In her left hand she held the Psalter, open at the words, "O let my soul live, and it shall praise Thee; and Thy judgments shall help me," 119:175.

A lost sheep . . . Thy servant, 119:176. Imploring help from the great God, David closes his magnificent Psalm in deepest self-humiliation, begging to be sought out like a lost or perishing sheep. Says F. B. Meyer, "It is touching to notice the closing minor cadence, for the loftiest flights of holy rapture must ever come back to a lowly confession of sin and unworthiness. 1 Peter 2:25." Wandering from so kind a Shepherd, so rich a pasture, and so good a fold, testifies to the mark of *inattention* Jesus warned His own against. We must never let Satan find us at a distance from the Lord, or he will assuredly be too much for us. We must, with all purpose of heart, cleave, not unto the dust (verse 25), but unto the Lord—as the ivy to the oak, or the child to the mother's breast.

Some writers feel that probably this final verse refers more to the condition of a community rather than the experience of an individual. Ellicott points out that "the word rendered *lost*, literally 'perishing' is used in Isa. 27:13 of the exiled Hebrews, and is rendered 'outcasts'; the emphatic, 'I do not forget Thy commandments,' which is the real close of the Psalm, seems to make this view imperative." We prefer to believe, however, that this *finale* was David's personal confession and that "in accordance with a true religious character that even at the end of a long protestation of obedience to the Divine law the Psalmist should confess his weakness and sin."

This closing minor cadence presents us with another triad of truth—a threefold cord not to be broken—

> *Regret*—"I have gone astray"
> *Request*—"Seek thy servant"
> *Remembrance*—"For I do not forget thy commandments."

It is imperative to keep David's confession about straying as a lost sheep in true perspective. He was not astray when he penned these words but had in mind past deviations from the practical precepts, instructive doctrines, and heavenly experiences set before him. The original word for *astray* signifies either the turning of the foot, or the turning of the heart, or both, out of the way. As the last clause of the verse precludes the idea of straying as deep sin, we must assume that the Psalmist was confessing heart-wanderings from the Shepherd of Israel. This is why he exhorts the saints in this Psalm to cleave to His commandments.

Within the best of us there should be the ever-clinging sense of our propensity to wander, and the realization of our inability to find our way back without the Shepherd's guiding hand to restore, and then to keep us near Himself. Each of us have need to pray—

> Thou know'st the way to bring me back,
> My fallen spirit to restore,
> Oh, for Thy truth and mercy's sake,
> Forgive, and bid me sin no more:
> The ruins of my soul repair,
> And make my heart a house of prayer.

The blessed truth to note, however, is that although a straying *sheep*, David was still God's *servant*, and as such he desired Him to seek him out, and bring him back to the fold. Had he been only a lost *sheep* he would not have prayed to be sought; but being also a *servant* he had the deep desire to pray for restoration, forgiveness, and taken into service again by his gracious Master.

In spite of his past and present failures, the Psalmist presented a most forcible argument, "For I do not forget thy commandments." With a loving memory of them, and a longing to know and obey them better, he knew that he was not utterly lost but was still under the Shepherd's eye. He had left the King's Highway for By-path meadow, but yearned to be back in full fellowship with the King.

> Though like a sheep estranged I stray,
> Yet have I not renounced thy way.
> Thine hand extend; thine own reclaim;
> Grant me to live, and praise thy name.

SONGS OF DEGREES: PSALMS 120–135

As we have now reached a group of 15 Psalms, Psalms 120-134, known as "Songs of Degrees," or "Lyric Songs of Going-up, or Ascents," a word or two is necessary as to the significance of such a title for these exquisitely beautiful odes. After the long gnomic Psalm 119, it is a relief to be back again in the region and air of these lovely lyric songs. "Suddenly we have left the continent of the vast 119th Psalm for the islands and islets of the Songs of Degrees," wrote Spurgeon. "It may be well to engage in protracted devotion upon a special occasion, but this must cast no slur upon the sacred brevities which sanctify the godly life day by day. He Who inspired the longest Psalm was equally the Author of the short compositions which follow it."

Many and varied are the explanations of the grouping and naming of these *Songs*—each of which bears the inscription, *A Song of Degrees*. Such an inscription was plainly intended to describe either the purpose for which these 15 Psalms were composed, or some use to which they were adapted. Some writers affirm that as "Degrees" or "Ascent" means "Going up" that the Psalms were composed to celebrate the return of the Jews from captivity in Babylon, or the "going up from Babylon," and sung as the Ark was being brought home to its resting place. Others regard them as referring to the yet future return of Israel from their long dispersion. Yet others spiritualize all the expressions in these *Degree* Psalms, making them to illustrate and interpret the experiences of the Church of God at all times, and in the present day, a method which is quite justifiable *after* the direct, historical association of each Psalm has been sought.

Much is made by some expositors of the term "Degrees," as implying "Steps," as well as "Ascents" and "Goings up"; and that these 15 Songs were sung as the people ascended the 15 steps of the Temple. In Ezekiel's Temple, Ezek. 40:22, 31, the number of steps is mentioned, 7 steps in the *outer* court, and another 8 steps in the *inner* court, but this Temple is the subject of prophecy, and away in the future. As four of these Psalms bear David's name as composer, and almost all the other Psalms in the group have evident references to his time and circumstances, he wrote in the time of the *Tabernacle* which had *no steps*. As renowned expositor, Dr. John Jebb, of the 18th century wrote—

> No trace in history, or authentic tradition can be found of these *steps*, which owe their construction solely to the accommodating fancy of the

Rabbins, who, as usual, imagined facts, in order to support their preconceived theories.

Bullinger in his remarkable *Companion Bible* identifies the 15 Songs of Degrees solely with the 15 added years God gave to King Hezekiah. Emphasis is placed on the definite article, "*The* Degrees," and the question naturally asked is *What* degrees? The only "degrees" we read of in the Bible are *the degrees* on the sundial of Ahaz, by which the shadow of the sun went backward in the days of his son Hezekiah, as a sign from Jehovah that he should recover from his sickness, while Jerusalem was surrounded by the armies of the king of Assyria, and Hezekiah was under sentence of death from the King of Terrors, 2 Kings 20:8-11; Isa. 36-39.
On recovering from his sickness Hezekiah said—

> Jehovah was ready to save me.
> Therefore we will sing MY SONGS to the stringed instruments
> All the days of our life
> In the house of Jehovah.

Thus the number of Psalms corresponds to the 15 years added to the king's life, while the number written by Hezekiah himself—10—corresponds with the number of "the degrees" by which "the shadow of the sun went backward." Then Dr. Bullinger goes on to make the claim that Hezekiah called the Psalms—*MY SONGS*, and that there was no need to put his name to the ten unnamed, as given in Scripture, out of the fifteen, but he put the name to the other five—one by Solomon is in the center with two by David on each side. Bullinger then goes to find the counterpart of these 15 Psalms, exclusively, in the life of Hezekiah.

Personally, we feel that this great Hebrew and Greek scholar (which he was), erred in affirming that Hezekiah wrote ten of the Psalms, when there is *no* Scripture record that he did. Bishop John Lightfoot, an equally gifted Bible scholar who died in 1675, had the most sensible approach to the association of Hezekiah and the *Songs of Degrees*. He wrote—

> Hezekiah liveth these fifteen years, in safety and prosperity, having humbled himself before the Lord for his pride to the ambassadors of Babel. The degrees of the sun's reversing, and the fifteen years of Hezekiah's life prolonging, may call to our minds the fifteen Psalms of Degrees: namely, from Psalm 120 and forward. These were Hezekiah's songs that were sung to the stringed instruments in the house of the Lord, Isa. 38:20. Whether these were picked out by him for that purpose may be left to conjecture.

The most simple and satisfactory explanation of the use of these Psalms is that they were sung by pilgrims as they journeyed from all parts of the country to attend the yearly Feasts at Jerusalem, and are thus well fitted for pilgrim songs, either for the Jew to Jerusalem, or for the Christian to that heavenly Zion whose builder and maker is God. Perhaps the 15 Psalms existed in a separate book as a kind of special hymnal, and known as *Pilgrim Psalms*. We have the expressions "*go up* to appear before the Lord thrice in the year," and "*go up* to do sacrifice," Exod. 34:24; 1 Kings 12:27. *Going up* is the meaning of "Degree." We can imagine how the devout pilgrims toiling up the long ascent would relieve the tedium of the way by changing these brief but blessed Psalms.

"*Go up, go up,* my soul!" must be the motto of those who would enter into the inner meaning and message of these Psalms, which are as a Jacob's ladder whose foot is fixed on the earth, but the top reaches up to the "heavenly Jerusalem." As to peculiar characteristics of the *Songs of Degrees* it has been suggested that nearly all of them have "sweetness and tenderness, a sad pathetic tone; brevity, an absence generates of the ordinary parallelism; something of a quick, trochaic rhythm." Witton Davies says of their poetical features, "They are all brief, bright, and beautiful." May our hearts mount up on these songs as on wings as we continue our earthly pilgrimage!

Psalm 120

Tremellius wrote of this Psalm that it is a most excellent song, and so indeed are the fourteen following it, for their form and manner of expression, which is wondrous short and sweet, is the very epigram of the Holy Spirit Himself, wherein each verse may well stand for an oracle. *A man of degrees* is put for an eminent excellent man, I Chron. 17:17.

This prayer for deliverance from the tongue of slander and from treacherous men is addressed to *Jehovah*, Who is twice mentioned in the opening verse. In fact, in each of the seven Psalms—on either side of the central Psalm—the name *Jehovah* occurs 24 times, and *Jah*, contraction of *Jehovah*, twice, once in the third Psalm of each seven. In the central Psalm—the eighth of the group, Jehovah occurs three times. Further, the five sections consisting of three Psalms each, revolve around a particular theme—

> The first of each group has *Distress* for its subject.
> The second has *Trust in Jehovah.*
> The third has *Peace and Blessing in Zion.*

The Psalm before us is a cry for help to Jehovah in sore distress, some say uttered by an exile under foreign oppression, perhaps during Sennacherib's siege of Jerusalem, 1 Kings 19. But as so many of David's Psalms seem to refer to Doeg, or a man of his calibre, whose lies had brought untold mischief to the sweet Psalmist of Israel, 1 Sam. 22:9, the old summary of the translators seems to be apt—*David prayeth against Doeg.* "If this be the scope of the Psalm, we see at once why it suggested itself to David at the station where the Ark abode, and from which he had come to remove it. He came to fetch the Ark, and at the same place where he found it he thought of Doeg, and poured out his complaint concerning him. The author had been grievously calumniated, and had been tortured into bitterness by the false charges of his persecutors, and here in his appeal to the great Arbiter of right and wrong, before whose judgment seat no man shall suffer from slanderous tongues."

In my distress . . . Deliver my soul, O Lord, 120:1-3. The safe and sound expositor, Samuel Cox, says of this Psalm that "the pilgrims were leaving home; and lying lips attack the absent. They were about to join the pilgrim caravan; and in the excitement of social intercourse their own lips might easily deviate from the truth." It is with this in mind that the Psalm begins with a plea for deliverance from the depressing and distressing influence of lying lips. The first verse presents us with the triad of Distress, Prayer, Deliverance. Such a reminiscence on David's part excited hope, stimulated prayer, and aroused gratitude.

Because of the promise, "I will hide thee from the scourge of the tongue," we can all pray the Psalmist's prayer against slander, for none but Jehovah can protect us from it or deliver us out of it. What a precious phrase this is—*And Jehovah heard me!* Here we have a rehearsal of a God Who hears and answers prayer; Whose ear is not deaf, nor even heavy. He ever hears, and responds to, the cry of the righteous. Lying lips are bad enough for they suck away the character of the one lied against, downright falsehood is worse than a lie. Deceitful tongues that fawn and flatter but are ready to destroy a life are to be feared, even as the Devil is when he appears as an angel. Lips that lie and deceive form the chariot of the Devil wherein he rides in triumph. Psalms 109:4; 119:75.

"Lying lips" tried to bear false witness against David, and the "deceitful tongue" sought to ensnare him, and to draw something from him on which they might ground accusations. A slander is a vile sin. James warns us against it, James 3. See Psalm 52:1-4. Because God had answered prayer, the poet found ground for his prayer of the second verse for a particular deliverance—which prayer is short, and to the point. No words are wasted. There was the plea for what was needed and what must be had, and until our tongue lies silent in the grave when deliverance will be no longer needed, our daily cry, whether in the same distress as David or some other kind, must be "Deliver my soul, O Lord." And our personal testimony will be, "He heard me." May grace be ours, then, to rest upon His promise, "Call upon Me in the day of trouble. *I will deliver thee!*"

In verse 3, the Psalmist turns from praying about lying and deceitful tongues to challenge and pronounce judgment upon those who are guilty of using their *little member* in such a dishonoring way. He felt that "the strongest punishment is not too much to be meted out to those who forge or circulate untrue statements, or statements the truth of which they have not verified." The margin gives the translation, "what shall the deceitful give unto thee?" or "what shall it profit thee?" The substance of the questions seems to be, *"What more can be added to thee* (that is, in the way of epithet) besides *lying lips* and *false, thou deceitful tongue?"* The usual metaphors of malicious speech are "the warrior's sharpened arrows," Jerem. 9:8; Psalm 57:4; and "fire," James 3:6.

David seems lost to suggest a fitting punishment to equal the crime, or what form the chastisement should take. "O, liars and deceivers, what shall be given unto thee?" The only reward they could expect for their false and malicious tongues was the terrible condemnation Jehovah alone could heap upon them as the next verse illustrates.

Sharp arrows . . . coals . . . Woe is me, 120:4,5. In these two verses we have the deserved punishment in reserve for liars and slanderers. If the rendering of the previous verse is accepted, "What shall Jehovah give thee, and what more shall He give thee, O thou deceitful tongue?" then Jehovah supplies the answer. *Sharp arrows of the mighty*, can be given as *Jehovah, The Mighty One*. Both figures of arrows and fire are expressive of Divine judgments. See Psalm 140:10. Shafts of calumny may miss the mark, but not so the arrows of God. The coals of malice may cool, but not the fire of justice.

Sharp arrows of the Almighty. It will be observed that these arrows are described as *sharp*, and not in any way blunt, and therefore able to pierce when hurled with great violence. Correspondence is frequently observed between the *transgression* and the *retribution* it receives. The law of correspondence by the use of similar figures to express the offense and the punishment of the wicked is often found in Scripture. "They bend their tongue like a bow," "Who whet their tongue like a sword, their bows to shoot in secret at the perfect." Now they are paid back in their own coin. Arrows sharp and swift and sent from the bow by the arm of Omnipotence. As sure as the sharpened, whetted poisoned arrow of the expert or warrior takes its victim, so revenge overtakes offenders against God and His saints. The arrow of Jehovah pierces the tongue of slanderers.

Coals of Juniper. Juniper-coals long retain their heat, are quick in burning, fierce in blazing. The Juniper, or Broom, supplies the root which is used for the manufacture of charcoal, the ordinary fuel among Arabs, which makes the hottest and most enduring fire. The answer to the question, "What shall be given thee?" is further in the fierce, and most lasting wrath of God Whose "lips are full of indignation, and his tongue as a devouring fire." Those who delighted, as if by fire, to destroy innocent lives, will themselves be burnt up in the fiercest fire. Liars are excluded from Heaven and have their dwelling with everlasting burnings. Jehovah alone can outmatch the fiery darts of the wicked one himself, the father of all lies and malicious slander.

David then goes on to express his lament at having to live in a land where haters of truth and of peace dwell. *Woe is me*! The Psalmist was ill-at-ease having to remain among lying neighbors which was as bad as if he was living among savages and cannibals. Those who seek to defame and destroy the righteous are "worse than cannibals, for they only eat men after they are dead, but slanderers eat them up alive."

Mesech and *Kedar* are used figuratively of the poet's sad loss in having to dwell among a cruel and barbarous and treacherous people. As only the wicked can be at home with the wicked, David found his dwelling among them most trying and distasteful. Yet Jehovah permitted His servant to remain among the unrighteous, not to enjoy their company but to live among them as His righteous child, and to rebuke them by life and lip of their ungodly deeds. Jesus prayed that His own might not be taken out of the world, but kept in it with lives unworldly in character.

The two names used, then, are typical of those who are cruel and merciless and inhospitable peoples among whom many of the Jews had been exiled, and among whom the Psalmist found himself. *Mesech* was from the north and *Kedar* from the south—a selection poetry dictated. Ellicott comments that "it is quite possible that the circumstances amid which the poet wrote made it necessary for him to veil in this way his allusion to powerful tribes, from whose violence his nation was suffering. At all events, the two concluding verses leave not doubt that some troubled state of affairs, in which the choice of course was not easy, and affecting the whole nation, not as an individual, is here presented."

It is most interesting to compare David's *Woe is me!* with that of the same lament Isaiah made. In fact, the similarity between Psalm 120:1-5 and Isaiah 6:10 is most unique. "Woe is me! for I am undone: because I am a man of unclean lips (verses 1 and 2 of Psalm 120 describes others as having lying, slanderous lips—here Isaiah confesses his own lips), and I dwell in the midst of an unclean people" (which is the lament of David in verse 5 of Psalm 120). Purging by live coal purged the mouth that had sinned (this we compare with verses 3 and 4 of the Psalm).

As we have already indicated, the power of the Psalm was strongly marked in the career of Oliver Cromwell. In 1636, he moved his home to Ely from St. Ives and from here he wrote one of his first extant letters, addressed to his cousin, Mrs. St. John, the wife of the celebrated ship-money lawyer. In it he speaks of himself and his lot in life—

> Truly then, this I find; that He giveth springs in a dry, barren wilderness where not water is. I live, you know where,—in Mesech, which they say signifies *prolonging*; and in Kedar, which signifies *blackness*, and yet the Lord forsaketh me not. Though He do prolong, yet He will, I trust bring me to His tabernacle, His resting place. Psalm 120.

This 5th verse is quoted in Bacon's *Essays*, "Nature and Men," *My soul hath long dwelt among them that are enemies unto peace.* When Thomas Carlyle sets down his half-humorous, half-bitter contempt for the trivialities of society, he quotes the same verse with which the *judicious* Bishop Hooker protested against his wife's shrewish tongue, Psalm 120:5. Returning in 1835 from a London dinner-party where Carlyle had met Sydney Smith—"a man of fat and muscularity . . . with shrewdness and fun, not humor or even wit, seemingly without soul altogether," he closed the note with the words—

"The rest babble, babble, Woe's me that I in Mesech am! To work." *Him that hateth peace . . . They are for war*, 120:6, 7. David continues his woe at having to dwell for so long among those who were warmongers. Opening his Psalm with a tribute of the gracious treatment

received at the hands of Jehovah, Who responded to his cry of distress, he closes it with a contrasted reference to man's ill-treatment of him. He yearned for peace—his enemies desired war. Are not Christians today frequently made conscious of this "contradiction of sinners," Heb. 12:3?

The term *long* is an emphatic word, and means "too long," just as the *they* is emphatic. David's enemies loathed the thought of peace, and these turbulent tribes fond of war, wearied his serene soul. See Psalm 109:3. As a man after God's own heart, David was a man of peace. Amesius said, "I would not give one hour of brotherly love for a whole eternity of contention, and the Psalmist felt the same for he said, 'I *am for* peace.' He sought to overcome evil with good."

It will be noticed that the words *am for* are in italics, implying that they are not in the original, but supplied by the translators to carry the sense of the clause. But the phrase is emphatic, and means, *I, even I*, or *I peace*. The writer was *Peace* personified, and loved peace and sought to promote it. He was all for peace, but when he said, *Shalom*, his foes returned war for his good wishes. Peace-makers are a blessing in the world, but Peace-haters are ever a curse. How fitting a conclusion to a Psalm set in a mournful key are the lines—

> Woe's me that I in Mesech am
> > A sojourner so long;
> That I in tabernacles dwell
> > To Kedar that belong.
> My soul with him that hateth peace
> > Hath long a dweller been;
> I am for peace: but when I speak,
> > For battle they are keen.
> My soul distracted mourns and pines
> > To reach that peaceful shore,
> Where all the weary are at rest,
> > And troubles vex no more.

Psalm 121

What a different atmosphere this well-loved Psalm provides! The previous one was so joyless, but this is so jubilant. David turns from the sinful, warlike people surrounding him to the hills with their calm serenity and majesty. "I will lift up mine eyes unto the hills where peace reigns." Bearing no other title than *A Song of Degrees*, it is several degrees in advance of the Psalm just considered, seeing it tells us of the peace of God's house and also of His guardian-care. "Psalm 120 bemoans the departure of peace from the good man's abode, and his exposure to the venomous assaults of slanderous tongues. In the first instance his eyes looked around with anguish, but here they look up with hope. From the constant recurrence of the word *keep*, we are led to name this song: *A Psalm to the Keeper of Israel*. Were it not placed among the Pilgrim Psalms we should regard it as a martial hymn, fitter for the evensong of one who slept upon the tented field. It is a soldier's song as well as a traveller's Psalm. There is an ascent in the Psalm itself which rises to the greatest elevation of restful confidence."

What a vivid contrast the final words of the last Psalm and the opening phrase of this Psalm present—*For war . . . The Hills*! The Psalmist leaves the tumult for tranquility. It is true that the glorious, unoffending, peaceful hills are sometimes ravaged by shells and bombs, but they never fight back and are always for peace. Their gaping wounds are so patiently borne, and once war ceases they try to cover them over with a robe of velvet green, or of wild foliage, and thus hide the hatred of man. A further contrast is seen in David himself as the two Psalms are compared. He sheds the spirit of heaviness, so prominent in Psalm 120, for the garment of praise in Psalm 121. Then after being compassed about by the malicious adversaries, David turns from them to the Almighty One, and in the Psalm before us, has no mention of his war-like foes but is obsessed with the greatness and goodness of Jehovah, Whom he mentions 5 times in 8 verses.

The very many biographical incidents in connection with this Psalm prove its abiding influence in the lives of saints through the ages. "What a history were that, if it could be written, of the countless thousands of Christians who have been consoled in trouble or sickness by this Psalm! Among others it was read at the death-bed of Julius Hare." Ellicott then goes on to add, "It is in this Psalm that the step-like progression of the rhythm is most plainly marked." David Livingstone, the Scottish missionary, read the 121st Psalm and the 135th, and prayed with his old father and sister, as he set out from Blantyre for Africa; and his mother-in-law, Mrs. Moffat, wrote him at Linyardi, on the threshold of his perilous journey, that the 91st and 121st Psalms were constantly with her as she thought of and prayed for him. She wrote, "Unceasing prayer is made for you. When I think of you, my heart will go upwards—Keep him as the *apple of Thine eye*; *Hold him in the hollow of Thine hand*, are the ejaculations of the heart."

Edward the Black Prince chose, "My help cometh from the Lord," the first clause of verse 2 of Psalm 121, as the motto for coins struck in England in 1362. J. S. Watson, Rear Admiral U.S. Navy, and successor to Admiral Dewey who commanded the Fleet in the Philippines, said, "My favorite chapter is the Traveller's Psalm, 121, the 7th and 8th verses mean more to me than any other." It is said that Romaine the celebrated French author read this Psalm every day because he felt that every word in it was calculated to encourage and strengthen our faith and hope in God.

Among the Scottish Covenanters Field-Conventicles were accounted with triumph and much Psalm-singing. At Craigmad, between Falktill and Moranside, the hills were crowned with mist-covered worshippers who were singing Psalm 121. A milk-white horse with a blood-red saddle on its back appeared among them, and was looked upon as an omen of the persecution that would follow the preaching of the Gospel.

William Edwards, of Budson, who was with Henry Havelock during the Indian Mutiny in 1857, writing on August 27, Edwards said, "Nothing new settled about our plans, and we are much harassed. Heavy guns firing at Turruckabad today, we know not for what cause; but they reminded us painfully of our fearful proximity to that place where are so many thirsting for our lives. Amidst it all, today Psalms are most consoling, and wonderfully suited to our ease, especially the 121st, *I will lift up mine eyes unto the hills, from whence cometh our help*, etc."

As this precious Psalm is so well-known among believers, many of whom can recite it from memory, and also because its comforting verses speak for themselves, we are not seeking to expound any of them, but simply record historical associations with almost all of them.

I will lift up mine eyes unto the hills, 121:1. As it is always wise to look to the strong for strength, David of old knew that when at the mercy of foes, a sure method of escape was to flee to the strongholds upon the mountains. The second clause, "Whence cometh my help," should be set as a question, *Whence cometh my help*? and the next verse supplies the answer. The strength and help the Psalmist required came not from the hills but from Jehovah Who made them, and all else in the heavens and the earth.

Historically, this opening verse suggests that the Psalm was designed to be sung in view of the mountains of Jerusalem, and is manifestly an evening song for the sacred bands of pilgrims, to be sung in the last night-

624   Psalms: *A Devotional Commentary*

watch, the figures of which are also peculiarly suitable for a pilgrim song; and with the next Psalm which, according to the express announcement in the introduction, was sung when the groups of pilgrims had reached the gates of Jerusalem and halted for the purpose of forming up in order for the solemn procession into the Sanctuary. See Psalm 134.

In his *Caravan and the Temple* E. Jewitt Robinson wrote in 1878, he tells of a dear woman, a pilgrim faint at the close of life's pilgrimage, who repeated the line

> Will he not his help afford?

She quoted it several times, trying to recall the song in which it occurs, and I refreshed and comforted her by reading Charles Wesley's spirited paraphrase, beginning—

> To the hills I lift mine eyes,
>   The everlasting hills;
> Streaming thence in fresh supplies,
>   My soul to Spirit feels.
> Will he not his help afford?
>   Help, while yet I ask, is given:
> God comes down; the God and Lord
>   That made both earth and heaven.

The natives of India used to say that when Sir Henry Laurence looked twice to heaven and then to earth he knew what to do when help and guidance were necessary. It has been suggested that by the marginal note—"Shall I lift up mine eyes to the hills? whence should my help come?" the poet may have had in mind the contrasting confidence with which a worshiper of Jehovah might look up to the sacred city on the crest of the holy hill with that superstition and idolatry which was associated with so many hills and high places in Canaan. The best commentary, both on the poetry and religion of this Psalm is to be found in John Ruskin's fascinating discourses on mountains in his *Modern Painters*, in which he describes their influence on the ancient, medieval, and modern mind, and the part they have played alike in the mythology of the pagan times and the religion of the Christian World. Ruskin, as we know, was a great lover of the Psalms.

Doubtless Wordsworth had in mind the feeling of the Jew who thought of the hills as a barrier of defense, and as heights of observation from which to watch for the messengers of peace, Psalms 125:2; Isa. 52:7, when he wrote—

> In the mountains did he feel his faith
> . . . and there his spirit shaped
> Her prospects.

Dante, in *Purgatorio* has many references to the Psalms. Cheered by St. James, Dante lifts up his eyes, heretofore bent on the ground with their over-heavy burden—*To the hills from whence cometh my help.* Thus help and hope came to him—

> From him who sang
> The songs of the Supreme, himself supreme,
> Among his tuneful brethren. "Let all hope
> In Thee," so spake his anthem, "Who have known
> Thy name."

Bishop James Hannington, who followed in the train of David Livingstone through Africa, every morning throughout his toilsome, dangerous journey, greeted the sunrise by reading, or repeating his *Travelling Psalm*, as he called it, "I will lift up mine eyes unto the hills."

He will not suffer thy foot to be moved . . . not slumber, 121:3. "Among the hills and ravines of Palestine the literal keeping of the feet is a great mercy: but in the slippery ways of a tried and afflicted life, the boon of upholding is of priceless value, for a single false step may cause us a fall fraught with awful danger." This verse is a choice stanza in a pilgrim song. *God is the convoy and body-guard of his saints.* Ancient families sought their motives in the Psalms. For instance, the Coghills chose, *Non dirmit qui custodil*—"The Lord is thy keeper."

Neither slumber nor sleep, 121:4. St. Francois de Sales, Bishop of Geneva, who died in 1622, was a devotee of the Psalms. The rule of life he laid down for himself when he was only 20 years of age was founded upon their language. He promised to hear Mass at all times. If midnight fears beset him, he would remember, "He that keepeth Israel shall neither slumber nor sleep." When one asked Alexander the Great how he could sleep so soundly and securely in the midst of danger, he replied that Parmenio, his faithful guard, watched. How securely we should sleep when it is God, Who never slumbers nor sleeps, watching over us.

An Eastern story has it that a poor woman came to the Sultan one day, and asked compensation for the loss of some property. "How did you lose it?" asked the monarch. "I fell asleep," was the reply, "and a robber entered my dwelling." "Why did you fall asleep?" said the Sultan. The woman answered, "I fell asleep because I believed you were awake." The Sultan was so delighted with such an answer, that he ordered her loss to be made up. Those who have the God of Jacob as their help can sleep safely because of the ceaseless care of Divine providence.

Commentator Albert Barnes says, "Man sleeps; a sentinel *may* slumber on his post by inattention, by long-continued wakefulness, or by weariness, a pilot *may* slumber at the helm; even a mother *may* fall asleep by the side of a sick child; but God is never exhausted, is never weary, is never inattentive. He never closes his eyes on the condition of his people, on the wants of the world."

> He who keepeth thee will not slumber,
> Behold, he who keepeth Israel
> Doth not slumber or sleep,
> Jehwah is thy keeper.

The sun shall not smite by day, nor the moon by night, 121:6. All protection is ours seeing that "the Lord is thy shade," verse 5. *Shade* is the image of protection, and one peculiarly attractive to the Oriental. See margin Num. 14:9; Psalm 91:1; Isa. 25:4; 32:2. This mention of shade leads to the amplification of the smiting power of the sun and the moon. The evil effects of *sunstroke*, often mentioned in the Bible (2 Kings 4:18, 20; Jonah 4), are too well known to need comment. As for the moon smiting by night, we read of those being *moon-struck*. It is a fact that temporary blindness is often caused by moonlight. Tennyson speaks of the moon being *keen with frost*, and probably the injurious effects of cold night air are implied. Possibly there is allusion in this verse to the belief, so common in old times, of the harmful influence of the moon's light—a belief still recalled in the word *lunacy*, from "lunar," meaning "moon."

Shakespeare, in *The Midsummer Night's Dream,* captures the supposedly power of the moon in the lines—

> The moon, the governess of floods,
> Pale in their anger, washes all the air,
> That rheumatic diseases do abound.

Preserve thee . . . thy soul . . . thy going out and thy coming in, 121:7, 8. We should read instead of *preserve,* "keep," the persistent dwelling on this one word making one of the chief beauties of the hymn. The triad in these concluding verses "thee," "thy soul," "thy going out and coming in," indicates the completeness of the Divine protection vouchsafed, extending to all the believer is in himself and to all that is associated with every phase of his life. Comforting to know that God always keeps watch for us in our *going out* to public responsibilities, and *coming in* to more private affairs.

Even for evermore. This last verse is a common Hebrew expression for the whole of life, Deut. 28:6; 1 Thess. 5:23. Jehovah has not helped, kept, and blest us all through life to forsake us at the very gate of Heaven. "Soul-keeping is the soul of keeping," and is an eternal security. The benediction of John Keble makes a fitting end to our meditation of this *Jehovah* Psalm—

> God keep thee safe from harm and sin,
> Thy spirit keep; the Lord watch o'er
> Thy going out, thy coming in,
>   From this time, evermore.

Psalm 122

In his *Book of Martyrs*, Foxe records how when Wolfgang Schuch, of Lothareng in Germany, heard the sentence that he was to be martyred by burning, began to sing this 122nd Psalm, the song of ascent to the city of God. In the flames he sang Psalm 51, and continued singing till the smoke and heat took from him voice and life. James Hogg, the renowned *Ettrick Shepherd* of Scotland, could repeat, before as a child he could read or write, the 122nd Psalm. His godly mother would read the metrical versions of the Psalms to him.

Gregory Nazianzea, who became the poet of Eastern Christendom, and one of the greatest of its orators and theologians, had a father who was a pagan. But Gregory's mother, Nonna, was a most godly woman and constantly prayed that her husband might become a Christian. Evidently he had some knowledge of the Psalms, for he dreamed one night that he was singing the words of this Psalm, "I was glad when they said unto me, we will go into the House of the Lord." The impression was too deep to pass away, and when he awoke he sought the Lord, was baptized, and eventually became, for 45 years, Bishop of Mazianzus, where he died in 374.

We have already seen how, during the French Wars of Religion, the Psalms became the Huguenot *Marseillaise*. Sentries were posted and relieved to the chant of Psalms. The singing of Psalm 3 gave the signal of danger—"Lord, how are they increased that trouble me." When victory was secured, the hymn of thanksgiving was raised in Psalm 122, from the walls of Huguenot strongholds, like Montauban or La Rochelle, as the soldiers of the League drew off their beaten forces.

As with the previous Psalm, so with this brief but spirited Psalm before us, the few verses are so clear and explicit, and speaking for themselves require little exposition. We are, therefore, confining ourselves to the historical background of the Psalm and to biographical incidents in connection with some of its verses. The title of the Psalm, *A Song of Degrees of David*, tells us that he was its author, and the historic occasion he wrote it for. It is on this Psalm that the tradition of the 15 Degree Psalms becoming known as *The Pilgrim Odes* is based.

David, cognizant of the ordinance directing every male Israelite to visit the Holy City three times a year, wrote this Psalm for the people to sing at the time of their goings up to the Holy Feasts at Jerusalem; and it appears to be suitable to be sung when the people had entered the gates, and their feet stood within the city. The pilgrim journey is over, and at this moment the excitement and joy with which it was commenced are lovingly recalled. "As they stood within the triple walls of the city, all things around the pilgrims helped to explain the words which they sang within her ramparts of strength. One voice led the Psalm with its personal '*I*,' but ten thousand brethren and companions waited with the first musician and swelled the chorus of the strain."

Amid the emotions of such an experience, the prayer for Jerusalem's welfare rises—"a prayer which is nonetheless real because it reproduces literally the formal Oriental greetings which at such a time would be passing to and for among the excited groups." Jerusalem means "Habitation of Peace," and *Peace* used 3 times, is the key word of the Psalm. Serene times were desired that the people might enjoy sincere worship without disturbance. In the original, *Prosperity* is related to Shalom, meaning "peace." Strange though it may seem to us, *peace* and *prosperity* were wished on *The City of Peace*.

Our feet shall stand within thy gates, O Jerusalem, 122:2. A renowned traveller, writing on his journeys through the Holy Land, describes the companies travelling from the East to Jerusalem. The long procession, after climbing over the extended and heavy range of hills that bounded the way, reached the top of the last hill and, stretching up their hands in gestures of joy, cried out, *The Holy City! The Holy City!*—and fell down and worshipped. Is this not the experience of the child of God as he reaches the last summit of life and in his last moments catches a glimpse of the Heavenly Jerusalem and cries out to be among its glories? Torquato Tasso, spiritual poet who died in 1595, left us the stanza—

> Lo, towered Jerusalem salutes the eyes!
> A thousand pointing fingers tell the tale;
> *Jerusalem!* a thousand voices cry.
> *All hail, Jerusalem!* hill, down and dale,
> Catch the glad sounds, and shout, *Jerusalem, all hail!*

Edward Payson, devotional writer of the 18th century, recorded for posterity his last hours before entering the New Jerusalem above—

> The celestial city is full in my view. Its glories beam upon me, its breezes fan me, its odors are wafted to me, its sounds strike upon my ears, and its spirit is breathed into my heart. Nothing separates me from it but the river of death, which now appears but as an insignificant rill, that may be crossed at a single step, whenever God shall give permission. The Sun of Righteousness has been gradually drawing nearer and nearer, appearing larger and brighter as he approached, and now he fills the whole hemisphere; pouring forth a flood of glory, in which I seem to float like an insect in the beams of the sun; exulting, yet almost trembling, while I gaze on this exces-

sive brightness, and wondering, with unutterable wonder, why God should deign thus to shine upon a sinful worm.

Thrones of Judgment, 122:5. A. P. Stanley in his *Lectures on the History of the Jewish Church*, informs us that a throne of ivory, brought from Africa or India, the throne of many an African legend, the Kings of Judah were solemnly seated on the day of their accession. From its lofty seat, and under the high gateway, Solomon and his successors after him developed their solemn judgments. Stanley then goes on to remind us—

> That *porch* or *gate of justice*, still kept alive the likeness of the old patri-archal custom of sitting in judgment at the gate; exactly as the Gate of Justice still recalls it to us at Granada, and the Sublime Porte—*The Lofty Gate* at Constantinople. He sat on the back of a golden bull, its head turned over its shoulder, probably the ox or bull of Ephraim; under his feet, on each side of the steps, were six golden lions, probably the lions of Judah. This was the *Seat of Judgment*. This is the throne of the house of David.

Pray for the peace of Jerusalem, 122:6. In the early days of Methodists when followers of the Wesleys were known as "Wesleyan Methodists," much opposition came to them from Anglican quarters. The incident is recorded of a group of Wesleyans opening a chapel at Painswick, England. Preacher Hoskins, Independent minister of Castle Green, was invited to preach the sermon. On the morning the new chapel was opened the first to enter the building was the Anglican Vicar, Cornelius Winter, who seated himself near the pulpit. At the end of the service he met the preacher at the foot of the pulpit steps, and shaking him with both hands, said aloud, "I thank you cordially, my dear brother, for coming to my help—here is room enough for us both; and work enough for us both; and much more than we can both accomplish; and I hope the Lord will bless our co-operation in this good cause." What a difference it would make to Church unity today if only a like spirit of brotherliness prevailed among churches fighting against each other instead of fighting together against one common foe. How the Church needs "Peace within her walls!"

Josephus tells us that there were at Jerusalem three ranges or rows of walls. The sense in verse 7 is, "Let no enemy approach so much as to thy out-works to disturb thee." The Church should be a walled-town situated among her enemies, but alas! her walls are broken down, and the enemies are within the city.

My brethren and companions, 122:8. In his *Gems from the Coral Islands*, published in 1869, William Gill relates an occasion when an elderly native, formerly a cannibal, addressing the Church members, said, *Brethren*, and, pausing for a moment, continued "Ah! this is a new name; we did not know the true meaning of that word in our heathenism. It is the *Evangelia a Jesu* (Evangelist of Jesus) that has taught us the meaning of Brethren."

Psalm 123

Matthew Henry, whose Bible Commentary is one of the best a lover of the Word could possess, has left us an account of the godly home in which he was reared, and which is one of the fairest pictures we have from the Puritan time, and might serve for the *Chamber Peace* in the palace *Beautiful* described by John Bunyan. Every Sunday evening, Matthew's father, Philip, would conclude the day with his family at Broadoak kneeling around him to receive his blessing. Psalm 123 was always read by Philip Henry, and then after meat and thanks, the usual song of the family and guests was Psalm 23.

Abounding in assonance, this ode has been called the *Rhyming Psalm*, and also beautifully named *Oculus Sperans*—THE EYE OF HOPE. (Rhyme, exceedingly rare in Biblical poetry, is more abundant in this Psalm that in any other commensurate part of the Old Testament. Rhyme abounds in the poetry of the Arabs, none of which is older than A.D. 500). Opinions as to its historical setting differ. Ellicott says that "it reflects the feelings of Israel under foreign oppression, but there is no indication of precise time, unless we are to adopt the Hebrew margin and seek the concluding word a reference to the *Ionians*, which would bring the Psalm within the Macedonian period."

As for Spurgeon, he says, "It has been conjectured that this brief song, or rather sigh, may have first been heard in the days of Nehemiah, or under the persecutions of Antiochus. It may be so, but there is no evidence of it; it seems to us quite probable that afflicted ones in all periods after David's time found this Psalm ready to hand. If it appears to describe days remote from David, it is all the more evident that the Psalmist was also a prophet, and sang what he saw in vision, knowing that doubtless it would be a favorite song among the people of God."

F. B. Meyer contends that "this Psalm must be internal evidence he carried, as to its authorship, to a much later date than the preceding one. It was probably composed after the return from the Captivity, when Israel was suffering so much from the Samaritans and others, Ezra 4; Neh. 2:19." As for John Calvin, he shows the application of the Psalm to the Church of all ages and says, "The Holy Spirit, by a clear voice, incites us to come to God, as often as—not one and another member only, but—the whole Church is unjustly and haughtily oppressed by the passions of her enemies." Is this not particularly so today, especially in Communist countries?

The double nature of the Psalm is that of eyes turned in faith to Heaven, and prayer for help in distress caused by scornful and contemptuous proud oppressors. The Psalmist looks up steadfastly to God and expresses his confidence in His ability to deliver His people. Without doubt, this is *A Psalm of the Eyes*, for "eyes" occurs 4 times, and "look up" twice—three, if we include "lift up." John Milton in *Il Penserosa* describes a church service that greatly impressed him, of which he wrote—

> Dissolve me into ecstasies
> And bring all Heaven before mine eyes.

It is evident that Heaven was before the Psalmist's eyes all through this brief Psalm. William Collins, 17th century poet, wrote of one "With eye up-rais'd, as one inspired"—and this certainly was the experience of the man who wrote this Psalm. As for Shakespeare, in *Romeo and Juliet*, he has the phrase, "Mei eyes were made to look—let them gaze," and the Psalmist's gaze must have been an absorbing one. Tennyson has the expressive line in his *In Memorium*, "Her eyes were homes of silent prayer," but in his nation's distress, the Psalmist's eyes were a home of heart-felt vocal prayer, and he could have said—

> God be in my eyes
> And in my looking.

The poet's assertion, "Unto thee do I *lift up* mine eyes," poses the question, "Why do Jews, Moslems, and Christians look up when they pray, as if God were in that direction more than in any other?" To those living in Australia "down under"—our *up* is their *down*. The suggestion is that looking up when praying is a survival of astral religion. Yet Jesus looked upward when He prayed, Matt. 5:34, and taught His disciples to emulate His example, seeing that God's throne is in Heaven. Visual direction, however, matters little. What is all-important is the gaze of the heart at Him Who fills Heaven and earth. If words and sentences cannot be articulated, an inner look can express our desire. Robert Green, poet of the late 15th century, left us the line—"Within mine eyes he makes his nest"—and when the eyes or our understanding are His nest, we are indeed thrice blest.

> Prayer is the burden of a sigh,
>   The falling of a tear,
> The upward glancing of an eye
>   When none but God is near.

The eyes of servants . . . the eyes of a maiden . . . our eyes, 123:2. Although the Psalmist used his eyes and his voice in the expression of his entreaty, he goes on to give us two homely metaphors of how a look without the lips moving brings necessary help, and introduces his illustrations with a *Behold*. Ordinarily, a word of *attention*, used for the stirring up of our audience and admiration, it is here employed to excite, not man but God, and to draw His eyes to how men and women re-act to a look, and to imitate them.

"The eyes of servants—slaves—look unto the hand of their masters." Slaves depend on what the master hands them, but here it is not the hand as *giving* but *commanding* that is implied. A very slight gesture is enough to indicate the master's will. A traveller to the East wrote, "I have seen a fine illustration of Psalm 123:2 in a gentleman's house at Damascus. The people in the East do not speak so much or so quick as those in the West, and a sign of the hand is frequently the only instructions given to the servants in waiting. As soon as we were introduced and seated on a divan, a wave of the master's hand indicated that coffee should be brought, and another hand signal, that we are ready for dinner. The slave watched his master's eye and hand, to know his will and do it instantly."

In the Psalm before us the hand of God is the *oculus sperans*, the eye which waits, and hopes, and is patient, looking only to Him and none other for help. There was also the expectancy of Divine interference to deliver from the tyrant. There is, of course, a larger application one would make, for it has been said that the servant looks to the master's hand for several things—

> For direction,
> For the supply of needs,
> For protection,
> For correction,
> For reward.

If only we could be so incessantly occupied with our heavenly Master as to need but a sign! See Genesis 16:6-9.

"As the eyes of a maiden unto the hand of her mistress." In this second illustration, taken from the duty of domestic servants, we come to maidservants, which implies that both sexes can express their confidence in God, with women knowing that help will be theirs because they are more frail than men. Deborah and Jael were certainly worthies, and courageous in God. The force of this second metaphor, however, is seen in the fact that Eastern women are even more thorough than the men in the training of their servants. It is usually thought that women issue more commands, and are more sensitive of disobedience, than the sterner sex. Female slaves of Roman matrons had a sorry time of it as they strove to be guided by the eye of a mistress. Blessed to know that in Christ there is neither male or female, and that all are satisfied whose eyes wait upon the Lord.

It will be noted that in the case of the slaves and female servants they *look* at the *hand* of their masters, but with the believer it is not *look* to, but *wait* upon the Lord. The Psalmist suggests that the eye *waits*—for to *wait* is more than to *look*; to *wait* is to look constantly, with patience and submission by subjecting our affections and wills and desires to the Divine Will: that is to *wait*. True, this word is printed in italics, meaning that it is not in the original but added by the translators for the supply of the sense of the passage. This does not imply that the Holy Spirit, in leading the Psalmist to write this Psalm, left it imperfect by not adding such a word of necessity. He left it more perfect in that He put not in His own verb but left it to every man's heart to supply a verb to his own comfort, and a better word than *wait* could not be found.

What was begged was worth waiting for, *Have mercy upon us.* Truly, this is a precious, most necessary gift to wait for, and in this case it was not a call for God to be merciful because the people had grievously sinned, but because they were "filled with contempt." *Exceedingly filled,* implies "to be saturated," and indicates that the people of God had had so much scorn heaped upon them, they could take no more. Godless ones of the world regarded the Temple Pilgrims and their faith in God with the quiet smile of disdain, thinking them a queer lot to concern themselves about an unseen God and an unknown Eternity.

Contempt is hard to bear: but we are taught to expect it as followers of Him Who was despised of men, Who passed through storms of contumely, but Who despised such shame, Heb. 12:2-4. If we are being ridiculed for Christ's sake, we must fix our hearts on the joy set before us and "rejoice inasmuch as we are partakers of Christ's sufferings," 1 Peter 4:13. In the last verse of the Psalm, the scorners described as being *at ease* and *proud* were heathen oppressors living in careless security. For an illustration of these proudest of oppressors, see 2 Kings 18:19-35. The use of the article in the Hebrew is more demonstrative and reads "*this* scorning." To give a better sense to the passage we can state it—"Let our desire be satisfied to the full with the scorn for those at ease, and the same contempt for the proud." Ellicott asks us to notice how the figure is retained. The oppressors are *masters and mistresses,* living in luxury while the slaves wait. Gesenius quotes Sallust in illustration of the wantonness of secure and luxurious power. As we read the verse, we seem to feel—

> The whips and scorns of time,
> The oppressor's wrong, the proud man's contumely.

Psalm 124

Because this Psalm is such a paeon of praise for a Divine deliverance, it has ever been precious to the saints of succeeding ages who found themselves hemmed in on every side by adverse foes and circumstances, but out of which the Lord brought them out. Andrew Bonar relates in his entrancing volume, *Christ and His Church in the Book of Psalms*, which was published in 1859, an incident in the year 1582, when this Psalm was sung on a remarkable occasion. John Curie, Minister first at Leith, then in Edinburgh, was suspended for his plain speaking against the Duke of Lennox. Set free from prison, he was met and welcomed on entering his home town by 200 of his friends. The number increased till he found himself in the company of some 2,000 who began to sing, as they moved up the long High Street, Edinburgh, *Now Israel may say*. They sang in four parts with deep solemnity, all joining in the well-known tune and Psalm. They were much moved themselves, and so were all who heard; and one of the chief persecutors is said to have been more alarmed at this sight and song than at anything he had seen in Scotland.

This same Psalm had a place in Swiss history similar to that of John Durie. John Key in *Psalms in History and Biography* tells the story. After Geneva had gained its freedom and become the head to the Reformed, the Dukes of Savoy, who were leaders of the Romish party, made many attempts to crush the new movement. One of the most noted was in 1602, known as: *Escalade*. The inhabitants, lulled to security by peaceful professions, had neglected all precautions.

On a dark night in December, 200 Savoyards, the advance part of a large force, scaled the walls and were about to admit their associates. The assailants were so sure of their prey that they despatched a messenger to their commander announcing their complete success. A sentinel going his rounds lighted on them and was killed; but a discharge of his pistol, before he fell, aroused the citizens. They flew to arms, each man with the nearest weapon, and after a desperate conflict the towns and walls were cleared of the enemy.

An iron pot with which an old woman knocked down a soldier was long preserved in the town arsenal; and a monument to the Genevese who fell, with their names inscribed, stands in the cemetry of St. Gervias. When the conflict was over, the venerable Theodore Beza, 80 years old, returned solemn thanks, and gave our Psalm 124 to be sung. Every year since, on December 12th, the same Psalm has been sung in Geneva. The French version of Psalm 124 was composed by Beze himself, and was sung to the same tune as the old Scottish version, which was fashioned after the old Reformation Psalter and was made by Whittingham, who succeeded John Knox as Pastor of the English exiles in Geneva, and who was married to John Calvin's sister.

The learned and pious theologian, Tholuck of Halle used to tell a story of his father-in-law who was a convert from Roman Catholicism. As it occasionally happens though the mind may be entirely emancipated, the desire for priestly absolution returns and his son-in-law asked him before the old man died, if he had any such feeling. The dying man expressed his sole confidence in the Great High Priest, and, giving a wave of triumph with his hand, said in the words of Martin Luther's version of Psalm 124—

> Broken are their nets, and thus escaped we.

Andrew Bonar, close friend of Robert Murray McCheyne, and his biographer, gives this account of his death: "Next day he continued to sink in body and mind, till about the time of his people met for their usual evening prayer-meeting, when he requested to be left alone for half-an-hour. When his servant entered the room again, McCheyne exclaimed with a joyful voice, 'My soul is escaped as a bird out of the snare of the fowler; the snare is broken, and I am escaped.' As he spoke, his countenance bespoke inward peace, and ever after, until he died, he was observed to be happy."

On August 22, 1900, The American Board of Commissioners for Foreign Missions received a cablegram from Che-Foo, China, where the missionaries were being massacred and undergoing the worst persecution of the century. It read *Psalm 124*, the names of missionaries that were saved and their stations being added. The comment of the daily press was that it was better than a code. As for the Psalm itself, it was sung at the Feast of Purin to commemorate a deliverance probably from Hamen, the Jews' worst enemy. It is a gladsome lyric, thanking Jehovah for escape from heathen destruction, and in its formation illustrates a particular rhythmic effect, namely the ascending scale of a series of phrases.

As to it authorship, its title reads *A Song of Degrees of David*, but some writers are reluctant to uphold the ascription of the Psalm, arguing that the LXX Version does not carry the title, and that because its imagery recalls Davidic poems before the inscription came into being. Spurgeon, dealing with the superfine critics who pounce upon the title as being inaccurate, goes on to say—

> The critics declare there are certain ornaments of language in this little ode which were unknown in the Davidic period. It may be so; but in their

superlative wisdom they have ventured upon so many other statements that we are not bound to receive this dictum. Assuredly the manner of the song is very like to David's, and we are unable to see why he should be excluded from the authorship. Whether it be his composition or no, it breathes the same spirit in that which animates the unchallenged songs of the royal composer.

Although the Psalm is ascribed to David, no reference is made to any specific danger and deliverance he experienced. There is a delightful universality in this language, which suits it admirably as an anthem of the redeemed, in every age and in every clime, who find themselves living in a hostile territory. One expositor suggests that the progression referred to was the triumphant return of the King and his loyal army to Jerusalem, upon the overthrow of the dangerous rebellion to which the great mass of the people had been excited by Absalom and his powerful band of confederates. Compare Psalms 45 and 60. Martin Luther says, "We may well sing this psalm, not only against our enemies who openly hate and persecute us, but also against spiritual wickedness." Compare Psalm 124 with Jonah's song of thanksgiving, 2:3-10.

A characteristic feature of this Psalm is the repetition of certain phrases, a mark common to many of the Psalms, e.g. 93:4; 96:13; 122:4; 135:12. Here we have two, *If it had not been the Lord Who was on our side*, verses 1, 2; *Waters, Stream, Waters*, verse 5; *Snare, Snare*, verse 7. Martin Luther said of the repetition of verses 1 and 2, that same was not in vain, "For whilst we are in danger, our fear is without measure; but when it is once past, we imagine it to have been less than it was indeed. And this is the delusion of Satan, to diminish and obscure the grace of God. David therefore with this repetition stirreth up the people to more thankfulness unto God for His gracious deliverance, and amplieth the dangers which they had passed. Thereby we are taught how to think of our troubles and afflictions fast, lest the sense and feeling of God's grace vanish out of our minds."

If . . . If., 124:1, 2. Readers will be aware of Rudyard Kipling's great poem on *IF*. Then Shakespeare in *As You Like It*, has the line, "your *if* is the only peace-maker, much virtue is *if*." Yet in his King Richard III, the same famous bard wrote—

> Talk'st thou to me of *ifs*? Thou art a traitor:
> Off with his head.

David talks of *ifs*, and there is much virtue in them, although there was no *if* in the matter of the Lord being on the side of His people. The repeated phrase *it had not been* is printed in italics, implying that it was supplied by the translators to patch up the passages and give them better sense. Had they left them in their abrupt, broken gandeur, they would have read—

Had it not been Jehovah! He was for us, oh let Israel say!
Had it not been Jehovah! He was for us when men rose against us!

The Lord is ever at the side, and *on* the side of his own to interpose for their protection against all the leagued hosts of adversaries. What *IFS*, then, are these—our "peace-makers." We shudder to think what would have happened to Israel if the preserving, delivering hand of the Lord had not been upon them. Weigh these two phrases in the balance, "The *Lord* on our side . . . *Men* against us." *Jehovah* and *Men*! Then how unworthy fears of Divine help appear. See Psalms 56:11; 94:17.

But Israel could repeat twice over, with deep gratitude of heart, *The Lord who was on our side*. What would have happened if He had not been their Defender, Provider, and Guide? Every child of God, no matter how poor and humble he or she may be has the assurance of Scripture that the mighty God is ever on the side protecting them from all destructive hordes; and, blessed be the name of Jehovah, *one* with *Him* is ever in the majority.

Then . . . Then . . . Then, 124:3-6. The first three verses are bound together by the most expressive triple *Then*—a three-fold statement of what would have happened to Israel without Jehovah's timely help.

"*Then* they had swallowed us up quick." *Quick* is an old English term for *alive*. Wild beasts swallow up their prey as they devour it. The enemy of God's people is described under the same figure in verse 6 of the Psalm. There may be an allusion here to the company of Korah being swallowed up alive by an earthquake, Num. 16:30-33 where the same verb and adjective occur together. See Prov. 1:12; Psalms 35:25; 55:15. Such language describes the ravenous rage of the adversary.

"*Then* the waters . . . the stream . . . the proud water had gone over our soul." The sudden transition in the imagery of being swallowed up by an earthquake to being drowned by floods is characteristic of Hebrew poetry. By *waters*, so overwhelming, we can understand "floods." See Psalms 18:4, 16; 69:1, 14, 15; 145:7. "The devastating effects of the wild mountain torrents of Palestine, and especially the loss of life and property caused by the rushing overflowing Jordan, often supplied the Psalmists with a figure of ruin due to foreign and native oppressors, Isa. 8:7, 8; Lam. 3:34."

By the *stream*, the torrent swollen with the winter rain. In Palestine these streams become suddenly swollen after a storm. The repeated phrase "over our soul," implies the possibility of the life being overwhelmed by the storms of life if God is not on our side. Psalm 107:18, 19.

Floods, Swollen Rivers, now *Proud waters*. The word for "proud" is given as *surging* or *swelling*. This epithet has an echo in the lines of Aeschylus—

And you will reach the scornful river—well it deserves the name.

There may be an allusion here to the destruction of the Egyptians who perished in the Red Sea because God was not on their side, He was on the side of Israel protecting them against the overflowing waters. Saints have been sorely tried and threatened by the proud waters surging to engulf, but there has always been a "Hiterhto shalt thou come, but no further," Job 38:11. God makes of soft sand a strong bar to the sea, and His voice on high is ever greater than the voices of the deep. Job 38:8; Psalm 93:3, 4.

Before he died on December 7, 1834, Edward Irving was one of the strangest and most pathetic figures in the ecclesiastical history of the 18th century. Friend of Thomas Carlyle, Irving began to preach in a small London church, and high and low thronged to gaze upon his remarkable figure and to listen to his eloquent and prophetic outflowings. Caught up in the movement of "unknown tongues" and brought before the Presbytery of Annan, he was found guilty of heresy and cast out of the denomination, then went on to found his own Apostolic Church. Before sentence was pronounced upon him by the Presbyters, he cried to the crowd around him, "Stand forth! Stand forth! What! will ye not obey the voice of the Holy Ghost? As many as will obey the voice of the Holy Ghost, let them depart." He was spared the pain of hearing himself deposed by the Church which disowned his service, and said, "I sang in my heart, 'Blessed the Lord, Who hath not given us as a prey to their teeth,'" Psalm 124:5.

Blessed be the Lord! These sudden outbursts of praise to God are so characteristic of the sweet Psalmist of Israel, Psalms 28:6; 31:21. *Blessed* means happy or prosperous in the external sense, Matt. 5:3-11. It was indeed something to be happy about that God had preserved His people from being chewed to death by the teeth of their oppressors. The jaws of the wicked have no threat for those who have God on their side Who, for Daniel, kept the mouths of hungry lions closed.

The homely poet, Robert Herrick, who died in 1674, left us these stanzas on verses 4-6 of this Psalm—

> When winds and seas do rage,
> And threaten to undo me,
> Thou dost their wrath assuage,
> If I but call unto thee.
>
> A mighty storm last night
> Did seek my soul to swallow;
> But by the peep of light
> A gentle calm did follow.
>
> What need I then despair
> Though ills stand round about me;
> Since mischiefs neither dare
> To bark or bite without thee.

Our soul is escaped . . . Our help is in the name of the Lord, 124:7-8. While in exile in America the persecuted Huguenots were summoned to meetings by the singing of a Psalm. In the language of the Psalms was commemorated the escape of those who fled from their old country. An old seal, still in existence, once the property of a Huguenot refugee, bears as its device a net below, and above, a bird soaring upwards: and its motto, the words, "My soul is escaped even as a bird out of the snare of the fowler," Psalm 124:7.

In his praise for deliverance in verses 6 to 8, David makes a rapid transition from swollen rivers to the favorite figure of a hunter's net, Psalm 10:9 etc. By the *snare* some kind of a trap-net for catching birds is to be understood. Thus, the thought of verse 7 is, "we were ensnared as a bird, but we escaped as an ensnared bird sometimes does," Lam. 3:52. The pronoun *we* is emphatic in Hebrew: *and we—we are escaped.* How we marvel at the way the Evil One tries to ensnare us!

> Satan, the fowler who betrays
> Unguarded soul a thousand ways.

Quite unexpectedly this satanic trapper begins to weave the meshes of some net around the soul, and seems about to hold it captive. Then, all suddenly, and blessed be the moment, the strong deft hand of the Jehovah, Who is on the side of the ensnared one, interposes, as we sometimes interpose on behalf of a struggling insect in a spider's web. It is as easy for Him to deliver those bound by Satan as it is for us to break a thread-net a bird is caught in. When He provides the way of escape the snare falls into a tangled heap, and the soul is free. As the gates of the Celestial City opened for Robert Murray McCheyne, he joyously exclaimed, "My soul is escaped as a bird out of the snare of the fowler: the snare is broken, and I am escaped."

Our help . . . the Lord, who made heaven and earth, 124:8. Both parts of this final verse occur frequently in the Psalms. See Jonah 2:9, for the latter part of the verse. This is the verse the French Protestant Church always commenced its public worship with—a verse which well became the children of the Huguenots. Alfred Edersheim, a renowned expositor of the Psalms of a past generation, wrote of verses 1, 2, 8 as a *three-fold* he held in his hand, or rather was held by it, and therefore could never be fainthearted—

> "The Lord *was* on our side"—this for the *past.*
> "The snare *is* broken"—this for the *present.*
> "Our help *is* in the name of the Lord"—this for our *future.*

"The name of the Lord" implies Jehovah Himself. The Lord's name is the Lord Himself as revealed, and so the phrase *the name*, is simply another way of saying the Lord Himself, Psalm 83:16. May grace be ours to lean back on the truth that all the help of Omnipotence is pledged on the side of the weakest of the saints! *Blessed be Jehovah!* Proof of His Almightiness is seen in the making of heaven and earth. Because of His creative power He can create the deliverance of His people as well as their preservation. He made the *earth*, where the floods rage and snares are hidden, and so can command them to cease their fear for His own children. He made the *heaven*, the true sphere of the soaring wings of those He delivers from the hatred and cruelty of the godless. The Lord Jesus in whose name is our help, came down to *earth* that He might break the snare of Satan and returned victorious to *Heaven*, that we might fly "as the doves to their windows," Isa. 60:8. Says a devout writer of the 18th century—

> The Romans in a great distress were put so hard to it, that they were fain to take weapons out of the temples of their gods to fight with them; and so they overcame. And this ought to be the course of every good Christian in times of public distress, to fly to the weapons of the Church, Prayers and Tears. The Spartans' walls were their spears, the Christian's walls are his prayers. His help standeth in the name of the Lord who made both heaven and earth.

Psalm 125

It was this Psalm the Scotch frequently sung in the hours of danger during the Reformation Period, the accompanying tune being St. Andrews—

> They in the Lord that firmly trust
> Shall be like Zion hill;
> Which at no time can be removed,
> But standeth ever still.

This same Psalm was in constant use also among the French Protestants when hiding from the *dragonnades* of Louis XIV and fleeing to the frontiers for escape. Every verse and word of the Psalm seemed made for such emergencies. As to the historical background of the Psalm itself, it seems to bring prominently before us the constant danger to which Israel was subjected from heathen rule—a danger of being seduced away from the political and religious principles of the restored nation.

Hengstenberg in his great work on the Psalms says of this 125th Psalm—

> The Church first sang it under the oppression of heathen rule (verse 3): but in her own land: from the natural features of which the figures of her security in Divine protection are taken. Struggling with manifold troubles, which might have led her to doubt as to the protecting favor of God, she here rises above those in faith. While many of her members were true, others had departed from the living God (verses 4,5.) These circumstances are exactly those which existed after the deliverance from Captivity; at the time when the building of the temple was interrupted. Compare Psalms 120, 126.

Some writers, however, argue that as the Psalm does not date itself it is useless speculating when it was written; that like other Psalms, it might have been composed for use in worship with no reference to any historical situation. What the Psalmist set out to emphasize was the fact that those who remain faithful to Jehovah are secured, as Jerusalem itself is secured, by the strength of its geographical situation. Thus the prominent theme of the Psalm is the perpetual preservation and peace of the people of God.

As a further step in *The Songs of Degrees*, this Psalm marks another station reached in the pilgrimage upwards, for here we have a still higher form of assurance. Faith has praised Jehovah for just deliverances, now she rises to a confident joy and peace in the present and future security of believers. Pilgrims chanting this song as they encircled the city walls must have been thrilled as they sang of being eternally secure.

The Psalm carries no author's name, and we cannot therefore dogmatically assert that David wrote it. But as Spurgeon expresses it, "We have as much ground for saying David did write it as others have for declaring that it was written after the Captivity. It would seem probable that all the Pilgrim Psalms were composed, or, at least, compiled by the same writer, and as some of them were certainly by David, this is no conclusive reason for taking away the rest from him."

As the Psalm makes clear that Jehovah is the bulwark of His people, but evil-doers shall perish, it has the two-fold division—

1. Safety for all who trust in Jehovah, 1-3.
2. Prayer on behalf of the righteous, 4-5.

Mount Zion . . . The mountains round about Jerusalem, 125:1, 2. The key opening the door of perpetual security hangs on the front door of the Psalm, *They that trust in the Lord.* The "stability" of verse 1, compared to that of Mount Zion, and the "security" of verse 2, like that of a city girt with hills, are only the possession of those whose trust links them to God, enabling them to acquire something of His stability, as the limpet, sticking to the rock, partakes of the nature of the rock. Such trust must be always, altogether, and for all things. The greatest service we can render God is to trust Him implicitly. Then comes the infallible object of trust— *Jehovah!* What a privilege it is to be allowed to repose our trust and confidence in Him!

The result of such Spirit-begotten faith is a life as stable as the Mount where David lived and the Ark had its abode. Zion was the image of eternal steadfastness, and, according to the Hebrew, *sits to Eternity*, meaning that its removal is impossible; that is never moves to and fro, and therefore, a fitting emblem of Divine restfulness, or a mirror of heavenly tranquility. Mount Zion has its roots deep down in the earth and cannot be moved or changed, and as the believer is compared to such, so Jehovah is likened in verse 2 to those mountains encompassing Jerusalem which, in times of war, proved its best defense. As the sacred city is mountain-bound, so all who trust in Jehovah are compassed on all sides. See Zech. 2:5.

The first two verses of the Psalm, then, prove the eternal safety of the saints who must, of necessity, abide where God has placed them if they would be protected from all evil. What an exquisite picture these verses give us of the believer—God-encompassed; God-encircled; God-girt! As the mountains round about Jerusalem made the city well-nigh inaccessible and impregnable, so God is within, round about His people, warding off the attacks of foes who cannot get through to His own except through Him. How more restful we would be if only our eyes were opened to see the invulnerable walls surrounding us (2 Kings 6:17)! Zechariah likens the protecting care of Jehovah to a *wall* about a city, instead of the rampart of mountains, as here. Zech. 2:4,5.

The wicked . . . The upright . . . The workers of iniquity, 125:3-5. We group these remaining verses together because they remind us that although our faith and confidence are rooted in God, suffering and tyranny imposed by the wicked does not cease. Throughout our pilgrimage, the hostility of "the wicked one" himself and his wicked workers will be levelled against us. The sorrow of the poet's time was, that, although the majority of those trusting in the Lord remained faithful, a few had departed from Him, verses 4, 5. Continued oppression led them to give way to sin and doubt in the reign of righteousness.

The word for *rod* means scepter—"the scepter of wickedness." By the *righteous* we are to understand "Israel." The scepter of the wicked, or the presence of their tyranny, had been upon the Holy Land, but God will not allow such tyranny to last, lest those who were weak should be forced into connivance with practices alien to trust in the Lord. Thus verse 3 can be rendered, "Surely He will not let the scepter of the wicked man rest upon the land allotted to the righteous." The implication, then, of the last part of the Psalm is that heathen dominion shall be broken off lest in doubt and despair the righteous be tempted to turn to wicked practices; and that those who do hesitate between serving Jehovah and worldliness will be swept away with heathen idolaters.

We know only too well that the tendency of oppression can drive the best of men into some hasty action for self-deliverance or vengeance. "If the rack be too long used the patient sufferer may at last give way. But here we are taught that the Lord puts a limit to the tyranny of the wicked. Did He not ordain that an Israelite who deserved punishment should not be beaten without limit, but given 40 stripes save one as the appointed limit?" Persecution of the righteous may appear stable, but God sees to it that it is not continuous. Athanasius said of Julian the Apostate, as he died, "That little cloud has quickly passed away."

Trial is to improve trust not injure it, and God watches lest a saint be overcome by impatience or is drawn aside by the world's *allurements* or *affrightements*. Said Chrysostom, "God acts like a lutanist, who will not let the strings of his lute be too slack, lest it mar the music, nor suffer them to be too hard stretched or screwed up, lest they break." A safeguard against sinful compliance is personal goodness and the constant experience of the goodness of Jehovah.

Do good is one word in the Hebrew and means "show kindness, or favor to"—a virtue God shows towards those who do not turn aside to the crooked ways of the wicked. This fourth verse expresses the favorite thought of Nehemiah, "Remember me, O my God, for *good*," Neh. 2:8, 18; 5:19; 13:14,31. Believers are described as *good*, but they can only be good if their heart is *good* or right with good. When the heart is bad, all is bad. They must be "upright in heart," or straightforward, as opposed to all moral obliquity whatever if God is to do them good. Does not this note in this pilgrim song express the anxiety of a true pastor over those who turn their ways of life aside from what is right, making them crooked? David's distress was that all in Israel were not true Israelites, and the heart-break of a shepherd is to find some of the sheep of his flock forsaking the straight way. See 1 Sam. 6:12.

Crooked ways are usually by-paths, or private ways, apart from the highways. "The commandments of God are on the public road, and to travel along with them is peace, but certain misery to those who diverge from them." So we have the wonderful conclusion of the Psalm, *Peace shall be upon Israel!* Taking the first and last verses together, Israel trusts in the Lord—Israel has peace. And what peace have they who believe God is in them, with them, and round about them on every side so that no evil can come nigh their dwelling. If peace, "the sweet gift of God's love" is ours, then we can enjoy peace concerning all things. See Psalm 119:163.

Psalm 126

Some 900 years after the dirge of St. Cuthbert had been sung on the Northumbrian shores, in Psalm 60, James Melville, the famous Presbyterian champion, wrote in his Diary, 1585, how he and other Scottish exiles, returning home with "the bountiful and gracious of their God upon them," and reaching Alnwick on their homeward journey, were constrained to sing Psalm 126 many times—"When the Lord turned again the captivity of Zion." William Keith, a native of the North of Scotland, and one of the exiles at Geneva in the time of John Knox, wrote the version of this Psalm then in use, the first verse of which reveals the variety of rhythm employed—

> Full true it is
> > That they who sow with tears indeed,
> A time will come
> > When they shall reap in mirth and joy.
> They went and wept,
> > In bearing their precious seed,
> For that their foes
> > Full oftentimes did them annoy;
> But their return
> > With joy they sure shall see;
> Their sheaves home bring
> > And not impeded be.

The theme of this further Pilgrim Psalm seems to be that of past joy and present sorrow. This exquisite little poem is conspicuous for its sudden, abrupt transition from deliverance to distress, from triumph to tears, melody to murmuring, and songs to sobs. There is the assumption that at some not distant period in the past, Jehovah turned the tide of the nation's affairs, making the people once more joyful and prosperous. But then comes another change, this time for the worse, for we seem to have the petition and hope that Jehovah may again bless and prosper the nation after its captivity. "The recollection of the exuberant burst of joy at the first news of the return from the Captivity, enables the Psalmist to anticipate a similar change from gloom to gladness now. The words of the song are too deeply enshrined in the heart of the whole world to make us very anxious to recover the precise time which gave expression to the nameless poet's feelings." Thus the six verses are equally divided between—

1. Praise for a former time when prosperity returned after captivity, 1-3.
2. Prayer and hope for a renewal of that prosperity after another experience of captivity, 4-6.

When the Lord turned again the captivity . . . The Lord hath done great things, 126:1-3. The term *turn*, used twice, would seem to be the key-note of this Psalm which is a song of turning, of conversion from a condition of sore bondage. The repeated phrase, "turned again the captivity," verses 1 and 4, does not require an actual removal into exile to fill out the idea expressed. The phrase "turn again the captivity" means to make a change in things, then "to restore the fortunes." See Job 42:10. Thus the opening line of the Psalm can be rendered, "When Jehovah restored the fortunes of Zion, we were like them that dream." "Indeed, the passage is not applicable to captives in Babylon, for it is in Zion itself which is in captivity, and not a part of her citizens; the holy city was in sorrow and distress; though it could not be removed, the prosperity could be diminished. Some dark cloud lowered over the beloved capital, and the citizens prayed, *Turn again our captivity, O Lord*." See Isa. 52:8.

There are times when the soul seems to dwell in a captivity, hindering both its joy and devotion. Then suddenly and unexpectedly the captivity is turned, and the soul restored, and is as in times past. We know the release was the Lord's doing, and we found ourselves as in a blessed dream, Acts 12:9. It was so with new ecstacy of the Zion-dwellers, the gracious pilgrims in trouble but whose national woe seemed to vanish and left them in a trance. Their deliverance was great because the great God Himself had wrought, but it all seemed too good to be actually true. *We were like them that dream.*

> If this is a dream? O if it be a dream,
> Let me sleep on, and do not wake me yet.

Such unexpected and sudden emancipation from national distress left the people laughing, singing, glad, and testifying to God's gracious interference on their behalf. Note the *when* and the *then* used in these verses. "God's *when* is not *then*." The moment He turns the captivity, the heart turns from its sorrow, and irrepressible mirth found vent in laughter and lyrics. Mere speech is too dull an expression of such joy. So we can paraphrase the reaction to a Divine deliverance: "We could hardly think of the fact of our deliverance real, so delighted were we. We thought we must be dreaming." Sudden joy and sudden sorrow have often this stupefying effect. See Isa. 29:7; Luke 24:41. But when the consciousness of reality dawned upon the people of Zion, they laughed and sang. Job 8:21.

> When God reveal'd his gracious name
>   And changed our mournful state,
> Our rapture seem'd a pleasing dream,
>   The grace appeared so great.

Robert Estienne, the famous printer, was sustained by this Psalm throughout his long struggle with the theologians of the Sorbonne, who vetoed his editions of the Bible in the vulgar tongue.

> "Whenever," he said, "I recall to mind the war that I have waged with the Sorbonne, these twenty years and more, I have been astonished that so small and frail a person as myself could have had strength to continue the strug-·gle. Yet every time that memory reminds me of my deliverance, that voice in Psalm 126, celebrating the redemption of the Church, strikes an echo in my heart: *When the Lord turned again the captivity of Zion, then we were like unto them that dream.*"

"Then was our mouth filled with laughter, and our tongue with singing,"—the expression of ecstatic joy at the triumph of freedom and a righteous cause,—gave language to Fowell Buxton when he heard of the Abolition of the Slave Trade. It was deep religious feeling which nerved the men who stood in the van of that battle.

The dreaming and singing, however, resulted in a public witness to Jehovah Who alone was responsible for their dramatic and delightful change of fortune. "Then was it said among the heathen, The Lord hath done great things for them," and those foreigners were no dreamers. They could plainly see what had happened to the Jewish population, and ascribed the transition from gloom to gladness to the great Giver of all Good. Then the community of Zion took up the words of the heathen and made them their own—"God multiplied to do great things" Joel 2:21. But, as Lancelot Andrews expressed it—

> It is a pity the *heathen* said it and that the Jews themselves spake not these words first. But now, finding the *heathen* so saying, and finding it was all true that they said, they must needs find themselves bound to say at least as much; and more they could not say; for more cannot be said. So much then, and no less than they. And this addeth a degree to the *dicebant*—that the sound of it was so great among *the heathen* that it made an *echo* even in Jewry itself.

Streams . . . Tears . . . Seed . . . Sheaves, 126:4-6. In these last three verses we have a change of tempo and of metaphorical language. We go from *dreams* to *streams* and *sheaves*, from singing to weeping. Just what

Psalms: *A Devotional Commentary*

is implied in this further turning is not easy to decide. Several writers feel it applies to exiles still in captivity, and the prayerful desire to return and re-join their already delivered brethren. Thus, Ellicott comments, "The joy of the great Return was too great not to last on through many vicissitudes. But the poet now thinks of the many exiles still dispersed among the nations, and prays for another manifestation of Divine favor and power." F.B. Meyer, in his study on *The Psalms* concurs, and says, "Much had been done for the exiles: but a large portion of the nation was still in bondage, and heavy disabilities remained on those who had returned. When God has done much for us, we may venture to ask more."

Other expositors, however, think that this concluding half of the Psalm is a prayer on the part of those already saved from what held them captive for the perfecting of the deliverance, for the turning of the dried-up experiences into stream; for the turning of an ocean of tears into a harvest of joy. Having had great things accomplished for them by Jehovah, the people would not let Him go until He had given them beauty for their ashes, or to change the emblem, a harvest of delight for the seed-tears they had sown. What was previously said in the plural—*they*, is here repeated in the singular—*he*. Thus the general assurance of a joyful reaping is applied to each one in particular. An old proverb has it—

> He that believes what he doth not see—this is the seed:
> Shall one day see what he hath believed—this is the harvest.

Sow in tears is an arrestive phrase illustrating the afflictions of God's people, with many of them weeping more than others over their own shortcomings, over the lost around them, over a world so corrupt, violent and doomed. In verses 4 and 5 we have as streams of tears, which are somewhat different from "the streams of the South" which is full deliverance from bondage as described.

The allusion is to the sudden filling of the dry torrent-beds of the Southern district of Palestine in the rainy season, and the poet prays that the same rapidity, with which the torrents pour into the desolate and deserted country, may be experienced in a spiritual way by the people of God who had been so desolate.

Reap in joy. Both the sowing and the reaping are figurative expressions for the commencement of undertakings and their results. "Those who sow in tears begotten of labor and anxiety, have joy when the reaping comes. Israel had toiled and wept enough; surely the time of joyous reaping has arrived." Probably, the verse, "They that sow in tears shall reap in joy"— *singing*, as the margin has it, may have been a current proverb which the poet "touched with the consecrating hand till it has become only less precious than the saying of the Divine lips—*Blessed are they that mourn, for they shall be comforted*."

A somewhat cryptic saying of Chrysostom, was, "If thou wouldest be cheerful, be sad"—which was but another way of confirming the quotation from St. Basil that "holy mourning is the seed out of which the flower of eternal joy doth grow." Tears over lost souls are never *lost*; and the tears of penitence on the part of the lost become seals of comfort as God pours in the joy of sins forgiven. This 5th verse was a favorite one of Philip Henry, father of the renowned Matthew Henry, who used to say that "weeping should not hinder sowing," and his death brought about a fulfillment of it. Philip died suddenly on the morning of a fast for public danger, when he was to have preached. Some members wished to postpone the service, but the text was quoted for having the special service, and his son Matthew preached in his father's stead from 2 Kings 13:20, "And Elisha died . . . and the bands of the Moabites invaded the land."

As those delivered by Christ from him who held us captive at his will, we must not count as lost the seeds we sow, or the tears in which we steep them. We must rest on the Psalmist's *doubtless*, which is God's guarantee of a harvest of joy. Precious tears! Precious seed! Precious reward! See Jer. 31:9, 14. The original of the final verse of the Psalm is very expressive and reads—

> He shall walk, and walk and weep,
> Bearing the handful of seed;
> He shall come, and come with singing,
>   Bearing his sheaves.

Ellicott says that "we must certainly see here an extension and not a mere repetition of the former figure, for the very form of the expression suggests the long patient labor of the sower, and the reward which patience and perseverance always brings—a harvest in proportion to the toil and trouble of seed-time. Haggai 1:10, 11; 2:19 . . . The contrast is so beautifully painted in this 6th verse of the Psalm was certainly realized when *the priests and Levites, and the rest of the children of the captivity, kept the dedication of the house of God with joy*, Ezra 6:16. See Ezra 6:2 and Neh. 12:42." Without doubt, the last two verses of this pilgrim Psalm remain vivid in our minds through the constant singing of Sankey's great hymn based on them—*Sowing in the morning*.

Psalm 127

This center Psalm of the 15 Songs of Degrees has many interesting historical and biographical associations. During the Crusades when there was a fierce struggle between the temporal and spiritual powers of the time, the Psalms were often in use. For instance, on October 3, 1187, Jerusalem was again taken by Saladin, and Pope Clement III urged the bishop to preach another Holy War, having Psalm 127 as their text, "Except the Lord build the house, they labor in vain that build it." Baldwin, Archbishop of Canterbury, was one who responded to the appeal, and, downing the White Cross of England, raised the banner of St. Thomas and preached the Crusade in Wales, chanting this Psalm and others as war-songs of his recruits. At the head of his troop, he left England for Jerusalem March 6th, 1190, eager to win back "the sepulchre of Christ," and, as Shakespeare expresses it in *Henry IV—*

> So chase these Pagans, in those holy fields,
> Over whose acres walked those blessed feet,
> Which fourteen hundred years ago were nail'd
> For our advantage on the bitter cross.

The inscription of the Psalm should be, as the margin suggests, "A Song of Degrees *of* Solomon," and not *for* Solomon. It was not written by another for him, but by the illustrious King himself, seeing that he was the great *human* builder of the Temple. Then the word "his beloved" in verse 2, is *Jedidiah* in the original, which was Jehovah's name for Solomon, 2 Sam. 12:25. To his credit he confessed that he could never have built the Temple without Jehovah's inspiration and guidance. Further, Psalm 127 has a resemblance to the Book of Proverbs both in form and sentiment. Proverbs 10:22, for example, sums up the prevailing thought of Solomon's Psalm.

Spurgeon, however, has a slightly different approach to the authorship of the Psalm. "Probably David wrote it for his wise son, in whom he so greatly rejoiced, and whose name Jedidiah, or 'beloved of the Lord,' is introduced in the second verse. The spirit of his name, *Solomon*, meaning, 'peaceable,' breathes through the whole of this most charming song." If Solomon himself was the author, it comes fitly from him who reared the house of the Lord. Psalm 72 is another connecting the title with the name of Solomon. In the LXX Version of Psalm 127, Solomon's name does not appear.

It is clearly seen that the Psalm is in two parts leading some critical scholars to affirm that the Psalm is made up of two smaller ones without any special connection with each other. But we believe that it was written by the one hand at the same time as a spiritual ode to declare that human effort or success is impossible without Jehovah's power and protection, verses 1 and 2—that godly children are the joy and defense of their father, verses 3 to 5. The repeated phrase, *Except the Lord*! is most arrestive, and proves along with a few former Degree Psalms that the heart must be fixed upon Jehovah only. Think of those other opening catch-phrases—*I cried unto the Lord. I will lift up mine eyes. Let us go into the house of the Lord. Unto thee will I lift up mine eyes. If it had not been the Lord.*

As the pilgrims paused in their ascent, Jehovah alone was exalted, and our pilgrimage is thrice blessed if each halting pace suggests a new song unto the Lord, and brings us to this, *The Builder's Psalm*, with its message that "Every house is builded by some man, but he that built all things is God," which applies to churches and empires, houses and cities. As *sons* are called "builders" in the Hebrew, the last part of the Psalm also extends the thought of Jehovah as the Builder of The Temple, and Watchman of the City, as the One Who overrules in the building up of families under His grace and blessing. The thrice repeated *in vain* serves to remind us of the utter futility of attempting any undertaking without Jehovah's interposition or perfect help. Benjamin Franklin, in his 1787 *Speech to the Convention for forming a Constitution for the United States*, said to the large assembly gathered, "If a sparrow cannot fall to the ground without God's notice, is it possible that an empire can rise without His aid?"

Affirming that the rhythm of this Psalm is fine and varied, Ellicott further comments on its most prominent feature common to Hebrew literature, namely, God's over-ruling providence covering both the greater purpose of human activity, and the homeliest duty of everyday life—

> Man's toil, and skill, and care would be all unavailing were there not a "Divinity shaping our ends" . . . All fall under the same benign and watchful purveillance. The smallest details, as the largest concerns of life, are objects of the Divine regard; and in little things, as well as the great, the great lesson to learn is that man cannot of himself command success, though it awaits the weakest who has the Divine blessing. If any particular set of circumstances must be sought for this expression of a truth so firmly planted in Israel, it is natural to look for them during the troubles and anxieties which accompanied the restoration and rebuilding of Jerusalem. Possibly the haste to rebuild the private houses before the public necessities were supplied (see Haggai 1:2, 4) may have given the motive for this poem, though it is but in the most delicate way, and under figures universally applicable, that the people are reminded that home, and a family, and property alike depend on God.

Build ... Keep ... Eat ... Sleep, 127:1, 2. The opening verse of this
Psalm has greatly appealed to builders of houses, institutions, and empires.
We shall more fully see this was the verse that Benjamin Franklin used in
1787 when he brought before the American Convention the formation of an
independent nation. Ancient families sought their Mottoes from the Psalms,
and that of the Beauchamps is *NISI DOMINUS FRUSTA*, Psalm 127:1. The
verse chosen by Smeaton for the Eddystone Lighthouse he built was, "Except
the Lord build the house, they labor in vain that built it." Inscriptions over the
doors of houses still indicate the homes of the Huguenots. At Zainton, for
example, is the motto taken from Psalm 127, verse 1. This same verse is
inscribed on the front of the Town Hall, Ripon, England.

The *house* can mean any house, and not necessarily the Temple, the
building of which, some writers feel, may have been in Solomon's mind
when he wrote this Psalm. The thought expressed is a common one, and
the lesson to be taken from it is that even in the common labors of men,
it is the Divine blessing which contributes the success; that in all our
undertakings there must be dependence on the blessing of God which is
the only true source of prosperity, and which should be sought on the
threshold of every undertaking.

These first two verses do not teach that we are not to build and watch,
leaving *all* to God, but that condemnation is ours if in our building and
watching we act independently of God, or have any hope of permanently
succeeding apart from Him. We must be fellow-workers with Him,
Proverbs 10:22. The verb for *labor* means *to work oneself weary*: but even
this avails not if God does not build with us or bless us. The same thought
applies to the *watchman* or "keeper," 121:4—one who acts the part of
keeper. The Psalmist does not suggest that the watchmen should not be
always on the alert, or neglect their duty, or show their trust in God by
doing no watching. The order of Oliver Cromwell was, "Trust in God, and
keep your powder dry"; and "happy is the believer who hits the golden
mean by so working as to believe in God, and so believing in God as to
work without fear."

This was the truth Madam Guyon became assured of, and her entire
dependence on Divine Grace became her dominant witness, and she
wrote, "I became deeply assured of what the Psalmist hath said, *Except
the Lord keep the city the watchman waketh but in vain*. When I looked
to Thee, O my Lord, Thou wast my faithful keeper: Thou didst continually defend my heart against all kinds of enemies. But, alas! when left
to myself, I was all weakness, how easily did my enemies prevail over
me! ... It is to Thee O God, my Deliverer, that I owe everything! And it
is a source of infinite satisfaction, that I am indebted to Thee!" Phineas
Fletcher, who died in 1650, left us the following expressive stanzas on the
two opening verses of this Psalm—

> If God build not the house, and lay
>   The groundwork sure—whoever build,
> It cannot stand one stormy day.
>   If God be not the city's shield,
> If he be not their bars and wall,
> In vain is watch-tower, men, and all.
> Though then thou wak'est when others rest,
> Though rising thou prevent'st the sun,
> though with lean care thou daily feast,
>   Thy labor's lost; and thou undone;
> But God his child will feed and keep,
> And draw the curtains to his sleep.

Extending his proverbial exhortation, Solomon warns us against giving overdue and anxious labor to the accomplishment of our purposes. Artificial lengthening of the day to work beyond our physical and intellectual ability and beyond the hours nature allots is implied in the uselessness of rising early or sitting up late, and of eating "the bread of sorrows," or of the bread of long, wearisome toil. The artificial prolonging of the day at either end brings little good. As Charles F. Beams wrote in his helpful volume *The Study*—

> Early rising, eating one's breakfast by candlelight, and prolonged vigils, the scholar's *midnight oil*, are a delusion and a snare. *Work while it is day.* When the night comes, rest. The other animals do this, and as races, fare as well as this anxious human race.

Spurgeon uttered a similar warning when he wrote, "Some deny themselves needful rest; the morning sees them rise before they are rested, the evening sees them toiling long after the curfew has tolled the knell of parting day. They threaten to bring themselves into the sleep of death by neglect of the sleep which refreshed life." Witton Davies has the note at this second verse, "The idea is: Jehovah gives the needful to those whom He loves even if they cannot move a hand to toil—as it were when they are asleep. The lesson is simply, 'Be not anxious; He provides': there is no encouragement here for idleness or carelessness; we are to labor, but to trust as if all depended upon God. See Matt. 6:25-34; Prov. 10:22."

No need to eat such bread of toil, when *in* peaceful sleep, God gives what is suitable and sufficient. Let others toil early and late, worry and vex themselves, and make little progress; for us, God's loved ones, there is prosperity even when we take the sleep He gives, Mark 4:27. An alternative reading has it, "He giveth unto His beloved *in* sleep," implying that while others wear themselves down with labor and sorrow, the blessing of God comes to the faithful even when they are resting and asleep. They are not slack as to their toils, but relief of the over-pressure of the nightmare of care is theirs. They have done their best, and leaving the results to God, sleep peacefully. Solomon, who wrote these words about *sleep*, received the desire of his heart from God as he slept. Peter, although in prison, bound with fetters, guarded by soldiers, and under sentence to die the next day, was fast asleep, and it took an angel's rough handling to wake him and take him out of prison, Acts 12:6, 7. The original "giveth sleep," implies a quiet rest without care or sorrow. Such was the undisturbed sleep Peter experienced.

A Greek proverb has it, "The net catches while the fisher sleeps," and a German saying goes, "God bestows His gifts during the night." See Mark 4:27. Solomon's beautiful proverb "makes sleep the gift of God, and if there is one thing which seems to come more direct from Heaven's bounty than another, that is its character as more benign, in its effects more akin to the nature of God, it is the blessing of sleep. In the times men have rendered thanks to Heaven for this boon. The ancients spoke of sleep as 'most grateful of known gifts,' but made itself as God."

Often *in* sleep, noble hearts have had dreams of ventures, plans, and achievements, and in the morning, remembering what they dreamt have recorded same, and then went on to make the dream a reality. It is said that Spurgeon would occasionally preach in his sleep, and that his diligent wife was always ready with pencil and pad to capture her husband's sublime, unconscious, yet God-given thoughts, thereby supplying him with material for a Sunday sermon. Elizabeth Barrett Browning, who died in 1861, at the age of 52, gives us the stanza—

> Of all the thoughts of God that are
> Borne inward into souls afar,
>   Along the Psalmist's music deep,
> Now tell me if that any is,
> For gift or grace surpassing this -
>   *He giveth his beloved—sleep.*

Heritage . . . Fruit . . . Arrows . . . Quiver full of them, 127:3-5. On the surface it would seem as if this remaining section of the Psalm presents an abrupt and sudden change of thought, yet it is not so. We are simply passing from the building and defense of houses and cities to rearing of those who live in them. Children are the heritage of Jehovah and the defense of their parents. According to Jewish belief children are one of God's greatest blessings, yet given without the laborious thought and care of men, as sleep is given. As an "heritage of the Lord" implies that a home receives children from Jehovah as they in turn inherit property from their earthly parents. Then there is a change of figure from *heritage* to *reward*, for the fruit of the womb is payment for uprightness of life.

Family life, like sleep, is God's gift. See Gen. 30:2; 33:5. Of old, children were reckoned to be a heritage *from* Jehovah, or a promise granted by Him, just as Israel herself was a possession He made for Himself.

Doubtless there are some parents who look on their children more of a burden than a blessing. But if there are "doubtful blessings," it is only because of their doubtful parents. To the children of God, children are chiefly a blessing. John Howard Hinton's daughter said to the famous Baptist leader as she knelt by his death-bed: "There is no greater blessing than for children to have godly parents." "And the next," said the dying father with a beam of gratitude, "for parents to have godly children."

Solomon adds yet another emblem for children for he speaks of them as *arrows*, and the parents are happy who have a *quiver* full of them. A 15th century writer says that children are "well-called *arrows*, for if they are well bred, they will shoot at their parents' enemies, and if evil bred, they shoot at their parents." *Arrows* go the way we aim them, and our children are what we make them. In a collection of Chinese Proverbs, there is one that reads—"When a son is born into a family, a bow and arrow are hung at the gate"—to which the following note is appended—"As no such custom appears to be literally observed, this should seem to be a metaphorical expression, signifying that a new protector is added to the family."

"Children, or sons, of the youth," implies those who are born when their parents are young, or who have an early marriage. See Genesis 37:2, 3; Isa. 54:6. The allusion is not only to the vigor of the children themselves, Genesis 49:3, but to their value to their parents in declining years, or able to protect them when they are old, verse 5. Sons stand up in a just cause and appeal for justice from enemies.

> This is the pride, the glory of a man,
> To train obedient children in his house,
> Prompt on his enemies to avenge his wrongs,
> And with the father's zeal in honor high
> To hold his friends.

No wonder Solomon said, "Happy is the man that hath his quiver full," of such children! The great Dr. Thomas Guthrie who had eleven children, once remarked, "I am rich in nothing but children." Moses Browne, a renowned Baptist minister of the early 18th century, replied to a friend who said to him, "Sir, you have just as many children as Jacob"—"Yes, and I have Jacob's God to provide for them." A clan of true and noble sons are well able to meet foes of their parents both in law and fight. "He speaks to purpose whose own sons make his words emphatic by the resolve to carry out their father's wishes."

> Therefore men pray to have around their hearth,
> Obedient offspring, to requite their foes
> With harm, and honor whom their father loves;
> But he whose issue is unprofitable,
> Begets what else but sorrow to himself,
> And store of laughter to his enemies.

Tate and Brady have also expounded in rhyme the last two verses of this Psalm.

> As arrows in a giant's hand
>   When marching forth to war,
> E'en so the sons of sprightly youth
>   Their parents' safeguard are.
> Happy the man whose quiver's filled
>   With these prevailing arms;
> He needs not fear to meet his foe
>   At law, or war's alarms.

Alas! some parents have a *quiver* but no *arrows*, for they are childless, and have no sons or daughters to comfort and care for them in riper years. Had they had children they might have grown up to be godless and worthless, and a constant heart-break, instead of the promised happiness Solomon wrote of. Others have a *quiver* but it is not full of *arrows*—perhaps only a single *arrow*. Yet the lives of parents do not consist in the abundance of the children they possess but in living as the children of God, by faith in His beloved Son, and who have in God a heavenly Father, well able to protect and provide for them when they are old and grey.

Psalm 128

The Dauphin, who became Henry II, delighted in singing Marot's version of the Psalms to popular music. Sometimes he composed his own tunes and surrounded himself with musicians who accompanied his voice on the viol or the lute. Courtiers adopted their special Psalms, just as they adopted particular family mottoes. As Henry was yet without an heir, he sang to his own music Psalm 128 which promises to the God-fearing man a wife as the *fruitful vine* and children *like the olive-branches*. Afterwards when Catherine de Medici bore Henry ten children, Psalm 128 took on a new meaning for him.

Continuing the domestic strain of the previous Psalm, this one has been called *The Home, Sweet Home* of Judaism, seeing it depicts the blessedness of a man's family and of his work when he fears God. Ascent from the last Psalm is clearly apparent, for there we were shown how a house may be built up. Here, in Psalm 128, we have a picture of that house finished and adorned with domestic bliss through the Lord's own blessing. We go from children to children's children, and from their being as *arrows* to olive-plants. Psalm 127 closes with *enemies at the gate*—Psalm 128 with the benediction, *Peace upon Israel!* Although this Psalm is given no authorship because it continues the family idea of Psalm 127, it would seem that the writer of one was the composer for the other. Since its appearance it has sung its way through the world, refreshing the hearts of godly parents as streamlets running among hills, seeing its burden is the blessedness of true godliness in the entire range of human life. Made up of poetry of the highest order, this Psalm is "a family hymn—a song for a marriage, or a birth, or for any doing in which a happy household has met to praise the Lord." It would seem as if this Psalm was written for the commendation, instruction and consolation of those who were either married or about to enter such a bond, and so enumerates the various phases of home life in which children are found.

Ellicott, who says that the parallelism of this Psalm is perfect, has the most comprehensive and suggestive introduction of it that we have encountered in our perusal of many works dealing with it—

> The last Psalm taught in a homely way the great lesson of cheerful content, and this, while announcing the promises attached to fidelity to Jehovah, still confines itself to the domestic circle—with the implied truth that national prosperity is bound up closely with domestic happiness, and

depends on the cultivation of domestic virtues. And what an idyllic picture
is here of peace and happiness!—the natural effects of that spirit of simple
piety which often preserves itself through many generations under a humble roof. We see the father of the family, working hard no doubt, but
recompensed for all his pains by an honorable competence, and the
mother, instead of seeking distraction outside her home, finding all her pleasure in the happiness of her numerous children, who, fresh and healthy, as
young saplings, gather round the simple but ample board. Happy the family, poor or rich, whose annals tell such a tale! But the happiness could not
be real or sincere which did not look beyond the home circle, to the prosperity of the larger circle of the nation of which it forms part; and so, like
Burns' famous poem, which, in telling the story of the Scottish peasant's
home-life, has caught the very spirit of the old Hebrew song, The Psalmist
ends with a patriotic prayer.

Blessed . . . Thine hands . . . Thy wife . . . Thy children, 128:1-3. The
benediction—*Blessed*, and the exclamation—*Behold*, divide this Psalm
into equal parts of three verses each. In verses 1-3, we have the fear of the
Lord resulting in the prosperity of the daily occupation and of the home
of those who walk in His ways. Then in verses 4-6, we have the Lord's
benediction resting upon the God-fearing man with the added prosperity of his own family and nation 4-6.

The word *blessed,* used in the opening verse meaning happy or fortunate, refers not to the character nor even to the feelings, but to the outward
life of the one described. His lot is a privileged one, having prosperity and
a happy home life. See Psalm 84:4. Continuously throughout the Old
Testament we find blessedness associated with godliness, Deut. 7:12-14;
28:1-14; Job 1:10; Psalm 33:12 etc. Emphasis to this verse is on the words
everyone, implying that such a blessing is for all, Jews and Gentiles who
comply with the conditions—"feareth the Lord"—"Walketh in His
ways." As for the *fear*, same is not dread, but a reverential confidence born
of love and the inner temper of the devout heart, revealing itself as a consistent and obedient walk. We walk in Jehovah's ways when we walk in
the Spirit, Gal. 5:16, 25. The last Psalm ended with a blessing for the word
in 127:6 "happy" is the same rendered here as "blessed." Thus, the two
songs are joined by a catch-word, and the fear of the Lord as the corner-
stone of all blessedness is the subject of both songs.

It is useless speaking about fearing the Lord unless we are prepared to
walk in His ways. *Fear of the Lord* is the internal principle, but unless
there is a corresponding expression in the outward life, the existence of
the inner principle is to be doubted. But if such a fear is established in the
heart, then with God walking with us, we delight to walk in His ways.
Walking is a natural action, and those who truly fear Jehovah are spiritually natural—practical as well as devotional. See Prov. 2:3-5. *The labor*

of thine hands of the second verse presents us with a personal application of the opening verse.

The spiritual responsibility of the believer is to "fear" and "walk," and his practical responsibility is to "work" and to enjoy the sustenance and happiness it provides. He is not to be so heavenly-minded as to be of no earthly use. Being in God's hands, we have our daily bread by working with our own hands, and as we labor He labors with us, seeing that we are laborers together. As the narrative is taken up with the bliss of married life, the law of nature demands that the father must sustain his wife and children. Hesiod, the ancient poet, gave the counsel, "First thou shouldest get thee a house, then a wife, and also an ox to till the ground," and therefore able to maintain a home.

It is only thus that the man of God can be happy, or, as the original has it, "Happiness shalt thou have." Heaped up happiness in the plural belong to that man who fears the Lord, walks in His ways, and to whom labor is beneficial. Further, it is always well to those who live and do well. "It shall be well with thee" can be translated *good for thee.* Although the sweat of our face as we seek to produce bread to eat is one aspect of the curse pronounced by man because of his sin, yet God crowns the honest and faithful labor of His own with blessing. As James Montgomery put—

> Labor, the symbol of man's punishment;
> Labor, the secret of man's happiness.

It shall be well with thee! This pledge is met with often in Scripture, Deut. 4:40; 5:16; 6:3; Ephes. 6:3; and is one so true of the godly even amid calamity and sorrow, in the deepest, and best, and most permanent sense. See Isa. 65:18-25. The most prominent aspect of this prosperity is that of a happy and peaceful home wherein the godly, industrious man has a wife and children who bring him great joy. The general way in which the God-fearing man is mentioned is now personalized and so we read of "*thy* wife . . . *thy* children . . . *thine* house . . . *thy* table."

The two figures of speech from fruitbearing trees—*vine* and *olives*—are in Hebrew poetry frequently emblems of fruitfulness and of a happy, flourishing state. See Psalm 52:8; Jerem. 11:16. We recognize, of course, that not every man who fears the Lord and walks in His ways has a wife. Yet if he should find one, he finds a good treasure who will share in his blessedness. By "the sides of the house" is understood the inner part of the house, Psalm 48:2, the private section for the woman's use, Gen. 18:9, and in which the godly wife and mother is content to live and not waste her time in idle gossip "at the door of her house on a seat in the high places of the city," Prov. 9:14. Her apartment in tent or house would be farthest away from the main entrance.

Within such the wife was as a "fruitful vine," with children adding to the domestic bliss of the home. As a vine is planted to produce grapes, so the woman was created to bear children. The *vine* is an emblem chiefly of *fruitfulness* but perhaps also of dependence as needing *support*, both of which come to the godly wife of the God-fearing husband with the children of both becoming like *olive plants*. This comparison of children to the healthy young shoots of a tree is common to all poetry and latent in expressions like *scion of a noble house*, or a *sweet young shoot of children*. Jesus grew up as a *tender plant* in a godly home. What a blessed privilege it is to be born into and reared within a home where parents "walk in His ways." See Psalm 145:12 for the ideal home. The *olive* is a precious tree in Palestine and godly children of godly parents are a most valuable possession in their vigorous, healthy and useful years, so long as the home is intact. Before the fall of our first parents Paradise was their home; but through grace *home* can become a Paradise re-gained.

What a complete family picture the Psalmist gives us with husband, wife, children, house, rooms in the side, and the table, with all such domestic peace and happiness the peculiar blessing of piety. Godliness makes such relationships joyous and profitable, and produces a domestic peace the sweetest of human felicity. *Behold*! Take a note of this for it is worthy of observation—a charming picture of a domestic bliss and then the moral of same. "May Jehovah bless thee out of Zion: mayest thou see the good of Jerusalem all the days of thy life!" Jerusalem was the center of religious worship where the Temple stood as the focus for the religious life and thought of the nation, its prosperity being intimately associated with the lives and homes of the people. Thus the spiritual and temporal act and inter-act, Psalms 20:2; 122:2-6. "No people ever perceived more strongly than the Jews the connection between the welfare of the State and that of the Family."

The crowning joy of the man God blesses because he fears Him, is to see his *children's children*. This promise accords with other declarations of such a blessing, Psalm 103:17; Prov. 13:22. Ezekiel pictured restored Israel as having aged men and women looking with satisfaction on boys and girls of a third or fourth generation playing in the streets, Ezek. 37:25; See Zech. 8:4, 5. Happy are those who can claim the promise of Isaiah 59:21 here and now! The repeated phrase, *Thou shalt see*, expresses purpose and implies—"Do this that thou mayest."

A sweet and favorite benediction closes this charming Psalm. *Peace upon Israel*! The conjunction *and* spoils this last passage for such a concluding prayer stands by itself, and it is only connected with the grandchildren and great-grandchildren of the God-fearing in as much as godly homes contribute to the true peace of a nation. What a more peaceful and prosperous country ours would be if only we had more fragrant homes like those depicted in this Psalm! When home-life deteriorates through departing from God, the spiritual and moral life of the nation decays.

Psalm 129

What a striking contrast the previous Psalm and this one afford. Psalm 128 begins with a benediction and ends with one, but Psalm 129 commences with much affliction and trial yet ends with a double blessing, and is a mingled hymn of sorrow and yet of strong resolve. As a rustic song, full of allusion to husbandry, the Psalm before us reminds us of the Books of Ruth and Amos. This is the Psalm that had an important ministry in a peculiar crisis of the history of the ancient Church of the Waldenses. When Louis XIV, in 1685, revoked the Edict of Nantes, he succeeded by promises and threats in inducing Amadeus, Duke of Savoy, to expel the Vaudois of Italy from their valleys and to plant the Romanists in their stead. Thousands were sent to prison for refusing to renounce their faith while others were permitted to retire to Switzerland. But after two years the exiles yearned for the old home, and in the autumn of 1689, a band of 800 men resolved to regain their valleys or die.

In frail boats under cover of night, these brave men led by Henri Arnaud, their heroic Pastor and Colonel, crossed the Lake of Geneva, but an unfriendly population and hostile troops greatly hindered their return. At last, after fighting their way back to their homes, "the gallant patriots took an oath of fidelity to each other, and celebrated Divine service in one of their own churches for the first time since their banishment. The enthusiasm of the moment was inexpressible: they chanted the 74th Psalm to the clash of arms. Then Henri Arnaud, mounting the pulpit with a sword in one hand and a Bible in the other preached a stirring sermon from Psalm 129, and once more declared in the face of Heaven, that he would never resume his pastoral office in patience and peace, until he should witness the restoration of his brethren to their ancient and rightful settlements."

The Psalm before us has much in common with Psalm 124, both being alike in form and manner, with two strophes, the first celebrating God's protection of Israel in the past. The second line in both is identical, *Let Israel now say*: and in both the first line is repeated. Probably deliverance from Babylon gave rise to both Psalms. This song of deliverance in trouble and the overthrow of the wicked is another of the nameless Pilgrim Songs in the group we are considering. As we do not know the order of the stations on the pilgrimage to the Temple, we cannot explain the position of the 129th Psalm in the ascent. A lament of long suffering, it does not seem to be a step beyond the previous beautiful Psalm unless we reckon *Patience* to be the more difficult grace than domestic love. If we do, then the ascent or progress can be discerned, seeing the afflicted one remained heart-whole, and scorned to yield in the least degree to the enemy. "In the *Degrees* of Christian virtue, the Psalm corresponds to the tenth step, which is patience in adversity."

The two-fold division of the Psalm is clearly apparent—

1. The poet looks back on Israel oppressed and tortured in the past from which the Lord, in His mercy, had delivered His people, 1-4.
2. Faith concludes that, however proudly the enemy may bear himself, God will certainly visit him with utter ruin, hence, the imprecations, 5-8.

Past deliverances of Jehovah from the bondage imposed by foes is the guarantee that He will intervene again on behalf of His persecuted people.

Afflicted . . . Afflicted . . . The Plowers . . . The Wicked, 129:1-4. Beginning abruptly, the poet, who had been musing, now speaks, and so "may now say" what he has to say, namely that Israel had proceeded from tribulation to tribulation from his youth on. He was, of course, referring to Israel's repeated afflictions which had been hers from the time God called the nation into being. And it had been good for her to bear the yoke in her youth. See Hosea 2:15. Israel's bondage in Egypt is spoken of as *her youth*, Hosea 11:1. A long series of oppressions had been suffered by the race as passages like Ezek. 23:3; Jer. 2:2; 22:21 declare. The repeated words, *Many a time*, is one word in the Hebrew and means "long," "exceedingly," "abundantly," and "much." Here we can read, "Much have they afflicted me." Further, in the original there is no adverb of time— *now*, and the phrase reads, "Let Israel say," See Psalm 124:1.

But what a ring of triumph there is in the defiant declaration—"Yet they have not prevailed against me!" This *Yet* breaks in like a blast of trumpets echoing forth the note of victory. Israel was often "cast down, but not destroyed," as her long history proves. Such was her disdain of her cruel foes that Israel does not name them, but simply identified them by the pronoun *they*—and one can imagine the stinging emphasis with which it was uttered. They did not deserve to be named, even as the rich man was not who went to Hell, Luke 16.

It may be that some of us look back on our youth, so full of promise, but many afflictions we little expected overtook us. Yet the God of our youth was with us and brought us through to victory. We proved that there is always a *Yet*, See Isa. 44:1; 49:15; Jer. 3:1. Now, we do not dwell on our afflictions but on the revelation they afforded of the strong and tender care of God. Too often, it is only in affliction that God is *sought*, and only in affliction that God is *known*. See 2 Chron. 33:12, 13. The repetition of the words, *They have afflicted me* is not superfluous, but emphasizes the truth that the people of God had not merely once or twice to enter the conflict, but that their patience had been tried and found not wanting by continual exercises.

The next two verses reveal the extremity of the torture inflicted, and also Divine intervention on behalf of the afflicted. What a gruesome affliction it must have been to have the wicked, cruel foes to plow the back of Israel, and to make long furrows in her history! What a striking metaphor the poet uses to describe the nation so cruelly maltreated by her enemies! The verses are a grand piece of imagery condensed into few words and a figurative mode of expressing severe persecution. Alexander Peden, renowned leader of the Scottish Covenanters, when preaching in Kyle in the year 1682, used this text, "The plowers plowed upon my back, and drew long their furrows," and in the course of a lengthy and stirring sermon asked—

> Would you know who first yoked this plough? It was cursed Cain, when he drew his furrow long and deep, that he let out the heart-blood of his brother Abel . . . and that plough has and will gang summer and winter, frost and fresh-weather, till the worlds's end; and at the sound of the last trumpet, when all are in a flame, their threats (traces) will know, and their singletrees will fall to the ground; the plow-men will lose their grip of the plough, and the gade-men will throw their gades; and then, O the yelling and screeching that will be among his cursed seed, clapping their hands, and crying to the hills and mountains to cover them from the face of the Lamb and of Him that sits upon the throne, for their hatred of Him and malice at his people!

The lashing of a slave and the actual and terrible imprints of oppression form the combination of two prophetic figures given by Isaiah. See 50:6; 51:33; and Micah 3:12. The whip was in constant use in Egypt and Palestine, and oppressors would lash their captives until their backs were marked like plowed fields. As a plow turns up the earth, so the scourge tore up the back, leaving long furrows of torn, bloody flesh. This, then, is illustrative of the persecution Israel had endured, and her enemies laid on a scourge which showed how hearty was their hate of the people of God. Such scourging was also true of Him in Whom ideal Israel was fully personified. During His passion, the Lord Jesus experienced what is here presented. While in the hands of Roman soldiers, He was stripped of His raiment and bound with cords to a pillar and flogged. He gave His back to the smiters, and with his stripes we are healed, Matt. 27:26. His wounds and torment were for our salvation.

God, however, is not blind to the terrible suffering of His own, nor deaf to their cries for justice, seeing He is righteous, and cuts asunder the cords of the wicked—which expression of faith reveals the deeply-rooted religion of Israel. *Cords* properly denote thick twisted cords such as go to make the thongs of a whip, and represent dominion, tyranny, and violence. But God is able to cut such scourges, and so spoil the lashing of His saints by the wicked. Twelve times throughout the Bible this truth is declared in the same words, *The Lord is righteous*, and it is comforting to know that He is "righteous in all His ways." See Psalms 11:7; 145:17; John 17:25. Sooner or later, a righteous God interposes and cuts asunder the cruel cords wicked men have bound His own with. Spurgeon's comment on this fourth verse is assuring—

> Never has God used a nation to chastise Israel without destroying that nation when the chastisement has come to a close. He hates those who hurt His people even though He permits their hate to triumph for a while for His own purpose. If any man would have his harness cut, let him begin to plough one of the Lords's fields with the plough of persecution. The shortest way to ruin is to meddle with a saint: the Divine warning is—*He that touched you touched the apple of his eye.*

Turned back . . . the grave . . . the mower . . . The blessing, 129:5-6. Many radical critics of the Bible would cut out altogether the imprecatory Psalms within the Psalter. The famous Joseph Cook, in his renowned *Boston Monday Lectures* which attracted very large audiences, told a story of a German theological Professor who was exalted by radicals as having done more for New England theology than any man since Jonathan Edwards, the mightily used Evangelist. The modernistic Professor visited Boston at one time, and one morning had a walk with a Pastor of conservative faith and soon was raising his objections to an inspired Bible on the grounds of the imprecatory, or judgment Psalms. The Pastor replied that David expressed the Divine purpose in praying that his enemies might be destroyed, and that he gave utterance only to the natural righteous indignation of a Spirit-enlightened conscience against unspeakable iniquity.

On the two walked until at last their attention was drawn to a newspaper bulletin which read, "Baltimore to be shelled at twelve o'clock." Said the radical preacher, "I am glad of it! I am glad of it!" Replied his companion, "And so am I, but I hardly dare say so, for fear you should say that I am uttering an imprecatory Psalm." God would not be righteous if He were not a God of judgment. The Psalmist's imprecation was only a good confusion. "Let them be confounded and turned *backward*"—back to God! This is the kind of imprecation leading to repentance—a confounding resulting in turning from an evil way and in grace and glory. See Isaiah 37:29. *Backward* can also imply disappointed, foiled in evil designs. The double imperative found here—*Let them*, may be read as predictions—*They shall be.*

It is but justice that those who hate and harass and hurt the people of God and who have turned back from God should be made to turn back to Him. There is no personal ill-will in praying for the confusion of those who hate Zion and in the expression of the wish—

> Confound their politics,
> Frustrate their knavish tricks.

Do you not agree with Spurgeon's blunt comment?—"Study a chapter from the *Book of Martyrs*, and see if you do not feel inclined to read an imprecatory Psalm over Bishop Bonner and Bloody Mary. It may be that some wretched nineteenth century sentimentalist will blame you: if so, read another *over him.*"

After using plowmen as emblematic of Israel's oppressors, the Psalmist changes metaphors and prays that in their just punishment they may be as *grass* withering up leaving the mower without sheaves to bind. *Afore it groweth up* means before it is unsheathed or shoots into blossom. Isaiah has an expansion of the illustration used here, 37:27. On the flat, almost hard much roofs of oriental houses, there is little soil, and any grass taking root there, having not depth of earth, is soon scorched by the fierce mid-day sun. Isaiah wrote of all the greatness of the world's empires as being like *grass,* 40:6, 7. See 37:27; 2 Kings 19:26.

The enemies of God's children are like such grass—soon up and soon down. Before they reach maturity, they are dead. An old proverb reads, *Soon ripe, soon rotten,* and the prosperity of the wicked is transient and their destruction is speedy. They may be up on *housetops,* but the very height of their position hastens their progress and hurries their doom. The wicked who afflict God's children are weak, rootless beings who come and go, and whose evil carries the seed of dissolution within itself.

Carrying the fact of their emptiness and final destitution still further, the oppressor has no wheat in his hand or sheaves in his bosom, symbolic language indicating their utter impoverishment. The grass looked promising but there was no fulfillment, nothing to cut and carry, nothing for the lap to gather. *The Century Bible* observes that "the representations—the Egyptian monuments show that the reaper used to hold his scythe with the right hand, laying hold with the left hand of what was cut, removing it out of the way. Behind him followed a man with a large girded garment, which above the girdle had open folds into which the grain or corn was placed: at intervals the latter was taken to be tied into sheaves." But useless and bad, the wicked described in the Psalm have nothing good or profitable to gather. Their aim is bad, their work is worse, and their end worst of all in that they are fit only to be burned.

Finally, they are exempt from all blessing. Nothing was more natural in ancient times for those passing fruit-trees or corn-fields loaded with a rich crop to exclaim—*Barak Allah!*—God bless you! We bless you in the name of the Lord. See Ruth 2:4. But such a customary salutation with which passers-by greeted the reapers could not fall upon the ears of those with no silvery note of love or blessing sounding over their decease. Perishing in their nakedness they die "unwept, unsung and unhonored." The ungodly cannot greet and bless each other in the name of the Lord, for there is nothing in their course and conduct to warrant the giving or receiving of a benediction. With the godly it is so different, for although roughly plowed by Satan and his emissaries, they are yet fruitful in their affliction and reap a harvest of great blessing.

Psalm 130

Prominent among the "Penitential Psalms," this 130th Psalm has brought hope and comfort to distressed, sin-conscious hearts all down the ages, and thus figures largely in the life and experience of so many outstanding saints of God. Richard Hooker, the pride of English theologians, whose *Ecclesiastical Polity*, by its massive dignity still retains its place in theological literature, when he came to his dying moments, was found meditating on Psalm 130. In the days of Henry II, Diana de Poitiers sang the *De Profundis*—Psalm 130—to the tune of a dance. John Wesley was another greatly influenced by this most prominent penitential prayer. On the afternoon of May 24th, 1738, he attended St. Paul's Cathedral and heard Psalm 130 sung as an anthem. Deep emotion was his, and the Psalm was one of the factors attuning his heart to receive the assurance of his salvation by faith. On the evening of that same day he visited a meeting of saints in a room at Aldersgate Street where his heart was *strangely warmed*. Soon after, the glorious truth of justification by faith laid hold of him through reading Martin Luther's work on Galatians. Out of these deep spiritual experiences there sprang the mighty movement that still bears his name.

After the French Revolution, at the end of the 18th century, religious worship returned to a simplicity of its primitive conditions. Crowds of armed peasants, fired by the arrow of a childlike faith, knelt at the feet of their prescribed and hunted priests who stood under the sky and woods by the bare rocks serving an altar of God. There as they commemorated friends who had died fighting for the Blues, the solemn words of Psalm 130 were repeated in alternate verses by priest and congregation, and as they sang *Out of the depths I have called unto Thee, O Lord*! the survivors renewed their vows to fight on for their king and their faith.

Martin Luther was another warrior who had a great delight in Psalm 130. Once asked what were his choice Psalms, the Reformer replied, *Psalmi Paulini*, and when pressed by friends to name these Psalms he gave psalms 32, 51, 130, and 143 as his answer. One of his greatest Psalm-Hymns, which he composed, was founded on Psalm 130 and was one which penetrated to the heart of the German people. *Lord, from the depths to Thee I cry*! If Luther's 46th Psalm furnished the *major*, this one gave the *minor* key among the sacred songs of Germany which he wrote in 1524.

The story behind Luther's hymn on Psalm 130 is associated with the 6th of May, 1524, when a poor old weaver sang it through the streets of Magdeburg and offered it for sale at a price that suited the poorest. The humble singer, however, was cast into prison by the Burgomaster for singing on the streets; but 200 citizens marched to the city hall and would not leave till he was released. The song returned to Luther's own heart, and during the Augsburg Diet when he was at the Castle of Coburg, he was buffeted by the devil and suffered much from inward and outwards and fainted away. When he came to, Luther said to his friend Philip Melancthon, "Come, Philip, and in defiance of the devil, let us sing the Psalm, *Lord, from the depths to Thee I cry.* Let us sing it in full chorus, and extol and praise God."

Psalm 130 was often used as a funeral song, and was sung at the interment of Frederick the Wise, the staunch friend and protector of Martin Luther, in 1525. Then, when Luther's own corpse was on its way from Eisleben, where he died, to Wittenburg, where he lies beside Melancthon and the two great Electors, Frederick and John, it remained a night in Halle, 20th Feb. 1546, in the *Lieb frauen Kirche* of which his bosom friend, Justus Jonas, was minister. This 130th Psalm in Luther's own version was given out by Jonas and sung by thousands who thronged and wept around the bier.

Let us now give ourselves to a coverage of this precious Psalm that has brought comfort and hope to a great number no man can number and is one that follows well upon its previous companion. In Psalm 129 the poet is taken up with the afflictions heaped upon him by the wicked. Here, in Psalm 130, there is no complaint about others—only about the writer *himself*—his own sins iniquities and desires. "*I* cried unto thee, O Lord" . . . "*I* wait for the Lord." "It is the soul of the people which here throws itself on the Divine forgiveness," comments Ellicott, "waiting for deliverance as one waiteth for the dawn . . . But the strong *personal* feeling breathed into it has made it even more the *De Profundis* of individuals than of nations or churches."

Out of the depths have I cried . . . Hear my voice, 130:1, 2. The opening words of the Psalm are used literally for the sea by Isaiah, 51:10, and are a recurrent image for overwhelming, personal distress, Psalms 18:16; 88:7; see 69:2. Hebrew poets often compared a condition of distress to being overwhelmed with böisterous waves. See 124:3; 42:7. Are there not items in our own personal experience when nothing suits as these initial words. "Out of the depths have I cried." Like Jonah, cast into the deep with God's billows and waves passing over us, we cried *De profundis Clamave.* Are we not encouraged to know that there is no depth so profound that we cannot cry therefrom, and that if we cannot pray, we can *cry* as "all Thy waves and Thy billows are gone over me?"

"Deep places beget deep devotion," says Spurgeon. "Depths of earnestness are stirred by depths of tribulation. Diamonds sparkle most amid the darkness. Prayer *De Profundis* gives to God *Gloria in Excelsis* . . . David had often been in the deep, and as often had he pleaded with Jehovah, his God, in whose hand are all deep places." Augustine, commenting on this first verse wrote, "But when he cried from the deep, he riseth from the deep, and his very cry suffereth him not to be long at the bottom." Often it is well worthwhile to go down into any *depth* to be taught how to *cry* and give voice to heart-felt *supplications*.

Deliverance out of the depths depends, of course, upon the one we cry to for help. The poet cried unto the *Lord*—JEHOVAH—the august name He gave to His people to confirm their faith in the stability of His promises, Exodus 3. Eight times over in the eight verses of the Psalm, the title *Lord* appears, which is either *Jehovah, Jah,* or *Adonai*. In verse two it is *Adonai*, declaring His Lordship over all hindrances in delivering those who cry to Him out of the depths. In verse 3 the original for "Lord" is *Jah*, another name of God which, although from the same root as *Jehovah*, is only used to intimate and express the terrible majesty of God. "He rideth on the heavens, and is extolled by His name *JAH*," Psalm 68:4. In the first part of the Psalm before us God is dealing with the guilt of sin and is thus represented to the convicted soul as the Great and Terrible One Who is yet merciful. Thus, by the use of these three names, all the qualities of God are conjoined for man's redemption. He were *JAH* only, no man would be able to stand before Him. But He is our *JEHOVAH*, the blessed name the soul loves to repeat again and again because of all the help and comfort it enshrines, and the name He immediately responds to as He hears the vice of distress.

Iniquities . . . Forgiveness with Thee, 130:3, 4. In verses 1-3, the needy one waits *on* Jehovah, but in verses 5-7, waits *for* Jehovah. When Theodore de Beza died on Oct. 13th, 1605, the text upon the lips of this veteran of the Reformation was, "If thou, Lord, will be extreme to mark what is done amiss, O Lord, who may abide it," Psalm 130:3. During one of his "grievous and dreadful" onslaughts of the Devil, John Bunyan found consolation as he pondered over verses 3 and 4 of this Psalm. It made his heart happy to know that God did not only notice his sins, but his tears and faith as well.

We pair these two verses seeing they contain the sum of all the Scriptures. *Iniquities . . . Forgiveness.* We come from Mount Sinai to Mount Zion where mercy is. Jeremiah tasted in his vision first a bitter fig out of the basket, then a sweet fig out of the other. In the days of Moses the waters were first bitter, then sweetened by the sweet wood. Elisha cast salt into the pottage of the sons of the prophets, thus it became wholesome. Great may be our iniquity, but there is forgiveness with Him we sin against. How Paul loved to ring the changes of the truths of *Sin* and *Salvation, Guilt* and *Grace*!

God is ever attentive to our supplicating cry for mercy, and as the One ever ready to forgive our trespasses, does not linger over the *marking* of them. The word *mark* used in verse 3 is the same word found as *watch* in verse 6. Thus the sense of the passage is, "Who could stand the test of being judged, if thou shouldest act as watchman, or keeper, in reference to men's sins." If the Lord were to watch for their lapses into iniquity, as one watches for the dawn, nothing but signal punishment would follow. Job actually believed that He did watch, 10:14; 14:16, as for both Jeremiah and Amos, they use the term *watch* in connection with the strict care taken that the consequences should follow the sin, Jer. 3:5; Amos 1:11.

Do you not question why the Psalmist said "*IF* thou, Lord, shouldest mark iniquity?" Does He not take note of every sin committed by men, especially by His own children? "Thou God seest *me*." Why, then, the emphasis upon *IF*? Here, again, to observe that the word rendered *mark* implies to watch with strictest diligence, and in the noun form means *watch-tower* in which the watcher can see all that is being done and take cognizance of all who approach. Then the word can signify to store and stock a memorial or record. See Genesis 37:11. So the understanding of the passage is that if the Lord eyed with vigor everything we do, or treasured up our sins in His memory and keep them by Him, who, then, could stand before Him?

The blessed *But* that follows sets forth the way by which we can stand before Him although His all seeing eye has seen the prevailing iniquities. "*But*, or *surely*, There is forgiveness, or a propitiation with Thee." Let iniquities be ready to crush the sinner by their weight, a free, full, and sovereign pardon is in the hand of the holy Lord sinned against, whose prerogative alone it is to forgive, cleanse the sinner, and receive him as a son. The word for *forgiveness* used here is only found again in Daniel 9:9; Nehemiah 9:17. Jesus Christ is the Great Propitiation or Ransom God provided, and it is only through Him that the sinner can hope to obtain forgiveness.

Forgiven we *Fear*—"That thou mayest be feared." Grace leads the way to a holy regard for the Lord and a fear of grieving Him again. "Gratitude for pardon produces far more fear and reverence of God than all the dread which is inspired by punishment." Thus, Divine forgiveness, called "the smile of God," binds the forgiven one to Him in a reverential trust and love, commending His grace to others who are yet in their sin. Forgiveness does not lead to lax living, but to a godly fear, and to a life well-pleasing to Him Who is ever ready to forgive. See Psalm 19:10. Dr. John Owen, the outstanding theologian of the 16th century, wrote *A*

Practical Exposition of Psalm 130, a series of discourses on this Psalm, nearly three-fourths of which is occupied with this fourth verse of the Psalm. Here is the story of how he came to write his illuminative commentary—

> Richard Davis, who afterwards became Pastor of a Church in Rowel, Northamptonshire, being under religious impressions, sought a conference with me," he wrote. "I put the question to him, "Young man, pray, in what manner do you think to go God?" Pastor David answered "Through the Mediator, sir," and I replied, "That is easily said, but I assure you, it is another thing to go to God through the Mediator than many who make use of the expression are aware of. I myself preached Christ some years, when I had by very little, if any, experimental acquaintance with access to God through Christ; until the Lord was pleased to visit me with some affliction, whereby I was brought to the mouth of the grave, and under which my soul was oppressed with horror and darkness; but God graciously relieved my spirit by a powerful application of Psalm 130, verse 4, *But there is forgiveness with thee, that thou may be feared*, from whence I received special instruction, peace, and comfort in drawing near to God through the Mediator, and preached thereupon immediately after my recovery.

Wait . . . wait . . . Watch . . . watch ..., 130:5, 6. The rest of the Psalm presents a strong hope of a full restoration and complete redemption. In the two verses before us we have a two-fold repetition, "I wait . . . my soul doth wait"—"Watch for the morning," "Watch for the morning." In the original the pronoun is emphatic "*I myself* doth wait." The repetitions of the writer are the reverse to *vain* repetitions in that they emphasize the desire to deal with the Lord intensely and earnestly with the whole heart. Blessed are all they that have this patient waiting *for* the Lord and upon Him. Such waiting itself is beneficial in that it tries faith, exercises patience, trains submission, and results in a full appreciation of the blessing when it comes.

God's people have ever been a *waiting* people. They waited in the depths and at last were delivered. They waited for the First Advent of the Savior, and multitudes of living saints now await His Second Advent. Thus the connection of the phrases—*I wait . . . I hope* is suggested Israel hoped in *His Word*, believing that no word of His can fruitless fall: that He cannot ever go back on any promise of His. Israel also hoped in the *Lord* Himself. Wrote William Cowper in *Work without Hope*, "Hope without an object cannot live." What spiritual and eternal life are ours when the Lord and His Word are the Objects of our hope! In these two verses, the poet makes mention of his hope, and the word he uses implies both a patient waiting and a hopeful trusting.

Too many of us wait and hope for circumstances, people, and things, meeting with frustration and disappointment because they are apart from the Lord Himself. But when we wait for Him, we cannot be ashamed for He alone is faithful Who hath promised, fulfilling His Word just *when* and just *as* He pleases. Then the Psalmist goes on to illustrate patient waiting and eager hope of the forgiven heart with a more expressive simile, "Wait—*more than they that watch for the morning.*" Not "as much as they that watch" but "*more* than they." Can we say that ours is the eagerness of the watch for the dawn as we wait for and upon the Lord? Jonathan Edwards, the much-used evangelist in early American history, had a peculiar affection for this sixth verse with its emphasis upon *watching*. In his *Journal*, he wrote—

> In September 1725, was taken ill at Newhaven, and endeavored to go home to Windsor; was so ill at the North Village that I could go no farther, where I lay sick for about a quarter of a year. And in this sickness God was pleased to visit me, again with the sweet influences of His Spirit. My mind was greatly engaged there on Divine pleasant contemplations and longings of the soul. I observed that those who watched with me would often be looking out for the morning, and seemed to wish for it, which brought to my mind those words of the Psalmist, which my soul with sweetness made its own language, *My soul waiteth for the Lord more than they that watch for the morning.* And when the light of the morning came in at the windows it refreshed my soul from one morning to another. It seemed to me to be some image of the sweet light of God's glory.

While the repeated word *watch* bears the interpretation of watching against a danger or coming evil, here the Psalmist gives a good and happy aspect of the term and implies that "it is a far higher, and better, and more filial thing to watch *for* a coming good than to watch *against* an approaching evil." Watch for the *morning*—not for the dark *night* with all its gloom and danger. It was in 1830 on the night preceding August 1st, the day the slaves in Britain's West Indian Colonies were to come into possession of the freedom promised them. That night, many of them never went to bed at all. Thousands of them assembled in their places of worship, praying and singing praises to God as they waited for the first streak of the light of the morning of that historic day of freedom. Some went to the hills from which they might obtain the first view of the coming day, and, by a signal, intimate to their brethren down in the valley the dawn of the day that was to make them *men*, and no longer, as they had been for so long, mere goods and chattels—men with souls that God had created to live for ever. How eagerly must those men have watched for that morning of emancipation!

For those of us, redeemed by the blood of Him Who bore our iniquities, we find in the fine poetical repeat—*Watch for the morning,* an expression of our ardent longing to see Him when He appears the second time for our deliverance from the entire presence of sin. As sentinels we may be weary at times, and long for an end to our tedious watch, but that bright and glorious morning will soon dawn.

> When wilt Thou come unto me, Lord?
>   Until Thou dost appear,
> I count each moment for a day,
>   Each minute for a year.

Mercy . . . Plenteous Redemption . . . Redeem, 130:7,8. Sir John Hayward published in 1625 a comforting, devotional book he named *David's Tears*. Dealing with these concluding verses of the Psalm, he wrote, "They containeth an evident prophecy of the Messiah in setting forth His plentiful redemption, and that He should redeem Israel, that is, the Church, from all their sins. Which words in their full sense were used by an angel to Joseph, in telling him that the Child's name should be *Jesus*, 'because he should save his people from their sins, Matt. 1:21.'" *Let Israel hope in the Lord*, and redeeming grace was her sole hope. Throughout the previous verses of the Psalm, the sorrows, prayers, penitence, awe, the waiting and watching were all personal and confined to the Psalmist himself. A change takes place, however, and it is no longer *I* but *Israel*, and *all* Israel at that. This is as it ought to be, for once a person has experienced a personal experience of redeeming grace and mercy, it is his duty and privilege to tell others the story. As Jehovah is *The God of Hope*, He expects all those He has forgiven to hope *in*, and *for* Him. The Psalmist, after speaking to God about himself, becomes the mouthpiece of the nation and preaches to it a plenteous redemption. See Psalm 131:3.

> Then, O my soul, still hope in God
> And plead thy Savior's precious blood.

As despondency does not become those whose iniquities are forgiven and banished, Israel must hope in God's mercy and in His plenteous redemption—a hope ever sure of fulfillment. The attribute of Mercy and the provision of a full salvation are two of the most sufficient reasons for trusting in Jehovah. Thus the Psalm, beginning with a cry out of the depths, ends with a chorale in the heights. And is it not better to cry out of the depths, hoping in God's mercy and grace, than standing on a mountain-top boasting in our own fancied righteousness?

Further, the Divine, personal pronoun, *He* is emphatic in the Hebrew, meaning, *He, and He alone*, for no other can redeem the soul of a nation, or a nation of souls, from *all* iniquities. Then, make a note of the verb *Shall*. Emblazon it across the sky, *He shall redeem*. It is as certain as His existence and as inevitable as His own glorious nature. If He made man without sin, but who, by his own volition became a sinner, He can, through His redeeming grace and mercy, re-make the sinner into a cleansed and unsinning son of His, delivering him not only from the consequences of sin, but sin itself; not only from the guilt of sin, but its government. The *Paradise Lost* becomes a *Paradise Regained.* Out of the dungeon we come into the palace of the King Who was crucified for our redemption. Thus this wonderful Psalm has a most graceful and appropriate conclusion in that, although it opens with *soul-depth,* it closes with *soul-height.* Hallelujah! What a Redeemer!

Psalm 131

One of the shortest Psalms to read, but one of the longest to learn, has been described as, "A song of child-like resignation of one committing himself to God in time of trouble." With its triad of verses, the Psalm is a humble answer to the demand, "My son, give me thine heart, and let thine eyes observe my ways," Proverbs 23:26. It is a beautiful expression of childlike humility and of trust and confidence, and loses its charm if the personal aspect is eliminated. The most perfect and sincere resignation breathes through this very short poem. Beginning with the Lord, it is a solitary colloquy with Him in which David uttered many things not proper for the ears of men.

The Psalm fittingly follows Psalm 130, which, as we have seen, is a Song of Forgiveness with Psalm 131 as a Song of Humility. The former celebrates the blessedness of the man whose transgressions are pardoned; the latter celebrates the blessedness of the man who is of a meek and lowly spirit. Being graciously delivered from the judgment our iniquities truly deserved should humble us. Having shed our filthy garments we should be found clothed in the garment of humility.

The title of the Psalm announces that it was written by David and therefore belongs to his time. "It is exactly in the spirit of that humble thanksgiving made by him, after the divine revelation by Nathan of the future blessings of David's posterity, 1 Chron. 22:9-11; and forms a most appropriate introduction to the following Psalm, the theme of which is evidently the dedication of the Temple." Among other introductions to a study of this further Pilgrim Song, we thought that by Spurgeon to be par excellence and herewith include it as our approach to the Psalm—

> It is both *by* David and *of* David: he is the author and subject of it, and many incidents in his life may be employed to illustrate it. Comparing all the Psalms to gems, we should liken this to a pearl: how beautifully it will adorn the neck of patience. It speaks of a young child, but it contains the experience of a man in Christ. Lowliness and humility are here seen in connection with a sanctified heart, as will subdued to the mind of God, and a hope looking to the Lord alone. Happy is the man who can without falsehood use these words as his own; for he wears about him the likeness of his Lord, Who said, *I am meek and lowly in heart*. The Psalm is in advance of all the Songs of Degrees: it is a short ladder, if we count the words; and yet it rises to a great height, reaching from deep humility to fixed confidence.

676 Psalms: *A Devotional Commentary*

Le Blanc thinks that this is a Song of the Israelites who returned from Babylon with humble hearts, weaned from their idols. At any rate, after any spiritual captivity let it be the expression of our hearts.

My heart . . . mine eyes . . . myself, 131:1-3. The cry of the child-heart expressed in the first two verses is one we should offer "in all times of our wealth," when pride and self-will lie in wait against us. See 2 Chron. 22:25. Evidently David composed them during that "morning without clouds" in which he ascended the throne of a united people, and thus before the dark clouds which overcast the close of his illustrious reign. In the opening verse David combines *heart* and *eyes,* for "pride has its seat in the heart, looks forth at the eyes, and expresses itself in the actions." See Psalm 18:27; Proverbs 6:17, R.V.

David begins with the confession, "Lord, my heart is not haughty," and rightly so, seeing it is the center of man's nature, and if pride resides there, it defiles everything just as mire in the spring causes mud in all the streams. The Psalmist did not have a "guid conceit o' himself," and called upon the Omniscient One Who alone knows the heart of man to corroborate his statement that he was not haughty. He asks God to witness that it was with all lowliness of mind that he left following "the ewes great with young to feed and govern They people." Such elevation did not make him proud in his opinion of himself, nor boastful and ambitious for the future. To keep as humble as a king and conqueror as when he was an obscure keeper of sheep is a tribute to excellency of character.

Matthew Arnold wrote of the *haughty scorn* that Byron, Scotland's famous poet, bore. But David, a far greater poet, was not guilty of such haughtiness. In his *Essays* on *Frederic the Great,* Macaulay says, "We hardly know any instance of the strength of human nature so striking, and so grotesque as the character of this haughty, vigilant, resolute, sagacious man." While David as a King, Poet, and Hero, was certainly vigilant, resolute, and sagacious," he certainly was *not* haughty. He knew, as his son Solomon was to write, that "Pride goeth before destruction, and a haughty spirit before a fall. Better it is to be of a humble spirit with the lowly, and to divide the spoil with the proud," Prov. 16:18.

From the *heart* we go to the *eyes,* "Nor mine eyes lofty." As the eye is the mirror of the soul, it reflects all within, whether good or bad. Pride is most clearly revealed in the eyes, hence, the frequent combination of the proud heart and the haughty look. "Him that hath a high look and a proud heart I will not suffer." Such a proud look is one of the seven things which are an abomination unto the Lord, "Thou wilt bring down high looks." Where there is a proud heart, there is commonly a proud look, Prov. 6:17. David calls upon Jehovah to witness that he had neither a scornful nor an aspiring look. Like the humble publican in the Gospel story, David could not so much as lift up his eyes.

The Psalmist then goes on to extend the range of his professed humility for, conscious of his limitations, he went on to say, "Neither do I exercise myself in matters, or in things too high for me." David knew his own size and never tried to look taller. The word *exercise* means to "walk with," or "to have to do with," or "bring oneself about," or "been in the practice of." In the past and in the present, he had not professed a knowledge of matters too *great* or *high* for him to grasp. Although he had "the promise of universal dominion, yet he took no step to secure it for himself. He resisted every subtle temptation to snatch for himself that which was nevertheless divinely assured." He was not foolish enough to tackle things beyond his power to accomplish. See Deut. 17:8; 30:11.

That godly divine of the 11th century, Anselm, emulated the spirit of humility of David when he prayed—

> I do not seek, O Lord, to penetrate thy depths. I by no means think my intellect equal to them: but I long to understand in some degree thy truth, which my heart believes and loves. For I do not seek to understand that I may believe, but I believe, that I may understand.

May grace be ours to keep within our own capacity and not stretch beyond our line! It is only too true that there are many things both *great* and *high* in Revelation, as well as in Divine Providence, and we are not forbidden to use our reason as we come up against them. What we must recognize is that God's thoughts and ways are higher than ours. He could not be God were it not so. Our true attitude, then, taught by the example of David, is one of childlike, loving trust, waiting to be taught and led; and in one the Spirit of Revelation responds by making clear mysteries which had baffled reason and left human genius faint and weary in its quest. Isa. 40:30, 31; Matt. 11:25.

As a child . . . as a weaned child, 131:2,3. What an appealing and beautiful emblem David used to describe his child-like trust in and dependence upon his heavenly Father! *Surely* was commonly used to express strong asseveration after an oath. While Israel, over which David reigned, is likened unto a "weaned child," Isa. 28:9, the King here used the expressive figure of himself as quiet as a child that is weaned. But what had he been weaned from? Was it not from any rebellion towards God and from haughtiness towards men; from all self-sufficiency, self-seeking, and self-exaltation?

The weaning process can be hard for both the child and its mother, until the sobbing child is soothed and forgets the breast. Often *soul* is spoken of as the organ of desire, of appetite. David was stilled and quieted, or silenced within, after being tempted to understand things too high for him to grasp. Now all longing after *great matters* had gone, just as a weaned child loses its desire for its mother's milk and is led to another source of supply, making for the maturing conditions of its life. The Targum has it, "As one weaned on the breasts of its mother, I am strengthened in the law." In a changing state, the weaned child learns to be submissive and content. See Phil. 4:11.

As the sucking period ends, the battle begins as the baby experiences its first real sorrow, not merely because of any minor pain it may feel, but because no further access is allowed to that which provided solace hitherto. So there are frets and sobs, but at last the child is quieted by a love which is powerful to soothe, even when it must deny. Once the weaned one finds nourishment at the table with others, there is no desire to return to the fountains once nourishing its life. Dear old George Herbert said of man, "If goodness lead him not, then weariness may toss him to God's breast." A more natural rendering would be weaned *on* his mother rather than *of*, or *from* her.

No longer sobbing for denial of what the mother had supplied, the child buries its head in the very bosom after which he had pined so sorrowfully. Thus, what David is saying of himself is that "Instead of fretting after what is too great for him, he quiets his ambition, and his spirit lies calm and gentle, like a child in its mother's arms, that after the first trouble of weaning is over is soothed and lulled by the maternal caress." When pride goes, submission follows. Springing out in gentle humility is a weaning from dependence upon self, and an utter reliance upon Him in Whom there is complete satisfaction.

> My soul doth like a weanling rest,
>   I cease to weep;
> So mother's lap, though dried her breast,
>   Can lull to sleep.

The last verse of this pearl of a Psalm reveals how lovingly a man who is weaned from self thinks of others—"Let Israel hope in the Lord from now and for ever." David loses himself in the care of the people he had been chosen to reign over, and sought to teach the nation that rest and peace can only be found where its King found it, namely, in lowliness of heart. Says F. B. Meyer, "The cure for inquietude is to be found in a hope which begins as a struggling ray, but expands into the *forever* of Eternity." This liturgical ending of the Psalm binds three Psalms together, 129:1; 130:7; 131:3. Israel's hope was not in her Divinely chosen King, but in Jehovah Himself and therefore it was to Israel's benefit to "hope, and quietly for the salvation of Jehovah." *Forever!* Only those who have been quieted by the soothing ministry of the Holy Spirit can look fearlessly into Eternity; and all that it holds for those whose hope was in the Lord, will fully justify such confidence.

Psalm 132

Here we have the longest Psalm in the group of the 15 Songs of Degrees. It has six times as many verses as the previous Psalm, and carries the theme that Jehovah promises to hear the people's prayer and, for David's sake, restore their fortunes. Evidently it was intended as a dedicatory song, composed for the completed Temple. Because of the happy event the Psalm celebrates it is a very joyful one, and one that all of us as pilgrims to the New Jerusalem can make our own and often sing. It is also a notable addition to *The Songs of Degrees* or *Ascents*, the "going-up" being very marked. The story of the Psalm ascends step by step from *afflictions* to a *crown*, from *Remember David* to *I will make the horn of David to bud.* "The latter half is like the over-arching sky bending above *the fields of the wood* which are found in the resolves, and prayers of the former portion."

There is a good deal of the dramatic element in the Psalm, and it is probable that its three sections were sung by at least three different parties—By a small section of the choir, verses 1-5. By a larger section, verses 6-10. By an individual, seeing we here have the answer of Jehovah, 11-18. Although it has been suggested that the Psalm is divided into four stanzas of ten lines, each of which contains the name of David, the translators, it would seem, have rightly divided it into three sections—

1. Purpose to build a house for the Lord, 1-7,
2. Prayer at the removal of the Ark, 8-10,
3. Plea for the fulfillment of Divine Covenant and Promises, 11-18.

Then, as *Parallelisms* are often necessary to bring out the meaning of Scripture, those of this Psalm should be traced with ease—

Verses 1-6, are answered by verse 12,
Verse 7 by verse 13,
Verse 8 by verse 14,
Verse 9 by verses 15, 16,
Verse 10 by verses 17, 18.

As to the authorship of the Psalm, although it carries no name, that of *David* occurs 4 times in it. Bishop Lightfoot ascribed it to David and supposed it to have been composed on the second removal of the Ark from the house of Obed-edom, 1 Chron. 15:4. But the appearance of David's name in verse 10 in the third person, and the terms employed, militate against his being the author. The general opinion is that it was written by Solomon, probably about the time of the removing of the Ark into the Temple he had built for it, or for the solemn services celebrating the dedication of the Temple, 2 Chron, 5:2. Verses 8-10 are almost identical with the closing words of Solomon's prayer, 2 Chron, 5:41. Ellicott's comment is, "Beyond question the Psalm is ideal in its treatment of history, and it is just conceivable that Solomon, who in 2 Chron. 6 is so careful to draw a contrast between his father's project and his own accomplishment of that project, might in a poem, have been entirely silent as to his share in the work."

Purpose to build a house for the Lord, 132:1-7. In the opening verse of this first section of the Psalm, the poet calls upon Jehovah to remember to fulfill the promises He had made to David, and also all his afflictions and anxious care for His work. The merits of David formed the basis of the plea for help for the nation he loved in the hour of its crisis. The word *affliction* here means, "his being hard worked," and doubtless refers to the zeal he had to build the temple and not to anything he *suffered*. See Psalm 137:7.

When the Lord was angry with the reigning prince, the people cried, "Lord, remember David;" and when they needed any special blessing, again they sang, "Lord, remember David." This was good pleading, but it was not as good as ours which runs on this wise—"Lord, remember *Jesus*, and all His afflictions." Still, when any design approaches completion, we should not forget those who were concerned in its first conception or gathered the materials. God never forgets them; and we should not, 1 Cor. 3:8. The names of the Apostles are not omitted from the stones, Rev. 21:14.

The next six verses go on to show David's anxiety to prepare all that was necessary for the temple, 2 Sam. 7:1, 2. Then the plea was enforced by the reminder of David's vow not to rest until the temple was built, and by the use of David's conception of God, as "Jehovah, the mighty God of Jacob." His name—*Jehovah*: his attribute—*mighty*: His special relationship—*mighty God of Jacob*, which was a title the patriarch used himself, Genesis 49:24. See 28:20. Such a mighty One of Jacob was worthy to have a temple built for Him.

David put the interests of God's House before concern for his own house when he declared that he would not be content to rest at home until he had found a home for God to dwell in among men. The Ark was in *the fields of the wood* at Kirjath-jearim, where in darkness and solitude it had been deposited after its return from the Philistines, 1 Sam. 7:1; 2 Sam. 6:3; 7:2. Thus David exhibited sacrificial energies in preparing the temple in which the Ark would have prominence. How could he enjoy sleep until he had done his utmost to have a home for the Ark!—the symbol of Divine presence. The Psalmist, of course, was writing poetically of David when he said of him that he could not give slumber to his eyes, and therefore such language is not what we would use in cold blood. The writer was all on fire and so pleads figuratively. It would be better for the cause of Christ if more of us were seized with sleeplessness over it.

By the plural—*Tabernacles*—the plural of majesty—we are to understand the sanctuary itself and all its enclosures and appendages. The plural is also found in Psalm 84:1. The burden, then, of the first division of the Psalm was that of David's tremendous project to give his generation a worthy place in which the people could worship Jehovah. Elaborate and costly preparations were made for He was deemed worthy of the very best. It is interesting to note the ascent in this part of this Psalm of Degrees—*We heard; We found; We will go; We will worship.*

Prayer at the Removal of the Ark, 132:8-10. The three verses forming the central portion of this Pilgrim Psalm are to be found in Solomon's dedicatory prayer at the opening of the temple, 2 Chron. 6:41, 42. See 1 Kings 8. Ellicott says of these verses, "All is blended together in the long perspective of poetry. As to the form of the words, they are of course themselves a reminiscence of the ancient battle-cry of the nation when the Ark set forward on the march. See Num. 10:35." The command for God to *Arise* seems bold and daring if it implied that He had been indifferent as to the Ark's welfare. See Psalm 68:1. There may be an allusion here to the watchword used when the Ark in the wilderness set forward—"Rise up, O Lord!" Num. 10:33, 35.

The Ark, long on the move, had now found a worthy resting place as "the Ark of Thy Strength," or "Thy Strong Ark," being deemed strong because by its presence the Israelites were enabled to conquer their foes, 1 Sam. 5:7; 6:19; Ps. 78:61. It was, of course, the presence of God with the Ark that gave it strength. It owed its origin to the belief that Jehovah was present with it in a very special sense—the image and pledge of His presence. Later on deeper reverence surrounded the Ark seeing it became the receptacle of the Tables of the Law. In Psalm 78:61—the only other place where the phrase "Ark of Thy Strength" is found—the word *strength* by itself denotes the *Ark.* The LXX Version has, "The Ark of Thy Sanctification."

Once the Ark was deposited on the most Holy Place, its staves by which it was borne were drawn out, indicating that its journeyings were complete, 2 Chron. 5:9. Applying this truth, F. B. Meyer says, "Oh weary tired builders, think of the strength of the true Ark of the Covenant, which is Jesus Christ! In Jesus, ascended and glorified God rests."

As neither David nor Solomon recognized a special order of Priests, those mentioned as being clothed with righteousness referred to those who

682# 682   Psalms: *A Devotional Commentary*

ministered unto the Lord, and who, in the next clause, are spoken of as "saints." In Anglican worship, the ninth verse is given as, "Endue Thy ministers with righteousness, and make Thy chosen people joyful." The original for righteousness used here is "salvation"—the term found in the repetition of the verse in verse 16. These repetitions in the Psalm, such as here, and in verses 2 and 5, etc., should be noted.

Under Grace, all *Saints* are *Kings and Priests*, wearing the robes of salvation, and, as Conquerors, shouting aloud for joy, Rom. 8:37; Phil. 4:4. God expects His chosen ones to be both holy and happy. Where holiness is found, happiness is round the corner. Where righteousness is the garment, joy may well be the occupation. Having prayed thus for the people, King Solomon finds himself being prayed for by the people that for his father David's sake, he may never be refused, as God's anointed one, an audience with Him Who was his father's God. Solomon wanted to be remembered as the far-off interest of David's prayers and tears. 1 Kings 8:25. To "turn away the face" from anyone who made a request was to send him away disappointed. Frequently God was urged to hear prayer for David's sake. 1 Kings 11:12, 13; 15:4; 2 Kings 8:19 etc. Respect for David's name is seen in this being put on a level with God. "Mine own sake, and for thy servant David's sake," 2 Kings 19:32-34. In the three verses considered, the temple, the ark, the saints, the people, and the king are prayed for.

Plea for fulfillment of Divine Covenant and Promises,132:11-18. Solomon is here found praying for himself and basing his intercession on the ground of God's partiality for David. The key to the whole of this last section is the clause, "The Lord hath sworn in truth unto David; He will not turn from it," verse 11. A more impressive rendering has it, "Jehovah hath sworn unto David, It is a truce oath; He will not depart from it." See Psalm 122:4, 5. The substance of this particular oath is found in 2 Sam. 7. In *truth* can be translated "in faithfulness," implying that having made the oath the Lord intended to keep it faithfully. It would be certain of execution.

While man's faithfulness was not allowed to interfere with Jehovah's faithfulness to His promise, Psalm 89:30, yet it was a condition of the vow that David's descendants should obey the Divine Law, 2 Sam. 7:14; 1 Kings 8:25. The grand covenant pleading of the kind in these final verses is always honored by the Lord, when the pleaders themselves have not turned in any way from the Divine covenant and testimony. Thus we have the *IF* of verse 12 which contains the condition of the Covenant as far as it concerned Kings of David's line before the coming of David's Greater Son to sit upon the throne for evermore. Born of the virgin Mary, Jesus came as the true Seed of King David, and is the King of Kings.

Multiple blessings characterize the Lord's rest in His chosen habitation—answer to the prayer of verse 8, just as verse 16 is the answer to verse 9. Observe the 3 *I wills*, and the 3 *Will I*. What better support for faith could we have? In the 6th century Gall, the Apostle of Switzerland as he was known, guided his life by the Psalms. Seeking to establish a monastery, he wandered through a forest until he came to a spot where the little river Steinach, falling from the mountain, hollowed itself a bed in the rock. Here Gall stumbled over a bramble and fell. His companions hurried to lift him up, but he told them to leave him for, "This," he said, "shall be my rest: here will I dwell, for I have a delight therein, Psalm 132:15." So was founded the great monastery of St. Gall, renowned for its library, its learning, and its cultivation of the arts.

A similar experience overtook Anselm in 1098, who visited the higher slopes of the neighboring mountains at Schlavia, to which the monks resorted in the summer months. It was on this beautiful spot in the crisp mountain air, free from his cares and surrounded by the simplicities of life and the charms of nature, that the old man's heart leaped within him, and he cried like Gall, "This shall be my rest for ever; here will I dwell, for I have a delight therein." It was here at Schlavia that he thought out and composed his famous treatise, *Cur Deus Homo*, in which he expounded his profound and original view of the Incarnation.

Chief among the promised blessings was the vindication of the promise of verse 11, regarding the progenitors of David. "There will I make the horn of David to bud." In fact, in the concluding two verses of the Psalm we have a four-fold promise, being—*Horn, Lamp, Enemies clothed with shame, Flourishing crown.*

The horn of David. The horn is the symbol of "honor," Psalm 112:9 and of "strength," Micah 4:13; Deut. 33:17, and is taken from a horned animal, 1 Sam. 2:1, 10, and, as used here, is an image of young, vigorous life. This, then, is a metaphor taken from those goodly creatures, as stags and such like, whose chief beauty and strength consists in their horns, especially when they bud and branch abroad. "To bud" means to "spring forth," and the implication is that the seed of David would prosper and be full of vigor. Having sworn to David, God did not forget His pristine promise for centuries afterwards. He spoke of it, Isa. 55:3. The partial realization was in the maintenance of a line of kings on the throne of Judah, 1 Kings 11:36, but its full accomplishment came in our Lord, and the Messianic application of this prediction comes out in Zechariah's Song, Luke 1:69.

I have ordained a lamp. The burning of a lamp in the house was a sign of the continuance and prosperity of the home, Psalm 18:29. See 1 Kings 11:36; 15:4; 2 Kings 8:19. Another translation reads, "I have trimmed a lamp for mine anointed," which suggests the keeping of the sacred lights by Aaron and his sons, Exod. 27:21; Lev. 24:2, 3. This last part of verse

17 is alluded to in the promise, "That David my servant may have a light always before Me in Jerusalem, 1 Kings 9:36." Such a light must continue to shine seeing it is *ordained* of God. The perfect fulfillment of this promise came in Jesus, that Lamp of God's grace shining in a dark world, John 8:12. See also Ezek. 29:21.

Paulinus, Bishop of Nola, who died in 431 as the hours for Vespers approached and the lamps were being lighted in the church which he had built, stretched forth his hands and died, repeating the words, "I have ordained a lamp for mine Anointed." Then, when Cyril, Archbishop of Alexandria, died in June 444, after a life-long struggle for the purity of the Christian faith, uttered the same words as Paulinus.

His enemies will I clothe with shame. This was the clause in Latin that was engraved on the shillings of Edward VI in 1549. God's saints are clothed with *salvation*, verses 9, 16, but His foes with *shame*. These enemies are spoken of as being David's, because he represented his successors. They were in him, and promises made to him were made to them. The feeling of solidarity prevailed in ancient times to a much greater extent than in our days, Psalm 109:9-15. God's enemies are not able to hide their shame and are thus covered with it. If they die in their sin then their shame will be "their convict dress to all Eternity."

But upon himself shall his crown flourish. The LXX Version reads "My crown"—shall flourish, or *glitter* in contrast to the *profaned crown* of Psalm 89:39. In Jesus, an horn of salvation was raised for us in "the house of his servant David," Luke 1:69. His enemies, however, crowned Him with thorns, but as the result of His death, resurrection and ascension, He is crowned with honor and glory, and His crown will ever flourish, or glow, with splendor. He, Himself, is the Source, Sustenance, and Center of the continuing prosperity of His kingdom, and thus His imperial glories cannot fade. Crowns become this Victor's brow. Is His the crown of your life and mine?

Psalm 133

The triumph of 1638 was the Bannockburn of Scottish religious liberty, the second Reformation. On a bright morning, to be followed by clouds and conflicts, but never forgotten, the famous Assembly was held in Glasgow with Alexander Henderson as Moderator. The Psalm sung that day was the 133rd, in the Scottish meter—

> Behold, how good a thing it is,
>   And how becoming well,
> Together such as brethren are
>   In unity to dwell.

With all our denominational divisions, we are in advance of that period, and every time the Psalm is sung it has a prophetic look and a prayer for the final happy issue.

Another historical association of this brief, ancient Psalm is connected with the American Greely Expedition of 1881, amid the eternal ice and snow of the Arctic Circle, during which the party had to spend 4 1/2 months in a winter house. The men arranged their reckoning of time so as to keep the Sabbath and have a religious service at which the Psalms were read. On their first Sabbath together, Psalm 133 was read, and the Commander brought before the men the duty of brotherly consideration, and his hope that every one would endeavor to cherish a friendly spirit and endeavor to reconcile those who might drift into an unpleasant controversy. The result may be found in the fact Greely recorded later on—

> For months without drinking water, destitute of warmth, with sleeping bags frozen to the ground, with walls, roof, and floor covered with frost and ice, deprived of sufficient light, heat, or food, they were never without courage, faith, and hope.

Although such fraternity inspired by this Psalm was most admirable, when David wrote it he had the blessed results of unity, when the children of God live harmoniously together, before his mind. To him, "the fellowship of kindred minds is like to that above," as a modern hymn expresses it. Psalms 127:2, and 128 were written to celebrate the blessings of large families. Psalm 133 sings the praise of good fellowship between brothers of the same family. During the three great Festivals of Israel, brothers of the same family would come together from widely separated parts of the world, and intercourse at such reunions must have been unspeakably sweet. Thus, the theme of the Psalm is the loveliness of brotherly union.

Dummelow says of the Psalm that it is "an exquisite gem of song describing the blessings of unity—suitable for a pilgrim song, when rich and poor, priest and peasant, might fraternize with Zion in sight." The truly Oriental unity eulogized in this beautiful little poem was not a mere brotherhood, but a *unity at Zion*, where God's blessing awaited those journeying there. Celebrating the love among God's people, it was probably written by David to celebrate the glad reunion of the nation after its long disunion during the times of the Judges and the opening years of his own reign. It was written then "all Israel" were united, "as the heart of *one man*," 2 Sam 19:9, 14. David knew by the experience the bitterness occasioned by divisions in families, says Spurgeon, and was well prepared to celebrate in choicest psalmody the blessing of unity of which he sighed.

Good and Pleasant Unity. The Psalm opens with the exclamation *Behold*! as if to suggest that the fragrant unity depicted is seldom seen, but admire it when it is. Perhaps there is an allusion to the previous jealousies and alienations in the family of Israel which were exchanged for mutual concord and affection as David ascended the throne. The exceeding excellence of such a united fellowship is found in the double *how* the poet uses to combine the two adjectives *Good* and *Pleasant*. Some things are *good* for us but not *pleasant*; while other things appear *pleasant* but are not *good* for us. But spiritual unity is both *good* and *pleasant*.

William Langland, Dante of the English people in the 14th century, in his *Vision of Piers Plowman*, has the paragraph—

> Finally truth takes the lute, and to it sings, Behold how good and joyful a thing it is, brethren, to dwell together in unity.

This verse was also quoted by the Roman legate at the meeting of Anselm and William II at Windsor, Whitsunday, 1095. It was likewise read at the reception of a new member in to the brotherhood of the Knights Templars, and was by St. Augustus quoted as the Divine authority for monastic life.

What, exactly, are we to understand by the expressed relationship, *Brethren*? It is certainly most agreeable to see brethren according to the flesh dwelling in unity, but experience proves that in many cases they get on better when they are apart. The brethren of Joseph dwelt together in envy. Here, the term implies those who are brethren in faith and spirit, who are bound together by the ties of love and surrender to God. If a gathering at a yearly Feast is implied, then the rendering of the verse can be, "How good and pleasant for those who are by race and religion brothers to unite for a sacred purpose."

If we profess to be brethren of Christ we must be brothers of each other, Mark 3:35; manifesting a continuing brotherly love. It is not enough to gather together as one in a church, we must take all opportunities of manifesting our unity to the world—*dwell together*—"dwell" being a word of residence, abode, and continuation. Such is a mark to the World around that we are His brethren and disciples. *Unity* does not mean uniformity, but oneness of heart, and feeling, and aim, 1 Cor. 12:4-6.

> Blest be the tie that binds
>   Our hearts in Christian love;
> The fellowship of kindred minds
>   Is like to that above.

> We share our mutual woes;
>   Our mutual burdens bear;
> And often for each other flows
>   The sympathizing tear.

The Precious Ointment, 133:2. The two short words given in italics were inserted by the translators as a fitting commencement of another verse, but in the original—*it is* does not appear, but the opening verse runs on "dwell together in unity, like the precious ointment upon the head," the idea being to emphasize the richness and fullness of life which spiritual brotherhood imparts. The fragrance of the oil poured on Aaron at his appointment to sacred office which overflowed on his beard and then down his official robe illustrates the *pleasant* side of spiritual unity, just as the *dew*, beneficial in its ministry, symbolizes the *good* effect of such unity.

The pleasure derived from the fragrance of the oil used is implied by David. Oil almost meets us as a standing symbol of joy and festivity and love, Psalm 45:7; Song of Sol. 1:3; Isa. 61:3. The precious ointment *ran down, went down*, from the head to the skirt of the garment, and brotherly love comes from the head, then falls at the feet. Love for the brethren condescends to men of low estate. Brotherly love cannot diffuse its fragrance unless it descends. Further, the oil was *precious*, not only because of its intrinsic nature but because of its typical character as symbolizing the nature and ministry of the Holy Spirit, 1 John 2:26, 27. It was with this Blessed Chrism that Jesus was anointed at His Baptism, and then copiously shed forth after His Ascension, Luke 2:21, 22; 4:18; Acts 2:33. "Moreover the results of that anointing have descended to ourselves, the weakest and furthest, who are but the skirts of His robes." Believer, be sure and avail yourself of the copiousness and wealth of our High Priests's enduement, John 3:34.

Dew Upon The Mountains, 133:3. Brethren dwelling together in unity is *good* even as "the dew of Hermon" and "of Zion." The particular *dew* was *one*, being the same copious summer night mist that descended on

Hermon in the south and upon Zion in the north. Thus an apt rendering would be "Like the dew of Hermon, which descend on Mount Zion." As the oil running down the beard was the same as that poured on Aaron's head, so the same dew is implied. "The dew of Hermon," as poetical synonym for *choice dew* "because of this freshness, abundance, and its connection with life and growth, is a symbol as the sacred oil is, of the covenant blessing in its *nature*." "Ran down," and "went down," should be given as *descended* as here in verse 3.

This descent is the point of comparison, for as the oil descends from Aaron's head over his face and beard and garment, so the dew of Hermon descends on Zion—low in actual measurement, but exalted by Divine favor above the loftiest hills. Thus, "it is not *unity* in itself which is the subject of the poem, but the unity of the *covenant* under which all blessings *flowed down* from above, rested on Mount Zion, and took outward shape and form there in the political and religious constitution." For almost half the year Palestine depends for its irrigation upon the refreshing and fertilizing dew which descends so copiously in the night that when morning dawns, the land looks as if a heavy shower had fallen. F. B. Meyer's comment on this last verse is finely expressed—

> The dew which fell on Mount Hermon is cited as being more lovely and holy than common dew. It is therefore employed as a further metaphor of the anointing oil, which had been referred to. And the Psalmist says that the love which was represented by the oil—which, in turn, was symbolized by the dews of Hermon—fell on Mount Zion as the dew on parched herbage, whenever the Lord's people met there in the exhibition of brotherly love. Love in the Spirit is the dew of this world of men; a symbol and channel of the eternal love and blessing of God.

Zion—such a holy place reminded David that God was thought in a special way to dwell and dispense blessings from there. "*There* Jehovah commanded the blessing." If Psalm 132 is blessing *FOR* Zion—Psalm 133, a blessing *IN* Zion, Psalm 134 is blessing *FROM* Zion. Wherever brotherly love reigns, God reigns. If we dwell together in loving unity now, we have already begun the enjoyments of Eternity, which are for evermore and can never be taken away from us. Precious and refreshing spiritual unity of the saints reaches its perfection in their gathering unto Him, Who is the Head of His Body—The Church.

Psalm 134

Made up of only 44 words, this beautiful little ode, equally full of sublimity and simplicity, brings us to the last Psalm in the group of Song of Degrees, or Songs of the Steps. As the finale of the Gradual Psalms, it depicts the Pilgrims going home and singing the last song in their Psalter. "They leave early in the morning, before the day has fully commenced, for the journey is long for many of them. While yet the night lingers on they are on the move." Then Spurgeon goes on to say in his introduction to this Psalm—"As soon as they are outside the gates they see the guards upon the temple wall, and the lamps shining from the windows of the chambers which surround the sanctuary; therefore, moved by the sight, they chant a farewell to the perpetual attendants upon the holy shrine. Their parting exhortation arouses the priests to pronounce upon them out of the holy place . . . The Psalm teaches us to pray for those who are continually ministering before the Lord, and it invites all ministers to pronounce benedictions upon their loving and prayerful people."

In the first two verses a night-greeting is addressed to the Priests and Levites in the Temple, with the last verse constituting their gracious reply in the form of a benediction. Martin Luther styled the Psalm—*Epiphonema Superiorum*—"I take this Psalm to be a conclusion of those things which were spoken of before." It would seem a if it is placed at the end of Songs of Degrees in order to take the place of a final blessing. *Bless* appears once in each verse.

The Servants, 134:1. This Psalm follows the last in that both begin with the demonstrative adverb—*Behold*! and indicates the reasons the Temple priests should bless Jehovah in the full provision He had made for the people to worship Him. Addressed to the sacred night-sentinels, it called upon the holy brotherhood to take care and be watchful through the night. They must not yield to sleep or idly waste their time, but perform all that was required of them until they were relieved by the morning guards. The exclamation, then, was necessary for evidently the matter was pressing, arising from the immediate circumstances of the moment.

After *Behold*, comes BLESS—the prominent word of the Psalm. Those addressed were called on to enter their service with praise. The first two references to *Bless* are connected with those urged to stir themselves up to bless Jehovah, but the last *Bless*, is Jehovah's blessing invoked upon

His people. The brief song, then, abounds in blessing. "May *blessed* and *blessing* be the two words describing our lives!"

It is the office of all "servants of the Lord" to bless or speak well of their Master. The term *servants*, as used here, is limited and defined by the next clause, "Ye which by night stand in the house of the Lord." The Temple ministrants, the Priests and Levites, and nightwatchmen are meant. Through grace we are all servants and should count it an honor to serve the Lord, whether it be in His House or in our own. We are to bless and serve Him at all times, even when the darkest hours overtake us.

We are told that the Levitical singers were "employed in their work day and night," 1 Chron. 9:30—the earthly sanctuary thus bearing a resemblance to the one above in which the redeemed "are before the throne of God, and serve him day and night in his temple," Rev. 7:15. Even by night the Lord is to be remembered and praised. It was the responsibility of the night sentinels to keep watch from sunset to sunrise over the hallowed precincts. Night vigils, while not as pleasant as those of the day, are yet necessary. Further, the day does not induce sleep as the night hours do. The Levites were urged to bless the Lord through the nightwatches. Jesus spent whole nights in prayer for His people.

God has still a relay of servants who come on duty and serve Him through the long hours of night. When night settled down on the Church, the Lord had His watchers and holy ones still guarding His truth. Wycliffe and his band in a dark period watched for the Reformation, as did the Waldenses. Coming down to ourselves, we have the sufferers from whose eyes sleep has departed—watchers by the bed-side at home and hospital—nurses on night-duty—all these, and others, maintain God's blessed worship when many of His active workers are recouping from their toils. At midnight, Paul and Silas prayed and sang praises unto God.

> Wake, and lift up thyself, my heart,
> And with the angels bear thy part,
> Who all night long, unwearied, sing
> High praise to the Eternal King.

Having to *stand* would prevent the Levites being overcome by drowsiness. "To stand before Jehovah" is a technical expression for the discharging of their official duties by the priests and Levites, Deut. 10:8; Heb. 10:11. But although *stand* was the customary word for sacerdotal service, the fact remains that there were no seats in the Tabernacle or Temple. The Rabbins say that the high-priest only sat in the sanctuary, as did Eli, 1 Sam. 1:9; the rest stood, as ready pressed to fulfill their office.

Another gesture of these priestly watchers was that of lifting up their hands in the sanctuary as they blessed the Lord. Such hands combined work and worship for they would be active at times dressing the Temple lamps and undertaking other necessary tasks, and then pausing in their hand-work, lifting up their hands in worship. The margin at verse 2 gives us "Lift up your hands in holiness." Paul speaks of "lifting up holy hands," 1 Tim. 2:8. To Israel, the lifted hand was the gesture of Prayer, an intimation of their expectations of receiving blessings from the Lord, and likewise an acknowledgment of the reception of same. Psalms 28:2; 62:4; 141:2. Combined with the lifting up of hands was the lifting up of voices in a further "Bless the Lord."

The last verse of the Psalm constitutes the reply of the leader of the Temple night-watchmen and was in the form of a benediction frequent in the Old Testament, 2 Chron. 30:27; 31:10; Psalms 12:2; 124:8; Ia. 37:16. The use of the singular instead of the plural, "bless *you*," addressed to the servants of the Lord as one person, is taken from the form found in the High Priest's blessing of the people, Num. 6:34. This answer of the priests, as they met the assembled pilgrims and return their salutations, reminds us that "we can never send up to God our adoration, but that it comes back to us again; as moisture drawn by sunshine from the earth returns to us again in showers."

What must not be forgotten in a consideration of this priestly benediction is its reference to the two-fold character of Jehovah, as the *Creator* "that made heaven and earth," and as the One condescending to dwell in "Zion," from which blessing flowed. Thus we see Him as the God of Nature and as the God of Grace. As we think of Him as Creator we have abundant evidence that He *can* bless us. Then as we meditate upon His dwelling among us as the Redeemer, we have abundant proof that He *will* bless us. Zion itself cannot bless us, only He Who dwells there. Thus we praise Him *from* Whom all blessings flow.

Psalm 135

It was with this Psalm along with Psalm 121 that David Livingstone bade farewell to his family and home at Blantyre, Scotland. Of this occasion, his sister wrote, "I remember my father and him talking over the prospects of Christian Missions. They agreed that the time would come when rich men and great men would think it an honor to support whole stations of missionaries, instead of spending their money on hounds and horses. On the morning of the 17th November, 1814, we got up at five o'clock. My mother made coffee. David read Psalms 121 and 135, and prayed. My father and he walked to Glasgow to catch the Liverpool steamer." David never saw his father again. His mother had told him that she "would have liked one of her laddies to lay her head in the grave." "It so happened," wrote David Livingstone in 1865, "that I was there to pay the last tribute to a dear good mother."

Coming immediately after the Songs of Degrees, they flow into the glorious Psalm of universal praise and find their response in it, just as rivers discharge their waters and lose themselves in the calm expanse of a beautiful lake. Ancient Jews looked on Psalms 134, 135 as one, with the latter being an expansion of the former. As the previous Psalm was used at shutting the Levites in at eventide, so Psalm 135 appears to have been a morning hymn they were called upon to sing at the opening of the gates of the Temple. The first two verses of this Psalm follow word for word the first verse of the last Psalm, and are now repeated with the view of keeping up the praise there commenced. It is a song full of life, vigor, variety, and devotion.

Made up of selections from other Scriptures, the Psalm claims no originality. A compound of many choice extracts, it has been called a mosaic and compared to a tesselated pavement. Put together, with very little art, for liturgic use, the repetitions yet have all the continuity and freshness of an original poem. Among the quotations called, the following are conspicuous—

> Verse 2 and 3 from Psalm 134.
> Verse 2, latter part, and start of verse 3 from Psalm 116:19.
> Verse 4, suggests Deut. 7:6.
> Verse 5 reminds us of Psalm 95:3.
> Verse 7 is almost identical with Jer. 10:13.
> Verse 13 can be found Exod. 3:15.

Verse 14 is from Deut. 32:36.
Verses 8-11 are in Psalm 136.
Verses 15-21, a repetition of Psalm 115.

Of these selected extracts it has been said that "the Holy Spirit occasionally repeats Himself; not because He has any lack of thought of words, but because it is expedient for us that we hear the same things in the same form. Yet, when our great Teacher uses repetition, it is usually with instructive variations which deserve our careful attention."

In our coverage of this Psalm we will not linger over its verses, seeing that we have already meditated upon some of them, and will review other verses quoted from future Psalms yet to be dealt with. Not only so, the verses speak for themselves and require little exposition. Let us, then, content ourselves with its broad outline. It is, indeed, a Psalm of *Praise*, the term Praise occurring 6 times; and also of *Blessing*, seeing that *Bless* appears 5 times.

1. Song of Praise to the Lord for His Power, Sovereignty and Goodness as the Lord of Creation, 135:1-7. The first verse presents us with a tirade of "Praise ye the Lord," and we cannot praise Him enough. "Let the Three-in-one have the praises of our spirit, soul, and body. For the past, present, and future, let us render three-fold Hallelujahs."

   In the time of Ambrose there were some strange theories as to Creation. It was held, for example, that earthquakes were explained from the 7th verse, by the winds being drawn out of God's secret treasuries.

2. Song of Praise for His Grace, Power, and Deliverance in respect to His ancient people, Israel. This section is an eloquent witness to the transcendence of Jehovah, 135:8-14.

3. Song of Praise for His Unity as the only true and living God, 135:15-21. The denunciation of the helplessness of all heathen deities is emphasized in verses 15-18. The concluding verses, 19-21, form a summons to praise Jehovah for all He is in Himself and in all His works. The concluding phrase *Out of Zion*, taken from 134:5, suggests a contrast for here Jehovah blesses the covenant people out of Zion—that is the place where the reciprocal relation is best and chiefly realized. This localization is made more emphatic by the addition of the name Jerusalem to Zion. See Psalms 76:2; 125:1,2. As Zion was the place where the people dwelt with God, it may represent the whole Church, or any place, however simple, where two or three meet in His name.

Psalm 136

The general theme of this Psalm, to which the LXX Version gives the title of *Hallelujah*, is the same as that of the previous Psalm, namely, a call to praise Jehovah on account of what He in Nature and in History revealed Himself to be. When, in 372, Athanasius was made subject to imperial tyranny, and fighting and slaughter surrounded his church, he sat down on the archbishop's throne and ordered the deacon to read Psalm 136 and all the people to respond with "For his mercy endured for ever"—which they did, and then withdrew to their homes.

When he was only 15 and already an undergraduate at Christ's College, Cambridge, John Milton was fascinated by the Psalms and translated into verse Psalm 136, which has been a much-loved hymn ever since—

> Let us with a gladsome mind
> Praise the Lord for He is kind,
> For His mercies aye endure
> Ever faithful, ever sure.

This is the only one of Milton's Psalms which has been taken into the public worship of the Church.

While we do not know who wrote this Psalm, we do know that it was sung in Solomon's Temple, 2 Chron. 7:3,6, and by the armies of Jehoshophat when they sung themselves into victory in the wilderness of Tekoa. It is a paean of praise to Jehovah for His delivering and protective mercy, and must have been popular among God's ancient people. Being tuned to rapture and rejoicing, it could only be fully enjoyed by those of a devoutly grateful heart. "O give thanks" is repeated four times, verses 1-3, 26, and implies that gratitude is the least we can offer God and should be freely and constantly offered Him for—

> When all those in changing within and around,
> In God and His mercy no change can be found.

The Mosaic pattern of the previous Psalm is traceable in this one which, like its predecessor, links itself to the Book of Deuteronomy. The first clauses *God of gods* and *Lord of lords*, verses 2 and 3, are taken from Deut. 10:17—*With a strong hand and stretched out arm*, verse 12, is from Deut. 4:34; 5:13—*To Him which led His people*, verse 16, is akin to Deut.

8:15. See Jer. 2:6. The first three verses contain three several names of the Deity, which are commonly rendered *Jehovah, God,* and *Lord* respectively.

1. *JEHOVAH* (given as *Lord*). This is His proper name and has reference to His essence as the *Self-existent One*, and as such is worthy of our praise and reverence to the highest degree.
2. *GOD OF GODS.* The heathen may worship their many tribal gods with zeal, but the God of Heaven is the only true, real, and living God. *God of gods* is a Hebrew superlative, because He is far above all man's created gods, whether they be so reputed or deputed. Being the Creator, He is infinitely higher than men or idols regarded as gods.
3. *LORDS OF LORDS.* "Lord" is from *Adoni,* representing Him as One with the power and authority to exercise rule. It is akin to *Governor.* And so with the three-fold Name is the three-fold doxology for all He is in Himself and in His work. See Num. 6:24-26.

Because of the particular and peculiar construction of this Psalm, we are not attempting a usual verse coverage. As for the initial clauses of all the verses, they tell their own story. What we want to dwell upon is the repetition, after each of the 26 clauses of the Psalm, the phrase, *For His mercy endureth for ever,* making the Psalm *An Oratio of Mercy.* The recurrence of this ancient liturgic refrain (Psalms 106:1; 118:1), indicates that it was prepared expressly for Temple service with the Levites repeating the initial clause of each verse, and then the people answering with the same refrain just as many of the favorite hymns today have the same chorus after each verse. "It seems like an inter-leaved Bible, and teaches us to interleave all things with the thought of the mercy of God." Because of its unique composition, the Jews included it in the *Great Hallel* covering Psalms 120-136, or, according to various sources, Psalms 134:4; 136. *Hallel* is an abbreviation of "Hallelujah"—*Praise ye Jehovah,* 136:1—and as Andrew Bonar suggested. *Praise* dominates the Psalm.

> Praise Him for what He is, 1-3.
> Praise Him for what He is able to do, 4.
> Praise Him for what He had done in Creation, 5-9.
> Praise Him for what He did in redeeming Israel from bondage, 10-15.
> Praise Him for what He did in His providence toward them, 16-22.
> Praise Him for His grace in times of calamity, 23, 24.
> Praise Him for His grace to the world at large, 25.
> Praise Him at the remembrance that this God is the God of Heaven, 26.

Poets all down the ages, like the Poets and Prophets of Bible days, have loved to praise the virtue of *Mercy,* both Divine and human. Of the qual-

ity of Mercy this Psalm extols in every verse, one instinctively feels that
William Blake's lines in The Divine Image are illustrative of it—

> For Mercy has a human heart,
> Pity a human face,
> And Love, the human form divine,
> And Peace, the human dress.

One wonders if Ebenezer Ellicott, who died in 1849, would have written his *People's Anthem* if he had prayerfully studied our *Mercy*
Psalm—

> When wilt thou save the people?
> Oh, God of Mercy! When?
> The people, Lord, the people!
> Not thrones and crowns, but men!

William Cowper, in one of his *Olney Hymns,* has a conception of
Mercy we can certainly apply to God's Mercy—

> Ev'ry door is shut but one,
> And that is mercy's door.

Shakespeare's description of Mercy is most expressive and illuminative when he makes *Portia* reply to *Shylock*—

> The quality of mercy is not strain'd,
> It droppeth as the gentle rain from heaven
> Upon the place beneath: it is twice bless'd;
> It blesseth him that gives and him that takes:
> 'Tis mightiest in the mightiest: it becomes
> The throned monarch better than his crown—

John Masefield, late Poet-Laureate, in his poem, *The Everlasting
Mercy*, has the stanza—

> The corn that makes the holy bread
> By which the soul of man is fed,
> The holy bread, the food unpriced,
> The everlasting mercy, Christ.

These and other poetic expressions of the intrinsic nature and value of
Mercy cannot out-match *God's Book of Mercy*, for on every leaf of the
Bible there is the seal of mercy. Even in the Ten Commandments which
are spoken of as "the ministration of death," there is an express mention
of mercy—"I will have mercy on thousands." In the Psalm before us we
have the rattling thunder-claps of mercy in every verse, with all 26 repetitions reminding us that God is both just and merciful, and that man

must not either despair of, or presume upon His mercy. No reason is given for such mercy but *mercy*, the Author of which is God. It is *"His mercy"*—the One offended by us, Who needed us not, Who gains nothing by us. This is the One Who is merciful.

Mercy follows mercy like links of golden chain through the Psalm, and if the end of one mercy was not the beginning of another, we would be altogether undone. Isaiah tells that, "In thy mercy is continuance," 64:5, and God's mercy is a treasure that can never be spent, never exhausted, for it is everlasting. Such mercy is the queenly grace that hath the keeping of the keys admitting us into every other Divine blessing. We, therefore, love the 26 repetitions before us, for they are not "vain repetitions," but express *fervency* and *zeal*. In Gethsemane, Jesus prayed three times using the *same* words, Luke 22:41.

Repetition means *emphasis*, and here in Psalm 136, there is a spiritual elegancy in it, seeing that it was the poet's purpose to show the unweariness and the unexhausted riches of God's free grace, notwithstanding all the efforts of men to thwart same. "He alone doeth wonders" and His most conspicuous wonder is the wonder of His mercy towards Adam's race, lost and ruined by the Fall. With all these thoughts of God's eternal Mercy in mind, then, let us take a parting look at its 26 applications in the Psalm. What were the 26 glorious aspects of Jehovah and His acts, eliciting the responses of the Temple chorus?

Response 1. Repeated, not after every verse but every clause, these responses do not appear once too often, for Jehovah's eternal mercy is the sweetest stanza any man can sing. The initial response was to His goodness. The Lord *is* good, and so *does* good. Having tested that the Lord was good, the people blessed Him as the Source, Sustainer, and Perfector of good.

Response 2. We cannot imagine the Godhead without mercy. What source of fear and terror it would be if Jehovah was not *the* God of gods. It is because He is the Highest that we should magnify Him in the highest style, for His works and words merit the gratitude of every heart.

Response 3. Lordship is His, and He rules with a strict impartiality. Mercy, however, is mingled with His justice seeing He delights more in mercy. As Lord over all, He can provide for and protect His own, and pardon the guilty who turn to Him in penitence and faith, pleading His mercy.

Response 4. Being the God of gods and Lord of lords, He alone can produce great wonders, Psalm 96:5. As the Wonderworker, He is unrivalled as the whole of His creative acts declare. But "the mercy of the wonder is the wonder of the mercy; and the enduring nature of that mercy is the central wonder of that mercy." May grace be ours ever to see the merciful in the wonderful, and the wonderful in the merciful.

Doing wondrous deeds alone,
Mercy sits upon the throne.

Response 5. The greatness and goodness of Jehovah appears in the wise way in which He fashioned an atmosphere suitable for man, bird, and beast to live in. Divine foresight and design are evident in the heavens above, and sprang from the Creator's merciful heart.

High as heaven his wisdom reigns,
Mercy on the throne remains.

Response 6. Who but the *God* of gods could have made earth such a fitting abode for man? And the power that fashioned it controls it. The waters are His, He made them, and they obey Him for He is the Master of ocean, earth and sky, as seen in His miracle when He said to the storm-tossed sea "Peace be still!" and there was a "great calm."

From the flood he lifts the land
Firm his mercies ever stand.

Response 7. The miracle worthy of our deepest gratitude is that of the creation of "great lights," identified for us in the next two verses. God's mercy gleams in the luminaries studding the heavens. How they declare both His greatness and glory as light bearers to the earth He created! His Son came as the most marvelous *Light* of all.

Lamps he lit in heaven's height
For in mercy he delights

Response 8. In each case it will be found that both the revelation declared and the response in praise and gratitude are specific. Here, for instance, we are informed of the precise function of the *Sun*, namely, *to rule by day*. Its untold benefits and influences are far too numerous to enumerate, and ever functions by the order of Him Who enthroned it as the lantern of the World. Pliny the Elder had the saying, "The sun chases sadness from the sky, and dissipates the clouds which darken the human heart." "Every sunbeam is a mercy, for it falls on undeserving sinners who else would sit in doleful darkness, and find earth a hell." John Milton gave us the lines of this 8th verse of the Psalm—

He, the golden tressed sun
Caused all day his course to run;
For his mercy shall endure
Ever faithful, ever sure.

Response 9. When the glory of the sun is absent, we have the many minor comforters of the moon and the myriads of stars to lighten our darkness, and mercy is seen in this numerous band as they shed their brilliance and influence on the tides or life-floods of earth. What else can we do but bless Him for His mercy in providing such tokens of His undying grace to men. Thomas Dick, who died in 1857, in his volume on *Celestial Scenery* reminded us that "in this nocturnal luminary, as in all other arrangements of nature, we behold a display of the paternal care and beneficence of that Almighty being Who ordained 'the moon and the starts to rule by night,' as an evidence of His abundant goodness, and of 'His mercy which endureth for ever.'"

Response 10. Expounding this 10th verse, Andrew Bonar says, "Remember His sovereign grace when righteousness would show itself upon the guilty. There was mercy even then to Israel—drops of mercy that forever endureth—at the very time judgment fell upon others. Should not this give emphasis to our praises? The dark background makes the figures in the foreground more prominent." The great design upon the affliction that fell upon Egypt was mercy to God's created favored nation, and through Israel to succeeding ages, and to all the World.

Response 11. The magnitude of Israel's emigration is staggering, and would have been utterly impossible had it not been for the over-ruling Providence overcoming the difficulties. "*He*—the mighty Jehovah—brought them out." The unfailing mercy of the Lord is gloriously seen in His separation of His elect from bondage, and henceforth the people were to show forth His praise and mercy.

Response 12. We have in this verse the channels of God's extraordinary power in the deliverance of Israel from Pharaoh's dominion and cruelty. It was by "a strong hand, and a stretched out arm." The figure of *an outstretched arm* is appropriate, says Calvin, for we stretch out the arm when any great effort is required: so that this implies that God put forth an extraordinary and not a common or slight display of His power in redeeming His people.

> See, he lifts his strong right hand,
> For his mercies steadfast stand.

Response 13. This and the next two verses describe the road God made across the sea-bottom, and arranged the waters so that His people could escape from Egypt, which they did awe-stricken, but quiet and confident that God's mercy alone had saved them. "God will do a new thing to keep His old promise. His way is in the sea, and He will make a way for His people in the same pathless region."

> Lo, the Red Sea he divides,
> For His mercy sure abides.

Response 14. God not only made a track through the fawning abyss for Israel to journey over, but *made* them pass over it. Mercy provided a deliverance, and the same mercy and power gave the people the courage to make use of the offered means of escape, and they marched dry shod through the heart of the sea. "Mercy cleared the road, mercy cheered the host, mercy led them down, and mercy brought them up again."

> Through the fire or through the sea
> Still his mercy guardeth thee.

Response 15. Mercy and Judgment are combined in the miracle of the Red Sea for what was *mercy* for Israel, was *misery* for Pharaoh and his host. Mercy defied and rejected ends in doom, for never had such a judgment overtaken a nation as it did Egypt on that momentous day. As for Israel, in united voice she could chant—

> Evermore his love shall reign,
> Pharaoh and his host are slain.

Response 16. Having brought His people *out* of Egypt and *through* the Red Sea, God now acts as the Guide to lead them *into* and through the wilderness. Because they were *His people*, He was pledged to lead them all the way to the promised land. Divine mercy was severely tested for 40 years, but it bore the strain and revealed its virtue in that it never ceased towards the pilgrims even when they transgressed. How expressive are the lines of Sir Walter Scott—

> When Israel, of the Lord beloved,
>   Out of the land of bondage came,
> Her father's God before he moved,
>   An awful Guide, in smoke and flame,
> By day, along the astonished lands,
>   The cloudy pillar glided slow;
> By night Arabia's crimsoned sands
>   Returned the fiery column's glow.

Responses 17, 18. In these two responses we have a general description of the royal foes of Israel, "Great kings"—"Famous Kings," and the next two verses specifically names two of them. *Great* though these rulers were, they could not hope to succeed when Divine Mercy was up in arms against them. Then *famous* they might have been in the eyes of men, but before God they were infamous, and their judgment increased the Lord's fame as the Protector of His own.

> Evermore his mercy stands,
> Saving from the foeman's hands.

Response 19. In battle Sihon had taken from Balak's predecessor the whole district between the Arnon and Jabbok, through which the

approach to Jordan lay, and transferred the capital from Boab-Ar to
Heshbon. Not only was Sihon great and famous, but valiant and powerful, and thus willfully refused to give Israel a peaceful passage through
his land. What the king forgot was that the merciful God of Israel was no
respecter of persons, and that neither his greatness nor fame could save
him once the sword of Divine justice was raised against him.

Response 20. What Og lacked in quality, he made up for in quantity
for he came of a race of giants, Deut. 3:11. Such was his enormous size
that he needed an *iron* bed to bear the strain of his weight, some 14 feet
long and 6 feet broad. Og looked more formidable than Sihon, so God
gave His people special encouragement as they encountered the giant,
Num. 21:34. Through Divine mercy, Israel was victorious over Og, who
was made to look like a pigmy, when forced to exchange his remarkable
bedstead of iron for a bed in the dust.

> Great kings before him yield
> Mercy everholds the field.

Responses 21, 22. Enduring mercy is further seen in that as the Lord
of the whole earth, He gave the land of conquered foes to the victors.
Repetitions are effective in poetry when they discover some unnoticed
feature. Thus, verse 22 explains who received the land for an heritage,
referred in verse 21—it was "Israel his servant." God speaks of His people as one man—*His servant*—because to Him they were one, His
first-born, Exod. 4:22. "Mercy fights for the land, mercy divides the spoil
among its favored ones, and mercy secures each man in his inheritance."

> For his mercy full and free,
> Wins us full felicity

Response 23. Divine remembrance is a Paradise from which no man
can expel God's redeemed ones. Israel, looking back over the past with
all its bondage and misery, experienced what it was to have His manifold
mercies to rouse the sweetest song—"He remembered *us*," even when
they were so low as captives in a strange land. His eye was ever upon
them, and His hand ready to deliver them in the hour of His appointing.
How could He forget those redeemed by blood? If you are low-spirited,
or in a low estate, let the truth lift you up to the highest joy that He Who
cares for the odd sparrow will not forget you.

Response 24. Remembrance and Redemption are vitally connected.
"Fear not, I have redeemed thee," and being redeemed from our sin and
enemies, the Redeemer could not possibly forget us. Having remembered
Israel in her low estate, God mercifully redeemed her from bondage and
blessed her with liberty. Is this not a forecast of the redemption Divine
mercy accomplished for us at Calvary?

> E'en to death upon the tree
> Mercy dureth faithfully.

Response 25. Further mercy is seen in that God not only redeemed His people, delivering them from poverty in Egypt, but replenished them. His providence cared for those He had redeemed. In spite of all the sin and failure in the wilderness, their testimony to unfailing mercy was that they lacked nothing. How bountiful is God's mercy as we think of the way He has given food to man, beast, and bird, all down the ages. The tragedy is that so few in comparison praise God from Whom all blessings flow, even daily bread.

> All things living he doth feed,
> His full hand supplies their need;
> For his mercy shall endure,
> Ever faithful, ever sure.

Response 26. The phrase *God of heaven* used here, is not met with in any other Psalm. It is found in other Old Testament books, particularly in Ezra, and is also found in Revelation 11:13; 16:11. What a sublime and appropriate designation of the true and mighty God this is to end the Psalm with! As the God of Heaven, He has provided Heaven for His people, and what an everlasting mercy this will prove to be. There are 26 *everlastings* in this one Psalm because God's mercy stretches from time into eternity. The sole cause of all we have below and above is the matchless mercy of Him Who is ever merciful to those who know themselves to be sinners in need of the mercy enduring for ever. The Psalm ends as it begins by giving thanks unto God. May ours be the grateful heart for all His mercy has provided, and provides!

Psalm 137

This plaintive ode, one of the most touching and charming compositions in the whole Book of Psalms for its poetic power in its description of Israel's captivity, love of Zion, and hatred for her foes, has found an echo in similar experiences of saints down the ages. It has also struck a key to many a song of the love of country. Lamoens, the national epic poet of Portugal, wrote of it as "The Psalm of pious patriotic memory." Released from prison in March, 1553, he sailed for India, was shipwrecked, and while waiting at Mekong for another ship, composed a paraphrase of Psalm 137, which is one of the finest metrical forms of the poem. Abbe Curie, great Oriental scholar, and author of a translation of the Old Testament into Italian and who was one of the few Roman Catholic clergy who took the side of Italy and freedom against the Papacy, had a preference for this Psalm. Lecturing in 1883 to an immense assembly in Rome, he expressed his love for the 137th Psalm, and said of it that "it was the first and grandest patriotic song which was ever written, linking God and country together."

The gifted but unfortunate Henri Heine, who submitted without heart-conviction to Christian baptism, was moved to the soul by this Psalm because of what he had suffered to his race in Germany. Writing to a Jewish friend, he said, "I remember me that the Psalm *We sat by the waters of Babylon*, was then your favorite, and that you recited it so beautifully, so nobly, so touchingly, that I would fain weep now, and not alone of the Psalm." Heine began a metrical version of a Psalm, inspired by his love for the 137th, but later on, parodied the verses he had written.

With pathetic force the lament of the people while exiles in Babylon appealed to the Puritans in New England and the exiled Huguenots in Canada, as they made this ode their own. Then, what memories of silent tragedies must the words of the Psalm have stirred in the hearts of the Covenanters, toiling among the slaves in the sugar plantations or rice-fields of West Indies and America, as they gave vent to song in its Scottish version!

In 1605, St. Vincent de Paul, one of the great figures in Roman Catholic history, was making his way from Toulouse by Narbonne to Marseilles, but the ship was seized by Barbary pirates, and both passengers and crew were carried to Tunis. Sold as a slave to a fisherman, Vincent passed after a time into the hands of an apostate Christian from

Nice, who carried him away to labor on an inland farm. As he dug in the fields under a burning sun, his Psalm-singing was noticed by one of the Turkish wives of his master. In a letter to his friend De Comment, Vincent wrote—

> "One day she asked me to sing to her some of the praises of God." The remembrance of the captive Israelites, *How shall we sing the song of the Lord in a strange land*? filled his heart, and he sang, "By the waters of Babylon," Psalm 137.

The woman told her husband that he had done wrong to change his faith, and she warmly praised the religion that Vincent had expounded to her. Her words sank into the renegade's heart and woke his slumbering conscience. He determined to escape and take Vincent with him. In 1607 they landed together at Aigues Mortes, and the captive was once more free.

The sorrowing words of the Babylonian exiles also rose to the lips of John II, King of France, a prisoner in England after the Battle of Poittiers, and a guest at a tournament. He looked on the brilliant scene with sorrowful eyes, and, when urged to enjoy the splendor of the pageant, answered mournfully, *How shall we sing the Lord's song in a strange land*? Psalm 137:4.

Jerome, born in 346, was another who loved the Psalms, and came to revise from the Septuagint their Latin version. In 385 he left Rome, where he had made both friends and enemies, convinced as he said, that he had tried in vain *to sing the Lord's song in a strange land*, and thus embarked for Palestine, where he labored with persistent energy till his death in 420. Many other appealing uses of this Psalm of tears could be given, but as John Knox expresses it, "In a still higher point of view than the love of the earthly land, this 137th Psalm may be regarded as the spring of the songs of the *Jerusalem above*, which, in all ages of the Church, have looked away from the banishment of exile in the final home"—

> For thee, O dear, dear country,
>   Mine eyes their vigils keep;
> For very love, beholding
>   Thy happy name, they weep;
>
> Even now, by faith, I see thee,
>   Even now thy walls discern;
> To thee my thoughts are kindled,
>   And strive, and pant, and yearn.

As to the background of this soul-gripping Psalm, Dr. F. B. Meyer says that "it reminds us of the emotions excited in an army on a distant march by hearing the strains of a home song. It was evidently composed by a returned exile. But it is also clear that the destruction of Babylon herself was imminent, verse 8. We are thus led to the conquest of Babylon by Darius, Daniel 5:31, whereby its entire destruction, as foretold in prophecy, was brought within a reasonable range."

While the Psalm is given with a title, the LXX Version has the curious one *The David of Jeremiah*, which is explained as meaning, "A David-like song by Jeremiah"—who is known as *The Weeping Prophet*. Without doubt, the Psalm is one of clearest records left in Hebrew literature of Captivity, but whether it dates immediately from it, or looks back with a distant though keen and clear gaze, is not easy to decide. We believe it to have been divinely inspired, but if it were not, it would still occupy a high place in poetry because of its highest degree of tender, intense patriotism.

Its nine verses fall into three strophes, each consisting of three verses, expressing these aspects—

1. The exiled Jews are requested by the Babylonians to sing and play, 1-3,
2. The captive Jews refusal and its reason, 4-6,
3. The vengeance invoked by Babylon and Edom, foes of Zion, 7-9.

The Request To Sing And Play, 137:1-3. The form of language used shows that the scene described belonged to past days, perhaps not far distant. These opening verses have caused the Psalm to be universally admired, and any soul capable of feeling must admit that there is nothing more exquisitely beautiful in literature than the picture of the loneliness of those broken-hearts as they say by the rivers of Babylon and wept and wept. As Stewart Perowne, in his masterly work on *The Psalms* expresses it, "This Psalm is a wonderful mixture of soft melancholy and fiery patriotism! The hand that wrote it must have known how to smite sharply with the sword, as well as how to tune the harp. The words are burning words of a heart breathing undying love to his country, undying hate to his foe. The poet is indeed"—

> Dower'd with hate of hate, to scorn of scorn,
> The love of love.

This lifelike memorial of the bitter experiences of the Jews in exile, with its strong expression of patriotism and an outburst of hatred against the enemies of their beloved Jerusalem, could not have begun in a more fitting way that it did, alongside the canals of Babylon with their coldness and solitude. The touching picture presented is a poetic way of expressing the silence during the exile of the religious and festal days. The very waters at which the captives sat seems to be in sympathy with their tears. They could see in the streams of Babel the image and symbol of their flood of tears. Their eyes were a fountain of tears as they wept day and night over the past. See Jer. 9:1; Lam. 2:18; 3:48.

The sitting posture was also in harmony with their sorrowful feelings for among poets *sitting* on the ground is a mark of misery and of captivity, as the sayings of Propertius indicate—

> With locks unkempt, mournful, for many days
> She sat.
> O might I sit a captive at thy gate.

This same posture can be found on old coins celebrating a victory of Lucius Verus over the Parthians and on several Judean coins of Vespasian and Titus in a sitting attitude indicative of sorrow and captivity. In servitude and helpless under a cruel enemy, Israel wept as she sat on foreign soil. See Job 2:8; Isa. 3:26; 47:1, 5.

We wept! But what was the cause of the tears of those strong men who were sweet singers? What was it that subdued their brave spirits? Cruelty, again, and poverty were theirs in Babylon, but the cruelties heaped upon them in captivity there did not cause their tears to flow. What they were enduring at the hands of their captors only made their hearts burn with wrath. No, they wept as they remembered Zion. The word *remember*, occurring 3 times, is the key-word of the Psalm. Zion was graven on their inmost hearts, and as they thought of their Temple where Jehovah dwelt, and of the great center of the national and religious life, and compared same with their captivity in a heathen land, their eyes could not refrain from floods of tears.

Further, the prolific weeping willows growing by the rivers and canals, causing Babylon to be known as "The Valley of Willows," seem to be in full sympathy with Zion's weeping worshippers. It was as if the exiles said, "The drooping branches appeared to weep as we did, and so we gave to them our instruments of music; the willows could as well make melody as we, for we had no mind for minstrelsy." Among those carried away captive were many singers, and these would, of course, carry their instruments with them for sacred use. What was the use of the most ancient of musical instruments as the harp is, if the heart is nigh to breaking? The phrases *Harps upon the willows* is a touching metaphor that has passed into all languages as an expression of extreme grief.

The question has been asked, why did the singers not leave their harps at home when expulsion came? The answer is that they needed them to accompany their Psalm-singing with. But refusing to sing, they hang up their harps on the willows simply because they were unwilling to sing their songs of Prayer and Praise for the mere amusement of their heathen captors who had unexpectedly captured them, as the next verse indicates. William Jay, in his exposition of this Psalm, has this somewhat appealing application of its second verse—

When the believer is in darkness, he hangs his harp upon the willows, and cannot sing the song of the Lord. Every believer has a harp. Every heart that has been made new is turned into a heart of praise. The mouth is filled with laughter—the tongue with divinest melody. Every Christian loves praise—the holiest Christians love it most. But when the believer falls into sin and darkness, his harp is on the willows, and he cannot sing the Lord's song, for he is in a strange land.

To the credit of the sweet singers of Israel, they preferred to be dumb and have silent harps rather than be forced to please her enemies with forced singing and music. They would not bring their talent into bondage to an oppressor's will. What cruelty it was to make a people sigh, and then require them to sing! *Mirth* also was required! The captives were asked not only to sing, but *smile*, and to cause their harps to add *merriment* to their music. This only added insult to injury, seeing Hebrew music was not so mirthful as the Babylonian. The fame of Hebrew Psalmody had travelled far and wide, and thus the demand for a song about Zion may have originated in such a reputation. Across the desert news of the sweetness of the Temple singing and music had reached the ears of the captors, and they were anxious to hear the same. Or, and F. B. Meyer suggests—

It may be their captors were anxious that the Israelites should reconcile themselves to their lot, and feel at home in their banishment. But in any case the treatment by those captors had made compliance with their demands impossible.

What made the request sound like mockery was that it came from those who had *wasted* the exiles—the word for *wasted* meaning plundered or robbed us of our country. Further, the insulting nature of the request is more conspicuous when we remember that the songs asked for in derision were those exalting Jehovah and His love towards His chosen people now in exile. These songs of Zion were the Temple ones such as the Psalter contains and to which the genius of the race was dedicated. Vibrating, then, with deep Hebrew religious feeling, how could the weeping hearts sing with the jollity asked one of these holy songs? The only place for the songs of Zion is in *Zion*.

The Reason the Request to Sing and Play Was Refused, 137:4-6. This further triad of verses contains a most emphatic indignant refusal. The margin at verse 4 reads, "How can we sing the Lord's song in the land of a stranger?" How could their hearts be in tune in such uncongenial company as the Babylonians were. *The Lord's Song . . . in a strange land* was the contrast, the incongruity gripping the hearts of these exiles in Babylon. How could they sing in loftiest adoration of their great Jehovah and of all His wondrous works in such a godless land? Why, the words would freeze upon their lips, and the harp refuse to sound! It would have sounded very strange indeed if they had sung the Lord's song in a *strange* land.

"The feeling expressed in this question is too natural to need any such explanation as that it was contrary to the Law to sing as sacred song in a strange land," comments Ellicott. "Nehemiah's answer offers a direct illustration, Neh. 2:2, 3. Of Jerusalem's choir in Babylon it might be truly said, as Tennyson expresses it"—

> Like strangers voices here they sound,
> In lands where not a memory strays.
> Nor landmark breathes of other days,
> But all is new unhallowed ground.

The imprecation following the request is just as explicit. *Hand* and *tongue* are mentioned in verses 5 and 6—on the one if it should be mis-employed in the skilled playing of the harp, and on the other in gifted singing. *Forget* is attached to the one, and *Remember* to the other. What pathos is in the phrase, *If I forget thee, O Jerusalem*! Jerusalem, the Golden, to which Jesus came to die for all who are strangers to grace. The word *cunning*, given italics, is an old Saxon word meaning skill. Thus, verse 5 can be paraphrased, "If at such a moment the poet can so far for-get the miserable bondage of Jerusalem as to strike the strings in joy, may his hand forever lose the skill to touch them." The tongue cleaving to the roof of the mouth carries the same implication. So the players on instru-ments and the sweet songsters were of one mind: the enemies of the Lord could have no mirthful tune or song from them. Jerusalem, the sacred city, was the head of their joy, first in their thoughts, queen of their hearts and crown of their joy, thus they could not dishonor sacred hymns by allow-ing their captors to ridicule their worship. May we never forget Him Who is the crown and chief joy of all who constantly remember His dying love!

The Vengeance Invoked on Israel's Foes, 137:7-9. The vindictive close of this fine song with its blending of tears and fire has received varying explanations from the theologians. What must not be lost sight of is the fact that this last section, containing as it does, a curse upon Israel's foes, begins with *Remember, O Jehovah*! In verse six the poet asked a kind of a curse upon his right hand and mouth if he failed to remember Jehovah. Now he calls upon Jehovah to remember the merited judgment of those who had ravaged the nation and driven the people into a cruel captivity. *Remember*—with a view to reciprocating the anguish received.

Edom took malicious pleasure in the destruction of Jerusalem. The phrase "in the day of Jerusalem," implies the day when the city was destroyed, Psalm 37:13; Obadiah 11-12. Thus the punishment of Edom is often referred to, 2 Kings 25:8; Jer. 49:7-22; Lam. 4:21, 22; Ezek. 25:12-14. The Edomites ought to have been friendly with the Israelites, seeing they were brethren and neighbors, but a deep hatred and cruel spite possessed them, Obad. 10; Amos 1:11; Mark 3:8; and in calling upon the Lord to undertake their just judgment, Israel left the matter in His hands, knowing that as the God of recompense, He would manifest justice without partiality.

Edom had razed Jerusalem to the ground, now the Psalmist prays for Edom to be razed out of memory, leaving no stone standing upon another in the city. *Raze it, raze it*, literally means "make it bare or naked," lay it bare of its houses and inhabitants, Hab. 3:13. Failing to remember any mercy towards those they hated and so destroyed, they deserved to be remembered by Divine vengeance. By "daughter of Babylon" we are to understand Babylon itself, to which the captives were taken. Proud and brutal Babylon must be made to pay for her crimes. "Happy shall he be that rewarded thee as thou hast served us." The cruel conduct must be measured back in their own bosoms. Having plowed iniquity, they must be made to reap the same, Job 4:8. Their wickedness must be recompensed in its own kind. The devastators must be devastated.

Because the Covenanters in the days of Claverhouse spared the lives of their prisoners, Sir Robert Hamilton supported his protest against such an act of mercy by quoting these last verses of Psalm 137. His contention was the enemy gave them no quarter but mowed them down mercilessly, so they should have destroyed them when they had them in the hand. "Yet we refused to be convinced that our sparing of the lives of these, when God has appointed to utter destruction, is one of the causes why our lives go for theirs."

Perhaps the most horrible part of the curse herewith pronounced was the happiness wished upon those who would batter babies to death. *Little ones* in this last verse means *sucklings*—babies at the breast. That this was a feature of barbarous cruelty associated with ancient wars is evident from other Scriptures, 2 Kings 8:12; Isa. 13:16; Hosea 10:14. Homer has the stanza, as found in Pope's translation of *Iliad*—

> My heroes slain, my bridal bed o'erturned,
> My daughters ravish'd, and my city burned,
> My bleeding infants dash'd against the floor;
> These have I yet to see, perhaps yet more.

Through two centuries of conflict and terrible persecution the Huguenots found great consolation in the Psalms. Their morals were austere, and their virtues were fostered by their love of the Bible. But from the same Book they justified their ferocity against their foes. To them *Rome* was Babylon, and the *Reformed Church* was Zion. Their enemies were God's enemies. They were His appointed instruments of vengeance, thus they made war in the spirit of John Calvin's commentary of Psalm 137:8, 9, and of his defense of its imprecations on the women and *children* of their foes.

The curse in this last verse had led some soft hearts to say that it would have been better if these last three verses could in some way be disjointed from the sweet and touching nature of the first two sections. "It sounds as if one of the strings on their well-tuned harp was out of melody, as if it struck a jarring note of discord." Says one expositor, "The dashing of little ones against the stones, reference to which is also made in Isa. 13:16-18, belongs to a Dispensation of Law and Judgment, and is not to be interpreted of the present dispensation of Grace." Similarly, F. B. Meyer says, "We can understand the spirit which breathes through them: but it is rather that of the Old Dispensation than of the New, Matt. 5:43-48." Another says of *the luxury of revenge* expressed here that "The Psalm is beautiful as a poem—the Christian must seek his inspiration elsewhere."

But what must not be forgotten is that it is the Lord Himself Who decreed the final desolation of Babylon, and the total destruction of those despots crushing virtue beneath their iron hell. In the siege and capture of Jerusalem, great atrocities were committed and—

> Many a childing mother then
> And new-born baby died.

If the children of such barbarous murderers of women and children were allowed to live and become grown men, their sin, if left alone, would be the continuation of parental cruelty. Better for the babies to die in innocency than to grow up as replicas of their cruel forbears. A just and equal retribution is thus called for, Isa. 47; Jer. 50. "As thou hast done," says God, "it shall be done to thee," Obadiah 15. Further, those who plead that such a curse is not Christ-like, should bear in mind that He said to the hypocrites of His day, "With what measure ye mete, it shall be measured to you again," Matt. 6:2. And what does this mean but, "you deserve to be paid back in your own coin?" One cannot do better than cite the sentiment of C. H. Spurgeon on the utterances of burning indignation—utterances, as righteous as they were fervent—

> Let those find fault with these curses, that were not causeless, who have never seen their temple burned, their city ruined, their wives ravished, and their children slain; they might not, perhaps, be quite so velvet-mouthed if they had suffered after this fashion. It is one thing to talk of the bitter feeling which moved captive Israelites in Babylon, and quite another thing to be captives ourselves under a savage and remorseless power, which knew not how to show mercy, but delighted in barbarities to the defenseless. The song is such as might fitly be sung in the Jews' wailing-place. It is a fruit of the Captivity in Babylon, and often has it furnished expression for sorrows which else had been unutterable. It is a gemlike Psalm within whose mild radiance there glows a fire which strikes the beholder with wonder.

Psalm 138

We have now reached another group of Psalms written by David, probably the last from the sweet Psalmist of Israel—Psalms 138-145. As all eight are written in the *first* person, and each bears the title, *A Psalm of David*, or better, *A Psalm By David*, we can expect the series to be Davidic in character as they are "exhibiting all the fidelity, courage and decision of that King of Israel and Prince of Psalmists." Several theologians with a critical approach to Scripture rob David of the authorship of these Psalms. For instance one writer, "Although the title of Psalm 138 ascribes it to David, it is generally considered to belong to the post-exilic period, of whose earnest piety, it is one of the best examples." Ellicott says that "because the tone and tenor of this Psalm bearing David's name suits the times of Ezra and Nehemiah, Zeribbabel or Nehemiah was its author . . . On the other hand . . . it may breathe the hope of the Maccabaean Period."

Dealing with the question of the Davidic authorship of these eight Psalms and of his belief in same, C. H. Spurgeon has the caustic statement about those rejecting the title, *A Psalm By David*—"Many modern critics are to the Word of God what blow-flies are to the food of men: they cannot do any good, and unless relentlessly driven away they do great harm." As to the correctness of the superscription of this first Psalm in the group, there can be no doubt as to David's authorship, seeing that it is a kind of commentary of the great Messianic promise of 2 Sam. 7 with David himself standing forth as its exponent. Further, as E. W. Hengstenberg states it—

> Proof also of David's authorship of Psalm 138 is found in the union, so characteristic of him, in bold courage, see especially verse 3, and deep humility, see verse 6. And in proof of the same comes, finally, the near relationship in which it stands with other Psalms of David, especially those which likewise refer to the promise of everlasting kingdom; and which David's thanksgiving in 2 Sam. 7, the conclusion of which remarkable agrees with the conclusion of our Psalm:
>
> And now, Lord God, the word which thou hast spoken upon thy servant and upon his house, that fulfill even to Eternity, and do as thou hast spoken.

David's desire to build a house of the Lord, and of the promised covenant of Jehovah, are dwelt upon with gladness both in 2 Sam. 7 and

Psalm 138. As we shall more fully see, idols, which could never compare with the promised blessing, retreat ashamed, verse 1—The Lord has done more to glorify Himself by it than by all His previous wonders, verse 2—All kings will one day praise the Lord on account of it, verse 4—It is the beginning of a chain of blessings that can never end.

As to a division of the Psalm, the following three aspects can serve as a guide—

1. Gratitude to Jehovah for His love and constancy, 1-3,
2. Prediction that all earth's kings will worship him, 4-6,
3. Confident Hope for the future, 7-8.

Gratitude to Jehovah for His love and constancy, 138:1-3. In these opening verses with their three *I WILL*'s, David expresses his determination to own his God before the gods of the nations, or before angels or rulers. A noticeable feature of these verses is that the Psalmist's mind is so taken up with God that he does not mention His name. "To him there is no other God, and Jehovah is so perfectly realized and so intimately known, that in addressing Him, David no more thinks of mentioning His name that we should do if we were speaking to a father or a friend. He sees God with his mind's eye, and simply addresses Him with the pronoun *Thee*."

Praise, mentioned five times if we include "shall sing," verses 1, 4, the equivalent, dominates the Psalm. In the first two verses, David praises Jehovah with all his being—praises Him before the gods—praises Him for His Word and virtues. Following Psalm 137, this Psalm is wisely placed for the apposition and contrast are striking. In the previous Psalm we have the need of silence before revilers, but in Psalm 138, we have the excellence of praise and a brave confession before all gods. There is a time to be silent lest we cast pearls before swine; and there is a time to sing and speak openly lest we be found guilty of cowardly non-confession.

David's praise of Jehovah was not of a formal or half-hearted nature, but with his *whole heart*. If the Psalmist had a broken heart over his great sin, he also had a whole heart to praise Jehovah Who forgave Him his transgression. By *heart* we are not to understand the seat of affection, but the whole being. Thus David actually meant, "With all that I am and have I will praise Thee." After silent hearts and harps, there is song once more unto the Lord, Psalm 9:1, and the verification of His Godhead before the false gods.

There is diversity of opinion as to the exact meaning of *gods* in the first verse of the Psalm. Was the praise before all the false deities in an idolatrous country? The LXX Version and Vulgate Versions give *Angels* instead of "gods." The Chaldee translates it *Judges*, the Syriac, *Kings*, while some of the Early Greek Fathers explained "gods" as a reference to the Priests and Levites. Many of the Rabbins interpreted the term as signifying "the great ones of the earth." See Psalms 8:5; 29:1, margin; 8:26; John 10:34-36; Heb. 2:7. Perhaps we should take the declaration as it stands and accept that David had in mind the images and false deities the Canaanites foolishly worshipped, and expressed his contempt of such professed adoration of dead idols who had no ears to hear the praise of men.

Although gorgeous temples had been reared to house idol gods, David turned in worship toward God's holy Temple, to the center of sacrifice and His own indwelling He had ordained. It is this mention of the *holy temple* that prompts critics to reject the Davidic authorship of the Psalm seeing it was not erected in the Psalmist's day. Having prepared abundantly for the building of the Temple, David was not allowed to erect it. But he could worship *toward* it, or look earnestly to the spot chosen of the Lord for His own sanctuary, as set forth in 2 Sam. 7. It has been indicated that "temple" here is properly rendered in the original as *mansion*—"the mansion of thy sanctity," and that this meaning destroys the critics' objection to David's composition of the Psalm.

Worship and Praise of Jehovah's being and virtues are conspicuous in David's approach to the sanctuary. Praising His *name* means extolling Him for all that He is in Himself, His character manifested in *lovingkindness* and *truth*, or His grace and His truth. P. B. Power in his most helpful volume on *The I Wills of the Psalms* says that two beautiful thoughts are expressed here, namely, "God's condescension in thought," and the other, "His tenderness in action," both being included in His "lovingkindness." God's promise made to David in 2 Sam. 7 was prompted by love and founded on truth, and was thereby a fuller manifestation of God's character than any previous revelation.

As to the last clause, "For thou hast magnified thy Word above thy name," is surely one of the most amazing and remarkable expressions in the whole of Scripture. Remember that *name* stands for all God's perfections, all He has revealed of Himself as having—justice, majesty, holiness, greatness and glory—then to affirm that He has magnified above all He is in Himself, His *Word* or *Truth*, surely implies that He has a *greater* regard for the words of His mouth than for the works of His hand; that His word or promise exercises a kind of sovereignty over all His attributes and prerogatives to which His word is never contrary. The faithful and complete performance of His promises surpasses the expectations which the greatness of His name has excited, Psalm 48:10.

There was a day, however, when David sobbed and could not sing, and on those days he cried, God answered him, and strengthened his soul, verse 3. Now he praises and worships God as the One Who hears and answers prayer. Every child of God can say *Amen*! to the Psalmist's experience—*In the day when I cried thou answeredst me.* Of course, God does not always answer our prayers in the way we request, but what He does for us is what He did for His beloved Son in Gethsemane, He strengthens us, Luke 22:43. One reading has it, "Thou hast enlarged me in my soul with strength." To enlarge with strength means, "to give one the feeling of freedom and strength." See Song of Sol. 6:5.

God granted David a speedy answer, for on the *very* day he cried he was heard; it was also a spiritual answer for as the Strength of Israel's God increased his strength, "Thou makest me brave in my soul with strength." If, when we cry for relief, the burden is not removed, as Paul's thorn in the flesh was not, yet sufficient strength and grace is given to bear the burden which is an equally effective method of help. By the continued pressure of the burden, we learn patience and also how sweet the uses of adversity are. The sufferings Paul endured produced an abounding consolation for other sufferers, 2 Cor. 1:5.

Prediction of Universal Worship of Jehovah, 138:4-6. That this central section of the Psalm heralds a prophetic pronouncement is evident from the fact that there has been a decade when *all* the kings of the earth were to be found praising the Lord for His Word and great Glory. But the forecast is that they "shall praise thee, O Lord." In David's own day, although he was a *King*, he sang wonderfully of the ways of the Lord and also of His great glory, as surrounding Heathen kings praised their dead idols. But the prediction is that earth's rulers will yet worship Israel's God, and David, knowing that His promises had been abundantly fulfilled in other directions, believed that the day would come when the same Divine Word will convince the Kings of the earth and bring them in confession and praise of Jehovah.

While surrounding monarchs beheld the wonderful dispensations of Divine Providence vouchsafed towards Israel and acknowledged same, the final conquests of the Messiah will only be witnessed when He returns as King of kings, as the princes and potentates receive His Word, learn by Divine grace to celebrate the glorious methods of His love, and see in the light of faith the greatness of Jehovah's glory as the God of Salvation. Not until King David's greater Son whom men crucified, as *King* returns to preach, will the monarchs of earth be converted and raise their voices in devout adoration. Then, and not till then, will princes throng to crown His head and "raise and bring peculiar honors to our King." What a day that will be when He reigns from shore to shore!

"All the kings of the earth"—What an assembly!
"They hear the words of thy mouth"—What a preacher!
"Shall praise thee . . . shall sing"—What a choir!

The glory of the Lord, overshadowing all the greatness and glory of

ON

earthly kings, will not only convict them of their need of His grace but constrain them to obey and adore, and to sing of His ways which are ever "ways of pleasantness," Prov. 3:17. *Ways* are His methods in dealing with men. The term is used of God's mighty works in Creation, Job 26:14; 40:18—of His action in history, Deut. 32:4; Ps. 18:30—of His righteousness, Micah 4:2. See frequent use of *ways* when combined with speaking and singing, Psalms 20:7; 44:8; 87:3; 105:2, etc.

High, mighty and proud though the kings of earth may be in the godless states, from His exaltation Jehovah looks down alike on the lowly and the proud, showing His gracious interest in the former, and His just negligence of the latter. Although the high and lofty One dwelling in the high and lofty place and high over all, in the person of His Son, Who was meek and lowly in heart, God humbled Himself. He views the humble with pleasure and thinks much of them because they think so little of themselves. "Lowliness and humility is the court dress of God; he who wears them will please Him well." To have *respect unto* means to "regard." God eyes with loving regard and pleasure those who exhibit Christ-like humility, but He is repelled from those whose hearts are so proud so as to look on them only from a distance, 2 Chron. 16:9.

God is never too high not to be concerned about the lowly, but the proud He sees from afar, but they are not hidden from His eye or beyond the reach of His justice. They are only kept at arms' length from Him. He has not need to come near the haughty, a glance from a distance reveals to Him their offensiveness, and has no fellowship with them. He knows the truth about and has no respect unto them. If they persist and die in pride of the flesh, then there is an eternal distance between God and all who haughtily reject Him.

Confident Hope for the Future, 138:7-8. David ends his Psalm on a personal note expressing his personal confidence in Jehovah to preserve him from his foes, and to complete His works in his life. Although he praised and magnified Jehovah with his whole being, such devotion did not guarantee immunity from trials. Walking in harmony with the will of the Lord he loved, David knew that there would be times when he would "walk in the midst of trouble," but his assurance was that the Lord would be with him, preserving and keeping him alive, even as He did for Daniel in the den of lions. How this 7th verse echoes passages like Psalms 23:4; 30:3; 71:20! Jehovah would not allow David's foes to compel his death, but kept him alive until God's plan for his life was complete.

Often has the Lord, Who is ever at hand to rout our foes, quickened us by our sorrows and revived us, and we do not regret the trouble experienced. The fact that revived fainting David was the confidence that the Lord would make short work of his foes and with one hand save him from them. Thus, the sweet singer of Israel rehearses his assurance of preservation and salvation, not only for Divine ears, but our own. May we be found clinging to David's boast in the Lord, *Thou wilt revive me*! "The revival of the soul is the gracious work of the Holy Spirit. How blessedly and unexpectedly these revivings steal into our hearts, and so often, when heavy trouble lies on us from without."

The concluding verse of the Psalm confirms the truth that all the interests of a believer are safe and secure in Jehovah's hand. His love will perfect all He planned. In spite of trouble, His purpose will not fail of completion. This is the Divinity shaping our ends, rough hew them as we, or others, may. When God builds a life, none is able to say, "He was not able to finish." He completes what he has begun in and for me, Phil. 1:6. See Psalm 57:2. "The works of Thine hands, do not leave them unfinished." Did not Jesus illustrate the confidence expressed here by David? Trials, foes, and sorrow could not keep Him from Calvary where, as He died in triumph, He cried—*It is finished.*

Our hope of final perseverance is the final perseverance of the God we love and serve. Because His mercy endureth for ever, His work in and for us will continue until we are perfected when we see Him in all His perfection. Queen Elizabeth, who knew what it was to walk in the midst of trouble during her reign, prayed, "Look upon the wounds of Thine hands, and forsake not the works of Thine hands." Martin Luther, whose life was also turbulent, had as his usual prayer, "Confirm, O God, in us that thou hast wrought, and perfect the work that thou hast begun in us, to Thy Glory." As F. B. Meyer so beautifully expresses it—

> There are no unfinished pictures on the walls of God's studio; no incomplete statues in His halls of sculpture. When He begins, He pledges Himself to complete. His mercy endures forever; so we cannot tire it or wear it out. But our assurance ought always to take on the language of pleading, that He will not forsake.

> The work which His goodness began,
> The arm of His strength will complete;
> His promise is Yea and Amen,
> And never was forfeited yet.

Psalm 139

This greatest and most noble and notable of the Psalms has many historical and biographical associations. Daniel Webster, the American statesman and orator who died in 1832, was a close student of Scripture, and made a most impressive use of Psalm 139 in one of his great cases which will be quoted as long as his name is remembered.

> A sense of duty pursues us ever. It is omnipresent like the Deity. If we take to ourselves the wings of the morning and dwell in the uttermost parts of the sea, duty performed or duty violated, is still with us for our happiness or our misery. If we say, "Surely the darkness shall cover us," in the darkness as in the light our obligations are yet with us. We cannot escape from their power, nor fly from their presence.

Villemain, the noted French critic, also extols this magnificent Psalm 139 in his Essays on the genius of Pindar: "I was seized with admiration the first time I read Plato's testimony to the omnipresence and providence of God—

> 'If you were hidden in the deepest caverns of the earth, if you were to take wings and fly to the height of the skies, if you were to seek the confines of the World, if you were to descend to the depths of Tarterus, or some more dreadful place, the Divine Providence would still be near you.'

His is higher than Homer's description of the movements of his gods in three steps to the end of the earth; but compare it with the Psalmist's—

> 'Whether shall I go from thy Spirit? or whither shall I flee from thy promise? If I ascend up to heaven, thou art there; if I make my bed in Sheol, behold thou art there. If I take the wings of the morning and dwell in the uttermost parts of the sea; even there shall thy hand lead me, and thy right hand shall hold me.'

If this poetry is man's, it is from a spirit transfigured by divine grace, as was the face of Moses when he came down from Sinai, shining with the brightness he had seen."

As soon as he was able to read and studied the Bible by his mother's side, John Ruskin learned by heart Psalm 139, along with other Psalms. Splendor of thought, as imagined by the Greek poet or philosopher, is only a pale reflection of the sublimity of idea as it is represented by David who, in Psalm 139, causes the beautiful blossom to burst into the full glory of the flower, and on his language is modelled one of the earliest fragments of missionary teaching German of the 9th century, which reads—

> O Lord, my thoughts cannot elude thy thoughts; Thou knowest all the ways by which I would escape. If I climb up into heaven, Thou dwellest there; if I go down to hell, there also I find Thy presence. If I bury myself in the darkness, Thou findest me there. I know that Thy night can be made clear as my day. In the morning I take flight; I flee to the ends of the sea; but there is no place in which Thy hand reaches me not, etc.

The teaching of this remarkable Psalm, even in an utilitarian, prosaic age, was embodied although coldly paraphrased in Thomson's hymn—

> Should fate command me to the farthest verge
> Of the green earth, to distant barbarous climes,
> Rivers unknown to song . . . 'tis nought to me;
> Since God is ever present, ever felt,
> In the void waste as in the city full.

Commendations of this Psalm, which is surely one of the sublimest compositions in the World, abound. Aben Ezra reckoned it to be "the most glorious and excellent Psalm in all the Book." A modern writer says, "No grander tribute has ever been paid to the omniscience and omnipresence of God. An author of the early 17th century has left us this unique tribute—

> Let the modern wits, after this Psalm, look upon the honest shepherds of Palestine as a company of *rude and unpolished clowns*; let them, if they can, produce from profane authors thoughts that are more sublime, more delicate, or better turned; not to mention the sound divinity and solid piety which are apparent under the expressions of the Psalms.

Of this sublime ode, Dr. John Ker says that it is, "A Psalm of wonderful power, in which the singer takes the sense of God's omnipresence first into his own heart, and then makes it flesh to the utmost bounds of the universe, and into the deepest secrets of being." As for Spurgeon, his tribute to the merit of the Psalm cannot be surpassed, "The brightness of this Psalm is like unto a sapphire stone, or Ezekiel's *terrible crystal*; it flashes out with such flashes of light as to burn night into day. Like a Pharos, this holy song casts a clear light even to the uttermost parts of the sea, and warns us against that practical atheism which ignores the presence of God, and so makes shipwreck of the soul."

The Psalm is inscribed to *The Chief Musician*, a phrase occurring 55 times in the Psalms, the meaning of which "one who has obtained the mastery," or "overseer" in musical matters, 2 Chron. 2:18; 24:12. This most conspicuous of the sacred hymns was worthy of the most excellent of singers to use in the solemn worship of the Most High God. Then the title also cites David as the author of the Psalm, but critics take it from him and give it to unknown sources. "The superscripture ascribing the Psalm to David must be abandoned in the face of not only the strong Aranaic coloring of the Psalm, but also of the development of its eschatology, which marks a late epoch." Critics make the Psalm the product of the Maccabean Age, during which Greek culture had much vogue in Palestine, hence Greek influence pervading the Psalm.

But the assignment to any other than David we reject on the ground that every line, every thought, every turn of expression and transition is his, and his only. The moral arguments for David's authorship are so strong as to overwhelm any such verbal, or rather *literal* criticism, were even the objections more formidable than they naturally are. The argument may be advanced as to how a poor shepherd has come to conceive so sublime a revelation as the Psalm contains, and to write of it in so sublime a strain. The answer is simple, "Holy men wrote as they were moved by the Holy Spirit," and therefore were inspired by Him to set forth, in no uncertain terms, the Divine attributes of Omniscience, Omnipresence, Omnipotence, Immutability and Eternity. Rather than accept the reasonings of critical minds whose minds of judgment are manifestly unreliable, we prefer to believe from the internal evidences of the style and matter of the Psalm that it came from the inspired pen of David who once declared, "The Spirit spake by me."

As to an outline of the Psalm, it seems to be made up of four stanzas, unequal in length but clearly marked—

1.   The Omniscience of God, verses 1-6,
2.   The Omnipresence of God, verses 7-12,
3.   The Omnipotence of God, verses 13-18,
4.   The Overthrow of God's Enemies, verses 19-24.

The Omniscience of God, 139:1-6. This initial section proves that Jehovah's omniscience is revealed in the perfect knowledge He has of man's outward and inward life. In earlier Psalms, David often reminds God's people of the love and mercy of God, which *endure for ever*: but in this Psalm he bids them take heed not to make such love and mercy an excuse for sin, because His eyes are as a flame of fire, See Heb. 4:12-16. Much as we would like to linger over all the verses of this admirable poem, because of the length of it, we must content ourselves with a casual glance at them. Preachers, however, can find sermons galore in the Psalm as a whole.

David felt that God knew him through and through. "Thou hast . . . known me." If his heart was closed to all else, it was open to Him, and He alone could detect the secret source of any spiritual disease, and cure it. What His search reveals, His grace can remove. "He knows all; but loves us better than He knows." The word the Psalmist used for *search* is associated with mining operations, Job 28:3, and with the exploration of a country, Judges 18:2. See also Psalms 17:3; 44:21; Jer. 17:10. Here, the term implies the ransacking of our entire life, a moral inquisition into guilt, and nothing escapes God's all-seeing eye. The Egyptians called God, *The Eye of the World*.

God knows all about our daily life, verse 2. *Downsitting*, time of quiet rest, silent hours of the night. *Uprising*, going forth in the morning to the toils of the day. The Targum interprets this of rising up to go to war; which David did, in the name and strength, and by the direction of Jehovah, Deut. 6:6; Ps. 127:2. *Thought afar off.* The aspect of the Divine knowledge of our entire life implies that God anticipates our thoughts and purposes before they are matured in mind, even the most intimate thoughts, wishes and inclinations. Though He has His home in Heaven, He knows what are the thoughts and feelings amid which a man habitually lives, Job 22:12, 13; Ps. 138:6; Prov. 21:1. "I know their imagination," *Thou knowest.* "Thou," in the original, is emphatic and means, *Thou—Thou alone knowest*, Deut. 31:21. *My path . . . lying down . . . all my ways.* The margin gives us *winnowest* for "compasseth." *Lying down* is equivalent to "downsitting," and *my path* to "uprising," going forth in the path of daily duty. To winnow or sift implies that God constantly applies the fan of His judgement to our active life and to thoughts chasing each other across our mind in sleep. It is suggested that the term "compassest" is connected with a word meaning *to lodge*, or *dwell*, implying that God is familiar with all one's life as our inhabiting the same house could be.

> About my path and bed thou art a guest,
> In all my ways thou dwellest.

Not a word . . . but thou knowest it altogether. Because of this aspect of God's knowledge how essential it is to set a watch upon our lips. This 4th verse can be understood in two different ways—

> My tongue cannot utter a word which thou does not altogether know.
> or
> Before my tongue can utter a word thou knowest it altogether.

Behind . . . Before . . . Upon. The word *beset* David used in verse 5 is a most interesting one. It suggests being *hemmed in*, and is employed to describe the action of an army besieging a town—"Thou hast besieged me—there is no escaping from Thee." *Behind*—that none may attack from the rear. *Before*—He searches out the path and meets our foes. *Hand upon me*, as if a child were to put one hand over the hollow of another to keep some frail insect from its pursuer, John 10:28, 29.

No wonder David cried out as he meditated upon God's omniscience searching every nook and cranny of his life, "Such knowledge is too wonderful for me!" The All-knowing is the All-present, and all the Psalmist could do was to worship, where he failed to comprehend the transcendent, unattainable knowledge of God of the past, present, and future. Compare this 6th verse with verses 17 and 18 of the Psalm and with Romans 11:33.

The Omnipresence of God, 139:7-12. The Divine pronouns of this section, or in the whole Psalm for that matter, prove that it could not have been written by a Pantheist, seeing that the writer describes God as a *Person* everywhere present *in* location, yet distinct *from* Creation. He is *everywhere*, but He is not *everything*.

Thy Spirit . . . Thy Presence. We must take the two clauses of this 7th verse as a parallelism, with the second line emphasizing the first. Taken together, of course, both lines declare that God fills all space. A heathen philosopher asked a missionary "Where *is* God?" The missionary replied, "Let me first ask you, where is He *not*?" The celebrated Linnaeus was always testifying to the greatest sense of God's presence, and so strongly was he impressed with God's omnipresence, that he wrote over the door of his library, *Live innocently; God is present.*

Spirit and *Presence*—which literally means *face*, and became one of the many names for God—both imply *God Himself.* How striking are the words, *Whither shall I go*? Where could he go and escape meeting God? Centuries ago it was said that the entire world was but one vast prison-house for the Roman Emperors, so complete was their power. What hope, then, can man have of escaping God? Jer. 23:24; Amos 9:2. Twelve years before his imprisonment for refusing the oath of allegiance to the Crown because of Pope Clement's pronouncement of the validity of the unlawful marriage of Henry VIII and Catherine, Sir Thomas More wrote a treatise on the words to Ecclesiasticus—"In all thy works remember thy last end, and thou shalt never sin." In a section dealing with Death, More wrote—

> Mark this well, for of this thing we be very sure, that old and young, man and woman, rich and poor, prince and page, all the while we live in this world, we be but prisoners, and be within a sure prison, out of which no man can escape. The prison is large, and many prisoners in it, but the JAILER can lose none: He is present in every place, that we can creep into no corner out of His sight. For as holy David saith to this JAILER, "Whither shall I go from Thy Spirit and whither shall I flee from Thy Face, Psalm 139:7, and who saith—*no whither.*

It was to his own thoughts that More's mind turned as he suffered months of cruel imprisonment in the tower of London where he was executed on July 5, 1535.

From God's *Spirit*, His creative and providential power, nothing can escape. As the Book of Wisdom expresses it, "The Spirit of the Lord filleth the World," which is tantamount to Christ's announcement to the woman of Samaria—*God is Spirit*, John 4:24. David enumerates possible avenues of escape from the all-pervading presence of the omnipresent God, but knew how hopeless his efforts to evade Him would be. If he tried to ascend to Heaven, as Enoch and Elijah did, he would find God ready to greet him. If he had tried to make his bed in Hell, or Hades, regarded as a place of rest, he would find God there. There was the conviction that the underworld was not exempt from the vigilance and even from the visitation of Jehovah, Psalm 86:13; Prov. 15:11; Amos 9:2; Job 26:6.

David then goes on to make a further, happy use of imagery in describing the impossibility of escape from the Face of God. Among the ancients the goddess of the dawn had wings with which she arose out of the Eastern Ocean, and, in the course of the day, covered the whole sky. We read of "wings of the sun," Mal. 4:2, and "wings of the wind," Psalm 18:10, but "wings of the morning," is an exquisite symbol, not only of "the pinions of cloud that seem often to lift the dawn into the sky, but also the swift sailing of the light across the world."

But if such strong wings carried David out to the uttermost parts of the sea, with the rapidity of light, God would be accompanying and protecting him. Thus, while guilty of trying to escape from Divine notice and observance, God overtakes the guilty one trying to hide from Him, taking him under His wings for loving care. As for *darkness* shielding David from the Divine Presence, God, as the *Light*, can cause darkness to shine as light, and thus expose him. The main thought in all the illustrations the Psalmist uses is that nowhere is there escape from God's sight in height, depth, distance, or darkness. No matter where we are, or may go, the words stand—*Thou God seest me*!—which is blessed to those who know Him as Father and Friend.

The Omnipotence of God, 139:13-18. In these remarkable verses we have a striking evidence of Jehovah's power and wisdom in the mystery of birth regarding as one of the greatest mysteries, Eccles. 11:5. Here, also, is a proof of God's omniscience. Verses 13 to 16 reveal what transpires in the secret workshop where nothing is concealed from the Maker Who knows all about man because He created him. The primary thought is that every birth is a Divine creation, and the language used of such is both delicate and beautiful.

The margin of the R.V. gives *formed* for "possessed," and *reins* imply the kidneys, the supposed seat of the emotions, desires, feelings, Psalm 73:2. Doubtless all the internal organs are embraced in this term. The margin of the R.V. also gives us "knit me together" for *covered me*, and the thought expressed is that of the inter-lacing of bones, sinews, and muscles, Job 10:11. "Thou didst weave me." "My mother's womb" is what is meant by being "made in secret, and curiously wrought in the lowest parts of the earth." This figurative description heightens the feeling of mystery attaching to the birth of a child. See Job 33:6.

The *substance*, seen by God, and made in secret, and "imperfect," meaning "undeveloped," is the embryo, as yet an unshaped mass, or an unfinished vessel, and *curiously wrought* within the womb. The Hebrew for this description means "embroidered with threads of different colors and seems to refer to the red vein marks on the body. The joint idea of weaving and of variegated colors lies in the root of the original word." As for the recording in the Divine book of the days associated with the development of the embryo, all ancient versions treat that which is written in God's book either the days of life, or men born in the course of these days, each coming into being according to the will of God. Before a man is born God has written down the exact number of days he has to live. Is He not "the length of our days?" Versified, these two passages can read—

> Thine eyes beheld my embryo,
> And in thy book were written
> All the days, the days
> Which were being formed,
> When as yet there were none of them.

No wonder, as he thought of the marvel and mystery of a human birth, David expressed his gratitude to God for His omnipotence and exclaimed, "I am fearfully and wonderfully made: Marvelous are thy works; and that my soul knoweth right well—or greatly." Some authorities render "fearfully and wonderfully" as, "thou art fearfully wonderful." Thinking of his own creation, and of all he possessed from his mother's womb, the Psalmist praises God for all His precious thoughts regarding his existence—thoughts that were as numberless as the sand. God's thoughts can neither be weighed nor numbered. The original has the plural *sums*—the large sum of them. "While the Divine penetration discovers the most intimate thought of man, man finds God's secrets incomprehensible."

The assertion of David after recounting God's omnipotence as seen in the birth of a child, *When I awake, I am still with thee*, suggests that while taken up with a mystery, he was in a king of a reverie. The original, more expressive, reads—

> Let me count them—more than the sand they are many: I have awaked—and still with thee.

As Ellicott comments, "With countless mysteries of Creation and Providence the poet is so occupied, that they are his first waking thought; or, perhaps, as the Hebrew suggests, his dreams are continued into his early thoughts." Tennyson has the lines—

Is not the vision *He*? tho' *He* be not that which He seems?
Dreams are true while they last, and do we not live in dreams?

The Overthrow of God's Enemies, 139:19-24. Another creation-song has a similar ending to this one before us, Psalm 104:35. There are those who feel that if this section could be removed, the rest of the Psalm would present a complete and charming poem. Some try to remove these last verses, indicating that they were tacked on to the Psalm for liturgical purposes in a time of bitter persecution. Such an "abrupt transition from a theme so profound and fascinating to fierce indignation against the enemies of God, would certainly be strange anywhere but in the Psalms." Yet is this so? Is not the doctrine of the punishment of wicked men the necessary outcome of Divine omniscience written plain in the whole of Scripture?

The eye of God, seeing man in the embryo state while he is yet without practiced sin, is still upon him after he is born and develops into a wicked man, and one of blood. The omniscient God Who sees all evil will slay all evil, for He will not suffer any creation of His defaced or defiled by those who break His moral laws, take His name in vain, and hate Him. Thus, the wonderful theme of God's perfect knowledge invariably leads the mind to the reality of evil, as well as to its origin and development. What is impressively evident in verses 19 to 22 is David's sympathy with the Divine abhorrence of wicked men, and with the judgment they deserve at the hands of the God sinned against. Commenting on these verses, Dr. Meyer has this personal application of them—

> When we are startled at these strong expressions of David, we may well ask ourselves whether, in our tender pity for sinners, we may not be losing something of his stern consciousness of the evil of sin, and the guilt of the wicked.

The prayer for a heart-searching for any wickedness therein forms a worthy termination of the Psalm. Returning to his opening theme of God's all-seeing eye, David asks that the same eye looking upon men speaking wickedly against God, might search his own heart for the discovery of any wicked way therein. God's inevitable scrutiny of his being, divinely created, is invited. David now prays that he may hate sin, not only when it is around, but when it is within him, anticipating thereby, the desire of Paul in Rom. 7:24. The striking contrast in the last six verses of the Psalm provide the key to many expressions found in what are called *Vindictive Psalms*. "Those who wrote them were men in conflict with sin which surrounded them, wounded them, sought to crush them; but they were taught by the Spirit of God to hate it also in themselves; and the completion of this lesson, as of the love of God, is reserved for the New Testament."

The advance in the meaning of the word *search*, verses 1 and 23, is worthy of note. David begins by confessing that the Divine examination has taken place—"Thou *hast* searched and known me." Then he ends the Psalm by asking God to do something already accomplished, "Search me, O God, and know my heart." The explanation seems to be that in respect to his outer life, his down-sitting and uprising, David had been searched and found upright. But he journeys on with God, meditating upon His omniscience, omnipresence and omnipotence, and also upon the clear vision the same gave him of his evil surroundings, and so turns from his outer, to his inner life. "Know my *heart* . . . . my *thoughts* . . . see if there be any wicked way *in* me." Blaise Pascal describes the Sisters of Port Royal, committing themselves to God, and praying with the Psalmist, "Look well if there be any way of wickedness in me."

None but the omniscient God can search the heart and lead us to abhor and forsake what He reveals, and when we see light in His light, the effect of such a revelation is the instant cry to Him for cleansing from any false way. "I am He that searcheth the hearts." Are we willing to have our heart searched and delivered from all that prevents the heart being right in His sight? If so then we are ready to be led in the way everlasting—the ancient way, Jer. 6:16; 18:15—the way planned from eternity by the Eternal and leading to the eternal home. In this concluding verse of the Psalm we have a mixture of figures, *Way of wickedness*, something within leading a man to choose that which issues in pain—*Way everlasting*, which if a man walks over it he will have length of life and peace.

The greatest poem ever written on David's masterly poem in this Psalm was by the gifted pen of James Montgomery who composed many of our best-loved hymns, such as *Prayer Is the Soul's Sincere Desire, Songs of Praise the Angels Sing, Hark the Song of Jubilee, Hail to the Lord's Anointed,* and *Forever with the Lord.* Montgomery's poem is made of seven long verses, of which we cite the first and the last.

> Searcher of hearts! to thee are known
>   The inmost secrets of my breast;
> At home, abroad, in crowds, alone,
>   Thou mark'st my rising and my rest,
> My thoughts far off, through every maze,
> Source, streams, and issue—all my ways ...
>
> Search me, O God! and know my heart;
>   Try me, my inmost soul survey;
> And warn thy servant to depart
>   From every false and evil way:
> So shall thy truth my guidance be
> To life and immortality.

Psalm 140

Sir Evelyn Wood, General in the British Army during the last century and honored with the *Victoria Cross* and other medals for bravery, was prominent in Indian, Egyptian, and African campaigns. He was severely wounded while carrying a scaling ladder at Redan. He dearly loved this 140th Psalm and said that the verse often in his mind while fighting was, "O Lord God, thou strength of my health: thou hast covered my head in the day of battle," Psalm 140:7.

It would seem as if there is no break between Psalm 139 and 140, seeing the closing section of the former with the description of wicked, blaspheming and cruel men, is given in greater detail in the latter in which 11 verses out of 13 are loaded with the particular aspects of those who are evil and violent. After calling down the judgement of God upon those who spoke and acted wickedly in Psalm 139, David now prays in Psalm 140 that he might be totally delivered from them. In fact, this Psalm bears a close resemblance to two early Psalms also by David, namely, Psalms 58 and 64. "The close of all these Psalms sounds very much alike; they all agree in the use of rare forms of expressions, and their language becomes fearfully obscure in style and sound, when they are directed against enemies."

Composed by David, the Psalm before us contains his prayer for protection against malignant and treacherous foes. The Syriac Version has the title, "A Psalm by David when Saul threw the spear," and the cause of the Psalm was probably the evil designs of jealous Saul and his dependence upon the tongues of traitors, like Doeg, for information about David's movements so that he could snare or trap him. The Psalm then, is not ascribed to David as one writer suggests, because it consists mainly of quotations from, and adaptations of, his early Psalms, but because its tone reflects his troubled days at court when his steps were taken with difficulty, seeing schemes and snares lined his pathway. In Psalm 138, David sets forth God's promise as the anchor of hope—In Psalm 139, God's omniscience our consolation in danger and motive for shunning evil—In Psalm 140, our danger from calumnious enemies, and our only safety in Jehovah our Strength.

Spurgeon calls the Psalm, *A Cry Of A Hunted Soul*, and says that David dedicated it *To the Chief Musician* so that such an experimental hymn might, under the care of the chief master of song, be sung in the best possible way with the best powers of heart and tongue, as a choice memorial of Jehovah's goodness in the deliverance of His servant. Few short Psalms are so rich in the jewelry of precious faith as this one. There can be little doubt that David wrote the Psalm in a time of exile and great peril. "David was hunted like a partridge upon the mountains, and seldom obtained a moment's rest. This is his pathetic appeal to Jehovah for protection, an appeal which gradually intensifies into a denunciation of his bitter foes. With this sacrifice of prayer he offers the salt of faith; for in a very marked and emphatic manner he expresses his personal confidence in the Lord as the Protector of the oppressed, and as his own God and Defender."

Two attractive features arrest our attention as we attempt to outline the contents of the Psalm. First of all, the prominence of the use of the name *Jehovah* which, under the English form of *Lord*, occurs 6 times, 4 of which are in the heart of the Psalm, verses 6 to 8. Then we have 3 *Selahs*. The word "Selah" occurs some 71 times in 40 Psalms of the Psalter. Authorities are not agreed as to its exact meaning. The LXX Version says that it represents a pause or interlude in the music, when singers and players would halt a little and meditate upon the truth of the song being sung. Thus, the word can mean, *Think of that!*—and wherever it occurs, there is a good deal to think about.

The precise terms David used of those who hated him and sought to slay him are most expressive—

1. Their Nature—*Wicked, Violent.*
2. Their Designs—Imagine mischiefs in their hearts.
3. Their Confederacy—Continually they are gathered together for war.
4. Their Accusations—They have sharpened their tongue like a serpent.
5. Their Objective—They have purposed to overthrow my goings.
6. Their Intrigues—They have set traps for me.
7. Their Overthrow—Cast them into the fire, into deep pits.

1. Prayer to be defended against violent and deceitful foes whose portrait is clearly drawn, with a *Selah* bidding us pause over the dark picture given, 140:1-3.
2. Prayer that the enemies' plans may come to naught in spite of the ways they spread their nets to trap the pursued. Another *Selah* speaks of David's thoughtful appraisal of evil intentions, 140:4-5.
3. Prayer of faith while enemies are laying their snares to capture the hunted one. In prayer he pauses, surveys the scene and then calmly sings, "I have said to Jehovah, My God art Thou!" 140:6-8.
4. Prayer for vengeance upon enemies, that they might be covered

with the reward of their own malice in evil speech and actions, 140:9-11.

5. Praise and Confidence that Jehovah will stand by the righteous, 140:12, 13. *I will maintain* is the motto of the great Defender of the rights of the needs. As surely as He will justly punish the wicked, so will He save those who were afflicted by the violence of their foes, and continue His protection of them until they come into His presence with its peaceful repose. "The righteous will give thanks." This is the only attitude they can take up. "Gratitude will be their one all-pervading emotion," as they walk and live in the manifested light of God's presence, Psalms 11:7; 16:11; Ephes. 5:20.

How cheerfully and confidently this Psalm ends! After all the perils, while being hunted here and there, the soul finds a sure dwelling-place in the light and favor of Jehovah. Of such a peaceful conclusion to such a turbulent Psalm, Spurgeon has this most appealing and impressive comment—

> The tremendous outburst at the end has in it the warmth which was so natural to David, who was never lukewarm in anything; yet it is to be noticed that concerning his enemies he was often hot in language through indignation, and yet he was cool in action, for he was not revengeful. His was no petty malice, but a righteous anger: he foresaw, foretold, and even desired the just vengeance of God upon the proud and wicked, and yet he would not avail himself of opportunities to revenge himself upon those who had done him wrong. It may be that his appeals to the great King cooled his anger, and enabled him to leave his wrongs unredressed by any personal act of violence. When most wounded by undeserved persecution and wicked falsehood he was glad to leave his matters at the foot of the throne, where they would be safe with the King of kings.

Amid all that we may be called upon to endure for Christ's sake, let us cling to the promise, "The Lord will maintain the cause of the afflicted." When foes make "inquisition for blood, *He* remembereth them," Psalm 9:12. See Psalm 18:27. God has the power to "undo all that afflict us," Zeph. 3:19. Praise Him! *Selah!*

Psalm 141

D uring the early days of Christianity because of Roman persecution, secretly, under cover of night or at early dawn, slaves oppressed by their masters, citizens suspected by their neighbors, subjects proscribed by their rulers, little companies of workers, as well as a few of higher rank and nobler birth, in danger of their lives would gather for prayer and praise in the catacombs of great cities. At these secret meetings the Psalms played a conspicuous part, and special Psalms were appropriated for particular occasions. The morning would open with Psalm 73, but for the Evening song, Psalm 141 was used. "Let my prayer be set before thee as incense, and the lifting up of my hands as the evening sacrifice," 141:2. In *King Henry the Eighth*, the words Shakespeare makes Buckingham repeat, refer to this 2nd verse—

> And, as the long divorce of steel falls on me, Make of your prayers one sweet sacrifice, and lift my soul to Heaven.

This calm floating of the fragrant cloud upward, the hands outstretched to God when the day's work was done, and the hunted saints gathered for worship would be in contrast to their morning prayer, full of purpose and aim, like an archer who fits his arrow to his bow, and then follows the mark—"My voice shalt thou hear in the *morning*, O Lord, in the *morning* will I direct my prayer unto thee, and will look up," Psalm 5:3.

As we approach a coverage of this further Psalm, of which it has been said that "few Psalms in so small a compass crowd together so many gems of precious and holy truth," the initial feature arresting our attention is the repetition of various expressions found in the previous Psalm. We are given a further glimpse of wicked, iniquitous men, of the snares and sins set to trap the righteous, and their cry for Divine deliverance. Psalms 140 to 143 form a group in which prominence is given to ever-present enemies and the cry for preservation from such, and Psalm 141 bears a striking resemblance to the other three.

The title tells us that it is another *Psalm by David*, but critics take it from him. As one arrests "The Davidic inscription cannot be for a moment maintained. There is no period of David's life which the Psalm could represent." But its many verbal and real coincidences, agreeing with other Psalms David composed, prove this one to be another of his compositions. Many past commentators, including John Calvin, were strongly of opinion that this 141st Psalm was written as a memorial of that appealing scene in David's life recorded in 1 Sam. 24, relating to his generous treatment of Saul at the cave of Engedi when he had the opportunity of slaying his cruel persecutor, but took from Saul only a cutting from his garment, and then demonstrated with his avowed enemy in the gentlest and most respectful language in regard to his injustice toward him.

As for Spurgeon, he had no doubt that this Psalm constituted David's cry to be preserved from sin and sinners—his evening prayer to be strengthened to resist temptation, and so escape the fate of evil men. "Yes, it is *A Psalm of David*, David under suspicion, half afraid to speak out lest he should speak unadvisedly while trying to clear himself; David slandered and beset by enemies; David censured even by saints, and taking it kindly; David deploring the condition of the godly party of whom he was the acknowledged head: David waiting upon God with confident expectation."

Far from being "one of the most obscure Psalms in the whole Psalter," as one critic states it, the Psalm, as it opens is "lighted up with the evening glow as the fragrant incense rises to Heaven: then comes a night of language whose meaning we cannot see; and this gives place to morning light in which our eyes are unto the Lord." As to an outline of the Psalm, perhaps the following can serve as a guide—

1. Prayer for Jehovah's help, verses 1-2,
2. Prayer to be kept from participation in prevailing sin, verses 3-4,
3. Prayer for the beneficial reproof and for intercessory ministry, verses 5-6,
4. Prayer for confidence for Divine preservation, verses 7-10.

Prayer for Jehovah's Help, 141:1, 2. Here we have cries for acceptance of prayer—a prayer that prayer might be heard and answered. The three key-phrases in the opening verse are *I Cry!—Make Haste!—Give Ear*. The repeated clause, "I cry unto thee," gives emphasis to David's appeal. *Cry*, or call, continually occurs in Scripture, Psalms 17:6; 22:2, and Psalm 3:4, shows the answer. For *make haste* see Psalms 38:22; 40:13; 70:1; and for *Give Ear*, Psalms 17:1; 55; 86:6. A different tense is to be noted, *I have cried, When I cry*, which signifies the Apostolic injunction of "Pray without ceasing." The double *cry* speaks of the earnest perseverance of the saint in prayer, never ceasing, so long as trouble will last. *Unto me* is answered by *unto Thee*. "Our prayer and God's mercy are like two buckets in a well; while the one ascends, the other descends." In need, prayer is our only and last resort, for it never fails. It is our sure refuge at all times and our confidence is that the *Ear* hearing our voice belongs to the One Who will make haste to help us.

> That were a grief I could not bear,
> Didst thou not hear and answer prayer;
> But a prayer-hearing, answering God
> Supports me under every load.

David then goes on to describe the nature and gesture of earnest prayer, which, first of all, must be set forth before God as incense. In Tabernacle and Temple of old *incense* had to be carefully prepared, kindled with holy fire, and devoutly presented unto God. Thus should it be with *Prayer*. Too often, we tumble into the presence of the Almighty with no clear idea of what we want to speak to Him about. Doubtless the reference is to the sweet-smelling savor which arose from Jewish sacrifices in general, Psalm 65:15. The offering of incense morning and evening, under the Levitical dispensation, symbolized prayer, Exod. 30:7, 8. In the last book of the Bible the prayers of saints are again identified with the offering of incense, Rev. 5:8; 8:3, 4.

As for the *lifting up* of the hands, or "spreading forth of the hands," Isa. 1:15, same is parallel to "making many prayers." This symbol of prayer—spreading forth our hands in believing and fervent prayer—is the only way of grasping mercy. There is a hand-prayer as well as a heart-prayer. Prayer without words can be presented by the motions of our bodies: bended knees and lifted up hands are tokens of sincere, expectant prayer. Tennyson in his *Morte d'Arthur* has the stanza—

> For what are men better than sheep or goats
> That nourish a blind life within the brain.
> If, knowing God, they lift not hands of prayer,
> Both for themselves, and those that call them friend

Prayer to be kept from participating in prevailing sin, 141:3, 4. The Psalmist then goes on to define how his voice and mouth should not be used. Having been vehicles of expression prayer, it would be a shame if they were defiled in any way and so he prayed, "Set at watch, O Lord, before my mouth: keep the door of my lips." As *watch* is an image drawn from the guard set at city gates at night, use of the figure may indicate the evening as the time when the Psalm was written. If the Lord is the Guard of our mouth and lips then the whole man is well garrisoned. David longed above all else to be a door-keeper for God, and now prays that God will be the door-keeper of his mouth. As he made our lips the door of our mouth, He can enable us to keep the door shut when we should. Said Xenocrates: "I have often repented of having spoken, but never of having been silent."

If this Psalm was written while David was hiding from Saul in the cave and felt that God was guarding the mouth of it, then it was apt that he used God's watchful care as an illustration of a watch before his mouth.

What must not be lost sight of is that, while the tongue is the principal instrument in the service of God, it is likewise the chief instrument of Satan—give him our mouth and lips, and he asks no more. If we desire to be preserved from lip-sins, then we must ask God to be the door-keeper, preserving us from a *froward mouth* and *perverse lips*, Prov. 4:24.

After praying about what comes *out* of his mouth, David then prays about what goes *into* it, "Let me not eat of their dainties." Different aspects of desire are to be distinguished in the intercession found in these two sections. Having prayed about his lips, he now prays about his heart, that appetites might not be his to turn it in the wrong direction. If both tongue and heart are guarded by God then all is well. The first clause, "Incline not my heart to evil," is equivalent to "Lead us not into temptation." David wanted not only to be preserved from a sinful utterance, but also from sinful works.

The word *incline* means "to bend—this way or that," and what the Psalmist wanted was to go straight on in the right direction. Thus he prays, "Leave me not lest my heart leans towards evil and evil men." No man can keep himself from being taken with the allurements of a wicked world, no matter how pleasantly enticing it may be, except the Lord preserve him. If *dainties* are all it can offer, then it would be better to starve. "Come out from among them and be ye separate, saith the Lord."

Those who practice wicked works are to be shunned as an infectious disease, for if we unite with them we shall soon be eating their sweet morsels and find ourselves bound to them by means of our palate. The word for *dainties* is from the same root as *sweet* or "pleasant" in verse 6. Sin is not only meat, but sweet meat, not only bread, but pleasant bread. For weeks Daniel ate no pleasant bread, but only that kind keeping body and soul together. Feasting was shunned. The enemies of David were sensual and luxurious, and would have gladly admitted him to share in their licentious banquets, but he prayed for deliverance from them and any inclination for those pleasures catering to the lust of the eyes and the lust of the flesh. Refusal to participate in the corrupt deeds of the wicked would enable the Psalmist to scorn their luxuries. Thus, a free rendering of the clause reads, "I will not taste of their sweets," which means "I will not listen to their allurements: what finds favor with them will not tempt me."

For those of us who have tasted of the heavenly bread, there should be no desire to "touch the unclean thing," or long after the *dainties* of a wicked world. Separation may bring us ridicule and trials, yet amid tribulation we do sit at a banqueting table, anointed as guests with oil, Ps. 23:5.

Prayer for beneficial reproof and the exercise of intercessory ministry, 141:5, 6. Many commentators speak of verse 5 as being "obscure as to be almost unintelligible"—"extremely obscure"—"corrupt to a degree;"

and of verse 6, as being "full of obscurities." Yet, as Spurgeon puts it, "The meaning of this Psalm lies so deep as to be in places exceedingly obscure, yet even upon its surface it has the dust of gold." When David encouraged the righteous to smite him, doing him a kindness thereby, he implied that he would be rather illtreated by the righteous than feasted by the wicked. "Faithful are the wounds of a friend." Such a faithful rebuke possesses the healing of "excellent oil." Ungodly smiles hide a cruel flattery, but when the righteous smite us their faithfulness is kind.

The sentiment of the context seems to be that the poet "rather than join in the wicked mirth of a profane banquet, he would be the object of continued rebuke and chastisement from one of the godly—his prayer meanwhile still rising for protection against the allurements held out to tempt him." But the rebuke of the righteous being as "excellent oil, which shall not break the head," is not easy to explain. One rendering of verse 5 has it, *Let a righteous man smite me, it is a kindness; and let him reprove me, it is oil for the head: my head shall not refuse it though it continue; yet my prayer is against their wickedness.* Job, we read, "prayed for his friends," who had reproved him without cause.

The R.V. gives this desirable correction of friends "as oil upon the head, let not my head refuse it . . . Even in their wickedness shall my prayer continue." Oil, a natural emblem of benefit, *Head* is first used for "hair," then for the *whole person.* The alternation in this verse is worthy of notice. The oil lavishly used with the *dainties* of wicked revellers was not excellent, but the oil of loving rebuke breaks no head or does no harm. "My friend must love me well if he will tell me of my faults; there is no unction about him if he is honest enough to point out my faults." While we accept the verse as referring to that loving care which one believer may exercise over another is admiration, there are some writers who suggest that *the righteous* refers to God, Who alone, in its full sense, deserves the appellation, 2 Sam. 7:14, 15.

The next verse also is not subject to a single explanation. Does it refer to the very remarkable occurrence in David's history when he encountered Saul in the cave around the mouth of which many judges or rulers had been destroyed by physical force, as if hurled down from the precipitous face of a ravine? See 2 Chron. 25:12. The verb *overthrown* is used of Jezebel in 2 Kings 9:23—"Throw her down. So they threw her down." Judgment overtook the rulers or leaders of David's enemies, and, too late, they perceived how reasonable his words had been, and sighed that they had not hearkened unto them. The words of David were sweet, particularly in the Psalms in which he had much to say about the Messiah, the rich experiences of the covenant of grace, and other doctrines he proclaimed. Truly, his words of courageous hopefulness remain sweet in our ears.

As already indicated the word for *sweet* is akin to *dainties*, and, says Ellicott, "the expression is ironical. They shall hear my words, how dainty they are." The ungodly, with their power broken, instead of being entertained by the poet at a licentious banquet, will listen to his words—shall hear a "dainty song from him, namely, *a song of triumph*." As for the Lord, His words are ever sweet to our taste, having an intrinsic daintiness commending them to our hearts.

Prayer of Confidence for Divine Preservation, 141:7-10, *Mine eyes are unto thee* .... The key phrases of these last verses are, *In thee is my trust ... Keep me*. See Psalm 25:15. What tragedy scattered bones plowed and cut up in pieces conveys! Doubtless the primary reference is the slaughter of priests by the command of Saul as related in 1 Sam. 22:16-19. This God-rejected King of Israel ruined the nation and scattered all its parts, and the Divine cause became as "a dead thing, even as a skeleton, rotten, shrivelled out of the grave, to return as dust to dust."

The people only existed as an unorganized whole. They had no cohesion and were destitute of a godly leadership, and their cause seemed to be at death's door, with David himself like one of the dried bones he describes. *Wood*, in italics, can be left out, for the figure used relates to cleaving or plowing the earth, and not to logs cut up by the woodcutter. If the figure refers to the righteous, and we compare it with Psalm 129:3 where plowing is used as an image of affliction and torture, as *harrowing* is with us, then this verse might be paraphrased: "We have been so harrowed and torn that we are brought to the brink of the grave."

Such a graphic illustration of national decline, however, can be applied to the many massacres of believers like that of the dreadful slaughter on the Eve of St. Bartholomew which marked the passage of the martyrs from this godless world to a better, where the blood of the slain calls out for the judgment of their murderers. Further, who can watch the digging of a grave and view the ruins then disclosed, without exclaiming, "*Our bones are scattered at the grave's mouth, as when one cutteth and ploughed up the earth.*" But such dissolution is a necessary means of a glorious resurrection. In Jehovah is One Who can re-unite a divided people and resurrect them as they seem to be spiritually dead. As for those who actually die in the Lord, He will bring up their dead bones from the grave.

But amid all this desolate, dead condition of Israel, David expresses his confidence in that he looked away from such a doleful scene of Jehovah. *Mine eyes are unto Thee*! Certainly his eyes saw the lifeless condition of things around him, but he looked away from surroundings to Him Who was his *God* and *Lord*. *In thee—in thyself alone—is my trust.* The bones of the righteous had found rest in God, so would David. The snares, schemes, and nets of the wicked might be all set to trap him, but

his eyes were not fixed on the ground, but upon the Throne, Psalm
119:110. Previously, the Psalmist had prayed that the door of his
mouth might be kept, now he prays "Keep *me*," because he realized that
nobody save the Omniscient and Omnipotent One was able to preserve
him.

The righteous might smite him, calamities overtake him, and Saul seek
to slay him, but David prayed that God would not leave his soul destitute
and remember His promise never to leave him alone. While he left without friends, he had the Friend sticking closer than a brother, Who would
care for his safety, and Who would likewise see to it that the wicked fell
into their own nets, as Israel witnessed in what happened to the Wicked
Haman. Sooner or later, the guilty reap the harvest of their own malice.
"The Lord shall keep thy foot from being taken," Prov. 3:26. The lesson
of all this is that nothing can prosper sin or hurt godliness. What better
ending to the verses just considered could there be than the expressive
stanzas of John Keble?—

> O pour not out my soul, I pray,
> From the dark snare preserve my way,
> The chambers of the blind entangling net,
> Which by my path to powers of evil set.
>
> Behold them laid, the godless crew,
> Low in the toils they darkly drew:
> The while, with gathering heart and watchful eye,
> I wait mine hour to pass victorious by.

Psalm 142

St. Francis of Assisi, who died Oct. 3, 1226, was one of the gentle and blameless of mankind—the saint and the poet of a poetic people. From the moment he took *Poverty* to be his bride, he remained faithful till death parted them. He dearly loved the Psalms, and when he came to die many were sung to him. As he had lived, so he died—in the arms of his *Lady Poverty*, stripped of clothing, and laid on the bare ground. At nightfall, as the voices of his brethren sang, Francis, with his special fondness for Psalm 142, would add his quivering voice, "I cried unto the Lord with my voice, yea, even unto the Lord did I make my supplication." Because of his inviolate chastity, he was preserved from the condemnation he pronounced in his *Canticle*, "Woe to those who die in mortal sin!"

This Psalm with its seven verses, provides us with a perfect illustration on how to pray for help against all persecutors. *Maschil* means "instruction," and as the margin puts it, *A Psalm of David, giving instruction.* The disciples of the Son of David one day asked Him, "Lord, teach us to pray," and this is what David himself does in Psalm 142. This needful, practical, and effectual part of our spiritual education did not come from a priest in the cloister who knew little about distress, but from a fugitive hiding in a cave from those who wanted to kill him. Probably it was in the cave at Engedi where David was a supplicant at the throne of grace in time of need. "Caves made good closets for prayer; their gloom and solitude are helpful in the exercise of devotion. Had David prayed as much in his palace as he did in his cave, he might never have fallen into the act which brought such misery upon his later days."

The most useful art of praying is described in several ways by the Psalmist. *I cried . . . I made supplication . . . I poured out my complaint . . . I shewed before him my trouble . . . Bring my soul out of prison.* The originality of the prayer-poem before us is an originality shown rather in passion and feeling as, for instance, in the lament, "Refuge failed me; no man cared for my soul," rather than in a poetic figure expression. The description of David's deep feelings cannot fail to move the tender affections of all who know what it is to pour out their heart unto the Lord.

Although the godly scholars who gave us both the A. V. and the R.V. translations of the ancient Scriptures entitled this Psalm as being, "The Prayer of David when he was in the Cave," some theologians have no compunction of conscience in robbing David as the one who offered and recorded his earnest prayer. Quite blatantly, *The Century Bible* says of the authorship of the Psalm, "No scholar now defends its Davidic authorship." As for *The One-Volume Bible Dictionary*, its verdict is, "Ascribed to David *in the cave*, but not likely to be by him." Ellicott's *Commentary of The Whole Bible* says that although, "This is one of the eight Psalms assigned by their inscriptions to the time of David's persecution by Saul, there is nothing in the contents of this Psalm either to support or controvert the title."

This author, however, although not as scholarly as he would like to be, agrees with those spiritually minded expositors, that every part of Psalm 142 shows the propriety of its inscription or title; that it was David himself who was in the condition of no one to plead his cause, or to protect him in the dangerous circumstances he was placed in, but who found heart-relief in voicing his pleadings with Jehovah, and who would have us learn the lesson he learned in the dark cave. We say a hearty *Amen*! to Spurgeon's affirmation of the Davidic authorship of the Psalm—

> There can be little doubt that this song dates from the days when Saul was sorely persecuting David, and David himself was in sore trouble, probably produced by that weakness of faith which led him to associate with heathen princes. His fortunes were evidently at the lowest, and, what was worse, his repute had fearfully fallen; yet he displayed a true faith in God, to whom he made known his pressing sorrows. The gloom of the care is over the Psalm, and yet as if standing at the mouth of it the prophet-poet sees a bright light a little beyond.

F. B. Meyer expresses a similar sentiment, "The prison and the persecutor oppress the soul of the sweet-singer, who yet towards the close catches sight of a brighter and better time." Is this not one of the lessons to learn from this Instruction Psalm?

As this brief Psalm seems to present one continuous prayer, a division of it is not visible or necessary. But to help us understand its teaching more fully, the two sections of *Complaint*, verses 1-4, and *Cry*, verses 5-7, may guide us—

The Complaint, 142:1-4. The R.V. renders each clause in the present tense so we read, "I cry unto the Lord." See Psalm 3:4. Twice over David used the phrase, "with my voice," and to use audible words is often a great incentive stirring up the spirit to more vehemency and concentration. So we can render the opening verse, "I cry aloud unto Jehovah; Loudly do I pray for favor." What the Psalmist is calling attention to is not the loudness of his prayer as such, but to the passion or earnestness which the loudness implies. It found great relief to David's heavy heart to use his voice in his complaint to Jehovah. "There was a voice *in* his prayer when he used his voice *for* prayer." Says Hosea, "Take with you *words*, and turn unto the Lord: *say* unto Him," 14:2. Had David not *cried* he would not have *said*.

Then how explicit is the substance of his voiced supplication—

"I pour out my complaint before him;
I shew before him my trouble," or distress.

David could not keep what troubled him bottled up in his heart, but through his voice poured out the wormwood and the gall. The substance of his *complaint*, or "meditation," as the word literally means, seeing his mind was meditating on his condition, is found in the next 2 verses. The Psalmist, it will be observed, did not complain *of God*, but *to* Him. We should take care where we outpour our complaints. If before men, they may receive an ill return, but if before God, He will hear and act. The next phrase, "I shew before him my trouble," implies that he exhibited his grief to One Who would understand his display of affliction. David was not afraid nor ashamed to open out before God his trials and exigencies. He was particular in his petition.

God, of course, knows all about our complaints before our voice pours them out; but is it not our privilege—and a great relief—to unbosom ourselves to Him? A further lesson we learn from David's prayer is that we reap so little benefit in prayer because we deal too much in *generals*, and do not enough dwell on the *particulars* of our need. To meditate upon specific matters as we pray prevents the mind from wandering. Voicing our thoughts and showing our trouble before the Lord merit His help on our behalf. Such aspects of supplication are necessary, not for Him to see our trouble, but that we may see *Him* as our only Refuge and a very present Helper in our trouble.

Is not this truth emphasized in the next verse, "Thou *knowest* my path"—yes, even before we told Him about it. What a comfort it is to know that the all-knowing God knows what we do not know! His eternal mind is always clear and cognizant of what is hidden from us. David was a hero and could smite a giant, but was not able to keep himself up. His trouble seems to smother, or muffle, his spirit, for his complaint literally means, *In the muffling upon me of my spirit*. Dejection of the *spirit* represents a still more sorrowful and downcast condition than the fainting of the soul, Psalm 143:3, 4. "Jesus was troubled in *spirit*," John 11:33; 13:21.

When heavy, like a veil of woe,
My spirit on me lay.

Because of fightings without and fears within, David's spirit was so wrapped in trouble and gloom, or "muffled with woe," as to be distracted and unable to discern what perils surrounded him in the snares his foes had set to trap him. But his trust is emphasized even in his trials, "Thou knewest my path." In the original the pronoun *Thou* is emphatic, Psalms 61:2; 77:3. "I know not what awaits me, and no man knows me, but *Thou*, and Thou alone, knowest everything about me." Is there not an echo here of the omniscience of God as recorded in Psalm 139, "Thou art acquainted with all my ways . . . Thou knowest altogether?" How apt are the lines of Charlotte Elliott on this third verse—

> From human eyes 'tis better to conceal
> Much that I suffer, much I hourly feel;
> But, oh, this thought can tranquillize and heal,
>   All, all is known to thee.

> Nay, all by thee is ordered, chosen, planned,
> Each drop that fills my daily cup, they hand
> Prescribed for ills, none else can understand,
>   All, all is known to thee.

A further complaint was that in the midst of those who did not openly assail him but sought privately to ensnare him, was the consciousness that there was no man who seemed to be concerned about his predicament. "No man would know me." Ignorance, of course, was wilful, for there were many who did know David and all about his trials. The Psalmist looked on his "right hand" for succor—the right hand reckoned as the post of a protector. In ancient Jewish courts of judicature, the advocate, as well as the accuser, stood on the *right side* of the accused. Psalm 110:5; 121:5. But David's lament was that there was no one to plead his cause or to protect him in the danger he faced.

Further, the beautiful opposites found here are most suggestive of spiritual truth, *Thou knowest . . . No man would know me. Refuge failed me . . . Thou art my refuge.* How sad must the spirit of David have been when he complained "Refuge failed me" or *perished* from me, Job 11:20; Jer. 25:35; Amos 2:14; and "No man cared for my soul." Not only had he become as a stranger to his brethren but an outcast, for in his dire calamity he could find no harbour of safety, as he felt Jehovah knew all about, as the imperative he used indicates—"*Look . . . refuge hath failed me.*"

No man cared for my soul follows *No man knoweth.* Those who don't want to know us have little care for our well-being, Jer. 30:17. "No soul cared for my soul," David seems to say. "I dwelt in No-man's land, where none cared to know, have and protect me." What a tragedy to see this man after God's own heart without a friend to give him a place to lay his head in peace! Of David's greater Son it is said, "They all forsook Him and fled." But the Psalmist knew how hopeless *looking around* him for deliverance, safety, and friendship were, so, as we shall now see he tried *looking up* instead.

The Cry, 142:5-7. The opening phrase of the Psalm is repeated at the introduction of this last division. *I cried unto Jehovah . . . Attend unto my cry*. By the term *cry* we are to understand "call." David had called unto Jehovah, and still called, and would continue to call until attention was given. Calling upon Jehovah, David said to Him, "Thou art my refuge and my portion in the land of the living." See Psalms 16:5; 22:8; 31:3; 46:1. The word for *refuge* in the 5th verse is a different one from that so translated in verse 4. In the latter, the prominent idea is that of *escape*, but in this 5th verse the word implies specially a place of *security* as such. What the Palmist failed to find in man, he discovered in God. Here David speaks to God about Himself, and confesses that he found not only a Refuge, but God Himself. *Thou art!*

Fleeing to God alone, and sheltering 'neath the wings of the Eternal, the outcast from men also found in Him his *Portion*. In this one sentence we have two steps of a ladder, the second rising far above the first. "It is something to have Jehovah for our Refuge, but it is everything to have Him as our Portion. If David had not *cried* he would not have *said*; and if the Lord had not been his *Refuge*, He would never have been his *Portion*. The lower step is as needful as the higher; but it is not necessary always to stop on the first rung of the ladder."

In his Poems the Poet of Israel often eulogized God as his *Portion*, 16:5; 73:26; 119:57, but here the figure carries a very personal application for it was only when David was banished from his portion in the land, and cut off from the portion of goods which he by right inherited, that he truly discovered that God *was*, indeed, his unfailing Portion. As F. B. Meyer reminds us in *Reading On The Psalms*—

> The loneliness and isolation of the soul from all human love often makes it turn the more urgently to God Himself, Who can be loved without satiety, and Whose love is unchangeable, unselfish, and eternal. How often does God diminish and break off our portion in this life that we may be driven to seek it again in Himself, Lam. 3:24.

The sixth verse seems to have a mosaic pattern seeing that its clauses are words and phrases borrowed from other Psalms. See 7:1; 17:1; 18:17; 31:25; 79:8. If the only way up is down, then David was brought very low as he hid in the cave while Saul, his pursuer, was very high as the head of the powerful army. The proverb has it, "He that is down need fear no fall." David was down in the dumps, but his plea for attention carried with it the grand confession of faith that God was able to raise him up from his prison-like cave, and once again set him among princes—"Bring my soul out of prison, that I may give thanks unto thy name." In his present low, impoverished condition, David's persecutors were in a much stronger position than he was, but his faith was in God, strongest of all as the Strength of Israel. So consoled by the truth that God cared for his soul, David cast all his care upon Him, and his trust sustained him.

By *prison* we are not to think of a literal *place* of confinement, such as the cave in which David hid, because he prays that his *soul* may be brought out of prison. Therefore, a *condition* of misery is to be understood by the term. Brought low, his was a prison-like misery, but as he came to prove, "Man's extremity is God's opportunity." See Psalms 107:6, 10; 143:3, 11, and Isa. 42:7. When he escaped as a bird from the fowler, David praised his Deliverer. "Soul-emancipation is the noblest form of liberation, and calls for the highest praise: he who is delivered from the dungeons of despair is sure to magnify the name of the Lord"—even although he may be suffering in an actual prison. Paul and Silas were cast into prison, but their spirits were not fettered for they "prayed and sang praises unto God."

The concluding phrases of the Psalm depict a sweet experience after all his distress, for David welcomed the gratitude of the righteous as they heard how God had dealt so bountifully with him, Psalm 116:7, 8. In the original, "compass me about" signifies not *in a circle, but a crown.* The Targum translates it, "For my sake the righteous will make to thee a crown of praise." Delivered from all his trials, the righteous gathered around David, congratulated him as a miracle of mercy, and joined him in praising God for deliverance, both his physical and spiritual bondage—his *body* out of the cave, and his *soul* out of prison. God's bounty to him was a source of joy to the righteous, who would bind the story they had heard from David on their brows as a festal crown. So the Psalm beginning with a sob, ends with a song. The cry going up to God in the voice of prayer is changed into a carol in the voice of praise.

Psalm 143

D r. Herman Adler, one-time Chief Rabbi of Britain when it was an Empire, had, as a Jew, a great love for the Psalms. He left it on a record that his favorite verse was Psalm 143:8, "Cause me to hear thy loving kindness in the morning: for in thee do I trust: cause me to know the way wherein I should walk; for I lift up my soul unto thee."

Savonarola, who was executed on May 22, 1498, by the Papal authorities for his fearless preaching of the truth, was the great dominican preacher who for five years held within the hollow of his hand the destinies of Florence and stands out as one of the most fascinating figures in history. That he had a deep affection for the Psalms is proved by his written meditations on many of them. As a hard-featured youth, he often pondered over the sin and misery of the world, praying, as he would tell his father, in the words of Psalm 143, "Shew Thou me the way that I should walk in, for I lift up my soul unto Thee." Seeking to escape the stifling atmosphere of wickedness surrounding him, Savonarola fled to the cloister and remained a man of unsullied morality.

Another historical association of this Psalm is related to Thomas Bilneg who was burned to death for his faith during the reign of Henry VIII. At first, Bilneg had a great fear of death, but rose above it, and his behavior at the stake had a profound influence on the crowd assembled. The historian of the time tells us that "Bilneg made his private prayer with such elevation of his eyes and hands to heaven, and in so good and quiet behavior, that he seemed not to consider the terror of death, and ended at last his private prayers with Psalm 143, beginning, 'Hear my prayer, O Lord, consider my desire!' Then he repeated the second verse, in deep meditation, thrice: 'And enter not into judgment with thy servant: for in thy sight shall no man living be justified.' And so, finishing this Psalm, he ended his prayers."

A further historical feature of this Psalm is that it was chosen by the Church for us on Ash-Wednesday, and placed seventh and last in the so-called *Penitential* Psalms, sometimes known as *Special Psalms*. These have long been used in the Church as the completest and most spiritual acts of repentance which she possesses. They have sometimes been thought of as the most appropriate condemnation of the seven deadly sins—

Against Wrath, Psalm 6.
Against Pride, Psalm 32.
Against Gluttony, Psalm 38.
Against Impurity, Psalm 51.
Against Covetousness, Psalm 102.
Against Envy, Psalm 130.
Against Indifference, or Carelessness, Psalm 143.

We doubt whether the Ecclesiastical Fathers were right in pressing their 143rd Psalm into their group of *Penitential Psalms*, seeing it hardly contains a penitential tear for sin. It appears to be more war-like and aggressive than sorrowful over any form of iniquity—"a supplication for deliverance from trouble rather than a weeping acknowledgement of transgression."

As for the theme of the Psalm as a whole, these aspects are apparent in its twelve verses.

A Supplication For Righteousness,
A Lamentation Over Injuries,
A Petition For Deliverance and Grace.

What is clearly evident is the way the devout poet could turn alternatively from *spiritual* to *temporal* subjects. He first confesses his unjustified state and begs for mercy; then he complains of his persistent enemies and seeks wisdom, then prays for their destruction. When his foes trouble him, he becomes martial; but lamenting his own spiritual darkness he prays for holiness and a fuller knowledge of the will of God. Another aspect of the Psalm is its resemblance to the previous Psalm. Repetitions are evident. In Psalm 142, twice over, the Psalmist said that he prayed, "I cried unto the Lord," and twice over in the Psalm before us we have "Hear my prayer, O Lord." Psalm 142: 2 we have, "My spirit was overwhelmed within me"—Psalm 143:4, "My spirit is overwhelmed within me." See also 77:3; 107:5. "Deliver me from my persecutors"—"Deliver me, O Lord, from mine enemies," 142:6; 143:9—striking proof that the Psalmist who wrote the one Psalm, penned the other.

The spirit and language of the Psalm we have reached in our odyssey are so in unison with earlier Davidic Psalms as to confirm the genuineness of the superscription, *A Psalm By David*. But Ellicott rejects such authorship by declaring that "there is hardly a phrase which is not derived from some other source—a fact which at once *disposes of the inscription*." But we believe the Psalm to be David all over, with his history illustrating it, and his spirit breathing in it. A convincing argument for Davidic authorship is the two-fold use of the phrase, *Thy servant*, verses 2 and 12. In this octave of Psalms 138-145, this appellation often occurs. It was first used by Jehovah in the great promise of 2 Sam. 7:5, 9-21, 25-29. *Tell to*

My David, and David fastened on it when pleading with Jehovah. *I am Thy servant*, was not a boast of service but a desire to magnify God's electing grace, 2 Sam. 7:18.

As to an outline of the Psalm, the single *Selah* at the end of verse 6 provides a natural division into two divisions of six verses each, which consist of four stanzas, each of three verses. This solitary *Selah*, connecting and returning to prayer, verses 7 -12, as the consequence of the reflection inverses 5 and 6, in the last *Selah* of the 71 Selahs used in the Psalms.

1. Confession of personal causes for distress, verses 1-6.
2. Supplication for guidance and deliverance from foes, verses 7-12.

From such a division we can see that the Psalm is a mingled strain, a box of ointment composed of many ingredients, sweet and bitter, pungent and precious. As a whole it is *"the out-cry of an overwhelmed spirit*, unable to abide in the highest state of spiritual prayer, again and again descending to bewail its deep temporal distress; yet evermore struggling to rise to the best things. The singer moans at intervals, the petitioner for mercy cannot withhold his cries for vindication. His hands are outstretched to Heaven, but at his girdle hangs a sharp sword which rattles in its scabbard as he closes his Psalm." Who but David, worshiper and warrior, could have penned such an impressive ode!

Confession of personal causes for distress, 143:1-6. If the historical background is associated with Saul's intense hatred of David and intent to kill him, or with the deceit and treachery of his own son, Absalom, then we can readily understand the Psalmist's grievous complaint to God about the malice of those who knew him—which was more than enough to make his soul exceeding heavy. The opening phrase of the Psalm, "Hear my prayer, O Lord," and more strongly repeated in verse 7, "Hear me *speedily*, O Lord," emphasizes the urgent necessity of relief from both physical and spiritual distress. Throughout his life, David was a great pleader at the throne of mercy. Ever supplicating *he* became one continual *prayer*.

Hear . . . Give ear. Is there any difference between these commands? Hearing may be passive—in one ear and out of the other; but *give ear* is always active, answering the request it hears. David's earnest desire to be heard is found in these three phrases, *Hear my prayer . . . Give ear to my supplication . . . Answer me*. He wanted God to listen with both ears, attentively and readily and responsibly. The Psalmist then expects to be heard and answered because of the active attributes of *Faithfulness* and *Righteousness*. In His righteousness, God had promised to hear and answer prayer, and because of His faithfulness, He must fulfill such a promise. John grounds his appeal for forgiveness on the same pair of

Divine qualities, 1 John 1:9, and see Psalm 65:5. Now, in Christ, the sterner attributes of God are on our side. David then goes on to deprecate the Divine justice he had just invoked. Having entreated for audience at the *Mercy-Seat*, he had no wish to appear before the *Judgment Seat*. Conscious that, through mercy, he was the Lord's servant, and not a traitor or impenitent sinner, he does not claim perfection nor plead merit because of this relationship but realized that in himself or on the footing of the Law he was not worthy of being justified before God. Said St. Bernard of Clairvaux, "So far from being able to answer for my sins, I cannot answer even for my righteousness." It seems as if, in this second verse, David anticipated the doctrine of universal condemnation by the law ages before Paul took his pen to expound the same truth.

The holiest of men have least confidence in themselves, Job 9:3; Phil. 3:7-9. If we are in Christ Jesus, then God will not *enter into judgment* with us, seeing our faith in, and acceptance of the Savior justifies us freely from all things, Rom. 5:1; 8:34. *Enter not into judgment*, or "do not let me be brought before Thy court," is a metaphor taken for the effort pursued by those who seek to recover the very utmost to which they are entitled by strict legal process, Job 22:4, 5. But through Christ, our debts have been cancelled, forgiven, and God does not enter a claim against us.

There is no escape from judgment through self-justification, as Jesus taught when He portrayed a self-righteous Pharisee.

> For merit lives from man to man,
> And not from man, O Lord, to thee.

Man can only stand acquitted before a righteous God if he is clothed in a Divinely-provided robe of righteousness.

> Thy servant also bring thou not
>   In judgment to be tried:
> Because no living man can be
>   In thy sight justified.

The preposition *For*, not only introduces a new sentence, but implies "because of," or "on account of," and introduces the ground of the earnest petition just offered. If trouble is a just cause for calling upon God for vindication, then surely David's cause could not be more just. If God would not enter into judgment with His servant, then He must deal with the enemy who had persecuted, smitten, and treated him as one long dead and forgotten, with not hope of a resurrection. The *dark places* may be a reference to the two caves of Adullan and Engedie in which, as a fugitive, David seemed to be buried alive. For those of us who are redeemed by the precious blood of Christ, although our bodies will dwell in darkness among the dead unless He returns in our lifetime to gather us unto

Himself, we travel from the darkness of death to light and life eternal.

There is no gainsaying that David was a great, brave soldier, as well as a man after God's own heart, yet he was ready to faint in the day of adversity. Thus, he repeats his woe of the previous Psalm, "My spirit is over-whelmed within me," 142:3; 143:4. *My heart within me* was the poet's way of saying, "I myself." Being human, David languished under the assaults made upon his character, as well as his body, knowing that the hostility of his enemy was both undeserved and unprovoked. Inner grief, loneliness, astonishment, made him feel as if he was forsaken of God. The mystery of his suffering greatly perplexed his heart.

Overwhelmed . . . Desolate! Can we plumb the depths of these two poignant words? David did, and so did his Greater Son, the Lord Jesus, and none of the ransomed will ever know how dark the night was that He passed through in order to redeem them. "He was tested in all points like as we are." But how unutterably the sorrow of the Psalmist's fainting and desolate heart! How true it is that those who are capable of the gladdest heights of joy are also capable of the saddest depths of depression! David was permitted by God to touch each, that he might be able to give expression to all kinds of emotion—to every phase of feeling.

The Psalmist, however, although persecuted, was not forsaken, cast down, he was not destroyed, for he knew how to betake himself to God and find in Him his relief, strength, and song. Thus, in the two verses left to us in this first half of the Psalm, we have five ways by which his agitated soul was calmed, and here are five points for a preacher to develop into a most impressive and fruitful sermon!—

1. "I remember the days of old"
2. "I meditate on all thy work"
3. "I muse on the work of thy hand"
4. "I stretch forth my hands unto thee"
5. "I thirst after thee"—verses 5 and 6.

In verse 5, *Memory, Meditation,* and *Musing* are linked together as three graces, ministering peace to David's troubled mind. As with his much-loved harp he had previously played the evil spirit from Saul, so now his own gloom is chased away from this desolate soul by blessed communion with God. The overwhelming of his spirit was eased, and his loneliness banished. David remembered the old days, and all Jehovah had accomplished for His people, and he was encouraged to believe that the same Deliverer would undertake for His servant calling upon Him. "We, too, have sunny, sacred and satisfactory memories, and these are as flowers for the bees of faith to visit, from whence they may make honey for present use."

Meditating and musing on the works of the Lord was a tonic to one

whose own works had not been altogether commendable and God-glorifying. All the Divine work of Creation, and activities in the history of
nations and men, must have been a cordial to the sinking spirit of David.
What God's hands had done for others, they were able to do for him in his
hour of need. The record of Divine mercy to those in the past when in
extremity was a guarantee that the same mercy would be displayed on
David's behalf. But hands must be stretched forth to appropriate all God
is able to offer. Remembrance of the past, meditation and musing on all
the wonders of old, are not sufficient. Hands and soul must go out to God,
as an evidence of sincere desire to be delivered by Him.

Thus, the meditating and musing are prayer's handmaid waiting on
them, both before and after the performance of the supplication. As the
hopper feeds the mill with grist, so does remembrance of the past supply
the heart with matter for prayer. Hands were stretched forth in hope that
the Divine hands that had accomplished so many mighty things, would lay
hold of them and draw the suppliant nearer to God. The outstretched
hands, then, were an outward, energetic expression of an inward longing,
See Psalm 44:20; Isa. 1:15; Lam. 1:17. Further, if David was still in the
cave when he thought of this Psalm, he must have experienced moments
of physical thirst. Now with a soul so parched and dry, he is conscious of
deeper thirst—*My soul thirsteth after thee*—Thee, only *Thee*!

Such a thirst as David descries is blessed, Psalm 42:1, 2; 52:1; Isa.
44:3, and to have it is to be satisfied. "There is no natural desire which has
not its satisfaction: in the woods, birds do not hunger for food which is not
to be had; and so the very existence of this thirst is a proof that the being
and sufficiency of Him for when it yearns, and in whom it is allayed." The
soul-thirst David wrote of answers to his previous Psalm, written as he
fled from Absalom, "My soul thirsteth for thee," Psalm 63:1. If we thirst
aright, God always refreshes and satisfies us. When Samson, in the bitterness of heart, cried, "I die of thirst," God opened a spring for him in the
jawbone of an ass, Judges 15:19. After all this traffic with God, how fitting is the concluding *Selah*, which is said to represent a pause in ancient
Hebrew music. After all his outpourings, it was time for David to pause
and ponder. Both his "harp-strings and heart-strings were strained, and
needed a little rest to get them right again for the second half of his song."

Supplication for Guidance and Deliverance from Foes, 143:7-12. In
this remaining section of the Psalm, David mixes together prayers for joy,
for guidance, and for sanctification, and begins by asking God for a speedy
hearing, and a quick delivery from his enemies. This was not the language
of sinful impatience, but of vehement yearning. "Hope deferred maketh the
heart sick." David's condition was low with faintness and failing of heart
and undelayed help was imperative. The petition for speedy relief did not
suggest any mistrust of God. David had often prayed, "Make haste, O Lord

to deliver." His thirst for God had become so intense that it admitted of no delay. How comforting it is to know that "Mercy has wings to its heels when misery is in extremity." See Psalms 69:17; 84:2; 102:2; etc.

Some of the phrases used here reveal the use made of them on other occasions, but "this does not detract from the reality of the feeling expressed by these ancient sobs and cries. The contrast with former times (verse 5) with the recollection of God's dealing then joined to thoughtful contemplation of the reality of His power as displayed in His works, makes the Psalmist's anguish the more intense, his longing the more consuming, his supplication the more urgent." Demanding requests fill up the last two stanzas of the Psalm, and are so prominent for a preacher to use for pulpit exposition—

> Hide not thy face from me—
> Cause me to hear thy lovingkindness—
> Cause me to know the way wherein I should walk—
> Deliver me, O Lord, from my enemies.

What a quartet of truth these three verses—7 to 9—contain for a Sunday morning sermon! David's unfailing longing was to bask in the sunshine of the Divine Face. He ever wanted to have God's smile. If such a smile was not his, then David felt he would be good as dead, for going *into the pit* means "to die." If God's countenance is lifted up upon us, we live, but if turned from us we live and labor in vain. Then, how appealing is David's double *cause*; "Cause me to hear," and "Cause me to know." God, the First Great Cause alone can cause us to hear and know. Spiritual senses are dependent upon Him, and lovingkindness and heavenly knowledge come from Him alone. David's sound and solid argument with God rested on his affirmation, "In thee do I trust." And He never disappoints true faith. The heaped up trial and sorrow the Psalmist had endured seem to drown the Divine voice, and he desired to hear it again with its assurance of unfailing lovingkindness.

In the morning, indicates the first dawning hour. See 90:14. Through his night a fugitive, David had wept much, now he wanted joy as a new day approaches. It may well be said we hear this lovingkindness in the morning, seeing it makes it morning to us whensoever we hear it. *Loving kindness* was his favorite and choice theme, and it is used more in the Psalms than in any other Scripture book. What is lovingkindness? Is it not love showing kindness—the sun of love shining with rays of kindness? This is what the Psalmist wished God's voice to echo forth in the *morning*, which was the season of devotion much prized by him. "In the morning . . . in the morning," Ps. 5:3. David knew from long experience the value of the morning watch. Inspired prayers will only be fully answered when the morning of Eternity breaks.

The second *Cause* is related to a knowledge of the right path he should follow, and the ground of such a plea was the lifting up of his soul to Him Who is the Source of all knowledge. When we are uncertain about our path of duty and safety, it is essential to lift up our soul into the presence of God until He shines upon it with His light and guidance saying unto us, "This is the way, walk ye in it." The second *Cause* arises from the first one. If we have obtained an assurance of God's favor and smile, then there will be the desire to conform our lives to the obedience of His Word and Will.

Having prayed for a knowledge of the way he should walk, David goes on to pray that it may be a path free from temporal danger. "Deliver me, O Lord, from mine enemies." Psalms 31:15; 59:1; 142:6. How Satan outwits himself when he drives a saint to hide in God's bosom, Psalm 27:5! The basis of David's appeal for safety is beautifully expressed in the phrase, *I flee unto thee to hide me!* Such a flight to Heaven was not a sign of cowardice, but a recognition that David had no might of his own to overcome his foes. The margin reading is suggestive, "I flee unto thee to hide me with thee," or, as some of the ancient Rabbins put it, "I have hid myself in thee." He did not want to hide *away* from Divine Presence, but *in* it. An ill-wind blows good when it carries us to God, in whom we are out of reach of harm, if we strive to be followers of that which is good. After praying, *Hide not Thy face*, David pleads, *Hide me in Thee*. "Thou blest Rock of Ages, I'm hiding in Thee."

In the concluding stanza of three verses we have further requests standing out as divisions of an effective sermon for some preacher to proclaim. *Teach me; Lead me; Quicken me; Destroy all that afflict me.* Each request is accompanied by a reason for the granting of same. *Teach me to do thy will.* Why? For thou art my God. See Psalms 25:4; 40:8. Having prayed for knowledge, David now prays for obedience, for it is more important to be taught to *do* than to know. Knowledge of the Divine will is, of course, necessary if we are to obey it. "Knowledge without obedience is lame, obedience without knowledge is blind; and we must never hope for acceptance if we offer the blind and the lame to God." Tuition asked for was Divine—"Jehovah . . . Teach me"—and, it is by the Spirit, Jehovah imparts such instruction. David's entreaty to be taught of God was backed by his personal relationship to Him, "For thou art *my* God." When we can truly say out of our heart, "Jehovah, thou art *my* God," then our mind is ready to know of Him, our will prepared to obey Him, and our whole man eager to please Him.

Another reason the Psalmist advanced as to why his request for guidance to do God's will was, "Thy spirit is good." The leadings of God's Spirit are always good to follow, Neh. 9:20; Ephes. 5:9. Some writers think that this phrase should be linked on to the next and the clause read, "May thy good spirit lead me over an even path," or "Let thy good spirit lead me." Paul certainly has much to say about being *led* by the Spirit, Rom. 8; Gal. 4, but we prefer to take the phrase as it stands at *Thy Spirit is good*.

The Holy Spirit of God is often called *good*, seeing He is the fountain of true goodness and of holiness. Is not "the fruit of the Spirit is all goodness?" Is He not the One Who inclines us to *be* good, and to *do* good? Goodness is His essence, and therefore He is perfectly qualified to teach, lead, quicken and deliver us. What greater good can He do to us than to respond to the next prayer, "Lead me in the land of uprightness." The word in Hebrew for "righteousness" means *what is level*, or *even*—a path free from pitfalls into which one may fall, and from rough stones over which one may stumble—a level tableland.

Low-spirited and languid, David then goes on to pray *Quicken me, O Lord*! He wanted not only light and leading but *life*, and he entreats Jehovah, for His name's sake, meaning that all He is as the revealed Lord and Giver of life, to renew and revive his drooping spirit. For the sake of His own glory, He must bring His servant out of his trouble. God's credit and glory are involved in the succor and deliverance of His saints. David might have brought such trouble *into* his life, but only He Who is "a very present help in trouble," can bring it *out*. Thus the Psalmist makes his plea for physical and spiritual invigoration on the basis of all God is in Himself. Psalms 23:3; 138:7; 142:7.

David further pleads with God, because of His mercy to deal drastically with all his enemies afflicting his soul. After all, is he not His servant and therefore as his Master, responsible for his safety? Earlier on in the Psalm, he speaks of himself as "*Thy* servant." Theodosius thought it a greater dignity to be God's servant than to be an Emperor. David had the same estimation of his Divine relationship and so entreated his Lord to protect him, and to make him victorious over all his foes. Psalms 18:40; 54:7. That his plea was granted is seen in the next Psalm where David praises God as His Deliverer, delivering "his servant from the hurtful sword," 144:2, 10.

Psalm 144

History records that the Psalms supplies many of the war songs of the Crusaders. St. Bernard made special use of Psalm 144 in the Crusade, declaring, "Blessed be the Lord my strength, which teacheth my hands to war, my fingers to fight." Not only did notable saints and scholars turn to the Psalms for inspiration, simple sailors found them a source of encouragement as they turned to them in peril from raiders or shipwreck. An historical illustration of this comes down to us from 1586, when five Turkey merchantmen equipped for trade and war, encountered on the high seas eleven Spanish galleys and two frigates. The English ships were summoned by the Spanish to surrender. On their refusal, a fight began, which is thus described by Philip Jones, who was on board—

> Although our men performed their parts with singular valor according to their strength, insomuch that the enemy as amassed therewith would oftentimes pause and stay, and consult what was best to be done, yet they ceased not in the midst of their business to make prayer to Almighty God, the Revenger of all evils, and the Giver of victories, that it would please Him to assist in that quarrel of theirs, in defending themselves against so proud a tyrant, to 'teach their hands to war and their fingers to fight,' Psalm 144:1, that the glory of the victory might redound to His Name, and to the honor of true Religion, which the insolent enemy sought so much to overthrow.

Their humble prayers were heard for at the end of four hours, the Spaniards drew off, and the English merchantmen pursued their voyage unmolested.

By passages taken from the Psalms, sundials all over the world enforce the solemn lesson of the passage of time. Thus at St. Brelade, in Jersey, is a dial bearing the inscription in French, "Man is like to vanity, his days are as a shadow that passeth away," Psalm 144:4.

A further biographical connection of this Psalm is found in the ministry of Bishop Bedell, one of the most devoted men of the early 16th century. He, it was who, after strenuous efforts, succeeded in getting the Bible translated into the Irish language. It was on Jan. 30, 1642, in the midst of the Civil War, that this 144th Psalm appeared in the Church reading for that day, and with singular appropriateness the Bishop preached from its first and last verses. The last sermon on this Psalm was preached by him in the house of a converted priest to which Bedell was allowed to retire

after his imprisonment in County Cavan. He died shortly after, and he lies
in a corner of Kilmore churchyard, close to a large sycamore tree which
he himself had planted.

Because of the references to the bountiful gifts of God in Nature, it is
felt that perhaps the Psalm was originally chanted at Harvest time, or
Festivals, or as *the help tune* of the reapers, as E. Browning depicts in
Saul—

> Their wine song, when hand
> Grasps at hand, eye lights eye in good friendship,
>   and great hearts expand,
> And grow one in the sense of this world's life.

What is apparent is that the Psalm, with its mingled tones of prayer and
praise, forms a fit connecting link between the supplicatory Psalms which
go before, and the strains of thanksgiving which follow it, or a point of
transition between previous *Prayer* Psalms and the *Praise* Psalms to follow. The cloud of former adversity is breaking; the beams of the sun are
struggling through. After the six foregoing Psalms with their cries of distress, we breathe a more exhilarating air in this noble Psalm.

Various forms of its structure have been suggested. One writer says it
is made up of three distinct parts—

1. Jehovah is praised for help in war, verses 1-4, and prayer is
   offered for further deliverance, verses 5-8.
2. Prayer of the King to be protected from treacherous barbarians,
   verses 9-11.
3. The Happiness of the people who worship Jehovah, verses 12-15.

Spurgeon's outline of the Psalm is helpful—

1. David praises God as the devout warrior, when he extols Him as
   his strength and stay, verses 1 and 2.
2. Man is held in small account, and marvels at the Lord's regard for
   him, verses 3 and 4.
3. Man turns in his hour of conflict to the Lord, Who is declared to
   be "a man of war," whose triumphant interposition he implores,
   verses 5-8.
4. Man again extols and entreats, verses 9-11.
5. A closing, delightful picture of the Lord's work for His chosen
   people, who are congratulated upon having such a God to be their
   God, verses 12-13.

Bullinger's massive, *The Companion Bible*, every student of Scripture
should possess, gives the following *repeated alternation* of the Psalm—

1. David's words. Praise and Prayer, verses 1-7.
   Words of foreigners. Vain and false, verse 8.
2. David's words, Praise and Prayer, verses 9-11.
   Words of foreigners. Vain and false, 12-15.
3. David's words. Right and true, 15—last part.

Evidently Bullinger indicates that the *strange children*, or aliens, guilty of *falsehood*, express in verses 12 to the first part of verse 15, the false view that happiness consists in outward prosperity, Psalms 4:6, 7; 146:3, 5.

As to the authorship of the Psalm, the title gives it to David. The LXX Version reads, *A Psalm by David concerning Goliath*. Doubtless this is because Psalm 8 which relates to David and Goliath has the same words in verse 4 as found in Psalm 144:3. The Psalm is peculiarly appropriate to that notable victory of David, 1 Sam. 17. Dr. J. A. Alexander, in his monumental work, *The Psalms Translated And Explained* well said that, "The Davidic origin of this Psalm is as marked as that of any in the Psalter."

Yet there are those critics who rob David of his Psalm, affirming that it is a *compilation of fragments* of some *lost Psalms* with their unknown authorship. But surely the language of the Psalm is of David, if ever language can belong to any man. "Nothing but the disease which closes the eye to manifest fact and opens it to fancy, could have led learned critics to ascribe this song to anybody but David." The objection brought against its Davidic authorship is its mosaic character, or fragments taken from other sources and pieced together as a whole, and that these borrowed parts were taken from older Psalms now lost. But this is no hotch-potch of a Psalm, but one with a perfect whole with a perfect design.

No sincere student of the Psalms can fail to notice that one of David's peculiarities was to draw from his earlier works a foundation for new productions. Thus it is only other Psalms of David which form the groundwork of this Psalm before us. Further, this transfer was never a dead borrowing, or the appropriation of previous sayings a sign of spiritual impotence or laziness for their repeated use are always given a fresh, spirited nature in their new setting. As one conservative expositor has so finely expressed it—

> It seems to us to be highly probable that the Psalmist remembering that he had trodden some of the same ground before, felt his mind moved to fresh thought, and that the Holy Spirit used this mood for His own high purposes. Assuredly the addendum is worthy of the great Hebrew poet, and it is so admirable in language, and so full of beautiful imagery, that persons of taste, who were by no means over-loaded with reverence have quoted it times without number, thus confessing its singular poetical excellence. To us the

whole Psalm appears to be perfect as it stands, and to exhibit such unity throughout that it would be a literary Vandalism, as well as a spiritual crime, to rend away one part from the other.

Praise for help, 144:1-4, Prayer for deliverance, 144:5-8. This first section is made up of three strophes—the first two containing two verses each—the last, four verses. As all the Divine attributes mentioned in the first two verses, transpired from David's earlier Psalm, the reader is referred to what we have already written of them in Psalm 18:2, 4, 6. The phrase, "Which teacheth my hands to war," is taken from David's song of deliverance in 2 Sam. 22:35. In fact this song colors many of his Psalms. See Psalm 18:34 in our previous notes. Further, as verses 3 and 4 are quotations from Psalms 8:4 and 39:5 respectively, attention is drawn to the exposition we have given on these quotations.

In the Prayer for Deliverance from enemies, verses 5 to 8, requests to God for help are stated as precisely as are His attributes in the previous verses—

> "Bow thy heavens, O Lord"
> "Touch the mountains"
> "Cast forth lightnings"
> "Shoot out thy arrows"
> "Send thy hand from above"
> "Rid me, deliver me out of great waters."

While there are touches of originality in the first two verses of this strophe, the theophany for which David prayed is described by him in his classic language for such manifestations in Psalm 18:9-45, with a reminiscence of Psalm 104:32, recognition of which will be found in our previous notes on these Psalms. The margin gives *hands*, and so the first clause of verse 7 should read, "Send thine hands from above"—both hands, or all God's power, David was in dire need of. As he praised God for teaching his hands to war, so now he prays that God's hands will war on his behalf against his foes.

"Rid me." The Hebrew word for "rid" means to loosen and then rescue or set free and is used only in this Psalm at verses 7, 10, 11. The verb implies "to tear asunder" and is used of the gaping of the mouth, Psalm 22:13. David asks God to repeat former deliverances. The disappearance of his enemies by Divine judgment would be a good riddance, especially as they are "strange children," or sons of a stranger. But what exactly is the significance of this classification used twice over, namely verses 7 and 11, which are expressed in the very same way? It is evident that they were David's open foreign adversaries, who treated treaties among nations as vain things. Perhaps they were not foreigners of every race, thus

strangers to God and His servant, but men of David's own nation of black hearts and traitorous spirit.

Isaiah has the phrase, "Your land strangers devour," 1:7, and Israel called all other nations *strangers* or aliens. Cicero, the Roman orator, is credited with saying, "He who is now called a stranger was called an enemy by our ancestors." These foes of David then were *strange*, not only in respect of generic origin, but also because of character and disposition. And the *Hand* from above could alone deliver the pleader out of their *hand*, and also from their empty speech and false ways. The clause, "Their right hand is a right hand of falsehood," requires explanation. *Right hand* is the equivalent of an oath. Among ancient Semites an oath was made by elevating the right hand toward a deity. Thus, the meaning of the above phrase is, "their oath is a false oath," implying that they could lie with dexterity. Lying mouths and hands of falsehood which go together, were perils God alone could save His servant from.

Prayer for Deliverance from treacherous barbarians, 144:9-11. The reference to false oaths in the previous and present parts forms a link between them, and proves a common authorship. The first verse here is a repeat of Psalm 33:2, 3, and the reader is directed to our observations there as to the significance of *the ten strings*, of "a ten-stringed harp." David was pleading for new mercies and these demand new songs. He wanted to give God freshly baked loaves for His table, 1 Sam. 21:6. The pronoun is commanding, "*I* will sing a new song unto thee." The song of others may be empty and false, but as for *me*, I will adore Thee with a new, true song. And it was a song for salvation given to *kings*. But David does not speak of himself as God's chosen, as King of Israel, but as "His servant," which to him was the highest title to bear. See Psalm 18:50.

Would that earthly kings and rulers could be found giving heed to the declaration "It is He that giveth salvation unto kings," realizing the utter folly of trusting to their own sagacity and armaments! How they need to learn that the Most High is Ruler among the nations and deals with kings according to the dictates of His own freewill. Ferdinand, King of Aragon, sending his son against the Florentines, warned him: "Believe me, son, victories are not secured by art or subtlety, but given of God." Although among the kings of his time, David does not name himself as one of them, but speaking in the present tense, *delivereth*, he confessed his indebtedness to the continuing mercy of God in preserving him from the hurtful sword with is thrust of death.

The Happiness of People richly blessed, 144:12-15. We do not believe as some critics affirm that this last section of the Psalm is "a mere fragment from a poem which is otherwise lost—a specimen so charming that one cannot but regret the loss of the rest of the song." Granted that the reminiscences or quotations principally from Psalm 18 suddenly cease, to be followed by this original and somewhat antique description of the lot of a happy people, the fact that the title makes David the author of the whole Psalm proves that by Divine inspiration he also composed these final verses. As Spurgeon so convincingly puts it in his foreword to the Psalm—

> Albeit that this Psalm is in some measure very similar to Psalm 19, yet it is a new song, and in its latter portion it is strikingly so. Let us accept is as a new Psalm, and not as a mere variation of an old one, or as two compositions roughly joined together. It is true that it would be a complete composition if the passage from verse 12 to the close were dropped, but there are other parts of David's poems which might be equally self-contained if certain verses were omitted; and the same might be said of many uninspired sonnets. It does not, therefore, follow that the latter part was added by another hand, nor even that it was a fragment by the same author, appended to the rest of the song merely with the view of preserving it.

While verses 12-15 contain a striking picture of a prosperous and happy nation with *masculine youth* as oaks of the forest; *young females* as the exquisitely polished corner-stones which adorn the walls of the palace or temple; *garners full*, implying an abundance of food for homes full of flourishing children; cattle and oxen in abundance; no robbers to break in and plunder the home of its plenty, nor foreign foes suddenly wrenching them from the happy homes; not any complaining, meaning no outcry of distress or sorrowful citizens, Jer. 14:2—the question is to whom do these verses apply?

The majority of devotional writers remind us that the Psalmist depicts, primarily, the happy condition of his nation when fully delivered from the devastation of war with all the hardships it inflicts, and doubtless the pleasurable and peaceful life he portrays was experienced through the goodness and mercy of God. But what must not be forgotten is the way David puts these glowing verses as coming from the mouths of "the strange children" who speak *vanity* and are guilty of falsehood. "Their right hand is a right hand of falsehood. That *our* sons may be as plants" etc. Certainly the people in such a case would be happy, but happy in what, in family life and material possessions? Do we not harbor a false view of happiness if we think that it consists *only* in outward prosperity? In a following Psalm we are told, "Happy is he that hath the God of Jacob for his help, whose hope is in the Lord his God," 146:5, 6.

Spiritual happiness then, is not in a *case*, but in Him from Whom all blessings flow. Thus the last phrase of the Psalm is David's own—his parting beatitude, "Happy people, whose God is Jehovah." This oft-repeated beatitude denies the vain and false words of the aliens, and declares the truth as to where real happiness is alone to be found. Our supreme joy is to be found not in blessings but the *Blesser* Himself.

My goal is God *Himself*, not joy, nor peace,
Nor even blessing, but Himself, my God;
'Tis His to lead me there—not mine, but His—
At any cost, dear Lord, by any road.

Psalm 145

What a rich historical background this *Psalm of Praise* by David possesses! Ancient Jews were accustomed to say that he who could pray this Psalm from the heart three times daily was preparing himself best for the praise of the world to come. The tradition about Psalm 145, which has been called the *TE DEUM* of the Old Testament, is that the *TE DEUM* itself, an ancient hymn of praise to God, the English version of which is, "We praise Thee, O God," was first sung by Amborse and Augustine, by Divine inspiration when they were together at Milan, in 387. As to the origin of the hymn itself, it was introduced into the West from the Eastern Church by Ambrose as a responsive Christian song, and used as a morning Psalm of praise, and began, "Every day will I bless thee and praise thy name for ever." The version of this germ of the widespread English version, appearing in the Scottish Psalmbook was composed by John Craig, the colleague of John Knox, and reveals his poetic taste.

Many of the early Lutherans, influenced by Martin Luther himself, based many of their hymns upon the Psalms. Paul Gerhardt, for instance, was inspired by Psalm 145 to compose his great hymn, "I was so oft in deep distress." In portions of *Paradise Lost*, John Milton, in the speech of Adam, apparently paraphrases Psalm 145 in the lines—

> Henceforth I learn, that to obey is best,
> And love with fear the only God, to wake
> As in his presence, ever to observe
> His providence, and on him sole depend,
> Merciful over all his works, with good
> Still overcoming evil, and by small
> Accomplishing great things, by things deem'd weak
> Subverting worldly strong, and worldly wise
> By simply meek.

Philip Doddridge, the renowned hymnist, recorded the conversion of a notorious rake James Gardiner. It was in 1719, while he sat in his room at Paris that he was wonderfully transformed by a vision, and thereafter, became a mighty soul-winner. Colonel Gardiner learned many of the Psalms by heart and would often repeat or sing them aloud to himself. In 1743, thinking that death was approaching, his mind dwelt with special delight on Psalm 145, and the version of it by Isaac Watts. He died two years later after being mortally wounded at the battle of Prestonpans. Further illustrations of the use of this Psalm will be found in the following treatment of several verses.

Psalm 145 is the last of the alphabetical Psalms, and as generally common to them all, this one has a somewhat looseness of thought making any logical outline difficult. The parts of the Psalm are bound by that which is external—the letters of the alphabet—rather than by thought. As we have already seen, acrostic Psalms have verses beginning in the Hebrew with the successive letters of the alphabet. Somehow the 14th letter *Nun* dropped out of the Psalm on its way down to us, but was inserted by the translators of the LXX Version. The omission reads, "The Lord is faithful in his words, and holy in all his works," and is placed between verses 13 and 14 in our English Bible. The majority of modern critics, however, reject the genuineness of the insertion.

Of this incomplete acrostic arrangement Andrew Bonar says that the omission of one letter in the structure of the Psalm may have been designed that we might be kept from putting stress on the mere form of the composition. Cassiodorus of ancient times, however, quaintly remarked that the Psalms in which the alphabetical order is incomplete, are especially fitted for the righteous in the Church Militant here on earth, as still imperfect, and needing to be purified from defect. As to the reason for this type of Psalm, Spurgeon's pithy observation is that, "this is one of the alphabetical Psalms, composed with much art, and, doubtless, so arranged that the memory might be aided. The Holy Spirit condescends to use even the more artificial methods of the poet, to secure attention, and impress the heart."

We have in the Psalm a wonderful tribute to Jehovah's bountifulness and compassion, in a lovely song of praise, described by one writer as "a bracelet in which one beautiful bead is strung on after another, making a yet more beautiful whole." It has been happily depicted as being the *New Song* promised in Psalm 144:9. The last Psalms of the Psalter, commencing with Psalm 145, have been described as the *Beulah* of the book, "where the sun shineth night and day, and the voice of the turtle is heard. Coming close after the mournful, plaintive, penitential, prayerful, varying notes, they unconsciously typify the joy and rest of glory." Although abounding in former familiar Psalm expressions, Psalm 145 deserves "the chain of originality from the insistence of its conviction of the Divine love and pity and care for all the world and all creatures."

It bears the title "David *Psalm* of Praise," and is the only Psalm to be named thus, and was likely coined from the last verse, "My mouth shall speak the praise of the Lord." This earnest desire to magnify God for His glory and majesty and love is expressed by various terms—*Extol, Bless,*

Praise, Declare, Speak of, Abundantly able, Talk, Make known. This designation "Psalm of Praise" has passed to the whole of the Psalter now commonly known as *the Book of Praises.* David singled out from the Psalms he penned, two on which he set his own mark as proper to himself—*The Prayer of David,* Psalm 86, and *The Praise of David,* Psalm 145. All the rest he composed for all in common, but these two he reserved peculiarly for himself. As to the distinction between Praises and Psalms, Augustine had this to say—

> Psalms are the praises of God accompanied with song; Psalms are songs containing the praise of God. If there be praise, but not of God, it is not a Psalm. If there be praise, and praise of God, if it is not sung it is not a Psalm. To make a Psalm there go these three—*Praise, God's Praise,* and *Song.*

Composed by David, the title is appropriate, because the Psalm wholly consists of praise as the result of this inspired, elevated frame of spirit to offer pure praise to God, without any touch of what was particular to himself. Although he had extolled God so often in his other Psalms, this one he regarded as his own crown jewel of praise. "It is not for any of us to render David's praise, for David alone could do that, but we may take David's Psalm as a model, and aim at making our own personal adoration as much like it as possible: we shall be long before we equal our model. Let each Christian present his own praise unto the Lord, and call it by his own name. What wealth of varied praise will thus be presented through Christ Jesus!"

Because of this unique feature of absence of any marked sections, and appearing as one and indivisible, an outline of contents is not easy to plan. Bullinger gives us the *Repeated Introversion,* as he calls it—

> Praise promised. For Jehovah. (David), verses 1, 2.
> Praise offered, verse 3.
> Praise promised. For His work (David and others), verses 4-7.
> Praise offered, verses 8—9.
> Praise promised. *For His kingdom* (The Works), verses 10-12.
> Praise offered, verses 13-20.
> Praise promised. David and all others, verse 21.

It is profitable to notice the appearances of *They shall, I will.* A convenient arrangement for exposition is that mapped out by some teachers of the Word. David praises God—

1. For His fame and glory, verses 1-7.
2. For His goodness, verses 8-10.
3. For His kingdom, verses 11-13.
4. For His providence, verses 14-16.
5. For His saving mercy, verses 17-21.

One characteristic word of this Praise-Song is the adjective *ALL*, which occurs 14 times. Gathering all their references together where this single, short word is found is to discover that such a wide outlook over the world is the object, with all it contains of the Divine pity and love, is a noble anticipation of our Lord's teaching in the Sermon on the Mount and is introduced in a similar manner. "Just as the subjects of the Kingdom of Heaven exceed the heathen in kindness and goodness, because they know the universal and impartial grace of the Father so here the *Saints*, the *numbers* of the Covenant, are to *bless* Jehovah, who shows them peculiar favor, but also lets His tender mercies flow in an unchecked stream over *all* His works. *All* Jehovah's works confess Him but His saints *bless* Him."

As the Psalm recalls in many expressions and phrases and thoughts and feelings of older songs, as, for instance, the first verse, a familiar strain opening other Psalms—see 30 and 34—*Greatly to be praised*—see Psalms 18:3; 48:1 etc., we are not to attempt any exposition of this Psalm, seeing that these repeated phrases have already been dealt with in previous notes. So the reader is urged to follow cross references given in the margin of the Bible, and check these for information we gave on such. We content ourselves, therefore, and conclude our survey of this remarkable Psalm vibrating with Praise to God, by gathering together historical sidelights on some of its verses.

William Law, who in his *Serious Call*, invites Christians to "live more nearly as they prayed," closes the most eloquent chapter of his work with a selection of Psalms adapted for devotional use. His choice for a morning hymn was Psalm 145, "I will magnify Thee, O God, my King, and I will praise Thy name for ever and ever."

In the *Confessions of St. Augustine*, the Psalms reveal their influence over the life of the saint. At the beginning of his *Confessions* can be found the quotation, "Great is the Lord, and great is His power; yea, and His wisdom is infinite," Psalm 145:3.

William Langland, poet of the 14th century, left us *Vision of Piers Plowman* in which he gave to his racy vigor and homely language something of spiritual intensity, clothed in the garment of the Psalms. In one of his *Sections*, Langland wrote, "Evil though the world is, Scripture bids men not to despair, no offence is beyond God's pardon, for *His mercy is over all His works*, Psalm 145:9."

Dr. William Carey, one of the greatest missionaries of the past, was also a scientific botanist and an ardent student of natural history. Yet, with him, science was always subordinated to his faith in God. It was a text from the Psalms that he prefixed to his edition of Roxburgh's *Flora Indica*, published in 1820—"All thy works praise Thee, O Lord!" 145:10.

Augustine's noble treatise, *The City of God*, written, as it were, in the glare of burning Rome, expresses with glowing eloquence his sense of the eternal destinies of the city of God. The same intense conviction of ever-lasting endurance amid decay, speaks in the inscription—*Thy kingdom is an everlasting Kingdom*, Psalm 145:13,—which is written in Greek char-acters, unobliterated by time or enemies, above the portal of the Church at Damascus, not a Mahomedan mosque.

Our last illustration, adapted from Prothero's great work *Psalms In Human Life*, from which much of the historical material we have used in our work on The Psalms was gathered, concerns John Howard whose name will be forever with the abolition of Slave Trade and with Prison Reform. Howard's visits to jails all over Britain and the Continent result-ed in the fevers he suffered because of the most noxious smell of the cells he met prisoners in. Gratitude for his recovery from these bouts were always expressed in the language of the Psalms. An entry in his Diary, when lying ill at the Hague in 1778, reads—

> *May 13th.* In pain and anguish all night . . . help, Lord, for vain is the help of man.
>
> *May 14th*—This night my fever abated, my pains less . . . "Righteous are thou in all thy ways, and holy in all Thy works," Psalm 145:17—bring me out of the furnace as silver purified seven times.

This remarkable, godly liberator, died at Kherson, in 1789. As we bid *adieu* to this God-glorifying Psalm it is with the feeling that its blithe spir-it will accompany us as we enter the five Praise-Psalms completing the Psalter. In fact, the last verse of this Psalm places in our hands the key admitting us into the five *Hallelujah* rooms, Psalms 146 to 150. "Speak the praise of the Lord . . . While I live will I praise the Lord," 145:21; 146:1.

Psalm 146

With this Psalm we begin the final group of Psalms known as the *Hallelujah* Psalms, because Psalms 146-150 each begin and end with that word which means, "Praise ye the Lord." It would seem as if these Psalms owe their origin to liturgical needs, namely, for use in the Temple worship. The LXX Version names them *The Psalms of Haggai and Zechariah*, as if they had been composed by them for the occasion of the dedication of the second Temple at the outset of the reign of Darius. In the original Hebrew, however, these Psalms have no title prefixed to them. As a whole, they sum up the joy of returned exiles and form a fitting conclusion to the Book of Psalms. After so many Psalms of grief, shame, tears, and various vicissitudes, it is comforting to be in the last series so full of the tones of Heaven—*Hallelujah—Praise*.

The English word "Praise" occurs some 44 times in these five Psalms in which kindred terms like *sing, thanksgiving*, and *joyful* are used. So, as Spurgeon reminds us, "We are now among the Hallelujahs. The rest of our journey lies through the Delectable Mountains. All is praise to the close of the book. The key is high-pitched: the music is upon high-sounding cymbals. O for a heart full of joyful gratitude, that we may run, and leap, and glorify God, even as these Psalms do."

Bullinger offers the suggestion that the five Psalms offer us a Pentateuch, as well as being an echo and reminiscence of all the Psalms.

> The first has *Genesis* for its subject—
> The second, *Exodus*—
> The third, *Leviticus*—
> The fourth, *Numbers*—
> The fifth, *Deuteronomy*.

The first Psalm, with its key-note of having God as our Helper, was the delight of David Hume of Wedderburn, who used to sing it to the accompaniment of his harp. Remarkable for his piety and integrity, he memorized whole Psalms, short portions of them being often in his mouth. This father of David Hume of Godscroft, author of the first Scottish family Latories, *The House of Douglas*, had a particular liking for the opening verse of this Psalm—"Praise ye the Lord. Praise the Lord,

O my soul. While I live will I praise the Lord; I will sing praises unto God while I have any being."

William Law, in *Serious Call*, wrote that "Psalms 34, 96, 103, 111, *146*, 147, are such as wonderfully set forth the glory of God, and, therefore, you may keep to any one of them at any particular hour as you like." Another who found consolation in Psalm 146 was the Earl of Strafford who was executed on Tower Hill, London, May 12th, 1641, for treason. Up to the last, he relied upon King Charles, his friend, to free him but without avail. As he died, it was to the Psalms that in bitterness of spirit he turned, for their expression, as quoted, "O put not your trust in princes, not in any child of man; for there is no help in them," 146:2. It was this quotation by Strafford, Shakespeare placed in the mouth of the fallen Wolsey—

> O how wretched
> Is that poor man that hangs on princes' favors!
> There is, betwixt that smile we would aspire to,
> That sweet aspect of princes, and their ruin,
> More pangs or fears than wars or women have;
> And when he falls, he falls like Lucifer,
> Never to hope again.

Ordericus Vitalis, the ancient chronicler, loved the Psalms, and his pages teem with quotations from them. At one point, he moralizes, "Put not your trust in princes, which are nought, of ye sons of men; but in God, the Living and the True, Who is the Maker of all," Psalm 146:3. But what should be recognized is the fact that the author of this Psalm does not castigate the caprice of princes, but their frailty as men that is declared unworthy.

The ten verses of the Psalm, however, proclaiming Jehovah alone as the unfailing Deliverer, do not lend themselves to marked divisions. They appear without a break—"one pearl, a sacred censer of holy incense, pouring forth one sweet perfume." Yet two aspects appear to be discernible—

1. Jehovah alone is to be trusted, and not man. All who trust the Lord are blessed by Him, 1-5.
2. The reason for same—all the Divine Perfections. Jehovah is Creator, Judge, Deliverer and King, 6-10.

Jehovah is our Helper, not man, 146:1-5. The first verse should be compared with Psalms 103:1; 141:1, 33, upon which this opening verse is likely based, but where the word *bless* is substituted for "praise." We here have both a general call and an individual summons to worship Jehovah. Primarily composed for congregational singing, "Praise *ye* the Lord," the personal note breaks out often, "Praise the Lord, O *my* soul . . . while *I* live will *I* praise the Lord." The Hebrew is emphatic, *O I myself!* The Psalmist not only exhorted others to bless the Lord, he aroused his innermost self, his *soul* to praise God. He calls upon the noblest element of his being to exercise its noblest function.

Hallelujah is the proper response to all Jehovah is in His attributes and acts. The ancient Britons, in the year 420, obtained a victory over the army of the Picts and Saxons near Mold in Flintshire. The Britons, unarmed, having Germanicus and Lupus at their head, when the Picts and Saxons came to attack, the two commanders, Gideonlike, ordered their little army to shout *Hallelujah* three times over at the sound of which the enemy, being suddenly struck with terror, ran away in the greatest confusion and left the Britons masters of the field.

While ours is to be the joyful privilege of praising the Lord throughout Eternity, the poet desires to consecrate his entire earthly existence to the exercise of praise—"While I live—While I have any being." The motion of personal praise must, like the motion of the pulse, last as long as life lasts. George Carpenter, the Bavarian martyr, being asked by some of his godly brethren, when he was burning to death at the stake, to give some sign of his constancy, answered—

"Let this be a sure sign unto you of my faith and perseverance in the truth, that so long as I am able to open my mouth, or to whisper, I will never cease to praise God, and to profess his truth"—which he did.

It is because there is no saving help in any other that God is praised as our "Help in ages past, our Hope for years to come." Thus we have the exhortation, "Put not your trust in princes, nor in the son of man, in whom there is no hope." We here have a distinct allusion to Gen. 2:7; 3:19, and Psalm 118:8, 9. This third verse with its warning against trusting in men, has the positive side of the truth enforced in verse 5. The Hebrew has it, "Confide ye not in a son of man," Jer. 17:5; John 2:25. The word rendered *princes* means liberal or bountiful ones, as they doubtless were, but even so they were not to be trusted. There is no hope or help in the strongest and richest. A prince of his Church, Pope Pius V, said, "When I was a monk I had hope of my salvation; when I became a Cardinal I began to fear; when I was made Pope I all but despaired of Eternity." See our notes on Psalm 118:8, 9.

Even princes are at the mercy of that ruthless tyrant, Black Prince—*Death!* They return to the earth, and any benign, benevolent or false thoughts they may have had perish with them. At the moment of death the most definite projects of prince and peasant are at an end, Luke 12:16-20. Their morning thoughts of larger barns perished that self-same night. *In that very day*, is the phrase Shakespeare may have had in mind when, in *Julius Caesar* he gave Antony the lines—

But yesterday the word of Caesar might
Have stood against the world; now lies he there,
And none so poor to do him reverence.

The two-fold designation of God, the writer goes on to describe, provide the reason why man should trust in Him alone—*The God of Jacob
. . . Jehovah his God.* What marvelous truths are wrapped in these two
titles, each of which has a fountain of joy in it. But the first will not cheer
without the second. "Unless Jehovah be his God no man can find confidence in the fact that He was Jacob's God." Emphasis is on the
pronoun *His*—His God. Happy indeed are all they who have this God of
Jacob as their God. He met Jacob when he had nothing, and deserved
nothing but wrath, Gen. 28:13; 32:10—and promised him everything.
This oft-used title answers to the New Testament title—"The God of all
grace," 1 Peter 5:10. The two-fold function of Jehovah provides another reason why man should trust in Him. He is *Our Help* and Our Hope.
He is "a very *present* help," meaning that He is with us day by day, meeting our every need. But being *Our Hope* we know that our future is
assured, for all that He *is*, He *will be* until travelling days are done. The
Hebrew word for *Hope* is rare in the Psalms expressing, as it does, earnest
"looking for" or "waiting for." See Psalms 104:27; 119:166. To the sincere Jew of old the coming Messiah was his hope; and for the saints
today, "the blessed hope," is the coming again of Jesus the Messiah to
gather His own around Him. *Happy* or *blessed*, used in this verse, constitutes the last beatitude of the Psalter.

Jehovah in all His Perfections, 146:6-10. What a marvelous number
of Divine attributes the Psalmist packs in these remaining five verses!
Within them God as Jehovah (Lord) is mentioned seven times. His
omnipotence shines forth in every clause in every verse. After such an
exhibition of what He has done, constantly does, and will yet do, can we
wonder at the Psalm concluding with a loud *Hallelujah*? Truly, there is no
other like unto Jehovah!

He is Creator. Because He is Maker of heaven, earth, and the sea, and
all that therein is, we should trust only in Him and not man. Think of it
like this—"He Who made heaven can make it a heaven for us, and make
us fit for heaven. He Who made the earth can preserve us while we are on
the earth, and help us to make good use of it while we sojourn upon it. He
Who made the sea with all its mysteries can steer us across the pathless
deep of a troubled life, and make it a way for His redeemed to pass over."

He is Faithful. Not only is God, Almighty, as the Creator of the
Universe, He is also the Covenant-keeping God Who "keepeth truth for
ever." Is not this *truth*, personified in His beloved Son, the most costly
jewel in His inexhaustible treasury, the sustaining power which preserves

the fabric of His Creation? That God does keep the truth from age to age is proved by the way His Holy Word is being more widely circulated than ever. God is ever true, and the Keeper of all that is true. Immutable fidelity is stamped upon Jehovah's nature.

He is Just. As the swift and impartial Administrator of Justice, "He executeth judgment of the oppressed," and as the Judge of all the earth can do that which is right. There is no need therefore, to avenge ourselves, for He stands ready to vindicate us if we are being unjustly treated by man, Psalm 103:6; Rom. 12:19; 1 Peter 2:23.

He is Bountiful. Are you not amazed to see the Creator and the universal Judge, not only displaying power and meting out justice but dispensing bounty? All food comes from God, but what the Psalmist would have us remember is the fact that the *hungry* are those He feeds. Those rich in food, He sends empty away. When Jesus came as this bountiful God personified, He fed to the full the hungry multitudes, John 6:14; See Psalms 103:6; 104:27; 107:9; 136:25; Isa. 65:1. The last part of this seventh verse, "The Lord looseth the prisoners," brings before us the marked feature of this line, and the next four each beginning with the Divine name, *Jehovah* (Lord), and that all five lines are associated with His creative power. These verses—7 to 9—are also an epitome of the mission of the Comforter, Psalms 69:5, 6; 107:10, 14; Isa. 35:5; 61:3.

Prisoners are liberated. For all who are bound whether by actual chains, as Paul and Silas were, or by sin, or adverse circumstances, the message is that the Creator can "open the prison to them that are bound," Isa. 61:1. And when He sets free the prisoner, he is free indeed. What a mighty Emancipator He is, whether spiritually, providentially, and nationally!

Blind are made to see. Often in Scripture, Blindness conveys the notion of general helplessness, Deut. 28:29; Job 12:25; 29:18; 35:5, and God can banish this form of blindness. Then there are those who are spiritually blind—blinded by the god of this world—but countless myriads in Heaven and on earth rejoice over having the eyes open to see in Jesus the only Savior. But Jehovah is able to give sight to those who are physically blind, as well as to those who are mentally or spiritually blind. What a true portraiture of the ministry of Jesus we have in this phrase, "The Lord openeth the eye of the blind," for in the days of His flesh He blessed many sightless eyes with the gift of sight, Luke 4:18, 19. As Co-Creator having made the eye, He can open it both for those born blind or smitten with blindness.

Bowed down are raised. Luke records how Jesus saw a poor woman who had been crippled for 18 years—"bowed together and could in no wise lift up herself," 13:11, but the compassionate One laid hands on her and "immediately was made straight," and just as immediately shouted her *Hallelujah*! for she "glorified God." All who are bowed down through one cause or another appeal to His lovely heart and He consoles the bereaved, cheers the defeated, comforts the despairing, and makes the crooked straight. See Psalm 145:14.

Righteous are loved. As the Righteous One, righteous in all His ways, and loving righteousness, God makes those who are clothed in the garment of His righteousness, His favored ones. How blessed we are if, as those made righteous by His grace, we are found basking in His love!

Strangers are Preserved. Hebrew legislation made provision for the stranger, the widow, and the orphan as orphans of compassion and beneficence, Deut. 10:8; 14:28, 29; Psalm 68:5. Jehovah made special laws for their shelter within His domain. He has a peculiar love for wanderers and pilgrims and for those, like Jacob, who are strangers in a strange land. His eye is upon their solitary and forlorn condition, and He alone knows how to preserve. Yes, and for all who are strangers to His grace, He offers an eternal preservation.

Orphans and Widows are relieved. What we have just said regarding the Mosaic Law for destitute persons applies here. Orphans are made the recipients of the tender love and provision of our Father in Heaven, and the widow bereft of her partner finds consolation in Him Who spoke of Himself as a Husband of the widow, as well as the Father of the fatherless.

Wicked designs are defeated. The term "upside down" means "to make crooked," giving the sense that "Jehovah causes the wicked to reach a goal which they had not in view; they seek happiness, but the way they walk in is made, by Divine over-ruling, to issue to misery." See Psalm 119:78, where the same word implies the same idea of interference, to thwart and impede a course of action, and is applied to an evil-disposed person who interferes, or turns upside down, the good designs of the righteous.

But in the clause, "The way of the wicked He—Jehovah—turneth upside down," we have the wicked man laying out his plans, but He, Who is high over all, looks as it were along a plain and level road of prosperity, bends the prosperous course aside; makes the path crooked, instead of straight; full of trouble and calamity, instead of successful and sure. And this is the eleventh reason given in the Psalm why those who put their trust in God and not man are blessed of Him. "All the preceding ten reasons lift up the poor saint, step by step, higher and higher," says Paul Palanterius. "At one word suddenly, like Satan falling as lightning from heaven, the wicked are shown dashed down the whole way from the summit of pride to the depths of hell." Is not this over-ruling Divine Providence illustrated for us in Joseph's brethren, Haman, and others?

Reigning For Ever. The Psalmist contrasts the Eternity of the reign of God with the brevity of man, verses 3 and 4; and His unending dominion is the final reason why we should have Him as our Help and our Hope; and also a perpetual theme for praise, because it carries with it the blessedness of all souls and all worlds. See Exod. 15:18; Psalm 99:1. Jehovah, as the Eternal King, cannot die, not abdicate, nor lose His crown by force. His throne, forever secure, can never be in jeopardy. In this final verse of such a Praise-Psalm, we have—

> A Cause for Praise—"The Lord shall reign for ever."
> A Center of Praise—"O Zion."
> A Cycle of Praise—"All generations."
> A Call to Praise—"Praise ye the Lord."

What else could we have at the end of this gladsome song but a resounding *Hallelujah*! But His praise does not end here. It ascends to Him from angels and saints forever.

Psalm 147

This further *Hallelujah* Psalm was also included by William Law in his *Serious Call* as setting forth the glory of God, and, therefore, used at any particular time as a fit hymn for devotion. Like Psalm 133, Psalm 147 is a Psalm of Brotherhood. Thus it was sung twice in seasons of Church union in Scotland, first in 1820 when two branches of the Secession were re-united, and again in 1847, when the United Secession and Relief joined to form the United Presbyterian Church. In the Scottish version of this Psalm, the second and third verses strikingly connect union with spiritual comfort and healing—

> God doth build up Jerusalem;
> And He it is alone
> That the dispersed of Israel
> Doth gather into one.
> Those that are broken in their heart,
> And grieved in their minds,
> He healeth, and their painful wounds
> He tenderly up-binds.

St. Augustine opens his *Confessions* with—"Great is our Lord, and great is His power, yea His wisdom is infinite," Psalm 146:3 down to verse 5. Shakespeare in *As You Like It*, has the prayer of Adam partly founded on the phrase, "He feedeth the young ravens that call upon him," 147:9.

> He that doth the raven feed,
> Yea, providently caters for the sparrow,
> Be comfort to my age!

In 1588, at the Market Cross, Edinburgh, Robert Bruce, the great preacher of majesty and power, when news reached him of the defeat and dispersion of the Spanish Armada, led the citizens in singing of Psalm 76, and from Psalm 147:18, he took the motto which was engraved upon the coins struck to commemorate the victory—*Affavit Deus*—God blew!

Without doubt, this Psalm deserves to rank high in the poetry of the Bible, and reveals the composer's powers in the keenness of his observation of Nature and in his sympathy with the life and movement of the world, as well as by the free play of his poetic fancy around each phenomenon attracting him. The theme of this song is Greatness of God, seen in what He has done, what He does, and what He can do. It is an eloquent tribute to the love and power of Jehovah as displayed in Nature and in Grace. Spurgeon speaks of it as "a specially remarkable song. In it the greatness and the condescending goodness of the Lord are celebrated. The God of Israel is set forth in His peculiarity of glory as caring for the sorrowing, the insignificant, and forgotten. The poet finds a singular joy in extolling one who is so singularly gracious. It is a Psalm of the city and of the field, of the first and second creations, of the commonwealth of the church. It is good and pleasant throughout. Let it be studied with joyful gratitude."

Those who are familiar with the language of the Psalms, will find that the Psalmist in his remarkable ode freely used existing material, quoting from the Book of Job, several Psalms, such as 33:1; 92:1; 135:3, and others, and Isa. 40:26, 28; 56:8; 61:1; Hosea 6:1. Where the marginal references to previous Psalms occur the reader is asked to turn to our notes on same. Because of its liturgical origin and character, a rigid outline of the Psalm is hardly possible. Bullinger has the following *Introversion and Extended alternation—*

> Hallelujah, verse 1.
> Praise. Kindness to Israel, verses 1-3.
> General operations. Nature, verses 4-5.
>> Contrast. What Jehovah does, verse 6.
> Praise. Kindness to Israel, verse 7.
> General operations. Nature, verses 8, 9.
>> Contrast. What Jehovah delights in, verse 10, 11.
> Praise. Kindness to Israel, verses 12-14.
> General operations. Nature, verses 15-18.
>> Contrast. What Jehovah has shown, verses 19, 20.
> Hallelujah, verse 20.

Beginning and ending with a *Hallelujah!* this Psalm is one of Praise in which the writer recounts the manifold ministry and mercy of Jehovah, as our analysis shows.

Restoration of Jerusalem and her exiled Inhabitants, 147:1-3. It is quite plain that in the opening verse of the Psalm the poet modelled it upon Psalms 33:1; 92:1; 135:3. To sing praises to God is *good, pleasant,* and *comely*—although the margin of the R.V. suggests a beautiful alternate reading: "For He is good; sing praises unto God, for He is gracious." But taking the appealing triad in the A. V., singing praises to God is *good* because He commands what is good, Micah 6:8, and, therefore, it is right to extol Him. It is also good because it is acceptable with God, beneficial to ourselves, and stimulating to fellow-singers. Certainly we are enjoined to make melody in our hearts unto the Lord, but singing both with *heart* and *voice* is more profitable, seeing such enables us to sing *of* God, and *for* God, as well as *to* God. Such expressed praise is also *pleasant*. How delightful it is to both hear and see a gathered assembly praising God in congregational singing! God is pleased with praise as the sweetest sacrifice offered Him, Psalm 50:23. Praise is not only pleasant and proper, but sweet and suitable or *comely*—the dictionary tells us means "decency" or "proper." There is therefore all the decency in the world in praise, for by it we express our gratitude to Him Who freely gives us all things.

Then there follows four reasons why we should sing praises to the God of all comfort—He builds, He gathers, He heals, He binds. A striking feature of this unique Praise-Psalm is the use of the personal pronoun *HE*, occurring some 20 times. He—Jehovah—is the Source of all power and grace. Thus His love for Israel is shown in His rebuilding of Jerusalem, the restoration of her exiled inhabitants, and the healing of the broken-hearted among them. Although Nehemiah and his companions were the visible builders, yet they realized that the Lord was the true Builder, Zech. 6:12; Matt. 16:18.

How those returned exiles must have rejoiced as they witnessed the upraising of their dearly-loved capital from its ruins! Desolation, like a fall, had weighed down every faithful heart, but what abounding praise as they saw the city rise in strength and beauty at Jehovah's will. By His power also all her scattered, broken-hearted exiles, thrust out of home and city by a cruel tyrant, were re-gathered and settled once again in their city as God's chosen ones, building them together in the city He re-built. The term *outcasts* is that which is used in Isa. 11:12 and 56:8, showing that the re-building of Jerusalem after the captivity is intended. The day is coming when the Lord is to "gather together as one the children of God that are scattered abroad." He will bring His elect from "the four winds," to build up a Jerusalem no man can ravage or destroy, Matt. 24:31; John 11:52.

What a marvelous contrast this section affords! The God Who can repair broken cities, likewise repairs broken hearts who are of more value to Him than material prosperity. Based upon Psalm 34:18; 137; Isa.61:1, Hosea 6:1, these touching lines of Jehovah as healer of broken hearts and binder-up of their wounds or griefs, brings Him very near to the lives of the disconsolate, Job 9:28; Prov. 15:13. The heavenly Physician is well able to cure, and care for, His patients.

> Thou wilt heal that broken heart,
> > Which, like the plants that throw
> Their fragrance from the wounded part,
> > Breathless sweetness out of woe.

Jehovah's skill is infallible, Whose goodness and care are equal to His skill. He never breaks the bruised reed, but tenderly binds up the painful wounds of the heart smitten with woe. He is the compassionate God as well as the creative One, Who "lays on the ointment of grace, and the soft bandages of love, and thus binds up the bleeding wounds of those convicted of sin." Let us have no fear in uncovering our broken heart and wounds to Him Who alone can make us whole again..

Revelation of Power and Grace, 147:4-6. Here, again, we have the combination of Jehovah's greatness and grace, for His is not only of "great power" to number and name the myriads of stars, but to bless the meek, or afflicted. With perfect ease He can journey from luminaries to the lowly. *Great power* implies "abounding in power," and proof of such is proven by His power to go beyond man's power to count, much more to name, the stars of heaven. To assemble the dispersed of Israel, however numerous and scattered, was easy to the Ruler of the hosts of heaven. Doubtless the original promise to Abraham was in the poet's mind, and still more the expression of Isaiah, when he penned these verses reminding us of Him Who is—

> Creator of the rolling spheres,
> Ineffably sublime.

As the stars, so the thoughts of His Divine mind, "His understanding is infinite," or as the margin puts it, "Of His understanding there is no number." See Psalm 145:3; Isa. 40:28. His kind and benevolent thoughts are as innumerable as the stars. Thus His love and power are manifested not only in inanimate nature, but in His treatment of the meek—and the wicked. The Creator is the Consoler—extremes Hannah and Mary, and a host of saints have celebrated in song, 1 Sam. 2:7, 8; Luke 1:48, 51-53. The fifth verse of this Psalm magnifies Him for three of His attributes—Greatness, Power, Knowledge.

The meek He raises on high and makes them princes and rulers after the lofty of earth are stripped of their gay robes and tinselled crowns. He can take the lowly from the dung-hill and place them among princes. He can reverse the evil order of things. The meek are down, and He lifts them up: the wicked are exalted and He hurls them to the dust. None of the wicked, if they remain wicked, can escape their deserved judgment. Of this sixth verse Spurgeon says—

> "Here we see the practical outcome of that character of Jehovah, which leads Him to count and call the stars as if they were little things, while He deals tenderly with sorrowful men, as if they were precious in His esteem. He is so great that nothing is little to Him. His infinite majesty thus naturally brings low the lofty and exalts the lowly"—and we can add, humiliate the wicked.

Rejoicing over God's natural provision for Beasts and Birds, 147:7-9.
With these verses the Psalm takes a new departure, with a fresh invocation to praise, going on to fresh proofs from nature to the Almighty Power.
One commentator thinks that with this new summons to praise God we
have the opening of a new Psalm. But its beautiful structure is against
such a view. Again we are exhorted to "sing unto Jehovah," but to have
in our praise the note of gratitude, "with thanksgiving" and "upon the
harp." He speaks to us in all His works, and by our lips and lives we are
to respond to His goodness and where possible blend music with song.
This omnipotent One is *our* God, and such a blessed fact is the one choice
joy as we praise Him with hearts and harp.

To the devout heart of the Psalmist there were no second causes, "*He*
covereth the heavens with clouds, *Who* prepareth rain for the earth, Who
maketh grass to grow upon the mountains." God is all, and in all, and for
all, Psalm 104:13, 14. The *clouds* are not caused by accident, or a mere fortuitous concourse of vapors, but a canvas the Great Artist's hand covers the
heavens with. *Clouds . . . rain . . . grass.* What a mutual dependence and
subordination between all second causes are herewith expressed! "The
heavens work up the elements, the elements upon the earth, and the earth
yielded here fruits for the use of Man," Hosea 2:21, 24.

When and *as,* God commands the rain-clouds part with their contents
to make grass grow upon mountains. What wise foresight was behind the
creative fiat of God, "Let the earth bring forth grass," seeing it suits almost
every soil and climate and is the most abundant and the most generally
diffuse of all vegetation. But what is so particularly appealing in the eighth
verse is the special providence of God in causing the grass to grow upon
mountains—in regions above the zone of man's cultivation. These mountain-grasses require no human cultivation, and are most suitable for those
beasts like mountain sheep and goats. Animals that live among men are
taken care of by men, but the wild beasts live upon the *mountains* and are
fed from heaven by Divine Providence.

A further manifestation of God's provision follows—"He giveth food
to the *young* ravens which cry." We sing, "The raven He feedeth, then
why should I care," but the emphasis here is on the *young* ravens which
cry. The stories told by Jewish and Arabian writers as to the raven's cruelty to its young in driving them out of the nests before they are quite able
to provide for themselves and so cry for food, are without foundation,
because no bird is more careful of its young than the raven. Doubtless the
reason for the raven being made as a special object of God's protecting
care can be traced to its habit of flying restlessly about in search of food
to satisfy its own appetite and that of its young ones. It is their cry God
hears and responds to. See Job 38:41; Psalms 104:14; 145:15; Luke 12:24.

Reminder of the objects of His pleasure, 147:10, 11. The works of God

Who is "mighty to make" and "great to grant," delight our hearts, causing us to express our pleasure in grateful song, but what delights the Creator's heart? First of all, we are told of two things He has no pleasure in, namely, "the strength of the horse," and "the legs of a man." This antithesis is thought by some to describe the *cavalry* and the *infantry* on which the military strength of a nation depends, but perhaps the poet had the more expressive passage found in Psalm 33:16, 17 in mind.

It is common knowledge that the horse is a type of strength and endurance, Job 39:19-25, and that Eastern nations naturally select fleetness of foot as the typical quality in a vigorous warrior—"a swift-footed Achilles," 2 Sam. 2:18; Psalm 18:33, but God's deliverances are not given to these but to those who trust Him utterly. Men are not favored by God if they are brainy, strong, and quick, but only if they are truly His, trusting in His mercy.

So, those Jehovah takes pleasure in are those who reverentially fear and trust Him, and hope in His mercy or "lovingkindness." *Fear* and *Hope* are the great *vincula*, or bond of union, in Old Testament theology, bracketing and including in their meaning all its ideas. A holy fear of God, and a pious hope in Him, afford Him much pleasure.

Rehearsal of Provision for Zion, and its People, 147:12-14. Praise is now urged for the power, peace, and plenty, Jehovah blessed His people with. A happy and prosperous state is portrayed in these verses. Mercies both temporal and spiritual were vouchsafed towards Israel. Throughout the rest of the Psalm the present-tense is maintained in twelve different connections commencing with *blessed*. In this further call to Jerusalem, built up by Jehovah, He assures the returned exiles of their security and peace as the result of the strengthening of the gates or the new fortifications of the restored city. See Neh. 3:3, 6, 13, 15. Thomas Adams, expositor of the 18th century, would have us remember that "Blessed is the city whose gates God barred up with His power, and openeth again with His mercy, There is nothing can defend where His justice will stride; and there is nothing can offence where his goodness will preserve." The only true security of a city is God's defense of it. These are days when evil men like revolutionists, vandals, and hooligans seem bent on destroying the bars and gates of city life.

The Psalmist then goes on to recite three reasons why Zion should praise God for its safe, secure city—

Benediction. "He hath blessed thy children within thee." See Isa. 60:17, 18. What is the use of external security, if there is not internal happiness and contentment? It was great of God to re-build and fortify the one-time ruined, wretched city, but greater still to bless its grateful inhabitants with His gifts.

Peace. "He maketh peace in thy borders." What hope this must have brought to the returned exiles after the horrors and unrest of war! What a great Peace-Maker is our God! Job 34:29; Prov. 16:7. The Hebrew expresses it, "Who makes thy boundary to be in a state of peace." The ancient Jews observed that all the letters in the name of God are *letters of rest*: and truly, God only is the Center where the soul can find rest. He alone can speak peace to a troubled city—or—troubled conscience. *Jerusalem*, means "Vision of Peace."

Abundance. "He *filleth* thee with the finest of the wheat." The present tense implies that God kept on filling them with the best of food. He continually gave both quantity and quality, the *most* and the *best* to the inhabitants of the peaceful city. The margin of the R.V. has "the fat of the wheat." See Psalm 81:16. With *protection*, and *peace*, there came *plenty*. And the marvel is that the best, and abundant food came from God's hands to the mouths of the people. What else could they do but sing praise unto God for all His bounty! After feeding beasts and birds, He feeds His saints.

Revolving Seasons obey His Word, 147:15-20. In these concluding verses of the Psalm, Jehovah's wonderful works in Nature and the power of His Word formed a pledge of His faithfulness to Israel. The reader should compare Psalm 33 with these verses, seeing this Psalm was likely in the thoughts of the poet as he combined God's work and Word—the latter being also described as *Commandments, Statutes, and Judgments*. In this section God personifies His Word. He sends out His commandment as His trusted messenger and representative, who runs swiftly to fulfill His purpose, both in Nature and Grace.

His Word runneth swiftly! What a captivating phrase this is! It runs and glorifies the One Who sent it out on its course. "He spake, and it was done," Psalm 33:9. After the temporal mercies eliciting grateful praise, we now have spiritual mercies God must likewise be praised for, namely, the accomplishments of His Word. In the day of the Psalmist, Oriental monarchs labored hard to establish postal communications by using the swiftest runners that could be found, but not even our modern means of quick conveyance of news can compete with Divine rapidity. No arrow makes so immediate an impression in the mark aimed at as the arrow of God's Word. What alacrity it has!

It would seem as if God is directly and personally at work in Nature, regulating revolving seasons by His Word. As Ellicott comments, "The Word of God is personified as a messenger who runs swiftly to do His bidding, at first binding the earth and sheaves up in a frost, then suddenly thawing and releasing them," verse 18. But let us take these arrestive phrases as they stand out so boldly with all their appeal.

He giveth snow like wool. Snow—Wool. What opposites! Yet the latter keeps us warm when the former appears in winter. Though snow is cold in itself, yet it is to the earth as wool, or as a woolen blanket keeping warm the body. The ancients used to call the snow, *wooly water.* Further aspects of the comparison between the two substances are the *whiteness, softness,* and *curled and tufted feature* of both, Isa. 1:18; Rev. 1:14. "He Who one day feeds us with the finest of the wheat, at another time robes us in snow: He is the same God in each case, and each form of His operation bestows a gift on men."

He scattereth the hoarfrost like ashes. In Creation, everything is traced back to the Creator. "The sea is His, He made it." So here, the snow, frost, ice, vernal breezes are *His.* The term *hoarfrost* comes from the Latin and implies "a rug of fire." This frost resembles the fine grey ash of wood burned in the open air. Thus it is likened unto "ashes" because it darkens the light, resembles the color of them, and has a kind of burning in it. Frost burns tender buds and blossoms, nips and dries them up. Unseasonable frosts in the Spring scorch the tender fruits. We speak of a *black* frost and a *white* frost, and the same colors are used of ashes. Thus God is behind every flake of snow and each particle of rime.

He casteth forth his ice like morsels. Notice the pronouns, *He* and *His.* Seeing He casts it forth it is *His.* Some writers think that there is an allusion here to Hail, Gen. 18:5; Judges 19:5. Morsels or crumbs can refer to the hail when it falls like crumbs of bread. Archbishop Leighton, writing one day to his sister and speaking of the season, said, "It is extremely severe, but God makes summer and winter." The arrestive phrases in this last section all indicates a very real presence of God in the phenomena of Nature.

Who can stand before His cold? Just as we cannot resist the vehemence of heat, so it is hard to bear the utmost rigors of cold. But as it is *His* cold, it must be for the benefit of the earth He created. As the Creator, He plans what is necessary and beneficial, even although we may not see the use of cold, bitter days when they overtake us. When one reads this clause they think of the tragic retreat of Napoleon's forces from Moscow in the depth of winter when untold numbers of men fell down, frozen dead, by the cold.

He sendeth out His word, and melteth them. The same Divine fiat causing snow, ice, and hail makes them to melt as Spring-time comes round. *He causeth His wind to blow, and the waters flow.* As warmer breezes blow, and the time of the singing of birds has come, this takes place in a general thaw, ice melts, and springs and rivers rise by the power of Him Who is the Ever-Potent One, the great First Cause in the natural world—and in the spiritual realm. *Word* and *Wind,* found here in the description of winter and spring, are terms attending each other in Grace. Christopher Wordsworth gives us this most apt application of these two Divine channels of power—

> Israel in the captivity had been ice-bound, like ships of Arctic voyagers in the Polar Sea: but God sent forth the vernal breezes of His love, and the

water flowed, the ice melteth, and they were released. God turned their captivity, and their icy chains being melted by the solar beams of God's mercy, they flowed in fresh and buoyant streams, like "the rivers of the south," shining in the sun, Psalm 126:4. So it was on the day of Pentecost. The winter of spiritual captivity was thawed and dissolved by the soft breath with spring-tide flowers of faith, love, and joy.

He sheweth His word unto Jacob, 147:19, 20. These last two verses present Jehovah as being worthy of all praise seeing that He is the Revealer as well as the Creator. Jacob and his seed were peculiarly favored in that He made them the recipients and custodians of His Word, Statutes, and Judgments. Israel alone, by Divine will, had a clear and exclusive revelation of God and knowledge of His attributes. In the Psalm, God is set forth as the Provider of all *creatures* in *general* in His common providence, and also to *Israel* in *particular*, for, "He hath dealt so with any nation." To the world, God gave light of nature, but to His chosen people, the light of Holy Scripture. Thus, the mighty Word of Jehovah, operative in nature, provided also a revelation for Israel. He manifested Himself unto His own as He did not unto the world. See Deut. 4:7; 32:32-41. Surrounding heathen nations had no knowledge of His *judgments*, which description of in Scripture does not imply a manifestation of wrath, but, as frequently expressed, the display of righteousness towards Israel, Psalm 119. Having thus dealt with His people in a singular way of electing grace and mercy, God expected singular praise and received it in another heart-felt *Hallelujah*!

Psalm 148

This is another Psalm prominent in the lives of saints down the ages. Here are some of the historical and biographical connections of the Psalm we have gathered to give it more prominence. St. Francis of Assisi, whose great love of the Psalms we have already noted, modelled his remarkable *Canticle of the Sun* on Psalm 148. In this *Canticle*, Francis sums up his love for all created things, and especially toward those in which he saw a figure of anything pertaining to God and religion. Francis, following the Psalm, closes with his *Hallelujah!* "Praise and bless my Lord! Give thanks to Him and serve Him with all humbleness of heart."

John Newman, in his *Dream of Gerontius*, has some striking passages as echoes from the Psalms. For instance, when Gerontius "quitted his mortal case," and was borne by an angel into the presence of the holy Judge, the soul and its guardian mount upwards, and the angelic choirs sing their Maker's praise in lines, whose opening stanza recalls Psalm 148, and also Psalm 150—

> Praise to the Holiest in the height,
> And in the depth be praise;
> In all His words most wonderful;
> Most sure in all His ways.

When medieval thought fell under the spell of the Psalms, science and literature as well as the history of the Middle Ages felt their sway. Medieval cosmogonists loaded their dissertations with quotations from the Psalms in which references to the created world are found. Thus, when they came to show that the air exhaled from the earth, formed lightning and hail, snow and vapors, wind and storm, they quoted Psalm 148:8 where these elements are mentioned. These cosmogonists also built some strange theories on the 4th verse, the phrase, "Ye waters above the heavens" was made to imply that Heaven was divided into two by the firmament which lay between our atmosphere and the Paradise of God.

Alexander Peden, the romantic figure who was the Prophet of the Covenant and leader of the Covenanters, in all his wanderings and escapes found the Psalms a perennial source of strength. Once, when hounded by his pursuers through bogs he knew so well and found a path of safety but in which his foes were drowned, he had the words of Psalm 148:8 very much in mind as he sought to escape to Scotland, but his boat was becalmed and he was in danger of capture, "Wind . . . fulfilling His word." So waving his hand to the west from whence he desired the wind, Peden prayed, "Lord, give us a loof-full of wind; fill the sails, Lord, and give us a fresh gale, and let us have a swift and safe passage over to the bloody land, come of us what will." Before he ended his prayer, the flapping sails filled like blown bladders, and he and his comrades were saved.

St. Bernard of Clairvaux, in his moving description of the death of his much-loved brother, not only by blood, but in the faith, says, "In thy last night below, thou didst invite us to praise God, when suddenly, to the surprise of all, thou, with a serene countenance and cheerful voice, didst commence chanting that Psalm," *Praise ye the Lord from the heavens; praise Him in the heights. Praise Him all ye angels; praise Him, all His hosts,"* Psalm 148:1, 2.

This splendid anthem, in which the Psalmist calls upon the whole creation to praise Jehovah for His Works, has also inspired both ancient and modern poets in their compositions. The model of countless hymns of praise, the Psalm is best appreciated and understood by comparison with some of them. The LXX Version of *The Song of Three Children*, as found in the Book of Daniel, is likely an imitation of this Psalm, but its lyric fire is lost in the artificial style of this *Song*. Then, writing of the tone of the anthems of the ancient church, I saw, Taylor says, "It is but feebly and as afar off, that the ancient liturgies—except so far as they are merely copies their originals—came up to the majesty and wide compass of the Hebrew worship, such as it is indicated in the 148th Psalm."

John Milton in *Paradise Lost* has elegantly imitated this Psalm by putting it into the mouth of Adam and Eve as the morning hymn in their state of innocency. On verses 3 and 4 of this Psalm in which God is praised for the constellations, Richard Mant has the lines—

> Praise him, thou golden-tressed sun;
> Praise him thou fair and silver moon,
>   And ye bright orbs of streaming light;
> Ye floods that float above the skies,
> Ye heavens, that vault o'er vault arise,
>   Praise Him, who sits above all height.

William Cullen Bryant, who died in 1878, revealed his poetic genius in his lines on verse 6 of the Psalm, "For ever and ever"—

> My heart is awed within me, when I think
> Of the great miracle which still goes on,
> In silence, round me—the perpetual work
> Of thy creation, finished, yet newed
> For ever.

On the passage in which Jehovah is praised for "fruitful trees, and all cedars," 148:9, the 15th century poet, Peter Pett, wrote this most expressive stanza—

> All creatures of the eternal God but man,
> In several sorts do glorify his name;
> Each tree doth seem ten thousand tongues to have,
> With them to laud the Lord omnipotent;
> Each leaf that with wind's gentle breath doth wave,
> Seems as a tongue to speak to that intent,
> In language admirably excellent.
> The sundry sorts of fragrant flowers do seem
> Sundry discourses God to glorify,
> And sweetest volumes may we them esteem;
> For all these creatures in their several sort
> Praise God, and man unto the same exhort.

Vapors, 148:8, or the driving mists of a storm, were regarded as smoke, as Tennyson confirms in his phrase, "The smoky mountain tops."

While the immediate occasion of the Psalm is not known, its motive is clearly evident. It is quite different from that sympathetic feeling for nature which figures so largely and powerfully into modern poetry—a feeling not entirely known to the Hebrew mind. In this Psalm, "it is not because the poet wants nature to join him in praise that he summons the universe to his choir, but that he may, in the last verse, enhance the glory and privilege of Israel. All nature has reason to praise the Creator who called it into being, and gave it its order so fair and so established, and poetically the universe may be imagined full of adoring creatures, but in reality, praise as a privilege belongs only to Israel. It is not here a contrast between inanimate and animate, rational and irrational . . . Expression is piled on expression to establish this fact. *His People; His saints;* A people near unto Him."

We are not going to attempt to divide the Psalm or expound its passages. "A living poem is not to be dissected verse by verse," says Spurgeon in his Preface to this Psalm, although he does give us a remarkable exposition of it *verse by verse.* The poem is one and indivisible. It is a song of nature and of grace. "As a flash of lightning flames through space, and enwraps both heaven and earth in one vestment of glory, so doth the adoration of the Lord in this Psalm light up all the universe, and cause it to glow with a radiance of praise. The song begins in the heavens, sweeps downward to dragons and all deeps, and then ascends again, till the people near unto Jehovah take up the strain. For its exposition the chief requisite is a heart on fire with reverent love to the Lord over all, who is to be blessed for ever." In his marvelous *Expositions of the Psalms,*

Spurgeon certainly reveals how his own heart was on fire with a reverent love for his Lord he constantly magnified.

For the preacher who would seek to use this Psalm for pulpit ministry, a model can be found in a sermon Canon Liddon preached on from Psalm 148:8 on the Sunday afternoon, December 23, 1883, in St. Paul's, London. He spoke of the Divine use of destructive forces found in this text, "Wind and storm fulfilling His word," and developed these points in his sermon—

1. In the *Physical World* we see the wind and storm fulfilling God's word.
   A. The Bible occasionally lifts the veil, and shows us how destructive forces of Nature have been the servants of God.
   B. Modern history illustrates this vividly.

2. In the *Human, Spiritual* and *Moral World*, we find new and rich application of the words of the text.
   A. In the *State* we see the storm of invasion and the storm of revolution fulfilling God's Word.
   B. In the *Church* we see the storm of persecution and the storm of controversy fulfilling God's Word.
   C. In the experience of *individual life* we see outward troubles, and inward storms of religious doubts fulfilling God's Word.

Psalm 149

T his lively song of triumph has been employed in the past as an excuse for the barbarities of fanatics inflicted upon their foes. Psalm 149 was used by Thomas Muntzer of the Protestant Church when he stirred up the German people to revolt against Catholic impositions. Then it was by means of this same Psalm that Caspar Scloppius, in his *Classicum Belli Sacri* which, as Bakius says, is written not with ink but with blood, inflamed the Roman Catholic princes to the Thirty Years' Religious War. It is to be regretted that the Psalm has become the watchword of the most horrible errors, especially in the religious realm. With the fuller and final revelation of the New Testament we recognize that "the weapons of our warfare are not carnal," 2 Cor. 10:4, and the Church of God cannot pray vindictively as the Jews of old did. Saints now live under the gentler dispensation of grace.

Of the last three Psalms in the Psalter, John Pulsford says that they form "*a triad of wondrous praise*, ascending from praise to higher praise, until it becomes 'joy unspeakable and full of glory'—exultation which knows no bounds. The joy overflows the soul, and spreads throughout the universe; every creature is magnetized by it, and drawn into the chorus . . . Man presses even dead things into his service, timbrels, trumpets, harps, organs, cymbals, if by any means, and by all means, he may give utterance to his love and joy as he meditates upon Jehovah's attributes and acts."

Such an expressed sentiment is true of this last but one *Hallelujah* Psalm with its tone exceedingly jubilant and exultant, and one in which all through the beat of drums, the music of timbrel and harp, are in harmony with the dancing feet of young maidens. It is a Psalm in which is joyfully blended religious and patriotic zeal. Evidently it belongs to the era of Nehemiah and Ezra, when the long-strained joy of the restored people broke into vigorous manifestation, Ezra 6:22. The praises of the *King* are, throughout, the theme and substance. And that it is a Psalm for saints to sing is found in the three-fold repetition of the epithet, *Saints*, verses 1, 4, 9. A possible division can be suggested, namely—

1. Rejoicing over deliverance from foes, verses 1-5.
2. Resolve to destroy all foes, verses 6-9.

Rejoicing over deliverance from foes, 149:1-5. With a *Hallelujah!* the Psalmist summoned Israel to bless Jehovah for the victory He had granted, but just what was the great event bringing the nation very much gladness cannot be traced. Perhaps it was the deliverance from Babylon and the rebuilding of the Temple.

Sing unto the Lord a new song. A new blessing calls for a new song, Psalms 33:3; 96:1. Jehovah is ever new in His manifestations, or like His mercies new every morning, and only those of new heart will sing a new song unto Him for His salvation. "Our new songs should be devised in Jehovah's honor, indeed all our newest thoughts should be towards Him." This fresh expression of reverent praise ascends to Him "in the congregation of the saints." Lonely songs are not so inspiring as those we sing when we gather with the Lord's people to share the enkindlings of common worship. We can render the phrase thus—"the assembly of the favored ones."

This song of renovation came from the lips of saints who had not forsaken the assembling of themselves together. Used three times over in the Psalm, the term *saints* meaning, beloved, or favored ones, indicates Divine workmanship. All who can sing the new song are saints, Ephes. 4:12. A saint in Christ Jesus is precious in God's sight, and an assembly of them is a treasure house of jewels. Saints above all people have a reason to praise Him Who is the Holy One because they are a new creation in the Redeemer.

Let Israel rejoice . . . Let the children of Zion be joyful. The object of Israel's new song was Jehovah, "their King." Rejoicing had to be *in Him*. We here have our first and our second creation. "He made him." *He made us and not we ourselves*. This is our natural life, and all that belongs to it is provision and nourishment for a theme of constant praise. But if *in* Him, then we are His children and He is our King—the King of Saints. This is our re-creation, our re-making when we received supernatural life, and we are therefore obligated to live in joyful obedience to our Sovereign Lord. Matthew Henry observes that in Psalm 148 we have "a hymn of praise to the Creator; this 149th Psalm is a hymn to the Redeemer."

This second verse has, of course, a direct association with Israel whose *Maker* was the Lord. He, it was, who formed of him a nation, then constituted the people a kingdom—truly a wonderful cause for rejoicing. It will be noted that the people were joyful, not for what the King had done for them, but in the King Himself. They did, indeed, praise Him for His works, but above all were joyful for His person. The Hebrew reads, "Let Israel rejoice in God *his makers*"—a reminder of the mystic ministry of the Trinity in the fashioning of a new creation.

Praise Him in the dance . . . with timbrel and harp. The next and final Psalm gives us a list of orchestral instruments used in Temple worship. The margin for "the dance" gives us "with the pipe," or flute. The Kingship of Jehovah was not a matter of terror, but of great and abound-

ing joy as bodies and music expressed in harmony "praises unto Him." It
is only when He holds court in the heart that the joy-bells ring, Psalm
118:15; Exod. 15:20. In primitive religions dancing played a very important part, but now, because of its associations and forms, dancing is far
from being a religious exercise, 2 Sam. 6:16. David danced before the
Ark, Judges 21:21. While the New Testament urges singing as a Gospel
ordinance, nothing is said of music and dancing. The Gospel edict for
songs of praise is to "sing with the spirit and with the understanding."
Modern dancers err when they justify their frivolous and lewd dances by
quoting the sacred dance of devout joy.

The blessed truth brought out here is that if God's people reveal their
pleasure in Him, then He takes pleasure in them and beautifies them with
salvation. How condescending it was for Jehovah to find "pleasure in His
people"—a people who sorely grieved Him at times. Many names and
titles are given to His people, but they are called *the meek*. The original
for "meek" means *poor and afflicted ones*, and afterwards was applied to
merciful persons. The question is, Are we meek enough to bring pleasure
to Him Who was meek and lowly in heart?

Another rendering of this fourth verse reads, *He adorns the oppressed
with salvation.* "Not only is the victory which achieves the deliverance of
the afflicted people a relief to them, but the honor won in the sight of the
world is like a beautiful robe, a figure no doubt suggested by the actual
triumphal dresses of the victors, or the spoils in which they appeared after
the battle," Judges 5:30; Isa. 50:5; 60:7.

As for the virtue of *meekness*, it not only imparts great peace of mind,
but beautifies the one manifesting it—a grand argument for exulting in
Him, seeing the fruit of meekness comes from Him, Gal. 5:23. A meek
and quiet spirit is called an *ornament of great price*, and certainly is part
of "the beauty of holiness."

Joyful in glory . . . upon their beds. The joyful saints in glory may
mean either the saints whose death was precious in God's sight and now
enjoy a foretaste of glory, or those who are glad in anticipation of glory.
The two clauses of this passage are directly parallel—

> Let the saints raise a cry in glory:
> Let them sing aloud upon their couches.

The saints in glory rest from their labors but not from their praise
which is more perfect than ever it was on earth. As for the latter part of
the verse, the nights of the exiles' grief were exchanged for nights of song,
Job 35:10. "Resting, free from fears and sorrow at night time, they *sing*
in their beds, not fearing the treachery of false friends, or the open hostility of avowed foes," Psalm 4:4; 6:6; Hosea 7:14. Upon our beds, when
no one else can hear us, even although they be beds of sickness, we can

make melody in our hearts unto the Lord. Many saints on beds of death and at the scaffold and stake had an outburst of joy their sufferings could not silence.

Resolve to destroy all foes, 149:6-9. The righteous, joyful over their victory, resolve to avenge their foes. Combined with their throated exaltations of celebration was a two-edged sword in their hand. They saw no contradiction between praise and punishment. While their mouths sing praises, their hands wield the sword, Neh. 4:10. The Maccabees thought they were fighting the Lord's battles (2 Macc. 15:26), just as Mohammed and Cromwell did. The original for "two-edged sword" is "a sword of mouths," meaning, an all-devouring sword, Judges 3:16. Sneeringly, the fighting Ironsides of Oliver Cromwell were called *Psalm-singers*; but God's Psalm-singers are always *Ironsides*, who sing not only at their work, but in the warfare against the world, flesh and the Devil.

Praises are called *high*, that is, Exalted, loud enough for others to hear, and are offered to God for His high, or conspicuous, excellent acts. His perfections, name, and majesty are constantly extolled or lifted up, Psalms 50:23; 68:4; 108:32; Luke 1:64. Thus with a song and sword kings are bound with chains, and nobles, with fetters of iron. The powers of evil could not bind Israel's *King* Who fought against his foes, covering them with shame and defeat. As a nation, Israel witnessed that vengeance was Jehovah's as He executed judgment upon His enemies.

The ancient Law was very stringent in its denunciation of kings and rulers refusing to acknowledge God, Deut. 7:2; 32:41. This is also a forecast in the last two verses of this Psalm of Messianic rule, Psalms 18:30-43; 83:10-13; Isa. 45:14; 49:7, 23; 60:3, when judgment preordained by God will be executed, Isa. 65:5; Job 13:26. When the Messiah returns, He will put down all rule, and authority, and power, for He must reign, 1 Cor. 15:24, 25. This Psalm may await the consummation John depicts, when we will sing of it, as Israel sang its song of deliverance at the Red Sea.

Under Grace, we are not executioners of justice, but heralds of mercy. We praise God with our lips, but the Word of God as a sharp two-edged sword is in our hands as we seek to imitate the servants of good Nehemiah, Neh. 4:17, 18. It is thus that our avowed enemy, the Devil, is overcome—the flesh crucified—and the world vanquished, Ephes. 6:17.

This honor have all the saints, or "This shall be the honor of all saints." What is the nature of such an honor for God's favored ones? Is it not the overthrow of all their enemies described by the Psalmist? All who were joyful in their heavenly King, and who were a people He had pleasure in and beautified with salvation shared in the victory of the King when He smote Israel's foes. The original is emphatic, *"His* saints," exclusively, have the honor of witnessing the overthrow of those who had caused them so much pain and sorrow and loss. The margin of the R.V. gives us a blessed change of this phrase—"He is the honor of all His saints." He is mine, my Heritage, my exceeding great Reward. Emphasis is on the tiny word *ALL*. The world of God's redeemed is a republic where the highest places are within the reach of each saint. I, poor, ineffectual, unworthy, may be peer and prince in His realm.

Stephen Gosson, who died in 1623 after a mighty ministry for God, wrote, "It was once the saying of Pompey, that with one stamp of his foot he could raise all Italy up in arms; and the mighty men of the World may have nations, kingdoms and commonwealths at their command, but yet God is more powerful than they all. If He did but arise, they shall all fly before Him. If He once fall to gettering princes, it shall be done so sure, that no flesh shall be able to knock off their bolts again." It was the honor of saints in Israel to witness such a Divine conquest. What a strong reason this was for glorifying the triumphant King with another *Hallelujah*—"Praise ye the Lord." Saints today have a great honor seeing they have been redeemed by the blood of the Lamb out of every nation, country, people and tongue, and made Heirs of God and joint-heirs with Jesus Christ. *Hallelujah!*

Psalm 150

A t last we have reached the end of our odyssey with a Psalm presenting a tumultuous outburst of praise. Alexander in his great work on *The Psalms* says, "There is nothing more majestic or more beautiful than this brief but most significant finale, as if in emblematical allusion to the triumph which awaits the Church and all its members, when through much tribulation they shall enter into rest." John Ker in *Psalms in History and Biography* expresses a similar sentiment—

> This last Psalm is the great *Hallelujah*, the triumphant acclaim to Him Who hath gotten the victory, after the manifold sorrows and conflicts through which the Church of God and the believing soul have passed. The temple thrills and throbs with the burst of gladness, as all the powers of man, and all creatures in the universe are summoned to aid the song. It seems as if this were the very summit and climax of the praise that can ascend to God, the loftiest wave of the many waters that break at the foot of His throne, and yet it yields to that joy of which the Apostle speaks which is "unspeakable and full of glory."

It was to the singing of this most jubilant Psalm 150 that the monks of old cast their bells as the brethren waited at the furnace for the metal to be poured into the mold. One can picture those swarthy sons of the furnace with the ruddy glow of the fire upon their faces as they stood around, while their deep voices rang forth this Hymn of Praise. Newman, in *Dream of Gerontius* describes how the departed soul and guardian mount upward, the angelic choir singing praise to the Maker in the language of most joyful Psalm. It was also by a verse from this Psalm that the first translation of the Scriptures into a language, "understanded of the people" was sanctioned by orthodox Christianity. Methodius and Cyril desired to construct an alphabet and to translate portions of the Bible into the Sclavonic tongue. Their request was referred to Pope John VIII in 879, and it was justified in his eyes by the words he quoted, "Let everything that hath breath praise the Lord," Psalm 150:6. And so in the Sclavonic language and in the rude alphabet, still witnessing to the Byzantine origin of Russian religion and literature, the whole of the New Testament was translated.

As we come to examine the Psalm with its connections and features, it is with the eulogy of Spurgeon in heart to urge us on—"We have now reached the last summit of the mountain chain of Psalms. It rises high in the clear azure, and its brow is bathed in the sunlight of the eternal world of worship. It is a rapture. The poet-prophet is full of inspiration and enthusiasm. He stays not to argue, to teach, to explain; but cries with burning words, *Praise Him, Praise Him, Praise ye the LORD*."

First of all, it is interesting to compare and contrast the first and last Psalms of the Psalter, both of which are made up of the same number of verses, and are both short and memorable. That Psalm 150 is an echo of Psalm 1 can be found in that the latter begins with *Blessed* and ends with *Blessed*, the theme of the initial Psalm being, "Blessed are all they that meditate on God's law to do it." And the fruit of that blessedness is displayed in the final Psalm which begins and ends with *Hallelujah*. Then the scope of these two Psalms is slightly different—

> Psalm 1 is an elaborate instruction in our duty, to prepare us for the comforts of our devotion.
>
> Psalm 150 is all rapture and transport, and perhaps was penned on purpose, says Matthew Henry, to be conclusion of those sacred songs, to show what is the design of them all, and that is, to assist us in praising God.

Another striking aspect of this concluding Psalm is its *thirteen* Hallelujahs in only six verses, with the greatest number of words between any two Hallelujahs being four, and that only once; in every other instance, between one Hallelujah and another there are but two words. It is as though the soul gave utterance to its whole life and feeling in the one word, *Hallelujah!* As Psalm 150 is one the Israelites sang, it has been suggested that the thirteen Hallelujahs were connected with the Tribes—Levi, Ephraim and Manasseh making three—one for each. Yet another writer says that this Psalm was sung by the people as they came with the first fruits into the sanctuary, with the baskets on their shoulders, and the Levites met them with singing, Ps. 30, and that the thirteen Hallelujahs praised God for His thirteen perfections or prosperities. The much vaunted Greek and Latin poetry of old looks pale alongside this sublime finale of the Psalter, sung by the sacred choir of the Universe.

As pointed out in our *Introduction*, the 150 Psalms are divided into Five Books, and each of the first Four Books ends with a *Benediction*, 41:13; 72:19; 89:52; 106:48, but the Fifth and last Book ends with a *Hallelujah* 150:6, which worthily closes not only the little Hallelujah group, but the Whole Psalter, and consequently has been called "The Finale of the Spiritual Concert." Thus "The Psalter, with all its cries from the depths, runs out in a *Hallelujah!* " As for a division of the miniature, merry Psalm, the following *three-decker* may help the preacher—

Where we are to praise Jehovah, 150:1. Two spheres are given, "In His sanctuary"—"In the firmament of His power." Some expositors take *sanctuary* and *firmament* to be parallel. In Psalm 148, the invocation to praise includes Heaven, where God's throne is, Psalm 11:4; 148:1-4, and Earth, 148:7. But in this final Psalm the order is reversed, the earthly sanctuary first, and the sublime things done on earth, then Heaven and the exalted greatness there. The sanctuary is the earthly temple, the firmament of His power the heavenly, with the former being formed on the pattern of the higher, Heb. 8:5; 9:23; 1 Chron. 28:11-19. In both realms, the thrice holy Jehovah is the object of adoration.

Why we are to praise Jehovah, 150:2. Two reasons are given—"His mighty acts"—"His excellent greatness." Excellent in His attributes and acts, His person and performances, He is worthy of the most excellent praise. *His mighty acts* are displayed on earth. As for *His excellent greatness,* or, as the Hebrew has it, "The abundance of His greatness," Heaven alone will bring us to a full realization of the perfection of Him Who is "great, and greatly to be praised."

As the female champion of Israel, Deborah arose and aroused Israel to shout a loud *Hallelujah!* as she "rehearsed the mighty acts of the Lord," Judges 5:7-11, so the Psalmist summons the people to magnify Him for all the miracles He performed on their behalf, an enumeration of which we recited in passages like Psalms 105, 106, or Col. 1:15-21. All His omnipotent acts in Creation, Providence, and Redemption call for our highest praise. Then Jehovah's excellent grandeur merits another heartfelt *Hallelujah* for He is the greatest to whom the greatest things are little things, nay, as nothing in His sight. Are not the great nations of the earth as a drop in a bucket to Him? Isa. 40:15.

With what we are to praise Jehovah, 150:3-6. What a stirring jubilant section this is with its *eight* Hallelujahs in *four* verses, in which no faculty is omitted but all are enlisted to extol and glorify Jehovah! Every kind of instrument known to the Hebrews, commandeered to praise the Lord, are mentioned, with the last verse calling upon all who had breath and voice to swell the Hallelujah chorus. *Breath* was employed, not only in blowing the trumpet, but in vocal praise—*fingers* were used in the playing of the psaltery, harp, timbrel, and stringed instruments—*feet* moved in the dance. Thus instruments and bodily expressions were harmoniously united to bless the Lord.

As it is not easy to determine the exact nature of the instruments referred to, we are not unduly concerned about them except to say that the Lord is worthy of the consecration of the highest musical talent. What we must remember is that each of our emotions and faculties may be musical instruments in the best sense. As F. B. Meyer says, we can "Praise Him with the sound of our love! Praise Him with hope and faith! Praise

Him with meekness and patience! Praise Him with courage and strength! Praise Him in Christian work! Praise Him when tied by pain and weariness to a sick-bed!"

The last verse of the Psalm, and of all the Psalms, exhorts us to pull out the mighty stops in nature's organ—

> Let every thing . . . Praise the Lord.
> Let the bright Seraphim in burning row,
> Their loud uplifted angel-trumpets blow.

Whether considered as a desire, a prayer, or an exhortation this climatic verse fitly concludes the Book of Psalms. Ellicott confines this sixth verse to Israel—"We naturally wish to give these words their largest intent, and to hear the Psalter close with an invocation, 'the earth with her thousand voices' to praise God. But the Psalm so distinctly and positively brings us into the Temple, and places us among the covenant people engaged at their devotions, that we are compelled to see here a hymn specially suited to the close of the collection of hymns of the covenant, as the first and second were to begin it. It is, therefore, not all breathing beings, but only all assembled in the sanctuary, that are here addressed; and the loud Hallelujah, with which the collection of Psalms actually closes, rise from Hebrew voices alone."

Needless to say, we disagree with such a limitation for the simple reason that the poet said let "*everything* that hath breath praise the Lord"—which surely includes all animate beings, whether on earth or in Heaven. The Vulgate Version puts it, "Let every spirit praise the Lord." Perhaps *breath* is used in contrast to the musical, material instruments previously mentioned. Those with breath are not lifeless instruments, but creatures able to offer vocal, articulate, and intelligent praise. Beasts and birds have breath and in their own way magnify their Creator. So, let the gnat make music with the vibrations of its wings! Let every creature which is in Heaven, and on earth, and under the earth, and such as are in the sea be heard singing, "Blessing, and honor, and glory, and power, be unto Him that sitteth upon the throne, and unto the Lamb for ever and ever." Hallelujah! Amen. Rev. 5:12, 13.

Then do you not love the way Joseph Addison, the remarkable Christian poet of the early 17th century, calls upon inanimate nature to express its Hallelujahs to Him Who brought her into being? In one of his Odes we have the stanzas—

> Soon as the evening shades prevail,
> The moon takes up this wondrous tale.
> And nightly to the listening Earth
> Repeats the story of her birth.

> While all the stars that round her burn,
> And all the planets, in their turn,
> Confirm the tidings as they roll,
> And spread the truth from pole to pole.
>
> In Reason's eye they all rejoice,
> And utter forth a glorious Voice,
> For ever singing as they shine,
> "The Hand that made us is Divine."

Surely there is nothing more majestic or more beautiful than this brief but most blessed significant *Finale* in which solemnity of tone predominates. It brings the Book of Psalms to an end with a glowing word of adoration from everything having breath. As we have breath may it ever be used to sing the praises of Him Who created and redeemed us. *Hallelujah!* Praise ye the Lord! Well, our odyssey is over, and as the author lays down his pen, he pauses for a moment to offer his personal Hallelujah to Him, Who enabled him to think His thoughts after Him.

> Praise God, from Whom all blessings flow;
> Praise Him, all creatures here below;
> Praise Him, above, ye heavenly host;
> Praise Father, Son, and Holy Ghost.